T0303853

'The natural system is not a stakeholder in our businesses; it is the ultimate foundation of the rules. This is law one of global responsibility. Law two states that everything, everywhere is linked in a single system, therefore every action must be considered in the context of its effect on the whole system. Forward-looking business leaders are those that help solve the dilemmas humanity face as a consequence of these two laws. The anthology *Business Strategies for Sustainability* is a timely and useful companion for business leaders and practitioners that realise the need and urgency to think, act and exist in a globally responsible mode – responsible to the self, the other and the whole.'

– John North, Executive Director, Globally
Responsible Leadership Initiative

'This book provides a detailed and extensive overview of how businesses can develop strategies for corporate sustainability. The team of editors has assembled an excellent group of academics who provide insights into the most relevant research issues of today. The book thus acts both as an introduction to the state of the research field and highlights the areas that will dominate academic debate in the coming years. In light of the Sustainable Development Goals, this book will be an important resource.'

– Prof. Kai Hockerts, Department of Management, Society and
Communication, Copenhagen Business School

'This book breaks new ground exploring the theory and practice of strategies for sustainability, an area which has been insufficiently addressed in management literature to date. The international team of researchers represented in this volume gives a comprehensive picture of both the particular problems that sustainability poses for business as well as examples of current research showing how business strategies can assist in addressing them. The various contributors unbundle the key topic of what corporate sustainability can mean for value creation, along with case studies of sustainability implementation in both developing and developed countries. In my view, the volume provides a means of introducing new readers to business sustainability challenges while providing an up-to-date summary of the field for those more familiar with some of the concepts.'

– Prof. Suzanne Benn, University of Technology Sydney

'This is a timely and comprehensive research anthology which contributes to the ongoing debate about the intersections between business strategies and sustainability. Too often, "strategy" and "sustainability" are lumped together without a deeper understanding of either concept. Moreover, "strategic" sustainability is sometimes reduced to a simple positioning game intended to make the company's products or services more attractive on the competitive marketplace. As demonstrated in this anthology, however, business strategies for sustainability can give rise to much more fundamental discussions about the role of business in society. Moreover, the anthology successfully combines theoretical perspectives and practical approaches to strategy/sustainability, which together deepens our understanding of the multiple drivers and determinants influencing businesses' initiatives toward current societal challenges.'

– Prof. Esben Rahbek Gjerdrum Pedersen, Copenhagen Business School

Business Strategies for Sustainability

Business Strategies for Sustainability brings together important research contributions that demonstrate different approaches to business strategies for sustainability. Many corporate initiatives toward what firms perceive to be sustainability are simply efficiency drives or competitive moves – falling far short of actual strategies for ecological sustainability.

To suggest true ecological sustainability strategies, this new research anthology adopts an interdisciplinary, or transdisciplinary, approach to discern what business strategies might look like if they were underpinned by environmental and ecological science.

The 23 chapters in this anthology reflect five main topic sections: (a) delineating sustainability challenges and visions; (b) contradiction, integration and transformation of business and sustainability logics; (c) innovating and developing strategic capabilities for sustainability; (d) assessing and valuing sustainability; and (e) toward multi-level engagement and collaboration.

Dr Helen Borland is Senior Lecturer in Business Sustainability at Aston Business School, Birmingham where she heads the Strategic Sustainable Business Research Unit. Dr Borland received her PhD from Cranfield University. She has published in the *Journal of Business Ethics*, *International Marketing Review*, *European Journal of Marketing*, and *Thunderbird International Business Review*, among others.

Dr Adam Lindgreen is Professor of Marketing at Copenhagen Business School, where he heads the Department of Marketing, and Extra Ordinary Professor at the University of Pretoria's Gordon Institute of Business Science. Dr Lindgreen received his PhD from Cranfield University. He has published in *California Management Review*, *Journal of Business Ethics*, *Journal of Product and Innovation Management*, *Journal of the Academy of Marketing Science*, and *Journal of World Business*, among others.

Dr François Maon is Associate Professor at IESEG School of Management where he teaches strategy, business ethics, and corporate social responsibility. He received his PhD from the Catholic University of Louvain. Dr Maon has published in *California Management Review*, *International Journal of Management Reviews*, and *Journal of Business Ethics*, among others.

Dr Joëlle Vanhamme is Professor of Marketing at Edhec Business School. Dr Vanhamme received her PhD from the Catholic University of Louvain (Louvain School of Management). Dr Vanhamme has published in *California Management Review*, *Industrial Marketing Management*, *International Journal of Research in Marketing*, *Journal of Advertising*, *Journal of Business Ethics*, *Journal of Retailing*, *Marketing Letters*, *Psychology & Marketing*, and *Recherche et Applications en Marketing*, among others.

Dr Véronique Ambrosini is Professor of Strategic Management at Monash University. She is Head of the Department of Management. She was previously Professor of Strategic Management at the University of Birmingham and at Cardiff University. Dr Ambrosini has published in journals such as *Journal of Management Studies, British Journal of Management, Long Range Planning, Journal of Business Ethics,* and *Human Relations, among others.*

Dr Beatriz Palacios Florencio is Associate Professor of Marketing at Pablo de Olavide University, Seville. Her main research is corporate social responsibility and tourism. She has published in *Journal of Business Research, Total Quality Management & Business Excellence, Management Decision,* and *Environmental Engineering and Management Journal*, among others.

Business Strategies for Sustainability

Edited by Helen Borland, Adam Lindgreen,
François Maon, Joëlle Vanhamme,
Véronique Ambrosini, and Beatriz
Palacios Florencio

Routledge
Taylor & Francis Group

LONDON AND NEW YORK

First published 2019
by Routledge
2 Park Square, Milton Park, Abingdon, Oxon OX14 4RN

and by Routledge
711 Third Avenue, New York, NY 10017

Routledge is an imprint of the Taylor & Francis Group, an informa business

British Library Cataloguing-in-Publication Data
A catalogue record for this book is available from the British Library

Library of Congress Cataloging-in-Publication Data
Names: Borland, Helen, 1964- editor.
Title: Business strategies for sustainability /
edited by Helen Borland [and five others].
Description: Abingdon, Oxon; New York, NY: Routledge, 2019. |
Includes bibliographical references and index.
Identifiers: LCCN 2018014885 (print) | LCCN 2018017904 (ebook) |
ISBN 9780429458859 (eBook) | ISBN 9781138311343 (hardback: alk. paper)
Subjects: LCSH: Management—Environmental aspects. |
Sustainable development.
Classification: LCC HD30.255 (ebook) |
LCC HD30.255 .B87965 2019 (print) | DDC 658.4/012—dc23
LC record available at https://lccn.loc.gov/2018014885

ISBN: 978-1-138-31134-3 (hbk)
ISBN: 978-0-429-45885-9 (ebk)

Typeset in Bembo
by codeMantra

Printed and bound in Great Britain by
TJ International Ltd, Padstow, Cornwall

For Mum and Dad, who have been beside me through thick and thin

—Helen

For Kjeld, for supporting me when doing my MSc, for Ian and Rod, for supporting me when doing my PhD, and for Mike, George, and Peter, for believing in me

—Adam

For my Sophia

—François

For my two lovely daughters, Vic and Zazou

—Joëlle

For my nieces Lucía and Julia and my nephews Manuel and Marco, who make me laugh when I need it most

—Beatriz

Contents

List of figures

List of tables

About the editors

Dr Helen Borland gained her first degree in environmental sciences at Plymouth University and her PhD in Marketing from Cranfield University. She is now Director of the Strategic Sustainable Business Group and the MSc Strategic Sustainable Business, and is Senior Lecturer in Business Sustainability at Aston Business School, Aston University where she is responsible for teaching strategic business sustainability to MBA, MSc, and PhD students. Dr Borland's research and teaching stem from her knowledge of the ecological sciences and the philosophy behind sustainability, and how these can be taught and researched in a business context. Her development of a unique strategic typology for business sustainability – transitional and transformational strategies – is gaining attention in a number of academic and commercial circles. Dr Borland has published in a number of leading international academic journals including *Journal of Business Ethics, International Marketing Review, Thunderbird International Business Review*, and *European Journal of Marketing*. She also speaks about business sustainability at public events, writes articles and book chapters for the popular press, contributes towards government policy documents and works on a number of consultancy and grant-awarded projects, including an EU Climate Change Leadership project.

Dr Adam Lindgreen After studies in chemistry (Copenhagen University), engineering (the Engineering Academy of Denmark), and physics (Copenhagen University), Adam Lindgreen completed an MSc in food science and technology at the Technical University of Denmark. He also finished an MBA at the University of Leicester. Professor Lindgreen received his PhD in marketing from Cranfield University. His first appointments were with the Catholique University of Louvain (2000–2001) and Eindhoven University of Technology (2002–2007). Subsequently, he served as Professor of Marketing at Hull University's Business School (2007–2010); University of Birmingham's Business School (2010), where he also was the Research Director in the Department of Marketing; and University of Cardiff's Business School (2011–2016). Under his leadership, the Department of Marketing and Strategy at Cardiff Business School ranked first among all marketing departments in Australia, Canada, New Zealand, the United Kingdom, and the United States, based upon the hg indices of senior faculty. Since 2016, he has been Professor of Marketing at Copenhagen Business School, where he also heads the Department of Marketing. From 2018, he has been Extra Ordinary Professor with University of Pretoria's Gordon Institute of Business Science, as well as Visiting Professor to University of Northumbria's Newcastle Business School.

Professor Lindgreen has been a visiting professor with various institutions, including Georgia State University, Groupe HEC in France, and Melbourne University. His publications have appeared in *Business Horizons, California Management Review, Entrepreneurship and Regional Development, Industrial Marketing Management, International Journal of Management Reviews, Journal of Advertising, Journal of Business Ethics, European Journal of Marketing, Journal of Business and Industrial Marketing, Journal of Marketing Management, Journal of the Academy of Marketing Science, Journal of Product Innovation Management, Journal of World Business, Psychology & Marketing*, and *Supply Chain Management: An International Journal*, among others.

Professor Lindgreen's books include *A Stakeholder Approach to Corporate Social Responsibility* (with Kotler, Vanhamme, and Maon), *Managing Market Relationships, Memorable Customer Experiences* (with Vanhamme and Beverland), and *Sustainable Value Chain Management* (with Maon, Vanhamme, and Sen).

The recipient of the 'Outstanding Article 2005' award from Industrial Marketing Management and the runner-up for the same award in 2016, Professor Lindgreen serves on the board of several scientific journals; he is co-editor-in-chief of *Industrial Marketing Management* and previously was the joint editor of the *Journal of Business Ethics*' section on corporate responsibility. His research interests include business and industrial marketing management, corporate social responsibility, and sustainability. Professor Lindgreen has been awarded the Dean's Award for Excellence in Executive Teaching. Furthermore, he has served as an examiner (for dissertations, modules, and programs) at a wide variety of institutions, including the Australian National University, Unitec, University of Amsterdam, University of Bath's Management School, University of Lethbridge, and University of Mauritius.

Professor Lindgreen is a member of the International Scientific Advisory Panel of the New Zealand Food Safety Science and Research Centre (a partnership between government, industry organizations and research institutions), as well as of the Chartered Association of Business Schools' Academic Journal Guide (AJG) Scientific Committee in the field of marketing.

Beyond these academic contributions to marketing, Professor Lindgreen has discovered and excavated settlements from the Stone Age in Denmark, including the only major kitchen midden – Sparregård – in the south-east of Denmark; because of its importance, the kitchen midden was later excavated by the National Museum and then protected as a historical monument for future generations. He is also an avid genealogist, having traced his family back to 1390 and published widely in scientific journals (*Personalhistorisk Tidsskrift, The Genealogist*, and *Slægt & Data*) related to methodological issues in genealogy, accounts of population development, and particular family lineages.

Dr François Maon received his doctoral degree in 2010 from the Catholic University of Louvain (Louvain School of Management). After a visiting scholarship at the University of California, Berkeley, he is now Associate Professor at IESEG School of Management, where he teaches strategy, business ethics, and corporate social responsibility. In his research, Dr Maon focuses mainly on topics linked to corporate social responsibility, learning, implementation, and change-related processes; cross-sector social partnerships; and stakeholder influence strategies. He has published in journals such as *California Management Review, European Journal of Marketing, European Management Review, International Journal of Management*

Reviews, *Journal of Business Ethics*, and *Supply Chain Management: An International Journal*. He has co-edited several special issues of academic journals and books, including *A Stakeholder Approach to Corporate Social Responsibility* (with Lindgreen, Kotler, and Vanhamme) and *Sustainable Value Chain Management* (with Lindgreen, Vanhamme, and Sen). He serves on the editorial board of *M@n@gement* and is the founder and coordinator of the IESEG Center for Organizational Responsibility (ICOR).

Dr Joëlle Vanhamme is Professor at the Edhec Business School. Dr Vanhamme received her PhD from the Catholic University of Louvain (Louvain School of Management). She has been Assistant Professor at Rotterdam School of Management, Associate Professor at IESEG School of Management, and a visiting scholar with Delft University of Technology, Eindhoven University of Technology, Hull University's Business School, Lincoln University, and the University of Auckland's Business School. Dr Vanhamme's research has appeared in journals including *Business Horizons, California Management Review, Industrial Marketing Management, International Journal of Research in Marketing, Journal of Advertising, Journal of Business Ethics, Journal of Consumer Satisfaction, Dissatisfaction and Complaining Behavior, Journal of Customer Behaviour, Journal of Economic Psychology, Journal of Marketing Management, Journal of Retailing, Marketing Letters, Psychology & Marketing, Recherche et Applications en Marketing*, and *Supply Chain Management: An International Journal*.

Dr Véronique Ambrosini is the Head of Department and Professor of Strategic Management at Monash Business School, Monash University. She was previously Professor of Strategic Management at the University of Birmingham and at Cardiff University. She started her career at Cranfield School of Management where she gained her PhD. Her research is conducted essentially within the resource-based and dynamic capability view of the firm and takes a strategy-as-practice perspective. Her research interests lie in strategy implementation, sustainability, knowledge, and management education. Her articles have been published in journals such as *Journal of Management Studies, British Journal of Management, Long Range Planning, International Journal of Human Resource Management, Journal of Business Ethics*, and *Human Relations*, as well as practitioner-oriented journals such as *European Management Journal* and *Management Decision*. She is the author of *Tacit and Ambiguous Resources as Sources of Competitive Advantage*, the editor of *Exploring Techniques of Analysis and Evaluation in Strategic Management* and a co-editor of *Advanced Strategic Management: A Multi-perspective Approach*. Professor Ambrosini is a former associate editor of *British Journal of Management* and of *Journal of Management & Organization*. She serves on the editorial board of *Journal of Management Studies, Academy of Management Learning and Education, British Journal of Management, Journal of Management Education*, and of *International Journal of Human Resource Management*. She is a past council member of the British Academy of Management and past chair of the Strategic Management Society Strategy Practice track.

Dr Beatriz Palacios Florencio, PhD in Business Economics and Associate Professor in the University Pablo de Olavide, has been working for more than eight years in a public university. She has been a visiting professor at prestigious international centres, such as the University Facsul Uniao Metropolitana-Unime and Cardiff Business School. She is a member of the research group REINTUR (Red Hispano-Lusa de Investigadores en Turismo) and area coordinator of Social Corporate Responsibility of the European Academia of Firm Management and Economics (AEDEM). Her main research has been developed through two principal lines: corporate social responsibility and tourism. She has published in journals such as *Journal of Business Research*, *Internet Research*, *Management Decision*, *Total Quality Management & Business Excellence*, and *Environmental Engineering and Management Journal*. She also has taken part in national projects, as well being an assessor in contracts with private firms.

About the contributors

Dr Pilar Acosta is Assistant Professor at the School of Business and Economic Sciences at Universidad Icesi, in Cali, Colombia. She earned her PhD at ESCP Europe and Université Paris 1-Panthéon Sorbonne in 2015. Her work has been published in international journals such as *Journal of Business Ethics*, *Supply Chain Forum: An International Journal*, book chapters and international conferences. Her research focuses on the evolution of Corporate Social Responsibility (CSR) and sustainability-related practices in Latin America across different organizational settings. She currently teaches corporate social responsibility and sustainability at both undergraduate and master levels. She holds an industrial engineering degree, a master's degree in organizations from the University of Paris-X and worked as an organizational consultant in France. Pilar Acosta is co-director of Kairós Observatory for corporate sustainability at Universidad Icesi.

Dr Aurélien Acquier (PhD, HDR – Habilitation for doctoral supervision) is Professor in the Department of Management at ESCP Europe Business School, at the Paris Campus. His research has been published in *Journal of Business Ethics*, *Business and Society*, *Revue Française de Gestion*, *M@n@gement*, *Supply Chain Forum: An International Journal*, among others. His research focuses on the social impact of corporations. More specifically, he explores how historical and contemporary organizational transformations (global value chains, platform capitalism) affect corporate responsibility. He created and manages the option 'Rethink: alternative business models, social innovation and sustainability'. He graduated from ESSEC Business School with an MSc in management. He also earned a joint MSc in organizational theory from University Paris-X, ESCP Europe, Ecole des Mines de Paris and Ecole Polytechnique and a PhD from Mines-Paristech. He holds a French Habilitation for Doctoral Supervision – HDR – from IAE – Paris 1 Sorbonne

Dr Elisabeth Albertini is Associate Professor at the Sorbonne Business School (Paris). Her research focuses on the measurement and the management control of the corporate strategies that address environmental issues. Her work uses the natural resource-based view to understand how companies can obtain a sustainable competitive advantage from the natural environmental. She is working on the issue of measuring and managing the environmental performance through this perspective. She received the Schneider Electric Sustainability and Business Strategy Chair Award delivered by IESE Business School, University of Navarra, and Schneider Electric in 2014. She teaches accounting, management control and CSR management and certification at master's degree level. Prior to academics, she worked for the Xerox Company as a Corporate Financial Planning & Accounting Manager.

Dr Debra Z. Basil is Professor of Marketing and a founding member of the Centre for Socially Responsible Marketing at the University of Lethbridge, Canada. She earned her PhD in Marketing from the University of Colorado at Boulder, USA. She has published in the *Journal of Business Research*, the *Journal of Business Ethics*, and the *Journal of Consumer Psychology*, among others. Research grants include funders such as the Social Sciences and Humanities Research Council of Canada, the Knowledge Development Centre, and Worksafe BC. Her research examines how companies and consumers coact for the betterment of society; specific focal areas include corporate social responsibility, nonprofit appeals, cause-related marketing, volunteerism, and social marketing.

Dr Julie Bastianutti is Associate Professor of Strategy and Management at the University of Lille (France) and a member of the LEM-CNRS research centre (UMR9221). She studied at École Normale Supérieure, la Sorbonne and obtained her PhD from the École polytechnique. She has been a visiting scholar at the University of Oxford (Merton College and Centre for Socio-Legal Studies) and at the Stockholm School of Economics (SCORE). She has published several books and papers about corporate social responsibility, sustainability, business models and managerial innovation.

Dr Frederick Bird is Distinguished Professor Emeritus at Concordia University (Montreal) where he previous held a Concordia University Research Chair in Comparative Ethics. At Concordia he was a professor in the Department of Religion and taught in both the Sociology and Management departments. He is an Adjunct Professor of Political Science at the University of Waterloo. He is the author, co-author, and editor of a number of books including *The Muted Conscience: Moral Silence and the Practice of Ethics in Business* (1996), *Good Management* (1992), *The Practices of Global Ethics* (2016), *Just Business Practices in a Diverse and Developing World* (2006), *International Business and the Challenges of Poverty in the Developing World* (2004), and *International Businesses and the Dilemmas of Development* (2004). Recent articles and chapters include the following: 'Learning from History: The Relevance of the History of Business Ethics for the Practice of Business Ethics', 'Out of Sorts: Ethical Reflections on the Financial Crisis and the Great Recession' and 'The Practice of Mining and Inclusive Wealth Development in Developing Countries'.

Dr Frank Birkin holds the chair in Accounting and Sustainable Development at the Management School of Sheffield University. He has published widely in such as the *Journal of Business Ethics*, *The Journal of Ecological Economics*, *Critical Perspectives on Accounting*, and *Sustainable Development*. His books include *Intrinsic Sustainable Development: Epistemes, Science, Business and Sustainability* (World Scientific Press, 2011). He has worked on a series of major projects including the European Union funded 'STEPS (Sustainable Tourism's Environmental Protection System) for Islands' and 'Building capacities for corporate environmental management: a study of experiences in the Yunnan and Jiangsu provinces of the People's Republic of China'. His research interests include accounting for sustainable development, environmental management accounting, culture and sustainability and episteme change. He is currently director of the 'Intrinsic Earth' social movement.

Dr Carl Brønn is Adjunct Associate Professor of Decision Science in the School of Economics and Business at the Norwegian University of Life Sciences. He teaches courses in business simulation methods, strategic decision-making, problem structuring, and environmental management. His research interests focus on applying the systems perspective on strategic organizational issues such as sustainability and corporate environmental management, studying the interactions between the firm's social and technological systems resulting from digital transformations, and organizational learning and knowledge management. His work has appeared in a number of books as well as in journals such as *Strategic Management Journal, Journal of Communication Management, Corporate Reputation Review, Engineering, Construction and Architectural Management* and the *Journal of Public Policy.*

Dr Peggy Simcic Brønn is Professor of Communication and Management in BI Norwegian Business School's Department of Communication and Culture. She is director of BI's Center for Corporate Communication and is co-responsible for the Master of Management in Corporate Communication Management. Dr Brønn's research areas include relationship outcomes, reputation and reputation risk analysis, corporate communication, motives for social engagement, and the strategic role of communication managers. She is an associate editor of *Journal of Communication Management*, sits on the editorial board of several journals and has published in such journals as *Journal of Business Ethics, European Journal of Marketing, International Studies of Management and Organisation, Corporate Reputation Review,* and *Business and Society Review.* She holds a Doctor of Business Administration degree from the Henley Management College.

Dr Valentina Carbone (PhD, HDR - French habilitation for doctoral supervision) is Professor of Operations and Supply Chain Management at ESCP Europe business school, at the Paris Campus. She is the author of several articles (published in *Journal of Business Ethics, International Journal of Production Economics, Journal of Business Strategy and the Environment,* among others), volumes, chapters and communications to international conferences. Her recent research deals with Corporate Social Responsibility (CSR), Sustainable Supply Chain Management, Sharing and Circular Economy Business Models. She is member of the board of the AIRL – the French-speaking International Association for research on logistics and SCM. Valentina has conducted research on sustainable supply chain issues with public sector bodies such as the European Commission, the French Ministry for Sustainable Development or the Italian National Research Council. She earned a business and economics degree, an MBA and a doctorate in logistics at ENPC Ecole Nationale des Ponts et Chaussées, Paris. She enjoyed three years of business experience (Procter & Gamble) and a four-year research fellowship at the French National Institute for Transport Research before joining ESCP Europe as a professor.

Dr Mônica Cavalcanti Sá de Abreu is Associate Professor for Business Management and Logistics at the Federal University of Ceará, Brazil. She holds a PhD in Industrial Engineering from the Federal University of Santa Catarina, Brazil and was a Visiting Researcher at the University of Cambridge, IfM, England. She has published in *Business Strategy and the Environment, Business Ethics: A European Review, Journal of Cleaner Production, International Journal of Human Resource Management, Journal of Environmental Management, Ocean and Coastal Management, Social Responsibility*

Journal, and *International Journal of Governance and Business Ethics*. Her research interests encompass corporate social responsibility, circular economy, industrial ecology, renewable energy, climate change policies and strategies.

Dr Amelia Clarke has been working on environment and sustainability issues since 1989, including as President of Sierra Club Canada. She holds a PhD in Management (Strategy) from McGill University. Dr Clarke is now an Associate Professor in the School of Environment, Enterprise and Development (SEED) at the University of Waterloo, where she is also Director of the Master of Environment and Business (MEB) executive-education programme. Her main research focuses are related to strategies for sustainable development, and include a half-million dollar team project on structuring cross-sector social partnerships to more effectively achieve local sustainability goals and other desired partner outcomes. Dr Clarke's work has been published in *Journal of Business Ethics, Business & Society, Organizations & Environment, Public Administration Review, Journal of Cleaner Production, Futures, Sustainable Development*, along with other journals, book chapters and practitioner reports. She is on the editorial board of the *Academy of Management Learning and Education (AMLE) Journal*.

Bénédicte Deryckere has more than 20 years of professional experience in IT and management consulting. She has led large business process re-engineering and IT projects for many multinational companies. She is currently a doctoral student at Grenoble Ecole de Management. Her research focuses on sensemaking, strategic management, and sustainability.

Dr Hervé Dumez is the director of the Interdisciplinary Institute for Innovation (i3-CNRS, Paris, France) and of the Research Center in Management Studies of the École polytechnique (i3-CRG). He studied at the École Normale Supérieure and at la Sorbonne (PhD). He has been visiting professor at MIT and at the Stockholm School of Economics (SCORE). He is associate editor of the *European Management Review*. His research programme is about strategy, market structures and regulation policies. He has published more than 60 papers (*Academy of Management Review, Journal of Business Ethics, European Management Review, M@n@gement*) and ten books (among them: *Comprehensive Research: A Methodological and Epistemological Introduction to Qualitative Research*, Copenhagen Business School Press, 2016).

Dr Mingyue Fan is Associate Professor of Management at Jiangsu University, China. Dr Fan received her PhD from Jiangsu University. She has published in *Science and Technology Management Research* (Chinese version), *Statistics & Decision* (Chinese version), *Technoeconomics & Management Research* (Chinese version) and *Information Science* (Chinese version). Her books include *Typical Case Study of Small and Medium Enterprise Growth Patterns* (Tianjin Academy of Social Sciences Publishing, 2015; Chinese version; with Xianyu Tian), and *Data Quality Control of Internet Survey* (Shanghai Joint Publishing Press, 2014; Chinese version; with Yin Feng). Her research interests include SME development, entrepreneurship and information quality.

Devon Fernandes is a Community Psychology master's student at Wilfrid Laurier University. His research interests include the intersection of sustainability and business, the circular economy, and organizational behaviour.

Dr Timothy Galpin is Senior Lecturer at the Saïd Business School, University of Oxford. He has published in Journal of Business Strategy, Corporate Governance, Journal of Corporate Citizenship, People & Strategy, and World Journal of Entrepreneurship, Management and Sustainable Development, among others. His books include Leading the Sustainable Organization (Routledge, 2012; with J. Lee Whittington and Greg Bell), The Complete Guide to Mergers & Acquisitions (John Wiley, 2014, 2007 and 2000; with Mark Herndon), Making Strategy Work (Jossey-Bass, 1997), and The Human Side of Change (Jossey-Bass, 1996). His research, consulting, and speaking interests are in strategy formulation and execution, mergers and acquisitions, organizational culture change, and leading sustainable organizations.

Dr Caroline Gauthier is Professor of Strategic Management at Grenoble Ecole de Management and Adjunct Professor at University Aix-Marseille (France). Dr Gauthier received her PhD from Toulouse School of Economics (France) and University College of London (UK). She has published in *Ecological Economics, Journal of Business Ethics, Journal of Cleaner Production, Organization & Environment*, among others. Her research interests include strategy for sustainability, sustainable marketing, and corporate social responsibility. She does consultancy for different institutions (EU, OECE, ONU, Ministries) on energy transition, environmental policy and innovation strategy.

Dr Bradley Googins is Executive Director Emeritus of the Boston College Center for Corporate Citizenship and Professor Emeritus in Organizational Studies at the BC's Carroll School of Management. He is co-author of *Beyond Good Company* and currently leads E4Impact to educate entrepreneurs throughout Africa. Googins holds a PhD in Social Policy from The Heller Graduate School at Brandeis University; an MSW from Boston College and a BA in philosophy and sociology from Boston College.

Merriam Haffar is a 2015 Vanier SSHRC Scholar, and a fourth-year PhD candidate at Ryerson University's Environmental Applied Science and Management Program. Her other research interests include context-based corporate sustainability reporting, and environmental resilience. Before joining her PhD programme, Merriam worked in the environmental testing industry for several years as an assistant branch manager and lead analyst.

Julia Hebard teaches social entrepreneurship and managerial finance at Colorado Mountain College. She also works as Advertising Director for the Steamboat Today, a subsidiary of Colorado Mountain News Media. Through this role she works with local businesses and organizations to develop comprehensive and engaging marketing solutions that help grow these organizations to their full potential. She is passionate about sustainable enterprise, the environment and working with businesses to create a positive change in the communities in which they operate. Additionally, Julia volunteers with numerous organizations throughout the Steamboat Springs, Colorado area. She holds an MBA in social and sustainable enterprise from Colorado State University.

Dr Tessa Hebb is a senior research fellow and past director of the Carleton Centre for Community Innovation, Carleton University, Canada. Her research focuses on responsible investment, impact investment, and impact measurement. This work has been funded by the Social Sciences and Humanities Research Council, Government of Canada. Dr Hebb received her PhD from the University of Oxford. Dr Hebb is the past chair of the steering committee of the UN-backed Principles for Responsible Investment (PRI) Academic Network and recently co-chaired the Province of Ontario's Social Enterprise Impact Measurement Task Force. She was a board member of the Responsible Investment Association (Canada) from 2011 to 2017. Dr Hebb is a frequent guest speaker on impact investment, responsible investment and impact measurement issues. She has published many books and articles on responsible investing and impact investing including the volumes *The Routledge Handbook of Responsible Investment*; *SRI in the 21st Century: Does it Make a Difference to Society?*; *Working Capital: The Power of Labor's Pensions*; *No Small Change: Pension Fund Corporate Engagement*; and *The Next Generation of Responsible Investing*.

Dr Andreas Hoepner is Professor of Operational Risk, Banking & Finance at the Smurfit Graduate Business School of University College Dublin, where he directs the MSc in Energy and Environmental Finance. Before joining UCD in June 2017, he was Associate Professor of Finance at the ICMA Centre of Henley Business School. Professor Hoepner has supervised eight PhD students to completion who all received instant placements at the ICMA Centre, MSCI, Sociovestix Labs (3x), University of Hamburg, and University of Oxford (2x).

Dr Johan Jansson is Associate Professor at Umeå School of Business and Economics at Umeå University and at Lund University School of Economics and Management, Sweden. He is also Adjunct Professor at University of Cape Town, School of Management Studies, South Africa. He has published in journals such as *Journal of Cleaner Production*, *Journal of Consumer Marketing*, *Business Strategy and the Environment*, *Journal of Consumer Behaviour*, *Energy Policy*, *Journal of Financial Services Marketing*, and *Sustainable Development*. His research interests include sustainable consumption and pro-environmental consumer behaviour, corporate social responsibility, sustainable transportation, eco-innovation adoption and marketing ethics. He has been awarded Umeå University's Excellent Teacher Qualification and has developed and taught courses widely at all levels in marketing ethics and sustainability.

Lena Judick is an external PhD student at the School of Business, Economics and Social Science of University of Hamburg and works as a consultant in the field of renewable energy, climate change and sustainability. She has published a guideline on how action on climate change can create added value for municipalities. Her research interests include corporate inaction on climate change, greenwashing and climate change denial.

Jennifer Liebetrau is a marketing instructor for the University of Lethbridge, Canada. She has a Master of Science degree in Management from the University of Lethbridge and a Master of Arts degree in International Business and Economics from the University of Applied Sciences Schmalkalden, Germany. Prior to earning her master's degrees, she worked as a marketing assistant for a mid-sized tool manufacturer in Germany with a focus on the design and execution of the company's communications and advertising plans, as well as PR and sponsoring activities. Her research focuses on company–charity alliances and their influence on consumer behaviour within cause-related marketing.

Dr Adriane MacDonald is Assistant Professor in the Faculty of Management at the University of Lethbridge, Canada. Dr MacDonald received her PhD from University of Waterloo. Her work has appeared in *Business & Society*, *Annual Review of Social Partnerships*, book chapters and practitioner reports. To date, Dr MacDonald's research emphasis has been on outcomes of multi-stakeholder partnerships in the context of community sustainability plan implementation. Her emerging research agenda is focused on tools that develop cross-sector collaboration skillsets and competencies. She is an associate editor for the *Annual Review of Social Partnerships*. Outside academia, she has worked as a consultant for a design firm and as a business analyst for the government of Canada.

Dr Joel Marcus is Assistant Professor of Management at York University's School of Administrative Studies. His research explores how individual differences, such as values and personality traits, impact one's propensity to engage in sustainability actions across the economic, social, and environmental domains. His work has appeared in *Business & Society*, *Entrepreneurship Theory & Practice*, and *Journal of Business Ethics*, among others.

Dr Will McConnell is Associate Professor of Interdisciplinary Studies at Woodbury University's College of Liberal Arts. Dr McConnell received his PhD from McMaster University, Hamilton, Ontario. He has published in *Handbook of Engaged Sustainability*, *Spirituality and Sustainability: New Horizons and Exemplary Approaches* and *European Legacy*, among others. His research interests include corporate social responsibility, marine protected areas and the science of global warming in ocean-based research, and community-based social marketing in environmental sustainability applications.

Philip Mirvis is an organizational psychologist and an advisor to companies and NGOs on five continents. He has written 12 books including, in the arena of sustainability, *Beyond Good Company: Next Generation Corporate Citizenship* and *Organizing for Sustainability: Building Networks and Partnerships*. Mirvis has a BA from Yale University and a PhD from the University of Michigan.

Dr Prashant Mishra is presently Professor of Marketing at IIM Calcutta. Professor Prashant has published recently in the *Journal of Business Ethics*, *Journal of Strategic Marketing*, *Marketing Intelligence and Planning*, and the *Journal of Media Business Studies*. His research interests include consumer psychology, digital marketing and sustainability and CSR. He serves as a reviewer for many reputed journals.

Frida Modig has a master's degree in business administration with a focus on service management from Umeå School of Business and Economics at Umeå University, Sweden. She has coordinated several research projects and published in *Business Strategy and the Environment*. She is currently working as brand manager at Haugen-Gruppen in Sweden.

Dr Jonas Nilsson is Associate Professor in Marketing at the School of Business, Economics and Law at the University of Gothenburg. His research interests include sustainable consumption, financial services and consumer behaviour and he has published his work in journals such as the *Journal of Business Ethics*, *European Journal of Marketing*, *Business Strategy and the Environment*, among others. He also serves on the editorial board of the *Journal of Financial Services Marketing*.

Eduardo Ordonez-Ponce is a PhD candidate in sustainability at the University of Waterloo. Eduardo has a bachelor's and a master's degree in engineering, and is focusing his PhD dissertation on organizations partnering for sustainability. He has extensive industry experience in sustainability, CSR, and environmental projects in developed and developing countries. He has academic and non-academic publications. His research interests include organizations and society, business ethics, corporate social responsibility, sustainability and strategic partnerships.

Dr Tatiana Rodionova is Lecturer in Finance and Deputy Director of the Sustainable Business Initiative at the University of Edinburgh Business School. Dr Rodionova received her PhD from the University of Edinburgh. Her main research interests are in the areas of corporate social responsibility, sustainability, responsible investment, governance, investment management and equity valuation. In 2015 her research (with Bill Rees) received the Best Paper award from *Corporate Governance: An International Review*. Before entering academia, she worked as an underwriter in cargo and marine insurance.

Dr Mary Runté is the founding director of Social Responsibility and Nonprofit Management, incumbent Chair of the Policy and Strategy Area and an Associate Professor in the Faculty of Management at the University of Lethbridge, Canada. Her research focuses on cross-sectoral organizational design and the intersection of work and non-work realms. She has been published in numerous academic journals, including the *Journal of Business Ethics, Journal of Business Research, Human Relations* and the *Journal of Nonprofit and Public Sector Marketing*. She was the founding chair of the Social Responsibility Division for the Administrative Sciences Association of Canada and has been recognized for her work as a mentor of young women as a YWCA Woman of Distinction.

Imelda Sánchez was born in Cordoba, Veracruz, Mexico, in 1991. She received a bachelor's degree in International Business from the Monterrey Institute of Technology and Higher Education, in Mexico 2013. In 2011, she was selected nationwide with nine other university students to receive an award for high academic achievements from Scotiabank, resulting in a one-semester exchange programme to the University of British Columbia (UBC). In 2013 she was awarded a Mitacs Global Scholarship, at Carleton Centre for Community Innovation, Carleton University working Responsible Investment topics. She began working for the multinational Unilever in Mexico City in February 2014.

Dr Runa Sarkar is Professor with the Economics Group at IIM Calcutta. She is an economist with a chemical and environmental engineering background, whose interests revolve around the domains of sustainable development, corporate environmental strategy and social impacts of ICT use in development. She is the chairperson of CTran Consulting Services, a leading climate change consulting business in India and serves on the board of the Basix Social Enterprise Group and Basix Consulting and Technology Services. She has published widely and her recent books include *Another Development: Participation, Empowerment and Well-being* (with Anup Sinha), *Environment, Business, Institutions, and Essays on Management and Sustainability: Emerging Perspectives* (edited with Annapurna Shaw).

Dr Anselm Schneider is Assistant Professor in Organization Theory at the Stockholm Business School. He holds a master's degree in economics (Freie Universität Berlin) and a PhD in business administration (University of Zurich). His research interests lie in the interface of organization theory, corporate social responsibility, sustainable development, and global governance. His work appeared in journals such as *Journal of Management Studies, Business and Society, Journal of Business Ethics*, and *Business Strategy and the Environment*, as well as in several edited volumes.

Dr Cory Searcy is Professor of Industrial Engineering and Environmental Applied Science & Management at Ryerson University. He currently serves as the Associate Dean, Programs in Ryerson's Yeates School of Graduate Studies. He has published in the *Journal of Business Ethics, Journal of Cleaner Production*, and *International Journal of Production Economics*, among others. His research interests include corporate sustainability reporting and sustainable supply chain management. He is currently a section editor at the *Journal of Business Ethics* and an associate editor at *Engineering Management Journal*.

Dr Natalia Semenova is Senior Lecturer in Accounting in the School of Business and Economics at the Linnaeus University in Sweden. Dr Semenova holds a doctorate in Accounting from the Åbo Akademi University in Finland. She has published in international journals, such as *Journal of Business Ethics, Journal of Applied Accounting Research, Sustainable Development, Finnish Journal of Business Economics* and *Journal of Modern Accounting and Auditing*. She has taken part in the Sustainable Investment Research Platform international research programme founded by Mistra, the Foundation for Strategic Environmental Research, in Sweden. She has been working in the area of sustainability/ESG since 2006.

Dr Bhaskar Sinha is a faculty in the ecosystem and environment management and the chairperson of the centre for climate change studies at the Indian Institute of Forest Management. Dr Sinha obtained his master's, MPhil and PhD degrees from the School of Environmental Science, JNU, New Delhi. He has more than 15 years of experience in interdisciplinary research, consultancy and teaching on issues related to integrated natural resource management, conservation and livelihood, the interface between social and ecological issues, climate change, adaptation and mitigation, CSR, sustainability and rural development. He has authored more than 25 papers in national and international journals, and three books. Dr Sinha has completed more than 20 research/consultancy projects and training programmes with the support of national and international agencies including UNDP, GIZ, MoRD, MoEFCC, DBT, GoMP, World Bank–WWF Alliance, Forest PLUS on various contemporary issues related to climate change adaptation, ecological sustainability and integrated natural resource management. Dr Sinha is actively involved in teaching various courses related to climate change and ecosystem management to the students at PG, MPhil and doctoral level.

Gabriella Hed Vall has a master's degree in Business Administration with a focus on service management from Umeå School of Business and Economics at Umeå University, Sweden. She has successfully founded and operated her own service firm for more than ten years and is currently also the event manager at Umeå municipality. She has published in *Business Strategy and the Environment*.

Ram Nayan Yadava is a doctoral student (environmental management) at the Indian Institute of Forest Management (IIFM) Bhopal. Before joining IIFM, he has worked as junior research fellow in environmental science division of CSIR-National Botanical Research Institute, Lucknow. He is working in the area of CSR and sustainability specifically focused on the nexus-based approach for sustainable development through energy-poverty-climate change vulnerability integration. He is the author of several research articles and book chapters in his research areas.

Foreword and acknowledgements

The purpose of this research anthology is to bring together important research contributions that demonstrate different approaches to business strategies for sustainability. The underlying premise is that all sustainability and sustainable development – be it economic, social, psychological, cultural or ecological – is underpinned by ecological sustainability, which provides the essential life support systems on which humans and all other species depend. From a position of ecological sustainability, we are better able to develop both integrated and separate strategies for economic, social, psychological, and cultural sustainability, as well as climate change and resilience to different settings, and thereby identify and help solve some of the most difficult challenges facing modern human society (Borland, Ambrosini, Lindgreen and Vanhamme, 2015; Borland and Lindgreen, 2013; Howard-Grenville, Buckle, Hoskins and George, 2014; Kelley and Nahser, 2014).

Ecological sustainability refers to a capacity for continuance in the long-term future, achieved by living within the constraints and limits of the biophysical world (Porritt, 2007). It represents a goal, endpoint, or desired destination for the human species, as much as for any other species, and it can be explained, defined and measured scientifically. Sustainable development instead refers to the process for moving toward sustainability; it implies trying to achieve sustainability but often seems poorly defined and difficult to measure. To achieve a sustainable human future, sustainable development generally entails economic, social and cultural factors, as well as environmental ones, though Porritt (2007) considers those latter elements secondary goals, because all else is conditional on living sustainably within the Earth's systems and limits. The pursuit of ecological sustainability thus is non-negotiable (Porritt, 2007; see also Mort, 2010), and attitudes, values and behaviours toward it need to evolve rapidly (Van der Werff, Steg, and Keizer, 2013).

The urgency of the ecological sustainability predicament also drives the search for new ways of living and conducting business (Hart, 1997; Mort, 2010). Yet many corporate initiatives toward perceived sustainability are simply efficiency drives or competitive moves (Unruh and Ettenson, 2010) – falling far short of actual strategies for ecological sustainability. To suggest true ecological sustainability strategies, we adopt an interdisciplinary or transdisciplinary (Gladwin, Kennelly, and Krause, 1995) approach and seek to discern what business strategies might look like if they were underpinned by environmental and ecological science. In particular, an ecocentric epistemology offers an alternative cultural and mental framework that focuses on the whole system or ecosystem and the balance of all species and elements (i.e. rocks, water and gases of the atmosphere). Humans move from their cosmologically central and egocentric position, in which the whole of nature exists only for their exploitation with no intrinsic value (Gladwin et al., 1995; Kilbourne, 1998, Kilbourne, Beckman, and Thelen, 2002; Purser, Park, and Montuori, 1995), to a more balanced site in the larger system that demands greater appreciation of and respect for other species and planetary resources (Borland et al., 2015; Borland and Lindgreen, 2013; Du Nann Winter and Koger, 2010; Porritt, 2007; Shrivastava, 1995; Whiteman, Walker, and Perego, 2013).

A systematic, interdisciplinary examination of business strategies for sustainability therefore is necessary, to establish an essential definition and up-to-date picture of the field. The 23 chapters in this anthology reflect five main topic parts:

- Delineating sustainability challenges and visions.
- Contradiction, integration and transformation of business and sustainability logics.
- Innovating and developing strategic capabilities for sustainability.
- Assessing and valuing sustainability.
- Toward multi-level engagement and collaboration.

Part I: Delineating sustainability challenges and visions

To start, Carl Brønn and Peggy Simcic Brønn call 'Sustainability: A wicked problem needing new perspectives'. These authors recognize that sustainability demands are deeply challenging and ongoing issues for managers who face highly complex and ill-defined conditions, such that historical and traditional business practices and ways of thinking are reactive at best and obsolete at worst. To succeed, managers and their organizations must develop skills and methods that are compatible with a sustainable business environment, so the sustainability challenge constitutes a 'wicked problem' that requires fundamentally different engagement approaches. This chapter suggests that for managers to adopt a complex adaptive systems perspective, they must focus more on interactions and higher system-level characteristics, which will leads to a learning-oriented, rather than solution-oriented, approach to effective engagement with sustainability challenges.

Next, in 'Addressing the global crisis of economic growth: An unavoidable ethical challenge,' Frederick Bird examines the modern global crisis associated with economic growth as an ethical challenge. That is, current economic growth threatens the Earth and aggravates inequalities, yet a lack of economic growth would threaten the nearly one-third of the human population living in poverty and potentially lead to economic instability in industrialized countries. To address this crisis, the author recommends moving beyond traditional notions of no growth, slow growth, or continued economic growth; instead, an alternative way to think about growth can establish several basic principles for fostering responsible forms. In this chapter, economic growth is defined in terms of the development and protection of generative economic assets, with an analytical distinction between the production and consumption of economic goods and services. Across public policies, firm activities, and household practices, this chapter calls for dedication to consuming sustainably, producing productively, and collaborating globally.

China's emerging eco-civilization may be a promising response to the world's environmental crisis, so in a chapter entitled 'Business and the emerging ecological civilization,' Frank Birkin and Mingyue Fan consider the broad sweep of civilization change relative to global and business responses to sustainability. They apply a Foucauldian epistemic analysis as a theoretical foundation, which helps account for how China's cultural background has supported steps toward an ecological civilization. A case study of Tianjin China Bio-Technology Group Co. Ltd. reveals how one Chinese company has managed and presented itself in an emerging eco-civilization. This evidence suggests the benefits of a business orientation dedicated specifically to the needs of an ecological civilization.

The final chapter in Part I 'Creating theory for business strategies for sustainability and climate change: transitional and transformational strategies and ecocentric dynamic capabilities' by Helen Borland, Adam Lindgreen, Véronique Ambrosini, and Joëlle Vanhamme reflects on the growing need to introduce new theory to the sustainability discipline. The authors argue that underpinning thinking needs to stem from knowledge of the physical sciences and, in particular, knowledge and understanding of sustainability, climate change and resilience. They identify business strategies that incorporate both ecocentrism and ecological sustainability before theorizing at the intersection of strategic management and strategies for ecological sustainability. With such an analysis at the intersection, the authors suggest, we can seek to transform the core of dynamic capabilities literature.

Part II: Contradiction, integration, and transformation of business and sustainability logics

Elisabeth Albertini starts the second part by reviewing 'What we know about business strategies for sustainability: An inductive typology of the research'. In the past decade, organizations increasingly have used a business case for corporate sustainability. Yet an unequivocal, established definition of business models for sustainability has remained missing, nor is there consensus about the indicators to use to measure the financial consequences of business models for sustainability. Therefore, this chapter offers an inductive typology of research pertaining to business strategies for sustainability that relies on a computerized content analysis of 58 articles published between 1995 and 2015. Four major research themes emerge: the relationship between corporate sustainability and financial performance, corporate sustainability under stakeholder engagement and institutional pressures, the strategic management of corporate sustainability, and increasing awareness of sustainable development issues. Thus the business case for corporate sustainability has evolved, from quantitative toward more managerial dimensions, such that sustainability performance has been integrated into corporate business strategies.

With the next chapter, Lena Judick seeks to identify the key reasons for corporate inaction on climate change. That is, despite extensive corporate activity related to climate change, most companies fail to reduce their greenhouse gas emissions or implement necessary measures, and prior literature has not conclusively identified the reasons for such corporate inaction or failure when it comes to climate change, whether at individual, organizational, or institutional levels. Therefore, 'Corporate inaction on climate change: A systematic literature review' provides an overview of 27 articles from business, sustainability, or management journals that analyse the reasons companies might remain inert rather than engage in climate change mitigation efforts. Beyond establishing the complexity of the reasons for corporate inaction, this chapter offers an outlook for further research.

Next, Prashant Mishra and Runa Sarkar examine the current state of customer-centric sustainability practices in firms operating in India in their article, 'Is customer centric sustainability an element of marketing strategy? Evidence from Indian firms '. Drawing on qualitative insights from in-depth interviews with senior executives, these authors determine that the amorphous, difficult-to-quantify benefits of sustainability prompt firms to take an easier, product-centric approach to integrating sustainability initiatives and marketing them, rather than a customer-centric approach. The respondents also acknowledge that marketing could revise its current focus: rather than managing customer relationships (and other stakeholders), marketing should manage the broader set of marketplace (economic, environmental, social) issues, such that it can cater to the needs and wants of multiple stakeholders.

In 'The importance of market and entrepreneurial strategic orientations among companies committed to sustainability values and practices,' Jonas Nilsson, Johan Jansson, Gabriella Hed Vall and Frida Modig argue that understanding why certain companies adopt sustainability initiatives, but others do not, is critical. To determine how sustainability links to core business strategies and concepts, this chapter focuses on corporate strategic orientations, adherence to an ecological worldview, and different measures of sustainability performance. The proposed analytical framework classifies companies according to their level of market and entrepreneurial orientation. In turn, this chapter reveals that companies that score high on these orientations integrate sustainability more closely into their corporate strategies and culture. That is, market and entrepreneurial strategic orientations are highly relevant for companies committed to sustainability values and practices.

The final chapter in this part introduces 'The emerging paradigm of enviro-ethical dialogism, corporate social responsibility, and consumer dynamism '. Will McConnell argues that increasing scrutiny devoted to accountability and transparency has shifted the role of ethics in relation to profitability, production and social issues. Therefore, this chapter offers an initial discussion of enviro-ethical dialogism, corporate social responsibility, and consumer dynamism that acknowledges the difficulty of environmental sustainability discourses, due to their inter- and transdisciplinary nature, lack of established metrics, persistent language games, and insufficient standards for establishing pollution baselines. For example, reduced pollution production rates are presented as 'good' for the environment, rather requiring the elimination of damage itself, in the current consumer enviro-ethos. With more nuanced, emergent models of corporate social and environmental responsibility, this chapter calls for a revised approach, with metrics that include comprehensive structures to enable consumers to make informed, responsible choices.

Part III: Innovating and developing strategic capabilities for sustainability

With an evidence-based framework, Timothy Galpin and Julia Hebard illustrate how external drivers can demand a strategic management approach to sustainability, such that firms can respond to external drivers by incorporating sustainability into their internal strategic management components. Aligned content across a firm's internal strategic management components also helps create consistency in its sustainability communication to various stakeholders. Managers often view the fluidity and diversity of external sustainability drivers with concern, but the framework proposed in 'Strategic management and sustainability' provides with an adaptive, context-related approach that can be tailored to the constantly changing sets of external sustainability drivers.

In 'Corporate social innovation: Top-down, bottom-up, inside-out, and outside-in,' Philip Mirvis and Bradley Googins explore various social innovations, drawing from a field study of more than 70 companies worldwide, many of which are known for their corporate social responsibility. These companies produce social innovations in different ways, from top-down to bottom-up and from inside-out to outside-in, and each space entails certain pitfalls. In turn, this chapter proposes four keys to successful corporate social innovation: compelling social purpose for innovating, an appropriate innovation process, strong partnering relationships, and clear definitions and expectations of the innovative payoff, in both commercial and societal terms.

With a dynamic capabilities lens, Aurélien Acquier, Valentina Carbone, and Pilar Acosta explore 'Dynamic capabilities for sustainable innovation: What are they?' They introduce the novel concept of dynamic capabilities for sustainable innovation (DCSI), defined as 'a set of capabilities that an organization can employ, in line with its governance structure, to purposefully create, extend or modify its resource base and its business ecosystem in order to address sustainable innovation issues '. The results of a study of 34 European firms reveal two DCSI types: ecosystem orchestration capabilities refer to an ability to guide how sustainable innovation ecosystems evolve, whereas organizational orchestration capabilities refer to an ability to identify appropriate governance and organizational structures, according to the degree of disruption caused by the sustainable innovations.

With a focus on 'Exploring challenges to developing corporate climate change strategies in Brazil,' Mônica Cavalcanti Sá de Abreu argues that when they seek to establish a particular strategy, managers respond to both external forces and internal capabilities. Climate change creates diverse risks and opportunities, perceived differently by different companies, which then determine the practices those firms adopt and consider appropriate. Four prominent strategies emerge: minimalist approach, regulation shaper, pressure manager, or greenhouse gas emission avoiders. Considering the magnitude of the risk associated with climate change, the evolution of climate change strategies by companies necessarily will suffer limitations until global and local regulatory systems are put in place.

With their literature review, Bénédicte Deryckere and Caroline Gauthier summarize recent literature pertaining to sustainable development and corporate social responsibility. Specifically, 'Sustainability: From conceptualization to operationalization: A literature review' highlights the emergence of business models as pertinent analysis units in research pertaining to how firms apply sustainability in their business models to achieve economic, social and environmental value. They also reveal that most research centres on (1) motivations for sustainable development as a managerial imperative, (2) conceptualizing the meaning of a sustainable organization, and (3) defining implications for firms' financial performance, without discussing the operationalization of sustainability within or across firms.

Part IV: Assessing and valuing sustainability

Anselm Schneider starts this section by acknowledging that corporate sustainability is a complex concept that challenges managers who seek to assess and thereby improve their firms' sustainability. In 'Unbundling corporate sustainability management and assessment,' the author seeks to disentangle different features of corporate sustainability (i.e. governance, values and identity), then analyses their interrelations to identify pre-conditions for corporate sustainability performance and thereby improve on the current methods used to assess and manage corporate sustainability.

In 'The value relevance of carbon disclosure strategies: A review of accounting research,' Natalia Semenova surveys accounting studies from 23 journals, related to the valuation implications of carbon disclosures, whether mandated by government regulations (e.g. emission trading schemes) or voluntary. Carbon performance can facilitate investor assessments of a company's financial risks and opportunities. That is, accounting literature provides important empirical evidence of the valuation impact of carbon disclosures, which communicate both strategy- and performance-related information that investors can use.

Next, 'Exploring the validity of corporate climate reporting under the global reporting initiative, carbon disclosure project, and greenhouse gas protocol' provides an examination of the validity of the three most commonly used voluntary reporting frameworks: the Global Reporting Initiative's (GRI) G4 guidelines, the Carbon Disclosure Project (CDP), and the Greenhouse Gas Protocol (GHG Protocol). Merriam Haffar and Cory Searcy define reporting validity as the degree to which disclosures accurately reflect a company's contribution to wider climate processes and thresholds. This study specifies the extent to which the three frameworks allow for valid climate disclosures, in terms of their comprehensiveness and connection to the company's sustainability context.

With two studies, Bhaskar Sinha and Ram Nayan Yadava propose 'Promoting sustainability through corporate social responsibility: An Indian perspective'. The first study identifies the impacts of different CSR activities by the Lupin Human Welfare Research Foundation (LHWRF) when it comes to improving the socio-economic conditions of the rural poor in the Vidisha and Raisen district, Madhya Pradesh, India. The second study compares sustainability reports by five Indian companies, according to the Global Reporting Initiative guidelines. Overall, reporting on social and environmental indicators is less comprehensive than reporting on economic dimensions. Because the CSR/sustainability programs have significant impacts on their beneficiaries, in terms of improving their socio-economic condition, synergies with other, related government initiatives offer promise for enhancing their effectiveness.

By examining successful environmental cause marketing campaigns – that is, winners of the Engage for Good's Halo Award from 2003 to 2015 – Debra Z. Basil, Mary Runté and Jennefier Liebetrau develop a framework for assessing them. Twenty-six winning or second-place campaigns provide the sample for 'Environmental cause marketing'. The assessment of each alliance involves the fit between the company and the cause, the form of the alliance, the trigger of a donation, and the benefits for the company and the cause. Most successful alliances feature good fitting partnerships, based on a natural fit. The alliance forms vary, though transactional and sponsorship formats are prominent. These complex campaigns also rely on multiple points of consumer contact, and various triggers lead to donations, often when linked to product purchases. The companies report benefitting from the positive publicity and often cite increased sales and market share benefits too; for the causes, the key benefits include donations, positive behaviours, media exposure, and new volunteers or members.

Part V: Towards multi-level engagement and collaboration

This final part begins with a comprehensive review of empirical research pertaining to individual-level sustainability issues. Joel Marcus and Devon Fernandes conduct a survey of articles published from 2005 to the present in 50 management and relevant niche journals, which identifies 65 pertinent studies. In addition to documenting relevant research and analysing key trends and themes, 'Motivating employees for sustainability: A comprehensive review of micro-behavioural research (2005-present)' provides an assessment of the current state of knowledge and its insights for sustainable management practice, as well as the gaps that suggest research opportunities. This review thus can be a reference for micro-level sustainability scholars and managers interested in encouraging sustainability among employees.

According to Tessa Hebb, Andreas Hoepner, Tatiana Rodionova and Imelda Sánchez, in their article 'Power and shareholder saliency,' shareholder activism affects company managers' attention to environmental, social and governance standards in their corporate decisions. Yet various shareholders do not receive the same levels of attention, and certain shareholder attributes appear necessary to attract managerial attention. Legitimacy is a key attribute associated with shareholder saliency; the quantitative analysis in this chapter also suggests that power is critical. Furthermore, in most cases marked by both shareholder engagement and one or more shareholder resolutions, a minority resolution precedes engagement and may be required to gain attention. Thus shareholder power appears to be a key determinant of shareholder saliency.

Julie Bastianutti and Hervé Dumez focus their analysis on industries that powerfully confront issues pertaining to CO_2 emissions and pollution in 'Environmental sustainability for industry legitimacy and competitiveness: The case of CSR collective strategies in the cement industry'. In such settings, non-market issues might be addressed by collective strategies that foster cooperation at various levels (industry, intra-industry, inter-industry). At the industry level, the view of CSR strategies emerges as an *ars combinatoria*, combining both intentions and forms. A case study in the cement industry reveals how perceptions of environmental sustainability have changed in recent decades. The diverse collective strategies provide a range of possibilities for enhancing industry legitimacy, with differential advantages. By collaborating, firms can reduce costs and transform threats into opportunities; accordingly, policy makers should be proactive in cooperating with businesses to come up with solutions and incentivizing collective designs.

Finally, 'Implementing community sustainability strategies through cross-sector partnerships: Value creation for and by businesses' suggests dealing with sustainability challenges by leveraging cross-sector partnership, such as when local governments partner with various stakeholders, including businesses, to formulate and implement community sustainability plans. Engagement at the community level enables these partnerships to assess actual sustainability progress, within ecosystem boundaries. Businesses also engage for reasons other than achieving sustainability goals; they seek learning, networking, reputation, and legitimacy opportunities, as well as improved relations with the community, channels to market their offerings, and greater financial performance. In this chapter, Amelia Clarke, Adriane MacDonald and Eduardo Ordonez-Ponce provide background information about community sustainability plans and cross-sector social partnerships, as well as the roles that businesses play to achieve community-wide sustainability visions. In particular, great value can be created by and for businesses that engage in community sustainability strategies.

Closing remarks

We extend a special thanks to Routledge and its staff, who have been most helpful throughout this entire process. Equally, we warmly thank all of the authors who submitted their manuscripts for consideration for this book. They have exhibited the desire to share their knowledge and experience with the book's readers – and a willingness to put forward their views for possible challenge by their peers. We also thank the reviewers, who provided excellent, independent and incisive consideration of the anonymous submissions.

We hope that this anthology stimulates and contributes to the ongoing debate surrounding business strategies for sustainability. The chapters in this anthology should help fill some knowledge gaps, while also stimulating further thought and action pertaining to the multiple aspects that surround business strategies for sustainability.

Helen Borland, PhD
Birmingham, England

Adam Lindgreen, PhD
Copenhagen, Denmark, and Pretoria, South Africa

François Maon, PhD
Lille, France

Joëlle Vanhamme, PhD
Lille, France

Véronique Ambrosini, PhD
Melbourne, Australia

Beatriz Palacios Florencio, PhD
Seville, Spain
1 July 2018

References

Borland, H., Ambrosini, V., Lindgreen, A. and Vanhamme, J. (2016). Building theory at the intersection of ecological sustainability and strategic management. *Journal of Business Ethics*, 135(2): 293–307.

Borland, H. and Lindgreen, A. (2013). Sustainability, epistemology, ecocentric business and marketing strategy: Ideology, reality and vision. *Journal of Business Ethics*, 117(1): 173–187.

Du Nann Winter, D. and Koger, S. (2010). *The Psychology of Environmental Problems*, 3rd edn. New York: Psychology Press, Taylor & Francis Group.

Gladwin, T., Kennelly, J., and Krause, T.S. (1995). Shifting paradigms for sustainable development: Implications for management theory and research. *Academy of Management Review*, 20(4): 874–907.

Hart, S. (1997). Beyond greening: Strategies for a sustainable world. *Harvard Business Review*, 75: 66–76.

Howard-Grenville, J., Buckle, S., Hoskins, B. and George, G. (2014). Climate change and management. *Academy of Management Journal*, 57: 615–623.

Kelley, S. and Nahser, R. (2014). Developing sustainable strategies: Foundations, method and pedagogy. *Journal of Business Ethics*, 123: 631–644.

Kilbourne, W.E. (1998). Green marketing: A theoretical perspective. *Journal of Marketing Management*, 14(6): 641–655.

Kilbourne, W.E., Beckman, S.C., and Thelen, E. (2002). The role of the DSP in environmental attitudes: A multinational examination, *Journal of Business Research*, 55(3): 193–204.

Mort, G.S. (2010). Sustainable business. *Journal of World Business*, 45(4): 323–325.

Porritt, J. (2007). *Capitalism as if the World Matters*. London: Earthscan.

Purser, R.E., Park, C., and Montuori, A. (1995). Limits to anthropocentrism: Toward an eco-centric organization paradigm? *Academy of Management Review*, 20(4): 1053–1089.

Shrivastava, P. (1995). The role of corporations in achieving ecological sustainability. *Academy of Management Review*, 20(4): 936–960.

Unruh, G. and Ettenson, R. (2010). Growing green: Three smart paths to developing sustainable products. *Harvard Business Review*, 95(3): 94–100.

Van der Werff, E., Steg, L. and Keizer, K. (2013). The value of environmental self-identity: The relationship between biospheric values, environmental self-identity and environmental preferences, intentions and behavior. *Journal of Environmental Psychology*, 34: 55–63.

Whiteman, G., Walker, B. and Perego, P. (2013). Planetary boundaries: Ecological foundations for corporate sustainability. *Journal of Management Studies*, 50(2): 207–336.

Part I

Delineating sustainability challenges and visions

1 Sustainability

A wicked problem needing new perspectives

Carl Brønn and Peggy Simcic Brønn

Introduction

The degree of structure inherent in a decision situation is often a consideration for classifying problem types. One common framework for distinguishing problem types uses the dichotomy 'well-defined' and 'ill-defined. At the extreme of ill-defined problems lies the special case of 'wicked problems'. For organizations, the issue of sustainability is clearly an ill-defined problem within the special case constituting wicked problems: it incorporates conflicting worldviews, it is dynamic, has unclear objectives, and it is important. It is a strategic problem where the central question is 'What shall we do?' rather than 'How shall we do it?'

Understanding sustainability as a wicked problem and the challenges this poses for business requires a broad perspective, one that the complex adaptive systems (CAS) view of organizations provides. The CAS perspective involves a different approach to leadership because it represents a significant shift in the mental models of both individual managers as well as the organization as a whole. It also has implications for leadership and communication. Leadership must be consistent with the constraints imposed by the dominant worldview employed in 'managing' the system. Thus, leaders must be aware of the importance of communication competencies when it comes to successful sustainability strategies.

Complexity and sustainability

The United Nations 2030 agenda for sustainable development outlines a plan of action for people, planet and prosperity. According to the agenda, 'the goals and targets will stimulate action over the next fifteen years in areas of critical importance for humanity and the planet'. From the perspective of business, 'sustainability' is a difficult concept. One common and traditional context for addressing sustainability in the corporate world is the so-called triple-bottom line concept constituting performance evaluations along three main dimensions: financial, environmental and social. The financial dimension may include costs, revenues and growth; the social dimension fair trade, donations or employee value; and the environmental dimension wastewater, resource use, consumption, etc. Firms are expected to manage the interaction of these dimensions in a manner that is sustainable, i.e. is good for people, the planet and prosperity, all within an ethical framework. Figure 1.1 schematically illustrates the managerial challenge that is presented by sustainability. In this figure, the triangle's vertices represent the sustainability dimensions. The three coils that connect the vertices to the

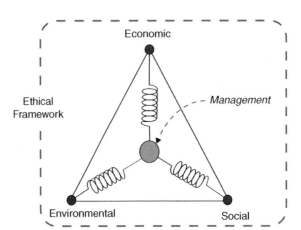

Figure 1.1 The sustainability triad and managerial dilemma.

circle are 'springs' that pull managerial attention towards each dimension. The result is an equilibrium position that depends on the relative strengths of the three springs. A relatively 'stiffer' spring will draw the circle towards that dimension, which results in a new equilibrium position with respect to the other dimensions.

Traditionally, the managerial 'equilibrium' point, i.e. balance, has been pulled much closer to the economic corner, with historically little attention paid to the environmental and social dimensions. While the three dimensions are naturally interrelated, the primary focus of business is on economic sustainability. Two elements, hyper-growth in production rates and the focus on short-term earnings, contribute to the dominance of the economic dimension. These measures capture the notion of scope and scale, respectively. Scope represents the variety of products as measured by stock keeping units (SKU). Scale can be indicated by firms' annual earnings.

The average urban New Yorker navigates through an economy estimated to contain 10^{10} SKUs (Beinhocker, 2007). This quantity represents an eightfold increase in the order of magnitude that has mostly occurred during the last 300 years. The scale of economic activity is equally impressive. Using 2011 data, Business Insider magazine (Trivitt, 2011) compared major corporations' annual revenues with leading countries' gross domestic products. In this ranking, Walmart Corporation's revenues were greater than the GDP of Norway, making Walmart the twenty-fifth largest 'country' in the world.

Naturally, there have been reactions to this growth. The effects of resource scarcity and increased pollution have resulted in the establishment of comprehensive environmental protection laws and institutions. Similarly, the consequences on the social dimension have resulted in calls for increased corporate social responsibility (CSR). Taken together, the interactions between these three dimensions define the scope of the sustainability challenge, and the daunting task facing managers.

Organizational objectives from the traditional economic perspective of maximizing shareholder wealth are clear: a manager's role is to identify and implement the course of action that most efficiently achieves the firm's goal. While there may be many alternative paths to achieving that goal, there is a clear primary stakeholder, the shareholders, and a limited set of action options available to accomplish the task. This problem may be complicated, but it is well structured, or 'tame'. When the objectives expand to include social issues such as outreach to local communities, donations to charities, codes of conduct, stakeholder inclusion, etc., managerial tasks become more difficult. There are several reasons for this. First, the lack of a clear understanding and consequently different interpretations of exactly what social issues entail stems partly from an increased set of stakeholders and their varied expectations. Most of these stakeholders do not share the shareholders' single objective of maximizing wealth. Second, the 'system' that management has direct control over, the firm, now needs to be understood with respect to how it interacts with other systems, for example the local community or other institutions. These new actors introduce additional objectives that may be in conflict with the shareholders' goals. Despite the increased complexity that social issues introduce, considerable progress has been achieved in adjusting business strategy to include it in managerial policymaking. The popularity and number of reputation measures is an indication that there is an emerging consensus on many important social performance measures.

The inclusion of the environmental dimension radically expands the complexity of the problem. While social issues in the form of CSR have the advantage of being conceptually closer to business activities, the traditional attitude towards the environmental dimension has been limited to seeing it only as a means to achieving an economic end. Extending the sustainability discussion beyond simply accessing resources to include ecological biosystems, with the attendant issues of biodiversity and the status of non-human stakeholders, introduces additional complications that are very distant from the managerial mindset and demands a view of sustainability within the special case constituting wicked problems.

Sustainability as a wicked problem

After almost 40 years, sustainability still defines itself by the statement of the UN World Commission on Environment and Development, Our Common Future (1987):

> *Sustainable development* is development that meets the needs of the present generation without compromising the ability of future generations to meet their own needs.

While this is an inspirational statement, the task of translating the spirit into strategy is not obvious. The absence of a more definitive expression of sustainable development has not been the fault of lack of effort. Writing in 2003, Parris and Kates (2003) reported that over 500 efforts had been devoted to developing quantitative indicators of sustainable development. They concluded that there were three primary reasons for the difficulty in achieving consensus: the ambiguity of the sustainability concept, the different purposes of measurement, and confusion over terminology and methods.

Given the nature of the sustainability challenge, these results are to be expected. This is because sustainability has all the characteristics of a class of problems called 'wicked problems', first categorized by Rittel and Webber in 1973. They identified ten criteria that are associated with this type of problem, all of which sustainability satisfies. See Table 1.2, which illustrates how the entire range of wicked problem characteristics affects sustainability. For example, a wicked problem is one that, among other things, has no definitive formulation. This is true for sustainability as multiple stakeholders have different values and objectives on the subject leading to different views/definitions. Wicked problems have no stopping rule; sustainability is dynamic and the time horizon is indeterminable. Every wicked problem is a symptom of another problem: issues around sustainability are consequences of nested and dynamic nature of the multiple systems involved.

Furthermore, there are no unique, clearly best solutions for wicked problems. For sustainability, the entire concept of a solution is meaningless and needs to be replaced with an appreciation that working towards a less unsustainable state (Ehrenfeld, 2005) is a continuous learning process.

Table 1.1 also clarifies that stakeholders play a prominent role in wicked problems. The effect of multiple stakeholders, all of whom are embedded in their own systems, is the tendency for everyone to be completely attentive to their own local needs, goals and actions. This intense focus, in conjunction with a simplified, event-oriented problem-solving perspective, tends to blind both external stakeholders and internal decision-makers to the unintended consequences of their actions. The result includes counterintuitive behaviours and policy resistance as other affected stakeholders attempt to meet their own objectives (Sterman, 2000).

Table 1.1 Characteristics of 'wicked problems' and their relationship to sustainability

Wicked problem characteristic (from Rittel and Webber, 1973)	Sustainability linkage
There is no definitive formulation of a wicked problem.	A consequence of multiple stakeholders with differing values and objectives.
Wicked problems have no stopping rule.	The context is dynamic, composed of many interacting systems operating under different constraints, including decision-making time horizons.
Solutions to wicked problems are not true-or-false, but good-or-bad.	Many of the needed choices are sensitive to the stakeholders' values and ethical perspectives.
There is no immediate and no ultimate test of a solution to a wicked problem.	A consequence of the process focus.
Every solution to a wicked problem is a 'one shot operation', because there is no opportunity to learn by trial-and-error, every attempt counts significantly.	A learning orientation is required, supported by an analysis paradigm based on systems thinking perspective.
Wicked problems do not have an enumerable set of potential solutions, nor is there a well-described set of permissible operations that may be incorporated into the plan.	The complex interactions of social, ecological and economic systems result in a high degree of causal ambiguity, making standard perspectives and approaches to decision-making less valid.
Every wicked problem is essentially unique.	This places weight on the ability to learn and to experiment because previous experiences generally do not extrapolate to new conditions.
Every wicked problem can be considered a symptom of another problem.	A consequence of the nested and dynamic nature of the many systems involved.
The existence of a discrepancy representing a wicked problem can be explained in numerous ways. The choice of explanation determines the nature of the problem's resolution.	Different stakeholders' mental models will selectively choose different information and process them in accordance with those mental models. There are no guarantees that these are co-oriented (see Newcomb, 1953).
The planner has no right to be wrong.	The consequences can be dramatic for one major stakeholder – people inhabiting the planet.

By itself, a wicked problem presents decision-makers with unique challenges that do not exist in well-structured or tame problems. Structured problems have stable parameters, clearly defined boundaries, relatively few and homogeneous stakeholders, and relatively well-understood causal relationships. These all lead to a clearly recognized optimal solution. Wicked problems, in contrast, have no clear stopping point, due in part, to the presence of multiple heterogeneous stakeholders who have different and/or conflicting viewpoints and interests.

Dealing with the wicked problem of sustainability

As noted previously, sustainability is a complex, wicked problem due to two primary influences: (1) the relationships between the economic, environmental and social dimensions shown in Figure 1.1; and (2) the presence of multiple heterogeneous stakeholders. The relationships between the economic, environmental and social dimensions are not simply complicated, as represented by the number of elements in each dimension; they are complex. Removing one dimension has enormous impacts on the others. As noted by Levin (1999), 'removing one such element destroys system behavior to an extent that goes well beyond what is embodied by the particular element that is removed' (p. 9).

The second influence is the presence of stakeholders (referred to as 'agents') in the systems that make up the three dimensions. In general, agents are individuals or entities that have the ability to collect and process information and adapt their behaviour in ways that enable them to maintain desired conditions (Beinhocker, 2007). For example, in the economic system are investors and customers, the social dimension comprises communities, activist groups or employees, and the environmental system comprises various kinds of ecosystems (marine, arctic, woodlands, etc.). Sustainability arises from the interactions of these numerous types of dynamic systems. The existence of these sometimes opposing 'agents' require organizations to be adaptive, to be able to change over time.

Simply put, these are all dynamic systems that, according to their internal logics, attempt to harmonize with their external environments. That is, they seek an equilibrium state. In the absence of competing external influences this state is generally achieved. Sustainability considerations arise when the success of one system comes at the expense of another one. Within each of the three dimensions this competition is resolved either by accommodation or by extinction of the weaker system. This is clearly seen in the economic dimension, where it is encouraged through market competition, and in the environmental sector with predator–prey dynamics. It is also found in the social sector with the rise and fall of philosophies and religions. However, when the whole system, comprising all three dimensions, is intimately connected and mutually reliant on each other, then accommodation is the only permissible outcome. As there are many subsystems under each dimension that are involved in this world, a single stable equilibrium does not exist. Consequently, the desired 'sustainability state' will continuously shift in response to the innumerable individual local actions taken within each dimension. The main driver is, of course, the overwhelming dominance of activities within the economic dimension and their effects on the whole.

A complex system, as described above, that can change its structure and behaviour over time in response to changes in its environment is a complex *adaptive* system (CAS). While many of the principles and theory of CAS developed in the physical and natural sciences, Eidelson (1997) provides a review of applying the CAS perspective in the behavioural and social sciences, of which management theory is a part.

Applying the CAS perspective to the wicked problem of sustainability suggests a way to engage with the multidimensional aspects of organizational performance. As noted by Clemente and Evans (2014), 'wicked problems take root and flourish precisely because they exist in a complex system that adapts to internal and external changes, and therefore wicked problems and complex adaptive systems are complementary frameworks of analysis' (p. 5). The complex adaptive systems view, however, is not a single encompassing theoretical perspective. It describes a worldview that enables business organizations to improve their mental models of how their activities affect the broader world of social and ecological stakeholders. The deeper understanding provided by the CAS approach can contribute to aligning business strategies with the realities of the natural and social worlds that lie beyond the firm's traditional boundaries.

Survival strategies and fitness landscapes

Organizations can no longer survive by simply adapting to today's world (landscape) or forecasting the future based on the current situation. New survival strategies are needed and these can only be developed through application of different mental models. In the case of sustainability, radical innovation is an imperative if the vision of the UN Agenda 2030 is to be met. The CAS view offers a way to map potential survival strategies that are available to the system through the concept of a *fitness landscape* (Kauffman, 1995).

A fitness landscape is an abstract representation of the search space in an optimization problem. Graphically it has the appearance of a topographical map, as shown in Figure 1.2. The optimization problem here is that of developing business strategies for the economic dimension that are compatible with the needs, constraints and goals of the social and ecological dimensions. Every business strategy traces a path through the landscape that is defined by the three dimensions. Similarly, activities in the other dimensions also define paths through the common landscape. The fitness landscape brings out the differences in the so-called fitness of a solution to the problem under study. Those solutions that are better than others are higher on the landscape. In the case where an optimal solution does exist, it will be the highest point on the landscape where the height of a peak indicates the fitness of the system: the higher the peak, the greater the fitness.

In the search for sustainability there is no one optimal solution and the best solution at any point in time will not necessarily be best the next time. Thus, the managerial task is that of engaging with a complex process in the hope of improving the situation.

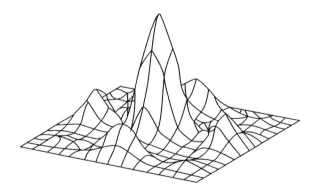

Figure 1.2 A fitness landscape (adapted from Chan [2001]).

The task is wicked, in part because there is no end in sight, but also because there is no agreement on what is an acceptable solution (despite the optimistic words of the UN 2030 agenda) and actions taken now will likely create new challenges in the future.

The development of a system and its evolution can be seen as a journey through a fitness landscape in search of the highest peak that provides greatest fitness and thus the greatest chance for survival. In this journey, it is possible that the system becomes stuck on the first peak it encounters. This represents a local optimal fitness level that is better than any of the nearest neighbouring peaks. However, this local peak may not be the best possible survival strategy because, over time, conditions may change enough to require a new strategy. If the system uses an incremental improvement approach, then it may not be possible to find better peaks that are farther away from the current location. The alternative is to 'jump' away from the current state to distant regions in the landscape. These strategies correspond to the strategic business management approaches of exploitation and exploration (March and Simon, 1958), respectively.

A complicating feature of the fitness landscape of a particular problem is that the landscape is also affected by the actions of other systems. Systems within the sustainability dimensions continuously change in response to internal and external influences. To the extent that the various subsystems are interrelated, the systems' landscapes coevolve and mutually affect their fitness. There are no optimal fitness solutions but despite the complications resulting from the interaction of multiple complex adaptive systems, there is frequently considerable order in the world; whether it is the biological or the social worlds.

Challenge of mental models

Management's basic purpose is to ensure the continued success of the organization by planning, directing, organizing and coordinating activities in the fitness landscape. The additional challenges imposed by demands for sustainable performance requires a re-evaluation of business strategy. Additionally, the new features in the business environment are such that incremental strategic changes will be insufficient to assure long-term success. Incremental changes imply only small-scale adjustments from an existing strategic position. This approach to decision-making implies that the underlying basis for the decision has not changes. That is, the mental model has essentially been unchanged by feedback from previous decisions.

In his studies of decision-making behaviour, Simon (1957) formulated the concept of 'bounded rationality' to describe the effect of the limited capacity of the human mind to access and process the enormous amounts of information that define many types of complex problems. In such cases, the decision-maker relies on simplified models of reality, called mental models, as the basis for structuring, diagnosing and taking action. Mental models are influenced by, for example, education, experiences, social roles and culture and assumptions regarding the cause and effect relationships relevant for the problem. As models, they are by definition wrong, but they can be useful (Box, 1976). They are simplifications that enable people to function in a seemingly rational manner (see Argyris and Schön (1978) for a comprehensive discussion).

In 1958, Ashby formulated the 'law of requisite variety' for complex systems. This law has several interpretations, but the most direct is that a model system or controller can only represent or control something (the focal system) to the extent that it has sufficient internal variety to represent it. In managerial terms, the controller (manager) must have a mental model (the 'model system') that includes all of the relevant aspects of the system to be controlled in order to be effective. The consequences of Simon's observations is on the decision-maker's limited cognitive attributes implies that he or she must rely on simplified models of the situation. Ashby's focus is on specifying the requirements for the content of the manager's mental models in order to be able to control the system.

Many factors shape mental models, but organizational culture and education are key drivers that influence individuals' worldviews. Mental models encompass the decision-maker's understanding of causality in the situation, as well as the underlying assumptions and beliefs. For example, if the dominant organizational mental model does not include elements from the non-business sustainability dimensions then one cannot expect effective organizational sustainability performance. For example, in cases involving environmental management, the prevailing mental models of key stakeholders may not be helpful. The relationship between business and environmentalists is frequently complicated as a result of each stakeholder's mental models being in complete in fundamental ways by not recognizing the mutual dependency of the economic and environmental dimensions. Environmentalists often do not acknowledge the importance of the market in making things happen; economists frequently have unrealistic assumptions regarding natural resource availability being only a function of price.

Consistent with the notion of systems leverage points (Meadows, 1997), the most effective method of ensuring significant systemic change is through changing the mindset or paradigm (mental models) from which the goals, rules and feedback structures that drive the system to be controlled are derived. Adopting the CAS perspective enables development of richer models of the relationships among the sustainability dimensions. Figure 2.3 relates different levels of abstraction with the theoretical perspectives that are commonly applied to organizational strategy and policy making. The theorizing perspectives are essentially formalized mental models of organizations. The range of application to organizations provided by the Complex mode indicates that this perspective supplies the requisite variety needed to inform managerial mental models.

Figure 1.3 shows how the complex adaptive systems perspective differs from the more traditional business modes of theorizing about organizational strategy and change. The theorizing perspectives and the levels of abstraction that frame the figure identify a

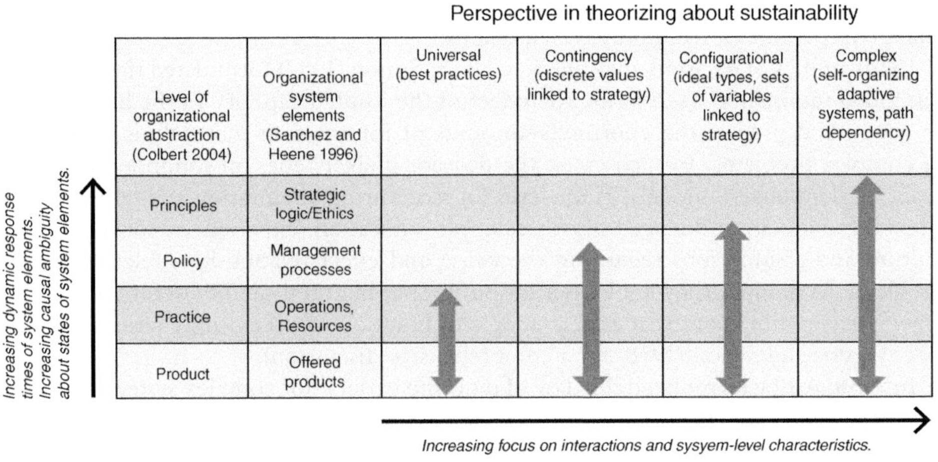

Perspective in theorizing about sustainability

Level of organizational abstraction (Colbert 2004)	Organizational system elements (Sanchez and Heene 1996)	Universal (best practices)	Contingency (discrete values linked to strategy)	Configurational (ideal types, sets of variables linked to strategy)	Complex (self-organizing adaptive systems, path dependency)
Principles	Strategic logic/Ethics				
Policy	Management processes				
Practice	Operations, Resources				
Product	Offered products				

Increasing dynamic response times of system elements.
Increasing causal ambiguity about states of system elements.

Increasing focus on interactions and sysyem-level characteristics.

Figure 1.3 Organizational abstraction and theories of sustainability (adapted from Colbert (2004) and Sanchez and Heene (1996)).

continuum of issues that distinguish important aspects of the organization's sustainability challenge. The continuum of theoretical perspectives spans the range from static reductionist theories (the Universal mode) on to the higher-level systems thinking model (the Complex mode). The other continuum combines the issues of dynamic response time of the system to perturbations and the causal ambiguity associated with different levels of abstraction, or organizational hierarchy. Conceptualizing the dimensions in terms of complex adaptive systems provides a common language with which to investigate the interactions among the sustainability dimensions.

As the level of abstraction increases, the nature of causality becomes more ambiguous due to the increased complexity of additional elements and their interrelations. The system's dynamic response time also increases. For example, it is much easier and quicker to make a production line change than it is to modify an organization's culture. In the former, there is no question about how a technical process functions and replacement is a physical operation. Changing an organization's culture, on the other hand, cannot be described in a handbook or through a set of equations.

High-level organizational change, on the other hand, is shrouded in causal ambiguity that opens for multiple, plausible interpretations of the causal relationships. Achieving a useful degree of agreement on the essential relationships is a delicate negotiation process, even when there is general agreement on the objectives. When the stakeholders' goals are contested and possibly in conflict, the process is elevated to an entirely different level. The change processes needed for systemic improvement now involves psychological process (See, for example, Flood and Carson (1993) and Casti (1990) for overviews of methods for working with complexity.).

Leadership for sustainability using CAS

Taking a CAS perspective on leadership is a relatively new approach where there is less reliance on managerial authority derived from formal hierarchical structures. Leadership that is confined to 'working within the system' is restricted by the formal rules and structures of the organization and consequently will not be as influential in shaping the firm's behaviour. The independence from direct formal authority suggests that distributed CAS leadership may directly influence the emergence of new behaviours in the adaptive organizational system.

Schneider and Somers (2006, p. 356) compare the term leadership and leader: leadership is used to 'connote the often indirect, catalytic process within organizations – which might be performed by people in rotation or in tandem – to the term "leader", which might falsely signal that there are individual and positional factors that strictly distinguish leaders from others'.

Management and leadership needed for engaging in the wicked problems of sustainability place new demands on the individuals responsible for these functions. Leadership and sustainability in organizations entails finding a balance between exploiting existing organizational competencies and competitive advantage, on the one hand, and exploration of new 'territory', on the other. The exploitation strategy prioritizes the short-term time horizon and the status quo. Exploration is riskier in that its time perspective is longer, the outcomes more uncertain, and the existing organizational skills may no longer be an advantage or even relevant. At worst, they may be counterproductive to the goal of improved performance. Exploration breaks with the status quo and often generates internal resistance to change.

The 'roads', or strategies, to improved sustainability performance involves the search for a higher peak in the fitness landscape. Since the Industrial Revolution the economic dimension, represented by business organizations, has found a relative peak in the sustainability landscape and expanded rapidly to take advantage of the benefits afforded by that location. Conditions have changed, however, due to a confluence of many factors and forces that indicate the need for change, which will require a leadership style that is compatible with this challenge. The historical success of strategies based on the priority of the economic dimension makes it very difficult to break out of this type of behaviour. Regardless of the diversity and individual differences exhibited by business organizations, their overall behaviour is generally similar. This similarity condition is called an 'attractor'. Given an organizational intervention (merger, acquisition, etc.) that changes the state of the organization, there will be a period of behaviour, a path, which differs from the pre-intervention patterns. This transient period ends when the organization returns to its 'normal' behavioural state. The final state may differ from the initial condition, but it will still conform to the conditions imposed by the larger economic system within which the firm operates. An attractor is said to have steep walls if it is difficult to escape from the conditions that define it. The cumulative effects of economic performance on the other dimensions have made it impossible to ignore the larger set of relationships. Stakeholder awareness and actions have introduced the need for broader measures of system performance. The triple-bottom line accounting and management tools like the balanced scorecard have broadened the set of state variables that are relevant for monitoring organizations. Introducing these variables has the effect of making the attractor walls less steep, thus easing the transition to alternate attractors that include variables from the social and environmental dimensions.

The leadership requirements in the transition from one attractor to another, seeking a higher peak in the fitness landscape, was described by Metcalf and Benn (2013) as a process of influence, following Yukl's (2001) definition of leadership. Unlike the traditional understanding of leadership as being associated with individual actors in hierarchical positions, the complex adaptive systems view is that leadership can be distributed among the agents involved with the system. These agents can be internal to the focal system, or external to it, such as stakeholders from other affected systems.

Metcalf and Benn's leadership theory involves the transition from the initial attractor, which is based on the logic of leadership of convergence and system stability achieved by social structures and rules. In this condition, the dominant strategy is probably based on exploitation of hard-earned organizational competencies. As conditions defining the system become more untenable, either through declining performance on normally accepted state variables or by the recognition and acceptance of new variables that were previously ignored, the need for change becomes more apparent. Eventually, the previous attractor becomes easier to escape and the search for a new attractor basin is initiated. Key in this phase is a leadership style that focuses on variety and innovation. This requires a strategy that emphasizes experimentation.

Finally, a new 'normal state', paradigm, is found. Business strategies that are compatible with the new paradigm will represent higher peaks in the fitness landscape. This new resting place will be characterized by an expanded set of state variables that will include elements from other sustainability dimensions. In this state, a new leadership orientation is needed. This one will require a focus on providing a new unity and consolidation. Throughout this dynamic process it is crucial to recall that the organization must continue to create value for its customers. The redesign process can be likened to the problem of rebuilding an airplane while it is flying. Stopping is not an option.

One of the central insights regarding managerial engagement from seeing the sustainability challenge as a wicked problem is the focus on the process. There is no optimal solution, nor is there a static solution. In addition, given the vast number of stakeholders, the likelihood of achieving a consensus with respect to what constitutes a sustainable state is very small. Consequently, the organization and its leaders should encourage an active learning environment within their organizations.

Learning is a dynamic feedback process that involves choice, action, observation, re-flection and choice. There are two modes by which learning takes place (Argyris and Schön, 1978): single-loop and double-loop learning. Single-loop learning disconnects decision-makers' mental models from the feedback loop. The result is that discrepancies between observations and expectations are resolved by incremental actions. The guiding mental model is unaffected by the differences and not updated in line with experience. Double-loop learning actually involves testing and updating the mental model as anomalous observations are detected. This process of revising the mental model expands the range of options from which to select. For a competitor, the resulting behaviour may be radically innovative, and different, and difficult to predict. This contributes to organizational fitness.

The organization's ability to reflect on its worldview and make changes is the key element for surviving and flourishing in a wicked problem environment. Experimentation is a basic characteristic of double-loop learning organizations. Successful learning is a function of having both an organizational culture that supports learning and managerial and leadership capabilities that facilitate the learning process (Nevis, DiBella and Gould, 1995). Among the specific facilitating factors, two stand out as having specific relevance for the leadership function. The first is to develop a climate of openness in the organization. This involves sanctioning and encouraging debate and conflict as acceptable ways to address and resolve problems. In this way, encouraging a climate of openness contributes to involving all organizational members to become engaged in the transition from the old to the new attractor, and enhances the experimentation required during the transition.

The second factor is having an involved leadership who interact frequently with organizational members and who are engage actively with the transformation process. Together these factors enable the development of the distributed leadership style that characterizes systemic leadership in complex adaptive systems.

Communication

Metcalf and Benn (2013) make the point that leading successful sustainability strategies or initiatives in organizations requires managers 'of extraordinary capabilities' (p. 381). One of these is the capability to engage groups both internally and externally, essentially by being a bridge-builder and interpreter. The interpreter role includes, among other things, linking through what the authors call stakeholder interviewing. Viewing sustainability as a wicked problem also emphasizes a much more active role by leadership in engaging with many and varied stakeholders through negotiating and effective communication. This implies additional extraordinary capabilities for interpersonal communication.

Communication comes from the latin *communicare*, to make common, to share. It is the activity of conveying information through the exchange of thoughts, messages or information, as by speech, visuals, signals, writing or behaviour. The interpretive view of communication sees it as a meaning-based process of coordinating and organizing actions. Communication is a dynamic process: the meaningful exchange of information between two persons or a group of people. People interact with and through symbols to create and interpret meanings (Wood, 2013) in a systemic process. Organizational communication as a field assumes that organizations are fundamentally communicative creations. This is because organizations are 'social units of people systematically structured and managed to meet a need or to pursue collective goals on a continuing basis' (Shockley-Zalabak, 2012). It focuses on general communication processes and dynamics within organizations.

Management communication fundamentally deals with how managers/leaders develop and disseminate knowledge. Focus is on how they as individuals build relationships with employees, with other managers and with important external organizational stakeholders. Objectives of management communication include developing a shared vision of the company/organization, establishing and maintaining trust in leadership, initiating and managing change processes, and empowering and motivating employees. It demands understanding of the importance of the movement of information and the skills that facilitate it, in addition to understanding language and the power it has. Management communication is seen as developing into leadership communication when individuals are able to use communication to create visions, to motivate, to instil new cultures, and to mobilize and focus energies (Shockley-Zalabek, 2012).

Mintzberg (1973) suggests that managers are almost constantly engaged in communication; most managerial roles are communication roles and all roles have communication elements. Interpersonal roles include those of figurehead, leader and liaison. The informational role is that of monitor, disseminator and spokesperson, and the decisional role comprises entrepreneur, disturbance handler, resource allocator and negotiator.

Leadership and management communication also 'influences decision-making, transmits communication rules and contributes to the shared realities that becomes the organization's culture or cultures helps organizational members' (Shockley-Zalabak, 2012, p. 213). It also helps organizations in setting priorities and determining what is needed. Management communication is tightly associated with theories of leadership and management, and personal traits, preferences for leadership styles or approaches, and responsiveness to leadership requirements have an enormous impact on managers' communication effectiveness and in the end the outcomes of their leadership.

Leadership style and communication that promote common understanding does not just happen. Leadership style and organizational success are tightly coupled with studies of organizational and leadership communication. Of fundamental importance is the notion of mental models, essentially a personal theory of how things work. Influential models include stakeholder theory, Argyris and Schön's mutual learning, and McLeod and Chaffee's (1973) co-orientation model. Lastly, because, we will look at the communication function and its role in supporting organizational leadership with respect to different aspects of sustainability.

McLeod and Chaffee's (1973) co-orientation model illustrates the need for mutually beneficial communication. A co-orientational approach includes four points of analysis: (1) the organization's view, (2) others' views (3) the organization's perception of others' views, and (4) others' perception of the organization's view. The interaction between these variables creates three measures of co-orientation – agreement, accuracy and congruency. 'Agreement' indicates the degree to which the organization's view matches the stakeholder's view. 'Accuracy' indicates the degree to which the organization correctly perceives the stakeholder's viewpoint, and vice versa. 'Perceived agreement' (or 'congruency') is the degree to which the organization's view matches its perception of others' viewpoint, and vice versa.

Dozier and Ehling (1992) suggest four co-orientation states: a state of true consensus, a state of dissensus, a state of false consensus, and a state of false conflict. True consensus exists when both parties have a similar understanding and agree on their view or evaluation of the issue discussed. Dissensus occurs when the parties hold conflicting views and are aware of their differences. A false consensus exists when the leader believes that a stakeholder agrees with him/her when in fact they do not. Managers may believe that someone defines something the same way they do, when in fact they do not. The same is true if stakeholder mistakenly believes that the firm leader holds the same view that they do. Similarly, this state also exists if both mistakenly believe that they agree on an issue when in fact they do not. A state of false conflict exists when the leader and stakeholders believe that they disagree on an issue, policy or action, when in fact they agree. The co-orientation model helps to remind organizations to check whether their perception of their stakeholders' views is accurate – or not. Those who take the trouble to check often find lack of accuracy between their perception of what the other party thinks and the actual position of the other party. This is when the need for better and more effective communication is revealed.

The danger in complex situations is that people have the natural tendency to assume that others see the situation in the same way as they do. This phenomenon is why the co-orientation model is useful; it clearly identifies the various states of misinformation that can arise between two or more agents (stakeholders) who do not clarify their interpretations of a complex situation of common interest. At the heart of the co-orientation framework is the notion of mental models (Senge, 1993) and the recognition that in order for any interaction to be effective, these models must be 'oriented' properly (Brønn and Brønn, 2003). The ability to communicate with others who share similar mental models and understandings of the world is easier than communicating with someone who does not share a common conceptual structure. Not having a common starting point on important factors leads to misunderstandings and disagreements between the communicating parties. However, the simple fact of having similar mental models in no way guarantees that this model is 'correct', i.e. a true representation of the situation. It only ensures that there is similarity in the conceptual structures that organize the world, the individual's particular worldview.

Three specific communication skills that enable communication managers to engage stakeholders in a meaningful dialogue, and thereby enhance the effectiveness of the organization's communication efforts are reflection, inquiry and advocacy (Brønn and Brønn, 2003). Reflection is an internally focused skill whose objective is to make the practitioner more aware of his or her own thinking and reasoning processes. Inquiry engages the two parties of the communication process in a joint learning process where the objective is to understand the thinking and reasoning processes of the other party. Advocacy is the process of communicating one's own thinking and reasoning in a manner that makes them visible for others. The reflective communicator seeks to find a balance between inquiry and advocacy. Too much advocacy results in one-way communication with little feedback, too much inquiry means being bogged down.

It is obvious that the incorporating the principles of co-orientation and advocacy and inquiry requires an organization-wide approach that considers the role of all individuals within the organization, particularly leaders. It is their interpretation of issues and their ability to be reflective that determine the success of organizational efforts. It is the leader's role to engage all stakeholders and to encourage everyone in the organization to communicate, with each other and with the outside world.

Conclusions

The business organization is a central element in the sustainability *problematique*. Much of the complexity of organizations is that they are formal systems that span the economic and social dimensions of sustainability, thus incorporating many of the aspects of these areas. The additional feature that they are purposive systems (Checkland, 2000) introduces a bias in the goals of the system. In the case of business organizations, the bias is towards the optimization of the economic dimension.

In terms of complex system behaviour, the concept of an attractor describes a set of values towards which a system tends to evolve for a wide variety of starting conditions of system variables. In this sense, economic factors dominate the attractor for business systems. This attractor 'basin' has relatively steep walls so that it is relatively stable. External forces may perturb the system, but not enough to move it out of the influence of the economic attractor. In a sense, the attractor is a metaphorical paradigm for organizational behaviour, in this case dominated by economic consideration. In the old paradigm, the values for environmental and social variables were set to zero; the dominant mental models did not include these influences.

An erosion of the economic attractor's walls is a result of changes in society and in the environment, influenced significantly by economic behaviour. As the walls erode, the slope becomes less steep, making it easier to escape the attractor, and making a leap to a new paradigm less arduous. Metcalf and Benn (2013) argue that different leadership styles are required for successful management of the system's evolution away from the outmoded paradigm, through a transitional phase, and finally to a new and more sustainable attractor basin. Ideally, a broader range of variables drawn from the previously underutilized sustainability dimensions would define this new attractor. This requires new thinking, new mental models and real jumps in innovation.

References

Argyris, C. and Schön, D.A. (1978). *Organizational Learning: A Theory of Action Perspective*. Reading, MA: Addison-Wesley.

Ashby, W.R. (1958). Requisite variety and its implications for the control of complex systems. *Cybernetica*, 1(2): 83–99.

Beinhocker, E.D. (2007). *The Origin of Wealth: The Radical Remaking of Economics and What It Means for Business and Society*. Boston, MA: Harvard Business School Press.

Box, G.E.P. (1976). Science and statistics. *Journal of the American Statistical Association*, 71(356): 791–799.

Brønn, P.S. and Brønn, C. (2003). Organizational implications of the coorientational model. *Journal of Communications Management*, 7(4): 291–303.

Casti, J.L. (1990). *Searching for Certainty: What Scientists Can Know About the Future*. New York: William Morrow and Co.

Chan, S. (2001). Complex adaptive systems. ESD.83 Research Seminar in Engineering Systems. (web.mit.edu).

Checkland, P. (2000). Soft systems methodology: A thirty-year retrospective. *Systems Research and Behavioral Science*, 17: S11–S58.

Clemente, D. and Evans, R. (2014). *Wartime Logistics in Afghanistan and Beyond: Handling Wicked Problems and Complex Adaptive Systems*. London: The Royal Institute of International Affairs, Chatham House.

Colbert, B.A. (2004). The complex resource-based view: Implications for theory and practice in strategic human resource management. *The Academy of Management Review*, 29(3): 341–358.

Dozier, D. and W.P. Ehling (1992). Evaluation of public relations programs: What the literature tells us about their effects. In J.E. Grunig (ed.), *Excellence in Public Relations and Communication Management*. Hillsdale, NJ: Lawrence Erlbaum Associates.

Ehrenfeld, J.R. (2005). The roots of sustainability. *MIT Sloan Management Review*, 46(2): 23–25.

Eidelson, R.J. (1997). Complex adaptive systems in the behavioral and social sciences. *Review of General Psychology*, 1(1): 42–71.

Flood, R.L. and Carson, E.R. (1993). *Dealing with Complexity: An Introduction to the Theory and Application of Systems Science*. New York: Plenum Press.

Kauffman, S. (1995). *At Home in the Universe*. Oxford: Oxford University Press.

Levin, S. (1999). *Fragile Dominion: Complexity and the Commons*. Reading, MA: Perseus Books.

McLeod, J.M. and Chaffee, S.H. (1973). Interpersonal approaches to communication research. *American Behavioral Scientist*, 16(4): 469–499.

March, J.G. and Simon, H.A. (1958). *Organizations*. New York: John Wiley & Sons.

Metcalf, L. and Benn, S. (2013). Leadership for sustainability: An evolution of leadership ability. *Journal of Business Ethics*, 112, 369–384.

Mintzberg, H. (1973). *The Nature of Managerial Work*. NY: Harper & Row.

Nevis, E., DiBella, A.J. and Gould, J.M. (1995). Understanding organizations as learning systems. *Sloan Management Review*, 36: 73–85.

Newcomb, M.T. (1953). An approach to the study of communicative acts. *Psychological Review*, 60: 393–404.

Parris, T.M. and Kates, R.W. (2003). Characterizing and measuring sustainable development. *Annual Review of Environment and Resources*, 28: 559–586.

Porter, E.H. (1962). The parable of the kitchen spindle. *Harvard Business Review*, 40(3): 58–66.

Rittel, H.W.J. and Webber, M.M. (1973). Dilemmas in a general theory of planning. *Policy Sciences*, 4: 155–169.

Ruhl, J.B. (2008). Law's complexity. *Georgia State University Law Review*, 24(4): 885–912.

Sanchez, R. and Heene, A. (1996). A systems view of the firm in competence-based competition. In R. Sanchez, A. Heene and H. Thomas (eds), *Dynamics of Competence Based Competition: Theory and Practice in the New Strategic Management*. Oxford: Pergamon, pp. 39–62.

Schneider, M. and Somers, M. (2006). Organizations as complex adaptive systems: Implications of Complexity Theory for leadership research. *The Leadership Quarterly*, 17: 351–365.

Senge, P.M. (1993). *The Fifth Discipline: The Art and Practice of the Learning Organization*. London: Random House.

Shockley-Zalabak, P. (2012). *Fundamentals of Organizational Communication, Knowledge, Sensitivity, Skills, Values*, 8th edn. Boston, MA: Allyn & Bacon.

Simon, H.A. (1957). *Administrative Behavior: A Study of Decision Making Processes in Administrative Organizations*, 4th edn. New York: The Free Press.

Sterman, J.D. (2000). *Business Dynamics: Systems Thinking and Modeling for a Complex World*. Boston, MA: Irwin McGraw-Hill.

Trivitt, V. (2011). 25 US Major Corporations: Where they rank if they were countries. *Business Insider*. www.businessinsider.com/25-corporations-bigger-tan-countries-2011-6?IR=T#walmart-is-bigger-than-norway-25 (accessed 3 April 2016).

United Nations (2015). Transforming our World, the 2030 Agenda for Sustainable Development. Resolution adopted by the General Assembly on 25 September 2015, available at:
https://sustainabledevelopment.un.org/post2015/transformingourworld.

World Commission on Environment and Development (1987). *Our Common Future, Brundtland
Report*. Oxford: Oxford University Press.

Yukl, G. (2001). *Leadership in Organisations*. Upper Saddle River, NJ: Prentice-Hall.

2 Addressing the global crisis of economic growth

An unavoidable ethical challenge

Frederick Bird

A complex and unavoidable challenge

The world now faces an unavoidable and fundamental challenge with respect to economic growth.[1] Without some form of economic growth, we condemn most of that third of all humans living below the poverty line to continued poverty. Without some form of economic growth these people will continue to live lives that are typically more than a dozen years shorter and filled with more malnutrition, ill health, and social conflict (Collier, 2007). Without economic growth, the economies of many industrialized countries will continue to sputter and tens of millions of their citizen will suffer from long periods of unemployment and under-employment. Without some form of economic growth globally we are likely to experience continued economic instability. However, if as a whole the global economy continues to grow as it has grown over the past 70 years, we place the Earth and the inhabitants of the Earth at great risk, as we deplete natural resources and pollute waterways and the Earth's atmosphere at disastrous rates. Continuing economic growth threatens the Earth's climate, endangers her forests and limited supplies of fresh water, and is using up the limited supply of arable land. Economic growth seems desirable and necessary, on the one hand, and dangerous and threatening, on the other hand.

How shall we find the appropriate means of balancing the integral yet opposing characteristic features of economic growth? Are their viable ways to foster, limit and reverse growth at the same time?

As generally understood, economic growth has been valuable in many ways. Historically, it has functioned as the primary means for reducing and overcoming poverty. As the North Atlantic countries industrialized, large portions of their populations that had been impoverished improved their economic status. More recently, hundreds of millions of people in China and India emerged out of poverty as the economies of these countries steadily expanded. Everywhere, economic growth has functioned to promote public education, improve health services and raise standards of living. As economies expand, countries are better able to defend human rights (Holmes and Sunnstein, 1997). Interestingly, during periods of economic growth, people tend to become more tolerant of diversity, more committed to freedom, and more inclined to resolve conflicts non-violently through negotiations and compromise (Friedman, 2005). Many countries with slow growth and no growth have experienced higher levels of social and political instability and civil conflict (Collier, 2009; Kaplan, 2016). In fact, there has been an often-cited correlation between economic development and the establishment of democratic political institutions (Lipset, 1959; Macpherson, 1977).

Continued economic growth holds out the prospect that as a whole people living on Earth will find ways of being able to meet their basic needs on a small planet as their population is expected to rise to over 9 billion by the middle of the current century.

However, as generally practised and understood, economic growth has been dangerous and destructive in many ways. As a result of economic growth humans have significantly depleted a number of natural resources from global fish stocks to arable lands, from many strategic minerals used in the production of metals to an assortment of rare earth minerals (Jackson, 2009, p. 18). Across the globe the processes of economic growth have aggravated deforestation as well as desertification. The activities associated with economic growth have increased the pollution of streams and oceans (Millennium Ecosystem Assessment, 2005; Sachs, 2015, chapters 6, 12, 13). As a result of continued economic growth global emissions levels have greatly increased the greenhouse gases in the atmosphere in ways that have irreversibly and adversely affected global climate. Moreover, if humans do not find effective ways of drastically reducing carbon emission within the next generation, climate changes will result in increasing the melting of polar ice packs, resulting in rising sea levels drowning coastal areas all over the Earth, and aggravating extreme weather conditions everywhere (Wijkman and Rockström, 2012, pp. 146–149). Economic growth has not only negatively impacted natural environments; it has had adverse impacts on social environments as well. Recently economic growth, as usually measured, has been associated with aggravated inequalities between the most well-to-do groups and those who are least economically advantaged (Milanovic, 2005; Piketty, 2014; Bourguignon, 2015; Brynjolfsson and McAfee, 2014). Economic growth characteristically undermines often highly valued traditional ways of life; in addition, it often occasions unrealistic expectations. Based on current practices, it would, for example, require the resources of several more Earths to make it possible for all people on Earth to live with the standard of those in North Atlantic countries (Brown, 1995). Many people correspondingly view continued economic growth as a threat to the planet and its inhabitants (Klein, 2014; Sachs, 2015; Wijkman and Rockstrom, 2012).

As generally understood, global economic growth has occasioned sharply opposing evaluations. It seems that now we cannot now live without it and we cannot now live with it. Economic growth occasions an unavoidable dilemma: it presents us with radically conflicting views both of which seem urgent and compelling. This is not a crisis we can ignore or hope that matters will be resolved by themselves over time. This crisis will become much worse over time if we do not find adequate ways of addressing it. This crisis cannot be effectively resolved by invoking many of the most highly regarded global ethical standards such as those embodied in the Universal Declaration of Human Rights or corresponding UN conventions. This crisis cannot be addressed by appealing either for the expansion of charity or for greater commitment to justice, as valuable as both are likely to be for addressing many other contemporary global issues (Singer, 2009; Pogge, 2008). Neither of these responses directly function to modify either the need and benefits of economic growth or its deleterious and destructive effects. Many have expressed confidence that humans will come upon technological discoveries that will, as similar discoveries have in the past, enable humans to limit their impact on the planet at the same time as their economies grow. One might point, for example, to ways in which the discovery of irrigation, modern organized work places, and solar energy each have played this kind of role (Lomborg, 2001). However, these kinds of discoveries often have had unanticipated negative impacts on environments and, more importantly, as a whole these kinds of inventions and their deployment in most ways only modify without fundamentally addressing the central crisis.[2] This crisis cannot be resolved by retreating into alternative intentional communities dedicated to living simple exemplary lives (Korton, 1995; Klein, 2014). While these kinds of communities have found ways of living prosperous and flourishing lives with little impact on the environment, these communities provide an alternative only for a few. Those involved hope that by setting these kinds of examples, many others will follow. In a world of 9 billion, this seems highly unlikely. Finally, this crisis will not be resolved by imagining that humans are likely in any basic ways to change the kind of creatures we have been for the past several thousand years or more. We are not likely to become more humane and more willing to adopt long range views of our lives in any fundamental ways.

This is not a crisis that can be easily resolved or resolved at all by fostering half way compromises. For example, it might be hoped that we could adequately address this crisis by promoting economic growth just for the least-developed countries and insisting on no growth or de-growth for the industrialized areas of the world. However, continued economic growth in the developing world in ways that have occurred over the past two centuries in the industrialized countries would still occasion disastrous environmental impacts. Moreover, as I will demonstrate in this chapter, there are ways that economic growth, rightly understood, is called for not only to help address economic problems in industrialized and developing countries but also to help address environmental problems globally. Finally, sustainable development, as this term is generally understood, does not fully and clearly address the crisis of economic growth. In a compromised way, sustainable development calls for restrained growth with much greater attention to environmental dangers but without re-thinking what we mean by economic growth, or, even, how restrained growth, as currently understood and practised, will address the ongoing problems of global poverty and increasing global inequality.[3]

Adequately addressing the crisis of economic growth is complicated by the widely shared, but taken-for-granted modern assumption that economic growth, as usually understood, is both normal and normative. Traditional societies viewed economic growth neither as something to be expected nor as an imperative. Characteristically, people enhanced their wealth by locating sources – such as conquered people, slaves, mineral deposits and valued items they could exploit directly or by trade – from which they could extract their wealth. Typically, those with control over the means of violence used these means both to gain and protect their wealth (North et al., 2008). However, for a number of reasons, in modern times economic growth has come to be regarded as both the desired and expected condition of economies and businesses.[4] Although people like Herman Daly have long advocated for a steady-state economics, they have been in a distinct minority (Daly, 1972; Daly, 1996). Because economic growth is viewed as normal and normative, lack of growth by firms and countries is viewed as problematic, as evidence that firms or countries are in economic trouble.

How humans address this crisis will affect and be affected by how we hold and understand the basic values by which we orient our lives. This is an intensely ethical crisis precisely because it touches upon not only national and international policies but also the ways we carry out our ordinary lives. As a whole, humans have let the genie of economic growth out of the bottle and we cannot now find an easy way to put this genie back. This is un-mistakenly a truly global crisis both in the sense that it affects us all and it affects how we live within the ecological limits of the Earth. I refer to this as an ethical crisis as well as a global crisis because it is unavoidable, deeply shapes how we live, and can only seriously be addressed by taking into account and ultimately engaging the fundamental values by which humans live.

In the remainder of this chapter I propose a way of thinking about and responding to this crisis that respects the imperatives and urgency associated each side of this dilemma. I begin by critiquing the usual ways of thinking about economic growth and proposing an alternative that, I argue, both more adequately identifies the core reality of genuine economic growth and provides the basis for a useful way of addressing the contemporary crisis. I argue that it is useful to distinguish between processes of production and consumption, although they are, to be sure, interrelated, and to examine the ways the present crisis calls for quite different imperatives with respect to each. I begin then by reflecting on the characteristic features of economic growth and on the current debates on how best to gauge it. I will move back and forth from analysing this crisis and responses to it from global, national, firm and household level perspectives.

Characteristic features of economic growth

What do we mean by economic growth and how is economic growth best measured? Often, we think of economic growth as economic changes that result in improved standards of living and we correspondingly gauge economic growth approximately in relation to higher levels of per capita income. While improved standards of living do in fact represent a by-product or consequence of economic growth and income level does represent a rough indicator of enhanced living standards, neither of these factors identify the components that especially make it possible for economies to grow. Sen has argued that per capita income is an inappropriate measure of economic growth because money income is simply a means, one of many, which people utilize to obtain those things which they have reason genuinely to value. What people really value and what enables them truly to live the kinds of lives they want to live, Sen argues, are means that allow them to gain an education, to live healthy lives, to work effectively in chosen forms of work, to participate in political processes, and to associate with whom they choose. Sen, and Nussbaum in parallel studies, refer to these means as human capabilities (Sen, 1999; Nussbaum, 2000, 2011). The capabilities approach does provide a fitting way of thinking about, and gauging, human development, an approach that does identify relevant ways of referring both to some of the most desired outcomes of economic growth as well as a few of the factors like enhanced education, improved health care systems, and reformed political processes that facilitate these developments. However, overall, the capabilities approach still tends to draw attention to by-products of economic growth rather than those factors that uniquely make it possible for economies to expand.

Typical discussions, such as Gordon's recent book on *the Rise and Fall of American Growth*, tend to view economic growth in terms of increases in productivity that result in higher standards of living (Gordon, 2016). In practice ordinarily we think about and measure growth in relation to higher levels of consumption. For example, per capita income basically is a measure of the capacity to consume. Alternatively, I maintain that economic growth is best understood as the processes that render productive processes more productive with the consequences of raising living standards and fostering wider ranges of opportunities. Gordon in fact makes a similar point by focusing on technological innovation that have especially enhanced living standards. As economies grow, people find means to make more effective use of human and natural resources so that they can produce more goods and services from limited human and natural resources to address their wants and needs. The key factor is this: economies are able to make more productive use of natural and human resources by developing what I refer to in this chapter as generative assets. What distinguishes generative assets is that they are both durable – long-lasting and not directly consumed – and they possess the capacity to generate flows of income and other economically valued benefits over time. Typically, generative assets have many different uses and help to occasion the development of other generative assets. For example, historically humans have discovered and made use of a number of such generative assets, including inventions of fire, the wheel, domesticated animals, literacy, educational systems, systems of credit, steam engines, electricity, the internal combustion engine, telephones and complex organizations. By developing these kinds of assets, humans have correspondingly discovered ways to utilize human and natural resources much more effectively and they have thereby fostered economic growth and also enhanced their capabilities to live the kinds of lives they have reason to want to live. Correspondingly, economies are more or less developed to the extent that they have been able to develop and make use of these kinds of generative assets. Underdeveloped economies have fewer and less productive generative assets than do more developed economies. Poorly performing firms have fewer and less productive generative assets than firms performing more effectively. Economic growth in general and industrialization in particular has been fostered by the development of a number of generative assets like the development of banking systems, institutions fostering trade and commerce, the spread of literacy, new inventions and investments as well as changing dispositions with respect to work and savings.

Economists use the phrase 'generally productive technologies' to refer the sub-groups of generative assets that involve physical technologies (Brynjolfsson and McAfee, 2014; Avent, 2016; Gordon, 2016). I use the term generative assets to include as well social technologies (Beinhocker, 2007) as well as changes in cultural values (Avent 2016, chapters 6 and 12; Weber, 1958), in so far as these factors occasion more creative and productive uses of natural and human resources.

Generative assets differ from resources in general, whether human or natural. Assets are deployable resources – that is: resources that have been transformed, organized or rendered so that they can be readily utilized in ways that can generate flows of income or other economic benefits. An untutored person who has not yet developed his or her physical, mental or social skills represents a potential economic asset. In contrast, an unorganized collection of potential workers when properly organized and trained can become a labour force capable of generating economic value. Water, soil, minerals, even domestic animals become generative assets only when they are appropriately accessed and cared for. Over time, as societies have learned more effective ways of accessing and utilizing these human and natural resources as generative assets, their economies have grown.

If a country finds and exploits oil, gas or mineral resources, that country then typically utilizes these resources as increased sources of income. Because these stocks of natural resources produce flows of income and other benefits, they are at least momentarily generative assets. However, if these assets are simply consumed and thereby depleted, they will correspondingly lose their value as generative assets. In contrast, if in the process of developing means to access and market these resources, countries and firms work to develop needed physical and social infrastructures not just as the immediate sites of particular operations but for the larger region and if they draw upon the earnings from these operations to establish other generative assets by investing in other businesses and other public institutions, then mining these resources can have a multiplier effect. In the first case, developing natural resources has little or no impact on economic growth because no continuing generative assets have been developed even though income levels have at least temporarily risen for some. In the latter case, extracting natural resources has genuinely fostered economic growth by utilizing the development of these resources to establish other generative assets in the form of infrastructures, other businesses, and at least some local networks of commerce.[5]

Assets may, of course, vary in the degree to which they are generative. Some stocks of personally held assets – collections of lands, households furnishing, objects of art, and unused saving accounts – may not be very generative at all. However, other assets – like new technologies, effective educational systems and active investment funds – may be very generative. Any assets that are used up by being directly consumed – like natural resources and overworked and abused labour forces – do lose value quite quickly. All assets gain or lose value as assets depending on how well they are respected and how effectively they are utilized as well as variable market conditions.

Increasingly over the past generation, there has been a growing recognition that capital assets and generative assets more generally do in fact assume a number of different forms. Already in the mid-1990s, a number of observers argued that the value of firms ought to be assessed not only in relation to the financial worth or financial capital but also in relation both to their productive, or what some observers refer to as their manufactured, capital – their technology, organization and physical investments – as well as their human capital – the skills, disposition, discipline and knowledge of their workforce (Blair, 1995, 1996). Increasingly, those concerned have recognized as well that the actual value of firms is affected by a number of intangibles: these include factors like a firm's access to relevant intellectual property, which has been described as intellectual capital, as well as its reputation, its overall milieu, and especially its capacity to foster trust and cooperation among those with whom it interacts, all of which have been described as social capital (Putnam, 1993; Avent, 2016). Other more environmentally concerned observers have added that the value of firms should also be assessed in relation to their access to, and the quality of, the natural assets or natural capital. Natural capital accordingly represents the sources and quality of the air, water, energy and other raw material they draw upon. A number of accountants and accounting organizations, including the World Bank, maintain that the economic value of both firms and overall economies must now be assessed in relation to multiple assets or capitals. In a recent book Gleeson-White refers to these as the 'Six Capitals:' that is, financial, manufactured, intellectual, human, social and natural capital (Eccles et al., 2011; Eccles, 2010; Hawkins et al., 1999; Gleeson-White, 2014).

From the perspective of our current discussion of economic growth, then, I further argue that economic growth takes place to the extent that particular economies have been able to develop generative assets generally and generative capital assets in particular in all of six of these forms. At the level of economies, it is appropriate to describe these capital assets in much of the same terms as they have been characterized in relation to firms but now in more general terms. Thus, financial capital includes stable currencies, the extent of credit available, the stocks of insurance, investment, saving, and property holdings, and the range of public and private institutions established to manage these financial assets. What I prefer to call productive (rather than manufactured) capital includes businesses, how effectively they are organized, technological developments, and the physical and economic infrastructures that facilitate business activity and commerce. Human capital refers to the extent to which workers are skilled and healthy as well as their dispositions to work effectively and creatively in addition to the social infrastructures that foster and facilitate these developments. Intellectual capital refers to the knowledge that people within societies draw upon to work and to innovate as well as the means of communication and rules with respect to copyright that both facilitate the diffusion of knowledge as well as the protection of appropriate property rights with respect to new knowledge. By social capital we refer to trust and social networks as well as the tacit as well as overt systems of security that allow people to cooperate freely and effectively. Finally, natural capital refers to natural resources that humans utilize in their private, public and working lives – including all of the ecosystem services humans benefit from; the condition of these resources – to what degree have been duly respected, protected and conserved; and the degree to which humans have found ways to gain greater benefits from these resources – by domesticating animals, the invention and modernization of agriculture, the utilization of solar panels, and so forth.

As societies have found ways to develop and not deplete these forms of capital – what I have referred to as generative assets – they have also, correspondingly, found ways to make more effective use of limited natural and human resources and they have as well experienced genuine and constructive forms of economic growth.

Although we often refer to economic growth in general terms, the characteristic features differ markedly depending upon whether we are focusing on the changes associated with quite primitive economic growth, the expansion of commerce, or industrialization. In approximate terms, there have been phases in economic growth associated in broad terms with the introduction of simple horticulture, the development of agriculture, various enhancements of agriculture associated with irrigation and the utilization of more recent technologies, the introduction and expansion of commerce – first local and then more distant, early stages of industrialization, advanced industrialization and the organization of economies associated with mass consumer societies, and the more recent changes associated with modern information technologies and communication systems.[6] Different factors have played decisive roles in relation to different phases of economic growth. A well-informed appreciation of the diverse but similar ways economies develop by passing through these kinds of phases is important for a number of reasons. In the process we are reminded, for example, that many current forms of development became possible because they presupposed and built upon prior developments. Advancements in commerce typically become more likely because of prior developments in agriculture. The possibilities for industrialization typically becomes more likely as a result of antecedent developments fostering economic growth in agriculture and commerce. Correspondingly, in so far as we are interested in fostering economic growth in underdeveloped areas, whether these be defined in relation to countries or regions within countries, then it becomes important to encourage forms of economic development that seem appropriate given the extent to which these areas have already developed. In some cases, as with the widespread adoption of mobile phones in Africa, it is possible to introduce quite advanced forms of technology in otherwise underdeveloped areas. However, in other instances, the construction of more advanced forms of mining and manufacturing in areas in which there has been little economic growth with respect to agriculture and commerce, leads to the creation of economic enclaves not well-integrated into these areas and of little benefit to the larger population of these areas. For instance, many of the investments from industrialized countries in developing areas have given rise to what observers have referred to as dual economies, as small pockets of externally oriented enterprises traded with foreign investors, while the remainder of the society pursued traditional patterns of exchange and production. In the process, inequalities between these sub-economies greatly increased further aggravating social and political tensions between them (Boeke, 1953; Lewis, 1979; Evans, 1979).

Industrialization represents a noteworthy and, historically, fairly recent phase of economic growth, introduced initially in northwestern Europe in the middle of the eighteenth century. What has been remarkable about industrialization has been the tremendous expansion of productive powers and the correspondingly greatly increased levels of consumption. As a result of industrialization, people have been able to live much longer, to produce noticeably more goods and services, to invest in much greater range of public services, and to eat better and to live more healthy lives. Since the late eighteenth century, industrialization has spread unevenly around the world. To-day some countries are much more industrialized than others. In the more than 100 least-developed countries and sometimes in large areas of otherwise economically de-veloped countries, there can be few traces of industrialization. Often when people dis-cuss economic growth, they are referring to industrialization, which is really only the latest phase in a much longer process of development. In term of the overall phases of economic development what many underdeveloped areas could benefit most from would be growth in the form of advancements in agriculture and local commerce.

If economic growth is best conceived of as the development of durable economi-cally generative assets, then how should we suitably and practically measure economic growth? In practice economic growth is frequently gauged by measuring gross domestic product on a per capita basis. This measure is widely used to estimate in general how well countries are performing economically, the extent of poverty within countries, and rates of economic development. Although pervasively utilized, this approach to gauging economic growth has also been strongly criticized. It is a mis-measure, many observers have argued, for a number of reasons. For example, it provides an account of overall market activity, without taking account of the depreciation of assets and the non-market contribution to the overall economy by households and civil society organizations. It understates the values that many businesses and households have gained at little expense by uses of modern digital technology (Brynjolfsson and McAfee, 2014). This meas-ure also overstates economic growth by failing to take account of the market failures connected with the under-utilization of able-bodied adults wanting to work but who remain unemployed or under-employed or who have for the time being dropped out of the labour force (Avent, 2016). As well it overstates rates of growth by failing to take account of long-term externalities of business practices, connected with slowly develop-ing adverse environmental and social damages (Nixon, 2007). By focusing on national averages, it fails to observe the distribution of incomes and the extent to which eco-nomic growth is inclusive or instead largely benefits small enclaves. (Stiglitz et al., 2010; IWR, 2012). By focusing on income, I have argued, it proximately gauges the ability to consume rather than productivity and the development of generative assets. Many have argued that it is a mistake to measure economic growth in terms of any single index because, after all, economic development is multi-dimensional, and takes place, as I have argued above, in relation to establishing and enhancing a number of different kinds of generative assets. These different kinds of assets are not fungible: they cannot easily be measured in relation either to a single index or in terms of the calibration used to gauge other kinds of capital assets.

Correspondingly, we need to develop different kinds of indices for the different types of generative assets, looking both for ways these assets have been typically enhanced as well as ways these assets have been typically degraded and depleted – for example, depending on the type of asset, by inflation, the abuse of work forces, or the excessive consumption of unrenewable limited natural resources. A number of groups are working to develop these kinds of gauges. For example, a number of different measures have been developed to take account of environmental impacts, including ones gauging environmental and/or carbon foot prints of economic activities as well as so-called 'green' measures of GDP, which subtract environmental costs from GDP figures. The European Council developed a multi-dimensional measure that includes a number of social, environmental and economic indicators. The International Commission on the Measurement of Economic Performance and Social Progress has proposed developing a hybrid measure of economic activity that variously attempts to look at levels of per capita income and consumption while taking account as well of the overall stocks of assets, including natural resources, which current generations are able to pass onto to future generations (Stiglitz et al., 2010). The World Bank has been working on what it refers to as WAVES: 'Wealth Accounting and the Valuation of Ecosystems Services'. (Gleeson-White, 2014, pp. 68–69) Robert Eccles and others in turn have been seeking to operationalize a system of integrated reporting that at once gauges the ways and the degrees to which economic activities affect financial, social, health and environmental assets (Eccles, 2010). What these several initiatives share in common is commitment to measure in relation to practical and relevant gradations economic activities in all their complexity. Accordingly, if we think it is fitting to describe economic growth as the development of generative assets, then it also seems possible to gauge both the degree and manner in which economies are growing roughly in relation to the development and/or degradation of this wide range of assets.

Norms for addressing the global crisis of economic growth

If we are to find a way of addressing the current global crisis with respect to economic growth, then we need to explore alternative ways of thinking about economic growth that encourage us to foster growth where it is needed while restraining growth as a whole – especially in areas where it is likely to have the most disastrous consequences.

As a guide for reflecting on this crisis, I propose modifying traditional guidance that John Wesley, eighteenth-century Anglican cleric and theologian, proposed long ago in a sermon on 'The use of money'.[7] Wesley argued that money itself was neither inherently good nor bad. 'In the present state of mankind, it is an excellent gift of God … food for the hungry, drink for the thirsty, raiment for the naked.' People have used money to feed their greed and to exploit others. They have also used money to care for others, to feed the hungry and clothe those without clothes. Money could be viewed as a generative asset, which humans might use beneficially or adversely. In itself money was morally neutral. What mattered, and mattered a lot, was the uses to which people put money. Wesley then proceeded to outline and explain three broad counsels regarding the responsible use of money. He urged his audiences to 'gain all you can', 'save all you can', and 'give all you can'. It is, of course, important to look carefully at how he explained and interpreted these three counsels. In relation to the first counsel to 'gain all you can', he spelled out a version of the work ethic, advising his listeners and readers to work hard, to respect other workers, to work safely, and to utilize resources effectively.

'Lose no time ... do it [your work] as well as possible ... learn from the experiences of others.' Wesley emphasized a consumer ethic in his second point, 'saving all you can'. Here he emphasized the importance of making effective use of what we have, minimizing waste, and fostering thrift. 'Not to use it effectively is to throw it away.' In relation to the third counsel about 'giving all you can', he set forth what we might today call a communitarian ethic, indicating that in so far as we had first properly cared for our families and we had the means, then we should act to support our neighbours and those in need. God has given us all we have. We should, Wesley declared, use what we have to care for ourselves, our households, and our communities, and others in need not as proprietors but as stewards of God's gifts (Wesley, 1944).

In broad terms Wesley's counsel regarding the responsible uses of money serves well as initial point of reference for thinking about the responsible uses of economic growth in relation to the current global crisis. Correspondingly, we begin by acknowledging that economic growth, appropriately understood (see previous section of this chapter) in itself is neither good nor bad: what matters is how we engage in economic growth. Following Wesley's lead, we start by advocating that we produce productively. Given the fact that human and natural resources are limited and that by mid–century more than 9 billion people will be living on the Earth, we are then appropriately counselled to make the most effective uses of these limited resources. Correspondingly, we might then re-interpret Wesley's second counsel to argue that we ought to consume these resources sustainably. Like Wesley, we can urge people not to abuse and waste these resources but to act to conserve and use them with respect. Finally, while using the language of charity, Wesley's third counsel urges people to view their lives broadly in relation to others with whom they have been called upon to live. Extrapolating this counsel to our current complex globalized world, we might then argue that we are called upon both to develop inclusive economies that benefit all and to collaborate globally as we seek to address this crisis. The Earth Charter, enacted in 2000 and adopted by civil society groups all over the world, affirms that as humans we should see ourselves as members along with other living things of the larger community of life on Earth (Bird et al., 2016, chapter 2: Brown, 2000).

In the remainder of this chapter, I will elaborate on these three principles. I will explore their normative and practical significance for the current crisis. I will call attention both to the widely based support for each of these principles and their practical relevance. I will argue that all three of these principles are important and that, while it is useful to distinguish among them, they must be honoured as a whole. After all, the practices of producing inherently involve forms of consumption and producers produce goods and services in large part in response to demands of consumers. Nonetheless, at least with regard to finding useful ways of responding to the current global crisis with respect to economic growth, it is useful to distinguish among these principles. I will begin with the principle of consuming sustainably, because endorsement of this principle has already gained considerable momentum.

Consuming sustainably

By consuming sustainably, I refer to intentional efforts to reduce the rates at which humans consume natural resources; to re-use, renew, re-store, and conserve resources where possible; to reduce especially the consumption of non-renewable resources; and to consume all resources in ways that respect the characteristic features of these resources. Consuming sustainably involves both a mind-set – a basic orientation to the Earth, its ecosystems, and its inhabitants – as well as an ever-enlarging set of practices. Consuming sustainably addresses the crisis in economic growth in three ways. First, to the degree that human consume sustainably, we thereby reduce adverse impacts of economic activity on the Earth and its ecosystems by using up/depleting valued resources and by discharging materials, fluids and emissions that pollute and contaminate. Second, as humans learn to consume sustainably, we also learn to use resources more effectively with less waste, thereby enhancing the productivity of production processes. Finally, as humans find ways to consume sustainably, we also increase the chances that these resources of the Earth will be 'enough and as good left in common for others' so all humans have reasonable chances for benefiting from them (Locke, 1952, p. 17; see also WCED, 1987).

There are severe limits to what humans can consume. There is only so much fresh water and arable land and in some places there are today insufficient quantities of both for the numbers of people living in these areas. As more and more countries economically develop, humans are consuming structural metals, like iron, bauxite, copper, and nickel at unsustainable rates (Jackson, 2009, p. 75; Rubin, 2012, p. 221). Although there are vast quantities of some minerals, there are limited supplies of many others. Although humans have continued to discover new sources of oil and gas, it costs much, much more to extract oil and gas from sources like tar sands and shale, and the supplies of these hydrocarbons still remain finite. By early 2014, the cost for oil had quadrupled over the past decade. This change occurred in part because of the added expenses associated with extraction and even more so because of the greatly increased demand for oil as countries like India, Brazil and China industrialize and as larger number of their citizens begin driving automobiles and manufacturing processes expand. The cost of these fossil fuels has since declined as the supply has momentarily expanded. However, more importantly, the known reserves of fossil fuels in any case far exceed the amounts of these fuels that can be consumed over the next 50 years if humans hope to limit the potential increases in global climate caused by emissions from burning these fuels to anywhere near the target rise of 2 degrees Celsius (Hansen, 2012; Klein, 2014, part 2) 350.org, the world-wide movement begun by Bill McKibben, has especially focused on ways to achieve this goal.

Because of the discovery of new sources of minerals and energy and because we have also discovered ways of utilizing these materials much more efficiently, in spite of the continued steep growth in human population, we have not yet reached the so-called physical limits to growth as soon as soon as authors of the 1972 *Limits to Growth* book predicted (Meadows et al., 1972). Nonetheless, those limits are real. There are finite mineral sources and minerals are a non-renewable resource. Although we have been able greatly to expand global food production, there are limits here as well. We are already exhausting some fish stocks. In many areas because of overuse, soil for growing crops has been seriously degraded. We have significantly depleted limited global supplies of ground water, especially in areas such as the Middle East, northern China, and central United States. All of these limits will become more challenging as the population of the Earth rises to more than 9 billion. The demands for these finite resources will increase both with the growth in population and as formerly underdeveloped countries industrialize and their citizens seek consumer goods and services associated with industrialized societies. More people will want to live in comfortable housing with plumbing, electrical services, and corresponding furnishings. They will want to buy their own cars. As a result of these steep increases in demand, prices are likely to rise. These trends may well aggravate the growing and troubling divide between economically advantaged and economically impoverished, especially in areas where water, land, or housing at affordable prices are severely limited.

Much attention has been addressed to the ways economic growth over time has had an adverse impact on the Earth's climate. Although estimates of this impact vary, among the scientific communities studying the climate there is universal recognition that human economic activity has not only increased air pollution in some areas to dangerously unhealthy levels but has also caused the overall temperature of the atmosphere to climb. As a result of human-occasioned global warming, glaciers and snow pacts have been melting near the Earth's poles as well as in high mountains from the Rockies in North America to the Himalayas in Asia. Melting ice and snow have occasioned fears that ocean levels will rise enough to threaten low lying populated lands all over the world. Global warming as well seems to be associated with changes in weather patterns, including increased drought in some locales and more violent storms in other locales (IPCC, 2014).

In response to these diverse problems, a widespread consensus has emerged that humans must undertake economic activity in the future in ways significantly different than we have in the past. We can no longer assume, as humans have frequently assumed for centuries, that there are unlimited supplies of land, water, air and minerals, which we can draw upon to address our needs and wants and into which we can dump our waste and emissions. We have to find ways of living within the ecological limits of the Earth. As we seek to measure economic activity, we must take account of how we are depleting or adversely altering the Earth's resources. Increasingly aware of these concerns, in 1984 the United Nations mandated the creation of an international commission to look at the relations between economic activity and the environment. As a guide for thinking about economic growth, that commission, chaired by Gro Brundtland, former Prime Minister of Norway, proposed that economic activity be guided by the norm of sustainable development. The commission argued that businesses and countries could continue to pursue economic growth so long as current economic activities provided the opportunities, and did not compromise the capacities, for subsequent generations to pursue corresponding patterns of growth (WCED, 1987). Subsequently, the principle of sustainable development has been variously interpreted, sometimes strictly in ways that would greatly restrict the non-renewable extractive activities and sometimes quite loosely focusing on the overall social and economic sustainability of societies and not just on limits of particular natural resources. For the purpose of this chapter, I propose to interpret this norm strictly in relation to patterns of consumption and then to gauge consumption patterns in relation to the Earth's ecological limits. As the Earth Charter, the Millennium Ecosystem Assessment report, Bill McKibben, and many others have argued: with respect to patterns of consumption, the relevant point of reference isn't the continued well-being of humans but rather the carrying capacity of the Earth (Earth Charter Commission, 2005; Millennium Ecosystem Assessment, 2005).

With respect to consuming sustainably, I will make three broad proposals to help address the current global crisis. These proposals are interrelated. Subtending these three broad proposals is the assumption there is no simple way of reducing consumption and rendering our consumer choices more responsible.

One, we need to find ways of limiting certain adverse industrial activities that endanger the Earth and its inhabitants either proximately or over the long term. Within this category we must include a number of practices, including the excessive emissions of carbon dioxide and other gases, the pollution of streams and ground water by careless industrial practices, as well as current patterns of fertilizer use because of the impact of this use on the water quality of streams and lakes. While there are certainly disagreements about the levels at which these activities become noxious or excessive, nonetheless, over the long term, all of these activities, and especially the emission of so-called greenhouse gases, must be greatly reduced. There is a growing sense of urgency about this matter. Industrial practices also endanger the planet by the ways they have acted to waste other valued but limited natural resources. These include the flaring of unused natural gases; the overuse and degradation of soils; the careless discarding of unmarketable fish catches; the exploitation of limited arable lands for non-agricultural uses; the enormous dumping of industrial wastes that might with a little extra effort be re-used, recycled or restored; and the less than efficient use of non-renewable mineral and energy sources. This list is just suggestive. Many other specific examples of the wasteful industrial uses of the Earth and its resources might be cited. In general, businesses aggravate the current crisis to the extent that they seek to augment their incomes primarily by finding and exploiting sites where they can extract wealth from given sources, whether these be poorly paid labourers, the excessive credibility of customers, increasingly depleted mineral sources, or over-cultivated lands (Nixon, 2007). Douglass North and colleagues argue that over the centuries prior to industrialization economic and political elites have typically adopted this kind of extractive approach to wealth creation. With industrialization, many businesses have realized how more wealth can be created by developing diverse assets that can in turn be utilized as ongoing sources of income (North et al., 2008; Acemoglu and Robinson, 2012; Diamond, 2008). In any case, too many businesses have been depleting the natural assets with which they work. These patterns of industrial abuse and wasteful use are unsustainable. They have put the Earth and the long-term viability of the global economy at great risk.

Recognizing the imperative to bring about appropriate changes, some governments and some businesses have begun to initiate fitting responses. Many governments have enacted laws to prohibit or greatly reduce the flaring of gases, to eliminate or greatly limit noxious emissions, and in particular to reduce carbon emissions. They have introduced extra taxes and fines to encourage compliance. Given the extent and urgency of the problem, current responses remain inadequate. Nonetheless, many resist these kinds of changes because they argue that these kinds of changes are not economically feasible at least in the medium and short term. Introducing these kinds of changes will, they contend, further threaten to cause economic slowdowns. In spite of these arguments, many businesses have begun to acknowledge the importance of these imperatives. No doubt, in large part because consumers have asked for changes, because requested changes have sometimes proven to be economically beneficial, and because of stricter governmental regulations, many businesses have found ways to make much more effective use of oil, gas, coal and other sources of energy, to limit pollution, and to reduce emissions. For example, as they have attempted to operate in ways that are safer, healthier, and environmentally less damaging, chemical producing firms through the internationally adopted, industry-wide Responsible Care programs have discovered that these initiatives actually foster the more efficient and therefore less costly use of chemical feed stock (Moffat et al., 2004). A number of the large petroleum extracting and retailing firms have been quite seriously repositioning themselves as energy companies, recognizing they can no longer put off not only the need to find and develop alternatives sources of energy, like solar power, but also the need to utilize all energy sources much more efficiently. In a recent publication, Royal Dutch Shell admitted that business as usual was no longer possible. Precisely because of the global crisis regarding economic growth, the world was likely to become more economically and political unstable. Therefore, it was important for firms like Shell to become far more flexible and far more responsible (Shell News Lens, 2013). Since 1994, Interface, a large firm making modular floor coverings, has found ways greatly to reduce waste, recycle products, greatly expand their use of solar power, and significantly reduce their consumption of fossil fuels. Having read Paul Hawkins book on the *Ecology of Commerce*, Ray Anderson, the founder and chair, encouraged a culture of experimentation that resulted in occasional failures but an overall significantly reduced environmental impact. The efforts by accountants to identify and measure the utilization of diverse assets/capital provide useful means for firms to gauge the degree to which their practices add to or deplete natural and human resources (Gleeson-White, 2014). Although these responses are not without merit, they remain as yet far too timid. It may well be that we cannot expect greater response until we are forced to introduce drastic changes as a result of environmental and/or economic crises which current practices will inevitably occasion.

Two, in our households and personal lives we need to find ways of consuming less and consuming more responsibly. If, as the world population expands and more and more people seek to live middle-class lives, we hope to reduce the overall consumption of limited natural resources, then we must explore ways to consume less. Developing effective public transportation systems will help to reduce both the ever increasing purchases of private cars and the amounts of energy consumed by these cars. We can revive traditional ideas about living simply. It is possible to explore ways of living fuller and happier lives that do not require us to consume more commodities, whether these assume the form of bigger houses, more clothes, greater use of personal means for transportation, or more entertainment. We can find ways of measuring our economic well-being not in relation to what we earn or buy but in terms of the quality of our lives. The challenge here is how to transition from current, deeply embedded habits of mind and heart that are also incorporated in taken-for-granted economic assumptions and move towards these alternatives viewed not simply as acts of personal virtue but as expressions of widely shared public purpose. However, if we hope to have even modest impact globally, we must translate these ideals into public policies.

We can take a couple of steps in this direction by instituting policies that encourage both the conservationist, non-wasteful use of resources as well as thrift. We can move in this direction in part by building upon existing initiatives. For example, many communities now foster the recycling and re-using of items that were formerly thrown into the garbage by the public collections of used plastics, glass, metals, paper and cardboard, and compostable wastes. In many communities, thrift stores sell used furniture, clothing and other household items and public food programs dispense meals prepared by using unsold items from both grocery stores and restaurants. We can take more serious steps, as the Danish did when they introduced a sales tax on automobiles equivalent to the cost of the vehicles (Rubin, 2012, chapter 6). This tax clearly discourages people from buying extra cars. Many countries have introduced hefty taxes on gasoline not only to pay for the upkeep of roads and the construction of public transits systems but also to use gasoline with greater restraint. As fuel prices continue to rise, these kinds of policies are likely to attract greater support. Nonetheless, we have a long way to go considering the hundreds of millions of gallons of oil consumed every day. It may well be necessary measurably to raise the level of value-added and consumption taxes not only to generate more public revenues to address public debts and to improve degrading public infrastructures but also to foster more conservative habits of consumption. In the industrialized nations, too many people have been living beyond their means. It would be very helpful, accordingly, to revive traditional views about the importance of thrift as a means of reducing household indebtedness, encouraging investments and savings, and also moderating excessive patterns of consumption.

These diverse efforts to foster reduced and more responsible patterns of individual and household consumption confront a major, not easily addressed challenge. People living in modern industrialized societies highly value consumption as an expression of their fundamental freedom of choice. Liberal societies treasure freedom of choice as this is expressed in our choices regarding where we might live, with whom we will live, where we will work, and how we will live. The latter is typically embodied in a series of consumer choices related to housing, leisure time, food, clothing, transportation and life style. The high valuation of consumer choice is further reinforced by the widely held economic assumption that the most effective means to overcome economic slowdowns is to encourage increases in consumer activity. As societies began to industrialize and they expanded their industrial capacity, it was widely assumed that economic prosperity was best fostered by encouraging hard, skilful work, new ideas, and financial investments. In late and post-industrial societies the critical factor has become consumption. It seems we can now produce more than enough goods and services. Correspondingly, it is argued, the economy may languish if not enough people choose to purchase what we produce. Therefore, through skilful uses of advertisements, it is assumed we need to encourage greater consumption (Bell, 1976; Galbraith, 1958 chapter 10 and 11; Cohen, 2003, chapters 2, 3, and 8). If these means seem inadequate, then, it has been argued, we may need to reduce taxes so that people will be encouraged to buy more.[8] Furthermore, if this latter initiative still seems to be ineffective, then others have proposed that we encourage people to borrow more so they can consume more, as in pervasive efforts to encourage families to make more credit card purchases.

It is clearly time to rethink the presumed priority which modern societies and modern economics have assigned to consumer choice. We may well need to revive the ancient traditions which encouraged us to exercise our freedom of choice in ways other than how we consume: through friendships, family life, patterns of thought, and leisure activities that we can pursue independent of consumer markets. We can also observe that how we consume has indeed become crucial for economic well-being, but not in terms of the volume of what we consume but in terms of the wisdom and restraint of our purchases as we recognize the possible adverse impact of our choices on the well-being of the Earth, its climate, and its inhabitants. In relation to the recent financial crisis and great recession, we can further recognize the adverse consequences of the uses of dubious means to increase the volume of consumption. I have in mind here practices of fostering highly risky home loan arrangements and tax cuts both of which aggravated the crisis and excessively reduced the capacity of governments to respond to the crisis and almost exclusively benefited the rich.

Three, in so far as possible we need to find ways of reducing population growth. The rapid and extensive expansion in global population over the past century has put an enormous strain on the Earth's carrying capacity. As the population of humans has grown, the number of people consuming finite human and natural resources has also grown. In many of the least-developed countries, the steady growth in population means that their slowly growing economies are unable to provide food and basic supplies to meet the needs of their own people. Most of these countries import food. Because of their often still underdeveloped character, in many settings rural lands cannot provide the jobs, food, sustenance needed by all the people born in these areas. Millions of these people every year move into the increasing large urban complexes. While the affluent do in fact consume far more than those who are economically impoverished, nonetheless the steady growth in global population aggravates all of these problems. It is now hoped that later in the twenty-first century global population will reach a steady state of between 9 and 10 billion people. Still, if there were viable ways of reducing the population growth sooner and reaching a steady with a smaller overall population size, then that would seem to be especially important. In fact, a viable solution to this problem seems to exist. It is not necessary to hope for wars and disease nor to introduce draconian population control measures. Over time, two factors have played especially instrumental roles in reducing the birth rates. One, as economies grow and as standards of living improve, birth rates tend to fall. People feel correspondingly less need for additional children, as they do when there are high mortality rates and when adult children provide the most reliable means for caring for their parents as the latter become older and more feeble. Both of these factors have been associated with less developed economies. Correspondingly, that is one of the reasons why some appropriate forms of economic growth seem important. Two, providing primary and secondary school education for girls has been particularly helpful in reducing birth rates. This education may be desirable on its own merit both as a way of providing humane opportunities for girls and as a way of augmenting at the national level the overall stock of human capital assets. In addition, as girls receive education, they become more aware of their opportunities and choices, they gain modestly but decisively in their capacity to shape the contours of their own lives, and they begin having babies at older ages. Anyone seriously interested in limiting the consumption of natural and human resources, and thereby helping to address the current global crisis with respect to economic growth, should therefore work to increase the global educational opportunities for girls (Banerjee and Duflo, 2011; Sen, 1999, chapter 4).

Producing productively

Producing productively is as important for protecting the carrying capacity of the Earth as consuming sustainably. Because we live on a planet with limited natural and human resources, it is vital that we find ways of utilizing these resources as effectively as possible. Producing productively aims to do just that. From this perspective economic growth takes places to the extent that people in a given generation are able to preserve, add to, and pass on to the next generation stocks of generative assets, which can in turn be drawn upon to foster the effective utilization of human and natural resources and corresponding flows of income. However, whenever humans act to destroy, deplete or degrade these diverse assets – as they do when they overwork labourers, pollute water supplies or exhaust mineral resources – then their actions must be regarded as unproductive and value-destroying no matter how much income they may produce in the process.

Societies gain in their capacity to develop useable economic assets to the extent that they have constructed the corresponding physical, social and economic infrastructures that both embody many of these assets and facilitate the creation and protection of others. As societies develop their physical infrastructures, they correspondingly create the conditions – roads, water systems, electricity grids and the like – that facilitate the expansion of local commerce, the growth of local industry, even the construction of schools – concomitant with increasingly productive utilization of their human and natural resources. The expansion of social infrastructures has had corresponding consequences: as societies develop educational services, health services, and social insurance programs, they correspondingly strengthen human and social assets, which in turn foster economic growth. The development of economic infrastructures plays an equivalently instrumental role, by expanding credit, institutionalizing market exchanges, fostering commerce and facilitating investments. In many respects, the best rough estimate of the extent and the ways in which developing countries are developing is to examine the degree to which they have been able to establish and to enlarge upon physical, social and economic infrastructures.

As societies develop their economic capital assets, by increasing both the scope of these assets as well as effectiveness of particular assets, they develop their ability to make more productive use of available resources and increase the accessibility of previously inaccessible resources. Understood in these terms, economic growth as the process of producing more efficiently and distributing raw materials as well as final products more efficiently remains a valuable objective for both developing and industrialized societies. Therefore, just as in response to the current global crisis regarding economic growth, it has become imperative to consume sustainably, so it has also become an imperative to produce productively. However, with regard to productivity the agendas facing the developing and industrialized societies differ in important ways.

Before examining these distinct agendas, we need to discuss briefly how we might at least approximately measure productivity. Accordingly, we need to measure productivity not just in relation to the extent to which given hours of labour are able to produce diverse goods and services, measured by current market prices adjusted for purchasing power parity. We also need to measure how effectively we have used and/or depleted and degraded natural resources, measured approximately both in relation to market values and the cost to replace or find substitute resources as particular resources are depleted or degraded. Of course, we will not be able to measure productivity as precisely as per capita income. Nevertheless, we can, as uses of the Human Development Index demonstrate, find some approximate measures that gauge various ways in which natural and human resources are utilized and/or abused. We can, for example, in approximate terms measure not only output per hours of labour as well as estimates of the lost hours of unemployed workers. We can gauge and we have gauged in approximate terms the extent and conditions of arable lands, forest reserves, fish stocks, accessible potable water, mineral lodes, and many other natural resources.

Additionally, we need to rethink the way we gauge labour productivity. Current practices make economies or businesses look more productive if newer technologies or workplace arrangements use fewer workers to produce the same amount of goods and services, thereby sometimes causing increased unemployment. To be sure, in many cases newer technologies and working arrangements have expanded economic opportunities for those seeking employment. Moreover, these kinds of changes characteristically make more effective use of those workers still employed. However, the productivity of economies in general as opposed to particular firms ought to be gauged with reference to all those able-bodied and qualified persons either working or actively seeking work not just with reference to those currently employed. A workforce becomes more productive both when it develops ways of utilizing the labour of given workers more effectively and when it finds ways of utilizing the labour of greater portions of able-bodied persons seeking to work. A labour force wastes the value-adding human resources of those potential workers for which no viable work opportunities exist.

Defined in relation to the development of economic assets and the productive uses of given resources, economic growth is an imperative for large parts of the world that remain underdeveloped. Economic growth becomes a means of reducing the poverty that still afflicts approximately one-third of all humans. Economic growth offers the promise for developing needed physical, social and economic infrastructures. There are a number of critical issues that we must address in order to foster fitting and effective patterns of economic growth in developing areas.[9]

First, it takes a long time for economies to grow, to establish and enlarge upon the economic assets – and the corresponding institutions and infrastructures – that constitute the basic building blocks of productive development. The economic arrangements associated with industrialization are best introduced in societies which have already found ways to make more effective use of resources through more modern methods of agriculture and have become more economically inter-connected through the expansion of local commerce. It is easier for firms to produce productively to the extent that they can utilize the economic assets embodied in developing corresponding physical, social and economic infrastructures. Marx once wrote that 'Men make their own history but they do not make it just as they please; they do not make it under circumstances chosen by themselves, but under circumstances directly encountered, given, and transmitted from the past' (Marx, 1963, p. 15). Correspondingly, if we hope to foster modern forms of industrial life in developing countries, we need first to work at establishing their preconditions, which include working to develop more productive forms of agriculture, more effective forms of local commerce, and the infrastructures that facilitate these developments. The work of Paul Polak provides a constructive example of what might be done. Polak has organized both International Development Enterprises and Windhorse International to help millions of small landholders in South Asia and Africa make more productive uses of their lands by growing in dry as well as wet seasons and by helping them markets their produce locally (Polak, 2008; Polak and Warwick, 2013).

In contrast, many investors from industrialized countries and many of the economic and political elites in developing countries seem to be especially interested in fostering developments that generate much wealth in the short term for those involved. Often these ventures focus on the extraction of minerals and energy, the growth of commodities for foreign markets, and the fabrication of products for export. Typically, the enterprises involved, like businesses in old company towns, build infrastructures almost exclusively for their own uses rather than collaborating with local agents to develop larger, more encompassing road systems, electricity grids, water systems, as well as educational and health services. In the process, both foreign investors and local elites augment their power and wealth. Since the 1980s, the expansion of supply chains in developing countries have operated mostly in this way (Avent, 2016, chapter 8). As a result, while over the short term these ventures do generate streams of income for those involved, they often only marginally help to establish and expand the generative economic assets associated with economic growth and producing productively. To be sure, in many developing countries some of the wealth produced by these ventures has ended up in government revenues and some of these funds have been utilized to fund infrastructure projects. Many observers argue that local business and political elites in many underdeveloped countries typically form patrimonial alliances that generate incomes for those immediately involved but lead neither to the development of effective systems of public administration nor to anything like thriving business sectors (Handley, 2008). Recently, a number of observers have criticized the failures of international aid programmes to foster economic growth in developing countries (Easterly, 2006; Moyo, 2009). One might make an equivalent critique of international business investments in so far as in many areas billions of dollars invested have had only marginal impact on developing the broad range of economic assets integral to the increasingly productive utilization of limited natural and human resources.

If least-developed countries are going to grow economically, then they must find ways of developing generative economic assets (broadly understood) and the corresponding infrastructures rather than increased but often short-term flows of income. Gleeson-White in her book *Six Capitals* makes reference to a number of indices by which these countries and businesses operating in them can gauge their development in relation to increases in financial, productive, intellectual social, human and natural capital (Gleeson-White, 2014). In the process they need to strengthen effective systems of public administration, encourage and support the expansion of local businesses, stimulate local commerce and foster the development of institutions that make these developments possible. Economic growth in this form is possible as we can see from examples of development in places as different as South Korea, Chile and Indonesia. However, as these examples well illustrate, recent economic growth in these countries benefited from the prior development of diverse social, productive and human assets and corresponding infrastructures. Before their recent and noteworthy periods of marked economic expansion, these countries had educational systems, comparatively reliable systems of public administration, many energetic local business enterprises, and modest but useable physical infrastructures (Maxfield and Schneider, 1997).

Second, in so far possible, it is important to foster inclusive patterns of economic growth in developing countries rather than growth that assumes enclave-like forms. The issue here concerns the degree to which any investment, government programme, or private enterprise broadly helps the society as a whole to develop or rather functions primarily to benefit particular groups. Often investments in developing countries have not been well-integrated into the economies of the host country. In part these enterprises remained isolated because they were developed to sell what they produced to foreign markets. Furthermore, these enterprises used few local businesses as suppliers. Many developing countries created export processing zones which, while they did offer employment opportunities for some workers and returns for a few local investors, played little or no role in developing economic assets and infrastructures for the host countries. In many cases foreign investments were not integrated in local economies simply because physical and economic infrastructures of these countries remained underdeveloped. Both host countries and foreign investors are accordingly challenged to find ways in which foreign investments can become more fully integrated in local economies and thereby have greater impact on the development of economic assets in these countries. One strategy for helping to realize this goal would be to require foreign investors to partner with enterprises from the host country to develop at a regional or provincial level and not simply at a site or local level the several infrastructural services that foreign investors do require simply to do business. As a condition of doing business, foreign firms would be expected to collaborate with partners from the developing areas to construct on a wider scale systems for providing electricity, water, transportation, garbage collection, health care and security which they need in order to do business. In the process, these ventures not only will produce income for investors and employees and taxes for governments but also will work to establish and strengthen generative capital assets, broadly understood, that will in turn render the overall economy more productive (IWR, 2012; Bird, 2006, chapter 7; Bird, 2016).

Third, efforts need to be made to limit the degree to which industrialized nations directly act to restrict the productive growth of developing areas. From this perspective, many developing countries suffer not just from the lack of development and not just from the legacy of past colonial and neo-colonial practices (Nixon, 2011). They suffer as well because of the ways they are currently impeded from productively developing their own financial, productive, human, social and natural assets. I will review several note-worthy examples. For instance, by virtue of price supports and tax credits they offer to agricultural enterprises in their own countries, industrialized countries in the European Community, North America, and Japan have acted to frustrate the efforts of farming enterprises in many developing areas to sell their produce both at home and abroad. In many developing countries agricultural sectors are correspondingly less developed than they might otherwise be (Stiglitz and Charlton, 2005). In addition, many international businesses operating in developing areas pay taxes much lower than they might be ex-pected to pay because they have made abusive use of transfer pricing practices, related to services and product they have acquired from foreign branches of their own companies (Baker, 2005). Although mining operations in Chile have greatly expanded since the 1990s and although these firms have extracted minerals worth billions of dollars, these firms have paid little or no taxes to the government of Chile because of their clever use of transfer pricing (Riesco, 2004). As a result, the Chilean government simply has had less revenue for upgrading the physical and social infrastructures of the country. Furthermore, to the extent that foreign enterprises invest in enclave-like projects in developing countries, they have also correspondingly occasioned and intensified ine-qualities in these countries in ways that have aggravated social tensions and undermined social capital.[10]

While continuing to be an urgent imperative, fostering the productive development of the economies of developing areas will not be easy. It will take much time. However, when we view economic growth as the development of generative capital assets, then at least we have a better sense of how we might most effectively proceed to achieve long-term, sustainable benefits. In keeping with the principle of consuming sustainably, we remain focused on establishing, expanding and protecting diverse economically generative assets.

The agenda for economic growth in the industrialized societies differs. We remain interested in producing productively. We maintain our focus on cultivating, refining and protecting generative capital assets. We continue to call attention to, and seek meas-urably to reduce, activities that seek to mine assets for current flows of income and thereby to deplete or degrade these assets, whether these are human or natural assets.

From the perspective of our model regarding the productive utilization of natural and human resources, two issues especially seem to call for concerted public attention. These issues are different but may be related in terms of how we choose to address them. One issue concerns the especially high rates of un- and under-employment, especially of young people. Although these rates have been climbing over the past three and half decades, they have become especially aggravated since the financial crisis of 2007–8 (Klein, 1999; *The Economist*, 2013; Avent, 2016). In some countries and some cities un- and under-employment as well as shadow unemployment (those who no longer are looking for work) rates for young males exceed 30 per cent. Un- and under-employment is in part a social problem because of the way this condition affects those involved and the degree to which some of those affected act in ways that are damaging to others. For example, many of those who are unemployed or under-employed over long periods are more likely to fail to support their families and dependents, engage in antisocial behaviour, acquire what they want or need by illegal means, and/or become easy recruits for militant terrorists or angry populist groups. However, from the perspective of our model of productive growth, those who suffer from high rates of un- and under-employment represent under-utilized and de-graded human resources. The presence of this supply of under-utilized population of labourers additionally functions to depress the wages of low-income fully employed workers. This is a huge social and economic problem. Effective labour markets ought to be able to help both those seeking workers to find employees and for those seeking employment to find work. To be sure, a small portion of those who lack regular full time work do so on account of normal imperfections in labour markets, the fact that some job seekers lack skills for available positions, many persons seeking work cannot easily move to places where there are job openings, or they lack information about these opportunities. However, in the present case, to a considerable degree, the high rates of unemployment and under-employment reflect the overall lack of demand. The current challenge, then, is to find ways of increasing demand for labour that are economically feasible, add to the productive capacity of society, and do so in ways that are sustainable in terms of finite natural and human resources.

For many, the situation with respect to under-employment and unemployment presents itself as an irresolvable conundrum that must be addressed effectively but cannot be easily resolved. Mindlessly fostering consumer spending by encouraging consumer borrowing not only represents a deeply flawed practice but also fosters over-consumption in ways that deviate from our standards of sustainable consumption. High rates of un-, under- and shadow unemployment are expressions of ongoing economic stagnation. For a number of years efforts have been made to stimulate economic growth by enacting diverse monetary policies. While these policies have helped to protect the economies of a number of industrialized countries from more aggravated forms of economic recession, increased monetary liquidity has not appreciably resulted in increased productivity and more employment opportunities (*The Economist*, 2016a). Some argue that we must simply get used to long-term stagnant growth, as growth is usually measured (Summers, 2016; Hill and Morris, 2016; Karabell, 2016).

Alternatively, a number of observers argue that low levels of economic growth results from an overall lack of demand (Stiglitz, 2012; Krugman, 2012) and that governments can act now, as they have in the past, to stimulate demand. While increasing their indebtedness, governments can act to stimulate the demand for more workers. While many would immediately object to this suggestion, we need to pause and reflect before we quickly dismiss this idea. Governments in many industrialized countries have already been engaged in activities like this. In the United States, for example, the federal government has been effectively investing to stimulate job opportunities indirectly both through the Earned Income Tax Credit, which adds to the incomes of otherwise low-paid workers, and the tax credit for mortgage interest payments, which indirectly works to subsidize the housing industry. The government subsidizes the agricultural industries with billions of dollars of price supports and tax benefits. The government also provides effective subsidies through the ways it undertakes contracts for defence spending and encourages explorations for new energy sources. Obviously many people overtly opposed to governments acting to increase demand for labour in practice avidly support policies, like those just named, that do just that. Nonetheless, moving people otherwise opposed to acknowledge their implicit support for these kinds of initiatives is not likely to be easy.

Much depends on what kinds of actions governments might undertake to stimulate increased demand for labour and how much these initiatives are likely to cost over time. Furthermore, much depends on whether government actions facilitate genuine growth, as in the increasingly productive use of natural and human resources, or the facsimile of growth, like purchasing otherwise unaffordable housing by taking out loans only repayable if the market prices continue to rise and the increasing value of the purchase allows one to repay for these loans. In relation to this question it is instructive to compare two programmes developed by the federal government in the United States during the depression of the 1930s. The better know of these was the Works Progress Administration (WPA), which funded all sorts of programmes including municipal improvement projects and theatre groups. To qualify for these positions, applicants had to apply through local welfare offices and they were paid welfare wages. Although the WPA gave rise to many civic improvements, many felt it largely consisted in make-work projects. The government also funded the Public Works Administration (PWA), which undertook a number of major construction projects especially involved in developing physical infrastructures in the form of electricity, water supplies, and roads for parts of the country, especially in rural areas, where these were missing. The PWA paid workers at going rates. In turn, as these workers spent what they earned in local communities, they helped to revive the economies in these communities. The workers themselves and their communities in turn were able to make larger tax payments. Although the PWA cost the government more per worker, it had a much larger and more permanent impact on the economic growth of the country (Galbraith and Johnson, 1940; Howard, 1943). The PWA helped to build infrastructures and foster genuine growth and the economic growth, in turn, eventually helped to pay off the cost of the initial investments.

In the paragraphs that follow I will discuss several ways by which industrialized countries and firms operating in these countries can address the problem of abundant labour, variously evidenced as unemployment, under-employment, shadow employment and continuing low wages among those working in low skilled employment occasioned by this abundant supply. The goal here is to expand sustainable employment positions and the remuneration to those positions in ways that are economically feasible, contribute to the well-being of society and the economy, and do not aggravate consumption of non-renewable natural resources. We are looking for the kinds of initiatives like the PWA that function to expand job-creating forms of consumption, address public needs, and overall help to rebalance the economy so that a greater portion of the earnings of businesses go to labour in the form of wages, salaries, deferred benefits, and services and smaller portion go to the increasingly disproportionate wealth of the wealthy. No one initiative is likely to make an appreciably difference by itself. However, instituting a number of related initiatives might well make a difference.

Interestingly, as we look for possible ways to address the under-development and under-utilization of labour, we confront a second major issue facing many industrialized societies, namely, the degradation and under-development of several different kinds of physical and social infrastructures. For example, in many industrial societies, as the demand for their services increases, physical and social infrastructures have been deteriorating. Road systems have become overcrowded and not always well-maintained.

Public system of transportation need to be expanded and upgraded. User complaints have increased. Many public school systems seem to be performing less well than they did in the past. Water systems are depleting limited sources. More demands are placed on healthcare services than they can address in a timely manner. Court systems grind along dispensing justice but doing so in ways that often waste the time of litigants and lawyers. Increasing numbers of elderly and handicapped people seem to need more services than are available. The overall quality of life seems to be deteriorating. At the same time, as we have already observed, diverse ecosystems from lakes and rivers to wetlands and marshes, from endangered species to over-used parklands, call for increased care and attention. While industrialized countries may not now experience what are usually called economic depressions, one might make a case that their physical and social infrastructures are experiencing something like the equivalent of depression. They just aren't working as well as they might. Much labour could be usefully employed to rehabilitate, expand and maintain the physical and social infrastructures of industrialized societies.

Additionally, much labour could be utilized greatly to expand the supply of moderate cost housing in urban areas. The prices for housing in urban areas have skyrocketed. The increased value of this housing has directly increased the wealth of property owners both because of rents they can charge and the market value of their properties. At same time many middle- and working-class households can no longer afford to buy urban housing. One way of addressing this problem is to find ways of greatly increasing the supply of moderate cost housing in urban areas. Several initiatives might facilitate this kind of housing market expansion, which include tax incentives for developers building multiple unit condominiums for first-time home owners, tax breaks for first-time home owners, and government subsidized plans for households to save for initial home purchases, along with favourable changes in zoning laws and expanded public and social services.

It is important to explore the ways that the increasing inequality of wealth in industrialized societies has aggravated both expressions of economic depression I have examined in this chapter. The additional wealth of the wealthy – variously resulting from greatly increased compensation packages for executives and some professionals, excess corporate profits of large firms, and inflated equity and property values – has not fostered the development of generative assets either in the form of enhanced social and physical infrastructures or in the form of increasingly productive firms and expanding labour markets. Rather, it has been recycled into a wide variety of financial vehicles including the sources of increased wealth just named as well as expanded insurance funds, funds held in tax havens, and the increased size and value of personal saving and property holdings of the rich (Frank and Cook, 1995; *The Economist*, 2016c; Lazonick, 2014; Piketty, 2014). If industrial societies are to become more productive, then they must reform tax policies to foster greater investment in genuinely generative assets.

It is possible to see how industrialized societies might benefit from economic growth both in general terms (i.e. as the more effective utilization of limited natural and human resources) as well as in specific forms (finding employment opportunities for under-employed and unemployed adults looking for work) designed to strengthen and invigorate social and physical infrastructures. Because we live in a world of limited resources, economic growth, understood as the process of asset development, remains a desirable objective for industrialized as well as developing societies.

At the level of the firm, there are a number of steps businesses can take to foster increased productivity in ways that create benefits for themselves, workers, and the goal of consuming more sustainability. For example, in the ways they organize their workforce, businesses can reduce tardiness, absenteeism, turn over, and careless and inefficient work practice, thereby measurably increasing productivity. The key here is fostering commitment to organizations through practices that extend to workers, often though work teams, and fostering a work culture in which workers exercise greater influence over the pace and character of their own work (Mowday et al., 1982). Likewise, reforming corporate governance patterns so that firms focus more on the good of the business as a whole – and not just the interests of the most powerful stakeholders – has been associated with fostering enhanced, mutually beneficial – and correspondingly more productive – interactions with all stakeholders. Finally, finding ways to reduce the aggravated inequalities in compensation not only will result in enhanced workplace morale but result in either or both marginally reduced consumer prices and/or higher pay for ordinary workers (*The Economist*, 2016b).

Collaborating globally

In order to address responsibly the current global crisis with respect to economic growth, I have argued we should not look for a position midway between the current champions of economic growth, like most professional economists, and the champions who call for limits to growth or the end of growth, like Daly, Klein and McKibben. Rather, as I have indicated, we need to rethink the nature of economic growth in ways that allows us to respond effectively both to the most compelling arguments for restraint as well as to those arguments that favour economic growth in targeted areas redefined in terms of the development of durable generative assets.

If we have any hope of addressing the current global crisis with respect to economic growth responsibly, then we must do so by collaborating globally. It is not enough to produce interesting and incisive analyses and/or to articulate eloquent and fact-laden warnings. For appropriate actions to take place, we need to engage in reciprocal conversations with people who are likely to disagree with us. We need to listen to and talk with both those sympathetic to our concerns and those likely to resist any meaningful efforts to address this crisis. At the same time as we work to develop realistic agendas to address these concerns in timely ways, we need to reach out globally to involve all relevant players in ongoing conversations about these matters. These conversations must include those who are likely to have divergent interests and harbour distrust. We will not be able to address this crisis adequately with agreements just among democratic countries, or industrialized countries, or African countries, or Muslim countries, or even among diverse proponents of alternative economies.[11] We won't be able to address this crisis if we are able to reach understanding among trade unions and environmentalists but not among business enterprises or understandings among businesses and environmentalists that exclude representatives of labour, or understandings among critics of modern markets but not supporters of market economies.

If we are unable to collaborate globally to address this unavoidable crisis, then the crisis is likely to get much worse. Many will suffer from continuing poverty, from adverse climate, from stalled economies, from increasingly high prices for many scare minerals as well as energy over the long haul, from under-employment and degraded infrastructures, and from rising sea levels. Conflicts will become exacerbated between those fostering particular forms of economic growth as this furthers their interests and those opposing any forms of growth because of adverse impact on the planet. We must work to make conversations about this crisis as inclusive as possible, so those with effective decision-making power, whether they are governments or businesses, faith communities or trade unions, indigenous communities or environmentalists, not only voice their concerns but listen attentively to those who voice divergent views.

It may be impossible to reach any kind of lasting resolution regarding this global crisis, given the deeply held divergent views of a number of contemporary groups. Eventually, the crisis may become so exacerbated, that it will be impossible to ignore. However, in that case, our responses are likely to be forced and the self-interests of those most powerful are likely to determine actions that are taken. It would be far better to find ways of responding before the current crisis becomes too severe. Still, there are reasons to hope. People from diverse and differing backgrounds have at times found ways of reaching workable normative agreements to guide their interactions with respect to other global issues. In spite of the continuing resort to the use of armed force, people from diverse nations have agreed to the Geneva Conventions regarding the rights of the wounded, prisoners and civilians in situations of armed conflict. Although these conventions continued to be violated on occasion, as do all normative standards, they have also over time gained both in official endorsement and in practical application. Likewise, in spite of their disagreements, people from diverse nations have endorsed a number of declarations and covenants spelling out basic human rights. While support is not universal, still many who dissent from particular clauses, not only embrace the broader notion of human rights but have voiced their commitment to most of the rights invoked by these United Nations documents. We can point to a number of examples where people from diverse cultures and political persuasions have reached other normative agreements regarding global issues. Consider, for example, the agreements on trade of endangered species, the international ban on land mines, the law of the Seas, the Equator Principles which have established normative requirements with respect to how development projects funded by loans from a number of international banks ought to proceed, the recently adopted Sustainability Principles, and the Paris agreement on the climate. Some of these agreements have gained wider assent than others. All have gained considerable compliance from countries that otherwise differ on many issues. Elsewhere I have referred to these kinds of global agreements as examples of the practices of global ethics (Bird et al., 2016). They represent examples of people from diverse backgrounds developing workable frameworks to address particular global problems in spite of deeply held disagreements about others matters.[12]

What matters is that people concerned about the global crisis with respect to economic growth find ways of engaging in some kinds of serious conversations with each other. Whether they begin from the perspective of those who continue to view growth as imperative – whether as a means of overcoming economic slowdowns or as a means of alleviating poverty – or they begin from the orientation of those who point with alarm at the ways economic growth, as it has been typically understood, has already adversely affected the Earth, they need to enter into thoughtful dialogues. At the extremes both groups have developed a range of arguments about why and how the concerns raised by their opponents ought to be dismissed or treated as comparatively of little importance. At both ends, proponents feel that their own arguments are not being taken as seriously as they ought to be taken and that too many people are being persuaded by others either because they haven't really thought about these matters realistically or because it simply serves their self-interests. In the process too many of those concerned have been engaging in by-passing monologues rather than genuinely reciprocating conversations. At the outset, what is required is that those concerned attempt to listen more attentively to others with whom they are inclined to differ and to see what elements of their opponents' arguments they might thoughtfully consider and might in some instances propose ways of re-stating to fit more closely with their own concerns. I doubt whether these kinds of conversations will be easy or will result in quick resolutions. However, over time they can be educational.

As they seek to engage globally in these kinds of reciprocating conversations, it is important to keep this point in mind. As we engage in these conversations, we are not simply trying to win debates. Hopefully, we are also trying to learn, to gain a better sense of what is happening and what is likely to happen. Therefore, it is very important that these conversations proceed on the basis of reliable information. It is important to seek out relevant analyses by trained investigators, who are studying the impacts of economic activities on social and natural environments, examining the viability of alternative energy sources, and exploring in particular and global ways how to consume more sustainably and how to produce more productively (Miller and Edwards, 2001).

This third basic principle, which I have referred to as collaborating globally, may be more important as a means of addressing the global crisis with respect to economic growth than the first two about consuming sustainably and producing productively. After all, any agreement or normative understanding worth anything must be one in which people from diverse nations, economic philosophies, political persuasions and faith communities seek to reach by seriously conversing with each other.

Conclusions: we must act now

If the proposals made in this chapter are followed, the result will lower levels of growth measured with respect to per capita income but not with respect to productivity, defined as the effective use of natural and human resources. Appropriately understood, the economies of the developing countries will be growing and the economies of the industrialized countries will continue to grow in sustainable and productive ways as overall we seek to make more effective use of limited and in many cases vulnerable natural and human resources.

In this chapter I have proposed three fundamental normative principles that serve as universal imperatives. This chapter describes how these principles can variously be put into practice in both industrialized and developing societies, in firms as well as households. I have argued that these principles, although rooted in widely shared traditional values, can, when appropriately understood, serve as practical ways of addressing the otherwise seemingly unresolvable crisis associated with economic growth. These principles become especially relevant when we rethink our understanding of economic growth, now understood as the development and protection of generative assets and when we distinguish between the inevitably interrelated processes of consumption, which we should undertake sustainable (or conservatively as in conservation), and the processes of production, which we should undertake productively.

There are multiple good reasons why we should adhere to these three principles. Briefly stated, one, these principles duly respect the good of the Earth, its vitality, its power, its grandeur, its vulnerability and its carrying capacity. The Earth has been here long before humans and will be here long after humans no longer exist on Earth. This argument has been voiced by many, including James Lovelock, the UN environmental conferences, the Earth Charter, and the Millennium Assessment Report. The Bible sums up this view by declaring in the initial chapter of Genesis, five time before there is any references to humans, that the heavens and the Earth are 'good' (Genesis 1: 4, 12, 18, 21, 25) and by acknowledging that 'the Earth is the Lord's'. (Psalm 24) Two, these principles provide a way of resolving the crisis of economic growth by affirming the value and urgency both of those who seek to foster economic growth, now appropriately understood and pursued, on the one hand, as enhanced productivity, and of those who seek to restrain growth, now appropriately understood, on the other hand, as limited and sustainable consumption. These principles, along with a new and more fitting way of understanding economic growth, allow us to work to honour both goals without seriously compromising either. Three, to the extent that governments and firms, communities and households seriously act to honour these principles, a strong case can be made that they will as a result be able to realize a number of utilitarian benefits. To be sure, considerable costs are indeed entailed in pursuing these ends. Moreover, many groups, organizations, and individuals are well-positioned to resist proposed changes. Nevertheless, many more people will benefit over long and short terms to the degree these principles are appropriately honoured. We can in the process find ways to help developing countries develop, reduce wasteful consumption, manage climate threats, explore ways to listen to and collaborate with ideological opponents, and address the root causes of at least some of the critical sources of social unrest and conflict. Still, normative principles, no matter how relevant, do not by themselves create changes. They offer useful frameworks for decision-making. What is critical is that we, as individuals, community groups, firms, and governments, find ways to exercise both judgement – balancing evidence, values, costs, and other considerations – and imagination, not allowing ourselves to be imprisoned by taken-for-granted assumptions.

What especially characterizes the current crisis of economic growth is the sense of urgency and timeliness. This crisis must be addressed now, and followed through across the next several decades if we have any chance of addressing it effectively at all. Otherwise, both the problems of poverty and under-employment associated with the lack of economic growth and the problems of adverse climate change and growing inequality associated with continued economic growth, as ordinarily described, will inevitably become worse. Except, perhaps on a smaller scale with respect to the Second World War, humans have never faced another crisis like this one that calls for everyone's attention. So, we must add a fourth principle: we must act now.

To be sure, some countries, businesses, civil society groups are more prepared to act now and act in ways appropriate to this crisis than others. However, we need both radicals – ready to assert uncompromising commitments both to caring for and protecting the Earth and its ecosystems and to helping and defending the most economically disadvantaged – and liberals/moderates, who will seek to build bridges of collaboration and engage in at least temporary compromises with those less ready to act. We need to take steps towards a future that both builds upon what has been constructive about economic growth – namely, the development of a wide range of generative assets – while also working to reduce what has been especially destructive about past patterns of economic growth – namely our excessive, careless, and wasteful consumption of human and natural resources. Most importantly, we must begin and continue to take these steps now.

Notes

1 An earlier version of this chapter was published as chapter 7 in a book edited by Gary Badcock (2016). This chapter was rewritten for this publication. I am grateful to anonymous

readers for their criticisms and suggestion for changes in this chapter. The basic argument of this chapter was initially presented in a public lecture at Wilfred Laurier University in February 2013.

2 A number of authors, such as Ray Kurzwell, have argued that the development of artificial intelligence at accelerating rates will result in the increasing availability and utilization of sustainable technologies for producing energy from renewable sources at low costs (Kurzwell, 2005). Referring to this possibility as the 'singularity', in 2009 along with others Kurzwell founded a Singularity University along the shores of the San Francisco Bay. While these developments are, no doubt, genuinely promising, scepticism about their overall impact seems fitting for several reasons: one, because these developments are likely to aggravate the problems unemployment, under-employment, and shadow unemployment, they do not address the other half of the basic challenge associated with economic growth; two, these technological developments do not address the needs for developing countries to develop basic social, physical, and economic infrastructures; and, three, these technological developments fail to address the other limitations of the natural environment in addition to energy.

3 The principles associated with sustainable development in critically important ways do call attention to the fact that the quality or character of economic growth is decisive. I address this concern as part of this chapter.

4 The assumption that economic growth is both possible and imperative grows out of a number of overlapping developments. These included the widely shared Enlightenment belief in progress as both the mark and goal of modernizing societies. Variously based on their high regard for triumphs of science, their broadly held adherence to humanism, and their corresponding commitment to civility, Enlightenment thinkers and those they influenced viewed progress as the characteristic feature of modern as opposed to traditional societies. Modern societies were correspondingly expected to economically progress (Friedman, 2005; Pinker, 2010). The view of economic growth as a normatively-valued process emerged as well as the by-product of efforts of diverse groups of people especially in Europe and North America to develop self-organizing (and often self-governing) associations in the form of religious communities, voluntary associations, business enterprises, as well associations of workers (de Tocqueville, 1954, vol. 11, book 2, chapters 4, 5, and 6; Weber, 1946). Furthermore, the processes of industrialization themselves rendered ideas about economic growth both credible and desirable. People witnessed dramatic changes in their own lives and those of others. Many people found themselves living much better than their ancestors. They experienced economic growth as good and they expected their descendants to enjoy enhanced growth as well. In addition, modern economic theory treats lack of growth as a symptom of economic dysfunction. Firms or countries that are not growing are correspondingly regarded as malfunctioning (Summers, 2016, Karabell, 2016).

5 In so far as any person, organization, or government owns any asset and can lay claim to it as form of property, we think of these assets as wealth. We often refer to those assets that are owned and can be sold or purchased as capital assets or wealth as capital (Piketty, 2014). However, many assets – like the skill level of a work force, the credit level of an economy, or air quality of the climate – are not directly owned and cannot be marketed. Many assets are publicly owned or managed, such as school systems, health care systems, and legal systems, all of which have played significant instrumental roles in economic development.

6 A number of different models of the phases of economic growth have been proposed. See Karl Marx (1973), pp. 471–514; Karl Marx and Frederick Engels (1947); W. W. Rostow (1961) and Talcott Parson (1977). In his *General Economic History* (1961) Max Weber outlined a similar although much more complex overview. One might criticize all of these models for imposing too restricted views on much more complex historical processes, for assuming excessively linear causal connections, and for overlooking quite different ways in which economies have developed in different areas and eras. Nonetheless, in broad terms these models remind us that economic growth has assumed different forms and that subsequent processes of growth characteristically presuppose and build upon prior processes of growth.

7 By referring to Wesley's sermon, which Weber cited as an example of the 'practical ethic of worldly asceticism' (The Protestant Ethic), I am arguing that these traditional values are able to provide a viable framework for thinking about ethical standards relevant for addressing the current crisis with respect to economic growth.

8 See Garfinkel et al. (2010), Michelmore (2012), and Bartlett (2012). While the Kennedy/Johnson tax cut of 1964 seemed to foster economic growth through modest increases in spending, subsequent tax cuts introduced in the 1980s and 2000s did not have the same noticeably positive effect.

9 There has been much debate about what factors have played and are likely to play the most decisive role in fostering industrialization in the past and in the present. Without attempting to resolve this ongoing discussion, we can note the important role played at different times and places by a number of distinct factors, including accessibility of new technologies and sources of energy; changes in the organizational forms by which people engage in manufacturing and commerce; the construction of physical, social, and economic infrastructures; the development of the rule of law; and the cultivation of dispositions favouring thrift, hard work, and the effective and not wasteful use of resources. See, for example, Gregory Clark (2007), part 2; Ferdinand Braudel (1980, 1982, and 1984); and Easterly (2002). See the debates occasioned by Max Weber's *The Protestant Ethic and the Spirit of Capitalism* (1958). Weber's account is far more complex than most of his critics realize. He not only called attention to the role of cultural factors – what he referred to as 'Practical Ethics of Worldly Asceticism' – but also indicated the decisive role played by the development of commerce, changes in legal understandings and institutions (see also *Economy and Society* (1978), the chapter on the Sociology of Law), as well as his discussions of various technological discoveries and political developments.

10 Concerted efforts to enhance the productivity of developing societies must also address the ways economic growth has also typically occasioned social and economic disruptions. While it has produced many benefits, economic growth has always been costly in a number of quite different ways. As a result of economic growth, old ways of life are left behind. Traditional customs are often forgotten or simply treated with diminished respect. Frequently, traditional structures of authority lose legitimacy. Old patterns of power are frequently overcome as new centres of power emerge. Because most processes of economic growth foster increased horizontal as well as vertical mobility, kinship bonds are typically loosened. These changes characteristically occasion conflicts as some groups take quicker and greater advantage of these changes than others. While many people have clearly benefited from processes of economic growth, others clearly have not. With industrialization, the pace of these changes often quickens. Moreover, while the process of industrialization greatly enhances the opportunities for increased wealth, it also introduces increased economic risks, connected with the loss of income and investments associated with work-related accidents, unemployment, retirement, bank failures, bankruptcy, and economic depressions. Correspondingly, economic growth has challenged societies to find effective and humane ways of responding to these disruptions and risks. In modern times states have developed a wide range of public social insurance and public welfare institutions, like deposit insurance for banks, workmen's compensation plans, and relief programs to manage these risks. Whether these programs adequately address these disruptions and risks is an ongoing concern.

11 Klein documents the growing support internationally for environmentally responsible consuming and producing practices among a wide range of indigenous groups, alternatives communities, and citizen groups protesting against the practices of big industrial corporations. As a whole she refers to these diverse groups as 'Blockadia', because of their efforts to block the further development of enterprises that result in increased carbon emissions (Klein, 2014, part 3). While Klein correctly argues for an end to the extractive mind-set (p. 447), she criticizes any attempts to address this crisis by attempting to build collaborative relationship either with big businesses, moderate liberals, or established governments. She argues that we have to unlearn the key tenets of the 'stifling free market ideology' (460), which has in any case 'been discredited by decades of inequality and corruption' (461) and 'continues to suffocate the potential for climate action' (120). She concludes that 'only mass social movements can save us now' (450).

12 In our co-authored book on *The Practices of Global Ethics*, we discuss and refer to a number of these international agreements, such as Universal Declaration of Human Rights and subsequent conventions on human rights, the Geneva Conventions, The Declaration on the Rights of Indigenous Peoples, the Earth Charter, the Extractive Industry

Transparency Initiative, various environmental accords, the World Bank's Performance Standards, the Parliament of the World's Religions' document 'Towards a Global Ethic', The UN Global Compact, The Sustainability Development Goals, and many more (Bird et al., 2016).

References

Acemoglu, D. and Robinson, J.A. (2012). *Why Nations Fail: The Origins of Power, Prosperity, and Poverty.* New York: Crown Publishers.

Avent, R. (2016). *The Wealth of Humans: Work, Power, and Status in the Twenty-First Century.* New York: St. Martin's Press.

Badcock, G. (ed.) (2016). *God and the Financial Crisis.* Cambridge: Cambridge Scholars.

Banerjee, A. and Duflo, E. (2011). *Poor Economics: A Radical Rethinking of the Way to Fight Global Poverty.* New York: Public Affairs.

Bartlett, B. (2012). *The Benefit and the Burden: Tax Reform – Why We Need It and What It Will Take.* New York: Simon & Schuster.

Beinhocker, E.D. (2007). *The Origins of Wealth: The Radical Remaking of Economics and What It Means for Business and Society.* Boston, MA: Harvard Business School Press.

Bell, D. (1976). *The Cultural Contradictions of Capitalism.* New York: Basic Books.

Bird, F. (2006). Perspectives on global poverty. In F. Bird and M. Velasquez (eds), *Just Business Practices in a Diverse and Developing World.* Basingstoke: Palgrave-Macmillan, chapter 7.

Bird, F. (2011). Rethinking the bottom line: International business and global poverty. *Management and Organization: A Multidisciplinary Journal of Business,* 2(2): 109–120.

Bird, F. (2016). Mining and inclusive wealth development in developing countries. *Journal of Business Ethics, 135(4): 631–643.*

Bird, F., Twiss, S., Pedersen, K., Miller, C. and Grelle, B. (2016). *The Practices of Global Ethics.* Edinburgh: Edinburgh University Press.

Blair, M.M. (1995). *Ownership and Control: Rethinking Corporate Governance for the Twenty-First Century.* Washington, DC: The Brooking Institution.

Blair, M.M. (1996). *Wealth-Creation and Wealth-Sharing: A Colloquium on Corporate Governance and Investment in Human Capital.* Washington, DC: The Brookings Institution.

Boeke, J.H. (1953). *Economies and Economic Policy of Dual Societies.* New York: Institute of Public Relations.

Bourguignon, F. (2015). *The Globalization of Inequality.* Princeton, NJ and Oxford: Princeton University Press.

Braudel, F. (1980, 1982, and 1984) *Civilization and Capitalism,* 3 vols. New York: Harper & Row.

Brown, L.R. (1995). *Who Will Feed China? Wake-Up Call for a Small Planet.* New York: W. W. Norton & Co.

Brown, P.G. (2000). *Ethics, Economic, and International Relations: Transparent Sovereignty in the Commonwealth of Life.* Edinburgh: Edinburgh University Press.

Brynjolfsson, E. and McAfee, A. (2014). *The Second Machine Age: Work, Progress and Prosperity in a Time of Brilliant Technologies.* New York: W. W. Norton & Co.

Clark, G. (2007). *Farewell to Alms: A Brief Economic History of the World.* Princeton, NJ: Princeton University Press.

Cohen, L. (2003). *A Consumer's Republic: The Politics of Mass Consumption in Postwar America.* New York: Random House.

Collier, P. (2007). *The Bottom Billion: Why the Poorest Countries are Failing and What Can Be Done About It.* Oxford: Oxford University Press.

Collier, P. (2009). *Wars, Guns, and Votes: Democracy in Dangerous Places.* New York: HarperCollins.

Daly, H.E. (1972). *The Steady State.* London: W. H. Freeman and Co.

Daly, H.E. (1996). *Beyond Growth: The Economics of Sustainable Development.* Boston, MA: Beacon Press.

Deaton, A. (2013). *The Great Escape: Health, Wealth, and the Origins of Inequality.* Princeton University Press.

Diamond, J. (2005). *Collapse: How Societies Choose to Fail or Succeed.* New York: Viking Press.

Earth Charter Commission (2005). *The Earth Charter.* Earth Charter Commission.

Easterly, W. (2002). *The Elusive Quest for Growth: Economists' Adventures and Misadventures in the Tropics.* Cambridge, MA: MIT Press.

Easterly, W. (2006). *White Man's Burden: Why the West's Efforts to Aid the Rest Have Done So Much Ill and So Little Good.* New York: Penguin Press.

Eccles, R.G. and Krzus, M.P. (2010). *One Report: Integrated Reporting for a Sustainable Strategy.* Hoboken, NJ: John Wiley & Sons, Inc.

Eccles, R.G., Herz, R.H., Kegan, E.M. and Phillips, D.M.H. (2011). *The ValueReporting™ Revolution: Moving beyond the Earnings Game.* New York: John Wiley & Sons, Inc.

Evans, P. (1979). *Dependent Development: The Alliance of Multinational, State, and Local Capital in Brazil.* Princeton, NJ: Princeton University Press.

Frank, R.H. and Cook, P.J. (1995). *The Winner-Take-All Society.* New York and London: Penguin Books.

Friedman, B.M. (2005). *The Moral Consequences of Economic Growth.* New York: Vintage Books, Random House.

Galbraith, J.K. (1958). *The Affluent Society.* Cambridge: The Riverside Press.

Galbraith, J.K. assisted by Johnson, G.G. Jr. (1940). *The Economic Effects of the Federal Public Works Expenditures.* Washington, DC: National Resources Planning Board, U.S. Government Printing Office.

Garfinkel, I., Rainwater, L., and Smeeding, T. (2010). *Wealth and Welfare States: Is America a Laggard or Leader.* New York: Oxford University Press.

Gleeson-White, J. (2014). *Six Capitals: Can Accountants Save the Planet: Rethinking Capitalism for the Twentieth-First Century.* New York: W. W. Norton and Co.

Gordon, R.J. (2016). *The Rise and Fall of American Growth: The U.S. Standard of Living since the Civil War.* Princeton, NJ: Princeton University Press.

Handley, A. (2008). *Business and the State in Africa.* Cambridge: Cambridge University Press.

Hansen, J. (2012). Game over for the climate. *New York Times*, May 9.

Hawkins, P., Lovins, A., and Lovins, L.H. (1999). *Natural Capitalism: Creating the Next Industrial Revolution.* Boston, MA: Little, Brown and Co.

Hill, J.T. and Morris, I. (2016). Can central banks goose growth? *Foreign Affairs*, 95(2): 10–17.

Holmes, C. and Sunnstein, C. (1997). *The Cost of Rights: Why Liberty Depends on Taxes.* New York: W.W. Norton & Co.

Howard, D.S. (1943). *The W.P.A. and Federal Relief Policy.* New York: Russell Sage Foundation.

IWR *(Inclusive Wealth Report: Measuring Progress toward Sustainability)* (2012). Cambridge: Cambridge University Press. A project sponsored by the United Nations University, The International Human Dimension Program on Global Environmental Change, and the United Nations Environmental Program.

IPCC (Intergovernmental Panel on Climate Change) (2015). *Climate Change 2014: Synthesis Report.* Geneva: World Meteorological Organization.

Jackson, T. (2009). *Prosperity without Growth: Economics for a Finite Planet* (2009). New York: Earthscan.

Kaplan, R.D. (2016). Eurasia's coming anarchy: The risks of Chinese and Russian weakness. *Foreign Affairs*, 92(2): 33–41.

Karabell, Z. (2016). Learning to live with stagnation: Growth is not everything: Just ask Japan. *Foreign Affairs*, 92(2): 47–53.

Klein, N. (1999). *No Logo.* London: HarperCollins.

Klein, N. (2014). *This Changes Everything: Capitalism versus the Climate.* Toronto: Vintage Canada.

Korton, D.C. (1995). *When Corporations Rule the World.* West Hartford, CN: Kumarian Press.

Krugman, P. (2012). *End This Depression Now.* New York: W. W. Norton & Co.

Kurzwell, R. (2005). *Singularity is Near*. New York: Penguin Group.

Lazonick, W. (2014). Profits without prosperity. *Harvard Business Review*, (September): 46–55.

Lewis, A. (1979). The dual economy revisited. *The Manchester School*, 47(3): 211–229.

Lipset, S.M. (1959). Some social requisites of democracy: Economic development and political legitimacy *American Political Science Review*, 53 (March).

Locke, J. (1952). *Second Treatise of Government*. New York: The Liberal Arts Press, Inc.

Lomborg, B. (2001). *The Skeptical Environmentalist: Measuring the Real State of the World*. Cambridge: Cambridge University Press.

Macpherson, C.B. (1977). *The Life and Times of Liberal Democracy*. Oxford: Oxford University Press.

Marx, K. (1963). *The Eighteenth Brumaire of Louis Bonaparte*. New York: International Publishers.

Marx, K. (1973). Forms which preceded capitalist production. In *Grundrisse*, translated by Martin Nicolaus. London: Allen Lane, pp. 471–514.

Marx, K. and Engels, F. (1947). *The German Ideology*, Part I. New York: International Publishers.

Maxfield, S. and Schneider, B.R. eds. (1997). *Business and the State in Developing Countries*. Ithaca, NY and London: Cornell University Press.

Meadows, D., Meadows, D., Randers, J., and Behrens, W.W. III (1972). *The Limits to Growth: A Report of the Club of Rome*. New York: Universe Books.

Michelmore, M.C. (2012). *Tax and Spend: The Welfare State, Tax Politics, and the Limits of American Liberalism*. Philadelphia, PA: The University of Pennsylvania Press.

Milanovic, B. (2005). *Worlds Apart: Measuring International and Global Inequality*. Princeton, NJ: Princeton University Press.

Millennium Ecosystem Assessment (2005). *Living beyond our Means: Natural Assets and Human Well-Being*. Washington, DC: Island Press.

Miller, C.A. and Edwards, P.N. (eds) (2001). *Changing the Atmosphere: Expert Knowledge and Environmental Governance*. Cambridge: MIT Press.

Moffat, J., Bregha, F., and Middelkoop, M.J. (2004). Responsible care: A case study of a voluntary environmental initiative. In K. Webb (ed.), *Voluntary Codes: Private Governance, the Public Interest, and Innovation*. Carleton University: Carleton Research Unit for innovation, Science, and Environment.

Mowday, R., Park, W. and Steers, R. (1982). *Employee-Organizational Linkages: The Psychology of Commitment, Absenteeism, and Turnover*. New York: The Academic Press.

Moyo, D. (2009). *Dead Aid*. New York: Farrar, Straus, and Giroux.

Nixon, R. (2007). *Slow Violence and the Environmentalism of the Poor*. Cambridge, MA: Harvard University Press.

North, D.C., Wallis, J.J., and Weingast, B.R. (2008). *Violence and Social Order: A Conceptual Framework for Interpreting Recorded Human History*. Cambridge: Cambridge University Press.

Nussbaum, M.C. (2000). *Women and Human Development: The Capabilities Approach*. Cambridge: Cambridge University Press.

Nussbaum, M.C. (2011). *Creating Capabilities: The Human Development Approach*. Cambridge: Cambridge University Press.

Parson, T. (1977). *The Evolution of Societies*, ed. J. Toby. Englewood Cliffs, NJ: Prentice-Hall.

Piketty, T. (2014). *Capital in the Twenty-First Century*, translated by A. Goldhammer. Cambridge, MA: Harvard University Press.

Pinker, S. (2011). *The Better Angels of Our Nature: Why Violence Has Declined*. New York: Viking.

Pogge, T. (2008). *World Poverty and Human Rights, Cosmopolitan Responsibilities and Reform*, 2nd edn. Malden, MA: Polity Press.

Polak, P. (2008). *Out of Poverty: What Works When Traditional Approaches Fail*. San Francisco, CA: Barrett-Koehler.

Polak, P. and Warwick, M. (2013). *The Business Solution to Poverty: Designing Products and Services for Three Billion New Customers*. San Francisco, CA: Barrett-Koehler.

Putnam. R. (1993). *Making Democracy Work: Civic Traditions in Modern Italy*. Princeton, NJ: Princeton University Press.

Riesco, M. (2004). Pay Your Taxes! Corporate Social Responsibility and the Mining Industry in Chile Draft Report Prepared for the United Nations Research Institute. Santiago, Chile.

Rostow, W.W. (1961). *Stages of Economic Growth*. Cambridge: Cambridge University Press.

Rubin, J. (2012). *The End of Growth*. Toronto: Random House.

Sachs, J. (2015). *The Age of Sustainable Development*. New York: Columbia University Press.

Schumacher, E.F. (1973). *Small is Beautiful: Economics as if People Mattered*. London: Blond and Briggs.

Sen, A. (1999). *Development as Freedom*. New York: Anchor Books.

Shell News Lens (2013). Scenarios: What might the future hold? www.shell.com/global/futures-energy/scenarios.

Singer, P. (2009). *The Life You Can Save: Acting Now to End World Poverty*. New York: Random House.

Stiglitz, J. (2012). *The Price of Inequality*. New York: W. W. Norton & Co.

Stiglitz, J. and Charlton, A. (2005). *Fair Trade for All: How Trade Can Promote Development*. New York: Oxford University Press.

Stiglitz, J., Sen, A. and Fitoussi, J.-P. (2010). *Mis-Measuring Our Lives: Why GDP Doesn't Add Up: The Report by the Commission on the Measurement of Economic Performance and Social Progress*. New York: The New Press.

Summers, L.H. (2016). The age of secular stagnation: What it is and what to do about it. *Foreign Affairs*, 95(2): 2–9.

The Economist (2013). Generation jobless: Youth unemployment. *The Economist* (April 27, 2013), pages 58–60.

The Economist (2016a). Out of ammo? and Fighting the next recession. *The Economist*, February 20, pp. 9, 16–19.

The Economist (2016b). Doing less with more: Low wages are both a cause and a consequence of low productivity. *The Economist*, March 19, p. 80.

The Economist (2016c). The problem with profits and business in America: Too much of a good thing. *The Economist*, March 26, pp. 11, 23–28.

Tocqueville, A. de (1945). *Democracy in America*, vol. 2. New York: Vintage Books.

WCED (World Commission on Environment and Development) (1987). *Our Common Future*. Oxford: Oxford University Press.

Weber, M. (1946). The Protestant sects and the spirit of capitalism. *From Essays in Sociology*, ed. H.H. Gerth and C. Wright Mills. New York: Oxford University Press, pp. 302–322.

Weber, M. (1958). *The Protestant Ethic and the Spirit of Capitalism*, translated by T. Parson. New York: Charles Scribner's Sons.

Weber, M. (1961). *General Economic History*, translated by F.H. Knight. New York: Collier Books.

Weber, M. (1978). *Economy and Society*, ed. G. Roth and C. Wittich. Berkeley, CA: University of California Press.

Wesley, J. (1944). The use of money. In *Forty-Four Sermons*. London: The Epworth Press.

Wijkman, A. and Rockström, J. (2012). *Bankrupting Nature: Denying our Planetary Boundaries*. London and New York: Routledge.

3 Business and the emerging ecological civilization

Frank Birkin and Mingyue Fan

Introduction

For Captain Nemo, global travel in the luxurious underwater accommodation of the Nautilus submarine was, of course, a fiction realized only in the novel *20,000 Leagues under the Sea*. When Jules Verne published this book in 1870, the world could dream of the promise of a better world made possible by technological progress. It could also rely upon a bountiful nature for Captain Nemo merely had to don a diving suit, step out of his underwater home and wander, a sophisticated hunter-gatherer on the sea-floor, to obtain all the food and materials needed to support his extravagant lifestyle.

The nineteenth century could rightly dream of increasing scientific knowledge and technological benefits taking mankind ever closer to a utopian existence. The natural world then appeared big and so resource-rich that any limits to progress were deemed local for there was always far-horizons where abundant resources lay waiting to be used by brave and enterprising souls. Planet Earth then had room for economic expansion with a global population at the close of the nineteenth century of around 1.6 billion.

In the twentieth century, two world wars, a distorted Nazi utopia, nuclear bombs and the polarization and armed opposition of political means either side of a wall – conceptual across the globe but real in Berlin – tarnished that nineteenth-century dream. But the impetus and direction of development that had been established in the previous century was not to be abandoned: the economic and industrial growth that had made Victorian Britain enormously rich in material means and assets was eagerly replicated, rolled out around the world and facilitated by the distillation and enforcement of a refined, economic essence, Capitalism-and free-markets.

So strong is the belief in the nineteenth-century vision of civilization based on the inventions of technology and theories of economics that it appears unassailable to this day. But why not? Why should this be a problem? Technology and economics have delivered health, wealth and prosperity for many people. For this we, the beneficiaries, should be grateful.

But those visions of civilization are problematic because they have no future on a planet being dangerously stressed by the needs and wants of a human population of approximately 7.3 billion people in 2015. Captain Nemo's bountiful and limitless world no longer exists. Hence the twentieth century is having to wrestle with an expectations gap between on the one hand, the promises of a 200-year-old vision that is deeply entrenched in our institutions and aspirations and, on the other hand, dismal reports of degradation caused by the wider consequences of that vision.

In 1992, humanity tried to face up to this gap. The United Nations Conference on Environment and Development (UNCED) was held with the intention of implementing more sustainable ways of developing. At this conference, a comprehensive agreement was signed by 178 countries who adopted a 700-page action-programme known as Agenda 21 to close the gap.

But that expectations gap persists in spite of our efforts. At the Rio+20 Summit on Sustainable Development convened in Brazil in June 2012 by UNDP (United Nations Development Program) and UNDESA (UN Department of Economic and Social Affairs), it was recorded that: 'The evidence from the reports is overwhelming that a gap exists between stated commitments to sustainable development and the reality of implementing sustainable development policies and programmes in all countries and regions reviewed' (UNDP/UNDESA, 2012).

Also in 2012 a review of Agenda 21 implementation was undertaken by the Stakeholder Forum for a Sustainable Future under the direction of the United Nations Division for Sustainable Development and the European Commission (Stakeholder Forum for a Sustainable Future, 2012). This review reported that on-target progress had been made in key areas of Agenda 21 including the management of toxic chemicals, the involvement of multiple stakeholder groups, improved governance processes and active engagements with NGOs. However, many targets had not been reached. In some critical aspects, results were classified as being 'far-from-target' and 'regressive'. Protection of the atmosphere was one such bad performer and changing consumption patterns was another.

The review concluded that the world had failed to deal with changing consumption patterns because the 1992 agreement had not addressed the 'interconnectedness of the various goals'. More specifically, the agreement '… was not 'allowed' to examine the economic system itself' (ibid., p. 8). Of course not, for to recognize the interconnected of various goals and to examine the economic system itself is approaching very close to an examination of the roots of Western civilization; if we examine those too closely, civilization itself would change.

Yet if we are to have a future on this planet, it is very likely that we do need to deal effectively with changing consumption patterns and the other issues in our economics system. These are likely to be far harder tasks than dealing with climate change for they reach deep into modern identities and ask existential questions of ourselves. They challenge the viability of Captain Nemo's vision, the dream of limitless technological harvesting of boundless resources. They would indeed mark an end to the dreams and aspirations of a civilization.

Many people believe that the business models we now employ need ongoing economic growth for businesses themselves to survive. To achieve such growth, our civilization has prospered not merely by meeting people's basic material needs – which are limited – but by exceeding them, by creating endless wants without limit.

But our living planet, 'Gaia', does not pay attention to either human needs or wants. Gaia represents a concept of the biosphere on Earth that has manipulated the atmosphere to suit her own interdependent, autonomous needs and limitations (Lovelock, 2000). If we wish to have a future living within Gaia, we need to know what her needs are and we need to learn how to live within them. We do indeed need a new civilization.

In this new civilization, the human economy is itself a subsystem of Gaia and as such it cannot outgrow her. The very need for sustainable ways of developing is a testament to this fact. If the resources at our disposal are limited then we need a kind of economic development that recognizes and works within this new home truth; we need a steady-state economy which is '... defined by constant stocks of physical wealth (artifacts) and a constant population, each maintained at some chosen, desirable level by a low rate of throughput, in other words by low birth rates equal to low physical depreciation rates ...' (Daly, 2014, p. 9).

But is the need for a new civilization really so surprising? Diamond (2006) shows us how civilizations have come and gone throughout history; their departures frequently being attributable to environmental causes. We now have ample archaeological evidence to refute arguments that civilizations do not come and go. It is therefore in-defensible to argue that our civilization will not change. Pertinent questions are hence not about will but how our civilization will change and about what exactly changes. If we can start to answer such questions, we may anticipate the new kinds of business models that will evolve.

How will our civilization change?

The famous French social theorist Michel Foucault has already identified how European civilizations have change. He did so using the concept of an 'episteme' (Foucault, 1970).

An episteme is the fundamental assumption that makes it possible to know anything at all in a particular age (Birkin and Polesie, 2011). It may also be thought of as the basic beliefs that underlie the rationalizing process. For example, if you believe in a wholly God-given world then the world may be understood as a kind of book in which His words may be literally read (in accordance with Foucault's recognition of the Mediaeval episteme, mediaeval Europe to around 1650). If you believe that God made a rationally ordered world, then a more scientific, mathematicized approach will be required to construct knowledge (Foucault's Classical episteme from approximately 1650 to 1800). If you believe that the world made itself largely without God's direct intervention, then you need to look for the origins of things (Foucault's Modern episteme from around 1800 to perhaps the year 2000).

Episteme change is not of only historic interest. Western civilization may have been within what Foucault identified as the Modern episteme for some 200 years but there is strong evidence that the Modern episteme is now being replaced. This newly emerging possibility of knowledge may be called either 'Ecological' since it is based on relations, or 'Primal' since these relations constitute the origins of the human sciences and our measures of performance need to relate better to their foundations or primal roots.

During the Modern episteme in the nineteenth and twentieth centuries, scientists looked for and found the origins of many phenomena from evolution to DNA, from sedimentary deposits to mountains, from electromagnetic fields to galactic clusters and from coal to nuclear power. This scientific quest for origins is ongoing.

However, Foucault (1970) argues that the modern search for origins was unsuccessful in the human sciences such as psychology, sociology and economics. Other sciences grew in accordance with newly found empirical evidence; and if the evidence did not fit the theory then the theory was wrong. But in the human sciences, this kind of em-pirical evidence was not available during the Modern episteme. Evidence of origins was looked for in modern psychology, sociology and economics but all that was found was man looking back at himself. So modern human sciences were necessarily reflexive, self-referential; a knowledge created about man, by man and for man (ibid.; Birkin and Polesie, 2011). The great modern psychologists such as Freud, Adler and Young based their studies on man's mind. Modern sociologists studied our own societies as separate entities. The foundation of modern economics is human choice.

Without the censure of independent empirical evidence, modern human sciences had to grow with reference to their own, man-made, internal rules and regulations alone. The verification of modern economics for example is dependent solely upon the coherence and validation of its own abstract, logical belief system (Ellis, 2002).

Only after Foucault's death in 1984 would this situation begin to change. The modern human sciences became challenged by new thinking based not on self-referential theory but on evidence from sources far more independent of mankind. Psychology became increasingly based upon non-human origins in evolution (*Psychology Today*, 2015) and the environment (De Young, 2013). Similarly, the new discipline of Ecological Economics is grounded in thermodynamics and ecosystem behaviour (Costanza, 1991; Daly, 2014). In addition, whereas the Modern episteme is distinguished by the strong separation of human science disciplines (due to their growth only in accordance with their own internal rules and regulations), the emerging episteme is marked by a flowing together of knowledge (Wilson, 1998). We are beginning to recognize how much the real world is inextricably joined-up; a situation formally acknowledged in the new science of complexity (Mitchell, 2009).

Such episteme change requires a different attitude to our knowledge and to ourselves. The extent of the impacts of this on our businesses and ways of living are hard to grasp. It is hard, if not impossible for the occupants of one episteme to accept and live within the rationale of another – there is literally no sense to be found in such crossovers. This is why Bruno Latour stresses the need for 'diplomacy' when working with change at the level of a new possibility for knowledge.

Working within the same French academic tradition as Michel Foucault, Latour rejected the modern era in 1993 with his book entitled *We Have Never Been Modern* (Latour, 1993). He has emphatically rejected the abstract theory-building of modern social sciences and economics in his widely used actor-network theory (ANT) (Latour, 2005). But it is in his book *An Inquiry into Modes of Existence* (Latour, 2013) that Latour may be seen to be working entirely within the emerging episteme. He argues that the modern mistake has been to take 'economic matters' as an object to study (ibid., p. 464) and that we need to change 'operating systems' from 'modernizing' to 'ecologizing' (ibid., p. 479). For Latour, it is the recognition of Gaia that finally puts an end to the modern era. We must, he argues, prepare for the coming ecological civilization and notably reject the dominance of modern economics in our social and business lives.

What exactly changes for business practice?

The preceding section identified the role of the Primal episteme in the mechanics of changing from a modern to an ecological civilization. In this section, we consider what business practice may be like in an ecological civilization.

In some ways, the term 'ecological civilization' appears as an oxymoron. After all, 'civilization' implies development and progress away from wild nature whilst 'ecological' has a sense of integrating with the natural. We could go so far as saying that civilization exploits nature to meet human demands (Fernandez-Armesto, 2001). But both 'civilization' and 'ecology' are relational terms. They imply knowledge of the relations between living things and their environments.

The key feature then of the emerging ecological civilization is that we recognize and work with the relations between all living things and their environments – there is no longer an 'us' and a 'them'; there is no longer a possibility of knowledge in the human sciences that is constructed only about, by and for man. It is in many ways a homecoming to more traditional wisdom.

In the episteme that Foucault called Classical, Linnaeus understood nature, God, the material world, people and society to be interconnected in an 'economy of nature'. It was the German zoologist Ernst Haeckel (1834–1919) who constructed the term 'ecology' using the Greek *oikos* for a home and *logos* for science. The new term 'ecology' was to expand the scope of the 'economy of nature' to include such as geographic distribution, biogeochemical cycles, nutrition chains and habitats. For Haeckel 'ecology' captures the great complexity of relations that makes life what it is.

So in an ecological civilization, there will no longer be an abstract, self-contained economy of overriding principles which we must slavishly follow: instead there will be an economy of people buying and selling within a gamut of relations between themselves, their businesses, the rest of life and indeed the whole universe of existence in which we find ourselves; and upon which we ultimately depend.

Management has already developed a range of approaches and tools derived from an ecological understanding of interdependence. These include life cycle assessments, environmental management, the triple bottom line (Elkington, 1997), the triple top line (McDonough, 2002), ecological footprint analysis (Wackernagel and Rees, 1998), the natural step (2010) and Benefit Corporations who are changing US legislation state by state to permit themselves to generate benefits for society and the environment as well as for shareholders (Benefit Corporations, 2015).

Taken together, all the above initiatives take business closer to the deep transformation that Hawken (1993, pp. viii–ix) called for: 'Rather than a management problem, we have a design problem, one that runs through all business. We will need a system of production where each and every act is sustainable and productive.' But the use of the above initiatives is far from universal. So whilst the 'Phoenix Economy Report' (Volans, 2009) identifies 50 pioneering companies who are enacting significant, transformative change towards sustainability, the same report calls for more widespread change including a whole new 'Phoenix Economy' with a generic 'ecosystem of change' (ibid., p. 28).

To spread the change wider, to become generic, simple principles need to emerge and gain acceptance. The lack of the recognition and acceptance of such simple principles is no doubt an obstacle restricting wider use of the new approaches. Indeed, the use of interactive, interdependent and uncertain ecological relations leads us directly to the science of complexity which is not per se easy to use (Mitchell, 2009) and is likely to require a whole new business vocabulary.

Three principles that would help to establish a changed world are 'No Quittance', 'Comprehensive Optimum' and 'Teleology not Causation'. The three are inter-related but do distinguish three important aspects of the world that we now know to exist.

'No Quittance' means that businesses acknowledge and abide by all the relations that we now recognize. Ultimately, there is no longer a 'contract', either legal or theoretical, to which businesses may resort to avoid responsibility. A business may break no laws and contravene no economic principles yet there remains an overriding duty to protect and enhance life on Earth.

An ecological understanding emphasizes the interdependence of species and mankind is no exception – the destruction of the habits of other species will finally result in the destruction of the human habitat. We are all in this new world together.

A *Guardian* (2014) newspaper article made for an attention-grabbing headline, 'Nasa-funded study: industrial civilisation headed for "irreversible collapse"?' and placed the blame on individual greed. But the social epidemiologists Wilkinson and Pickett (2010) have already provided detailed statistics as to why more equality is better for everyone. They also argue that there will be no sustainability without equality. So in the emerging ecological civilization there can be no such thing as *quittance* – that closing of the books of account that says this is where our responsibility ends – for, as Latour argues, you are no longer quits at all (Latour, 2013, p. 474).

'Comprehensive Optimum' means that an optimum still needs to be pursued in an ecological civilization but it is no longer a purely economic one. This new optimum needs to be calculated even though it contains incommensurable parts. The economic optimum works by reducing all values to a common monetary denominator as if this were a straightforward matter of fact. The comprehensive optimum contains the full range of the world's beings and they do not reduce to a single measure but nonetheless the optimum must be calculated and pursued. Once again Latour expresses it well: 'Goods and evils cannot be weighed against one another and *yet they must be weighed!*' (ibid., p. 461).

Given the no quittance and the comprehensive optimum, it is clear that simple, discrete cause and effect relationships may no longer be established. Vallega (2005) takes up this point and argues that business performance can no longer be *explained* and that it should be *comprehended* in the sense of its etymological root which is *cum-prehendere*, a bringing together. In this understanding, ecological and human systems interact with each other and their external environments as they move towards holistic targets such as the comprehensive optimum, balance, harmony or maturity. This, Vallega argues, means that cause and effect relationships have to be replaced by goal-orientated understandings: teleology replaces cause and effect.

Finally for this section, two summaries of the transition are presented to bring together some of the ideas dealt with above and present them in a memorable, communicable format. The first consider companies as moving from a 'Bulldozer' stereo-type to a 'Dinghy' one, Figure 3.1.

The second is a statement of fundamental elements of the transition as we cross from crisis to sustainability over the bridge at the edge of the world:

being, not having
needs, not wants
better, not richer
connected, not separate
ecology, not economy
part of nature, not apart from nature.

(Speth, 2008, p. 236)

Move from: "BULLDOZER COMPANIES" in Modern episteme

- Passive Nature Attitude
- Deterministic/Predictable
- Independent
- Forcing a way forward

Move to: "DINGHY COMPANIES" in Primal episteme

- Active Nature Attitude
- Indeterminate/Unpredictable
- Interdependent
- Sensing a way forward

Figure 3.1 From bulldozer to dinghy companies (Birkin and Polesie, 2011, p. 291).

The emerging Chinese eco-civilization

The People's Republic of China (PRC) has made a commitment to develop an ecological civilization. China has existed in a 'civilized' state for over 3,000 years which suggests that the Chinese must know at some level something about sustainability. Indeed, the first of the Chinese characters for 'China' is *Zhong* which means middle, between, among, average and balanced. Hence the name of China is itself representative of their concept of harmonious development.

In addition, the culture and belief systems of China may draw on a tradition argu-ably more amenable to sustainable development than those of the West. Taoism and its amalgamation with Confucianism and Buddhism weave a complex interdepend-ence between mankind and nature. Taoism as *The Way* establishes the autonomy and transcendence of nature and details man's ultimate dependence on its unknowable vagaries, on natural fortune. Buddhism regards the function of work not just to produce but to engage a person and society in ongoing development. Buddhist work is to:

i   give man a chance to use and develop his faculties;
ii   enable him to overcome his ego-centeredness by joining with other people in a common task; and
iii bring forth the goods and services needed for a becoming existence.

(Schumacher, 1973)

This Buddhist transcendence of self resonates with the Chinese expression of 'Tian Xia' which literally means 'all under heaven'. Zhao (2005) proposes that Tian Xia could be an alternative that the world could consider to overcome the separation caused by strong individualism and discrete nation states. For Zhao, Tian Xia has three levels of meaning: (i) the Earth in the traditional Chinese triad of Earth, heaven and people; (ii) all the people on Earth and under heaven; and (iii) an ethical-political mix wherein everybody treats everybody else like members of a single family.

In spite of their cultural heritage that appears to have all the elements for a sustainable society, recent decades have shown China to be very adept at economic development with little apparent heed of social, environmental and ecological consequences. This is partly attributable to the Chinese need, still evident, to catch up.

China was for many centuries a world leader. In the eighteenth century, Adam Smith identified that for a long time China had been one of the richest, most industrious, most prosperous and most urbanized countries in the world. After the isolationism of Maoism, Deng Xiaoping pursued policies to 'Reform and Open Up' China with a 'Socialism with Chinese Characteristics'. This saw the introduction of free market principles to China, an influx of foreign investment and a new generation of entrepreneurs starting their own businesses free, more or less, of state control. At that time in the 1980s, the Chinese state still owned most industries so privatization policies were implemented through the 1990s. Many industries then contracted out of state-ownership. Certain key sectors were kept under state control, including banking and petroleum, but by 2005 Engardio (2005) estimated that 70 per cent of the Chinese gross domestic product was being produced by the private sector. This is supported approximately by Changhong (2014) who estimated that the 'non-public' sector of the Chinese economy dropped from 69.74 per cent in 2008 to 67.59 per cent in 2012.

However, in their desire to mimic and catch up with the West, ancient Chinese harmony was sacrificed in that rush for economic success. Towards the end of the twentieth century, environmental and ecological devastation was endemic in much of China and could not be ignored. In typical Chinese style, the solution would be to create a whole new civilization.

The Chinese ecological civilization officially commenced at the 16th National Congress of the Communist Party of China in 2002. It then took some five years before detailed strategic plans could be drawn and presented at the next, the 17th National Congress of the Communist Party of China in 2007. It was from 2007 onwards that the concept and practice of ecological civilization began to catch the attention of the Chinese people and businesses.

But even basic definitions are still in a state of flux. It was as recently as 2013 that *Qiushi*, the official journal of the Central Committee of the Communist Party of China, argued that 'ecological pertains to the state in which nature exists, whereas the term civilization refers to a state of human progress. Thus ecological civilization describes the level of harmony that exists between human progress and natural existence in human civilization' (Kai, 2013). Chinese harmony is becoming the goal once more.

Of course, the creation of an ecological civilization in China is still in initial stages and experimentation and innovation play main roles. Initial responses may be classed principally as 'Ecological Modernization' in which the PRC is very visible doing something about environmental degradation but not challenging core economic development assumptions. For example, the 11 Five-Year Plan regulated that in the years up to 2010, the unit of GDP energy consumption must be reduced by 20 per cent; and the total discharge of major pollutants must be reduced by 10 per cent. To achieve these targets, the Chinese government imposed 45 policies to control production, circulation, consumption and distribution within their economy. These policies were implemented in more than 1,000 regions and cities.

The 12 Five-Year Plan up to the year 2015 had similar environmental protection targets including:

- The emission of major pollutants should be significantly reduced.
- The environmental safety of drinking water sources in both urban and rural areas should be better protected effectively.
- Heavy metal pollution should be effectively controlled, especially for persistent organic pollutants, dangerous chemicals and hazardous waste.
- The construction and operation level of urban environmental infrastructure should be improved.
- The regulation ability of nuclear and radiation safety should be enhanced.

However, the 13 Five-Year Plan moved beyond modernization to a make a start on a proactive ecological restoration programme:

- Most strict policy of environmental protection will be carried out.
- The atmosphere, water and soil pollution prevention action plan will be thoroughly implemented.
- The ecological protection and restoration project of forest and lake will begin.
- A large-scale afforestation, improving the natural forest protection system and the rectification action of blue bay will be enhanced.

Hence over a period of less than ten years, successive Chinese policies have moved from environmental protection to ecological restoration. The reforms now address many of the country's major environmental and ecological concerns and include: protection of natural resource rights; establishment of a national parks system; better and stricter systems for protection of arable land and water resources management; establishment of a green financing system; and improvement of environmental compensation mechanisms.

In addition to using policy directives and regulations to implement the proposed reforms, the Chinese are running trials of a system of natural resources audits to be conducted when senior local officials leave their posts. If officials fail to heed the environmental and ecological aspects in their areas of jurisdiction, it is the intention that the audits will reveal their shortcomings and then the official concerned will be personally held responsible to the detriment of their careers. Pilot natural audit schemes will be carried out in five different locations, including Hulunbuir in Inner Mongolia. These trials will take place in three stages: a launch, an expansion phase, then in 2017 full audits in the trial locations. Regular audits will be commencing in 2018.

However, implementation of the audit scheme will be difficult. There will be many practical obstacles to overcome when calculating responsibility for deteriorating natural resources which, as discussed above, do not have simple cause and effect relations. The interconnectedness and varying time horizons of man-made and natural factors will make the amount of blame attributable to any one official difficult to calculate.

Nonetheless China is earnestly and urgently pursuing its vision of an ecological civilization. As a world first, it will inevitably face many difficulties but the Chinese people are nothing if not determined and able … and, in the long term, sustainable.

Finally, in the midst of such social upheaval, what are Chinese businesses doing? Whilst not under direct control from the PRC, they will depend upon the support of local officials for many aspects of their businesses and hence they too will need to pay close attention to national policies and the forthcoming natural resource audits.

Case study of Tianjin Chunfa Bio-Technology Group Co., Ltd

This company is located in Tianjin that is one of China's exemplar 'eco-cities' located not far from Beijing. However, the product of the Tianjin Chunfa Bio-Technology Group is mainly food flavourings which are notably neither environmentally friendly nor ecologically desirable. The company does not therefore possess inherent, good 'eco-credentials' so the question may be asked 'How does it manage and present itself in an emerging eco-civilization?'

The company was formerly 'Tianjin Chunfa Food Ingredients Co. Ltd '. and had been established in 1992. In July 2011, the company restructured itself and the Tianjin Chunfa Bio-Technology Group was established with three subsidiaries: Tianjin Chunyu Food Ingredients Co., Ltd., Tianjin Chunsheng Muslim Food Co., Ltd., and Tianjin Chunfa Environmental Protection Equipment Co., Ltd. It then had a new manufacturing base in Binhai with an investment of more than 200 million yuan. The company at this time, 'Chunfa' in short, had not only updated its name to include 'bio-technology' and expanded into environmental protection but also possessed one of the most advanced automatic manufacture system in the world. Research and development of natural products were regarded as the key strategic response for the future of Chunfa.

From the time when Mr Xin Haiming established Chunfa, its core values had been open, progressive and notably not singularly economic. These values had been summarized as 'first virtue, then business'. By choosing 'virtue' as a core value, Chunfa was not merely conducting good Chinese PR. The imprecision or ineluctable component of 'virtue' will always be difficult to pin down and translate into practice – we all know to where the road of 'good intentions' goes. So Chunfa supported its values with three searching questions: 'Who am I?', 'What should I do?' and 'where could I go?' These three questions guided Chunfa for more than 20 years and directly supported its development.

In 2012 Chunfa sales revenue was 310 million yuan. Its profit and taxes paid for the year were 31 million yuan and 37 million yuan respectively. It is a very successful company that explains its success in terms of quality, reputation and responsibility.

Chunfa quality

In 20 years, Chunfa established itself as an 'invisible champion' by maintaining a healthy, high-quality development of itself and its ecological environment in both technological and managerial innovations. The enterprise now has 104 R&D staff representing more than 30 per cent of its total employees. These key personnel include experts from home and abroad for Chunfa has engaged in long-term cooperation with research institutions and universities including the China Agricultural University, the prestigious Chinese Academy of Science, Tianjin University of Science and Technology, Lanzhou University and Tianjin Institute of Industrial Biotechnology.

Chunfa exports quality. In 2009, the food flavour testing laboratory of Chunfa was certificated by appropriate authorities and its testing facilities can now be used in more

than 50 countries and regions. Chunfa now has some of the most advanced fully au-
tomated production equipment in the world based on its own innovative designs and
intellectual property rights.

Its innovations are the product of a 300-million-yuan investment programme, representing an annual investment of over 5 per cent of turnover, designed to make food additives
less artificial and more natural. This strategy avoids synthetic chemical processing which in
turn protect the natural environment.

To support its innovation strategy, Chunfa pays attention to the balance between
management practice and technological advance. With regard to production process
management, Chunfa has adopted a maxim of 'thinking well and doing early'. As early
as 2002, Chunfa had installed an ERP production management system which improved
production efficiency and reduced waste costs by 750,000 yuan in that year alone. It was
in fact the earliest manufacturing factory to implement such a system in China consequently Chunfa became a demonstration company for industrial information management in Tianjin city.

Chunfa has also obtained HACCP (Hazard Analysis Critical Control Point) system
certification that is the global preventive food safety control system. With an integration
of ERP, Lean Production and HACCP certification, Chunfa pursues another of its max-
ims to 'supply people with high quality products'.

Chunfa reputation

Chunfa's reputation in the food-flavouring sector rests upon strict quality control. It
operates a two-hour food safety traceability system and has an ongoing management
programme for quality and safety system improvements.

Today, Chunfa is the clear leader in the Chinese food-flavouring sector. It is a principle for drafting national standards for the salty-flavour industry and it participates in
setting up more than ten other industrial standards. Chunfa owns 38 patents and has 160
patent applications pending. In the USA, Chunfa has FDA (Food and Drug Administration) and AIB (American Institute of Baking) certification. It also has Halal and Kosher
food certification. Chunfa is the largest, hi-tech salty-flavour manufacturing companies
in the world.

Chunfa is a highly conscientious company. Strict quality control management means
that Chunfa can be trusted and it never uses defective materials. Throughout its history, Chunfa has sought the highest moral ground in all aspects to truly implement the
maxim 'first virtue, then business'. In the rapidly changing Chinese society, there have
been many internal and external threats and challenges to Chunfa's integrity but it resisted these and witnessed its market share rise steadily for 20 years.

In the early years, Chunfa allowed no grey area between its business and the law.
Although some customers would request to have no invoices to avoid taxes, Chunfa
would always issue them and pay its taxes in full. A clean history in a Chinese society
that could have cut many corners is a matter of some pride for Chunfa.

Chunfa has always complied with Chinese national environmental policies. Indeed,
the company has always associated quality products with environmental protection.

The company has its own charitable foundation and has built three 'Chunfa Hope' primary schools; one in each of Tianjin city and the provinces of Sichuan and Ningxia. It has
also provided support to hundreds of poor students at the China Agricultural University,

the Tianjin Normal University, the Tianjin University of Science and Technology and the Tianjin Foreign Studies University.

Chunfa's benevolence is not used as a PR asset by the company. For example, all the students it funds have to sign confidentiality agreements to promise not to broadcast Chunfa's support. Neither does the company respond to the many requests from the media regarding its charitable work. It has a policy of not benefiting from charitable work.

Conclusions

The world is in flux – it has to be for either we manage change or change will manage us. Such change has happened before for history reveals that civilizations come and go.

Present day 'reality' will become yesterday's fantasy. The dominance of abstract, logical belief systems grounded in nineteenth-century science and its view of the world no longer work. We now know that events in the world are far more interdependent, interactive and uncertain than previously thought and that our planet has its own needs and limits. We live and work in a world of complex ecological relations.

Some things change and some endure. For China, the principle of harmony has endured so has the inclusive openness of Tian Xia, all people under heaven. For business management everywhere, the quaint charm of Chunfa's mission 'first virtue, then business' may become the most solid of paths to the future.

References

Benefit Corporations (2015). A new class of corporation. Benefit Corporations, USA. Available at http://benefitcorp.net/ (Accessed August 2015).

Birkin, F.K. and Polesie, T. (2011). *Intrinsic Sustainable Development: Epistemes, Science, Business and Sustainability*. Singapore: World Scientific Press.

Changhong, P. (2014). Quantitative estimation of the leading position of China's public ownership and its developmental trends. *Social Sciences in China*, 1: 4–29.

Costanza, R. (1991). Ecological economics: A research agenda. *Structural Change and Economic Dynamics*, 2(2): 335–357.

Daly, H.E. (2014). *From Uneconomic Growth to a Steady-State Economy*. Cheltenham: Edward Elgar.

De Young, R. (2013). Environmental psychology overview. In S.R. Klein and A.H. Huffman (eds), *Green Organizations: Driving Change with IO Psychology*. New York: Routledge, pp. 17–33.

Diamond, J. (2006). *Collapse: How Societies Choose to Fail or Survive*. London: Penguin.

Elkington, J. (1997). *Cannibals with Forks: the Triple Bottom Line of 21st Century Business*. Oxford: Capstone.

Ellis, B.D. (2002). *The Philosophy of Nature: A Guide to the New Essentialism*. Chesham: Acumen.

Engardio, P. (2005). China is a private-sector economy. *Bloomberg Businessweek*, 21 August.

Fernandez-Armesto, F. (2001). *Civilization*. London: Pan Books.

Foucault, M. (1970). *The Order of Things: An Archaeology of the Human Sciences*. London: Routledge.

Guardian. (2014). Nasa-funded study: Industrial civilisation headed for 'irreversible collapse'? *The Guardian*. Available at www.theguardian.com/environment/earth-insight/2014/mar/14/nasa-civilisation-irreversible-collapse-study-scientists (Accessed August 2015).

Hawken, P. (1993). *The Ecology of Commerce*. London: Harper Collins.

Kai, M. (2013). Committing to the development of an ecological civilization in China. *Qiushi*, 5(4).

Latour, B. (1993). *We Have Never Been Modern*. Cambridge, MA: Harvard University Press.

Latour, B. (2005). *Reassembling the Social: An Introduction to Actor-Network-Theory.* Oxford: Oxford University Press.

Latour, B. (2013). *An Inquiry into Modes of Existence.* Cambridge, MA: Harvard University Press.

Lovelock, J. (2000 [1979]). *Gaia: A New Look at Life on Earth*, 3rd edn. Oxford: Oxford University Press.

McDonough, W. and Braungart, M. (2002). Design for the triple top line: New tools for sustainable commerce. *Corporate Environmental Strategy*, 9(3): 251–258.

Mitchell, M. (2009). *Complexity: A Guided Tour.* Oxford: Oxford University Press.

Natural Step. (2010). *The Natural Step.* Stockholm: The Natural Step. Available at www.naturalstep.org/ (Accessed December 2010).

Psychology Today. (2015). *Evolutionary Psychology.* New York: Sussex Publishers. Available at https://www.psychologytoday.com/basics/evolutionary-psychology (Accessed August 2015).

Schumacher, E.F. (1973). *Small is Beautiful: Economics as if People Mattered.* London: Blond and Briggs.

Speth, J.G. (2008). *The Bridge at the Edge of the World: Capitalism, the Environment, and Crossing from Crisis to Sustainability.* New Haven, CT: Yale University Press.

Stakeholder Forum for a Sustainable Future. (2012). *Review of the Implementation of Agenda 21 and the Rio Principles.* New York: United Nations Department of Economic and Social Affairs.

UNDP/UNDESA. (2012). *Synthesis of National Reports for Rio+20.* New York: United Nations Publications.

Vallega, A. (2005). Diversity: A multi-faceted concept. In G. Bellezza, L. Ayo and D. Bissell (eds), *International Workshop Cultures and Civilisations for Human Development.* Rome: International Geographical Union.

Volans. (2009). *The Phoenix Economy: 50 Pioneers in the Business of Social Innovation.* London: Volans Ventures.

Wackernagel, M. and Rees, W. (1998). *Our Ecological Footprint: Reducing Human Impact on the Earth.* Gabriola Island: New Society Publishers.

Wilkinson, R. and Pickett, K. (2010). *The Spirit Level: Why Equality is Better for Everyone.* London: Penguin.

Wilson, E.O. (1998). *Consilience: The Unity of Knowledge.* London: Little, Brown and Co.

Zhao, T. (2005). The *Tianxia System: An Introduction to the Philosophy of a World Institution.* Nanjing: Jiangsu Jiaoyu Chubanshe.

4 Creating theory for business strategies for sustainability and climate change

Transitional and transformational strategies and ecocentric dynamic capabilities

Helen Borland, Adam Lindgreen, Véronique Ambrosini and Joëlle Vanhamme

Introduction

We reflect on the growing need to introduce new theory to our discipline. Thus far, much of our academic endeavour has been phenomenon-driven focusing directly on specific issues to do with sustainability, climate change and/or resilience, and our human ability to combat them. We recognize the need to develop good theory that can address successfully practical business needs, but that is not so dependent on existing business management literature and its conceptual thinking. Rather, we believe, the underpinning thinking needs to stem from knowledge of the physical sciences and, in particular, knowledge and understanding of sustainability, climate change and resilience. Thus, we seek to contribute to the development of theory that builds on our knowledge of the related science and provides us with new business concepts and theories that can be taught and researched within business schools to help enhance business performance for the future in an environmentally changed world.

In setting up such theory, Borland et al. (2016) make three important points. The first point is that we need to move away from the Brundtland-style definition of sustainability and move towards a more inclusive, ecocentric definition. The authors identify Porritt's (2007) definition as inclusive of all species, including the human species. The second point is that the authors identify the importance of thinking about philosophical perspectives when establishing theory development for sustainability and climate change. They posit that it is important to move our perspective from an anthropocentric (human-centric) towards an ecocentric (all species–centric) perspective if we are to move our thinking towards an understanding of sustainability, climate change and resilience. The third point is that although these two perspectives may be seen as different and possibly incompatible, the perspectives also can be viewed as two ends of a continuum, with developmental steps in-between, which create an opportunity for individuals – and, in our case, organizations – to travel along as part of an integrated process of changing thinking and strategy towards sustainability and climate change (Borland et al., 2016). Borland and Lindgreen (2013) provide a strategic grid exercise that acts as a simple-to-use audit tool to help organizations identify which business activities are currently anthropocentric and which ones are ecocentric.

In developing new theory, it is also important to acknowledge the difference between incremental anthropocentric, change where extensions to existing theory and concepts are put forward; and transformational theory change where radically new ideas are brought into being, born out of ideas from different disciplines and fields. Zahra and Newey (2009) focus on a high impact contribution of theory-building research, which they refer to as a 'transforming the core' category that goes beyond simply borrowing and domesticating theories from one field (Oswick et al., 2011). Instead, it borrows concepts/theories from one field and intersects them with concepts from another field in a way that extends one or more of the intersecting theories, but also transforms the core of those fields and their disciplines. The outcome is a transformation of ideas in the parent domain, based on lessons learned from its extension into the focal domain. When interdisciplinary research takes this approach, it likely makes a greater impact, such that it should be more useful to practice.

Attempting to incorporate ecological sustainability thinking into management theory and practice is a complex, multifaceted exercise; we also believe it is necessary. Developing business strategies that incorporate ecological sustainability both extends intersecting theories and disciplines and also potentially transforms the core of a dominant perspective in strategic management, namely, the dynamic capabilities view (Mellahi and Sminia, 2009).

On the basis of this extant literature and the two philosophical perspectives of sustainability, we identify business strategies that incorporate both ecocentrism and ecological sustainability. Building on contributions from Hart (1995, 1997), Hart and Dowell (2011), McDonough and Braungart (2002), and Stead and Stead (2004, 2010), we theorize at the intersection of strategic management and strategies for ecological sustainability. With such an analysis at the intersection, we can seek to transform the core of dynamic capabilities literature.

Business strategies for sustainability

We begin theorizing about ecological sustainability by proposing two strategic alternatives, transitional and transformational strategies, which offer distinct levels and approaches to ecological sustainability. To build our argument, we explicate three types of business strategies. First, traditional business strategies are not concerned with ecological sustainability. We compare these traditional strategies with transitional strategies for sustainability that embrace anthropocentric assumptions and with transformational strategies that embrace ecocentric assumptions. Second, we combine the dynamic capabilities framework with an ecocentric perspective and thereby propose an ecocentric dynamic capabilities framework that goes beyond the boundaries of the firm's business ecosystem, with emphasis on the importance of managerial perceptions about the firm's environment and performance (Klettner et al., 2014) and core psychological beliefs about ecological sustainability (Wright et al., 2012).

Traditional strategy

A fundamental assumption for firms that use traditional business strategies is that the economy is a 'closed circular flow in which ever-abundant resources, products and services can, forever, flow from businesses to households without stressing the Earth's social and ecological systems' (Stead and Stead, 2010, p. 491). Such strategies are not concerned with ecological sustainability; examples of firms that adopt this approach include Netto and Aldi. Traditional frameworks embedded in industrial organization economics, such as the five forces (Porter, 1980) or the value chain model (Porter, 1985), emerge from such assumptions. The processes involved in applying these frameworks are linear and static (Teece, 2007). For example, the process of selling a product and making a profit begins with procuring component parts and finishes with the use of the product by the end consumer, without any consideration of the disposal process or the exploitation of raw materials that make up the product. This linear process is thus a cradle-to-grave process; it also can be described as an open loop, because it does not close the circular loop of life and leaves used products as waste, from a human perspective. Nature lacks a concept of waste though, so high entropy, waste materials become a problem; because natural processes do not recognize them, natural processes cannot break the waste materials down (Stead and Stead, 2004). The firm and its business economy operate as though it were a separate, closed system, without any interaction, interrelationship or responsibility toward society or natural ecosystems.

(a)

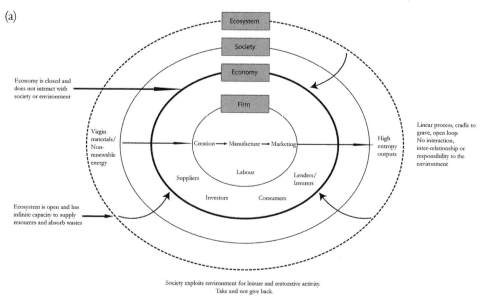

(Adapted from Stead & Stead, 2004)

(b)

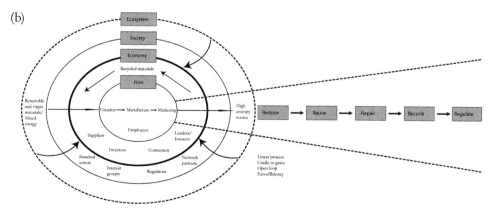

(Adapted from Stead & Stead, 2004)

Figure 4.1 Traditional, transitional and transformational strategy.

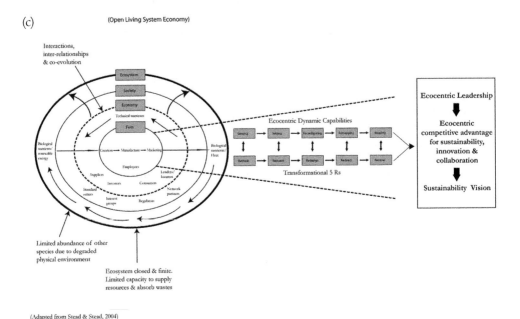

(Adapted from Stead & Stead, 2004)

Figure 4.1 (Continued)

Transitional strategy

Transitional business strategies reflect anthropocentric assumptions and can be identified readily in today's corporate arena, with examples such as Marks & Spencer, Procter & Gamble, Unilever, and Tesco. These strategies operate in a linear, cradle-to-grave, open loop fashion, but with the assumption that eco-efficiency should be pursued (McDonough and Braungart, 2002). Unlike traditional strategies, this strategy introduces the 5Rs: reduce, reuse, repair, recycle, and regulate (see Table 4.1). In one respect, this positive approach encourages reductions in the use of precious commodities (e.g. metals, fuels, electricity, gas), and also the approach considers what should be done with waste materials, such as recycling them. However, these assumptions do not change fundamentally how firms make products or how consumers dispose of the products. Most recycled products eventually end up in landfill sites or incineration plants, because recycling generally downgrades the fibres and materials to the point that ultimately they become useless for making new products.

Businesses that use transitional strategies still operate within a closed business system with very little interaction, interrelationship or responsibility toward society or natural ecosystems. The products still are made conventionally, with little consideration for raw materials, the environment whence they come, the disposal process, or the environment to which they go (Martin and Kemper, 2012). Therefore, 5R activities are add-on options to deal with the problems of waste and toxic material from products, after they have been created, sold and used. This eco-efficiency process (McDonough and Braungart, 2002) implies that firms are trying to be less bad than others operating according to the traditional mode. Businesses try to reduce their negative impact on the environment rather than eliminating it, such as by not creating

Table 4.1 Transitional and transformational 5Rs

Transitional 5Rs	Transformational 5Rs
Reduce Reduce the quantity of material used in manufacturing certain products, and domestically reduce the quantity/number of products used.	**Rethink** This first stage requires completely rethinking the concept of what the product is: is a car a car, or is it a means of getting from A to B? After determining the function of the product, we can think of different ways to satisfy the function in an environmentally, closed-loop way.
Reuse Wherever possible, reuse materials and products so that the overall volume demanded is reduced and the product is used to its fullest extent.	**Reinvent** Make way for reinvention: This creative, innovative, brainstorming process identifies completely new concepts that may or may not be based on existing products. Alliances and clean technology may be required.
Repair Some products can be repaired and reused, rather than being disposed of, thus extending their useful life and reducing demand for new products.	**Redesign** Once new concepts have been identified, redesign needs to embrace ecological requirements as its primary position so that products (and services) are designed to be made from biological material or technical materials only, eliminating waste and toxic residues. For example, an upcycled vehicle might run on water and release no dangerous residues, but instead contribute positively to the environment by cleaning air or water as it runs.
Recycle If a product cannot be repaired or reused, recycling options exist, whether domestically, municipally, or through a corporate recollection scheme. Conventional recycling is a finite process for most products, because the elements ultimately become degraded beyond usefulness, leading to down-cycling and disposal in a landfill or incineration.	**Redirect** Redirect and recover affect the product at the end of its life. Redirect refers to the need to have two clear channels for waste materials: one where *all* waste materials go back into the industrial cycle so that nothing is wasted and pollutants are not released to damage the environment, thus creating a closed loop, and another for biodegradable materials that can go back to nature without causing any physical or chemical damage. These two channels need to be kept separate. Sophisticated, productive, profitable channels need to exist to make it a reality, so that industrial materials can be infinitely cycled without loss of quality. This step also addresses the increasing scarcity of some raw materials (e.g. copper).
Regulate Increasingly companies and individuals are subjected to laws, restrictions and regulation that control activities associated with waste material. These restrictions are set to increase in the future.	**Recover** To recover scarce (and not so scarce) elements and materials and use them in new production and market opportunities, thus maintaining their market value (industrial symbiosis) and again closing the loop. This cycle then operates as an infinite, circular system with no end. Only increases in end-user demand generate the need for virgin resource extraction.

toxic materials in the first place. The end result thus remains a physical environment cluttered by waste products and damaged by toxic production processes. Transitional strategies slow down the rate of damage and destruction to the environment, other species and soil, water and atmosphere – and thus to homes, leisure places, workplaces and the quality of life.

Because the emphasis of this strategy is on resources and 5R activities, a transitional strategy reflects the resource-based view of the firm (Barney, 1991; Levitas and Ndofor, 2006; Lockett et al., 2008), and more specifically a natural resource-based view of the firm (Hart, 1995). Hart (1995) argues that firms can achieve superior performance by managing their relationship with the natural environment and thereby developing valuable, rare, difficult-to-imitate, non-substitutable resources related to pollution reduction, product stewardship and sustainable development. These 5R activities, with their focus on limiting damages, reflect an argument about whether it is worthwhile, from a profit perspective, to adopt an environmental strategy. Although the natural resource-based view embraces the idea of the natural environment, it is essentially static and designed to minimize firms' impact on the environment, then enjoy the advantages of doing so; it does not embrace the quest for no or a positive impact on the environment. As duly noted by Hart and Dowell (2011, p. 1476), this version may not be sufficient anymore:

> most firms continue to focus on incremental strategies such as eco-efficiency, pollution reduction, product stewardship, and corporate social responsibility. As important as these corporate initiatives have been, it is now clear that such incremental sustainability strategies will simply not be sufficient. Companies and management scholars are being challenged increasingly to develop breakthrough strategies that actually resolve social and environmental problems, rather than simply reducing the negative impacts associated with their current operations.

Transformational strategy

The assumption behind transformational strategies differs: these strategies develop from ecocentric assumptions (Purser et al., 1995) and embrace ecological sustainability, working within the constraints of natural ecosystems (Wittneben et al., 2012). The assumption is that business strategies should seek to eliminate waste and toxic chemicals from ever being created or deposited in the environment. Businesses seek to achieve eco-effectiveness (McDonough and Braungart, 2002) by cycling continually only safe, bio-materials in the ecological system while keeping anything that nature does not recognize and cannot break down, or techno-materials, out of the ecological system and circulating them solely in the industrial system. To achieve eco-effectiveness, a different set of 5R activities thus may be required: rethink, reinvent, redesign, redirect and recover (see Table 4.1). Rather than closing the economic and business system off from society and nature, the aim is to open it and thereby integrate, emulate and mimic natural cycles, which would allow materials and nutrients to pass through ecosystems. Such cycles are cradle-to-cradle and closed-loop. For example, when a leaf falls from a tree in autumn, it is broken down by worms and soil microbes, which release nutrients into the soil that become available for reuse in exactly the same form in which they were released. In spring, the nutrients may be taken up by the tree and made into new leaves. This process is a perfect closed-loop, cradle-to-cradle cycle, with no waste and no unrecognizable chemicals, which makes it sustainable: trees only grow if enough nutrients, water, soil and sunlight are available. Discarded nutrients get taken up and used again and again, with no waste. The assumption for businesses that opt for a transformational strategy thus is that resources are finite and limited meaning that to become eco-effective these firms must use the resources again and again, without downgrading them, discarding them or producing toxic compounds that nature cannot process.

Moreover, a successful transformational strategy requires the organization to adopt a sustainability vision (Hart, 1997; Hart and Milstein, 2003). Managers need a long-term mindset, in which the planet's homeostatic balance is the most important consideration and there is no separation between the social and the biophysical world. Managers must believe that nature and humans together form ecosystems and that their business organizations have roles to play in sustaining and enhancing those ecosystems. Therefore, the businesses must engage creatively with physical and human ecosystems to sustain competitive advantages for the future and achieve ecological sustainability.

Commercial benefits become apparent from such a transformational strategy, including the reduced need for and reduced cost of purchasing raw materials. The increasing costs of purchasing virgin, raw materials worldwide makes it more attractive for firms to find a position in which they do not need raw materials or at least need very limited quantities. In addition, such firms reduce their costs of disposal of waste materials and, particularly, toxic waste materials, which represent an increasing expense for most firms. Another benefit stems from the positive effects on corporate image and reputation. With a transformational strategy, firms can claim genuine sustainability status for their products rather than greenwashing. Finally, firms can adjust their business model from a model for selling products to one for renting products, and for such service-based firms, product return at the end of its life is an integral step. Thus, a television manufacturer would sell 10,000 hours of viewing, rather than a television.

The emphasis of a transformational strategy thus is on operating in an open living system economy (business interacts directly with ecosystems without harming them) (Stead and Stead, 2010). Sustaining and enhancing ecosystems in an eco-effective way implies a managerial mindset toward ecological sustainability and a quest for a sustainability vision that develops out of transformational strategies that encourage ecocentric leadership, innovation, collaboration and a competitive advantage based on sustainability. This proactive environment strategy, to use Aragón-Correa and Sharma's (2003) term, is a dynamic capability: It allows the firm to refresh and renew its resource base (Ambrosini and Bowman, 2009; Helfat et al., 2007; Wang and Ahmed, 2007; Zahra et al., 2006).

In the next section, we provide a practical example that illustrates a move from a traditional anthropocentric approach to a transformational ecocentric approach; we also examine the 5Rs of transformational strategies using a dynamic capabilities lens and illuminate ways to enhance the dynamic capabilities framework to transform it into an ecocentric dynamic capabilities framework. That is, we borrow and extend in an effort to transform dynamic capabilities literature (Zahra and Newey, 2009). We examine the transformational strategies instantiated by one firm: Ricoh UK.

Ricoh UK

We elaborate on the above theoretical development by reporting empirical data gathered from interviews conducted with Ricoh's environment officer and internal and external documents that summarize firm-specific facts and figures. This illustration allows us to provide an example of transformational strategies while further developing our conceptualization of ecocentric dynamic capabilities.

In 1994, Ricoh UK changed its corporate philosophy from an anthropocentric approach to one that is more ecocentric. Figure 4.1 illustrates Ricoh UK's new closed-loop business approach, including uptake of a zero waste-to-landfill programe, applied to remanufactured photocopiers. In 2000, this programme was rolled out across the whole firm and all its activities. Other streams of activity also were incorporated into this ecocentric model, including remanufacturing, harmonizing with the environment, biodiversity and energy and carbon reduction. Although the firm has not reached the far end of the continuum, it is proximate to the ecocentric end and perceives itself as on a journey toward ecocentrism. The environmental officer for Ricoh UK was responsible for leading and embedding this new programme within the organization. In spearheading the programme, the environmental officer made leadership and personal responsibility key themes for employees to adopt, at work and in the community.

As a result, Ricoh UK has earned itself an enviable reputation among its peers and competitors for its practical application of environmental activities, including awards and accolades, a tripling of turnover and increased profits. The firm also gained a position as a role model and exemplar for its industry. Furthermore, Ricoh UK transformed a loss-making waste stream activity into a profit-making activity (−£46,000 to +£59,000) because the firm identified and employed appropriate

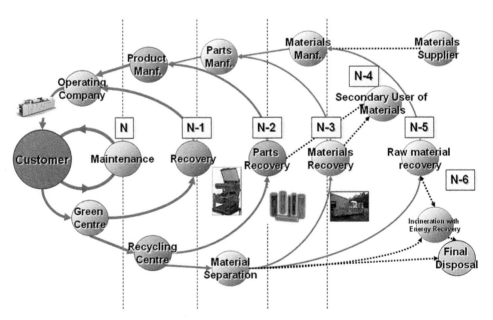

Figure 4.2 Lifecycle: Comet circle deployment.

recycling channels for its card and plastic waste and began reusing the material without downgrading. Since 2011, 95 per cent of its manufacturing waste is recovered and reused in the remanufacturing of photocopiers (almost transformational); only 5 per cent undergoes incineration. In terms of energy and carbon reduction – a transitional rather than transformational activity – the firm's UK site has managed to reduce its energy bill by £500,000 annually and its carbon output by 50 per cent. The firm's biodiversity activities include swales of phyto-remediation plants that absorb excess rain runoff and any production spillages. These swales provide a more pleasant physical environment for staff, visitors and wildlife; they also save the firm approximately £50,000 a year in wastewater management (transformational). Projects seek to provide homes and monitor wildlife on the site (transformational). Finally, in harmonizing with the environment, the Ricoh UK site works with educational institutions, other companies and charitable organizations to implement environmental activities elsewhere.

In 2013, Ricoh UK's head office in Japan announced a European reorganization, such that the manufacturing of photocopiers would move to a French site, while ink cartridge manufacturing would stay in the UK. At that point, the UK environmental officer had developed, drawn on and exploited internal knowledge and capabilities to move Ricoh from a traditional business approach to a nearly ecocentric one. With the reorganization, the environmental officer needed to adapt the knowledge, skills, and capabilities that the UK team had developed and reconfigure them to support a new business activity, in an ecocentric way, while still ensuring profits for the firm (all units must turn profits).

The first step was to determine whether ink cartridges could be remanufactured, with 95–100 per cent recovery (transformational), which likely involves rethinking, reinventing and redesigning the cartridges. This remapping exercise required the environmental officer to draw on previous experience and capabilities, then close the loop for producing cartridges, as well as apply previous knowledge about reducing energy and carbon emissions (or generating green energy to use in the remanufacturing process). The positive outcome for Ricoh UK would be reaping the benefits, both financial and non-financial, previously enjoyed from the remanufactured photocopiers, such that the success of the cartridges activity would become embedded into its ecocentric business model. Next, the challenge for Ricoh UK would be to rethink inks and paper associated with the cartridge business and examine whether they could also become ecocentric (e.g. paper that is biodegradable, that creates zero toxic residues as it biodegrades, or infinitely reusable paper and ink). Such efforts would, once again, create opportunities for ecocentric transformational strategies.

Ecocentric dynamic capabilities

The dynamic capabilities view is an appropriate theoretical framework for grounding business strategies for ecological sustainability (for reviews of the dynamic capabilities view, see Ambrosini and Bowman, 2009; Barreto, 2010). Teece (2007, pp. 1319–20) suggests that dynamic capabilities constitute a three-stage process: 'the capacity 1) to sense and shape opportunities and threats, 2) to seize opportunities, and 3) to maintain competitiveness', such that they 'embrace the enterprise's capacity to shape the ecosystem it occupies'. The sensing, seizing and reconfiguring dynamic capabilities are salient for ecocentric strategies, because they explain how firms can transform themselves. We illustrate this application using the Ricoh case and reveal how three of the 5Rs – rethink, reinvent and redesign – map onto Teece's (2007) dynamic capabilities of sensing, seizing and reconfiguring. However, the framework as it stands may be too restrictive because an ecosystem refers to a business ecosystem, which Teece (2007, p. 1325) defines as 'the community of organizations, institutions and individuals that impact the enterprise and the enterprise's customers and suppliers'. For firms to be eco-effective and ecologically sustainable, their ecosystem, even in a dynamic capabilities framework, must extend to a global, natural ecosystem that embraces both human and biophysical worlds. Thus, we propose an ecocentric dynamic capabilities framework to help businesses become ecologically sustainable.

Taking an ecocentric view means that the manufacturing and value chain process becomes a closed loop, which in turn demands additional steps in the dynamic capabilities framework. The dynamic capabilities also must allow for the final two steps of the 5Rs, redirect and recover. We describe these additional dynamic capabilities as remapping and reaping, as illustrated in Table 4.2 and with the Ricoh example.

Table 4.2 Development of ecocentric dynamic capabilities

Transformational 5Rs	*Ecocentric dynamic capabilities*
Rethink This first stage requires completely rethinking the concept of what the product is: is a car a car, or is it a means of getting from A to B? After determining the function of the product, we can think of different ways to satisfy the function in an environmentally, closed-loop way.	**Sensing** Sensing requires managers or individuals within the firm to be alert to changes in the business and natural environment and to sense changing consumer demands as society, at large, becomes more sensitized to global ecological phenomena and the plight of other species.
Reinvent Make way for reinvention: This creative, innovative, brainstorming process identifies completely new concepts that may or may not be based on existing products. Alliances and clean technology may be required.	**Seizing** Seizing requires managers and individuals within the firm to seize new ecocentric business opportunities by brainstorming new creative and innovative processes, products, structures and systems that can be adopted by the firm and are not damaging to the physical environment. If large projects are adopted, alliances and/or clean technologies may be required.
Redesign Once new concepts have been identified, redesign needs to embrace ecological requirements as its primary position so that products (and services) are designed to be made from biological material or technical materials only, eliminating waste and toxic residues. For example, an upcycled vehicle might run on water and release no dangerous residues, but instead contribute positively to the environment by cleaning air or water as it runs.	**Reconfiguring** Reconfiguring requires managers, individuals, and the firm as a whole to embrace the closed-loop, cradle-to-cradle requirements of ecosystems and allows for products, from their inception, to be designed and produced using only biological or technical materials; the two types of materials are kept separate at all times in the production process, during consumer use, and for return at end of life.

Redirect

Redirect and recover affect the product at the end of its life. Redirect refers to the need to have two clear channels for waste materials: one where *all* waste materials go back into the industrial cycle so that nothing is wasted and pollutants are not released to damage the environment, thus creating a closed loop, and another for biodegradable materials that can go back to nature without causing any physical or chemical damage. These two channels need to be kept separate. Sophisticated, productive, profitable channels need to exist to make it a reality, so that industrial materials can be infinitely cycled without loss of quality. This step also addresses the increasing scarcity of some raw materials (e.g. copper).

Remapping

This new ecocentric dynamic capability embraces the ability of managers to imagine their products and processes as inputs and resources for the next generation of products, services and processes, then find profitable, ecologically appropriate channels for these materials. This remapping will become essential as virgin resources become scarcer and more expensive, and the need to eliminate waste and pollution from the industrial system becomes a competitive necessity for continuing business activities into the future, as the financial and environmental cost of polluting increases. Remapping also refers to the ability of managers to transfer ecocentric transformational product creation strategies to other products in the firm's portfolio, so an ecocentric approach becomes embedded within the firm/business unit and applied to all products.

Recover

To recover scarce (and not so scarce) elements and materials and use them in new production and market opportunities, thus maintaining their market value (industrial symbiosis) and again closing the loop. This cycle then operates as an infinite, circular system with no end. Only increases in end-user demand generate the need for virgin resource extraction.

Reaping

This new ecocentric dynamic capability addresses the ability of managers to benefit from the circular flow of materials, find new (profitable) channels for their waste materials, and reap the benefits in terms of financial gain (reduced costs and/or increased profits), as well as non-financial ways, such as peer group/industry recognition, accolades and awards, societal approval, improvements in reputation, or improved physical environments.

Remapping is part of closing the loop; it requires managers to understand the difference between the biological and technical cycles of materials, the nature of the chemical make-up of those materials, and how to keep them separate. Remapping also demands that managers find ways to re-channel waste materials 'correctly' from earlier generation of produced products to reuse those materials (with the same quality as virgin materials) or dispose of them safely without chemical damage to the environment. This remapping dynamic capability extends to the capability to embed an ecocentric business model into the manufacturing of other products in the firm's portfolio; as illustrated in the Ricoh example, the embedding also might involve another product line as a result of reorganization.

The reaping dynamic capability impresses on managers the notion that pursuing an ecocentric agenda needs not be a sacrificial or profit-negative activity. As with any new initiative, there are implementation costs attached, but the return on investment and profit opportunities (or cost reductions) arise from both ecocentric and traditional product and process developments. If cost reduction and profit opportunities exist for both traditional and ecocentric developments, why should a manager opt for the ecocentric opportunity? At the very least, does this argument involve an appeal to the 'better nature' of the managers? Yet, such opportunities exist in addition to the primary profit opportunities associated with the product being sold (which, if a genuine ecocentric and sustainable product, should command a price premium). Therefore, these features constitute additional profits or cost-reducing activities, and they also provide non-financial advantages, in the form of awards, accolades, recognition, reputation, exemplar status-, and helping others. As the Ricoh example shows, the features bring about a new kind of competitive advantage: an ecocentric competitive advantage or competitive advantage for sustainability.

The two new dynamic capabilities of remapping and reaping, similar to sensing, seizing and reconfiguring, highlight the importance of leaders and managers in organizations. The leadership of a firm and its ability to take risk, engender trust-, or create an organizational culture that embraces change is essential (Pablo et al., 2007; Rosenbloom, 2000; Salvato, 2003). Because of the anthropocentric assumptions, ecocentric leaders and individuals who deploy dynamic capabilities must be embedded ecologically (Whiteman and Cooper, 2000). The argument that leaders and managers are critical determinants of the deployment of dynamic capabilities already is widespread in dynamic capabilities literature (Adner and Helfat, 2003; Ambrosini et al., 2009; Eisenhardt and Martin, 2000) as emphasized by the expression 'dynamic managerial capability', which refers to 'the capacity of managers to purposefully create, extend or modify the resource base of an organization' (Helfat et al., 2007, p. 24). Specifically, it is managers who must sense the environment and changes in technology, customers, suppliers, and so forth. This sensing ability, and their subsequent choice of dynamic capability deployment, depends on managers' motivation and experience (Zahra et al., 2006, 2011), their beliefs and mental models (Adner and Helfat, 2003; Bruni and Verona, 2009), and their willingness to change and break from old paths (Zahra et al., 2006). Using our explanation of the difference, compared with the anthropocentric logic, of ecocentric beliefs that underlie ecocentric dynamic capabilities, we argue that the role of cognitive framing is critical for predicting which strategies for ecological sustainability managers likely choose. Developing an ecocentric mindset represents the first step toward deploying ecocentric dynamic capabilities.

Conclusions

To conclude and complete the previous section on theory building, we suggest that intersecting the dynamic capabilities and ecological sustainability perspectives entails more than just borrowing from one field (ecological sustainability) and extending its insights to the other (dynamic capabilities) (Oswick et al., 2011). We have borrowed and applied existing principles from the dynamic capabilities view of the firm and strategies for sustainability literature, specifically its ecocentric perspective; we also have contributed to dynamic capabilities view research and the dynamic capabilities framework by extending it to include remapping and reaping, arguing that the boundaries of an enterprise are not the business environment but the natural environment. By acknowledging the role of managerial beliefs, we go beyond traditional anthropocentric perceptions of performance or competition to embrace a wider basket of measures that includes managers' fundamental beliefs about the relationship between humans and nature. Thus, we highlight that knowing how to change dynamic capabilities is a salient issue that demands further investigation. To reflect on these extensions of the framework boundaries, we propose a new concept, the ecocentric dynamic capabilities framework.

For this argument, we consider ecological sustainability literature as the parent discipline and strategy literature as the child, such that by applying ecological sustainability principles to dynamic capabilities literature, we extend the concept of dynamic capabilities. Our goal has been to contribute to strategy literature and develop a better understanding of how to integrate ecological concerns at a strategic level – an area that, despite increased public and firm concern for environmental problems, remains woefully atheoretical and academically underdeveloped (Corley and Gioia 2011). In starting to fill this gap, we hope to encourage more scholars to address this field and develop insights to help leaders and managers begin to understand, categorize and adopt strategies that will assist them in making conscious, strategic choices that reflect their informed beliefs about ecological sustainability.

Furthermore, extending extant strategic management literature and scholarly thinking into the realm of ecocentrism and eco-effectiveness represents an interesting challenge, because existing management literature is not consistent with ecocentric thinking. We believe that to develop genuine strategies for ecological sustainability and ecocentric dynamic capabilities, it is imperative to change the way business strategies are construed. Transitional and transformational strategies are grounded in extant literature and can be generalized to theoretical and practical levels, then applied universally to firms in first-world economies, emerging economies, developing economies and base-of-the-pyramid societies around the world. They can be applied regardless of the size of the firm, whether it is new or incumbent, and to both product- and service-based businesses. Transformational strategies are progressive, developmental and dynamic, as well as positive toward ecosystems, human development and welfare. Ecocentric transformational strategies require a change in ethos, comprehension and core values, moving toward sustainability through heightened understanding, combined with an identification with and desire to change things for the future. They are not transitional strategies, focused on incremental change created by market forces. By providing this insight into the development of business strategies for ecological sustainability, and thus a sustainability vision, we hope practitioners benefit from renewed clarity and understanding of the ways they can combine business success with ecological responsibility. Academics also have a new framework from which to observe, examine and measure firms' business strategies for ecological sustainability (Markóczy and Deeds, 2009).

On a practical level, managers and academics can use our descriptions of strategies for ecological sustainability and ecocentric dynamic capabilities to assess where an enterprise stands and how to develop a transformational strategy, should they embrace ecocentric views. They also can identify which parts of their business's value chain operates in eco-effective or eco-efficient manners. For example, Ecover, the European manufacturer of domestic detergents, has gone a long way toward creating a transformational business. Its products, made from natural plant materials and extracts, as well as its production methods, buildings, energy consumption and water-treatment approaches are all regarded as transformational; its packaging, waste prevention, transport and machinery use are transitional. This business thus can re-examine its value chain activities relative to ecological sustainability and implement steps to shift its transitional activity to transformational forms. Interface, which manufactures carpeting and provides carpeting services, offers a transformational product, waste strategy and energy use; its use of transportation is transitional (www.interface.co.uk). Improved ecocentric dynamic capabilities can help leaders and managers in these and other companies achieve their transformational strategy goals.

Finally, we envision theoretical research opportunities for refining and developing transitional and transformational strategies and our ecocentric dynamic capabilities framework. Empirical research should work to observe and measure business activities to distinguish between the transitional and transformational strategies that firms adopt. Research must measure both qualitative and quantitative improvements, including ecological enhancement, societal benefits and financial uplift; qualitative research approaches may yield more informative outputs, at least in the early stages of research (Edmondson and McManus, 2007), because of the interdisciplinary, integrative, systems-based nature of sustainability research, whereas quantitative research approaches may continue down a reductionist path. Testing the ecocentric dynamic capabilities framework may be challenging, because of the need to find firms willing to adopt a transformational approach. However, as the increased costs of doing business associated with resource depletion, problematic waste disposal, environmental degradation, species extinction and devastating weather patterns become more widespread, firms willing to adopt, as well as those actively seeking, new strategic approaches likely will increase in number.

Acknowledgement

This chapter has not undergone the traditional reviewing process, as parts of the chapter (including figures and tables) have appeared in previous publications, namely Borland and Lindgreen (2013) and Borland et al. (2016).

References

Adner, R. and Helfat, C. (2003). Corporate effects and dynamic managerial capabilities. *Strategic Management Journal*, 24: 1011–1025.
Ambrosini, V. and Bowman, C. (2009). What are dynamic capabilities and are they a useful construct in strategic management? *International Journal of Management Reviews*, 11: 29–49.
Ambrosini, V., Bowman, C. and Collier, N. (2009). Dynamic capabilities: An exploration of how firms renew their resource base. *British Journal of Management*, 20: 9–24.
Aragón-Correa, J.A. and Sharma, S. (2003). A contingent resource-based view of proactive corporate environmental strategy. *Academy of Management Review*, 28: 71–88.
Barney, J.B. (1991). Firm resources and sustained competitive advantage. *Journal of Management*, 17: 99–120.
Barreto, I. (2010). Dynamic capabilities: A review of past research and an agenda for future research. *Journal of Management*, 36: 256–280
Borland, H. and Lindgreen, A. (2013). Sustainability, epistemology, ecocentric business and marketing strategy: Ideology, reality and vision. *Journal of Business Ethics*, 117(1): 173–187.
Borland, H., Ambrosini, V., Lindgreen, A. and Vanhamme, J. (2016). Building theory at the intersection of ecological sustainability and strategic management. *Journal of Business Ethics*, 135(2): 293–307.
Bruni, D.S. and Verona, G. (2009). Dynamic marketing capabilities in science-based firms: An exploratory investigation of the pharmaceutical industry. *British Journal of Management*, 20: S101–S117.
Corley, K.G. and Gioia, D.A. (2011). Building theory about theory building: What constitutes a theoretical contribution? *Academy of Management Review*, 36: 12–32.
Edmondson, A.C. and McManus, S.E. (2007). Methodological fit in management field research. *Academy of Management Review*, 32: 1155–1179.

Eisenhardt, K. and Martin, J. (2000). Dynamic capabilities: What are they? *Strategic Management Journal*, 21: 1105–1121.

Hart, S. (1995). A natural-resource-based view of the firm. *Academy of Management Review*, 20: 986–1014.

Hart, S. (1997). Beyond greening: Strategies for a sustainable world. *Harvard Business Review*, 75: 66–76.

Hart, S. and Dowell, G. (2011). A natural-resource-based view of the firm: Fifteen years after. *Journal of Management*, 37: 1464–1479.

Hart, S. and Milstein, M. (2003). Creating sustainable value. *Academy of Management Executive*, 17: 56–67.

Helfat, C.E., Finkelstein, S., Mitchell, W., Peteraf, M.A., Singh, H., Teece, D.J. and Winter, S.G. (2007). *Dynamic Capabilities: Understanding Strategic Change in Organizations*. London: Blackwell.

Klettner, A., Clarke, T. and Boersma, M. (2014). The governance of corporate sustainability: Empirical insights into the development, leadership and implementation of responsible business strategy. *Journal of Business Ethics*, 122: 145–165.

Levitas, E. and Ndofor, H.A. (2006). What to do with the resource-based view: A few suggestions for what ails the RBV that supporters and opponents might accept. *Journal of Management Inquiry*, 15: 135–144.

Lockett, A., O'Shea, R. and Wright, M. (2008). The development of the resource based view: Reflections from Birger Wernerfelt. *Organization Studies*, 29: 1125–1141.

Markóczy, L. and Deeds, D.L. (2009). Theory building at the intersection: Recipe of impact or road to nowhere? *Journal of Management Studies*, 46: 1076–1088.

Martin, R. and Kemper, A. (2012). Saving the planet: A tale of two strategies. *Harvard Business Review* (April): 48–56.

McDonough, W. and Braungart, M. (2002). *Cradle to Cradle: Remaking the Way We Make Things*. New York: North Point Press.

Mellahi, K. and Sminia, H. (2009). Guest editors' introduction: The frontiers of strategic management research, *International Journal of Management Reviews*, 11: 1–7.

Oswick, C., Fleming, O. and Hanlon, G. (2011). From borrowing to blending: Rethinking the processes of organizational theory building. *Academy of Management Review*, 36: 318–337.

Pablo, A., Reay, T., Dewald, J.R. and Casebeer, A.L. (2007). Identifying, enabling and managing dynamic capabilities in the public sector. *Journal of Management Studies*, 44: 687–708.

Porritt, J. (2007). *Capitalism as If the World Matters*. London: Earthscan.

Porter, M.E. (1980). *Competitive Strategy: Techniques for Analysing Industries and Competitors*. New York: The Free Press.

Porter, M.E. (1985). *Competitive Advantage: Creating and Sustaining Superior Performance*. New York: The Free Press.

Purser, R.E., Park, C. and Montuori, A. (1995). Limits to anthropocentrism: Toward an ecocentric organization paradigm? *Academy of Management Review*, 20: 1053–1089.

Rosenbloom, R.S. (2000). Leadership, capabilities, and technological change: The transformation of NCR in the electronic era. *Strategic Management Journal*, 21: 1083–1103.

Salvato, C. (2003). The role of micro-strategies in the engineering of firm evolution. *Journal of Management Studies*, 40: 83–108.

Stead, W.E. and Stead, J.G. (2004). *Sustainable Strategic Management*. New York: M.E. Sharpe, Inc.

Stead, J.G. and Stead, W.E. (2010). Sustainability comes to management education and research: A story of co-evolution. *Academy of Management Learning and Education*, 9: 488–498.

Teece, D. (2007). Explicating dynamic capabilities: The nature and microfoundations of sustainable enterprise performance. *Strategic Management Journal*, 28: 1319–1350.

Wang, C. and Ahmed, P. (2007). Dynamic capabilities: A review and research agenda. *International Journal of Management Reviews*, 9: 31–51.

Whiteman, G. and Cooper, W. (2000). Ecological embeddedness. *Academy of Management Journal*, 43: 1265–1282.

Wittneben, B., Okereke, C., Banerjee, S.B. and Levy, D. (2012). Climate change and the emergence of new organizational landscapes. *Organization Studies*, 33(11): 1431–1450.

Wright, C., Nyberg, D. and Grant, D. (2012). 'Hippies on the third floor': Climate change, narrative identity and the micro-politics of corporate environmentalism. *Organization Studies*, 33: 1451–1475.

Zahra, S. and Newey, L.R. (2009). Maximizing the impact of organization science: Theory building at the intersection of disciplines and/or fields. *Journal of Management Studies*, 46: 1059–1075.

Zahra, S., Sapienza, H. and Davidsson, P. (2006). Entrepreneurship and dynamic capabilities: A review, model and research agenda. *Journal of Management Studies*, 43: 917–955.

Zahra, S.A., Abdelgawad, S.G. and Tsang, E.W.K. (2011). Emerging multinationals venturing into developed economies: Implications for learning, unlearning, and entrepreneurial capability. *Journal of Management Inquiry*, 20: 323–330.

Part II

Contradiction, integration and transformation of business and sustainability logics

Part II

Contradiction, integration and transformation of business and sustainability logics

5 What we know about business strategies for sustainability

An inductive typology of the research

Elisabeth Albertini

Introduction

The recent global economic and financial crises have raised fundamental questions about the impacts of existing corporate business model on the ecological sustainability of the global economy and society. Hence, the role of business in society has been a concern for both scholars and managers for a long time. Recently business case for ecological sustainability has increasingly been used by consulting firms and non-governmental organizations to enhance the integration of a sustainability perspective in the companies' strategies (Stubbs and Cocklin, 2008; Whetten, Rands and Godfrey, 2002).

Since the publication of the Brundtland report (WCED, 1987), the concept of sustainable development has become a leading goal of policy makers and scientific researchers. Indeed, sustainable business models seek to preserve the environment, while continuing to improve the quality of human life (Garetti and Taisch, 2012). These models are seen to create competitive advantage through superior customer value and contribute to a sustainable development of the company and society (Lüdeke-Freund, 2010).

Even if the scope of issues and methods in this field is expanding continuously, an unequivocally supported definition for sustainability is still missing (Schaltegger, Hansen and Lüdeke-Freund, 2015). Furthermore, the literature on sustainability and corporate responsibility remains vague when it comes to what constitute a 'sustainable business model' (Boons and Lüdeke-Freund, 2013). The lack of common definition on sustainable business models makes it difficult for researchers and practitioners to gain an overview of the scope of business model innovation for sustainability (Bocken, Short, Rana and Evans, 2014). Furthermore, different indicators have been used to measure the financial consequences of the business models for sustainability leading to an unclear vision of business model for sustainability.

How far has academic research covered the full complexity of the business case for sustainability in its multiple dimensions? Since academic research has linked 'sustainability' closely to 'business models', we question the extent to these two notions have been considered jointly. To answer this research question, I propose an inductive typology of the academic work on this topic through a content analysis of the abstracts of 58 articles that contain the key words 'business case' or 'business model' or 'business strategy' **and** 'sustainability' in either the titles or the abstracts. Indeed, content analysis is a systematic, objective, quantitative analysis of message characteristics (Berelson, 1952; Neuendorf, 2002) that allows us to identify authors' points of view and describes the research trends in this field (Weber, 1990).

The aim of this literature review is to draw up an exhaustive and objective classification of the academic work on the multiple dimensions of business case for sustainability. The remainder of the chapter is organized as follows. In the next section, the main academic frameworks of the business case for sustainability are presented, and follow this with a description of the research method used (section 3). The findings are presented in section 4 followed by the typology of the research on business model for sustainability in section 5.

Review of present research

Since the Brundtland report has been published (WCED, 1987), the concept of sustainable development, defined as 'development that meets the needs of the present without compromising the ability of future generations to meet their own needs' (WCED, 1987, p. 41), has become a leading goal of policy makers and academic researchers. On the organizational level, the vision of sustainable development has led to concepts such as sustainability management, corporate sustainability (Dyllick and Hockerts, 2002; Schaltegger and Burrit, 2005), sustainable innovation and sustainable entrepreneurship (Halme and Korpela, 2014) or social business (Yunus, Moingeon and Lehmann-Ortega, 2010).

Many definitions of sustainability are based upon the 'triple bottom line' concept, covering the three aspects, which are environmental performance, societal responsibility and economic contribution. Nowadays, many companies recognize and monitor these three parallel aspects using sustainability indicators, which provide information on how the company contributes to sustainable development (Milne and Gray, 2013). Sustainability reports are emerging as a new trend in corporate reporting, integrating financial, environmental and social performance of the company in one report. Moreover, several institutional frameworks such as the Global Reporting Initiative (GRI), the 'triple bottom line' (TBL) or more recently the integrated reporting (IR) have deeply enhanced the sustainable reporting of the companies while the ecological systems is still deeply threaten by the companies' activity. Hence, sustainability management refers to approaches dealing with social, environmental and economic issues in an integrated manner to transform organizations in a way that they contribute to the sustainable development of the economy and society within the limits of the ecosystem (Schaltegger and Burrit, 2005; Whiteman, Walker and Perego, 2013).

Dozens of frameworks of sustainability assessment that focus on the performance of companies have been suggested by now. Important development for the issue of sustainability reporting were the foundations of the World Business Council for Sustainable Development (WBCSD, 1997), the Global Reporting Initiative (GRI, 2002a, 2002b), and the development of standards for environmental management systems, such as ISO and EMAS standards (OECD, 2002). In that context, academic research has used numerous and diverse sustainability performance indicators focusing either on the results of corporate responsible management (objective measures) or on the sustainability practices themselves (non-objective measures) (Krajnc and Glavic, 2005).

Objective measures of sustainability performance

Academic research presents sustainability indicators as observable and quantifiable variables, reflecting the different ways in which environmental and social impacts can be caused by a given activity (Dixon-Fowler, Slater, Johnson, Ellstrand and Romi, 2013; Ilinitch, Soderstrom and Thomas, 1998; Xie and Hayase, 2007). These variables are given in physical, chemical and biological units and expressed as either absolute or relative values. These data can measure resources consumed during the manufacturing process or the pollution generated by company's activity (Molina-Azorin, Claver-Cortés, Lopez-Gamero and Tari, 2009). These indicators also reveal a company's past behaviour, thus making it easier to compare companies and/or activities. However, they do not allow forecasting, which would enable polluting behaviour to be monitored (Tyteca, 1996; Xie and Hayase, 2007). Furthermore, the results of these empirical studies are ambiguous and contingent upon different factors such as the time period, the size of the companies, industries studied. All in all, results are largely inconclusive since they are subject to research bias and ambiguous regarding the causal relationship between the 'sustainability' and financial performance (Cochran and Wood, 1984; Griffin and Mahon, 1997).

Non-objective measures of sustainable performance

Academic research has shown that 'sustainability' performance is related to the business models implemented by the firm (Salzmann, Ionescu-Somers and Steger, 2005). In this context, academic research uses non-objective indicators to measure environmental and social performance, revealing the efforts companies make to reduce the impact of their activities on the environment (Molina-Azorin et al., 2009; Schultze and Trommer, 2012). Case studies have been extensively used as a research method to describe stories about successful pollution prevention projects and cost savings. They also refer to other issues, such as risk avoidance and corporate sustainability as part of business excellence (Banerjee and Bonnefous, 2011; Benijts, 2014). The implementation of business models for sustainability, the integration of sustainability objectives in the firm's planning, eco-design, the product life-cycle analysis, the development of 'green' products, and the company's voluntary participation in responsible programmes, are all measures of companies' sustainability performance (Johnson and Suskewicz, 2009; Roome and Louche, 2015). Yet, case studies have two main withdraw-backs. First, the evidence presented is often not hard enough, since it is based on non-objective indicators; and, second, they are only valid for a specific sector or company, hence their applicability is limited. Nevertheless, these non-objective measures highlight the practices implemented by firms, their goals with regard to their sustainable responsibilities (Wagner and Schaltegger, 2003). It is less a question of measuring or reducing pollution, and more about giving an account of the organizational changes these sustainability strategies require.

Hence, business models for sustainability is a very complex research field since it is contingent on a number of parameters that vary between industries, plants, countries and different point in time. Moreover, the business case for sustainability exists to a certain extent but may be often marginal in practice and/or difficult to detect. The economic value of more sustainable business strategies is a lot more elusive, since it only materializes in the long term. Although the scope of issues and methods in this field is expanding continuously (Bocken et al., 2014), an unequivocally supported definition of business models for sustainability is still missing (Roome and Louche, 2015; Schaltegger et al., 2015).

Research methodology

The aim of this study is to survey the research related to business cases for sustainability, which results from the intelligent design of voluntary or mainly voluntary social and environmental management that creates a positive business effect (Bocken et al., 2014; Salzmann et al., 2005; Schaltegger et al., 2015).

A search in academic reference databases (EBSCO, EconLit, JSTOR, Academic Search Premier) of the keywords 'business case' or 'business model' **and** 'sustainability' in titles and/or abstracts generated a sample of 58 articles published in peer-reviewed journals in the management field. For each of these references, the following characteristics were noted: publication date, journal title, track of the journal review, geographical zone of the university of the author(s), type of sustainability indicator and type of research method. Each paper was read carefully in order to collect other useful information, such as theoretical background, research question, research design, types of indicators used in the study and the main contributions of the paper.

The scope of the study is based on the content analysis of the abstracts of these 58 articles. The choice of abstracts as an analysis sample is justified by the fact that they were written by the authors themselves in order to interest readers by presenting the main points of their work. Their compactness requires authors to select their words carefully. Thus, it is reasonable to presume that the analysis of words used in titles and abstracts will give a representative image of the whole article (Lesage and Wechtler, 2012).

As the aim of this study is to provide an inductive typology of the academic research relating to the business case for sustainability, a computer-based content analysis of these abstracts was carried out. This research method uses a set of statistical procedures to make valid inferences from the text itself (in our case the abstracts of the articles), the author or its audience. Content analysis can be used to identify the intentions and other characteristics of the communicator, reveal the focus of individuals, groups, institutional or societal attention, and describe trends in communication content (Weber, 1990). This method uses the verbal unit, as the database is particularly well suited to the case of longitudinal studies (Kabanoff, Waldersee, and Cohen, 1995).

Given the large number of texts and the aim of meeting the requirements of replicability, we selected the computer-aided approach (Kabanoff et al., 1995) as it reinforces face validity. We used the SPAD-T-V8 software, which provides useful frequency distributions of words, or analysis of words in context, and performs statistical analyses of textual data. This software suits quantitative narrative analysis, as it provides useful analytical tools for mapping clusters of words graphically (Franzosi, 2010). This methodology relies on textual statistics and allows the analysis of important texts on the basis of particular lexical contingencies, where the individual statistic is made up from the occurrence of a textual unit (word, lemma, segment, repeated segment) (Lebart and Salem, 1994).

The computer-based content analysis comprises several steps. First, the software generates a dictionary of all the words present in the database as well as their frequency (the 58 abstracts contain 1,373 different words with 9,275 occurrences). Then filters are applied to eliminate tool-words and articles in order to confine the dictionary to main words. In the case of homonyms, the software allows the user to consider the context of the word in order to decide whether or not to keep it. The lemmatization process that follows allows the user to bring together complex words related to the same semantic group. In this way, groups of words with the same roots can be formed around a significant keyword (Bolden and Moscarola, 2000).

Indeed, lemmatization depends on correctly identifying the intended part of speech and meaning of a word in a sentence, as well as within the larger context surrounding that sentence, such as neighbouring sentences. Finally, a second elimination phase allows the removal of words that appear infrequently. In this case the final dictionary is made up of 49 keywords representing 32.49 per cent of occurrences.

Moving on from studying the words alone, the contingencies table (item*words) was used to run a factorial correspondence analysis (FCA) with 'business model' as an active variable and the other variables as illustrative variables. This factorial correspondence analysis is completed by a classification of the keywords using a hierarchical cluster analysis. This last phase reveals a typology of four classes of significant keywords. The study of these classes reveals the characteristics of the academic research. The use of these statistical methods makes it possible to carry out an exploratory study of the content of the texts (Guerin-Pace, 1998) and present a typology of the significant keywords (Franzosi, 2010).

Findings

One major theme stands out in this typology (Table 5.1). 'The relationship between sustainability performance and financial performance' represents almost 35 per cent of the academic literature. Initially academic research tried to reassure shareholders, the principal providers of resources for the firm, through empirical studies of the relationship between sustainable business model and financial performance. Objective indicators have been widely used to test Porter's win–win hypothesis (1995) and verify how far 'sustainability' performance improves financial performance and creates shared value (Porter and Kramer, 2011). In the light of these studies it seems that the relationship between 'sustainability' performance and financial performance is positive (Campbell, 2006; Davis, 2009; Freeman, 1984; Useem, 1996; Waddock and Graves, 1997) even if some studies tend to prove the opposite (Aupperle, Caroll and Hatfield, 1985; Friedman, 1970) while others maintain it is impossible to prove (Barnett and Salomon, 2006; McWilliams and Siegel, 2001). Despite a number of limitations, such as the diversity of sustainability indicators or the variety of research methods, these works show that environmental and social performance improves financial performance to a certain degree (Margolis, Elfenbein and Walsh, 2007; Orlitzky, Schmidt and Rynes, 2003). In the environmental field of the sustainability business case, researchers have shown that environmental practices or strategies implemented by companies can lead to improve the financial performance of the companies. Indeed, pollution prevention activities that are carried out within the framework of an environmental strategy imply that production processes should be modified in order to reduce energy consumption; production costs would be reduced, too, leading to competitive advantages (Al-Najjar and Anfimiadou, 2012; Lopez-Gamero, Molina-Azorin and Claver-Cortés, 2009; M. Wagner, 2005). Moreover, the sale of environmentally friendly products allows companies to obtain a leading position in emerging markets for 'green' products (Hart, 1995). Nevertheless, this relation has to be placed in a long-term context since it relies on very heavy investments, which tend initially to penalize profitability before eventually serving companies' purposes. Yet, some authors have pointed out that the lack of a theoretical background does not allow for efficient testing of the link between environmental and social performance and financial performance (McWilliams and Siegel, 2000; Roome and Louche, 2015; Salzmann et al., 2005).

Two further themes emerge from this typology, each representing almost 24 per cent of the vocabulary.

The first is 'Sustainability management and institutional pressures', highlighting the two main kinds of pressure from civil society and government. The academic research on institutional pressures shows how much the firm is at the heart of a set of relationships with partners that include shareholders as well as actors interested in its activities and decisions (Bocken et al., 2014; Hall and Wagner, 2012; Romero, Lin and Jeffers, 2014). The research highlights the determining roles of government, civil society, certification organizations, media and other companies in the same sector in the disclosure of sustainability practices and in the introduction of sustainability activities in the corporate strategies (Escobar and Vredenburg, 2011; Pedersen and Gowozdz, 2014; Sharma and Henriques, 2005). Among these pressures, environmental regulations require companies regularly to communicate information on their ecological footprint and greenhouse gas monitoring in order to satisfy environmental standards (Delmas and Toffel, 2004; Sharma, 2000). A significant increase in sustainability reporting leads academic research to study its possible exploitation by companies as a way of managing public impressions or of increasing legitimacy (R. Hahn and Lülfs, 2014). The need to reassure worried stakeholders motivates companies to disclose very detailed reports that encourage stakeholders to give more rapid approval to a polluting industrial activity (C. Cho, Laine, Roberts, and Rodrigue, 2015). The optimistic tone adopted by companies in their annual reports or on their websites may mask poor ecological performance and does not allow the classification of firms according to their 'sustainability' performance (Azlan, Keat, Riduan Toani and Susela, 2015).

The other theme that represents almost 24 per cent of the vocabulary is 'Increasing awareness of the sustainability business case issue'. The research focuses on very concrete topics such as sustainability and ecological issues through objective indicators used in empirical studies. In the context of 'process' issues, researchers refer to the need for a more sustainable way of manufacturing that seeks to reduce the carbon footprint. These studies mention regulatory or voluntary approaches to pollution control implemented by companies in order to reduce pollution levels. The keyword 'sustainability' refers to the preference for a sustainable development approach rather than a financial approach. These studies insist that corporate sustainable performance should meet economic performance goals.

The final theme emerging from this typology is 'Strategic sustainability management and reporting' and represents a little less than 18 per cent of the vocabulary. These articles, within the resource-based-view theory, try to identify the dynamic and inimitable organizational capacities that enable a company to gain a strong competitive advantage through a proactive sustainability business case (Chakrabarty and Wang, 2012; Hart and Dowell, 2011; Hofmann, Theyel and Wood, 2012). This competitive advantage relies on the company's capacity to bring together all its resources (human, financial, material) by applying knowledge and know-how within the framework of a sustainability strategy (van Kleef and Room, 2007). It allows firms to invest in new and unexplored markets for 'green' products in advance of their competitors and sometimes even influences future regulations by presenting their expertise to the government (Amini and Bienstock, 2014; Lockrey and Bisset Johnson, 2013). This research theme is based on non–objective indicators that highlight innovations, staff training, setting up a dedicated department and planning the roll out of responsible practices (Taneja, Sewell and Odom, 2015; van Bommel, 2011). The research underlines the association of the reporting of sustainability performance and the management of this performance for companies that interact with external actors, such as their supply chain strategies (Darnall, Jolley and Handfield, 2008; Handfield, Sroufe and Walton, 2005). Sustainability indicators may have an external value for sustainability reporting purposes or an internal value for managing the sustainable business strategy. This corresponds to two logics of the representation of environmental and social performance (Gond, Grubnic, Herzig and Moon, 2012).

Table 5.1 Typology of the research relative to the sustainable business case

Theme	No. of words	Theme characteristics	Theme keywords (in bold: most characteristic and maximum contribution)
The relationship between sustainability performance and financial performance	17	Empirical studies, objective indicator, organization and production reviews	**Company, financial,** implementation, **implications,** improvement, **indicators,** innovation, integration, **leadership,** manufacturing, **measurement, performance,** proactive, relation, **shareholder,** reduction **proactive**
Sustainability management and institutional pressures	12	Non-objective indicator, case study, normative study, agriculture and environment reviews	**Certification,** framework, **green,** legitimacy, **management,** market, practices, production, **quality, regulation, stakeholder, disclosure**
Increasing awareness of the sustainable issues	12	Objective indicators, empirical studies, Asian and US study area, management reviews	**Sustainability, benefit,** capability, **control,** cost, decision, **effective,** increase, information, investment, **process, value,** achievement,
Strategic sustainability management and reporting	8	Objective and non-objective indicators, strategy management reviews	**Board,** commitment, **competitive, goal,** business case, **policy, resource-based, strategy**

Discussion and conclusions

To sum up, research on the business case for sustainability centres around four major themes: (1) the relationship between sustainability performance and financial performance; (2) sustainability management and institutional pressures; (3) toward an increasing awareness of the sustainable issue and (4) strategic sustainability management and reporting. This typology illustrates the varied contexts in which business cases for sustainability have been studied by the academic research, and the efforts made by researchers to cover the full complexity of the sustainability business model issue. Academic research shows that an increasing number of companies use objective and non-objective indicators to measure their sustainability performance with the aim of managing this performance internally and reporting the information to institutional stakeholders in conformity with increasing regulations. In addition, the joint use of objective and non-objective indicators by academic research underlines the interdependence of these indicators to measure environmental and social performance.

From this typology, we can draw some conclusions about what we know about the business case for sustainability literature.

First, the research questions as well as the context of the studies have determined the different uses of sustainability performance indicators. Numerous empirical studies of the relationship between business models for sustainability and corporate financial performance have caused the academic research to digress from a crucial question, which is how to measure the impact of corporate activities on the natural environment. The same goes for academic research that studies sustainability disclosure as a way for companies to gain or maintain their legitimacy. These studies use sustainability indicators not to measure the negative externalities caused by companies but rather to determine the financial consequences of environmental and social practices or the extent to which companies are practising 'greenwashing' (C.H. Cho, 2009). Furthermore, studies about the relationship between sustainability performance and the financial performance have not reached a consensus about the strength of the relationship. Even if the overall relationship is positive, the kind of indicators chosen to measure either sustainability performance or financial performance deeply influences the strength of the relationship (Margolis et al., 2007; Orlitzky et al., 2003) This lack of consensus on how to measure sustainability performance and its consequences on financial performance contributes to the lack of theoretical foundation, calling into question the knowledge convergence (Boons and Lüdeke-Freund, 2013; Salzmann et al., 2005; Schaltegger et al., 2015).

Second, the different theoretical backgrounds chosen by researchers clearly influence the way the business model for sustainability issue is studied. The stakeholder perspective highlights conflicting pressures from internal (customers, employees, stockholders) and external (regulators, environmental activists, non-governmental organizations) stakeholder groups (Amit and Zott, 2012; Johnson and Suskewicz, 2009). Institutional theory suggests that rules, customs or beliefs guide and constrain the behaviour of organizations (Caprar and Neville, 2012). Hence, studies in these academic streams have often posited the sustainability commitment of companies as an answer to stakeholders' demands or institutional constraints in a reactive rather than a proactive way.

Third, the definition of business model for sustainability is still missing since its nature is extremely complex and contingent to the technology that varies between industries, plants and countries. Furthermore, in the academic field, the business models for sustainability refers to the management of the environmental and social performance as well as the results of its management. Yet, these two notions are independent of one another (Dobers and Wolff, 2000). The business models for sustainability do not lead systematically to a reduction in pollution caused by a company's activities. Indeed, some environmental practices stimulate financial incomes, allowing companies to increase their profitability without reducing the impact of their activities on the natural environment (Bansal and Knox-Hayes, 2013). Furthermore, companies take advantage of this multiple definition of business models for sustainability. They can disclose significant information about their sustainable practices through their annual reports, even if these practices are inadequate when it comes to reducing the pollution caused by their activities. The lack of audit of their environmental and social results allows companies to disclose their sustainability management practices with the aim of maintaining or increasing their legitimacy (Banerjee and Bonnefous, 2011). Thus, the ambiguous definition of business model for sustainability prevents not only a clear understanding of this issue but also the development of a theoretical foundation (Bocken et al., 2014; Boons and Lüdeke-Freund, 2013).

Fourth, this study underlines the different contexts in which the indicators have been used in academic research to measure sustainability performance. There is no doubt that this performance is quantified with the aim of measuring the relationship between sustainability performance and the financial one and determining its significance.

Nevertheless, the research has evolved little by little towards a more managerial dimension of sustainability business model, as shown by the increasing use of non-objective as well as objective indicators. This may highlight a significant change in research question. Indeed, after studying why companies implement sustainability business strategy and how far this impacts financial performance, it seems that research is more about how companies address the consequences of climate change or north–south inequalities that impact their corporate business strategy. Even in developed countries, the increasing scarcity of certain resources obliges companies to modify their manufacturing process in order to make them more energy efficient. Indeed, physical impacts from climate change pose major challenges for organizations (Winn, Kirchgeorg, Griffiths, Linnenluecke and Günther, 2011) and determine the business strategies for sustainability (Hahn, Pinkse, Preuss and Figge, 2015).

Fifth, limits to the indicators themselves can be highlighted. This typology demonstrates that some research features indicators of questionable accessibility and reliability. Moreover, these objective indicators do not allow us to attribute improvement in business models for sustainability performance to any one specific responsible practice because the connections between a company's activities and the natural environment are complex. As for the non-objective indicators mobilized during the research, they are directly linked to the company and its activity, making generalization and repeat studies very difficult. Moreover, the validity of the use of non-objective indicators to measure the sustainability performance of companies has still not been established empirically (Whiteman et al., 2013).

From this typology based on the business models for sustainability literature, we can know suggest an agenda for future research.

First, as this typology has highlighted, sustainability performance indicators seem to be a significant communication tool in the relationship between a company and its external stakeholders. Indeed, firm's corporate sustainability reporting enhances the quality of the analysts' information context, which ultimately allows them to make better forecasts (Renzo, Best and Cotter, 2014). It would be interesting to study the extent to which corporate sustainability reporting is a part of integrated reporting for companies and what types of indicator are used in this specific reporting (Jensen and Berg, 2012). Furthermore, it may be interesting to determine the extent to which a company can comply with mandatory external reporting and manage sustainability performance internally using the same indicators. In other words, can environmental and social performance indicators be used to report sustainability performance to external stakeholders and at the same time be used to manage that performance internally to satisfy shareholders?

Second, sustainability performance is measured through objective indicators that highlight the consequences of corporate activities on the natural environment and non-objective indicators that enhance knowledge about the business practices for sustainability implemented by companies. It might be interesting to study the extent to which the joint use of these indicators through a management control system could help companies to obtain a permanent competitive advantage from their business models for sustainability.

Third, the lack of consensus about the relationship between sustainability performance and financial performance seems to show that this relationship may be indirect rather than direct (McWilliams and Siegel, 2001). Thus, there is a need to study the potential moderator or mediator of this relationship, such as corporate strategies (Stubbs and Cocklin, 2008), environmental innovation (Forsman, 2013) or organizational capabilities and resources (Aragon-Correa and Sharma, 2003; Dangelico and Pontrandolfo, 2015). Indeed, technological capital such as innovative capacity, relational capital such as relationships with customers and business partners, or human capital such as training could be significant mediators in the relationship between business practices for sustainability and financial performance. Furthermore, as the strength of this relationship differs according to the type of financial performance indicators used in empirical studies, further research might question a financial indicator that could reflect the long-term return on investment of these business practices for sustainability and the competitive advantage they provide to the company as well.

Fourth, as these capabilities provide a sustainable competitive advantage, further research might seek to enhance knowledge about the kind of capabilities and resources that need to be developed from a contingent resource-based perspective (Aragon-Correa, Hurtado-torres, Sharma and Garcia-Morales, 2008). Since the success of business models for sustainability rely on organizational capabilities such as a shared vision of the ecological issues within the company, stakeholder pressure management, business redefinition, environmental product innovations and new processes (Aragon-Correa et al., 2008), further research could study how companies enhance the development and the implementation of these capabilities. Indeed, qualitative studies, such as case studies, might enhance significantly our knowledge of these deeply embedded organizational capabilities (Salzmann et al., 2005; Schaltegger et al., 2015).

Fifth, since academic research has mainly focused on the top managers' role in the commitment of the firm to a business case for sustainability, research on the specific role of the employees in the ecological and responsible decision-making process could enhance the knowledge of the microfoundations of the sustainability policy success (Morrow and Mowatt, 2015). Indeed, organizational citizenship behaviours for a sustainable future, based on individual and voluntary initiatives, are increasingly considered as an essential ingredient of a corporate strategy for sustainability (Dyllick and Hockerts, 2002; Temminck, Mearns and Fruhen, 2015). In that context, research can study to what extent employees of a proactive responsible company generate a positive 'word of mouth' influencing consumers' way of purchase.

To conclude, this typology highlights four major themes around which the academic research is organized: the relationship between sustainability business model and financial performance; sustainability management and institutional pressures; toward an increasing awareness of the sustainability issues and strategic sustainability management and reporting. From this typology, several future research questions could be addressed such as the possible connection between the sustainability disclosure made by companies and the integrated reporting, the influence of mediators or moderators on the relationship between business models for sustainability and financial performance, the extent to which a management control systems can enhance the efficiency of the sustainable corporate strategy and the resources and the capabilities that need to be developed to improve the competitive advantage generated by an business model for sustainability. Yet, it worth highlighting that the demands of growing the business, making increased profits, and securing the financial viability of the business lead to increasingly damage the environment moving us toward greater levels of unsustainability.

References

Al-Najjar, B. and Anfimiadou, A. (2012). Environmental policies and firm value. *Business Strategy and the Environment*, 21(1): 49–59.

Amini, M. and Bienstock, C.C. (2014). Corporate sustainability: An integrative definition and framework to evaluate corporate practice and guide academic research. *Journal of Cleaner Production*, 76, 12–19.

Amit, R. and Zott, C. (2012). Creating value through business model innovation. *MIT Sloan Management*, 53(3): 41–49.

Aragon-Correa, J.A., Hurtado-torres, N., Sharma, S. and Garcia-Morales, V.J. (2008). Environmental strategy and performance in small firms: A resource-based perspective. *Journal of Environmental Management*, 86(1): 88–103.

Aragon-Correa, J.A. and Sharma, S. (2003). A contingent resource-based view of proactive corporate environmental strategy. *Academy of Management Review*, 28(1): 71–88.

Aupperle, K.E., Caroll, A.B. and Hatfield, J.D. (1985). An empirical examination of the relationship between corporate social responsibility and profitability. *Academy of Management Journal*, 28(2): 446–463.

Azlan, A., Keat, O.S., Riduan Toani, M. and Susela, D.S. (2015). The impact of business strategies on online sustainability disclosure. *Business Strategy and the Environment*, 24(6): 551–564.

Banerjee, S.B. and Bonnefous, A.-M. (2011). Stakeholder management and sustainability strategies in the French nuclear industry. *Business Strategy and the Environment*, 20(2): 124–170.

Bansal, P. and Knox-Hayes, J. (2013). The time and space of materiality in organizations and the natural environment. *Organization and Environment*, 26(1): 61–82.

Barnett, M.L. and Salomon, R.M. (2006). Beyond dichotomy: The curvilinear relationship between social responsibility and financial performance. *Strategic Management Journal*, 27(11): 1101–1122.

Benijts, T. (2014). A business sustainability model for government corporations: A Belgian case study. *Business Strategy and the Environment*, 23(3): 204–216.

Berelson, B. (1952). Content Analysis in Communication Research. New York: Hafner.

Bocken, N.M. P., Short, S.W., Rana, P. and Evans, S. (2014). A literature and practice review to develop sustainable model archetypes. *Journal of Cleaner Production*, 65, 42–56.

Bolden, R. and Moscarola, J. (2000). Bridging the quantitative-qualitative divide: The lexical approach to textual data analysis. *Social Science Computer Review*, 18(4): 450–460.

Boons, F.A. A. and Lüdeke-Freund, F. (2013). Business models for sustainable innovation: State-of-the-art and steps towards a research agenda. *Journal of Cleaner Production*, 45, 9–19.

Campbell, J.L. (2006). Institutional analysis and the paradox of corporate social responsibility. *American Behavioral Scientist*, 49(7): 925–938.

Caprar, D.V. and Neville, B.A. (2012). 'Norming' and 'conforming': Integrating cultural and institutional explanations for sustainability adoption in business. *Journal of Business Ethics*, 110(2): 231–245.

Chakrabarty, S. and Wang, L. (2012). The long-term sustenance of sustainability practices in MNCs: A dynamic capabilities perspective of the role of RandD and internalization. *Journal of Business Ethics*, 11(2): 205–217.

Cho, C., Laine, M., Roberts, R.W. and Rodrigue, M. (2015). Organized hypocrisy, organizational façades and sustainability reporting. *Accounting, Organizations and Society*, 40, 78–94.

Cho, C.H. (2009). Legitimation strategies used in response to environmental disaster: A French case study of total SA's erika and AZF incidents. *European Accounting Review*, 18(1): 33–62.

Cochran, P.L. and Wood, R.A. (1984). Corporate social responsability and financial performance. *Academy of Management Journal*, 27, 42–56.

Dangelico, R.M. and Pontrandolfo, P. (2015). Being 'green and competitive': The impact of environmental actions and collaborations on firm performance. *Business Strategy and the Environment*, 24(6): 413–430.

Darnall, N., Jolley, G.J. and Handfield, R. (2008). Environmental management systems and green supply chain management: Complements for sustainability. *Business Strategy and the Environment*, 17(1): 30–45.

Davis, G.F. (2009). *Managed by the Markets: How Finance Reshaped America*. New York: Oxford University Press.

Delmas, M. and Toffel, M.W. (2004). Stakeholders and environmental management practices: An institutional framework. *Business Strategy and the Environment*, 13(4): 209–222.

Dixon-Fowler, H.R., Slater, D.J., Johnson, J.L., Ellstrand, A.E. and Romi, A.M. (2013). Beyond 'Does it pay to be green?' A meta-analysis of moderators of the CEP-CFP relationship. *Journal of Business Ethics*, 112(2): 353–366.

Dobers, P. and Wolff, R. (2000). Competing with 'soft' issues: From managing the environment to sustainable business strategies. *Business Strategy and the Environment*, 9(3): 143–150.

Dyllick, T. and Hockerts, K. (2002). Beyond the business case for corporate sustainability. *Business Strategy and the Environment*, 11(2): 130–141.

Escobar, L. and Vredenburg, H. (2011). Multinational oil companies and the adoption of sustainable development: A resource-based and institutional theory interpretation of adoption heterogeneity. *Journal of Business Ethics*, 98(1): 39–65.

Forsman, H. (2013). Environmental innovations as a source of competitive advantage or vice versa? *Business Strategy and the Environment*, 22(5): 306–320.

Franzosi, R. (2010). Quantitative Narrative Analysis: Quantitative Applications in the Social Sciences. Thousand Oaks, CA: SAGE.

Freeman, R.E. (1984). Strategic Management: A Stakeholder Approach. Boston, MA: Pitman.

Friedman, M. (1970). The social responsability of business is to increase its profits. *The New York Times Magazine*, 33, 123–126.

Garetti, M. and Taisch, M. (2012). Sustainable manufacturing trends and research challenges. *Prod. Plann. Control*, 23(2–3): 83–104.

Gond, J., Grubnic, S., Herzig, C. and Moon, J. (2012). Configuring management control systems: Theorizing the integration of strategy and sustainability. *Management Accounting Research*, 23(3): 205–223.

GRI. (2002a). The Global Reporting Initiative: An Overview. Boston, MA: GRI.

GRI. (2002b). Sustainability reporting guidelines 2002 on economic, environmental and social performance. *The Global Reporting Initiative: An Overview*. Boston, MA: GRI.

Griffin, J.J. and Mahon, J.F. (1997). The corporate social performance and corporate financial performance debate. *Business and Society*, 36(1): 5–30.

Guerin-Pace, F. (1998). Textual statistics: An exploratory tool for the social sciences. *Population*, 10(1): 73–95.

Hahn, R. and Lülfs, R. (2014). Legitimizing negative aspects in gri-oriented sustainability reporting: A qualitative analysis of corporate disclosure strategies. *Journal of Business Ethics*, 123(3): 401–420.

Hahn, T., Pinkse, J., Preuss, L. and Figge, F. (2015). Tension in corporate sustainability: Towards an integrative framework. *Journal of Business Ethics*, 127(2): 297–316.

Hall, J. and Wagner, M. (2012). Integrating sustainability into firms' processes: Performance effects and the moderating role of business models and innovation. *Business Strategy and the Environment*, 21(3): 183–196.

Halme, M. and Korpela, M. (2014). Responsible innovation toward sustainable development in small and medium-sized enterprises: A resource perspective. *Business Strategy and the Environment*, 23(8): 547–566.

Handfield, R., Sroufe, R. and Walton, S. (2005). Integrating environmental management and supply chain strategy. *Business Strategy and the Environment*, 14(1): 1–19.

Hart, S.L. (1995). A Natural-resource-based view of the firm. *Academy of Management Review*, 20(4): 996–1014.

Hart, S.L. and Dowell, G. (2011). A natural-resource-based view of the firm: 15 Years after. *Journal of Management (Invited Editorial)*, 37(5). 1464–1479.

Hofmann, K.H., Theyel, G. and Wood, C. (2012). Identifying firm capabilities as drivers of environmental management and sustainability practices: Evidences from small and medium-sized manufacturers. *Business Strategy and the Environment*, 218(530–545).

Ilinitch, A.Y., Soderstrom, N.S. and Thomas, T.E. (1998). Measuring corporate environmental performance. *Journal of Accounting and Economics*, 17(4–5): 383–408.

Jensen, J.C. and Berg, N. (2012). Determinants of traditional sustainability reporting versus Integrated reporting: An institutionalist approach. *Business Strategy and the Environment*, 21(5): 299–316.

Johnson, M.W. and Suskewicz, J. (2009). How to jump-start the clean tech economy. *Harvard Business Review*, 87(11): 52–60.

Kabanoff, B., Waldersee, R. and Cohen, M. (1995). Espoused values and organizational change themes. *Academy of Management Journal*, 38(4): 1075–1104.

Krajnc, D. and Glavic, P. (2005). How to compare companies on relevant dimensions of sustainability. *Ecological Economics*, 55(4): 551–563.

Lebart, L. and Salem, A. (1994). *Statistiques textuelles*. Paris: Dunod.

Lesage, C. and Wechtler, H. (2012). An inductive typology of auditing research. *Contemporary Accounting Research*, 23(2): 487–504.

Lockrey, S. and Bisset Johnson, K. (2013). Designing pedagogy with emerging sustainable technologies. *Journal of Cleaner Production*, 61, 70–79.

Lopez-Gamero, M.D., Molina-Azorin, J.F. and Claver-Cortés, E. (2009). The whole relationships between environmental variables and firm performance: Competitive advantage and firm resources as mediator variables. *Journal of Environmental Management*, 90(10): 3110–3121.

Lüdeke-Freund, F. (2010). Towards a conceptual framework of business models for sustainability. Paper presented at the ERSCP-EMU Conference, Delft, the Netherlands.

Margolis, J.D., Elfenbein, H.A. and Walsh, J.P. (2007). Does it pay to be good? A meta-analysis and redirection of research on the relationship between corporate social and financial performance. *Ann Arbor 1001*, 48109–41234.

McWilliams, A. and Siegel, D. (2000). Corporate social responsibility and financial performance: Correlation or misspecification? *Strategic Management Journal*, 21(5): 603–609.

McWilliams, A. and Siegel, D. (2001). Corporate social responsibility: A theory of the firm perspective. *Academy of Management Review*, 26(1): 117–127.

Milne, M. and Gray, R. (2013). W(h)ither ecology? The triple bottom line, the global reporting initiative and corporate sustainability reporting. *Journal of Business Ethics*, 118(1): 13–29.

Molina-Azorin, J.F., Claver-Cortés, E., Lopez-Gamero, M.D. and Tari, J.J. (2009). Green management and financial performance: A literature review. *Management Decision*, 47(7): 1080–1100.

Morrow, J. and Mowatt, S. (2015). The implementation of authentic sustainable strategies: i-SITE middle managers, employees and the delivery of 100 per cent pure New Zealand. *Business Strategy and the Environment*, 24(7): 656–666.

Neuendorf, K.A. (2002). *The Content Analysis Guidebook*. Thousand Oaks, CA: SAGE.

OECD, O. f. E.C.-o. a. D.-. (2002). *An Update of the OECD Composite Leading Indicators*. Available at www.oecd.org.

Orlitzky, M., Schmidt, F.L. and Rynes, S.L. (2003). Corporate social and financial performance: A meta-analysis. *Organization Studies*, 24(3): 403–441.

Pedersen, E. and Gowozdz, W. (2014). From resistance to opportunity-seeking: Strategic responses to institutional pressures for corporate social responsibility in the Nordic fashion industry. *Journal of Business Ethics*, 119(2): 245–264.

Porter, M.E. and Kramer, M.R. (2011). Creating shared value: Redefining capitalism and the role of the corporation in society. *Harvard Business Review*, 89(1–2): 62–77.

Porter, M.E. and van der Linde, C. (1995). Toward a new conception of the environment-competitiveness relationship. *Journal of Economic Perspectives*, 9(4): 97–118.

Renzo, J., Best, P. and Cotter, J. (2014). Sustainability reporting and assurance: A historical analysis on a world-wide phenomenon. *Journal of Business Ethics*, 120(1): 1–11.

Romero, S., Lin, B. and Jeffers, A. (2014). An overview of sustainability reporting practices. *CPA Journal*, 84(3): 68–71.

Roome, N. and Louche, C. (2015). Journeying toward business models for sustainability: A conceptual model found inside the black box of organisational transformation. *Organization and Environment*. doi:10.1177/1086026615595084.

Salzmann, O., Ionescu-Somers, A. and Steger, U. (2005). The business case for corporate sustainability: Literature review and research options. *European Management Journal*, 23(1): 27–36.

Schaltegger, S. and Burrit, R. (2005). *Corporate Sustainability*. Cheltenham: Edward Eldar.

Schaltegger, S., Hansen, E.G. and Lüdeke-Freund, F. (2015). Business models for sustainability: Origins, present research and future avenues. *Organization and Environment*, 1–8.

Schultze, W. and Trommer, R. (2012). The concept of environmental performance and its measurement in empirical studies. *Journal of Management Control*, 22(4): 375–412.

Sharma, S. (2000). Managerial interpretations and organizational context as predictors of corporate choice of environmental strategy. *Academy of Management Journal*, 43(4): 681–697.

Sharma, S. and Henriques, I. (2005). Stakeholder influences on sustainability practices in the Canadian forest products industry. *Strategic Management Journal*, 26(2): 159–180.

Stubbs, W. and Cocklin, C. (2008). Conceptualizing a 'sustainability business model'. *Organization and Environment*, 21(2): 103–127.

Taneja, S., Sewell, S.S. and Odom, R.Y. (2015). A culture of employee engagement: A strategic perspective for global managers. *Journal of Business Strategy*, 36(3): 46–56.

Temminck, E., Mearns, K. and Fruhen, L. (2015). Motivating employees toward sustainable behaviour. *Business Strategy and the Environment*, 24(6): 402–412.

Tyteca, D. (1996). On the measurement of the environmental performance of firms: A literature review and a proactive efficiency perspective. *Journal of Environmental Management*, 46(3): 281–308.

Useem, M. (1996). *Investor Capitalism: How Money Managers are Changing the Face of Corporate America*. New York: Basic Books.

van Bommel, H.W.M. (2011). A conceptual framework for analyzing sustainability strategies in industrial supply networks from an innovation perspective. *Journal of Cleaner Production*, 19, 895–904.

van Kleef, H. and Room, N. (2007). Developping capabilities and competence for sustainable business management as innovation: A research agenda. *Journal of Cleaner Production*, 15(1): 38–51.

Waddock, S. and Graves, S. (1997). The corporate social performance-financial performance link. *Strategic Management Journal*, 18(4): 303–319.

Wagner, M. (2005). How to reconcile environmental and economic performance to improve corporate sustainability: Corporate environmental strategies in the European paper Industry. *Journal of Environmental Management*, 76(2): 105–118.

Wagner, M. and Schaltegger, S. (2003). How does sustainability performance relate to business competitiveness? *Greener Management International*(44): 5–16.

WBCSD (1997). *Signals of Change: Business Progress Toward Sustainable Development*. Geneva: WBCSD.

WCED. (1987). *Our Common Future: World Commission on Environment and Development*. Oxford and New York: Oxford University Press.

Weber, R.P. (1990). *Basic Content Analysis*, 2nd edn. Newbury Park, CA: SAGE.

Whetten, D.A., Rands, G. and Godfrey, P. (2002). What are the responsibilities of business to society? In A. Pettigrew, H. Thomas and R. Whittington (eds), *Handbook of Strategy and Management*. London: SAGE, pp. 373–409.

Whiteman, G., Walker, B. and Perego, P. (2013). Planetary boundaries: Ecological foundations for corporate sustainability. *Journal of Management Studies*, 50(2): 307–336.

Winn, M., Kirchgeorg, M., Griffiths, D., Linnenluecke, M.K. and Günther, E. (2011). Impacts from climate change on organizations: A conceptual foundation. *Business Strategy and the Environment*, 20(3): 157–173.

Xie, S. and Hayase, K. (2007). Corporate environmental performance: A measurement model and a new concept. *Business Strategy and the Environment*, 16(2): 148–168.

Yunus, M., Moingeon, B. and Lehmann-Ortega, L. (2010). Building social business models: Lessons from the Grameen experience. *Long Range Planning*, 43(2/3): 308–325.

6 Corporate inaction on climate change

A systematic literature review

Lena Judick

Introduction

Climate change is one of the most urgent problems of our time. The Fifth Intergovernmental Panel on Climate Change (IPCC) report states that anthropogenic greenhouse gas emissions are now higher than ever and that 'their effects ... are extremely likely to have been the dominant cause of the observed warming since the mid-20th century' (p. 4).[1] Decarbonizing the global economy is a prerequisite to limiting the impact of global warming that threatens to have irreversible consequences for the Earth. The historic Paris Agreement of December 2015 raises gradual expectations that steps will actually be taken. Nevertheless, despite the pressing need for joint action, major industries worldwide continue to emit roughly the same amount of carbon dioxide every year. Energy-intensive industries, in particular, are major contributors to global CO_2 emissions and play a special role in cutting emissions by mitigating the effects of climate change and changing their business models. The results of the Carbon Disclosure Project (CDP) illustrate that several companies in these sectors fail to reduce their overall greenhouse gas emissions.[2]

In the literature, a synopsis of the many reasons of corporate inaction on climate change is lacking. The majority of the literature on business and climate change concentrates on company strategies on climate action.[3] This literature review aims to contribute to a better understanding of the sources of organizational inaction on climate change, and to show why companies remain inertial in reducing their emissions and neglect the pressing need for action. In order to do so, key papers from the field will be examined and a summary of the main reasons for corporate inaction will be given. In a further step, the author analyses the complexity of reasons at the individual, organizational and institutional levels. The examination aims to deepen the understanding of the sources of corporate inaction on climate change, in order for a contribution for further research to be made.

Analysis of the various reasons for corporate inaction on climate change contributes to research on corporate sustainability, as well as organizational research on climate change. Furthermore, it sharpens our understanding of the absence of adequate corporate responses to the challenges of climate change. The systematic collection of reasons for corporate inaction along different categories allows future research to understand the complexity of their interplay and to further analyse how to overcome them.

Defining corporate inaction on climate change

Thus far, corporate inaction on climate change has not experienced the attention it deserves in corporate sustainability literature. The majority of studies examine corporate strategies on climate action and show how firms respond to climate change issues.[4] A clear conceptualization of firms' inaction on sustainability issue is lacking.[5] Corporate inaction on climate change can be defined as 'the failure of companies to reduce absolute greenhouse gas (GHG) emissions due to a lack of effective measures' (p. 2).[6] Wade-Benzoni et al. refer to the asymmetry between action and inaction as a reason for the lack of intensive research on inaction. They view inaction as a unique phenomenon due to the fact that people have 'the tendency to consider harmful acts to be worse than equally harmful omissions' (p. 45).[7] A person can be made responsible for harms that are caused by an action; however, establishing a causal link between inaction and harms occurred seems more difficult.[8] This is the core problem of corporate inaction.

Considering the growing demands of globalized markets, organizations and stakeholders, it can be expected that the reasons for inaction are complex and interwoven. What has to be examined is the reason for the paradox that a growing number of business actions on climate change are not achieving meaningful results (when it comes to CO_2 reduction).[9]

Methods

The methodical literature review followed the guidelines of a systematic and structured approach suggested by Fink to offer a thorough review of the research landscape on organizational inaction on climate change.[10] To detect relevant articles, the review began with a research question based on the objective to identify key reasons for corporate inaction analysed in the literature so far. The objective was to present an overview of the current state of research on corporate inaction on climate change on three levels: the individual, organizational and institutional levels. This structure has been chosen as one of the most recent papers on corporate inaction on climate change by Slawinski et al. has also taken this approach.[11] Following this, the second step was to include the identification of relevant databases. The databases Social Science Citation Index and the EBSCO Business Source Complete were used, as they ensure substantial validity with high-impact, peer-reviewed journals.[12]

Thirdly, specific search terms were defined according to the idea that corporate inaction occurs at the individual, organizational and institutional levels. As a result, various reasons of corporate inaction will be illustrated along these three categories. Due to the inadequate conceptualization of corporate inaction on climate change in the literature thus far, the author expected only a few results upon searching for corporate inaction. As a result, the following search terms[13] were applied in order to secure an appropriate first enquiry in September 2015: 'corporate inaction on climate change', 'organi*ational inaction on climate change' as well as 'corporate inertia on climate change' and 'organizational inertia on climate change', followed by 'corporate inaction' and 'climate change', 'organi*ational inaction' and 'climate change', 'corporate inertia' and 'climate change', 'organi*ational inertia' and 'climate change', 'organi*ational barrier(s)' and 'climate change', 'corporate barrier(s)' and 'climate change'. Based on a preliminary analysis on the topic, search terms were validated in a discussion with two colleagues from the field. Further search terms have been added according to this discussion, such as the combination of 'corporate strategy*' and 'climate change' and 'inaction or inertia', 'business strategy*' and 'climate change' and 'inaction or inertia', 'business respons* or corporate respons* or organi*ational respons*' and 'climate change' and 'inaction or inertia'. The results were scanned, and in reading their abstracts, a verification on whether the paper was eligible

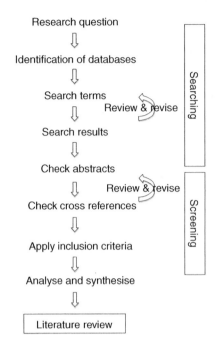

Figure 6.1 Systematic approach of the literature review

for inclusion has been conducted. The selected search terms led to seven papers[14] after the first validation round, which illustrated reasons for inaction. Consequently, further literature with a focus on inaction, and which was cross-referenced within the identified papers from the initial search, was included. The review required a number of iterations to ensure that papers which were within the scope of the review were captured. In sum, the combination of different keywords (and wildcards) resulted in the search terms mentioned above, leading – together with the cross-reference check – to a selection of 65 papers.

At the fourth stage, these 65 papers were screened based on practical and qualitative criteria in order to include or exclude papers from the study. The author assessed whether the papers were illustrating specific reasons for corporate inaction or not. In order to cover only the relevant studies acknowledged within the scientific community, priority was given to English peer-reviewed articles and papers, excluding news pieces, editorial notes, comments or even book reviews. Additionally, only papers from the field of sustainability, management, economy or environmentalism were included. Results were screened in a preliminary phase, and in order to ensure validity, the selection was discussed and validated with the above-mentioned colleagues from the field. The screening process led to a final selection of 27 journals as a basis for the literature review. Journals include those in the field of sustainability, such as *Energy Policy, Global Environmental Policy and Climate Policy*, as well as the following strategy and business journals: *Academy of Management Journal, Business and Society, Business and Politics, California Management Review, Organization Studies, Journal of Management Studies*, and *European Management Journal*. Included are the *Review of International Political Economy* and a journal of ecosocialism: *Capitalism Nature Socialism*. With regards to the applied research methods, the majority of the articles are empirical (17), including quantitative analyses of published reports and data (2) and qualitative approaches such as interviews, case studies or experiments (15). Ten articles represent theoretical work.

For the fifth and last step, papers were analysed with a focus on recurring patterns of reasons for corporate inaction in the research. The intention was to show common reasons indicated by various authors and to group and systematize them accordingly. The patterns built the basis of the research categories along the three levels of inaction. It became obvious that the different authors handle reasons for inaction differently. In some papers, these reasons were explained precisely; however, in other papers authors remained vague with regards to the allocation of inaction to the three levels mentioned earlier. In order to contribute to a more systematic approach to the various reasons for inaction, the author searched for recurring patterns and developed clusters accordingly. It became evident that these patterns could be matched to the previously defined categories.

Findings

Individual level

Managers have a significant influence on a company's behaviour. Senior leaders, in particular, play a crucial role as they determine whether to invest in new technologies, energy management or production methods (or not to invest). Together with their lobbying activity, they either initiate a change in the organization or stick to existing carbon-focused processes.[15] Environmental and social aspects are being probed for potential economic benefits.[16] Action on climate change will fail if managers are missing the support of their senior management. As DeCanio illustrates it, the behaviour of the firm is the result of the interaction of different individual motivations.[17] That being said, it is not only the managers who influence a firm's behaviour, but also other stakeholders involved with a diverse level of influence such as experts, engineers and geoscientists (for special branches). In the following section, a summary of the major reasons of corporate inaction that can be traced back to an individual resistance to change is given.

Present-time perspectives of managers

Climate change requires a sustainable and visionary attitude that goes beyond short-term goals. This is contradictory to the mindset of managers striving for short-term success as their compensation is linked to current performance and as they rotate within the company frequently. The individual time perspective highly affects decision-making.[18] Slawinski et al. look at the impact of a present-time perspective, especially under the condition of uncertainty. They argue that present-oriented managers will be less likely to consider an environmental impact and will estimate present costs over future benefits.[19] For these managers, possible benefits of action on climate change seem to be distant, lacking the importance and urgency. According to the study of Slawinski et al., the reasons for this conflict lie in the relationship between time and uncertainty. As a result, the authors assume that 'the greater the managers' present-time perspective and the lower their tolerance for uncertainty, the more an organization will be disposed to inaction on climate change' (p. 10).[20] Top management gives low priority to relatively small cost–cutting projects (particularly energy-saving).[21]

Cognitive barriers supporting the resistance to change

When it comes to personal resistance, one has to look at individual behaviour and the reasons that lie behind it. There are several cognitive barriers to action which earlier research has identified. In their analysis of cognitive barriers to action, Hoffman and Bazerman explain that sustainability and competitiveness are framed in a win-lose relationship where competitiveness wins. Hoffman and Bazerman discern a win-lose relationship between sustainability and competitiveness – also called the mythical fix bias – as a reason for inaction.[22] There is also the problem of information cascades. Information cascades entail that some individuals tend to follow the actions and behaviour of preceding individuals without considering their own set of information.[23] Decision-makers tend to imitate their peer groups in order to minimize research costs as well as avoid costs of experimentation. Consequently, they run the risk of copying the mistakes of others.[24] Climate change also faces the problems of a group failure. According to Ostrom, climate change suffers from a classic collective action problem. Distorted private incentives are more likely to lead to inertia, Ostrom postulates.[25] 'The individuals making up a business firm may all be rational seekers after their own interest, but the outcome of their collective action may be suboptimal' (p. 907).[26]

Complexity of environmental issues

Environmental issues are characterized by the difficulty to understand their whole impact in a simple manner and by the involvement of various stakeholders from numerous dimensions. The complexity of issues increases and requires cross-functional communication.[27] Environmental strategies follow the economic objective and will not have the needed effect. What is lacking is performance standards being assessed against environmental parameters to ensure that the environmental strategies of firms lead to a reduction of environmental effects.[28] When it comes to climate change, the economic consequences of action are hard to foresee. Kolk and Levy argue that managerial discretion is higher within these unforeseeable situations and therefore leads to inaction.[29] As Banerjee formulates it, managers might be challenged within these situations. He calls for further analysis on what the decision-making of managers in these challenging situations defines.[30]

The role and influence of experts

Within the field of corporate political activities, research indicates a variance in experts' opinions that can subvert legislative processes and regulation.[31] Experts can either influence organizational decision-making directly (via their hierarchical position) or indirectly when they act as advisers to decision-makers. 'In matters such as climate change, organizational decision makers and policy makers must turn to scientists and experts to justify their lines of action' (p. 1499).[32] Nevertheless, the influence of individual experts on company decision-making depends on how embedded they are within the organization. Findings show that more defensive experts occupy senior positions within an organization compared to activists. This manoeuvres defensive experts closer to the decision-making within the company, hindering the required change, and may even contribute to the reluctance to develop and implement suitable strategies to act on climate change. Engineers and geoscientists, on the other hand, can have major influence within their industry to affect national and international policy.[33] Lefsrud and Meyer point out that within the petroleum industry, expert positions are staffed with opponents to the IPCC and anthropogenic climate change, resulting in defensive institutional work.[34]

The role and influence of corporate scientists

Corporate scientists can influence a company's perception on climate change due to their interaction with the scientific community. Corporate (internal) scientists become the first employees aware of climate change as a potential risk. Depending on the extent to which the scientists are more embedded within the scientific world or the corporate world, this determines the degree of adherence to a more sceptical perspective on climate science. DiMaggio and Powell argue that the greater the level of accountability of the scientific staff to other functions such as product management, marketing and government affairs; the stronger the institutional pressures to match the climate sceptic position.[35] Rothenberg and Levy found that the less embedded the scientist is within the external scientific profession, the greater the likelihood that organization's institutional frames shape the translation process.[36]

Regional differences

European and American companies show contrasting behaviour when it comes to climate change.[37] This difference is also remarkable at the management level. It can be attributed to the managers' home country having an impact on the managers' behaviour, thus resulting in different corporate strategies. Levy and Kolk underline that personnel at the senior management level responsible for developing a corporate climate strategy, typically build upon the conditions of the company's home country.[38] In the 1990s, according to Jones and Levy, senior managers of European companies saw climate change more seriously, whereas US managers were sceptical about it. European managers, in comparison to US managers, estimated regulation of emissions as inevitable and were more optimistic about new technologies.[39]

Organizational level

Corporate responses to climate change have been changing over the years. In the 1990s, companies had political and non-market strategies, whereas now they strive towards product and process improvements and emission trading as a way to reduce emissions.[40] As Levy and colleagues argue, business responses for North American companies have been massively ineffective, only touching reputational and brand management issues. Fossil fuel industries, in particular, have a high stake in opposing further regulation, and consequently, build the spearhead of resistance.[41] Firms' responses to climate change depend on various factors, such as their exposure to climate risks, their industry classification, and individual capabilities or specialties of particular business leaders.[42] Inaction at the organizational level is a result of cross-level interactions.[43] Firms do not behave like individuals. 'The behavior of the firm is the outcome of the interplay of motivations of the individuals comprising it ...' (p. 906).[44] The following section offers an overview of the reasons of corporate inaction from an organizational point of view.

Short-termism and uncertainty avoidance

Slawinski et al. apply the theoretical concepts of short-termism and uncertainty avoidance to explain corporate inaction on climate change. From their research findings, both concepts reinforce each other and result in corporate inaction. They explain how firms with business models that focus on short-term financial returns are less likely to invest in order to reduce their GHG emissions.[45]

Corporate investments have different time horizons: either having a short-term impact or representing longer-term solutions.[46] Time shapes organizational responses. In their studies, Slawinski and Bansal emphasize that the temporal perspective of firms demonstrates a disconnected view of time in which the distant past and future are not considered in decision-making with regards to climate change. This disconnected perspective on time relates to each firm's low tolerance for uncertainty, as a lack of certainty may lead to significant decisions being delayed. According to Slawinski and Bansal, focused firms consider investments that go beyond their compliance obligations as too risky, and will wait for a planning reliability before investing. These types of firms demonstrate a low tolerance when it comes to uncertainty. Integrated companies, on the other hand, invest in a broad range of activities to reduce their GHG emissions and appear to make a greater connection between the firms' past, present and future activities. Nevertheless, they do not have the competency to respond quickly. The two patterns (categories) in firms' responses to climate change reflect two different time perspectives. Their study offers insights into the tension between speed and breadth of responses in addressing climate change.[47]

Fear of losing competitive advantages

For the survival and competitiveness of a company, economic goals are pre-eminent.[48] Environmentalism is still associated with economic losses. This also refers to the win-lose relationship, mentioned earlier, by Hoffman and Bazerman; the mythical fix bias. Both authors point to organizational barriers, such as the over-reliance on regulatory standards, to explain compliance activities instead of effective solutions for sustainability challenges.[49]

In terms of investments in alternative technologies or research and development, companies need to be sure not to waste money.[50] Some companies suffered from losses when investing in renewable energy, and therefore have scarcely a positive view on alternative energy.[51] According to Jones and Levy, firms place a greater emphasis on management processes, policy influence and market image than on major investments in low-emission technologies.[52] DeCanio illustrates an 'efficiency paradox', in that companies sometimes decide not to maximize their profits, not even investing in profitable energy-saving measures.[53] Carbon-save technologies might include costs that can make their adoption economically untenable.[54] In the field of corporate environmentalism, environmental strategies seem to remain dominated by financial benefits. Environmental issues are framed as quality issues, which leads to companies focusing on the implementation of standards such as the ISO 9000 family of quality management systems standards. Only environmental approaches following productivity improvement or costs savings are being implemented.[55]

The market dominance of the fossil fuel industry

Many authors focus on the oil industry, as it contributes a major part of emissions due to fossil fuels being the basis for their business models. Its resistance to change is extremely high as it is one of the most powerful global business sectors in the world. Radical changes would be necessary to alter the current global balance of forces.[56] Newell and Paterson point out how fossil fuel companies manage to secure their positions with regards to climate change policy. According to the authors, it is clear that 'when the centrality of fossil fuels in producing global warming is combines with the centrality of fossil energy in industrial economies ... the fundamental interests of major sectors of these economies are threatened by proposals to limit greenhouse gas emission' (p. 682).[57]

Kolk and Levy analyse developments in the oil industry over the past few years, and have observed remarkable shifts in corporate climate strategy. They explain the divergent behaviour of oil companies in terms of company-specific factors such as the profitability and location of the company, market assessments, the degree of centralization and the presence of climate scientists. They present an analytical framework, in which they analyse the sources of corporate strategy choice in consideration of the fact that the oil industry is heavily affected by regulatory measures to cut GHG emissions.[58] Skjærseth and Skodin assume that according to the logic of their corporate actor model, oil companies with more emphasis on coal than on gas might be more likely to adopt a reactive climate strategy, and not vice versa. Also, companies having experienced societal concerns and pressure are likely to respond to an enhanced public concern for climate change.[59]

Kolk and Levy illustrate that the economic situation of oil multinationals plays a role in their inaction on climate change. In the previous decades before the 2000s, oil multinationals experienced years of diversification in the mid-1970s, divestments and focus strategies in the 1980s and large-scale mergers and acquisitions in the 1990s. Based on their review of alternative energy, companies came to the conclusion that renewables symbolize only a niche market, where a company will only invest if substantial profits can be expected.[60]

Le Menestrel et al. argue that climate change poses an ethical dilemma to oil companies, explaining their inaction on climate change. Reflecting on the ethical dilemma that climate change creates for the oil industry helps to understand their reactive behaviour and strategies. For the oil industry, the business ethical dilemma symbolizes 'a trade-off between a socially detrimental process (emitting greenhouse gases, hence inducing a risk of climate change) and a self-interested consequence (profits)' (p. 3),[61] explaining business behaviour that chooses business interests over social responsibility. 'From a business standpoint, corporations ... consider that climate change policies represent a threat to their business and, as such, should be fought against' (p. 12).[62]

Levy and Egan apply the neo-Gramscian framework for corporate political strategy in order to analyse responses to climate change by firms in the US and European oil and automobile industries. The corporate political strategies of these companies are defined by their struggle to defend their hegemonic position, thus leading to corporate inaction on climate change. The fossil fuel industry tries 'to preserve its hegemonic position in terms of market dominance, autonomy and policy influence' (p. 824).[63] 'In particular the neo-Gramscian approach points to the crucial role of civil society, the significance of political struggle over climate science and economics and the ultimate weakness of ... the ... industry' (p. 824).[64]

Structural power of capital

Newell and Paterson look into the lobbying efforts of the fossil fuel industry and show the dependency of capitalist societies on capital accumulation. This fundamental feature of capitalist societies explains why governments have been more sympathetic to the concerns of fossil fuel industries than too many other pro-action coalitions. Lobby groups demonstrate a wide influence and work at various levels, supporting the inaction on climate change. Their involvement ranges from influencing legislative procedures, to actively participating in international climate conferences to campaign for climate change denial and to influence the public's perception on that topic.[65] Kolk and Pinkse see corporate lobbying as one barrier that hinders the implementation of more ambitious regulations.[66] Oil multinationals fund non-governmental organizations in order to strengthen climate change sceptic lobby groups and policy think tanks that can attack the science of climate change.[67]

Regional differences

In their analysis of corporate strategies of oil multinationals (MNCs), Levy and Kolk highlight that the MNCs formulate their climate strategies in the context of cognitive frames and regulatory systems reflecting home country environments. The MNCs must deal with the specialty of both home and host country. The host-country aspect is most notable in the case of non-EU firms having to deal with the European emissions trading scheme (ETS). Levy and Kolk indicate that the country of origin effect supports institutional pressures and strategic heterogeneity. MNCs are a subject of conflicting strategic pressures, as the institutional environment depends on the home or host country as well as the global industry. They argue that due to this, MNCs develop unified, company-wide positions that make it challenging to act on climate change.[68]

According to Bonardi and Keim, firms from countries with considerable institutional constraints and a lack of government pressure will elect for self-regulation to pre-empt more binding legislation.[69]

Kolk and Pinkse define climate change as a multi-domestic issue. According to their results, multinational companies are not opposed to action on climate change itself, but rather strongly prefer market-based policies and voluntary initiatives. Firms attempt to steer policy makers in the direction of their preferred policy types. Corporate effort to sway the opinions of experts who have influence on the evolution of the issue and its degree of saliency, are dominated by firms from the United States where there are fewer institutional constraints.[70]

The two authors also examine market strategies and their impact on responses to climate change. They emphasize that a decade of business interests in climate change has led to a clear shift in strategies. In the first half of the 1990s, political and non-market strategies dominated the scene. At the time of writing their article, market strategies became more dominant on the scene. Additionally, globalization and companies operating in different states brought further multi-domestic and non-market strategies to the table.[71]

Uncertainty in the planning process

Companies navigate in an exceedingly uncertain business environment when it comes to climate change. Based on regulatory forecasting, economic analyses of the costs and benefits and the uncertainty of the climate regime; many companies refrain from omitting greenhouse gas reduction equipment in new plants.[72] According to Kolk and Pinkse, companies face more uncertainty about the competitive effects of possible (upcoming) regulatory measures.[73] This applies globally and within Europe. Okereke explores the motivations, drivers and barriers to carbon management, and identifies three barriers to efficient carbon management: firstly, there is a lack of a strong policy framework that could create long-term value for carbon emissions reductions technology; secondly, companies must deal with uncertainty regarding governmental action and the issue of climate change. These include the role of international institutions and regulations as opposed to national and local regulations. There are also uncertainties about the political stability of major oil supplying blocs and its effect on energy prices. Third, there is uncertainty about the marketplace. There is no guarantee in forecasting the price of carbon. It is exceptionally impossible to predict what consumers would pay for low-carbon products.[74]

Companies in mature markets with few opportunities for process or product substitutes are more likely to resist GHG reductions than those in evolving markets, where plenty of alternatives are available for achieving reduction goals. Furthermore, companies which supply industry sectors that embrace GHG reductions will hold a more favourable view of GHG reductions than those that service more resistant fields. Nevertheless, the strategic implications of GHG reductions remain uncertain.[75]

Institutional level

Companies have to cope with a more complex business environment than ever before. Globalization, growing requirements of the community of states, stakeholder pressure and increased public perception, symbolize only an extract of factors that influence corporate behaviour. Institutional logic combined with regulatory uncertainty can have a significant influence on corporate inaction on climate change. The following section gives a summary of the multilayered reasons for corporate inaction caused by external factors.

Time-perspective and uncertainty avoidance

The question for companies in taking action is when to take it (when interpreting the prospective future policy framework). Be it domestic or international, business is mindful of the importance of timing and the danger of pursing initiatives either too early or too late. If firms act too early, the price of carbon might be too low to achieve sufficient returns on investment. If they are too late, they fall behind their competitors with the loss of market share.[76] So far, business opportunities resulting from climate change are not sufficient to encourage the stepwise change necessary for climate stabilization. Levy and Egan argue that the lack of a strong regulatory framework that might generate strong profit incentives and penalties for non-compliance, leads to the lack of far-reaching corporate climate strategies. According to them, the lacking regulatory pressure is the most important non-market driver of corporate carbon strategies.[77]

Weak international climate policy

The international climate policy is marked by inconsistent positions among key actors. In the EU, initial attempts to implement climate policies and secure the stabilization of emissions can be observed in the early 1990s. That being said, the approach to implement an energy tax failed due to the strong opposition of key actors in the industry and member states. Many European companies were active in discussions after Kyoto in order to pre-empt stricter forms of regulation (more in the direction of voluntary initiatives). In the US, there was a lack of domestic pressure for companies to be more cooperative. The lack of a strong international climate policy provided companies such as ExxonMobil significant opportunities to further oppose climate change measures.[78] Skjærseth and Skodvin elaborate that the position of a major non-state actor (the oil industry) is crucial to US climate policy.[79]

Lack of political pressure

Okereke and Russell argue that corporate climate strategies are shaped and mediated by a complex interplay of internal and external drivers, ranging from leadership to social responsibility to pressure from non-governmental organizations, with a special emphasis on dynamics and regulatory pressure. Their research indicates that while the market remains a crucial driver, only strong governmental regulation can ultimately induce radical action of business actors. 'Without a strong political will, much of the change would likely be incremental rather than radical as companies attempt to stick as close as possible to their areas of traditional competence' (p. 121).[80]

Carbon lock-in and CO_2 markets

Unruh seeks to expand DeCanio's analysis of barriers for firms, which prevent them from investing in energy-efficient technologies. Unruh looks into the impact of a carbon-focused path-dependency that results in policy inertia towards action on climate change. He emphasizes the phenomenon of a carbon lock-in that creates systemic market and policy barriers to implementing carbon-saving technologies.[81]

Veal and Mouzas doubt the ability of the actual and intended CO_2 markets to mitigate climate change.[82] Bond underlines that the ETS has not provide the required incentives to invest in low-carbon technologies. Especially more effective approaches to move to low-carbon technologies are being prevented in order to not endanger the ETS.[83]

The over-allocation of CO_2 permits results in CO_2 costs that do not challenge businesses' existing behaviour. The European Trading Scheme (as it is currently being implemented) does not incentivize market participants to reduce their CO_2 emissions.[84]

Involvement of the state in the energy business

Newell and Paterson look at the mutual dependency of states and the energy sector to explain how fossil fuel companies have been able to secure their interests in state policies on climate action. This is due to the structural power of capital and the fact that states are extensively involved in the energy business in most capitalist countries. Maintaining capital accumulation as a primary goal plays a key role for the preservation of state legitimacy in capitalist societies. For most of the history of capitalism, fossil energy has been one such crucial resource. Such industries are highly capital-intensive and resistant to change, and they have even 'used threats against states to prevent the adoption of policies to limit emissions' (p. 683).[85]

Paterson and Newell argue that the political economy approach offers a better explanation of global climate politics within a regime framework. This approach provides an explanation for the limited nature of international policy on climate change to date, for example the failure of the EU CO_2 tax, and 'explains why governments seem to anticipate the energy companies' reaction to proposed policies and scale down proposals' (p. 694).[86]

Climate change as a non-salient issue

Whether an issue is seen as widely salient or non-salient determines whether stakeholders act upon it. When climate change is seen as a salient issue, and the public views the problem as serious, it is more likely that climate change policy is adopted. Companies striving for self-regulation rather than supporting legislative action with regards to climate change, reveals an underlying intention to keep climate change a non-salient issue. Bonardi and Keim examine how an issue becomes salient, as a key determinant of successful corporate political strategy is identified by the prominence of the issue. Companies find ways to prevent an issue from becoming salient, e.g. via massive public operations.[87] Hoffman makes it clear that 'many companies still see climate change as a scientific or social issue' (p. 39).[88]

Regional differences

Skjærseth and Skodin argue that US companies have exhibited weaker responses to climate change due to weaker societal demands. According to them, environmental non-governmental organizations have lesser influence in the US compared to Europe. The American approach to climate policy provokes a confrontation between regulation agencies and target groups, and therefore complicates attempts for cooperation. 'In the US, a legalistic tradition and the exclusion of the oil industry in climate policy has stimulated an adversarial process characterized by mistrust and intense lobbying efforts' (p. 60).[89] Different climate policy strategies from major European and American oil multinationals can be observed. '... A number of studies have shown that Europeans have been much more receptive to proactive measures on climate change than North Americans' (p. 55).[90]

Discussion

The following table summarizes key findings of the literature review. It underlines the complexity of the reasons for corporate inaction on climate change and its systematic nature which makes it so challenging. In the following section, conclusions from the findings will be drawn.

The analysed literature reveals the complexity and manifold reasons for corporate inaction on climate change. Although the literature shows various reasons for inaction, their interdependencies remain uncertain. In particular, the impact of each factor (and their interaction) in fostering inaction is not well studied and, thus, remains vague. It can only be suggested that the interwoven connectivity between and especially within the different levels of inaction makes it difficult to determine the relevance of individual sources of inaction. Although a significant amount of progress has been made with regards to corporate engagement for climate change, the results with respect to reductions in CO_2 emissions remain unsatisfactory. Even companies that have implemented carbon-related strategies often demonstrate an opposition against (further) regulatory measures.

Table 6.1 Overview of the reasons for inaction at the individual, organizational and institutional level

Individual	Organizational	Institutional
Present-time perspective of managers	Short-termism and uncertainty avoidance	Time-perspective and uncertainty avoidance
Cognitive barriers supporting the resistance to change	Fear of losing competitive advantages	Weak international climate policy
Complexity of environmental issues	The market dominance of the fossil fuel industry	Lack of political pressure
The role and influence of experts	Structural power of capital	Involvement of the state in the energy business
The role and influence of corporate scientists	Regional differences	Climate change as a non-salient issue
Regional differences	Uncertainty in the planning process	Regional differences

Conclusions

The allocation of reasons for inaction within the three categories (individual, organizational and institutional) helps to group and systematically analyse corporate inaction on climate change. It becomes apparent that inaction occurs at all three levels, indicating that strategies to overcome barriers of inaction must address each category appropriately.

On the individual level, there are cognitive barriers, which hinder individuals to act upon climate change. Senior managers, in particular, have a significant influence on a company's strategy to act on climate change.[91] Apart from them, the role of experts and corporate scientists must be considered as well, and their influence should not be underestimated. What is key at the individual level is decision-making. Individuals are trapped in a dilemma of not being able to foresee the economic consequences of action they might take.[92] Climate change is a complex issue which requires the willingness to change – from each individual being involved.[93]

At the organizational level, the literature indicates that firms prefer to focus on setting goals, targets, carbon accounting or monitoring procedures voluntarily in order to avoid legally binding requirements.[94] Action on climate change requires long-term solutions. The long-term orientation necessary to implement climate change action is counterproductive to the typical short-term orientation of organizations. Companies demonstrate contradictory behaviour, expressing concern over the threat of climate change in some contexts, whilst actively working to weaken policy responses to climate change in others. There is proof of corporate influence on climate policy and scientific research in this field, with corporations using their influence to obscure science and block effective and ambitious climate policy.[95] Dependency on fossil fuels and the global oil industry fosters the systematic problem of corporate inaction. It is principally those companies with core business models reliant on fossil fuels that show a different behaviour from those less dependent on fossil fuels.[96] The continuously profound and interwoven structural power of the fossil fuel industry impedes companies from implementing green solutions. Firms have specialized competencies and assets and cannot easily change directions. Growth in production and sales take precedence over emissions reductions.[97] Companies face significant costs and incentives to leave old business models behind. Consequently, as they prefer to adhere to the old models, this unwillingness to change supports inaction.

At the institutional level, current regulations are too weak and do not reflect the required steps for long-term successful climate protection. The failure of key implementation tools to mitigate climate change, such as the European Trading System, show that regulations are not stringent and stable enough to incentivize far-reaching corporate action on climate change.[98] The global climate regime has not managed to set the required incentives in order to motivate companies to reduce their CO_2 emissions. Current legislative measures have not led to improvements in terms of absolute CO_2 emission reductions.[99] Uncertainty appears to weigh heavily at the institutional level, leading to defensive institutional work and a lack of incentives to change corporate behaviour.

Managerial implications

There are a number of managerial implications arising from the findings. A better understanding of why firms fail to act adequately on climate change can help tackle other sustainability issues, such as moving towards green products or energy efficiency. In particular, a deeper understanding of the interplay of various reasons for inaction supports the awareness that companies will need to take different reasons into consideration in order to effectively act on climate change. If only single reasons are changed, the impact of other reasons might hinder any positive development.

The results reveal the immense challenge managers have to meet facing the complexity of environmental issues. If they are able to transfer global environmental issues to their own company and extract their impact, effective solutions may be found in order to overcome inaction on climate change.

The findings identified the importance of long-term oriented management. If managers handle sustainability issues with their present-time orientation, they fail to implement sustainable solutions which come to effect far beyond their mandate. If organizations manage to encourage long-term engagement, and if they find the right incentives to foster sustainable behaviour, it may become possible to solve the weariness towards action on climate change.

Results of the analysis of reasons for corporate inaction on climate change may provide actors, such as policy makers and non-governmental organizations, suggestions for potential levers to overcome the barriers preventing companies from acting on climate change as they are expected to. What could be further evaluated is the impact a more stringent regulatory environment such as a revised ETS could have on the behaviour of companies, managers and policy makers.

Further research

Recurring in the literature are problems of short-termism and uncertainty which foster corporate inaction at all three levels of examination. Following the suggestion of Slawinski et al.,[100] the role of time in sustainability could be deepened in future research.

Corporate inaction on climate change can be traced back to economic, psychological and market-economic reasons. Therefore, in order to better understand the logic of the various sources of inaction and their interdependencies, future research could follow a stronger interdisciplinary and multi-actor approach, bearing in mind that apart from corporate management, there is additionally the potential influence of experts and corporate scientists on corporate behaviour. With regards to the structural power of the fossil fuel industries, further studies could evaluate to what extent developments such as divestments might contribute to a gradual phase out from fossil fuels.

With the adoption of the Paris agreement and the changing framework conditions in the field of climate change, it will be interesting to observe whether and how the agreement will support robust national mitigation targets. These targets may incentivize firms to act upon climate change and work further on emissions reductions. It remains to be seen whether the Paris agreement can overcome fatigue on the subject of climate change and increase the likelihood of policy makers to further regulate CO_2 emission reductions.

Table 6.2 Appendix: List of publications included in the review

1. Banerjee, S.B. (2012). A climate for change? Critical reflections on the Durban United Nations Climate Change Conference. *Organization Studies*, 33(12): 1761–1786.
2. Banerjee, S.B. (2001). Managerial perceptions of corporate environmentalism: Interpretations from industry and strategic implications for organizations. Journal of Management Studies, 38(4): 489–513.
3. Bonardi, J.P. and Keim, G.D. (2005). Corporate political strategies for widely salient issues. Academy of Management, 30(3): 555–576.
4. Bond, P. (2008). The state of the global carbon trade debate. Capitalism Nature Socialism, 19(4): 89–106.
5. DeCanio, S. (1993). Barriers within firms to energy-efficient investments. Energy Policy, 21(9): 906–914.
6. DeCanio, S. (1998). The efficiency paradox: Bureaucratic and organizational barriers to profitable energy-saving investments. Energy Policy, 26(5): 441–454.
7. Hoffman, A.J. (2005). Climate change strategy: The business logic behind voluntary greenhouse gas reductions. California Management Review, 47(3): 21–46.
8. Hoffman, A.J. and Bazerman, M. (2007). Changing practice on sustainability: Understanding and overcoming the organizational and psychological barriers to action. In S. Sharma, M. Strarik and B. Husted (eds), Organizations and the Sustainability Mosaic: Crafting Long-Term Ecological and Societal Solutions. Cheltenham: Edward Elgar, pp. 84–105.
9. Jones, C.A. and Levy, D.L. (2007). North American business strategies towards climate change. European Management Journal, 25(6): 428–440.
10. Kolk, A. and Levy, D.L. (2001). Winds of change: Corporate strategy, climate change and oil multinationals. European Management Journal, 19(5): 501–509.
11. Kolk, A. and Levy, D.L. (2002). Strategic responses to global climate change: Conflicting pressures on multinationals in the oil industry. Business and Politics, 4(3): 275–300.
12. Kolk, A. and Pinkse, J. (2004). Market strategies for climate change. European Management Journal, 22(3): 304–314.
13. Kolk, A. and Pinkse, J. (2005). Business response to climate change: Identifying emergent strategies. California Management Review, 47(3): 6–20.
14. Kolk, A. and Pinkse, J. (2007). Multinationals' political activities on climate change. Business & Society, 56(2): 201–228.
15. Lefsrud, L.M. and Meyer, R.E. (2012). Science or science fiction? Professionals' discursive construction of climate change. Organization Studies, 33(11): 1477–1506.
16. Le Menestrel, M., v.d. Hove, S. and de Bettignies, H.-C. (2002). The oil industry and climate change: Strategies and ethical dilemmas. Climate Policy, 2: 3–18.
17. Levy, D.L. and Egan, D. (2003). A neo-Gramscian approach to corporate political strategy: Conflict and accommodation in the climate change negotiations. Journal of Management Studies, 40(4): 803–829.
18. Newell, P. and Paterson, M. (1998). A climate for business: Global warming, the state and the capital. Review of International Political Economy, 5(4): 679–703.
19. Okereke, C. (2007). An exploration of motivations, drivers and barriers to carbon management: The UK FTSE 100. European Management Journal, 25(6): 475–486.
20. Okereke, C. and Russel, D. (2010). Regulatory pressure and competitive dynamics: Carbon management strategies of UK energy-intensive companies. California Management Review, 52(4): 100–124.

21. Rothenberg, S. and Levy, D.L. (2012). Corporate perceptions of climate science: The role of corporate environmental scientists. Business & Society, 51(1): 31–61.
22. Skjærseth, J.B. and Skodvin, T. (2001). Climate change and the oil industry: Common problems, different strategies. Global Environmental Politics, 1(4): 43–64.
23. Slawinski, N. and Bansal, P. (2012). A matter of time: The temporal perspectives of organizational responses to climate change. Organization Studies, 33(11): 1537–1563.
24. Slawinski, N., Pinkse, J., Busch, T. and Banerjee, S.B. (2015). The role of short-termism and uncertainty avoidance in organizational inaction on climate change: A multi-level framework. Business & Society, 56(2): 253–282.
25. Unruh, G. (2000). Understanding carbon lock-in. Energy Policy, 28(12): 817–830.
26. Veal, G. and Mouzas, S. (2012). Market-based responses to climate change: CO2 market design versus operation. Organization Studies, 33(11): 1589–1616.
27. Wittneben, B.B.F., Okereke, C., Banerjee, S.B. and Levy, D.L. (2012). Climate change and the emergence of new landscapes. Organization Studies, 33(11): 1431–1450.

Notes

1 IPCC, *Climate Change 2014: Synthesis Report*. Contribution of Working Groups I, II and III to the Fifth Assessment Report of the Intergovernmental Panel on Climate Change (Core Writing Team, R.K. Pachauri and L.A. Meyer (eds)). Geneva: IPCC, p. 4.
2 Carbon Disclosure Project/PricewaterhouseCoopers (12 September 2013). *Sector Insights: What is Driving Climate Change Action in the World's Largest Companies? Global 500 Climate Change Report 2013*. London. Retrieved from https://www.cdp.net/cdpresults/cdp-global-500-climate-change-report-2013.pdf.
3 Hoffman, A.J. (2005). Climate change strategy: The business logic behind voluntary greenhouse gas reductions. *California Management Review*, 47(3): 21–46; Kolk, A. and Pinkse, J. (2005). Business response to climate change: Identifying emergent strategies. *California Management Review*, 47(3): 6–20.
4 Hoffman (2005); Jones, C.A., Levy, D.L. (2007), North American business strategies towards climate change. *European Management Journal*, 25(6): 428–440; Kolk and Pinkse (2005).
5 Slawinski, N, Pinkse, J., Busch, T, Banerjee, S.B. (2015). The role of short-termism and uncertainty avoidance in organizational inaction on climate change: A multi-level framework. *Business & Society*, 56(2): 253–282.
6 Slawinski et al., 2.
7 Wade-Benzoni, K.A., A.J. Thompson, L.L., Moore, D.A., Gillespie, J.J., Bazerman, M.H. (2002). Barriers to resolution in ideologically based negotiations: The role of values and institutions. *Academy of Management Review*, 27, 41–57.
8 Wade-Benzoni et al.
9 Jones and Levy.
10 Fink, A. (2009). *Conducting Research Literature Reviews: From the Internet to Paper*, 3rd edn. Los Angeles: SAGE.
11 Slawinski et al.
12 Podsakoff, P.M., MacKenzie, S.B., Bachrach, D.G., and Podsakoff, N.P. (2005). The influence of management journals in the 1980s and 1990s. *Strategic Management Journal*, 26: 473–488.
13 Instead of climate change, the term 'global warming' has also been used for all search terms mentioned.
14 These papers were: Nos.5, 8, 11, 13, 24, 26 and 27 (according to the list in the appendix).
15 Wittneben, B.B.F., Okereke, C., Banerjee, S.B., Levy, D.L. (2012): Climate change and the emergence of new landscapes. *Organization Studies*, 33(11): 1431–1450.
16 Hahn, T., Preuss, L., Pinkse, J., Figge, F. (2014): Cognitive frames in corporate sustainability: Managerial sensemaking with paradoxical and business case frames. *Academy of Management Review*, 3(4): 463–487.
17 DeCanio, S. (1993). Barriers within firms to energy-efficient investments. *Energy Policy*, 21(9): 906–914.

18 Slawinski et al.
19 Slawinski et al.
20 Slawinski et al., 10.
21 DeCanio (1993).
22 Hoffman, A.J. and Bazerman, M. (2007). Changing practice on sustainability: Understanding and overcoming the organizational and psychological barriers to action. In S. Sharma, M. Strarik and B. Husted (eds), *Organizations and the Sustainability Mosaic: Crafting Long-Term Ecological and Societal Solutions*. Cheltenham: Edward Elgar, pp. 84–105.
23 Bonardi, J.P., Keim, G.D. (2005). Corporate political strategies for widely salient issues. *Academy of Management*, 30(3): 555–576.
24 Bikhachandi, S. Hirschleifer, D. and Welch, I. (1992). A theory of fads, fashion, custom and cultural change as informational cascades. *Journal of Political Economy*, 100: 992–1026.
25 Ostrom, E. (2009). *A Polycentric Approach for Coping with Climate Change*. Washington, DC: World Bank.
26 DeCanio (1993).
27 Westley, F. and Vredenburg, H. (1996). Sustainability and the corporation: Criteria for aligning economic practice with environmental protection. *Journal of Management Inquiry*, 5(2): 104–119.
28 Banerjee, S.B. (2001). Managerial perceptions of corporate environmentalism: Interpretations from industry and strategic implications for organizations, *Journal of Management Studies*, 38(4): 489–513.
29 Kolk, A. and Levy, D.L. (2002). Strategic responses to global climate change: conflicting pressures on multinationals in the oil industry, *Business and Politics*, 4(3): 275–300.
30 Banerjee (2001).
31 Bonardi and Keim.
32 Lefsrud, L.M., Meyer, R.E. (2012): Science or Science Fiction? Professionals' discursive construction of climate change. *Organization Studies*, 33(11): 1499.
33 Lefsrud and Meyer.
34 Lefsrud and Meyer.
35 DiMaggio, P.J. and Powell, W.W. (1983). The iron cage revisited: Institutional isomorphism and collective rationality in organizational fields. *American Sociological Review*, 48: 147–160.
36 Rothenberg, S. and Levy, D.L. (2012). Corporate perceptions of climate science: The role of corporate environmental scientists. *Business & Society*, 51(1): 31–61.
37 Kolk, A. and Levy, D. (2001). Winds of change: Corporate strategy, climate change and oil multinationals. *European Management Journal*, 19(5): 501–509; Jones and Levy.
38 Kolk and Levy (2002).
39 Jones and Levy.
40 Kolk and Pinkse (2005).
41 Jones and Levy.
42 Jones and Levy.
43 Slawinski et al.
44 DeCanio (1993).
45 Slawinski et al.
46 Weinhofer, G. and Hoffmann, V.H. (2010). Mitigating climate change: How do corporate strategies differ? *Business Strategy and the Environment*, 19: 77–89.
47 Slawinski, N. and Bansal, P. (2012). A matter of time: The temporal perspectives of organizational responses to climate change. *Organization Studies*, 33(11): 1537–1563.
48 Van der Byl, C.A. and Slawinski, N. (2015). Embracing tensions in corporate sustainability: A review of research from win–wins and trade-offs. *Organization and Environment*, 28(1): 54–79.
49 Hoffman and Bazerman.
50 Okereke, C. (2007). An exploration of motivations, drivers and barriers to carbon management: The UK FTSE 100. *European Management Journal*, 25(6): 475–486.
51 Rothenberg and Levy.
52 Jones and Levy.
53 DeCanio, S. (1998). The efficiency paradox: Bureaucratic and organizational barriers to profitable energy-saving investments. *Energy Policy*, 26(5): 441–454.
54 Unruh, G. (2000). Understanding carbon lock-in. *Energy Policy*, 28(12): 817–830.
55 Banerjee (2001).

56 Bond, P. (2008). The state of the global carbon trade debate. *Capitalism Nature Socialism*, 19(4): 89–106.
57 Newell, P. and Paterson, M. (1998). A climate for business: Global warming, the state and the capital. *Review of International Political Economy*, 5(4): 682.
58 Kolk and Levy (2001).
59 Skjærseth, J.B. and Skodvin, T. (2001). Climate change and the oil industry: Common problems, different strategies. *Global Environmental Politics*, 1(4): 43–64.
60 Kolk and Levy (2001).
61 Le Menestrel, M., v.d. Hove, S. and de Bettignies, H.-C. (2002). The oil industry and climate change: Strategies and ethical dilemmas. *Climate Policy*, 2: 3–18.
62 Le Menestrel et al.
63 Levy, D.L. and Egan, D. (2003). A neo-Gramscian approach to corporate political strategy: Conflict and accommodation in the climate change negotiations. *Journal of Management Studies*, 40(4): 803–829.
64 Levy et al.
65 Newell and Paterson.
66 Kolk, A. and Pinkse, J. (2007). Multinationals' political activities on climate change. *Business and Society*, 56(2): 201–228.
67 Wittneben et al.
68 Kolk and Levy (2001).
69 Bonardi and Keim.
70 Kolk and Pinkse (2007).
71 Kolk, A. and Pinkse, J. (2004). Market Strategies for Climate Change. *European Management Journal*, 22(3): 304–314.
72 Hoffman (2005).
73 Kolk and Pinkse (2005).
74 Okereke.
75 Hoffman (2005).
76 Slawinski et al. (2015).
77 Levy and Egan (2003).
78 Kolk and Levy (2001).
79 Skjærseth, J.B. and Skodvin, T. (2001). Climate change and the oil industry: Common problems, different strategies. *Global Environmental Politics*, 1(4): 43–64.
80 Okereke, C., Russel, D. (2010). Regulatory pressure and competitive dynamics: Carbon management strategies of UK energy-intensive companies. *California Management Review*, 52(4): 100–124.
81 Unruh.
82 Veal, G. and Mouzas, S. (2012). Market-based responses to climate change: CO_2 market design versus operation. *Organization Studies*, 33(11): 1589–1616.
83 Bond.
84 Veal and Mouzas.
85 Newell and Paterson.
86 Newell and Paterson.
87 Bonardi and Keim.
88 Hoffman (2005), p. 39.
89 Skjærseth and Skodvin.
90 Skjærseth and Skodvin.
91 Wittneben et al.
92 Kolk and Levy (2002).
93 Westley and Vredenburg.
94 Slawinski et al. (2015); Banerjee (2012).
95 Wittneben et al.
96 Newell and Paterson.
97 Banerjee (2012).
98 Bond.
99 Veal and Mouzas.
100 Slawinski et al.

7 Is customer–centric sustainability an element of marketing strategy?

Evidence from Indian firms

Prashant Mishra and Runa Sarkar

Introduction

Although considerable progress has been made to understand the importance of sustainable business practices in marketing and other management domains, more needs to be done to develop a meaningful and relevant framework that synthesizes the sustainability literature with prevailing trends in marketing. There is also a need to recognize that this framework itself may be different for the developing world, as compared to its Western counterpart where the concept of sustainability was first mooted. This is primarily because consumer awareness and expectations in the developing context can be quite different from that in the developed world. In the developing world, where sensitivity to price is very high, it would be interesting to see how consumers' view sustainability attributes. A look at extant literature indicates that the two key purposes of marketing strategy are (1) to influence consumer preferences and (2) to enable a company to attain and sustain competitive advantage (Varadarajan, 2010; Chabowski et al., 2011).

Further, while marketing efforts could be made in different domains, including, for example, a firms supply chain and R&D activity, what is clear is that the marketplace tends to appraise the impact of marketing efforts primarily by evaluating the marketing assets created by the firm. Externally focused sustainability measures that are 'visible' have the most influential position on marketing assets (Buysse and Verbeke, 2003). These include pricing, product introduction, promotions and advertising and distribution activities. Responsible product stewardship, especially after the consumer has already bought the product, is another visible marketing activity that can go a long way towards developing customer-centric sustainability. Theoretically, this is in line with the capabilities based resource perspective, where the value of your marketing assets reflects the quality of marketing capability in the firm and the extent to which the firm is embedded in the marketplace.

In this context, one of the six universal premises to which eco-centric marketing strategies should adhere is to educate people about their individual responsibility towards the environment and other species (Borland and Lindgreen, 2013). The impact that marketing strategy can have over consumer preferences implicitly puts the onus of environmentally responsible behaviour on the decision makers within a firm. One approach, proposed by Sheth et al. (2011), is the concept of customer centric-sustainability (CCS) as a metric of performance of the inclusion of sustainability concerns in marketing strategy. CCS outcomes are those that result from customer directed business actions and are personally consequential for customers. In other words, CCS is defined as the consumption mediated impact of marketing actions on environmental, social and economic well-being of the consumer.

The purpose of this chapter is to contribute towards the discourse on sustainability by advancing the understanding of the sustainability agenda in marketing with a customer-centric approach. To fulfil this purpose, we examined the current state of practice and strategic thinking concerning sustainability in organizations operating in an emerging market setting (India in this case) and explored whether the firms are responding to the customer-centric challenges of sustainability. India was chosen not only because of familiarity with the country but also as one of the largest emerging markets at the forefront of climate change debate, an understanding of how firms view and practice sustainability is of paramount importance. We interviewed senior executives responsible for sustainability agenda and marketing function together to gather first-hand insight into business decision making. Further, we also examined, from the firm's perspective, how their marketing strategies impact the Indian customers' sustainable consumption decisions. The outcome of the study contributes towards a better understanding of how firms in India view a customer-centric approach towards sustainability. In the process we have explored the factors driving or inhibiting the adoption of customer-centric sustainability (CCS) approach in emerging market firms.

The chapter is organized as follows. The next section provides the theoretical backdrop. Literature surrounding the interconnectedness of sustainability, strategic orientation and marketing theory followed by more marketing practice oriented studies is highlighted. Following this, the research methodology adopted for this study is discussed. Section 3 presents the findings of the study and attempts to draw some broad generalizations about the thinking and practice of Indian enterprise in general towards a customer-centric approach in addressing sustainability issues. The propositions posited would serve as the basis for further research, both in terms of depth as well as comprehensiveness, so as to draw more substantive conclusions. Finally, some concluding thoughts on the state of sustainability and marketing practice in India are presented for the reader to deliberate on.

Sustainability, marketing theory and practice

Sustainability is regarded as a critically important business goal by multiple stakeholders, including investors, customers and policymakers (Epstein and Roy, 2003; Nidumolu et al., 2009; Pfeffer, 2010). For the purpose of understanding sustainability in the context of business in a market based economy one has to inherently assume a philosophy of weak sustainability. This refers to an assumption that natural capital and man-made capital is fully substitutable and hence takes a middle ground between the neo-liberal economists and the eco-fascists (Hopwood et al., 2005). Furthermore, thoughts on the influence of corporate concern for sustainability on the development of marketing theory are not well documented (Kilbourne, 1998; Sharma et al., 2007). Part of the reason for this may be that sustainability is an interdisciplinary concept, rooted in several scientific disciplines and does not belong to any one. Researchers further noted that currently prevalent sustainability strategies have three major deficiencies: they do not directly focus on the customer, they do not recognize the looming threats from rising global over-consumption, and they do not take a holistic approach (Sheth et al., 2011). In the context of marketing strategy, they argue that differences in stakeholder orientation get reflected in the sustainability practices of companies, and this in turn influences the company's sustainability performance. In most sustainability initiatives of business, however, the customer is not in the foreground as a stakeholder, and as a consequence, strategic initiatives (including marketing strategy) also do not address customer-centric issues in sustainability adequately.

Based on an extensive review of sustainability-related issues and research streams in marketing a typology of sustainability capabilities was proposed based on their focus (internal vs. external), emphasis (social vs. environmental) and intent (discretionary, ethical or legal). They suggest that sustainability initiatives can have an influence on marketing assets (Chabowski et al., 2011). Other researchers have discussed the role of marketing in addressing sustainability through the environmental dimension, and through challenges such as responsible consumption (Cronin et al., 2011; Sharma et al., 2010; Huang and Rust, 2011).

The assertion that sustainable practices are critical for business profitability is strengthened by the notion that businesses can reduce environmental problems 'by finding new ways to produce, package, and deliver goods and services to consumers and disposing or recycling the wastes created in the production or consumption of these goods or services' (Menon and Menon, 1997; Varadarajan, 1992). Further, from the point of view of the marketing discourse, sustainability can be an effective way for a firm to differentiate its offerings and to achieve a position of competitive advantage (Porter and Van der Linde, 1995).

There are, however, several gaps and ambiguities which persist in the research on sustainability marketing. First, researchers often use the terms sustainability marketing with ecological marketing, green marketing and environmental marketing interchangeably although each has a different nuanced connotation (Fisk, 1974; Ottman, 1998; Coddington, 1992). Second is a relatively short-sighted understanding of sustainable organizational practices, where profit-orientation and survival goals in the long term are prioritized over socio-environmental concerns (Connelly et al., 2011). Third, often studies focus on some specific aspect of the sustainability agenda, such as, the environmental, economic or social dimension exclusively, which do not contribute significantly to the overall understanding of sustainability marketing (Nolan and Varey, 2014; Peattie and Peattie, 2009). These shortcomings result in raising doubts in the minds of marketing researchers and practitioners as to how to integrate the principles of sustainability successfully into marketing practice (Greenfield, 2004).

This approach is changing, with optimists leading the way, with research demonstrating that the number of consumers preferring to purchase from companies that care about sustainability is growing, thus emphasizing the need to restructure marketing to build in sustainability attributes (Kotler, 2011). However, there is sufficient counter-evidence that customer perceptions about sustainable products and services are not always equally positive, often due to their perceptions of certain trade-offs with the services the product is supposed to deliver (Barone et al., 2000; Olson, 2013). This is reiterated in other research where it is demonstrated that environmentally friendly products are perceived as less effective than regular products, and as a result, consumers expect to use (or actually use) more of the product as a means to compensate for their perceived lack in efficacy (Lin and Chang, 2012). Such consumer behaviour defeats the purpose of developing such products, aimed at reducing their ecological footprint.

It is of great concern that despite an increasing presence of initiatives to leverage marketing toward the promotion of sustainable practices, and servicing niche markets comprising environment-friendly customers, many papers continue to report strong consumer resistance to the purchase and consumption of products that reduce both the carbon footprint of their actions and current consumption patterns (Laroche et al., 2001; Chernatony et al., 2000; Cherrier, 2012). What is reported is that in most instances, products featuring sustainability attributes are attractive to a consumer only if the other more salient features of the product are not only present but also meet consumer expectations (Jagel et al., 2012; Lim et al., 2014). Further, a failure to account for such concerns could result in customers becoming more averse to the purchase of goods with sustainability attributes (Carrington et al., 2014; Vermeir and Verbeke, 2006). Thus, the challenge to bring together marketing and sustainability practices so as to bring out desirable consumer behaviour and influence consumer choices till the point that their preferences shift to the use of green products remains an area of considerable study (Rettie et al., 2012; Thogersen and Zhou, 2012). Marketing Strategy is probably the best means to try and achieve this change in consumer behaviour so as to achieve the sustainability agenda.

Academia has its fair share of sceptics who do not believe in the compatibility of marketing and sustainability. They continue to criticize the discipline of marketing for its role in driving the growth in global consumption (Jones et al., 2008). But as discussed above, the potential for marketing to contribute solutions driven by the growing synergies between sustainability and marketing strategy is evident (Ferdous, 2010). The issue of cost still needs to be addressed. Attaining sustainability may lead firms to increase costs to resource constrained end consumers, leading to affordability issues (Charter et al., 2002).

While there are two distinct arguments for bringing in the all-encompassing perspective of sustainability to marketing strategy, one ethical and the other pragmatic, the focus of the literature surveyed here and our chapter is on the pragmatic argument. This view posits that because the entire global society, planetary resources and economy is interlinked in a complex manner, outcomes in one area of interest cannot be delivered effectively and efficiently without accounting for other happenings in the rest of the 'system' – the social and environmental spheres (Elkington, 1999, Sutton, 2004). In this context, integrating sustainability into marketing efforts can be a win–win game, as it is about value co-creation that can be maintained over time, and about influencing consumer tastes in the right direction (Vargo and Lusch, 2004).

A second pragmatic argument for integration of sustainability into marketing is that sustainability strategies are best delivered through marketing because facilitation of sustainable production and consumption efforts are the inherent responsibilities of the marketing department. Since marketers are often in direct contact with all stakeholders of an organization, they can focus on understanding and changing organizational behaviour, through internal marketing, or consumer behaviour, through marketing campaigns and marketing mix strategies (Merrilees et al., 2005; Clulow, 2005; Andreasen, 2002; George, 1990; Yoo et al.; 2000). Further, as the many theories and practices in marketing are evolve to address new trends and events in the marketplace, both locally and globally, they can easily also incorporate sustainability concerns (Doyle, 1995; Lusch, 2007). As it develops strategies on the basis of analyses of consumers, competitors and other environmental forces, which it then combines with other strategic inputs (e.g. financial, research and development, and human resources) to arrive at an integrated holistic strategic blueprint (Jobber, 2010), marketing presents itself as a natural home for the advancement of greater sustainability through the development of increasingly sound marketing strategies. Finally, arguments about changing behaviour and harnessing creativity and innovation are typically couched in growth jargon, which is often considered one of the hallmarks of marketing (Jones et al., 2008; Hauser et al., 2006; Schmitt, 1999). Arguably, the co-integration of sustainability and marketing would enable consumers and firms to advance the global initiatives for sustainability. To conclude, marketing could conceivably play a major part in moving society toward a more self-sufficient and sustainable future.

Thus, the challenge is to understand the role of marketing in changing consumer behaviour, such as by influencing perceptions, attitudes, beliefs, actual behaviour and business perspectives, to move toward sustainability. While these are all logical reasons why marketing as a function should play a pivotal role in sustainability strategy, there is little research, especially in the developing world context, which documents actual practices of leading firms.

Research methodology

The objective of our study is to further the understanding of the state of sustainability practice and its linkages with customer-centric thought in leading Indian organizations. Eight leading firms, operating in different industries with relatively large market shares in their industry were chosen for the exercise, while keeping in mind a need for variety, so as to arrive at conclusions that are robust and applicable to a developing economy. In addition to reviewing the sustainability reports and websites of the chosen firms to get detailed insights into their profitability, marketing initiatives and sustainability practices, we conducted in-depth interviews with ten senior executives from these diverse set of corporations. They were directly responsible for the firm's sustainability initiatives and had a top-down view of the firm's sustainability practices. The respondents for the interviews were serious, and more than willing to share their views despite fairly busy schedules, given the objectives of our research, outcomes of which they believed would help them. The target participants were selected through a process of purposive sampling in which we tried to interview executives from those Indian firms which are at forefront in implementing sustainability based initiatives in Indian setting. Table 7.1 gives the description of companies that were interviewed in this research. Efforts were made to interview companies from diverse business areas so that they were representative of the business scenario in India. For example, for some of these sustainability departments were embedded within the firm and for others they were standalone divisions.

In-depth interviews, using a semi-structured questionnaire were considered as a method for research as it combines structure with flexibility and this structure is sufficiently flexible to permit topics to be covered at the convenience of the interviewee to allow responses to be fully probed and explored (Legard et al., 2003). The interviews were undertaken between October 2015 to February 2016 and covered companies with sustainability initiatives and individuals who were connected with the initiatives.

A semi-structured questionnaire was followed so that the respondents had the opportunity to give as much detail as possible and create a narrative that was not dictated by just the research objectives. Wherever possible, face-to-face interviews were the preferred mode of interaction. However, most interviews were conducted over the telephone as this was more convenient. For one firm, the interviewee completed the questionnaire over email. Transcripts of the interviews were shared with the interviewees, and a sign-off obtained, to ensure that there was a minimal chance of misinterpretation. We

Table 7.1 Descriptions of the firm covered in the study

Organizations in India	Industry	Description of business
Firm 1	B2C – FMCG	Indian consumer goods arm of a global FMCG giant
Firm 2	B2B – Automotive	Tyre supplier to the automobile industry
Firm 3	B2C – Fast food	Among the world's largest chain of fast food restaurants
Firm 4	B2C – Finance	Among the world's largest banking and financial organizations
Firm 5	B2B (evolving to B2C) – Finance	Specialized infrastructure finance group of firms, which have recently diversified into commercial banking
Firm 6	B2C – FMCG	Multi-business enterprise with a footprint in fast moving consumer goods, hotels, paper, packaging, agribusiness and information technology
Firm 7	B2C – Finance/ e-commerce	Startup in the online money payment transaction platform domain
Firm 8	B2B – Steel	Large business conglomerate, operating in the steel, cement, energy and infrastructure sectors in India and abroad

B2C – Business to Consumer.
B2B – Business to Business.

interviewed the respondents on a range of issues including their firm's view on sustainability, different stakeholders, firm's sustainability initiatives, business linkages of sustainability initiatives, linkages with financial and non-financial performance outcomes, etc. Interviews were content analysed using key words based on which underlying themes emerged leading to the propositions (Chachamu, 2015). The evidence collected in these interviews is presented in the next section.

FMCG – Fast Moving Consumer Goods.

Findings and discussion

As already discussed, the objective of this study was to understand how firms operationalized their sustainability objectives into marketing strategy, in general, and a customer-centric sustainability approach in particular. We started with exploring the firms' understanding of, attitude towards and practice of sustainability. This was followed by an attempt to gain insights as to what these market leaders perceive to be their sustainability challenges, and whether they are industry or firm specific. This would help us understand the thrust of sustainability initiatives of the firms. The link between sustainability and firm strategy was explored next, to assess the extent of integration of sustainability into the firm's business decisions. Finally, we zeroed in on the objective of our study, that is, whether market leaders in India have adopted a customer-centric sustainability approach, and understanding the drivers for the same.

Our qualitative analysis led us to classify our findings into four broad themes, starting with how the firms operationalized the concept of sustainability within their domain, sustainability challenges identified by the firms, strategic orientation of sustainability initiatives and finally customer-centric sustainability. What follows are the findings related to the link between customer-centricity and sustainability initiatives of the firms. Four broad propositions are presented, which could serve as research hypotheses to be tested in future studies with appropriate methodology and data.

Customer-centricity relates to the role of the firm in influencing the consumer to display more responsible behaviour in the context of sustainability. Literature laments that the firm is not doing enough in this regard, considering the current situation of global over-consumption (Epstein, 2003). This could be due to 'sustainability marketing myopia', a distortion stemming from an exaggerated focus on the socio-environmental attributes of a sustainable product at the expense of customer benefits and values, thus distorting the marketing process and likely leading to product failure (Belz and Peattie, 2009). Researchers in the past contended that the main reason consumers do not buy into sustainability products and practices is the belief that they require sacrifices, such as inconvenience, higher costs and lower performance, without any added perceived benefit of significant socio-environmental conservation and advancement[41]. Hence there is some resistance on the part of firms to be customer-centric. The disconnect between marketing and sustainability as noted by studies such as Roper (2002) was evident in our study as well, best expressed by Firm 4, when it said:

> Corporate Sustainability is a separate function in itself. It is not a part of Marketing, HR or Corporate Affairs. It is recognized as a separate function … For example, when we are working on skill or when we are working on water, it is through community investments which are grants, there is no lending to it. Sustainable finance is the only initiative where we facilitate business. In that too the facilitation part remains with the Corporate Sustainability, the business remains with business.

It was apparent from our discussions with the firms that while there are is niche set of consumers who value sustainability, and are willing to pay a premium for products and services that embody an element of sustainability in them, the marketing strategies of the firms are formulated keeping the average consumer in mind. The average consumer is not necessarily sensitized to and aware of sustainability issues, and often has the misconception that an environmental friendly product has lower quality attributes as compared to a regular product. As Firm 1 shared with us,

> We find that the consumer is reasonably isolated and on an island compared to all the work that's happening on sustainability. We have a formulation of a product that is a shower gel concentrate which uses lesser product, less water allowing you to have a bath of a quality of a regular bath when we were looking to market this product, consumers who were willing to buy this product for its sustainability intent was limited. We found consumers will not compromise on the quality of their bath – despite agreeing that sustainability is important. Intent and action are different there … While sustainability is a big word, I think it is something which has yet to catch on with the consumers. Consumers are still guided by the experience they

have with the product, the value they get it at rather than the sustainability benefits it provides them. It's different in the West, and possibly gradually changing here but we have a long way to go.

As a result of this, most firms tend to separate out customer experience from their sustainability initiatives. For a customer-centric firm like Firm 3,

> The customer will never find a change as for him it is completely business as usual with expectations having been met. But expectations have never been compromised but we have made whatever changes as a backend to ensure that our footprint doesn't grow beyond what it is already. How much of it is optic and how much of it is real only God knows.

Firm 6 summarizes the outlook of the average consumer as the unwillingness of markets, whether financial or product, to reward sustainability. In their words,

> See the first challenge is the fact that markets still do not reward sustainability. Ultimately, if no one is giving you any premium for being sustainable, there is no incentive provided by markets and therefore, you are depending on corporate conscience, not on a value proposition. If markets rewarded sustainability, that would become a value proposition for marketing to customers. So if we can make markets work for sustainability, the point is how can you get consumers to support sustainable companies? If the power of consumer franchise drives sustainability, then there is a financial dimension and investors will also go there. However, how would you distinguish a sustainable company from someone else? For consumers to make an enlightened consumer choice, there has to be education. So we are talking about creating a 'trustmark' for customer choice … Unless markets reward such practices, no one differentiates you as sustainable.

Based on the outcomes and analysis of our interviews, we put forward the following proposition:

P1: Firms first prioritize customer experience, and then sustainability, when it comes to marketing practice.

As a result of the myopic outlook of consumers, Firm 1 commented that:

> you know sustainability for me is something which may not essentially be consumer facing in a very large way, because the customer may not be ready.

This probably points to the maturity of the Indian consumer market, but this is a research issue for future study. An outcome of this understanding has been to adopt a product-centric approach to sustainability. For instance, when the Firm 8 group was asked to provide an example of a sustainability initiative it has taken up, it provided the following as one of many instances:

> One could be in the setting up of a subsidiary company to manufacture value-added products as a 'downstream' operation to meet unmet needs of customers rather than

sell intermediates that they would need either further processing, or items that would be imported. These coated metals (galvanised, or vinyl coated metals) that are used in manufacture of white goods.

Firm 7, the newest firm that we interviewed (it has been around for less than a year) said:

> Okay, for example, the social media handle; all of it, we experiment with a new app or a new technology. We use it to gather feedback from all our users. And those feedbacks are considered and much more cost effective measures are developed. That's how we are using customer centricity in our marketing process.

Thus we can conclude that:

P2: Firms tend to adopt a product-centric approach rather than a customer-centric approach to sustainability.

Over time, however, as sustainability initiatives mature in a firm, then regardless of the level of maturity of the consumer, firms tend to move closer towards customer-centric sustainability.

Firm 3, which is relatively new in India, practises all the sustainability initiatives that its parent company has adopted. Yet it has not really adopted a customer-centric approach for which it believes one needs to be in the business for a longer period of time. In its words,

> The time frame of the limited number of years in the business is such that whatever we do at our backend may not be translated right now into front end consumer awareness ... Product A has done it only in the past 7 years till then they were also selling us as much soaps as it could. How does this (sustainability initiatives) change into a consumer proposition, that is something we have not yet come to.

Firm 1 traced it trajectory from product-centricity to customer-centricity as follows:

> Around 2008, internally from a company point of view there was an emphasis on having a sustainability goal to meet all the challenges of the company. The Firm was keenly aware that if we wanted to build a business for the future, it was imperative that Sustainability needed to sit at its heart. Till now a lot of the work on Product A we were doing on sustainability was largely around ensuring that formulations and innovations were environment friendly, that they did not lead to an increased carbon footprint and so on; things we still continue to do today through our practices, our formulations. There are certain ingredients we do not use because we know they are not good for the environment, even though our competitors use them to their benefit. And we constantly seek to innovate around sustainability. Seven years ago we explored the possibility of impacting sustainability through consumer behavior change. That has now led us to deploy programmes on the ground that help change the hygiene behaviours of a million people. We envelop this under the campaign of 'Help A Child Reach 5', and have proven to change the handwashing behaviours of over 250mn people in India itself. With this our sustainability agenda spans the spectrum of being product centric to consumer centric.

Further, to provide evidence of its customer-centricity, it provided the following anecdotal evidence:

> And just to give you an idea, typically in a category like laundry, only 8% may be our impact, in say water will be in our manufacturing operation, and the larger impact, about 60% of the impact, environmental impact will be at the consumer use stage. So, we have taken responsibility end-to-end.

Firms with a longer history of taking sustainability initiatives (such as Firm 6 or Firm 1 in our data set) tend to be more consumer-centric in nature, evolving from a product approach to begin with. These firms focused on the potential of marketing and distribution networks to find solutions to the sustainability problems created by business in the past, as proposed in literature (Belz and Peattie, 2009). Firm 6 explained to us how, almost two decades back, the deeds of sustainability were sown into its decision making.

> There are two parts to it. One is what would be the competitive business strategy of the firm, and second, what would be the way of conducting our businesses. These were two different things that we looked at. So in the first phase of what we called as business re-structuring, business portfolio rationalization and augmentation were done. This was in 1996, when we were already an 80 year old company. It was not a new company and had gone through lots of upheavals already. Our business re-structuring stemmed from a superordinate vision, a vision of becoming an engine of growth for the Indian economy. The mission was to make a significant and growing contribution to the Indian economy, while simultaneously continuing to serve society. This was the important part, as it made societal value creation, not just mere shareholder value creation, the primary purpose of business. I think it was a very important departure. The purpose of companies across the world has and will be shareholder value creation. How to make your societal value creation your goal and still meet the purpose of shareholder value creation was an important part of our sustainability innovation.

Based on our findings, we propose that:

P3: Firms with a longer history of sustainability initiatives are more customer-centric in nature.

Among firms, the belief was well entrenched that visible sustainability measures have a direct impact on the brand value of an asset. This is in line with the arguments put forth by researchers in the past (Jones et al., 2008). In other words, the market evaluates the impact of sustainability initiatives based on how it has influenced the marketing assets created by the firm. Firm 7, for example, has kept this in mind, even as it tries to build its brand, develop customer loyalty and try to make a profit in its fledgling business.

> I mean, sustainable and competitive advantage, speed is the key. Next is all about tie ups, our business is deeply integrated with the end user. Banks they have not been able to adapt themselves to this change, the digital one. We are there to serve the consumer, and they are the ones whose convenience matters and banks will not

allow their systems to be changed to meet the end consumers' needs So the other competitive advantage is building that kind of trust in the ecosystem, in terms of people, terms of technology, the kind of past relationships that can help you sustain a network and relationship. Other is deep integration with the customers by reaching out to them and trying to service their needs from their point of view.

Firm 1 recognizes how the Parent Company Sustainability Plan has positively impacted its brand value across countries.

The Parent Company Sustainable Living Plan has made a big difference in really embedding sustainability in the company, in our everyday business. This is not separate from the business; it's not that we have a separate set of people who are driving the sustainability agenda, no. The core team of marketing and brand managers, who have the responsibility of the business and the brand, that's the team that is responsible for its sustainability agenda

Further, it explains how sustainability is completely integrated into its marketing strategy.

so it's absolutely at the heart of marketing, Globally about 50% of the Parent Company's growth comes from brands which contribute to sustainable living. And these brands are growing, much faster than other brands. And its easy to see why. For a brand like Product A, every bar of soap sold impacts business, obviously, it also has a positive impact on the health and hygiene in a community. Business and sustainable impact go hand in hand.

Firm 6 has successfully bridged the gap between being a responsible consumer, minimizing her use of resources and indulging herself in the luxuries of life by promoting 'responsible luxury'.

for example, for the entire hotels branding, we went through a lot of processes. The primary task of the sales function was to sell premium luxury accommodation. Now a green element to them at that point in time was like selling an ecotel, which is completely different. Essentially, the challenge for the marketing team was that if we pegged our hotels as green hotels, it would take away from the luxury proposition to consumers. Now, here my proposition is that I am not just selling rooms, I am selling luxurious sleep, so I am investing in, say, giving you a choice of 20 pillows. However, the challenge was how to deliver the best of green practices and still give that kind of luxury. So we defined the concept, 'Responsible Luxury'. Therefore, while luxurious sleep is still what we market, we also highlight that you can sleep with a clear conscience as I am not burdening you with the fact that your lifestyle choices could be polluting the environment, because the hotel is compensating for that in other ways.

Further, to address the challenge it pointed our previously about markets not rewarding sustainability, Firm 6 has taken several initiatives to enlighten the consumer, so as to obtain its brand loyalty.

So how do you help the consumer make an enlightened choice? I'll give you an example of notebooks. We had put on the back cover that every rupee you are going to spend on the notebook, a certain amount would go into education of underprivileged children. Even now, after so many years, people write saying that they buy notebooks because of this. But cause-based marketing doesn't work in everything in India. It didn't work for us in every area. How do you develop a kind of trustmark for consumers which is based on not just the green performance but entire triple bottom line performance?

It was evident from our discussions that:

P4: Firms understand and leverage the idea of strengthening their marketing assets using sustainability initiatives.

Conclusions

This study on the marketing practices of firms considered to be sustainability champions in their respective domains in India goes a long way in understanding the how they view a customer-centric approach towards sustainability, and what the ground realities are. It is evident that the customer experience cannot be compromised at any cost, even if it means taking compensating action for over indulgence, as conveyed by the term 'responsible luxury'. Further, owing to its amorphous nature and difficulty in quantifying the benefits accruing from sustainability, it is usually easier to take a product-centric approach towards implementing sustainability initiatives and marketing them rather than a customer-centric approach. This is in line with the earlier findings reported by Buysse and Verbeke (2003), who argued that visible sustainability measures including pricing, product introduction, promotions and advertising and distribution activities are most favoured by the firms. The implications of this in the long term could be the implementation of several disjoint measures, which may not add up as effectively as a customer-centric approach would. However, as the sustainability initiatives of a firm mature, their strategies evolve from being product-centric to more customer-centric in nature. This is primarily because the sustainability initiatives start having a positive impact on the marketing assets (brand) of the firm, and the adoption of the CCS approach is the best way to leverage that strength.

One of the key concerns that emerge from our study, however, is that, overall, customer-centricity is an attribute of exemplary practice, used only by sustainability leaders rather than the norm among firms in emerging markets. This appears to be primarily because of the belief that markets do not reward sustainability, that is, while the average customers does appreciate sustainable attributes, they are far more demanding of the utility that the product or service is designed to produce. Olson (2013) in his study of Norwegian consumers came to a similar conclusion. He argued that customer perceptions about sustainable products and services are not always equally positive leading to 'value–action gaps that are created by green attribute tradeoffs, which limit the market share and environmental impact of green products'. However, there are others who believe that there is a trend towards increasing demand for products or services that have better environmental and social attributes (Frenkel and Scott, 2002). This is a challenge for any firm that aspires to adopt a CCS approach, as well as for policy makers, who must improve consumer awareness and initiate a change in consumer behaviours that their relative valuation of sustainability in terms of their willingness to pay improves. Firms in emerging markets are also constantly exploring about how marketing function in a firm can influence the changes to individual consumption practices so that sustainable consumption practices become central and not peripheral to individual and communal consumption. This theme needs more exploration and can be a significant area of research for future efforts.

The study also indicates that marketing as a discipline and practice has an opportunity to contribute significantly to the understanding of sustainability, its boundaries, its merits and its viability as a focus for organizations' future operations. One significant thought which emerges from this study is the view that customer-centric sustainability depends on effectively building and managing relationship with various stakeholders. This could also relate to internal stakeholders. Thus, the narratives from Firm 1 and Firm 6 clearly demonstrate how sustainability has become a shared value across the organization. Such enterprises are referred to as transparent organizations where cross-departmental communication results in a high level of empowerment among employees to implement the sustainability goals of the organization (Baldassarre and Campo, 2016). The organizations studied as part of this study acknowledge the need to manage a wider set of stakeholders rather than attending to the financial performance goals of the firm as perhaps their sole responsibility. Though 'customers' are seen as the firm's most important stakeholders, there is growing recognition of the fact that strategically managing relationships with multiple stakeholders is important. A closer look at interactions with the firms as part of this study also indicates that marketing has potential to remodel its current focus from managing customer relationships (and other stakeholders) to managing a broader set of marketplace issues involving economic, environmental and social dimensions and thus catering to the to the needs and wants of multiple stakeholders.

An element of hope emerging from this study arises from the attitude of firms in emerging markets towards sustainability that is best summed up by Firm 6 as:

> we practice sustainability, not just because it's the right thing to do, but because that is what is going to make it a future ready organization, because we believe that we will not be able to survive in the long run without it.

References

Andreasen, A.R. (2002). Marketing social marketing in the social change marketplace. *Journal of Public Policy and Marketing*, 21(1): 3–13.

Baldassarre, F. and Campo, R. (2016). Sustainability as a marketing tool: To be or to appear to be? *Business Horizons*, 59(4): 421–429.

Barone, M.J., Miyazaki, A.D. and Taylor, K.A. (2000). The influence of cause-related marketing on consumer choice: Does one good turn deserve another? *Journal of the Academy of Marketing Science*, 28(2): 248–262.

Belz, F.M. and Peattie, K. (2009). *Sustainability Marketing: A Global Perspective*. Chichester: Wiley.

Borland, H. and Lindgreen, A. (2013). Sustainability, epistemology, ecocentric business, and marketing strategy: Ideology, reality, and vision. *Journal of Business Ethics*, 117(1): 173–187.

Buysse, K. and Verbeke, A. (2003). Proactive environmental strategies: A stakeholder management perspective. *Strategic Management Journal*, 24(5): 453–470.

Carrington, M.J., Neville, B.A. and Whitwell, G.J. (2014). Lost in translation: Exploring the ethical consumer intention–behavior gap. *Journal of Business Research*, 67(1): 2759–2767.

Chabowski, B.R., Mena, J.A. and Gonzalez-Padron, T.L. (2011). The structure of sustainability research in marketing, 1958–2008: A basis for future research opportunities. *Journal of the Academy of Marketing Science*, 39(1): 55–70.

Chachamu, N. (2015). Stephanie Taylor, *What is Discourse Analysis?* and Reiner Keller, *Doing Discourse Research: An Introduction for Social Scientists*. *Qualitative Research*, 15: 405–406. doi:10.1177/1468794114535049.

Charter, M., Peattie, K., Ottman, J., et al. (2002). *Marketing and Sustainability*. Cardiff: BRASS Centre.

Chernatony, L., Harris, F. and Riley, F.D. (2000). Added value: Its nature, roles and sustainability. *European Journal of Marketing*, 34 (1/2): 39–56.

Cherrier, H., Szuba, M. and Ozcaglar-Toulouse, N. (2012). Barriers to downward carbon emission: Exploring sustainable consumption in the face of the glass floor. *Journal of Marketing Management*, 28(3/4): 397–419.

Clulow, V. (2005). Future dilemmas for marketers: Can stakeholder analysis add value? *European Journal of Marketing*, 39(9/10): 978–997.

Coddington, W. (1992). *Environmental Marketing*. New York: McGraw-Hill.

Connelly, B.L., Ketchen Jr, D.J. and Slater, S.F. (2011). Toward a 'theoretical toolbox' for sustainability research in marketing. *Journal of the Academy of Marketing Science*, 39(1): 86–100.

Cronin, J.J., Smith, J., Gleim, M., Ramirez, E. and Martinez, J. (2011). Green marketing strategies: An examination of stakeholders and the opportunities they present. *Journal of the Academy of Marketing Science*, 39(1): 158–174.

Doyle, P. (1995). Marketing in the new millennium. *European Journal of Marketing*, 29(13): 23–41.

Elkington, J. (1999). *Cannibals with Forks: The Triple Bottom Line of 21st Century Business*. Oxford: Capstone Publishing.

Epstein, M.J. and Roy, M.J. (2003). Making the business case for sustainability. *Journal of Corporate Citizenship*, 2003(9): 79–96.

Ferdous, A.S. (2010). Applying the theory of planned behavior to explain marketing managers perspectives on sustainable marketing. *Journal of International Consumer Marketing*, 2: 313–325.

Fisk, G. (1974). *Marketing and the Ecological Crisis*. New York: Harper & Row.

Frenkel, S.J. and Scott, D. (2002). Compliance, collaboration, and codes of practice. *California Management Review*, 45(1): 29–49.

George, W.R. (1990). Internal marketing and organizational behavior: A partnership in developing customer-conscious employees at every level. *Journal of Business Research*, 20(1): 63–70.

Greenfield, W.M. (2004). In the name of corporate social responsibility. *Business Horizons*, 47(1): 19–28.

Hauser, J., Tellis, G.J. and Griffin, A. (2006). Research on innovation: A review and agenda for marketing science. *Marketing Science*, 25(6): 687–717.

Hopwood, B., Mellor, M. and O'Brien, G. (2005). Sustainable development: Mapping different approaches. *Sustainable Development*, 13(1): 38–52.

Huang, M.H. and Rust, R.T. (2011). Sustainability and consumption. *Journal of the Academy of Marketing Science*, 39(1): 40–54.

Jagel, T., Keeling, K. Reppel, A., et al. (2012). Individual values and motivational complexities in ethical clothing consumption: A means-end approach. *Journal of Marketing Management*, 28(3/4): 373–396.

Jobber, D. (2010). *Principles and Practice of Marketing*. Maidenhead: McGraw-Hill Education.

Jones, P., Hill, C.C., Comfort, D., et al. (2008). Marketing and sustainability. *Marketing Intelligence and Planning*, 26(2): 123–130.

Kilbourne, W.E. (1998). Green marketing: A theoretical perspective. *Journal of Marketing Management*, 14(6): 641–655.

Kotler, P. (2011). Reinventing marketing to manage the environmental imperative. *Journal of Marketing*, 75(4): 132–135.

Laroche, M., Bergeron, J. and Barbaro-Forleo, G. (2001). Targeting consumers who are willing to pay more for environmentally friendly products. *Journal of Consumer Marketing*, 18(6): 503–520.

Legard, R., Keegan, J. and Ward, K. (2003). In-depth interviews. In J. Ritchie and J. Lewis (eds), *Qualitative Research Practice: A Guide for Social Science Students and Researchers*. London: SAGE, pp. 138–169.

Lim, W.M., Yong, J.L.S. and Suryadi, K. (2014). Consumers' perceived value and willingness to purchase organic food. *Journal of Global Marketing*, 27(5): 298–307.

Lin, L. and Chang, C. (2012). Double standard: The role of environmental consciousness in green product usage. *Journal of Marketing*, 76(5): 125–134.

Lusch, R.F. (2007). Marketing's evolving identity: Defining our future. *Journal of Public Policy and Marketing*, 26(2): 261–268.

Menon, A. and Menon, A. (1997). Enviropreneurial marketing strategy: The emergence of corporate environmentalism as market strategy. *The Journal of Marketing*, 6(1): 51–67.

Merrilees, B., Getz, D. and O'Brien, D. (2005). Marketing stakeholder analysis: Branding the Brisbane Goodwill Games. *European Journal of Marketing*, 39(9/10): 1060–1077.

Nidumolu, R., Prahalad, C.K. and Rangaswami, M.R. (2009). Why sustainability is now the key driver of innovation. *Harvard Business Review*, 87(9): 56–64.

Nolan, T. and Varey, R.J. (2014). Re-cognising the interactive space: Marketing for social transformation. *Marketing Theory*, 14(4): 431–450.

Olson, E.L. (2013). It's not easy being green: The effects of attribute tradeoffs on green product preference and choice. *Journal of the Academy of Marketing Science*, 41(2): 171–184.

Ottman, J.A. (1998). *Green Marketing: Opportunity for Innovation*. Lincolnwood, IL: NTC Business Books.

Peattie, K. and Peattie, S. (2009). Social marketing: A pathway to consumption reduction? *Journal of Business Research*, 62(2): 260–268.

Pfeffer, J. (2010). Building sustainable organizations: The human factor. *Academy of Management Perspectives*, 24(1): 34–45.

Porter, M.E. and Van der Linde, C. (1995). Green and competitive: Ending the stalemate. *Harvard Business Review*, 73(5): 120–134.

Rettie, R., Burchell, K. and Riley, D. (2012). Normalising green behaviours: A new approach to sustainability marketing. *Journal of Marketing Management*, 28(3/4): 420–444.

Roper (2002). *Green Gauge 2002: Americans Perspective on Environmental Issues, Yes … But*. New York: Roper ASW and NOP World.

Schmitt, B. (1999). Experiential marketing. *Journal of Marketing Management*, 15(1–3): 53–67.

Sharma, A., Iyer, G.R., Mehrotra, A. and Krishnan, R. (2010). Sustainability and business-to-business marketing: A framework and implications. *Industrial Marketing Management*, 39(2): 330–341.

Sharma, S., Starik, M. and Husted, B. (2007). *Organizations and the Sustainability Mosaic: Crafting Long-Term Ecological and Societal Solutions*. Cheltenham: Edward Elgar.

Sheth, J.N., Sethia, N.K. and Srinivas, S. (2011). Mindful consumption: A customer-centric approach to sustainability. *Journal of the Academy of Marketing Science*, 39(1): 21–39.

Sutton, P. (2004). *A Perspective on Environmental Sustainability?* Victoria: Research and Strategy for Transition Initiation, Inc.

Thogersen, J. and Zhou, Y. (2012). Chinese consumers' adoption of 'green' innovation: The case of organic food. *Journal of Marketing Management*, 28(3/4): 313–333.

Varadarajan, P.R. (1992). Marketing's contribution to strategy: The view from a different looking glass. *Journal of the Academy of Marketing Science*, 20(4): 335–343.

Varadarajan, R. (2010). Strategic marketing and marketing strategy: Domain, definition, fundamental issues and foundational premises. *Journal of the Academy of Marketing Science*, 38(2): 119–140.

Vargo, S.L. and Lusch, R.F. (2004). Evolving to a new dominant logic for marketing. *Journal of Marketing*, 68(1): 1–17.

Vermeir, I. and Verbeke, W. (2006). Sustainable food consumption: Exploring the consumer 'attitude-behavioral intention' gap. *Journal of Agricultural and Environmental Ethics*, 19(2): 169–194.

Yoo, B., Donthu, N. and Lee, S. (2000). An examination of selected marketing mix elements and brand equity. *Journal of the Academy of Marketing Science*, 28(2): 195–211.

8 The importance of market and entrepreneurial strategic orientations among companies committed to sustainability values and practices

Jonas Nilsson, Johan Jansson, Gabriella Hed Vall and Frida Modig

Introduction

In the last few decades it has become ever more evident that humankind faces many serious environmental challenges (Rockström et al., 2009; Steffen et al., 2015). Here, the corporate world is often considered to be a key actor as corporate activity could both be argued to be the *cause* of many of the problems (Hopwood et al., 2005), but in various ways also hold the *solutions* to many of the challenges involved with establishing a sustainable economy (Hult, 2011; Porter et al., 2011). In the sustainability domain, however, individual companies differ greatly, and while some companies work in a genuine manner with sustainability issues, others are less attentive to devoting resources and time to these issues (EC, 2012; OECD, 2007). From a sustainability perspective, understanding the roots of these differences, and thereby allowing policy makers to design relevant regulation to increase sustainability, is therefore of utmost importance.

From a research perspective, one of the potentially important avenues that could be used to understand the differences in sustainability in the corporate sector is how individual companies, or their key decision-makers, relate to overall paradigms or worldviews. According to Shafer (2000) it has been argued for more than two decades that Western societies are undergoing a fundamental shift away from the old 'Dominant Social Paradigm (DSP)' towards a "New Environmental Paradigm'. Cotgrove (1982) as cited in Shafer (2000) suggests that the core values of the dominant social paradigm such as economic growth and domination over nature are being displaced by the realizations that the natural world possesses intrinsic value and that man must live in greater harmony with nature, i.e. the new environmental paradigm. Similarly, Dunlap and his colleagues (Van Liere and Dunlap 1980; Dunlap et al., 2000), argue that the core beliefs underlying the dominant social paradigm are being gradually displaced as it becomes more widely acknowledged that there are limits to economic growth, that humanity has the ability to upset the balance of nature, and that humanity does not possess an undisputable right to dominate and control nature. Indeed, a large body of literature has developed over the past three decades that question the assumptions underlying the economic, political and technological dimensions of the dominant Western worldview or paradigm (e.g. Jackson, 2005; Jackson, 2009; Shafer, 2000; Varey, 2010).

However, while an understanding of how decision-makers in companies relate to an ecological worldview could generate an understanding of drivers and barriers for corporate sustainability initiatives, few studies on ecological worldviews focus on how these values impact the decisions of corporations. On a more general level, when previous research has addressed the issues of corporate strategy and sustainability (Cassells and Lewis, 2011; Revell et al., 2010), it has often treated sustainability efforts as an add-on that companies do, in *addition* to focusing on their core business models. Less research has focused on how sustainability related concepts, such as the new environmental paradigm, are linked with core business strategies that companies develop to survive in the marketplace (Borland and Lindgreen, 2013; Hult, 2011). As integration of sustainability into day-to-day business practices (as opposed to just adding sustainability 'on top' of a business model) is likely to be one of the keys for a genuine transformation into a sustainable society (Borland and Lindgreen, 2013), this lack of focus on the relationship between current business models and strategies and sustainability is troubling.

One particularly important concept to understanding a company's business model and strategies is that of strategic orientation. In general, strategic orientation refers to 'the guiding principles that influence a firm's marketing and strategy-making activities. These activities represent the elements of the organization's culture that guide interactions with the marketplace, both with customers and competitors' (Noble et al., 2002, p. 25). Both in the general management literature and in the marketing literature, a firm's strategic orientation has been widely discussed. However, to date, few studies explore the connections between a firm's strategic orientation and how the company chooses to work with challenges revolving around sustainability and environmental issues.

Against this background, the purpose of this chapter is to classify companies using their strategic orientations and then compare them on their degree of *ecological worldview integration of sustainability concern, and sustainability* practices. In doing so, this chapter extends and complements the results of a previous paper (Jansson et al., 2017), where the main focus was on analysing relationships among the variables, rather than comparing and contrasting companies with various orientations. Values of individual managers are used in this study to gauge the entire organizations' sustainability commitment which is the primary analytical focus.

The chapter proceeds as follows. First, the theoretical framework is presented. Here, the concept of strategic orientation as well as the ecological worldview is presented and explained, and an analytical framework is presented. After this, a short presentation of the survey method ensues. Based on the analytical framework, we then discuss the different types of orientations in relation to how the company deals with sustainability in their strategies, culture and practical sustainability practices. Finally, these results are discussed and conclusions of the study are drawn.

Theoretical framework

Corporate strategy: market and entrepreneurial orientations

Strategy is about making choices (Porter and Kramer, 2006), and strategic orientation is an overarching direction focusing on the 'organization's culture that guide interactions with the marketplace' (Noble et al., 2002, p. 25). As such there are several different types of strategic orientations. Grinstein (2008) highlights the main strategic orientations as being: market, innovation, learning, entrepreneurial and employee orientations. Two of the most commonly studied orientations, are the market and entrepreneurial orientations (e.g. Baker and Sinkula, 2009; Miller, 1983; Oakley, 2012). These two orientations are also the focus of the present study, and discussed further below.

Market orientation and entrepreneurial orientation in relation to company sustainability initiatives

In many ways, both market- and entrepreneurial orientations are central concepts within the broad business and marketing literature, albeit in different ways. Market orientation is usually used to indicate a company that is focused on the customer, and bases its decisions on information about customers (e.g. Baker and Sinkula, 2009). However, while the focus of the customer is a key tenet of market orientation, there are numerous more specific definitions in the literature, such as the one by Kohli and Jaworski (1990, p. 6) who state that market orientation is '… the organizationwide generation of market intelligence pertaining to current and future customer needs, dissemination of the intelligence across the departments, and organizationwide responsiveness to it' and Narver and Slater (1990, p. 21) who define market orientation as '… the organizational culture that most effectively and efficiently creates the necessary behaviors for the creation of superior value for buyers and, thus, continuous superior performance for the business'. Oakley (2012) combines these definitions and considers market orientation to have three components: customer focus, coordination and planning, and an external focus. These three components form the basis of the present study.

Turning to entrepreneurial orientation, the emphasis is more internal. Here, the focus is usually on the company's ability to be innovative and proactive towards the market (Lumpkin and Dess, 1996). In a frequently cited paper, Miller (1983), outlines three components of entrepreneurial orientation; innovativeness, proactiveness and risk-taking. Here, innovativeness has been characterized as 'the firm's tendency to engage in and support new ideas, novelty, experimentation and creative processes that may result in new products, services, or technological processes' (Lumpkin and Dess, 1996, p. 142), while proactiveness has been described as '… the ability of firms to seize the initiative in the pursuit of marketplace opportunities' (Baker and Sinkula, 2009, p. 447). Finally, risk-taking is usually thought of as a measure of willingness to take risks to generate new opportunities (Baker and Sinkula, 2009; Miller, 1983;Lumpkin and Dess, 1996). In all, the entrepreneurially oriented company is one that is characterized by support for new products and solutions, that takes marketplace initiative and is willing to take risks to succeed.

While these two strategy concepts have been frequently addressed in the literature, few attempts have been made to highlight their possible relationships with sustainability performance. However, there are both conceptual grounds and some empirical insight that highlight the relevance of these concepts as to how the company addresses sustainability. For example, it is frequently argued that customers increasingly are demanding products that are more in line with long-term environmentally and socially sustainable development. From this perspective, market-oriented companies may be encouraged to adapt to customers and offer products that take environmental consideration, while entrepreneurially oriented companies may see potential for developing innovations that could be environmentally more sound than other products (e.g. Aragón-Correa., et al. 2008; Crittenden et al., 2011; Menguc and Ozanne, 2005).

Dominant and ecological worldviews

Human activity, such as business operations, is today the main force shaping the ecological system on planet Earth. Ecological sustainability has been defined as the capacity for continuance into the long-term future, by living within the constraints and limits of the biophysical world (Porritt, 2007). The planetary boundary concept, developed by Rockström, Steffen and colleagues, tries to estimate the boundaries for a safe operating space for humankind on the planet (e.g. Rockström et al., 2009; Steffen et al., 2015). Since the industrial revolution the planet has been used as a source for raw materials and a sink for waste. Little attention has been paid to how this approach has impacted the resilience of the fragile systems that all life depends upon. Even when environmental and sustainability issues have been considered, epistemologically an anthropocentric grounding, taking human dominance over nature for granted, has been at the core (Borland and Lindgreen, 2013). This anthropocentric view has been related paradigmatically to the dominant social paradigm which is built on reductionist, rational and competitive thought pillars. As such this paradigm has also been termed business as usual, i.e. the current state of affairs where economic growth is at the centre of most societal assumptions and activities (Borland and Lindgreen, 2013; Daly, 2005; Varey, 2010). Lately the dominant social paradigm has been tested among business students (Kilbourne et al., 2002), and also been related to materialism in seven industrial market-based economies (Kilbourne et al., 2009).

As a contrast to the dominant social paradigm stands the new environmental (or ecological) paradigm. From a business perspective, according to Jonker and Marberg (2007), this paradigm holds that the production, consumption and employment practices that are currently being carried out by business are unethical and environmentally unsustainable in the long run. According to the overview provided by Borland and Lindgreen (2013), the new ecological paradigm for example builds on an ecocentric grounding with ecologically rational and holistic values, a holistic scientific approach and transformational strategies. Although discussed in academic circles for quite some time now, and also to some extent in the general sustainability debate, this worldview or its cousins, have not had much echo in the business world according to several researchers (e.g. Hahn et al., 2015; Varey, 2010). Relatedly, much of the work on the ecocentric or ecological paradigm is based on case studies where adherence to paradigms is discussed in general terms and that there in general is a lack of empirical research that explores how organizations link paradigms and what assumptions are held by organizational key decision-makers (Barter and Bebbington, 2012). Thus exploring adherence to an ecological worldview in organizations is still a largely unexplored territory.

In terms of measurement of an ecological worldview Dunlap and Van Liere (1978) specified the elements of the ecological (then environmental) worldview in some detail and developed an instrument for its measurement; the NEP scale. The NEP has since then been updated and is referred to as the New Ecological Paradigm (Dunlap et al., 2000). In addition to contrasting to the DSP, the NEP recognizes the innovative capacity of humans, but argues that humans are still ecologically interdependent with other species (Dunlap and Jones, 2002). Accordingly, the NEP notes the power of social and cultural forces but does not profess social determinism. Instead, humans are impacted by the cause, effect and feedback loops of ecosystems. Further on, the Earth is perceived to have a finite level of natural resources and waste capacity. Thus, the biophysical environment can impose constraints on human activity such as consumption (Dunlap and Jones, 2002). In an empirical study of these concepts, Shafer (2000) found that there is a negative correlation between the DSP and the NEP. Most studies utilizing the NEP analyse individuals and behaviours such as purchasing of different products, transportation and recycling. However, as pointed to above, there are few empirical studies that relate the NEP to the business arena.

The analytical framework

For the purpose of this study, an analytical framework was constructed to depict how the strategic orientations relate to the various sustainability measures. Here, companies

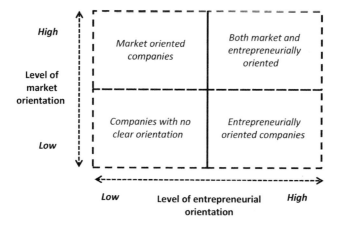

Figure 8.1 The market orientation/entrepreneurial orientation matrix.

are classified according to their combined levels of market orientation and entrepreneurial orientation, as presented in Figure 8.1. As displayed in the figure, the result of
classifying companies in the market orientation/entrepreneurial orientation matrix is in
essence a four-group structure consisting of (1) the *market-oriented* companies, (2) the *entrepreneurially oriented* companies, (3) the companies who are *both entrepreneurially oriented
and market-oriented*, and finally (4) the companies *without a clear orientation*.

By using this framework, it becomes possible to compare and contrast different
types of companies with regard to their sustainability initiatives directly in connection to their overall strategic orientation. Here, the analytical framework also takes
a non-exclusionary view of market orientation and entrepreneurial orientation as is
discussed in the literature (Baker and Sinkula, 2009; Matsuno et al., 2002). As such
we recognize that various combinations of the two orientations can be present simultaneously and thus rated from low to high. For instance, just because a company can
hold a strong market-oriented view does not necessarily mean that the company in
question cannot be entrepreneurially oriented (Baker and Sinkula, 2009). Likewise,
some companies may not display any strong orientation at all due to a confused strategic orientation or lack of knowledge of the orientation when answering the survey.

Method

In order to compare companies of different orientations with regard to their ecological
worldview and sustainability initiatives we use a database generated from a web-survey
with 450 Swedish SMEs (response rate 10 per cent) located in northern Sweden (Also
used in Jansson et al., 2017). 79 per cent of the responses came from companies with
fewer than 10 employees while 18 per cent came from companies with 10–49 employees
and 3 per cent from companies with more than 50 employees. Compared to the average
of SMEs in Sweden, the sample was estimated to be representative. The survey, directed
to decision-makers within the organization contained questions on strategic orientation
(both market orientation and entrepreneurial orientation), based on recognized scales
(Baker and Sinkula, 2009; Oakley, 2012). Furthermore, the survey contained questions on how sustainability is integrated in overall market strategies, overall culture

and recycling activities (Karna et al., 2003). Moreover, the new ecological paradigm was measured using the NEP scale developed by Dunlap et al. (2000) and previously validated in the Swedish context (Jansson et al., 2011).

Based on the survey, companies were classified according to their level of MO and EO: 50 companies were classified as market-oriented, 37 as entrepreneurially oriented, 108 as both market- and entrepreneurially oriented, and 98 as companies with no clear orientation. Based on these groups we analyse the results of the survey next. The four different types of SMEs are evaluated, contrasted and compared, specifically focusing on the *integration of sustainability in market strategies*, the *integration of sustainability in corporate culture*, *recycling practices*, and, finally, *adherence to the ecological worldview*.

Results

Strategic orientation and integration of sustainability in market strategies

In order to be able to compare and contrast companies of various orientations with regard to their integration of sustainability in market strategies, three items based on Kärnä et al. (2003) were included in the survey. The questions focused on sustainability concerns integrated in product development, purchasing, and how to pick markets to prioritize are presented in Table 8.1.

As displayed in Table 8.1, there were several differences between the four groups of companies on the overall three-item scale and on the separate questions. On a general level the results indicate that there are connections between strategic orientation and the manner in which companies integrate sustainability into their operations. A similar pattern emerged in all three questions where the no orientation group displayed the lowest tendency to integrate sustainability into their product and market strategies. This was followed by the market-oriented group and the entrepreneurially oriented group. The group displaying the highest levels of both market orientation and entrepreneurial orientation, however, consistently had the highest levels of sustainability integration in their strategies.

Table 8.1 Sustainability in market strategies

	MO	EO	Both	No	Sig. All	Sig. MO-EO	Sig. MO-Both	Sig. MO-No	Sig. EO-Both	Sig. EO-No	Sig. Both-No
Scale★	3.17	3.41	3.69	2.79	.000	n.s.	.005	n.s.	n.s.	.002	.000
When making strategic product decisions, environmental friendliness is an important consideration for our company											
	3.18	3.57	3.81	2.77	.000	n.s.	.001	n.s.	n.s.	.000	.000
Environmental friendliness is important when we plan what products and markets to prioritize											
	3.20	3.46	3.63	2.77	.000	n.s.	n.s.	n.s.	n.s.	.002	.000
Environmental and social sustainability is important when we plan and execute our purchasing											
	3.12	3.22	3.61	2.83	.000	n.s.	.037	n.s.	n.s.	n.s.	.000

★Scale mean=3.24 (alpha=.88), Scale 1: disagree completely – 5: agree completely.
n.s.: Indicates non-significance at $p < .05$.
MO=Market-oriented firms, EO=Entrepreneurially oriented firms, Both=Both market and entrepreneurially oriented firms. No=No clear orientation.
Bold numbers indicate the highest row mean.

As can be seen, the results between the both market and entrepreneurially oriented group and the no orientation is significant for all items as well as the scale overall.

Strategic orientation and sustainability in overall culture

The second battery of questions regarded sustainability as a part of overall company culture. Here questions focused on whether sustainability was a part of overall company values, whether it is a prioritized matter for management and overall planning of the business model. The questions, again, were based on Kärnä et al. (2003).

In Table 8.2, sustainability in management and company culture are compared across the four company groups. The table indicates several significant differences regarding all the items as well as for the scale overall. For all questions, the company group lacking a clear strategic orientation had the lowest score and the group high in both entrepreneurial and market orientations received the highest score, indicating a positive and significant relationship between the orientations and integration of sustainability in corporate culture. This relationship, however, was not as substantial for market-oriented companies as it was for the entrepreneurially oriented companies.

Strategic orientation and recycling activities

The third battery of questions looked more closely at self-reported actual sustainability activities. One such actual activity, that could be a sign of an overall commitment to sustainability, is that of recycling. Thus, three questions were included on recycling; whether the company has procedures in place to recycle office supplies, food and other waste.

In Table 8.3, the recycling activities are presented across the four groups of companies. As can be seen, the results were not as clear cut as they were for company culture and market strategies above. Instead it was found that the highest mean values varied between the strategic orientations and the items. In addition, the only significant relationship was found for recycling of office supplies, where the entrepreneurially oriented group had the highest level of recycling activities and the group without a clear strategic

Table 8.2 Sustainability in management and company culture

	MO	EO	Both	No	Sig. All	Sig. MO-EO	Sig. MO-Both	Sig. MO-No	Sig. EO-Both	Sig. EO-No	Sig. Both-No
Scale★	3.29	3.54	3.96	3.16	.000	n.s.	.003	n.s.	n.s.	n.s.	.000
Sustainability is an important part of our company's philosophy and values											
	3.44	3.76	4.08	3.35	.000	n.s.	.005	n.s.	n.s.	n.s.	.000
Sustainability is a prioritized matter for our company's management											
	3.34	3.51	3.95	3.18	.000	n.s.	.001	n.s.	n.s.	n.s.	.000
Sustainability issues affect planning of our business											
	3.08	3.35	3.84	2.96	.000	n.s.	.001	n.s.	n.s.	n.s.	.000

★Scale mean=3.55 (alpha=.94), Scale 1: disagree completely – 5: agree completely.
n.s.: Indicates non-significance at p <.05.
MO=Market-oriented firms, EO=Entrepreneurially oriented firms, Both=Both market and entrepreneurially oriented firms. No=No clear orientation.
Bold numbers indicate the highest row mean.

Table 8.3 Strategic orientation and recycling

	MO	EO	Both	No	Sig. All	Sig. MO-EO	Sig. MO-Both	Sig. MO-No	Sig. EO-Both	Sig. EO-No	Sig. Both-No
Scale*	3.81	3.86	**3.97**	3.52	.049	n.s.	n.s.	n.s.	n.s.	n.s.	.035
To what extent does your company recycle office supplies											
	3.80	**4.08**	4.05	3.47	.017	n.s.	n.s.	n.s.	n.s.	n.s.	.020
To what extent does your company recycle food/lunchroom waste											
	3.36	3.24	**3.53**	3.03	n.s.	n.s.	n.s.	n.s.	n.s.	n.s.	n.s.
To what extent does your company recycle other waste (packaging, etc.)											
	4.28	4.24	**4.34**	4.07	n.s.	n.s.	n.s.	n.s.	n.s.	n.s.	n.s.

*Scale mean=3.80 (alpha=.75), Scale 1: disagree completely – 5: agree completely.
n.s.: Indicates non-significance at p <.05.
MO=Market-oriented firms, EO=Entrepreneurially oriented firms, Both=Both market and entrepreneur-
    ially oriented firms. No=No clear orientation.
Bold numbers indicate the highest row mean.

orientation had the lowest score. The other two items, food/lunchroom recycling or other waste showed no significant differences.

Strategic orientation and the new environmental paradigm

Finally, the questionnaire also measured ecological worldview, through five questions from the Dunlap et al. (2000) NEP scale. Based on factor analysis in order to achieve a better fit, three of these items were used, presented in Table 8.4. Applied in our context, the NEP largely captures whether the decision-maker/manager adheres to the ecological worldview. This worldview largely challenges ideas associated with the traditional paradigm, such as the notion that mankind has an indisputable right to control nature and instead upholds ideas such as the notion that mankind must live in harmony with nature. It should be noted that the questions are reverse coded, but have been reversed so that a high score indicates adherence with the ecological worldview in Table 8.4.

In Table 8.4, the results of the three items are displayed. A low mean indicates a low adherence to the item. As can be seen in the table the Cronbach's alpha value is quite low (.64) which is not uncommon in the area (Hawcroft and Milfont, 2010), but indicates that interpretations should be done with care. This is further discussed below. It should also be noted that there are no statistically significant differences between the four groups, for any of the items. Descriptively, however, it can be noted that the companies high in entrepreneurial orientation, were ranked the lowest on all three of the items. This means that decision-makers/managers in this group had the lowest level of adherence to the ecological worldview although not statistically significantly different from the others. In contrast, market-oriented companies received the highest score of all groups on all three the items, indicating that they had the highest level of adherence to the ecological worldview. It should be noted, however, that while these descriptive observations are both noteworthy and interesting, they are not statistically significant. Thus, it is not possible to make any general statements about the groups concerning ecological worldview. As this is one of the first attempts to compare NEP score across groups of companies, however, this finding is interesting and warrants further discussion below.

Table 8.4 Strategic orientation and ecological worldview

	MO	EO	Both	No	Sig. All	Sig. MO-EO	Sig. MO-Both	Sig. MO-No	Sig. EO-Both	Sig. EO-No	Sig. Both-No
Scale*	4.29	3.96	4.15	4.10	n.s.	n.s.	n.s.	n.s.	n.s.	n.s.	n.s.
Humans have the right to modify the natural environment to suit their needs (RC)											
	4.48	4.05	4.33	4.24	n.s.	n.s.	n.s.	n.s.	n.s.	n.s.	n.s.
The balance of nature is strong enough to cope with the impacts of modern industrial nations (RC)											
	4.64	4.22	4.49	4.34	n.s.	n.s.	n.s.	n.s.	n.s.	n.s.	n.s.
Human ingenuity will ensure that we do not make the Earth unlivable (RC)											
	3.76	3.62	3.64	3.68	n.s.	n.s.	n.s.	n.s.	n.s.	n.s.	n.s.

*Scale mean=4.10 (alpha=.64), Scale 1: disagree completely – 5: agree completely.
n.s.: Indicates non-significance at $p < .05$.
MO=Market-oriented firms, EO=Entrepreneurially oriented firms, Both=Both market and entrepreneurially oriented firms., No=No clear orientation.
Bold numbers indicate the highest row mean.
RC = Reverse coded.

Analysis and discussion

The results section above highlights several interesting observations regarding the grouped companies' overarching strategic orientation, their adherence to an ecological worldview, and the integration of sustainability into their processes, strategies and practices. The results support the idea that there is a general relationship between overall strategic orientation and how companies deal with sustainability and environmental issues. Here, when comparing the different types of companies, in basically all indices and questions, the no orientation cluster of companies ranked the lowest of all categories. Thus, companies without a clear strategic orientation seem to take fewer measures when it comes to integrating sustainability in overarching market strategies, corporate culture and practices, such as recycling, compared to companies that are high in either strategic orientation. An implication of these findings is that by identifying companies with a lack of a clear business strategy or orientation it might be possible to also identify companies with a low or non-existent sustainability focus.

Turning to the other groups of companies, the results indicate that the entrepreneurially oriented group of companies was especially favourable to installing strategies and practices that take sustainability into account. Given that entrepreneurship and innovations are important components in aligning corporate activity with a sustainable development (e.g. Hall et al., 2010), this is encouraging. The results are also in line with previous research on entrepreneurial orientation and sustainability (e.g. Aragón-Correa, 2008). The fact that the entrepreneurial orientation group often ranked higher than the market-oriented group on most sustainability measures, however, may also be a bit of a surprise considering the market-oriented notion that companies adapt and respond to customer preferences, and that customers will prefer products and services that are environmentally friendly. This is likely a sign that customer demand for green products still is relatively low (at least as seen by companies). As such companies subscribing to a mindful way of doing business might have to become better at attracting the mindful consumers (e.g. Sheth et al., 2011).

The results also showed that the group that displayed a combination of being entrepreneurially *and* market-oriented, exhibited the most environmental consideration out of the four groups. In many ways this makes sense. The 'megatrend' (e.g. Lubin and Esty, 2010) of sustainability is likely to generate opportunities both in terms of new technologies and innovations, and in terms of demand for more sustainable solutions from customers. It also shows that companies that are open to both more internal (entrepreneurial) and more external (market) forces are more prone to pick up on the sustainability issues as business possibilities. Likely, they have a developed information handling system that collects and analyses data and as such sustainability is likely to emerge as a trend in those analyses. Whether this is a genuine sustainability orientation or more of a business as usual perspective, viewing sustainability and/or CSR as an add-on, rather than ingrained (Vallaster et al., 2012), is open for discussion. More research is necessary to connect these two strategic orientations to genuine sustainability work using a combination of methods less reliant upon (potentially biased) self-reports.

Turning to the ecological worldview, the results showed that there were no statistically significant differences between the four groups. Given that significant results were reached when it comes to strategies and culture, this is somewhat surprising. The conclusion we can draw from this is that the differences we observe as to how the different groups of companies integrate sustainability in overall market strategies and corporate culture is likely *not* due to differences in adherence to the ecological worldview. It should, however, be noted that the levels of the NEP in our study are, in an international comparison, high (summated mean above 4.00) on citizens (for a meta-analysis of the NEP scale see Hawcroft and Milfont, 2010). There may thus be a ceiling effect as the majority of the companies included in our study have a high degree of ecological worldview and as such the scale is unable to discriminate between the company groups. As few studies have been published as to adherence to the new ecological worldview among business managers, the possibility to compare our results on the scale is limited. The non-significant and also relatively high results raise questions whether the sample for this study is representative of Swedish businesses in general, but also whether there are different levels of adherence to the NEP among citizens and managers. Based on the meta-analysis by Hawcroft and Milfont (2010) where it was found that there was a positive correlation between white-collar workers and the NEP, but a negative one between blue-collar workers and the NEP, it might be the case that adherence to the NEP is more related to sociodemographic factors such as education, than actual sustainability work and strategic choices in the firm. Further research is necessary to clarify these different levels and how they are related to genuine sustainability work in the business sector. Research in that area might uncover how the ecological worldview can be used to connect the sustainability challenges with business strategies through education at different levels in companies depending on adherence to the worldview.

In all, by highlighting that the groups differ as to the manner in which companies deal with sustainability challenges, the results of this study support the notion that the road towards a more sustainable development is not necessarily reached by viewing sustainability as an 'add on' to regular business practices, but rather as an *integrated* part of general business strategies. In many ways, this integrated way of approaching sustainability in the corporate sector is likely to be of importance to the way regulators and policy makers approach regulation on sustainability performance. While sustainability as an 'add-on' to corporate strategies implies that regulators should focus on creating regulations that target the harmful and negative consequences of corporate conduct, the sustainability as integrated into corporate fundamental strategies implies that regulators could focus on creating positive market-based incentives to forming business strategies around sustainability. Here, understanding success factors for market-oriented and entrepreneurially oriented companies, and creating regulations that encourage offering sustainable market solutions or an entrepreneurial focus on sustainability, could be objectives for regulation.

Contributions and implications

Academic contribution

In reporting on the results of a large scale questionnaire targeted to Swedish SMEs, this chapter has provided a detailed analysis, based on a large dataset, of how groups with differing combinations of market and entrepreneurial orientations adhere to the ecological worldview, and relate to integrating sustainability in their market strategies and corporate culture. In doing this, the chapter contributes in several ways, both theoretically and practically.

Starting first with the sustainability perspective, this chapter provides an overarching contribution by exploring the relationships between various combinations of two general strategy concepts; market and entrepreneurial orientation, and how the company integrates sustainability into their strategies, practices and culture. Previous research has not addressed the overarching relationships between fundamental strategy and sustainability as an integrated (and not an 'add-on') component in any great extent. Our comparison of groups also highlights that companies who hold differing orientations indeed relate to sustainability challenges in different ways (practices and worldviews), indicating that a fruitful direction of future research may be to document fundamental strategy concepts as to how they relate to sustainability measures.

A second contribution of this chapter is more in line with previous research on strategic orientation. Here, an abundance of research has shown that entrepreneurial orientation and market orientation are of relevance for the financial profitability of the firm (Baker and Sinkula, 2009). This chapter extends this literature by highlighting other factors related to strategic orientation; specifically in terms of how the orientations correlate to how the company addresses environmental challenges.

Finally, this chapter also contributes by highlighting the new ecological worldview in a corporate context. The vast majority of previous studies that utilize the NEP have been focused on consumers and citizens such as students and environmentalists. While the NEP had little discriminatory power in the current study, this study provides insights into how an ecological worldview can be measured in relation to business strategies.

Managerial implications

For managers, the results of this chapter highlight that sustainability performance may not come as a consequence of separate initiatives alone. Instead, the core business policies and models are likely to be a major incentive or obstacle to sustainability performance. While managers who wish to maximize sustainability performance may do well in designating resources specifically for improving sustainability, they would also do well in evaluating the core business models that are actually used. In addition, it might be worthwhile to work with the ecological worldview among managers and personnel of the organization. This might lead to a heightened awareness among entrepreneurs, marketers and other co-workers of the necessity of sustainability for social and environmental reasons, but it might also mean that new business opportunities are realized (cf. Porter et al., 2011). With more firms recognizing the importance of sustainability and acting more in line with the NEP, and thus pushing out other firms from the market, the transition to sustainability might stand a better chance of being realized.

142   *Jonas Nilsson et al.*

References

Aragón-Correa, J.A., Hurtado-Torres, N., Sharma, S. and García-Morales, V.J. (2008). Environmental strategy and performance in small firms: A resource-based perspective. *Journal of Environmental Management*, 86: 88–103.

Baker, W.E. and Sinkula, J.M. (2009). The complementary effects of market orientation and entrepreneurial orientation on profitability in small businesses. *Journal of Small Business Management*, 47(4): 443–464.

Barter, N. and Bebbington, J. (2012). Environmental paradigms and organisations with an environmental mission. *International Journal of Innovation and Sustainable Development*, 6(2): 120–145.

Borland, H. and Lindgreen, A. (2013). Sustainability, epistemology, ecocentric business, and marketing strategy: Ideology, reality, and vision. *Journal of Business Ethics*, 117(1): 173–187.

Cassells, S. and Lewis, K. (2011). SMEs and environmental responsibility: Do actions reflect attitudes? *Corporate Social Responsibility and Environmental Management*, 18(3): 186–199.

Cotgrove, S. (1982). *Catastrophe or Cornucopia: The Environment, Politics and the Future*. New York: John Wiley & Sons.

Crittenden, V., Crittenden, W., Ferrell, L., Ferrell, O. and Pinney, C. (2011). Market-oriented sustainability: A conceptual framework and propositions. *Journal of the Academy of Marketing Science*, 39(1): 71–85.

Daly, H.E. (2005). Economics in a full world. *IEEE Engineering Management Review*, 33(4): 21–21.

Dunlap, R.E. and Jones, R.E. (2002). Environmental concern: Conceptual and measurement issues. In R.E. Dunlap and W. Michelson (eds), *Handbook of Environmental Sociology*. Westport, CN: Greenwood Press, 482–524.

Dunlap, R.E. and Van Liere, K.D. (1978). The 'new environmental paradigm'. *Journal of Environmental Education*, 9(4): 10–19.

Dunlap, R.E., Van Liere, K.D., Mertig, A.G. and Jones, R.E. (2000). New trends in measuring environmental attitudes: Measuring endorsement of the new ecological paradigm: A revised NEP scale. *Journal of Social Issues*, 56(3): 425–442.

EC (2012). *Flash Eurobarometer 342: SMEs, Resource Efficiency and Green Markets*. European Commission.

Grinstein, A. (2008). The relationships between market orientation and alternative strategic orientations: A meta-analysis. *European Journal of Marketing*, 42(1/2): 115–134.

Hahn, T., Figge, F., Aragón-Correa, J.A. and Sharma, S. (2015). Advancing research on corporate sustainability: Off to pastures new or back to the roots? *Business and Society, 56(2): 155–185.*

Hall, J.K., Daneke, G.A. and Lenox, M.J. (2010). Sustainable development and entrepreneurship: Past contributions and future directions. *Journal of Business Venturing*, 25(5): 439–448.

Hawcroft, L.J. and Milfont, T.L. (2010). The use (and abuse) of the new environmental paradigm scale over the last 30 years: A meta-analysis. *Journal of Environmental Psychology*, 30(2): 143–158.

Hopwood, B., Mellor, M. and O'Brien, G. (2005). Sustainable development: Mapping different approaches. *Sustainable Development*, 13(1): 38–52.

Hult, G. (2011). Market-focused sustainability: Market orientation plus! *Journal of the Academy of Marketing Science*, 39(1): 1–6.

Jackson, T. (2005). Live better by consuming less?: Is there a 'double dividend' in sustainable consumption? *Journal of Industrial Ecology*, 9(1–2): 19–36.

Jackson, T. (2009). *Prosperity Without Growth : Economics for a Finite Planet*. London: Earthscan.

Jansson, J., Marell, A. and Nordlund, A. (2011). Exploring consumer adoption of a high involvement eco-innovation using value-belief-norm theory. *Journal of Consumer Behaviour*, 10(1): 51–60.

Jansson, J., Nilsson, J., Modig, F. and Hed Vall, G. (2017). Commitment to sustainability in small and medium-sized enterprises: The influence of strategic orientations and management values. *Business Strategy and the Environment*, 26(1): 69–83.

Jonker, J. and Marberg, A. (2007). Corporate social responsibility: Quo vadis? *Journal of Corporate Citizenship*(27): 107–118.

Kärna, J., Hansen, E. and Juslin, H. (2003). Social responsibility in environmental marketing planning. *European Journal of Marketing*, 37(5/6): 848–871.

Kilbourne, W.E., Beckmann, S.C. and Thelen, E. (2002). The role of the dominant social paradigm in environmental attitudes: A multinational examination. *Journal of Business Research*, 55(3): 193–204.

Kilbourne, W.E., Dorsch, M.J., McDonagh, P., Urien, B., et al. (2009). The institutional foundations of materialism in Western societies: A conceptualization and empirical test. *Journal of Macromarketing*, 29(3): 259–278.

Kohli, A.K. and Jaworski, B.J. (1990). Market orientation: The construct, research propositions, and managerial implications. *Journal of Marketing*, 54(2): 1–18.

Lubin, D.B.A. and Esty, D.C. (2010). The sustainability imperative. *Harvard Business Review*, 88(5): 2–9.

Lumpkin, G.T. and Dess, G.G. (1996). Clarifying the entrepreneurial orientation construct and linking it to performance. *Academy of Management Review*, 21(1): 135–172.

Matsuno, K., Mentzer, J.T. and Özsomer, A. (2002). The effects of entrepreneurial proclivity and market orientation on business performance. *Journal of Marketing*, 66(3): 18–32.

Menguc, B. and Ozanne, L.K. (2005). Challenges of the 'green imperative': A natural resource-based approach to the environmental orientation–business performance relationship. *Journal of Business Research*, 58(4): 430–438.

Miller, D. (1983). The correlates of entrepreneurship in three types of firms. *Management Science*, 29: 770–791.

Narver, J.C. and Slater, S.F. (1990). The effect of a market orientation on business profitability. *Journal of Marketing*, 54(4): 20–35.

Noble, C.H., Sinha, R.K. and Kumar, A. (2002). Market orientation and alternative strategic orientations: A longitudinal assessment of performance implications. *Journal of Marketing*, 66(4): 25–39.

Oakley, J.L. (2012). Bridging the gap between employees and customers. *Journal of Marketing Management*, 28(9/10): 1094–1113.

OECD. (2007). *Small Businesses and Environmental Compliance: Review and Possible Application of International Experience in Georgia*. Paris: OECD.

Porritt, J. (2007). *Capitalism as if the World Matters*. London: Earthscan.

Porter, M.E. and Kramer, M.R. (2006). Strategy and society: The link between competitive advantage and corporate social responsibility. *Harvard Business Review*, 84(12): 78–92.

Porter, M.E., Kramer, M.R., Habip, A., Pigdon, J., et al. (2011). Creating shared value: *Interaction*, 89: 16–17.

Revell, A., Stokes, D. and Hsin, C. (2010). Small businesses and the environment: Turning over a new leaf? *Business Strategy and the Environment*, 19(5): 273–288.

Rockström, J., Steffen, W., Noone, K., Persson, A., et al. (2009). A safe operating space for humanity. *Nature*, 461(7263): 472–475.

Shafer, W. (2000). Social paradigms and attitudes toward environmental accountability. *Journal of Business Ethics*, 65(2): 121–147.

Sheth, J., Sethia, N. and Srinivas, S. (2011). Mindful consumption: A customer-centric approach to sustainability. *Journal of the Academy of Marketing Science*, 39(1): 21–39.

Steffen, W., Richardson, K., Rockström, J., Cornell, S.E., et al. (2015). Planetary boundaries: Guiding human development on a changing planet. *Science*, 347(6223). doi: 10.1126/science.1259855.

Vallaster, C., Lindgreen, A. and Maori, F. (2012). Strategically leveraging corporate social responsibility: A corporate branding perspective. *California Management Review*, 54(3): 34–60.

Van Liere, K.D. and Dunlap, R.E. (1980). The social bases of environmental concern: A review of hypotheses, explanations and empirical evidence. *Public Opinion Quarterly*, 44(2): 181–197.

Varey, R.J. (2010). Marketing means and ends for a sustainable society: A welfare agenda for transformative change. *Journal of Macromarketing*, 30(2): 112–126.

9 The emerging paradigm of enviro-ethical dialogism, corporate social responsibility and consumer dynamism

Will McConnell

In this chapter, a preliminary discussion on the emerging paradigm of enviro-ethical dialogism, corporate social responsibility and consumer dynamism focuses on an effort to redefine an interdisciplinary and international discussion. Environmental sustainability discourse is difficult to absorb in part due to its inter- and transdisciplinary nature, and in part due to the lack of agreed-upon metrics, language games and standards for establishing, and assessing improvements in, companies' pollution baselines; thus, any and all 'improvements' – usually reductions in the 'rate' of pollution production, rather than elimination of damage itself – in the production of waste or environmental damage is easily interpreted, in the current consumer enviro-ethos, and in the most broadly conceived of terms, as 'good' for the environment. The following analysis identifies more nuanced modes of constructing pathways towards 'best practices', investigates helpful models for measuring and analysing emergent models of corporate social and environmental responsibility, and concludes with a call to revise modelling such that metrics include a more comprehensive set of modelling and reporting-out structures from businesses, such that consumers can make the more informed, more responsible choices they clearly are attempting to make in the current marketplaces of environmental sustainability.

Introduction

In the last decade in the United States, the concepts and practices of accountability and transparency have received increasing scrutiny and revision, both within the business sector and, increasingly, in governmental (and more public) arenas. This scrutiny has rapidly shifted the role of ethics – enlarging and diversifying performance indicators, for example – in profitability, but also in production and social impact. Consumer decision-making behaviours have also shifted considerably. Numerous signs across business culture itself suggest that this rapid change will continue to interpenetrate business and consumer loci of decision-making.

In this chapter, a preliminary discussion on the emerging paradigm of enviro-ethical dialogism, corporate social responsibility and consumer dynamism focuses on an effort to redefine an interdisciplinary and international discussion. Environmental sustainability discourse is difficult to absorb in part due to its inter- and transdisciplinary nature, and in part due to the lack of agreed-upon metrics, language games, and standards for establishing, and assessing improvements in, companies' pollution baselines; thus, any and all 'improvements' – usually reductions in the 'rate' of pollution production, rather than elimination of damage itself – in the production of waste or environmental damage is easily interpreted, in the current consumer enviro-ethos, and in the most broadly conceived of terms, as 'good' for the environment. The following analysis identifies more nuanced modes of constructing pathways towards 'best practices', investigates helpful models for measuring and analysing emergent models of corporate social and environmental responsibility, and concludes with a call to revise modelling such that metrics include a more comprehensive set of modelling and reporting-out structures from businesses, such that consumers can make the more informed, more responsible choices they clearly are attempting to make in the current marketplaces of environmental sustainability.

Shifting business ethics and consumer behaviour

According to the Union of International Associations, '[t]he number of international non-governmental organizations that scrutinize the ethics of organizations has increased worldwide from 30,000 in 2000 to over 60,000 in 2007' (Union, 2008). Similarly, according to the Social Investment Forum, 'ethical and sustainable investing in the U.S. increased from $639 billion in 1995 to $2,159 billion in 1999 and from $2,290 billion in 2005 to $2,711 billion in 2007' (Social, 2007). These figures alone suggest that the grounding assumptions for understanding the constitution of ethical behaviour – in a business context, the construction of a relation between businesses and consumers – is also shifting rapidly. On the one hand, the demand on businesses is rising, from all quarters, for accurate, objective information about (internal, workplace) ethical performance; on the other, consumers themselves have also become more active in demanding evidence of the link between increased social awareness of environmental and social impacts and practices in business ethics. In a 2008 survey of consumer behaviours, for example, '57 percent of U.S. consumers currently say that their purchase decision could be influenced by whether or not a product supports a worthy cause' (Nielsen, 2008). This trend in supporting products and business with a 'worthy cause' has continued to grow across the last eight years. In more pointed language from a 2015 Nielsen survey, 30,000 respondents from 60 countries were asked, 'How much do you agree with the following statement: I am willing to pay extra for products and services that come from companies who are committed to positive social and environmental impact?' According to Nielsen's report *The Sustainability Imperative*, 'sixty-six percent of global respondents say they are willing to pay more for sustainable goods' – an increase from 55 per cent in 2014 and 50 per cent in 2013 (Nielsen 2015, p. 8). Further, this trend is backed by research in retail data: in 2014, 65 per cent of total sales measured globally were generated by brands whose marketing conveyed commitment to social and/or environmental value (Nielsen 2015, p. 6).

The problem posed by this business climate is daunting: how can businesses respond proactively to such a rapidly shifting, volatile set of metrics, actors, stakeholders, external organizations, communication demands, etc.? The emerging ethical climate requires much more of a dialogic positioning to maximize responsiveness between businesses and consumers. How can businesses better position themselves as 'going (ethical) concerns' in the face of rapid changes posed by what is likely to become the most intractable arena of business ethics: environmental ethics?

One tool that has been a mainstay in businesses' ability to address ethical considerations in the marketplace is the concept of corporate social responsibility (CSR). Although CSR has a long history of development and refinement, that history has been characterized by the definition of a set of performance measures whose primary aim is to represent more of a company's internal atmosphere – in particular, its internal climate of ethically based decision-making and action – than the relation of a company to its (potential) external audiences. Similarly, the primary goal of both historical and current ethics metrics and measurement systems reflects this less-than-accurate internal/external paradigm. Internally driven information, as a component of businesses' self-reporting, and externally produced analyses, offered by independent, information-gathering organizations, such as the National Business Ethics Survey of the U.S. Workforce (NBES), mirrors that same structure of 'internal/external' dichotomies in information gathering and reporting structures. The NBES reports capture data from multiple business sectors in a series of longitudinal studies; the NBES is the only research of its type to track patterns and trends in ethics in the American workplace since 1994. Even here, the internal dynamics of businesses are the almost exclusive foci. This focus on internal business issues is evident in the most recent NBES findings (2014). For example, although reports of misconduct by employees have shown a steady drop, incidents of reprisals from backlash effects of reporting ethical abuses have risen since the previous NBES findings report (2007). Like the NBES reports, the majority of businesses communicate their ethos as practised *within* the walls of that business, in order to indicate more of an internal environment than balance sheets and income statements can, and in more objective methodologies and findings, to its immediate stakeholders. Increasingly, this approach places businesses at a disadvantage in the marketplace of ethical responsiveness. How have businesses begun to respond?

Shifting definition of marketing

To date, communicating more effectively with external audiences – non-immediate, or not current, stakeholders – has largely been the provenance of marketing and public relations firms and activities. The American Marketing Association's (AMA) numerous, recent shifts in the definition of 'marketing' are indicative of the strategies most businesses adopt. In 1985, the AMA defined 'marketing' as 'the process of planning and executing the conception, pricing, promotion and distribution of ideas, goods, and services to create exchanges that satisfy individual and organizational goals' (Gundlach and Wilkie, 2009). By 2004, the definition had changed to '[m]arketing is an organizational function and a set of processes for creating, communicating, and delivering value to customers and for managing customer relationships in ways that benefit the organization and its stakeholders' (Gundlach and Wilkie, 2009). The emphasis is still on the benefit to the organization and stakeholders, but the introduction of creating and delivering 'value' to customers, and a focus on 'customer relations' signals a shift in the communicative environment now facing businesses.

According to Gundlach and Wilkie (2009), however, the 2004 definition was deemed too restrictive by marketing professionals, who found it 'overly narrow' in its focus on 'organizational function[s] and set[s] of processes' (2009, p. 259). Essentially, then, the 2004 definition of marketing reflected the limited and limiting approach of many businesses towards CSR to date, in which the focus remains on the internal dynamics of businesses' functioning, and the explicit, nearly exclusive targeting of current stakeholders, thereby excluding emerging forms of exchange with non-stakeholders (or potential stakeholders). As Gundlach and Wilkie note, the 2004 definition excluded 'the institutions, actors, and processes beyond the organization' (2009, pp. 259–60).

The current AMA definition, released in 2007, develops more concretely the meme of dialogism in customer – business relations: '[m]arketing is the activity, set of institutions, and processes for creating, communicating, delivering, and exchanging offerings that have value for customers, clients, partners, and society at large' (Gundlach and Wilkie, 2009, p. 260). This approach has also given rise to, for example, 'social marketing', defined by Lazer and Kelley (1973) as a concern 'with the application of marketing knowledge, concepts, and techniques to enhance social as well as economic ends. It is also concerned with the analysis of the social consequences of marketing policies, decisions and activities'.

Strategic integration of ethics and action

In many business enterprises, however, there remains a sense that 'social marketing', even if and when effective, is little more than an 'added-value' strategy, rather than one motivated by a consistent, coherent ethical strategy and lived culture evident throughout its operations. Consumers are wary of inconsistencies between businesses' messaging functions and the consistency or coherence signified in and by their operations. These are often now understood, or framed, by consumers as ethical shortcomings, rather than as the consequence of 'doing business'. In part, this demand for greater coherence across the entirety of business operations is due to the wider business and social climate. Recent historical events have kept the need for ethical review mechanisms a dominant feature of social and business discourse (and perpetuated the focus on communicating socially about ethical standards). In the wake of the Enron scandal, for example, the Sarbanes–Oxley Act (2002) established both more wide-ranging and more specific accountability and transparency standards for public companies; exacerbated by the more recent housing finance scandals of 2007–08 and the long recession that has followed, the ethical climate in which, and the connectivity with which, consumers themselves make purchasing decisions has undergone radical changes. As former Representative Michael Oxley, co-sponsor of the Sarbanes–Oxley Act of 2002 and chairman of the ERC board of directors, noted: 'Business ethics is one of the pillars of a strong economy and in today's environment, it is more important than ever that our nation's business leaders set and meet the highest standards of ethical conduct' (Ethics World, 2014).

At best, consumer confidence in the ethicality of behaviours exhibited by both public and private businesses has reached a curious, insistent crossroads. On the one hand, as Oxley recognizes, a strong ethical orientation forms the bedrock of most effective business strategies; on the other, business professionals and consumers often find themselves conflicted about the actualization of ethical decision-making processes, and its relation to strategic positioning for maximizing profitability in a global environment. In no business-consumer relation is this paradoxical crossroads more evident at present than in the conundrum represented by environmental ethics. The 'greening' of the business environment has received considerable attention in the last 15 years, with no signs of abating. But sustainability as a set of 'ethically motivated' ideas, behaviours and actions has produced a paralysing crossroads between business-based definitions of ethically motivated behaviour and a more robust, more widespread, ethically motivated eco-consumerism. For instance, most businesses have done little to produce the coherence or consistency necessary for an action–oriented ethic represented by 'sustainability' and most consumers have done little to shift their purchasing behaviours and attitudes, beyond demanding more 'green' solutions of businesses. As an ethical

orientation, 'sustainability' has produced plenty of actions, claims and misunderstandings, but no coherent action plan for best practices – either for businesses or consumers.
Each group seems to be poised to act on what they know, while waiting for the other
to lead although there is significant misinformation circulating about sustainable action.

As Selznick (1957) recognized long ago, however, '[t]ruly accepted values must infuse
the organization at many levels, affecting the perspective and attitudes of personnel, the
relative importance of staff activities, the distribution of authority, relations with outside
groups, and many other matters' (p. 136). The stakes of producing greater coherence
across a business' many levels of activity – as Selznick notes, to 'infuse' values with performance indicators – have never been greater.

Towards an understanding of integrated business ethics

Scholars such as McCoy (1985, p. 87) place ethics at the core of business activity. As
McCoy notes,

> Dealing with values required continual monitoring of the surrounding environ-
> ment, weighing alternative courses of action, balancing and (when possible) inte-
> grating conflicting responsibilities, setting priorities among competing goals, and
> establishing criteria for defining and evaluating performance. Along with these
> goes learning ways to bring ethical reflection directly and fully into processes by
> which policy is made, implemented, and evaluated. Increasingly, skills in dealing
> with values as integrated components of performance and policy-making are being
> recognized as central for effective management in a society and a world undergoing
> rapid change.

Both McCoy and Selznick recognize the importance of integrating 'values', 'performance' and 'policy' in today's business climate. Nowhere, for businesses and consumers
alike, is there more at stake in aligning 'values', 'performance' and 'policy' than in environmental ethics. Pressure on the environmental, ethical strategies and overall climate
of business activities continues to increase, increasingly from 'internal' stakeholders but
more so from 'outside groups', as trends in accountability, transparency, consistency of
performance and a host of other factors continue to drive now widely available, publicly
traded information. In fact, active groups previously understood as 'external' to business
operations and reporting systems are multiple as well as mobile in their configurations,
alliances and strategies for being heard. Trends in the growth of these often transitory
alliances indicate that the interaction of provisional groups of varying specific interests
will continue to bifurcate, reform and increase their viability and visibility as forces in
marketplace decisions.

What is sustainability and can businesses achieve it?

In part, the difficulty for businesses and consumers to move forwards stems from the
concept of sustainability itself, as inherited from the Brundtland Commission's Report
(1987, also known as *Our Common Future*). The Brundtland Report (1987) definition is
'Sustainable development is development that meets the needs of the present without
compromising the ability of future generations to meet their own needs.' It contains
within it two key concepts: the concept of 'needs', in particular the essential needs of

the world's poor, to which overriding priority should be given; and the idea of limitations imposed by the state of technology and social organization on the environment's ability to meet present and future needs (Brundtland Report, 2014). Not only does the definition of sustainability offer no discernible, distinct plan of action, but also this definition retains an anthropomorphic bias towards understanding and applying the idea of 'resources' in the context of a future-oriented discourse of human survival. That is, 'sustainability', as an ethically directed concept, plants the seeds of its own (ultimate) failure: if all planetary interactions are understood as, ultimately, 'resources' for human expropriation, extraction and waste, even the often cited ethically driven mantra of 'reduce, reuse, recycle' will likely be understood, by the very future generations in whose name we claim an ethical responsibility, as a form of rhetoric which not only maintained, but also perpetuated distinctly unethical behaviour.

Forging the difficult path forwards is made more complex still by what scholars have deemed a double (ethical) standard. Both consumers and business enterprises seem to understand the ethical conundrum represented by this form of 'progress', predicated on a 'future-oriented', ethically based thinking and action. But traditional models of business leadership, and meaningful, intentional dialogue with consumers has not, to date, led to any distinct pathways for redirecting behaviour whole-scale, either for consumers or for businesses. De Burgh-Woodman and King (2013) characterize this seeming ethical impasse as a 'paradoxical dynamic' in which many consumers 'have a passive connection to sustainability yet demand an 'ethical' outlook from corporations' (p. 162). The assumption that consumers perpetuate a double (ethical) standard in their relation to a business organization's activity is borne out by the work of Vermeir and Van Kenhove (2008), De Bock and Van Kenhove (2011), and De Paulo (1985, 1987): in empirically supported studies, these scholars demonstrated that consumers 'have a double standard when it comes to their own unethical behaviour compared to that of a corporation' (de Bock et al., 2013, p. 227).

The question of how to move forwards, then, seems the most pressing, both for businesses interested in maintaining strong strategic performance indicators, and for consumers, attempting to act in the absence of accurate information (or representation) of the emerging ethical climate of sustainability. In 1957, Selznick could not have foreseen the distinct ways that two of the most broadly articulated categories he presents – 'relations with outside groups, and many other matters' – would emerge to be equally as significant performance measures as those based on profitability. As far back as 1986, Chakravarthy noted that traditional measures of a business' health based on profitability alone were not adequate for evaluating the effectiveness of that business to position itself for strategic performance in the marketplace.

Increasingly included in Oxney's 'pillars of a strong economy' are largely unmeasured aspects of business climates, or aspects of CSR that are difficult to measure as well as anticipate. These seemingly invisible pillars of economic health and stability have become commodities in themselves, with a difference: these often intangible items of strategic performance can be, and often are, leveraged in the marketplace of public education and opinion. In today's business climate, then, there is no longer a clear distinction between the historical measures that produce an 'inside' and 'outside' of a business enterprise. A decision made in a boardroom in small town USA emerges quickly in other geographic and virtual locations to have significant impacts both within local economies of towns and cities across North America and abroad, in a global economy and environment. A business' ability to expand its operations in the current marketplace now increasingly depends not only on adopting Selznick's approach, but also on creating, continually refining and rapidly modifying that approach, as consumers' relation to businesses and business activities has shifted dramatically with the advent of modes of communication ushered in by such technological modalities as the Internet (and other, rapidly expanding forms of social communication). Consumers can now obtain, disseminate and mobilize information about themselves and businesses in ways unforeseen in the history of business enterprises – whether or not those consumers are recognized stakeholders in particular companies.

The emergence to prominence of the NBES reports also signals a shift in the general awareness of the significance of ethical standards in employees and consumers alike. To explore dimensions of the ethical climate, in order to mobilize that climate for effective ethical change (i.e. both to enlarge or expand the prevailing business definitions and reporting structures of 'ethical behavior'), a return to some paradoxical findings in the NBES data can help set a benchmark for developing an understanding of 'ethics' beyond the most widespread, currently defined measures. The most recent NBES report (2013) indicates that 'while misconduct overall is down [from 1994–2007 levels] … a significant amount of misconduct [reported by employees] involves continuous, ongoing behaviour rather than one-time incidents', and further, that senior level managers are responsible for a large share of workplace misconduct (60 percent). The findings suggest not only an increased awareness of ethical issues within individual businesses (and across businesses in the U.S. generally), but also the significance of strong leadership in reaching ethical goals within as well as outside business enterprises. The survey instrument also functions as an educational tool, and as such, signals arise in the understanding of ethical behaviour and the significance of experiencing ethical breaches in the workplace. These employees, in turn, are also consumers elsewhere. As Patricia J. Hamed notes in the foreword to the NBES study, '[t]rust and transparency also make a difference. Bottom line: workers who believe management communicates honestly and openly are less likely to break rules and more likely to report bad behavior when they see it' (Ethics Resource Center, 2014, p. 9).

This set of findings suggests a great deal about the current climate of ethics for both consumers and employees (and the businesses for which they work). Firstly, within a specific set of criteria included in the study, the US workforce understands ethical performance as well as ethical breaches as never before, according to the national survey instrument used by the Ethics Resource Center, which constructs the parameters of the study and produces the NBES reports. The instrument itself helps to create and/ or reinforce what is meant, in business circles, by 'corporate social responsibility' or 'business ethics'. Similarly, the study revealed that, despite the fact that both 'retaliation against workers who reported misconduct and pressure to compromise standards were at all-time highs' (p. 9), misconduct itself did not increase: it decreased. Perhaps more tellingly, the vast majority of ethical misconduct incidents were committed by managers. The findings from the study suggest that ethical behaviour, as well as the reporting of unethical behaviour, is valued by employees. As the report makes clear, 'ethical performance is becoming a new norm in many workplaces' (p. 12).

But 'ethical performance' is not only a normative workplace expectation, increasingly, consumers are seeking broadened applications of ethical performance. Many of these consumers are also demanding specific performance metrics in the reporting-out of ethical action *across* an enterprise's activities. Thus, ethics programmes within businesses 'consist of the measures, policies, and instruments an organization adopts to promote ethical behavior and deter unethical behavior' (Kapstein, 2010, p. 603). However, these same expectations are carried into the marketplace as elements of 'social responsibility' enlarged and shaped by social, political, historical and cultural events, and re-applied 'from without' a business to provide a more holistic account of both patterns of behaviours and metrics for measuring deeper levels of ethical engagement and performativity.

Environmental ethics: two cases

How is this shift in ethical responsiveness and expectations articulated in the current business climate of environmental ethics? Two examples of businesses positioning themselves on the forefront of the changing face of business ethics can situate the more prevalent, if divergent, strategies for moving environmental 'ethics' and business performance into closer alignment globally: Interface and Walmart. The recent work of Halme and Laurila (2009) can situate an analysis of the emergence of different types or categories of ethical awareness in the dialogic dynamism of the 'new' relation between consumers and businesses, as well as underscore the difficulty of 'fixing' categorical metrics for interpreting business activity in the emerging environmental ethics of the global marketplace.

Halme and Laurila create a simple metric for understanding a business' approach to CSR; however, they also acknowledge that 'the typology suggested ... is only one step towards a more elaborated understanding of corporate responsibility actions and their financial and societal outcomes' (p. 336). The provisional nature of the categories they offer mirrors the quickness with which concepts and practices of 'business ethics' are shifting. Nonetheless, the categories developed in their work suggest a language by which businesses and consumers can readily understand, and articulate, more concrete ethical pathways forwards – that is, categories that are easily remembered and readily applicable to anchor consumers' decision-making processes as well as business' claims of coherence or integration of their actions with social responsibility. The categories also mirror a workable template for better understanding how consumers actually have come to see a business' relation not only to CSR, but also to society itself.

Citing a lack of empirical studies that investigate the influence of the type of corporate responsibility on financial performance, Halme and Laurila rightly point to the work of Hillman and Keim (2001), who, using information from 300 of Standard and Poor's 500 companies, found that 'responsible management of primary stakeholder relationships accrues improved shareholder value, whereas charity-type CR (i.e. philanthropy), which is not related to primary stakeholders, is negatively associated with shareholder value' (as paraphrased in Halme and Laurila, 2009, p. 333). Further, Hillman and Keim (2001) note that philanthropy, when it is strategic, can accrue financial performance gains – but philanthropy seldom is strategic in implementation. That is, although there is little extant research on different types of benefit accruing from different categories of CR, philanthropy, as practised traditionally by businesses, is far less effective than strategically positioned investment in achieving socially aware forms of action that express core business values. The research of Husted and De Jesus Salazar (2006) supports Hillman and Keim's findings: a strategic rather than altruistic CR approach is more profitable for firms seeking greater impact for their investments in social responsibility.

Thus, given this current business context – a cultural context in which philanthropy is increasingly called into question as the best investment in CR – Halme and Laurila

(2009) posit 'philanthropy, integration, and innovation' (p. 326) as three categories for understanding a business enterprise's relation to its social context and responsibility. They define these categories as follows:

- Philanthropy (emphasis on charity, sponsorships, employee voluntarism etc.).
- CR Integration (emphasis on conducting existing business operations more responsibly).
- CR Innovation (emphasis on developing new business models for solving social and environmental problems).

(p. 330)

Halme and Laurila's categories for articulating structural dimensions of the emerging approaches to CSR can best be understood by applying them to two companies that have, relatively recently, attempted to shift their CSR portfolios. Both Interface and Walmart have expended considerable energy in formulating and actualizing a social ethic and ethically driven work culture based more concretely in principles of environmental sustainability. Walmart's struggles with what employees as well as wider society interpret as ethical breaches or missteps is well documented: the scope and tenor of their labour disputes (nationally and internationally) are now legendary, and the interpretation of their business model as an application of a ruthless economy of scale that drives out small businesses region by region, manipulates suppliers and producers around price-points, and irrevocably alters small town quality of life, is widely held. However, that same business model is now a key strategy in their environmental sustainability efforts. Similarly, Interface was, for its first 21 years, a major player in a pollution-intensive industry: carpet production and distribution. By 1994, however, founder Ray Anderson had radically shifted his understanding of a relation between his industry and the wider social world. That shift came through his understanding of the principles of environmental sustainability.

Even a cursory comparison of the two companies' mission statements shows clearly the contrast between the approaches they take in dealing with corporate social responsibility as environmental sustainability. First, the case of Interface. An investigation of their webpages, the inspiration behind Ray Anderson's fundamental change of world-view in 1994, and a rhetorical analysis of the company's vision statements and accompanying documentation of their efforts is revealing. A considerable element of their vision is to adopt and maintain a position as not merely stewards of the environment, but also leaders of business models designed through and guided by sustainable ideas. For these ideas, Anderson borrowed far outside the existing tradition of business ethics; for example, Anderson cites Paul Hawken's *Ecology of Commerce* as a fundamental source of inspiration (www.interfaceglobal.com/sustainability/interface-story.aspx). Anderson's drive moved Interface quickly beyond the traditional models of both business ethics and business-based versions of profitability (as limited to financial performance). The company's opening statement, across meticulously crafted web pages detailing their efforts and approaches, is 'Interface's values are our guiding principles'. In the vision statement, those values are mirrored rhetorically, in the arrangement of nouns. The suggestion in the wording of the mission statement is that the company inverts the normative hierarchies of value, as consumers and business enterprises have historically understood that hierarchy. Interface will be 'the first company that, by its deeds, shows the entire industrial world what sustainability is in all its dimensions: People, process, product, place and profits – by 2020 – and in doing so we will become restorative through the power of influence' (Interface, 2014a).

Interface's mission statement is detailed – suggestive of an approach that demarcates a set of *measurable*, reportable objectives behind that statement. In part, their mission statement reads, 'We will honor the places where we do business by endeavoring to become the first name in industrial ecology, a corporation that cherishes nature and restores the environment. Interface will lead by example and validate by results, including profits …' (Interface, 2014a). Again, the emphasis is on measurable, transparent results and 'profits' appears subsumed within other objectives, is presented as one of a number of equally important objectives by which the company will measure its overall (social and financial) capital. In such strategies, Interface signals its version of, in Halme and Laurila's terminology, 'integrative' and 'innovative' CSR without having explicitly to compel stakeholders or consumers to interpret their ethically integrated efforts as 'authentic'. This rhetorical approach articulates the company's integration of its principles across its entire network of global operations. As the company states elsewhere (in the 'Sustainability' section of the website), 'Interface®'s sustainability journey is made more focused by measuring our progress' (Interface, 2014b)

Equally suggestive of their integration between an ethical position statement and their actions is the innovative design of their own metrics for quantifying and measuring that progress:

> Our EcoMetrics™ measurement system is designed to quantify the 'metabolism' of our operations. In other words, how much we take, in terms of materials and energy, how much we make, in terms of product, and how much we waste, in terms of wastes and emissions.
>
> We also measure our impacts on people – our associates and our communities. Our SocioMetrics™ measurement system collects data on our investment in people, including training and education, volunteering and philanthropy (Interface, 2014b).

The company website serves to educate consumers as it details the link between its ethos and its activities, providing a crucial, often missing link between business leadership and consumer decision-making; the strategy combines concepts drawn from such disciplines as chemistry, engineering, biology, accounting, etc. For example, the claim to quantify the 'metabolism' of their operations – to remain aware of their products' 'life-cycle' from pre-production to end-of-use, raw material to landfill – borrows from theories of biomimicry as well as chemical exchange theories and architectural design (i.e. German chemist Michael Braungart and US architect William McDonough's *Cradle to Cradle*). Similarly, the positioning of the language in the SocioMetrics section also suggests a deeper integration of their activity and ethical positioning as CSR: 'philanthropy' appears last – as an additional way the company 'gives back' to communities in which it operates. If, as Halme and Laurila (2009), and Hillman and Keim's (2001) research suggests, traditional versions of philanthropy are not directly profitable when not directly or properly (i.e. strategically) integrated into a company's operations, such strategies lack the impact of 'integration' and/or 'innovation'. Interface seems poised between these two categorical descriptors: seeking a strategy of both integration and innovation, Interface reveals the relative limitations of Halme and Laurila's categories. Through even a cursory analysis of Interface's strategic positioning of their CSR initiatives, we could add a fourth category to their schema: 'transformative practice' – or perhaps, more in keeping with sustainability efforts that have to work 'on the ground' of preventing or eliminating, or even, reversing damage, a fifth category such as 'net zero impact' could be added to Halme and Laurila's schematic. These additions (see the conclusion for a more nuanced description of these based on Halme and Lauri-la's categories) could more accurately measure, for both consumers and companies, successes like those of Interface, which completely transformed their own company as they radically redefined the industry of which they are a part. Interface's success with this approach is now legendary: their version of transformative innovation has paid huge dividends, socially and financially. Although successful before 1994, 'Interface is [now] a billion-dollar corporation, named by Fortune magazine as one of the 'Most Admired Companies in America' and the '100 Best Companies to Work For" (Interface, 2014).

In contrast, the evaluation of Walmart provides the limit-case for environmental sustainability researchers. The company's size and organization pose considerable challenges to researchers, and consumers, who attempt to evaluate the effectiveness of Walmart's 'best practices' in reaching its stated environmental sustainability goals. The company's overall strategy is lacking transparency in key reporting areas; thus, Walmart's mission statement has the rhetorical effect of a slogan: 'People, Saving Money, Living a Better Live'. According to one critic, while the mission statement includes significant components – i.e. customers and self-concept – it lacks many other components, such as products and services, markets, technology, concern for survival, philosophy, concern for public image and employees. And a clearly identifiable, discernible stance on environmental sustainability. 'Therefore, it provides little information as to what is the core purpose of the business and addresses too few stakeholders' ('Mission statement of Walmart', 2014). Walmart's web pages reveal the limitation of 'integration' as a categorical, conceptual device: there appears far less integration of their ethical position and their actions than is evident in the Interface web presence, and it remains difficult to quantify, to accurately measure, the extent of 'integration'. Rhetorically, however, the lack of integration has the effect of suggesting that Walmart's ethical position is either inchoate, in transition or simply disingenuous.

Such is the emerging paradigm of consumer interpretation: if companies around Walmart can produce such integration of ideas, action, metrics, and, ultimately, profitability, then Walmart appears less than genuine in the marketplace of public (ethical) opinion and reception. CEO Lee Scott pledged three significant goals in his 'Twenty-First Century Leadership Speech' (Scott 2005); in large part, this thinking was a response to the profound environmental disaster caused by Katrina in New Orleans. At the time, Scott set out the following three broadly defined environmental goals for Walmart:

• To be supplied 100 per cent by renewable energy.
• To create zero waste.
• To sell products that sustain our resources and environment.

At the time, Scott noted that 'these goals are both ambitious and aspirational, and I'm not sure how to achieve them … This obviously will take some time'. (Scott, 2005). What has been the progress towards these goals?

Five years later, an advocacy group called the Environmental Defense Fund (EDF) that had been partnering with Walmart since 2005, produced a short critique of the efforts Walmart had made in the intervening five years. The group noted the 'sheer number and scope of the goals as 'notable, as is the actual progress that the company has made on most of them' (Sturcken, 2010). Sturcken noted three areas in which Walmart needed improvement:

- 'Avoiding waste'. As Sturcken argues, 'Walmart likes to talk about waste being redirected from landfills' but the company should also focus on avoiding waste produced that then must either enter the production stream as recycled material or be relegated to a landfill as waste.
- 'Progress on packaging is lagging'. Walmart set no goals (more specifically, metrics for measuring progress) five years prior, and five years into the programme, no goals are evident. As Sturcken notes, 'we should be able to see an actual baseline ... the goal of 'packaging neutral' is never defined'.
- 'Reporting progress in context'. Again, the project of measuring overall gains in a coordinated strategy is absent.

And yet, despite these issues in developing clearly defined metrics of improvement in their sustainability initiatives, most notably, Walmart has adopted environmentally based programmes in its attitudes towards its businesses in its vast, global supply chains. Clearly, the company can apply, and has leveraged, its size to dictate production methods in their supply chains, and further, to claim that such activity is a movement towards sustainable production (and consumption).

Kalfagianni (2014) notes that contemporary politics 'is characterized by an increasing trend toward experimental forms of governance' (307); in most cases, this means private forms of governance are increasingly outdistancing public, governmental forms of regulation and oversight in the global marketplace. This situation can be confusing for consumers while, at the same time, it can create marketplace leverage and opportunities – creating both positive and negative impacts on the environment and human health – for transnational corporations (TNCs). As Kalfagianni notes:

> a plurality of private standards, codes of conduct and quality assurance schemes currently developed particularly, though not exclusively, by TNCs replace traditional inter- governmental regimes in addressing profound global environmental and socio-economic challenges ranging from forest deforestation, fisheries depletion, climate change, to labor and human rights concerns. (Kalfagianni, 2014, p. 307)

Private standard-setting (Blowfield, 2005; Fuchs et al., 2011) has risen to prominence via claims to environmentally and socially sensitive marketing strategies. To simplify what is currently meant by 'standards' in business practices, standards are 'agreed criteria by which a product or a service's performance, its technical and physical characteristics, and/or the process, and conditions, under which it has been produced or delivered, can be assessed' (Nadvi and Wältring, 2002, p. 6). They can extend to customers and end users as a basis for attaching credence, or value, to particular claims made about a product's characteristics and specification or the ways in which it has been produced (Nadvi, 2008). Thus, 'standards' become, at once, marketing/branding differentiators as well as 'regulators' in, and set by, TNCs business holdings and dealings. Market forces, public scrutiny, and strategies that blur the distinctions between 'regulations' and 'standards' mark the emerging positionalities of companies seeking to increase their market share. As Kalfagianni (2014) recognizes, 'a central feature of private standards is an expanded role for the market' (p. 309). A disproportionate number of benefits from this emerging marketplace – uniform conditions for environmental protections, ecosystems and more socio-economic forms of sustainability – result in different proportionalities or regionalities across the globe. Mayer and Gereffi (2010) note that 'institutional and societal conditions allow for better functioning' of such standards in urbanized countries than they do in satellite, developing or 'third-world' areas. Examples of this differential price paid for business abounds across products and commodities (Gulbrandsen, 2010; Gullison, 2003; Neilson and Pritchard, 2007; Pattberg, 2006). Thus the rule-setters, such as Walmart, are among those who clearly benefit from existing inequalities in political, social, cultural and economic power structures, while those upon whom these privatized standards are exercised – often, developing businesses and regions – will absorb a disproportionately high cost in social, economic and political terms. As *Fortune* reported, 'if Walmart were a country, its sales would rank it 28th in the world in GDP' (Snyder, 2015). The company has the power to shape standards in its own image, and 'regulate' change – eternalized as 'supply chain' – at its own pace.

Walmart's 2015 Global Responsibility Report (Walmart, 2015) reveals some environmentally based successes – notably, the company claims to have doubled the fuel efficiency of its fleet since 2005; exceeded the 2010 goal to eliminate 200 million metric tons of greenhouse gas emissions from its global supply chain; the diversion of 82.4 per cent of its waste, by 2014, across stores, clubs, distribution centres and other facilities; 68 per cent waste diversion outside the U.S. All of these strategies accrue environmental conservation gains; however, at the level of cost structures in operations, these strategies tend to benefit the company's financial bottom line before other kinds of benefits accrue to reduce 'externalized' costs. However, any cost/benefit analysis can cut both ways in the case of an international operation such as Walmart enjoys: this set of figures does not, for example, take into account the damage done through materials sourcing in a *relative* measure of 'before' and 'after' extraction for first-use materials. Across its sustainability initiatives, there is no baseline measurement from which to accurately measure the reality of changes to environmental damage a result of the company's efforts – or lack thereof. The figures provided in these reports register and promulgate only incremental changes across discrete periods of time, with carefully defined parameters of measurement in the definition of 'metrics' for reporting out the company's changes. Thus, the company's claim to have eliminated 20 million metric tons of greenhouse gas emissions from its global supply chains can be, at best, interpreted as aspirational marketing and, at worst, as a deceptive dissimulation of 'actual' emissions eliminations relative to the total emissions across the entirety of the company's operations.

Such issues of benchmarking also appear elsewhere in the company's efforts. In 2009, the company launched a 'sustainability index', somewhat in the mode of Interface's 'EcoMetrics' and 'SocioMetrics' measurement tools. While the language of sustainability, on the surface, appears to be an impressive response to the lack of metrics by which to measure Walmart's environmental sustainability initiatives, the assessment tool is being used in just 1,300 of Walmart's direct or indirect involvement in hundreds of thousands of suppliers. Walmart does not disclose numbers in aggregates – another less-than-transparent marketing and reporting strategy: it remains impossible accurately to understand what 1,300 suppliers actually means, but this represents a small percentage of the total suppliers with whom Walmart contracts. Another problem with this metric: while seeming to measure the environmental impact of particular products suppliers are providing Walmart, the metric is actually a measure of more constrained impacts: the life cycle of *specific* products. The language in which Walmart characterizes their intended goals for 2017 are revealing: by 2017, in its US stores, Walmart will buy 70 per cent of the goods it sells 'only from suppliers who use the Sustainability Index to evaluate and share the sustainability of their products if they produce goods in categories *where the Index is available* [italics added]'. But what percentage of goods, or what specific goods or products the Sustainability Index actually 'covers' is never made clear. Similarly, Walmart leverages this index across its suppliers, rather than in its own, internal supply chains. The company's wording is suggestive: '[t]he Sustainability Index program is a powerful tool that is helping Walmart to understand, monitor, and enhance the sustainability of our products and supply chain. The program allows Walmart to integrate sustainability into our core business and to increase our customer's trust in us and the brands we carry' ('Walmart's sustainability index', 2014). Another issue here: the index remains largely voluntary, and suppliers report-out directly to the company rather than submit their findings to third-party analysis. As Cho (2010) notes, '[t]he responses are accepted in good faith, and since the survey doesn't examine actual products, it doesn't take into account toxic materials or the amount of water used in creating specific products, or the safety, energy efficiency and recyclability of products'. In other words, behind the language of 'sustainability index', there are a lot of sustainability initiatives missing.

The use of 'sustainability' here is markedly different from that in the Interface application of the same term – whereas Interface applies the concept's logic of 'closing the loop' on production and waste in clearly stated goals, measurements and outcomes, Walmart's language emphasizes 'integration' not for these direct sustainable outcomes, but to produce the outcomes in consumer affective dimensions ('trust in us and the brands we carry'). This language, too, suggests a less-than-integrated approach to achieving environmentally sustainable goals through an ethically motivated mandate. The use of sustainability in this context points to the confusion both consumers and businesses can perpetuate about how to qualify and quantify best practices in sustainable aspirations and achievements. The claim of sustainable action is made more problematic still in the admission that the use of the sustainability index across its suppliers is a 'voluntary program' – not an ethical position at the foundation of the company's CSR: 'While Walmart's corporate policy considers the Sustainability Index to be a voluntary programme, many merchant teams have made it a requirement to participate in the program' ('Walmart's sustainability index', 2014).

Whatever its purported gains in environmental sustainability, Walmart's economic and global reach points to another serious problem, and one that threatens to dismantle the very idea of 'economic sustainability' as currently understood and practised. Given our current economic models for production, global sourcing and distribution, and consumption and waste, 'environmental' strategies of 'reduction', 'reuse', and 'elimination' of waste entering landfills are absolutely crucial to develop and maintain, of course. But even these are not enough, considering the phenomenal growth model of international conglomerates such as Walmart: in the 12 years between former Walmart CEO Scott Lee's pronouncements about his company's leadership in the twenty-first century and now, given this growth model, the company has actually slipped backward in sustainability measurements, according to the Institute for Local Self-Reliance (ISLR), a non-governmental research group. Writing in 2015, Mitchell notes:

> despite making a public commitment to sustainability nine years ago, Walmart's efforts have failed to tackle substantive changes that will help consumers and the company reduce waste and protect the environment. [Walmart's statements] will not address the environmental impact of their products, leaving consumers without real tools to make meaningful decisions about their purchases.

Equally damaging to consumers' efforts to ensure transparency in their decision-making, the entire product-driven side of the company's sustainability enterprise depends on 'supplier surveys, rather than third-party evaluations' (Mitchell, 2015). Similarly, in their operations, Walmart continues to use large quantities of coal-fired electricity – in fact, the company remains one of the largest users of coal-fired electricity. The language of sustainability is fraught with rhetoric that can prevent consumer evaluation of 'real-time' gains or failures. For example, in its 2016 report on global responsibility activities of Walmart's operations, the following language is used to make a significant claim of emissions reductions: 'Over the period from 2005–2014, Walmart has limited our emissions growth to less than one third of our business growth rate during the same period' (2016, 60). Similarly, studies completed by ISLR, in contrast to Walmart's claim to have limited global emissions significantly, have found that, since Walmart launched its environmental campaign in 2005, 'the company's self-reported greenhouse gas emissions have increased by 14 percent' (2013, 5). The ISLR's report (*Walmart's Assault on the Climate: The Truth Behind one of the Biggest Climate Polluters and Slickest Greenwashers in America, 2013*) is damaging to the messaging and imaging emanating from Walmart's corporate offices, if the report is little read or understood outside relatively constrained environmental sustainability research circles. Walmart reported these findings to the CDP, formerly known as the Carbon Disclosure Project; as Mitchell notes, 'this figure only accounts for a fraction of the company's total emissions, as Walmart does not include large segments of its greenhouse gas pollution in these disclosures' (5). For example, greenhouse emissions 'external' to Walmart's calculations of its global impact include international shipping, ocean shipping, land and development construction, any increases in driving by consumers to get to Walmart locations, and manufacture of store-brand products, to name a few. To provide a single vector for the scale of construction implied above: in 2014–2015, Walmart had plans to build 516 new stores in the US. In 2016, it planned an additional 400 store openings in the US (*Vault: Rankings and Reviews*). None of this greenhouse gas production and environmental disruption and damage enters into Walmart's reporting of its global warming impact.

Ultimately, the message communicated here, despite the advances in environmental reduction of harm that Walmart's economies of scale supplier strategy creates, is that the company's environmental efforts actually are produced by 'merchant teams' with a tangential, and financially perilous, relation to the company itself. And, although the goals articulated are laudatory, the oversight processes remain at best difficult to regulate – and, if necessary, to enforce. In addition, Walmart can also take advantage of pollution's economies of scale in the social imaginary: provided consumers do not know the gross totals of pollution produced, any reduction reported by Walmart will appear environmentally 'sustainable'. For example, if Walmart reduces greenhouse gasses by 21 million metric tons, this can sound impressive; however, if the country is responsible for adding 100 million metric tons due to increased sales, the company has done little, whatever the difficulty of reaching the achievement of 21 million metric tons reduction, to engage in an environmentally sustainable contribution to reducing greenhouse gasses.

Conclusions

Interface and Walmart are two examples of thousands of businesses that struggling to balance traditional measures of profitability with the emerging ethical climate of production and consumption. Both companies are attempting to position themselves proactively by inverting or subverting traditional approaches to CSR, in part by positioning, or repositioning, their business operations through the ethics of environmental sustainability. Differences in their approaches are striking, but they point to two possibilities for businesses to position themselves, with varying levels of commitment and/or ability. In the current discursive fields of consumer decision-making and business ethics, there is an urgent need for businesses to shift the ways they think about, and report, corporate social responsibility as a relatively inert form of traditional or social marketing, or creating and supporting 'charity events' that display little integration with the core missions of their enterprises. Businesses must shift rapidly to a more integrated, holistic strategy for both conducting and reporting on their operations, as increasingly consumers are looking across businesses' activities for the codes of integrative operations – from input streams in production cycles to plant operations to waste reduction or elimination. Similarly, consumer communities are also more aware than ever before of the impacts businesses are having on both local and global communities. Although this chapter does not offer a single 'best practices' rubric, the author believes that there is a vital need to identify future research directions for moving both businesses and consumers towards more concrete, actionable strategies for articulating and practising environmental sustainability.

Absent in the delineation of best practices for consumers is a model that captures the difference, and highlights for consumers, the significant differences, in an oppositional metric, between 'aspirational' and 'actual' transformation; thus, a company such as Walmart can operate remarkably differently than a company like Interface, and still reap similar benefits in the marketplace of consumer belief that they are all working towards environmental sustainability consumption practices. In a revision of Halme and Laurila's model, for example, two additional categories could be developed, which would help define some measurement of the gap(s) between the rhetoric/marketing of sustainability offered by a company and the accompanying practice or process by which that company achieves specifically measured, and measurable, results in actually reversing environmental damage (rather than what often passes for environmental sustainability: reduction of the rate at which harm is produced, and which, furthermore, can result in an actual net increase of damage).

The two categories that can deepen Halme and Laurila's model are 'transformative practice' which, measures the changes a company undertakes that lead to significant resource reductions which can be benchmarked and measured, monitored and assigned a score within its own operations and supply chains (thereby leading to more specific modes of consumer tracking of a company's sustainability performance beyond statements it produces). Thus, in the case of Walmart, such measures as 'net decrease' in carbon emissions across its supply chain's operations would qualify as a 'transformative practice' that would highlight measurement of 'reduced damage' rather than qualify as 'sustainable practice', language which suggests the elimination of these forms of environmental damage. The second would be 'net zero impact', which measures pollution and environmental damage impacts relative to total production of damaging impacts across the life time of a company's history. The goal then becomes a more significant measure than the mere reduction of rates of damage independent of damage produced via increased sales or market share growth (which can offset any gains made in reduction strategies). With 'net zero impact', the metric of measurement would actually be the *improvement* of the earth's lived conditions. To meet the requirements of this rating, Walmart would then be required to document the measurement to zero impact in order to represent its efforts as 'successful' in meeting a more stringent measure of environmental sustainability. Thus, in applying these two categories to environmentally based activity, a company might get one rating for its rhetorical delineation of plans, projects and targets, and quite another for its actual performance in achieving these aspirations. The difference between the two would be captured in a 'net zero impact' coefficient. In the current modelling, the distinctions between 'projected' and 'achieved', 'speech' and 'speech-act', and perhaps most confusing and damaging, 'actual' and 'marketable' environmental sustainability efforts are easily collapsible in consumers' processing of a company's representations of achievement(s). Thus, consumers often unwittingly reproduce the very behaviour they are attempting to circumvent when they make decisions based on the environmental sustainability claims of the majority of businesses in the current enviro-dialogical marketplace. Nuancing Halme and Laurila's model of sustainability efforts could clarify both companies' approaches to environmental issues and consumers' approaches to purchasing behaviours – especially in a socio-economic climate in which so many claim to make purchasing decisions based on 'environmental' reporting of companies they support in the marketplace of consumer responsibility.

References

Blowfield, M. (2005). Corporate social responsibility: The failing discipline and why it matters for international relations. *International Relations*, 19: 173–191.
Brundtland Report. (1987). Retrieved from www.un-documents.net/ocf-02.htm-I (accessed April 2016).
Chakravarthy, B.S. (1986). Measuring strategic performance. *Strategic Management Journal*, 7: 437–458.
Chelli, M. and Gendron, Y. (2013). Sustainability ratings and the disciplinary power of the ideology of numbers. *Journal of Business Ethics*, 112(2): 187–203.
Cho, Renee (2010). Greening Wal-Mart's supply chains. *Inside Climate News*. Retrieved from https://insideclimatenews.org/news/20100101/greening-wal-mart%E2%80%99s-supply chains (accessed March 2016).
De Bock, T. and Van Kenhove, P. (2011). Double standards: The techniques of neutralization. *Journal of Business Ethics*, 99(2): 283–296.
De Bock, T., Vermeir, I. and Van Kenhove P. (2013). 'What's the harm in being unethical? These strangers are rich anyway!' Exploring underlying factors of double standards. *Journal of Business Ethics*, 112(2): 225–240.
De Burgh-Woodman, H. and King, D. (2013). Sustainability and the human/nature connection: A critical discourse analysis of being 'symbolically' sustainable. *Consumption, Markets and Culture*, 16(2): 145–168.
DePaulo, P. (1985). The ethics of deception in retail bargaining: Do consumers accept the game analogy? Paper presented at the 1985 Conference of the Southwestern Marketing Association, New Orleans, LA.

DePaulo, P. (1987). Ethical perceptions of deceptive bargaining tactics used by salespersons and customers: A double standard. In J. Saegert (ed.), *Proceedings of the Division of Consumer Psychology*. Washington, DC: American Psychological Association, pp. 201–203.

Environmental Defense Fund (EDF) (2016). The *power or partnerships*. Retrieved from http://business.edf.org/files/2016/02/EDF-Walmart-10-Year-Journey-Case-Study.FINAL_.pdf (accessed July 2016).

Ethics Resource Center. (2014). *National Business Ethics Survey of the U.S. Workforce*. Retrieved from www.ethics.org/downloads/2013NBESFinalWeb.pdf (accessed March 2016).

Ethics World. (2014). *Ethics Resource Center National Ethics Surveys*. Retrieved from www.ethicsworld.org/ethicsandemployees/nbes.php (accessed March 2016).

Fuchs, D., Kalfagianni, A. and Havinga, T. (2011). Actors in private food governance: The legitimacy of retail standards and multistakeholder initiatives with civil society participation. *Agriculture and Human Values*, 28(3): 353–367.

Gulbrandsen, H.L. (2010). *Transnational Environmental Governance: The Emergence and Effects of the Certification of Forests and Fisheries*. Cheltenham: Edward Elgar.

Gullison, R.E. (2003). Does forest certification conserve biodiversity? *Oryx*, 37: 153–165.

Gundlach, G.T. and Wilkie, W.L. (2009). The American Marketing Association's new definition of marketing: Perspective and commentary on the 2007 revision. *Journal of Public Policy and Marketing*, 28(2): 259–264.

Halme, M. and and Laurila, J. (2009). Philanthropy, integration or innovation? Exploring the financial and societal outcomes of different types of corporate responsibility. *Journal of Business Ethics*, 84: 325–339.

Hillman, A. and Keim, G. (2001). Shareholder value, stakeholder management, and social issues. What's the bottom line? *Strategic Management Journal*, 22: 125–139.

Husted, B. and De Jesus Salazar, J. (2006). Taking Friedman seriously: Maximizing profits and social performance. *Journal of Management Studies*, 43(1): 75–91.

Interface. (2014a). *Our Sustainability Journey*. Retrieved from www.interfaceglobal.com/Sustainability/Interface-Story.aspx (accessed March 2016).

Interface. (2014b). 2013 Manufacturing Highlights. www.interfaceglobal.com/Sustainability/Our-Progress/AllMetrics.aspx (accessed March 2016).

Kalfagianni, Agni. (2014). Addressing the global sustainability challenge: The potential and pitfalls of private governance from the perspective of human capabilities. *J Bus Ethics*, 122: 307–320.

Kapstein, M. (2010). The ethics of organizations: A longitudinal study of the U.S. working population. *Journal of Business Ethics*, 92: 601–608.

Lazer, W. and Kelley, E.J. (1973). *Social Marketing: Perspectives and Viewpoints*. Homewood, IL: Richard D. Irwin.

Mayer, F. and Gereffi, G. (2010). Regulation and economic globalization: Prospects and limits of private governance. *Business and Politics*, 12(3): 1–25.

McCoy, C.S. (1985). *Management of Values: The Ethical Difference in Corporate Policy and Performance*. Marshfield, MA: Pittman.

McDonough, William and Michael Braungart. (2002). *Cradle to Cradle: Remaking the Way We Make Things*. New York: North Point Press.

Mission Statement of Walmart. (2014). Retrieved from www.strategicmanagementinsight.com/mission-statements/walmart-mission-statement.html (accessed March 2016).

Mitchell, Stacy (2013). *Walmart's Assault on the Climate: The Truth behind One of the Biggest Climate Polluters and Slickest Greenwashers in America*. Retrieved from http://ilsr.org/wp-content/uploads/2013/10/ILSR-_Report_WalmartClimateChange.pdf (accessed July 2015).

Nadvi, K. (2008). Global standards, global governance and the organization of global value chains. *Journal of Economic Geography*, 8: 323–343.

Nadvi, K. and Wältring, F. (2002). *INEF Report, 58*. Duisburg: Institut für Entwicklung und Frieden.

Neilson, J. and Pritchard, B. (2007). Green coffee? The contradictions of global sustainability initiatives from an Indian perspective. *Development Policy Review*, 25(3): 311–331.

Nielsen. (2008). *Corporate Ethics and Fair Trading: A Nielsen Global Consumer Report.* New York: Nielsen.

Nielsen. (2015). *The Sustainability Imperative: New Insights on Consumer Expectations.* New York: Nielsen. www.nielsen.com/content/dam/nielsenglobal/dk/docs/global-sustainability-report-oct-2015.pdf (accessed January 2016).

Pattberg, P. (2006). Private governance and the south: Lessons from global forest politics. *Third World Quarterly*, 27(4): 579–593.

Scott, Lee. (2005). *Twenty First Century Leadership.* http://corporate.walmart.com/_news_/executive-viewpoints/twenty-first-century-leadership (accessed March 2016).

Selznick, N. (1957). *Leadership in Administration: A Sociological Approach.* Evanston, IL: Row, Peterson.

Snyder, Benjamin (2015). 9 facts about Walmart that will surprise you. *Fortune: Retail.* Retrieved from http://fortune.com/2015/06/06/walmart-facts/ (accessed March 2015).

Social Investment Forum. (2007). *2007 Report on Socially Responsible Investing Trends in the United States.* Washington, DC: SIF.

Sturcken, Elizabeth (2010). What's working and what's not in Walmart's sustainability efforts. Retrieved from https://www.greenbiz.com/blog/2010/05/12/whats-working-whats-not-walmarts-sustainability-efforts (accessed June 2015).

Union of International Associations. (2008). *Annual International Meeting Statistics Report 2007.* Brussels: UIA.

Vault (2016). Rankings and reviews. www.vault.com/company-profiles/retail/wal-mart-stores,-inc/company-overview.aspx (accessed July 2016).

Vermeir, I. and Van Kenhove, P. (2008). Gender differences in double standards. *Journal of Business Ethics*, 81(2): 281–295.

Walmart (2015). *Walmart 2015 Global Sustainability Report: Opportunity, Sustainability, Community.* Retrieved from http://cdn.corporate.walmart.com/f2/b0/5b8e63024998a74b5514e078a4fe/2015-global-responsibility-report.pdf (accessed June 2016).

Walmart (2016). *Walmart: Sustainability, Community, Community: Using Our Strength to Help Others. 2016 Global Responsibility Report* (2016). Retrieved from http://cdn.corporate.walmart.com/bc/7d/a1aeaa35455e888bfacd19dcb444/2016-global-responsibility-report.22.16.pdf (accessed November 2016).

Walmart's Sustainability Index Home. (2014). Retrieved from www.walmartsustainabilityhub.com/app/answers/detail/a_id/242/session/L3 RpbWUvMTQwODU2NzMxMC9zaWQvMzVB NDlsKmw%3D (accessed June 2015).

Part III

Innovating and developing strategic capabilities for sustainability

10 Strategic management and sustainability

Timothy Galpin and Julia Hebard

Introduction

Sustainability is creating a profound shift in people's awareness and worldview, and now appears to be *the* business imperative for firms of all sizes (Elliot and Webster, 2017). However, management teams often fail to connect sustainability to business strategy (Porter and Kramer, 2006). Therefore, this chapter proposes an evidence-based framework (see Figure 10.1) to help management:

1   Analyse and evaluate external strategic drivers to shape a firm's strategic approach to sustainability.
2   Respond to external strategic drivers by incorporating sustainability into a firm's internal strategic management components.
3   Create alignment among a firm's internal strategic management components.
4   Clearly communicate a firm's sustainability agenda to various stakeholders.

Before embarking on this discussion, we should clarify our use of the term sustainability, as the concept of sustainability is evolving and a single globally accepted definition for the term does not yet exist. The phrases Sustainability, Corporate Social Responsibility (CSR), Corporate Social Performance (CSP), Going Green, and the 'Triple Bottom Line' all refer to organizations enhancing their long-term economic, social and environmental performance. For purposes of our discussion, throughout this chapter we will use the term *sustainability* to refer to the concept generally and all of its related constructs.

There is an ever-expanding volume of literature underscoring the importance of sustainability to organizations and its positive impact on firm financial and environmental performance, as well as employee job satisfaction and organizational commitment (Asrar-ul-Haq, Kuchinke and Iqbal, 2017; Huang and Watson, 2015). However, the practice of integrating sustainability into a firm's strategy is not well understood. The preponderance of writing on the topic provides broad guidance about how firms can include sustainability as part of their business strategy (see for example Basu and Palazzo, 2008; Porter and Kramer, 2011 and 2006). In this chapter we attempt to provide more specific guidance by presenting a framework that can help management integrate external sustainability drivers into their firm's internal strategic management components.

Strategy should precede action (Mintzberg, 1990). Therefore, a firm's sustainability efforts should begin at the organization-wide *strategic management* level. Strategic management is not just the organization's strategic plan. Rather, it is the total sum of a firm's plans,

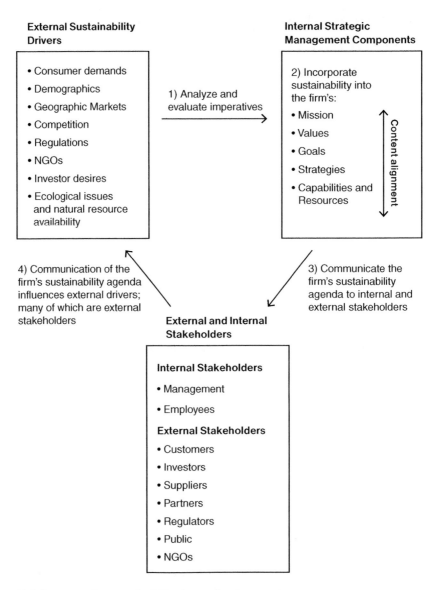

Figure 10.1 Incorporating sustainability into a firm's strategic management.

goals, capabilities, resources and actions leading to measurable results (Galpin, Whitting-ton and Bell, 2015). This more integrated view of the firm is in contrast to traditional strategic planning, which is characterized by the systematic formulation of strategies geared towards the achievement of organizational goals (Mintzberg, 1987). Research has demonstrated that firms which put strategic management into practice typically outper-form those organizations that do not, with strategic management providing: 1) a clearer direction for the company, 2) a sharper focus on what is strategically important, and 3) an improved understanding of a rapidly changing environment (Wilson, 1994).

External sustainability drivers

As Figure 10.1 illustrates, there are a number of external sustainability drivers that should be analysed and evaluated to determine the sustainability imperatives each driver may create for the firm. This analysis helps determine each driver's potential impact on the firm, and how the drivers might be incorporated into a firm's internal strategic management components. The drivers identified in Figure 10.1 were selected based on the pervasiveness of each driver appearing in the available literature about sustainability and its relationship to strategic management. The external drivers illustrated in Figure 10.1 are:

- Customer demands
- Demographics
- Geographic Markets
- Competition
- Regulations
- Non-governmental Organizations (NGOs)
- Investor desires
- Ecological issues and natural resource availability

Each of these drivers on their own can create a compelling case for a firm to implement sustainability into its strategic management approach. Together, they present a firm with an imperative to pursue a sustainability agenda. Due to the need for brevity, the following discussion of each of the sustainability drivers merely provides a brief overview of each driver and their potential effect on a firm's strategic sustainability agenda.

It should be noted that the drivers listed above are diverse and each driver is fluid. The diversity of the drivers can create conflicting sustainability imperatives for a firm (Laurenti, Sinha, Singh and Frostell, 2016). For example, customers may want to purchase environmentally safe products, which might be more expensive for the firm to produce, while at the same time, investors may demand the firm's sustainability efforts focus on maximizing profit through cost reduction by the firm using less energy and/or producing less waste. Beyond conflicts, similarities can also exist among the sustainability drivers, such as regulators, NGOs and investors all demanding safe working conditions for employees. Analysis of the set of sustainability drivers should highlight these similarities and conflicts, allowing management to evaluate the relative impact on the firm from each driver in an attempt to balance the sustainability imperatives across the set of drivers and/or prioritize which of the drivers is most impactful to the firm's brand, finances and future growth.

The fluid nature of each sustainability driver creates uncertainty about the potential changing sustainability demands placed up a firm. Regulations are often updated, new NGOs are formed, consumer demands change, competition introduces new products, services and methods, and natural resources become scarcer. This uncertainty can be a cause for concern on the part of management (Sharma and Sharma, 2011). However, regularly analysing and evaluating each driver for changes in content will help management adjust how sustainability is included in the firm's strategic management approach.

Consumer demands for sustainability

Customers are demanding sustainable practices from the companies they patronize. For example, in a recent survey, when considering a new beauty product, 70 per cent of women indicated they are more likely to buy a product from a company that supports a social issue. Moreover, the same survey found that 58 per cent are willing to pay more for products that support a social mission (61 per cent of women are willing to pay 10 per cent more for socially conscious products; 26 per cent between 11 per cent and 20 per cent more) (Herich, 2017). Another study revealed that consumers' perceived legal and ethical responsibilities of brands improve brand loyalty (He and Lai, 2014).

Demographics and sustainability

As an extension of consumer demands, firms also need to address the growing demand for sustainability being created by demographic trends. In a study polling more than 30,000 consumers in 60 countries throughout Asia-Pacific, Europe, Latin America, the Middle East, Africa and North America, almost two-thirds (66 per cent) of consumers are willing to pay extra for products and services that come from companies who are committed to positive social and environmental impact. When sorting by age, the study revealed that almost three-quarters of Millennials (age 20–34) stated they would pay more for sustainable products. Furthermore, 72 per cent of respondents under 20 (known as Gen Z) were willing to pay more. In comparison, 51 per cent of Baby Boomers (ages 50–64) said that they would pay a premium for sustainable products (MarketingCharts staff, 2015).

The same study found that female Millennials appear to be some of the most strident supporters of companies' sustainability programmes. Among the various Millennial segments identified in the study (by age, gender, affluence and parenthood), female Millennials emerged as the most likely to:

- Buy a product with a social and/or environmental benefit, given the opportunity (90 per cent, versus the 83 per cent adult average).
- Tell their friends and family about a company's sustainability efforts (86 per cent, versus the 72 per cent adult average).
- Be more loyal to a company that supports a social or environmental issue (91 per cent, versus the 87 per cent adult average).
- Geographic market drivers of sustainability

Another extension of customer demands is the rising demand across global geographic markets. Starting in 2008, *National Geographic* partnered with GlobeScan to develop an international research approach to measure and monitor consumer progress towards sustainability called the 'Greendex' survey. The first, 2008, survey encompassed 14 countries, 17 countries in 2009 to 2012, and 18 countries including 18,000 consumers in 2014. Respondents were asked about behaviours such as the relative use of sustainable versus conventional products, attitudes towards sustainability, and knowledge of sustainability issues. Their findings indicate that, compared to the study's 2008 baseline levels, sustainable consumer behaviour has increased in all countries tracked since the first study, with the exception of Brazil. Consumers in the large developing economies of India and China have scored highest on their sustainability measures. Canadians and

Americans, with their relatively massive environmental footprints as individuals, continued to score lowest (*National Geographic*, 2014).

In addition to the results of the National Geographic Greendex survey, Nielsen's 2015 global sustainability survey polled more than 30,000 consumers in 60 countries throughout Asia-Pacific, Europe, Latin America, the Middle East, Africa and North America. According to the survey, 55 per cent of the respondents indicated they are willing to pay more for products and services provided by companies that are committed to sustainability. The propensity to buy socially responsible brands is strongest in Asia-Pacific (64 per cent), Latin America (63 per cent) and Middle East/Africa (63 per cent). The numbers for North America and Europe are 42 and 40 per cent, respectively. Amy Fenton, Global Leader of Public Development and Sustainability at Nielsen states, 'Consumers around the world are saying loud and clear that a brand's social purpose is among the factors that influence purchase decisions' (Nielsen, 2015).

Competition and sustainability

Beyond consumers of various demographics and locations, competition compels companies to become more sustainable. Research has found that a competitive advantage can be accomplished through the inclusion of sustainability into a firm's operating model (Bernal-Conesa, de Nieves-Nicto and Briones-Peñalver, 2016). In addition to research, numerous examples exist of innovation driven by industry competition leading to sustainable solutions. In their supply chains several companies are working on innovative solutions to sustainable agriculture. Examples include Diageo and SAB Miller with barley production in Africa, Nestlé with milk supplies in Pakistan, and Cadbury's (now Kraft's) Cocoa Partnership to preserve vital supply chains in Ghana. In the distribution chain Coca-Cola's micro-distribution centres in Africa have developed new ways to employ local entrepreneurs to get their products 'the last mile' to small urban and rural outlets. While companies like these may be willing to share their initiatives outside the competitive context, with NGOs and companies outside their sector for example, in almost every case, these sustainability business models have been developed to improve the competitive positioning of each company, improve their brand value, and increase quality and quantity of sales (Baxter, 2013).

Regulation as a motivator for sustainability

Regulatory trends also drive companies towards sustainability. For example, in 2001, France implemented a requirement for sustainability reporting among all firms operating with the country. However, initial compliance with the statute was low. But, in an examination of the change in CSR disclosure from 2004 in comparison to 2010 for a sample of 81 publicly traded French firms, researchers found significant increases in the space allocated for sustainability reporting within company documents, as well as an increase in quality of the reporting due to stricter enforcement of the regulatory requirement (Chauvey, Giordano-Spring, Cho and Patten, 2015).

Regulatory compliance concerning sustainability is complex, with regulations varying by country, state, and often by city. For example, in 2007 San Francisco banned supermarkets from using plastic bags at checkout, while many other major cities have not. However, firms have found that there are competitive advantages to adhering to and even anticipating sustainability regulations. For example, companies that focus on emerging regulation gain time to experiment with materials, technologies and processes, *before* the regulations are put in place. Furthermore, regulatory compliance can actually save companies money. When complying with the least stringent standards, firms must manage sourcing, production and logistics separately for each market, because rules vary by country. However, Cisco, HP and other firms enforce a single standard across each of their facilities globally, gaining from economies of scale and optimizing their supply chains. To be successful with this approach, a firm's worldwide norm must be the strictest standard that the firm will encounter globally (Nidumolu, Prahalad and Rangaswami, (2009).

NGOs drive sustainability

It is claimed that NGOs help bring a multiplicity of perspectives, and principally the interests of the less powerful, to business regulation and new governance systems (Grosser, 2016). Firm's often partner with NGOs to enhance their sustainability and improve their corporate image (Grolleau, Ibanez and Lavoie, 2016). Sustainability research has extensively explored the role of NGOs' relationships with corporations (Rasche, De Bakker and Moon, 2013), and it is argued that NGOs, at least partially, compensate for the diminishing power of the nation–state in relation to corporations that operate transnationally (Burchell and Cook, 2013). Research has demonstrated that NGOs have had an impact on firms' approaches to sustainability with regard to environmental issues, labour rights and human rights, and gender equality (Grosser, 2016; Hoffman, 1999; Vogel, 2008).

Investor desires for sustainability

Investors are increasingly considering a firm's sustainability important enough that they are influencing firms towards more sustainable business models through their investing choices (Rajagopal, Dyaram and Ganuthula, 2016). Moreover, a study comparing Socially Responsible Investment (SRI) funds and conventional funds with regard to the impact of the global financial crisis of 2008 found that SRI funds better resisted the bankruptcy of the financial crisis than conventional funds (Nakai, Yamaguchi and Takeuchi, 2016). Interestingly, when examining the tactics of various groups in demanding firms' social change researchers found that different activists rely on different tactics. For example, NGOs rely upon boycotts and protests, whereas activist investors rely on lawsuits and proxy votes (Eesley, Decelles and Lenox, 2016).

Ecological issues and natural resource availability drive sustainability

Finally, firms are finding that they can no longer continue to exploit environmental resources and shirk their responsibilities by acting as separate entities regardless of the interest of the society (Krishna Murthy and Pitty, 2013). A number of ecological issues and resource scarcity are driving firms' sustainability agendas including climate change and greenhouse gas emissions, air and water pollution, limitations of oil and gas supplies, water scarcity, loss of natural areas, threatened species and toxic spills (Adamowicz and Olewiler, 2016; Brelsford and Abbott, 2017). Firms in various industries are responding to these issues by developing sustainability agendas based on their particular resource uses (Kajzer Mitchell and Walinga, 2017).

Internal strategic management components

The external strategic drivers described above create a persuasive argument for firms to include sustainability as part of their overall strategic management. Consequently, the second step identified in Figure 10.1 – incorporating sustainability into the firm's internal strategic management components – will be addressed in this section. The internal strategic management components illustrated in Figure 10.1 are the firm's mission, values, goals, strategies and capabilities and resources. Although seemingly straightforward, it should be noted that incorporating sustainability into a firm's strategic management components is often problematic. The difficulty is due to the fact that attitudes and actions regarding sustainability can vary widely among company leadership. Some leaders may identify sustainability as an important strategic imperative for a firm, while others may not. Likewise, even if they agree on sustainability as a priority, company executives' often hold conflicting views about how best to incorporate sustainability into the firm's strategic management components (Sharma and Sharma, 2011).

Building sustainability into the firm's mission

In general, a mission identifies how a firm defines its purpose and establishes the priorities of the organization. Furthermore, a well-designed mission statement can help differentiate a firm from other similar organizations. Mission statements are a powerful tool for setting the strategic direction and tactical actions of the company (Dermol, 2012; Jacopin and Fontrodona, 2009). Considerable research has shown that a well-articulated mission statement provides critical signals to organizational stakeholders regarding the aims of the organization and can ultimately lead to positive outcomes that benefit the entire firm (Atrill, Omran and Pointon, 2005; Desmidt, Prinzie and Decramer, 2011).

Initiating a company's sustainability efforts begins with a mission statement that strikes a balance between financial performance, social performance (e.g. workers' and women's rights, working conditions, fair pay, and so forth) and environmental performance; and seeks to achieve high performance in terms of each of these areas. When addressing sustainability, it is important that a mission convey the role of the organization in relation to society to the various stakeholders identified in Figure 10.1, including employees, customers, investors, and so forth (Castello and Lozano, 2009; Quinn and Dalton, 2009). Mission statements that adopt this balanced posture will convey to both internal and external stakeholders that the firm does not consider success in terms of the 'triple bottom line' (i.e. people, profit and planet) to be mutually exclusive. Instead, top managers will lead the organization in a way that reflects success in financial, societal and environmental terms. Examples of firms that have adopted a sustainability perspective in their missions include Patagonia – *Build the best product, cause no unnecessary harm, use business to inspire and implement solutions to the environmental crisis* (Patagonia, 2017a), and Whole Foods – *Whole People, Whole Planet* (Whole Foods Market, 2017a).

While including sustainability in a firm's mission statement is necessary to initiate sustainability efforts, it is far from sufficient. Indeed, if a firm that changes its mission to symbolize becoming more sustainable without subsequent efforts that are substantive in nature, they run the risk of being accused by external stakeholders of superficially employing sustainability merely as a marketing tactic. Therefore, to earnestly pursue their sustainability aspirations, firms should begin with their mission statements, and then proceed with instilling sustainability in their organizational value systems, goals, business strategy and capabilities.

Building sustainability into the firm's values

The mission statement is an effective tool for articulating the organization's values to the various external stakeholders identified in Figure 10.1, as well as setting expectations for the behaviour of internal stakeholders (i.e. management and employees) to align with those values (Klemm, Stuart and Luffman, 1991; Swales and Rogers, 1995). Organizational values refer to beliefs about the types of goals firm members should pursue, as well as ideas regarding standards of behaviour organizational members should use to achieve those goals. Values are the basis for the development of the organizational norms and expectations that define appropriate behaviour by employees in particular situations. Shared values can also provide a source of motivation and commitment among organizational members (Schein, 2010). A firm's values answer the question – *Who are we as an organization?* Shared values have been found to be a key component of aligning management and employee decision-making and behaviours with a firm's sustainability efforts (Hargett and Williams, 2009; Morsing and Oswald, 2009). A firm's sustainability values have also been found to have a positive impact on perceptions of other stakeholders including customers, NGOs and investors (Bhattacharya, 2016; Rajagopal et al., 2016; Rasche et al., 2013).

Examples of companies that have incorporated sustainability into their corporate values include Whole Foods – *Caring about our communities & our environment* (Whole Foods Market, 2017b), and Pacific Gas and Electric – *We are accountable for all of our own actions: these include safety, protecting the environment, and supporting our communities* (Pacific Gas & Electric, 2017).

Building sustainability into the firm's goals

Organizational sustainability goals should complement sustainability-centred missions and values. Goal setting provides the foundation for developing a roadmap of organizational activity (i.e. the company's strategy), as well as provides the basis for establishing the metrics which will be used to measure progress (Locke and Latham, 2012; Smith and Locke, 1990). A firm's goals answer the question – *What will the organization achieve?* Goals communicate to all stakeholders the direction the company is headed and the priorities of the firm. For example, Vail Resorts committed to 'Target 10' in 2008, a 10 per cent reduction in energy use by 2012. Hitting that number ahead of schedule in 2011, the company committed to 'The Next Ten', a programme aimed at yet another 10 per cent by 2020 (Vail Resorts, 2017).

As important as organizational level goals are, they are not adequate in themselves to create a comprehensive approach to sustainability. In order to insure that the firm's commitment to sustainability permeates the entire organization, it must be extended into the development of its business strategy.

Building sustainability into the firm's strategy

A global survey of more than 1,500 corporate executives found that a majority of respondents believe sustainability is becoming increasingly important to business strategy, and that the risks of failing to act on sustainability are growing (Berns et al., 2009). If a firm's sustainability efforts are to provide long-term value to both the company and society, sustainability must be integrated into the firm's strategy in a way that complements the firm's goals and overall mission. The link between a firm's strategy and its performance is well established, with additional empirical evidence demonstrating a strong link between an organization's strategy and the firm's performance in terms of social responsibility (Beard and Dess, 1981; Galbreath, 2010). Moreover, embedding sustainability in organizational strategy has the twin benefit of providing value to society as well as distinguishing the firm from competitors (Castello and Lozano, 2009; Siegel, 2009). Examples of firms that have adopted sustainability strategies include Patagonia's 'activist company' strategy (Patagonia, 2017b) and Coca-Cola's 'water stewardship and replenishment' strategy (Coca-Cola, 2017).

Building sustainability into the firm's capabilities and resources

Although it is necessary to instil sustainability into a firm's mission, values, strategies and goals, doing so is not sufficient to fully establish sustainability as a key element of a firm's strategic management. Strategic capabilities, those that differentiate a firm from its competitors, involve the patterning of activity, and investments are typically required to create and sustain such patterning; for example, in a firm's supply chain design, product development process or manufacturing methods. Consequently, capabilities cannot easily be bought and must instead be built (Winter, 2003). The reconfiguration of firm resources and capabilities enable the implementation of sustainability innovations. For example, Unilever recently undertook a product redesign and introduced compressed deodorant cans. The existing organizational processes to produce the deodorant can were reassessed and reconfigured, which made the deodorant cans half of their previous size. This resulted in each deodorant can using approximately 25 per cent less aluminium, requiring approximately 33 per cent less fuel for transportation and reducing the associated carbon footprint by 25 per cent (CanTech International, 2013).

Content alignment

Before being able to communicate a consistent purpose and direction to all stakeholders the content of a firm's mission, values, goals, strategy and capabilities should be in alignment with one another. Misalignment of the firm's strategic management components identified in Figure 10.1 can create confusion among both internal and external firm stakeholders about the firm's sustainability agenda, whereas it has been found that aligning the content of a firm's strategic management components creates consistency among management and employee behaviours (Longoni and Cagliano, 2015). Moreover, research has indicated that the overall alignment of strategic management components leads to improved firm performance (Wu et al., 2014). Examples of firms that have aligned their sustainability agenda across the strategic management components identified in Figure 10.1 include Patagonia (Patagonia, 2017a and b) and Whole Foods (Whole Foods, 2017a and b).

Communication of the firm's sustainability agenda

As Figure 10.1 indicates, once management has consistently embedded sustainability into the firm's strategic management components, the next step is communicating the firm's sustainability agenda to various internal and external stakeholders. Indeed, the increasing global awareness of sustainability has led to a significant proliferation in the publishing of firms' sustainability reports around the world (Guidry and Patten, 2010). Firms disclosing sustainability information are able to signal superior sustainability performance, which positively affects the market's view of the firm and potential future value (Prado-Lorenzo and Garcia-Sanchez, 2010). The positive effect of sustainability reporting on firm value can be explained by stakeholder theory. Stakeholder theory posits that business success lies in a firm's ability to maintain trustful and mutually respectful relationships with the various stakeholders identified in Figure 10.1 (Freeman, 2010). Interestingly, firms that publish sustainability reports have been found to possess higher market valuations than firms that do not provide sustainability reporting. Moreover, the same researchers found that among the firms that publish sustainability reports, those with high sustainability reporting quality and perceived credibility have higher market valuations than firms with low sustainability reporting quality and perceived credibility of sustainability reporting (Wang and Li, 2016). Examples of firms who regularly report sustainability results include Vail Resorts (Vail Resorts, 2017) and Pepsico (Pepsico (2017).

Lastly, as illustrated in Figure 10.1, communicating a firm's sustainability agenda also influences external drivers, many of which are external stakeholders. Examples of firms' influencing various sustainability drivers include, lobbying regulators (Funk and Hirschman, 2017), partnering with NGOs (Calveras and Ganuza, 2016), demonstrating ethical behaviour that in turn drives competitors to emulate ethical behaviours (Carson, Hagen and Sethi, 2015), and advertising sustainable practices which influences customer desires (Ülkü and Hsuan, 2017).

Implications for Management

The framework we present implies several key actions enabling management to take an adaptive and context-related approach to strategic sustainability management that can be tailored, as ever-changing external sustainability drivers require.

The first step is to conduct an external drivers analysis, collecting both quantitative and qualitative data, for each of the key external sustainability drivers. This external analysis will help management determine the sustainability requirements and constraints of the firm's customers, geographic markets, competitors, regulators, investors and natural resources. Data from the external analysis should then be used to incorporate sustainability into each component of the firm's internal strategic management, initially by clearly articulating sustainability as part of the firm's mission. Then, by developing organizational values that include sustainability, followed by establishing organizational goals focused on sustainability, incorporating sustainability into the firm's business strategy, and developing the firm's capabilities and resources to implement desired sustainability efforts. Once sustainability is incorporated into the internal strategic management components, the firm's sustainability agenda can then be clearly communicated to various stakeholders including customers, investors, suppliers, partners, regulators, the public and NGOs. Communication of a firm's sustainability agenda also enables management to proactively influence various external drivers, from lobbying regulators to partnering with NGOs, to influencing customer desires. Finally, management should continually monitor the external sustainability drivers, and regularly adapt the firm's internal strategic management components as sustainability imperatives change.

Conclusions

The evidence-based framework we offer illustrates how external drivers provide imperatives for a firm's strategic management approach to sustainability, and how a firm can respond to external drivers by incorporating sustainability into its internal strategic management components. Moreover, content alignment among a firm's internal strategic management components helps create consistency in a firm's sustainability communication to various stakeholders. While management may view the fluid nature of a diverse set of external sustainability drivers with concern, our framework provides them with an adaptive and context-related approach to strategic sustainability management that can be tailored, as ever-changing external sustainability drivers require.

References

Adamowicz, W.L. and Olewiler, N. (2016). Helping markets get prices right: Natural capital, ecosystem services, and sustainability. *Canadian Public Policy*, 42(1): S32–S38.

Asrar-ul-Haq, M., Kuchinke, P.K. and Iqbal, A. (2017). The relationship between corporate social responsibility, job satisfaction, and organizational commitment. *Journal of Cleaner Production*, 142: 2352–2363.

Atrill, P., Omran, M. and Pointon, J. (2005). Company mission statements and financial performance. *Corporate Ownership & Control*, 2 (3): 28–35.

Basu, K. and Palazzo, G. (2008). Corporate social responsibility: A process model of sensemaking. *Academy of Management Review*, 33(1): 122–136.

Baxter, G. (2013). Competition, not just collaboration, can push forward sustainability. *The Guardian*. Available from: www.theguardian.com/sustainable-business/competition-collaboration-push-forward-sustainability (accessed 6 January 2017).

Beard, D.W. and Dess, G.G. (1981). Corporate-level strategy, business-level strategy, and firm performance. *The Academy of Management Journal*, 24(4): 663–688.

Bernal-Conesa, J.A., de Nieves-Nieto, C. and Briones-Peñalver, A. (2016). CSR and technology companies: A study on its implementation, integration and effects on the competitiveness of companies. *Intangible Capital*, 12(5): 1529–1590.

Berns, M.A., Townend, Z., Khayat, B., Balagopal, M., Reeves, M.S., Hopkins, A. and Kruschwitz, N. (2009). Sustainability and competitive advantage. *MIT Sloan Management Review*, 51(1): 19–26.

Bhattacharya, C.B. (2016). Responsible marketing: Doing well by doing good. *Marketing Intelligence Review*, 8(1): 8–17.

Brelsford, C. and Abbott, J.K. (2017). Growing into water conservation? Decomposing the drivers of reduced water consumption in Las Vegas, NV. *Ecological Economics*, 13: 399–110.

Burchell, J. and Cook, J. (2013). CSR, co-optation and resistance: The emergence of new agonistic relations between business and civil society. *Journal of Business Ethics*, 115(4): 741–754.

Calveras, A. and Ganuza, J. (2016). The role of public information in corporate social responsibility. *Journal of Economics & Management Strategy*, 25(4): 990–1017.

CanTech International (2013). Aerosols: 'compressed' deodorant cans launched by Unilever. *CanTech International*, 20(6): 39.

Carson, S., Hagen, O. and Sethi, S. (2015). From implicit to explicit CSR in a Scandinavian context: The cases of HÅG and Hydro. *Journal of Business Ethics*, 127(1): 17–31.

Castello, I. and Lozano, J. (2009). From risk management to citizenship corporate social responsibility: Analysis of strategic drivers of change. *Corporate Governance*, 9(4): 373–385.

Chauvey, J., Giordano-Spring, S., Cho, C. and Patten, D. (2015). The normativity and legitimacy of CSR disclosure: Evidence from France, *Journal of Business Ethics*, 130(4): 789–803.

Coca Cola (2017). Water stewardship and replenishment report. Available from: www.coca-colacompany.com/stories/setting-a-new-goal-for-water-efficiency (accessed 7 January 2017).

Dermol, V. (2012). Relationship between mission statement and company performance. In *Proceedings of Management Knowledge and Learning 2012 International Conference* in Zadar, Croatia, pp. 891–899.

Desmidt, S., Prinzie, A. and Decramer, A. (2011). Looking for the value of mission statements: A meta-analysis of 20 years of research. *Management Decision*, 49(3): 468–483.

Eesley, C., Decelles, K.A. and Lenox, M. (2016). Through the mud or in the boardroom: Examining activist types and their strategies in targeting firms for social change. *Strategic Management Journal*, 37(12): 2425–2440.

Elliot, S. and Webster, J. (2017). Editorial: Special issue on empirical research on information systems addressing the challenges of environmental sustainability: An imperative for urgent action. *Information Systems Journal*, 27(4): 367–378.

Freeman, R.E. (2010). *Strategic Management: A Stakeholder Approach*. Cambridge: Cambridge University Press.

Funk, R.J. and Hirschman, D. (2017). Beyond nonmarket strategy: Market actions as corporate political activity. *Academy of Management Review*, 42(1): 32–52.

Galbreath, J. (2010). Drivers of corporate social responsibility: The role of formal strategic planning and firm culture. *British Journal of Management*, 21(2): 511–525.

Galpin, T.J., Whittington, J.L. and Bell, R.G. (2015). Is your sustainability strategy sustainable? Creating a culture of sustainability. *Corporate Governance*, 15(1): 1–17.

Grolleau, G., Ibanez, L. and Lavoie, N. (2016). Cause-related marketing of products with a negative externality. *Journal of Business Research*, 69(10): 4321–4330.

Grosser, K. (2016). Corporate Social Responsibility and multi-stakeholder governance: Pluralism, feminist perspectives and women's NGOs. *Journal of Business Ethics*, 137(1): 65–81.

Guidry, R.P. and Patten, D.M. (2010). Market reactions to the first-time issuance of corporate sustainability reports: Evidence that quality matters. *Sustainability Accounting, Management and Policy Journal*, 1: 33–50.

Hargett, T.R. and Williams, M.F. (2009). Wilh. Wilhelmsen Shipping Company: Moving from CSR tradition to CSR leadership. *Corporate Governance*, 9(1): 73–82.

He, Y. and Lai, K.K. (2014). The effect of corporate social responsibility on brand loyalty: The mediating role of brand image. *Total Quality Management & Business Excellence*, 25(3/4): 249–263.

Herich, D. (2017). Beauty is where the heart is. *Global Cosmetic Industry*, 185(1): 30–33.

Hoffman, A. (1999). Institutional evolution and change: Environmentalism and the US chemical industry. *Academy of Management Journal*, 42: 351–371.

Huang, X.B. and Watson, L. (2015). Corporate social responsibility research in accounting. *Journal of Accounting Literature*, 34: 1–16.

Jacopin, T. and Fontrodona, J. (2009). Questioning the corporate responsibility (CR) department alignment with the business model of the company. *Corporate Governance*, 9(4): 528–536.

Kajzer Mitchell, I. and Walinga, J. (2017). The creative imperative: The role of creativity, creative problem solving and insight as key drivers for sustainability. *Journal of Cleaner Production*, 140: 1872–1884.

Klemm, M., Stuart, S. and Luffman, G. (1991). Mission statements: Selling corporate values to employees. *Long Range Planning*, 24(3): 73–78.

Krishna Murthy, M. and Pitty, N. (2013). Corporate social responsibilities of Indian public sector enterprises: A case study of Bharat Heavy Electricals Limited (BHEL). *Proceedings of The International Conference on Management, Leadership & Governance*, pp. 194–202.

Laurenti, R., Sinha, R., Singh, J. and Frostell, B. (2016). Towards addressing unintended environmental consequences: A planning framework. *Sustainable Development*, 24(1): 1–17.

Locke, E.A. and Latham, G.P. (2012). *New Developments in Goal Setting and Task Performance*. New York: Routledge.

Longoni, A. and Cagliano, R. (2015). Cross-functional executive involvement and worker involvement in lean manufacturing and sustainability alignment. *International Journal of Operations & Production Management*, 35(9): 1332–1358.

MarketingCharts staff (2015). Global consumers willing to pay more for socially responsible products. *Sustainable Brands*. Available from: www.marketingcharts.com/traditional/will-consumers-pay-more-for-products-from-socially responsible-companies-60166/ (accessed 6 January 2017).

Mintzberg, H. (1987). Crafting strategy. *Harvard Business Review*, 65(4): 66–75.

Mintzberg, H. (1990). The design school: Reconsidering the basic premises of strategic management. *Strategic Management Journal*, 11(3): 171–195.

Morsing, M. and Oswald, D. (2009). Sustainable leadership: Management control systems and organizational culture in Novo Nordisk A/S. *Corporate Governance*, 9(1): 83–99.

Nakai, M., Yamaguchi, K. and Takeuchi, K. (2016). Can SRI funds better resist global financial crisis? Evidence from Japan. *International Review of Financial Analysis*, 48, 12–20.

National Geographic (2014). Greendex, consumer choice and the environment: A worldwide tracking survey. *National Geographic*. Available from: http://environment.nationalgeographic.com/environment/greendex/ (accessed 6 January 2017).

Nidumolu, R., Prahalad, C.K. and Rangaswami, M.R. (2009). Why sustainability is now the key driver of innovation. *Harvard Business Review*, 87(9): 56–64.

Nielsen (2015). The sustainability imperative. *Neilsen*. Available from: www.nielsen.com/us/en/insights/reports/2015/the-sustainability-imperative.html (accessed 6 January 2017).

Pacific Gas & Electric (2017). Core values. Available from: www.pgecorp.com/aboutus/corp_gov/coce/core.shtml (accessed 7 January 2017).

Patagonia (2017a). Environmental and social responsibility. Available from: www.patagonia.com/environmentalism.html (accessed 7 January 2017).

Patagonia (2017b). The activist company. Available from: www.patagonia.com/the-activist-company.html (accessed 7 January 2017).

Pepsico (2017). Our progress. Available from: www.pepsico.com/purpose/performance-with-purpose/planet (accessed 7 January 2017).

Porter, M.E. and Kramer, M.R. (2006). Strategy & Society: The link between competitive advantage and corporate social responsibility. *Harvard Business Review*, 84(12): 78–92.

Porter, M.E. and Kramer, M.R. (2011). Creating shared value. *Harvard Business Review*, 89(1/2): 62–77.

Prado-Lorenzo, J.-M. and Garcia-Sanchez, I.-M. (2010). The role of the board of directors in disseminating relevant information on greenhouse gases. *Journal of Business Ethics*, 97: 391–424.

Quinn, L. and Dalton, M. (2009). Leading for sustainability: Implementing the tasks of leadership. *Corporate Governance*, 9(1): 21–38.

Rajagopal, V., Dyaram, L. and Ganuthula, V. (2016). Stakeholder salience and CSR in Indian context. *Decision*, 43(4): 351–363.

Rasche, A., De Bakker, F. and Moon, J. (2013). Complete and partial organizing for corporate social responsibility. *Journal of Business Ethics*, 115(4): 651–663.

Schein, E. (2010). *Organizational Culture and Leadership*, 4th edn. San Francisco, CA: Jossey-Bass.

Sharma, P. and Sharma, S. (2011). Drivers of proactive environmental strategy in family firms. *Business Ethics Quarterly*, 21(2): 309–334.

Siegel, D.S. (2009). Green management matters only if it yields more green: An economic/strategic perspective. *Academy of Management Perspectives*, 23(3): 5–16.

Smith, K.G. and Locke, E.A. (1990). Goal setting, planning, and organizational performance: An experimental simulation. *Organizational Behavior and Human Decision Processes*, 46(1): 118–134.

Swales, J.M. and Rogers, P.S. (1995). Discourse and the projection of corporate culture: The mission statement. *Discourse & Society*, 6(2): 223–242.

Ülkü, M.A. and Hsuan, J. (2017). Towards sustainable consumption and production: Competitive pricing of modular products for green consumers. *Journal of Cleaner Production*, 14(2): 4230–4242.

Vail Resorts (2017). Caring about our communities & our environment. Available from: www.vail.com/mountain/environment.aspx#/EnergysavingsTab (accessed 7 January 2017).

Vogel, D. (2008). Private global business regulation. *Annual Review of Political Science*, 11: 261–282.

Wang, K. and Li, D. (2016). Market reactions to the first-time disclosure of corporate social responsibility reports: Evidence from China. *Journal of Business Ethics*, 138(4): 661–682.

Whole Foods Market (2017a). Declaration of interdependence. Available from: www.wholefoodsmarket.com/mission-values/core-values/declaration-interdependence (accessed 7 January 2017).

Whole Foods Market (2017b). Caring about our communities & our environment. Available from: https://www.wholefoodsmarket.com/mission-values/core-values/caring-about-our-communities-our-environment (accessed 7 January 2017).

Wilson, I. (1994). Strategic planning isn't dead-it changed. *Long Range Planning*, 27(4): 20–32.

Winter, S.G. (2003). Understanding dynamic capabilities. *Strategic Management Journal*, 24(10): 991–995.

Wu, T., Jim Wu, Y., Chen, Y.J. and Goh, M. (2014). Aligning supply chain strategy with corporate environmental strategy: A contingency approach, *International Journal of Production Economics*, 147(Part B): 220–229.

11 Corporate social innovation

Top-down, bottom-up, inside-out and outside-in

Philip Mirvis and Bradley Googins

Introduction

Social innovation in business

Innovation is a key driver of business growth and essential to sharpening and sustaining competitive advantage. But as core as innovation has been to the DNA of firms, it has not been an integral part of corporations' engagements with society. Today we find that some leading companies are bringing social innovation into their economic, social and environmental agendas.

These firms take a core competence of their business – its capacities to innovate – and apply it to pressing issues in their corporate ecosystem. In so doing, they draw on the talents of their employees and assets of their core business to co-create innovations with social sector (and other stakeholder) partners. Corporate social innovation (CSI) can be defined as:

> Corporate Social Innovation is a strategy that combines a unique set of corporate assets (innovation capacities, marketing skills, managerial acumen, employee engagement, scale, etc.) in collaboration with other sectors and firms to co-create breakthrough solutions to complex economic, social, and environmental issues that bear on the sustainability of both business and society.
>
> (Mirvis, Googins and Kiser, 2012)

Over the past five years, we have been studying practices in over 70 socially innovative businesses and exploring examples of 'shared innovation' involving cooperation among businesses, NGOs, community groups and various levels of government.

Innovation drivers

Several factors shape corporate interests and activity in social innovation:

- Societal challenges are prominent on the corporate radar screen. Chronic poverty and unemployment, declining education and infrastructure in communities, global warming and a deteriorating biosphere, worrisome consumption trends, industry-specific issues such as access to health care, banking, technology and more all register on the corporate radar screen as does continuing distrust of big business. The large companies we studied understand that stakeholders expect them to take responsibility to engage some of these issues (Browne, Nuttall and Stadlen, 2016). Several map the range of social issues relevant to their business and consult with stakeholders to set their social investment priorities.

- Traditional corporate responses are not sufficient. Companies have traditionally addressed societal challenges through their charitable giving and corporate social responsibility and sustainability initiatives. Now leading firms are taking a more robust approach with moves towards strategic philanthropy, development of a comprehensive green agenda and experimentation with 'shared value' principles in managing global supply chains and reaching consumers at the 'base of the pyramid'. These moves require new kinds of innovations and innovation processes (Hart and Christensen, 2002; Pfitzer et al., 2013; Kiron et al., 2013).
- Addressing social challenges requires 'innovation in innovation'. Many firms have well-developed innovation protocols and innovation teams that can encompass R&D, product and marketing units, and their sales force. But these processes and personnel are oriented to innovation in traditional corporate markets and in line with commercial criteria. Addressing social challenges requires outreach from firms beyond their traditional customer base into communities and populations in need. Social value propositions hinge on different kinds of investment and assessment criteria. In search of new ideas, companies we observed variously draw ideas 'bottom-up' from employees and 'inside-out' through open innovation platforms.
- Sustainable social innovation hinges on multi-party collaboration. Complex problems call for complex solutions and organizations from different industries and sectors bring unique and essential assets to the work of social change. Recognition of this is leading many companies to collaborate with NGOs, government, other companies, and/or social entrepreneurs to address social challenges (Kania and Kramer, 2011; Worley and Mirvis, 2013). Firms we studied often engage partners early on to refine their understandings of social issues and inform and shape an innovative response. Many also work with external parties in networks and collaborative arrangements that range from contracted services to full partnership.
- Employees are eager to be engaged in social innovation. Increasing numbers of young people worldwide aspire for 'something more' from a job. Many want to work for a company committed to social and environmental improvement (Cone, 2016). Several companies studied engage their employees in 'good work' through innovative pro bono service assignments where they travel to distant lands and work with local businesses, NGOs or government agencies to address social challenges. In others, employees are engaged locally with social entrepreneurs to accelerate their growth and enhance their capabilities. Select firms sponsor internal innovation contests whereby employee social intrapreneurs can vet and gain funding for social and eco-innovation ideas (Mirvis and Googins, 2018).
- Social issues are business opportunities. Management sage Peter Drucker once opined 'Every single social and global issue of our day is a business opportunity in disguise.' In this light, companies are devising social innovations that deliver value for both society and their business. Many promising social innovations, however, cannot generate financial returns equal to typical commercial investments. Socially innovative companies take account of relationship and reputational gains from social innovations and apply a longer-term horizon to expected financial payoff. Some support their innovations through 'blended-finance' – with funding from

the corporate foundation and the business, and sometimes from social investors and partners. Most important, the social investment decisions and management are conditioned on producing measurable 'social impact'.

Research sample

The findings and case material here comes from personal interviews, field observations, and in some instances corporate reports, internal communiques and blogs. The sample consists of 70 companies and select foundations or think tanks based in the US, Europe and Asia (see Appendix A for full list). Companies were identified based on their strong track records in corporate social responsibility and, in many instances, familiarity with the authors based on our prior research into their CSR profiles and performance (Googins et al., 2007). This is a sample of convenience and not representative of corporations worldwide or of any industry.

Field research involved face-to-face interviews with executives, CSR and sustainable leaders, and employee social innovators at their base sites and in some cases investigation at innovation sites in the field. Supplemental information was obtained from studies of select companies by scholars and professional service firms.

In this exploratory study, we were not 'testing' any specific hypotheses about CSI or conducting a rigorous evaluation of specific social innovations. Rather, research methods were inductive and aimed towards pattern definition. The focus in this chapter is on the range of social innovations produced by companies and key factors that influenced their production.

Range of social innovations

We identified a broad range of corporate social innovations that can be classified along two dimensions:

1   One dimension distinguishes innovations that are developed 'top-down' via structured corporate innovation processes versus 'bottom-up' from internal or community innovators.
2   The second differentiates between innovations generated primarily from a company for society (inside-out) versus from societal actors funded and/or supported by a firm (outside-in).

Naturally, many innovations identified have multiple sources and fit into the co-created or 'shared' innovation space (see Figure 11.1 on sources of social innovation).

Top-down, inside-out

In this quadrant, innovation is led by company experts and applied in society. Here companies often invest in basic or applied research and engineering projects to develop 'disruptive' solutions to social and ecological challenges. In the firms we studied, this encompassed a range of eco-innovations, new food ingredients and recipes, the introduction of 'smart' technologies, and some business model innovations. A primary emphasis in this quadrant is technical innovation. Users may provide informational inputs

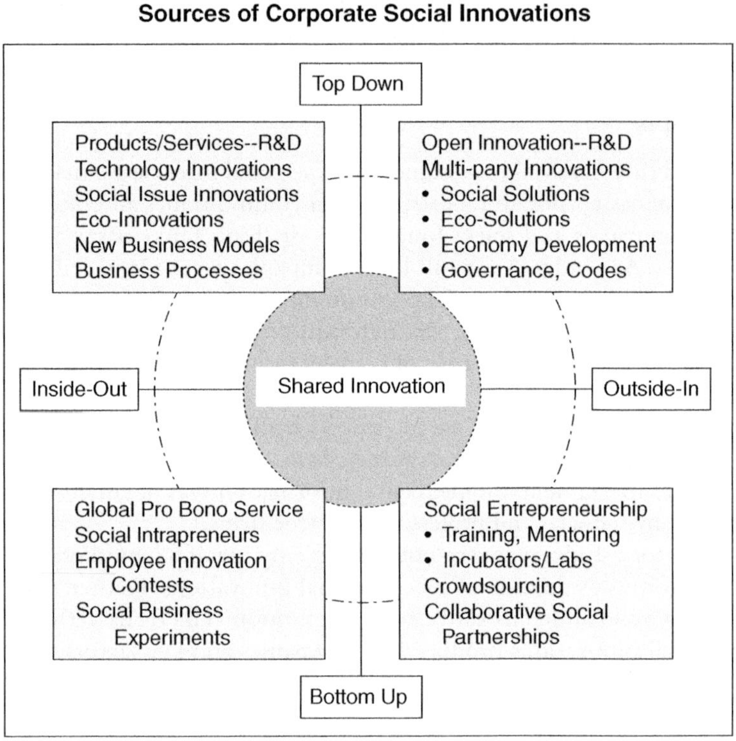

Sources of Corporate Social Innovations

Figure 11.1 Sources of corporate social innovations.

into product design and development but only more actively engage when it comes to marketing and distribution.

Solving world challenges. From 1996 to 2005, Dow Chemical focused internally on reducing its environmental footprint. Dow's EH&S performance in cutting energy use, water and waste over the ten years yielded $5.5 billion in savings, based on incremental investments of $1 billion. But reactions to continuing on this track for the next ten years were ho–hum. 'What makes Dow great', said a group of external advisers 'is to take your science and technology to solve world challenges.' This led Dow to repurpose its innovation engine and apply its core competencies to socially and ecologically relevant R&D.

Dow would shoot for a fivefold increase in sales of products using 'sustainable chemistry' (which maximizes energy use and material efficiency and reduces harm to the environment). And it embraced a truly audacious goal: deliver three breakthroughs from its labs that would help to solve world challenges. And Dow's R&D team delivered. First, Dow developed heart-healthy Omega 9 Oils (derived from canola and sunflower seeds) that have zero trans-fat and the lowest amount of saturated fat among commonly used cooking oils. Already, the use of Omega-9 Oils has eliminated more than one billion pounds of trans- and saturated fat from the North American diet. Second, it introduced a reverse osmosis water filter that yields significant savings compared to existing technology (40 per cent better purification with

30 per cent less energy use). Says Neil Hawkins, VP of sustainability at Dow, 'This innovation will help deliver a more sustainable water supply to the world, addressing global water scarcity in a very tangible way.' Finally, Dow developed a new type of structural adhesive for auto frames that improves safety and gas consumption.

Smart technology and big data. On the information technology front, IBM's Watson computer has moved from competing (and winning) on the game show *Jeopardy!* to treating cancers through cognitive computing. In an early application, Baylor College of Medicine used the artificial intelligence system to sift through 23 million scientific abstracts to identify, in weeks, six cancer-related proteins worth targeting. More recently, Watson has been used at Memorial Sloan Kettering Cancer Center to analyse patient records, medical studies and clinical-trial results to help physicians make treatment decisions. Here it connects patient's genomic data with 'evidence-based' treatment options and can also match patients with the best available clinical trials. In the future, Watson will act as a physician's assistant by examining a clinical case from different angles and then – using reference materials and its collaborative learning experiences – enable a physician to support or refute etiological hypotheses.

IBM positioned its analytic technologies to ameliorate a broad array of societal and environmental challenges through smart technology applications:

- A Kenyan school system works with IBM Research-Africa to use cognitive and mobile technologies to help identify which schools (and students) are most at risk of failure.
- Toulouse, France identifies and prioritizes citizens' most pressing issues using social media analytics.
- Ishinomaki City, Japan is revitalizing the local fishing industry by analysing fish species and location data.
- Singapore Land Transit Authority provides a more convenient transportation system using predictive tools and smart cards.

Eco-innovation. One of our favourite examples here is Ray Anderson, the late head of Interface Carpets, who transformed his entire industry through the development of carpet tiles (so you don't have to replace an entire carpet in the event of soiling and spills). Interface next innovations included using plastics and polymers, rather than petroleum-based materials, for carpet backing; that way, carpets can be recycled and produce less waste. It also made ingenious use of principles of biomimicry in carpet design. Interface mimicked nature by producing carpet tiles with natural leaf patterns that could be laid out on the floor in any order – just like leaves falling in the forest – with no time or materials wasted lining the carpet tiles up and matching seams. And, with nature in mind, the company also invented a way to tape the tiles together, like a spider web, rather than glue them to the floor surface – protecting both the people laying the carpet and the environment from toxicity.

Taking its zero waste mission to the full ecosystem, Interface is today reclaiming tons of abandoned commercial fishing nets – which kill fish trapped in them and pollute the oceans and beaches – and transforming them into carpet yarn. That yarn is featured in a new product line with 81 per cent total recycled content, and an industry-first 100 per cent recycled nylon face fibre. All of this furthers Anderson's ecological vision for Interface. He told us, one month before his death in August, 2011, that his hopes were to first reach sustainability and then become restorative – 'by putting back more than we ourselves take and doing good to Earth, not just no harm'.

Nutrition. Several of the global food makers have R&D projects to produce functional foods and beverages – or what some call 'nutraceuticals' as they offer nutritional and medical benefits. An early mover in this area, Unilever developed a low-cost iodized salt called Annapurna and introduced it into India. It has since made this available in sachet sizes as small as 100 grams and at prices the equivalent to 6 US cents to place it within the price reach of poor families. PepsiCo, in turn, has introduced an iron-fortified cracker in India that addresses iron deficiency and has cookies on offer in Mexico that are fortified with Vitamin A. But no big food company has yet done as much to blend food and medicine as Nestlé. In 2011 the company formed its Nestlé Health Science unit, which has since invested in companies that make products such as drinks for people with metabolic disorders and a medical food sold for the dietary management of Alzheimer's disease.

Danone has taken to field with its nutrition research. Danone's Nutriplanet group, drawing on nutritional, epidemiological, socio-economic and cultural data, has analysed the habits and health issues in 52 countries. After studying the diets of Brazil's youth, for example, Danone reformulated a best-selling cheese (reducing sugar and adding vitamins) and in Bangladesh, children eat 600,000 servings a week of Danone's Shokti-Doi, a nutrient-rich yogurt. R&D also extends into packaging. In Senegal, Danone developed a 'pouch', a carton composed of local grain and a little milk that can be stored at room temperature. And its Sari Husada line in Indonesia has offerings with different features and at different price points: its low-cost Gizikita line meets 50 per cent of vital daily nutritional requirements and is available as both milk for babies and porridge for infants and toddlers. In turn, Nutricia is targeted at high-end consumers and features a website and 'netzine' providing consumers with scientific information on nutrition for expectant mothers and infants.

Getting it wrong. As stimulating as these examples might seem, it is worth reminding, as several socially innovative companies did, that the 'hit rate' for successful innovation in R&D is quite low. We also found some cases where good ideas were not translated into effective products. For instance, PepsiCo launched the compostable bag for its SunChips product which the company had positioned as a healthy snack. Made of biodegradable plant material instead of plastic, the bag looked great and kept the chips fresh. There was one small problem: It was noisy – the bags made 'crinkly' and 'crackly' sounds when they were handled. A Facebook page on the noise called 'SORRY BUT I CAN'T HEAR YOU OVER THIS SUN CHIPS BAG' got more than 49,000 likes. Interestingly, PepsiCo acknowledged the noise and, in a tongue-in-cheek ad campaign, offered to send customers a free set of ear plugs. Note, however, that the company has not introduced compostable packaging in its other snack products.

More broadly, meta-analyses of studies of company-led product innovations find that a firm's market orientation and technological proficiency, its predevelopment activity, and specific product advantages and innovativeness are the best predictors of success (Evanschitzky et al., 2012). Apropos of Danone's experience, the meta-analysis documents that market research is especially important in cases where consumer interests are complex and unpredictable.

Bottom-up, inside-out

In this quadrant, innovation is led by employees of a firm. Several companies in our study have hosted employee innovation contests and support employee intrapreneurship with new venture funding, mentoring and rewards. Global pro bono assignments find employees, often in teams, developing solutions to social challenges with small businesses, government agencies and NGOs in developing nations. A few companies devised 'social businesses' within the corporate structure to support employees engaged in longer-term service projects.

The Zuritanken effect. Ferrovial is a Spanish multinational engaged in the design, construction, financing, operation and maintenance of transport, urban and services infrastructure. Well recognized for its innovation in smart technology, the company has also sought to engage its employees in the innovation game through an innovation contest. Manuel Martinez, Manager of Open Innovations, developed and titled the programme 'zuritanken', which is a combination of the Swahili term 'nzuri', meaning 'good' and the Swedish term 'tanken', or 'idea'. Ferrovial employees from all over the world are invited to offer solutions to challenges in each of the company's strategic business areas. Factors considered in evaluating their proposals are that the innovation should be novel, attractive to the business, feasible in application and have a high potential impact.

The winning idea at inaugural innovation contest was called 'Floor Power-Not a Step Wasted' and was implemented at Heathrow Airport (which Ferrovial manages). The project was devised by the four zuritankeners who created a floor surface that is capable of harnessing the kinetic energy generated by each footstep and converting it into electricity. Each year over 70 million passengers pass through London's Heathrow Airport and the project uses their footsteps to generate energy and identify transit patterns. Power Floor's appeal is that it is a sustainable, efficient innovation that minimizes energy consumption, provides information on foot traffic at the airport, and improves passenger satisfaction by making them feel part of the infrastructure. Other implemented innovations involve the use of GSM technology to collect tolls from mobile technology, a programme of job training for the disabled, and acoustic and illuminating warning device for use in a train cabin.

Activating intrapreneurship. There is growing interest in and more exemplars of social 'intrapreneurship' in companies (Elkington, 2008; Grayson et al., 2014). For example, Ericsson runs a grass-roots Collaborative Idea Management Program that enables employees to propose and build on innovative ideas in every region and layer of the company. Over 300 Electronic IdeaBoxes set up by employees have to date cumulated over 16,000 ideas and comments from over 10,000 users. These inputs are vetted, rated and enhanced by experts and coaches throughout the company and bundled into award winning innovations.

In rural Kenya, as one example, a network of employees launched a Community Power Project that uses 'off-the-grid' base stations, powered by wind and/or solar power, to share excess power among nearby communities. The base stations power mobile phone charging (which drives network usage) and in larger-scale deployment can electrify street lights, clinics and schools for an entire community. Of course, bringing such innovations to market takes money. A couple of years ago, Ericsson added Innova boxes to its programme that provide internal venture capital funding for employee ideas. This venture funding allows employee groups to experiment with their innovations, develop prototypes, and ultimately to launch them in the marketplace.

Grass-roots innovation partnerships. The Intel Environmental Excellence Awards recognize employees or employee groups that have created an environmental innovation. The company also offers Sustainability-in-Action Grants to allow employees to get funding for an innovative sustainability idea or project. The grants offer a few thousand dollars, and perhaps more importantly frees up employee's time to develop their sustainability-in-action project.

Signing on to this programme in Intel India, Sonia Shrivastava designed a low-cost hardware utility that helps visually challenged people communicate and access daily information. With Intel's financial and technical support, Sonia managed a team of internal and external experts who customized a set of freeware applications and utilities on a low-cost Intel® Atom™ based netbook computer and created a solution that was 85 per cent less expensive than any other solution in the marketplace. The idea is now being translated into a viable business model and a Delhi-based NGO, Saksham, is running with the project with continued support from Intel. How does sustainability-in-action work? 'Ideas from employees get reviewed, both by internal leaders and external experts from NGOs and academia, and we then provide them with technology and seed funding, similar to venture capitalists, to create a proof of concept,' says Praveen Vishakantaiah, president of Intel India.

Pro bono global service. Since 2008, IBM has sent 3,000 employees in over 275 teams to nearly 40 countries for one-month service assignments through its Corporate Service Corps. Modelled on the U.S. Peace Corps, the programme engages teams of volunteers in three months of pre-work, one month in country, and two months in post-service where they harvest insights for themselves and their business. In Tanzania, IBM teams collaborated with KickStart, a non-profit exploring new technologies to fight poverty in Africa, to develop modular e-training courses in marketing, sales and supply chain management for local entrepreneurs. What are IBM's motivations? To open new markets, develop a new generation of socially conscious global leaders, and bring to life its corporate commitment to 'Innovation that Matters – for Our Company and the World.' IBM's service corps work in Calabar, capital of the Cross River State in Nigeria, was done in partnership with Governor Liyel Imoke. One project funded by the World Bank provided support to pregnant women and children under 5. This led to a $1.2M services deal signed in March of 2010 – IBM's first services deal in West Africa.

Pxyera Global, an NGO supporting corporate volunteering, has identified 39 companies that sponsor pro bono global service programmes, but that number has doubled each of the past three years. Shell and Dow Corning have teams working with non-governmental organizations (NGOs) to develop and market affordable, safe and efficient cooking stoves for the world's poor (of whom nearly 2 million worldwide die per year due to prolonged exposure to smoke from traditional stoves). One team of ten employees from Dow Corning went to Bangalore, India to develop more energy-efficient cook stoves for street vendors and rural renewable energy products for rural housing. Confronting technical challenges, the Dow Corning team emailed, blogged and tweeted ideas with scientists and engineers back home, bringing the expertise of not just ten but hundreds of fellow employees to their partners

When intrapreneurship fails. As appealing as employee intrapreneurship sounds, it is also a challenge to manage. A major manufacturer, for instance, ran a series of design thinking workshops for employees and then 'unleashed' them to innovate in their areas of responsibility. Not surprisingly, many would-be innovators encountered resistance from managers and even fellow employees and lacked the political skills to create a coalition to support them. This reminds that personal passion and even a great idea are not sufficient to produce social innovation bottom-up in a company.

Top-down, outside-in

In this quadrant, innovative ideas are sourced from various actors in society and developed or bundled by a firm. Several companies in our study have open innovation platforms or sponsor competitions to draw in promising technologies or product ideas. Others work with government agencies, NGOs and other firms on large-scale projects to, for example, develop smart power grids, increase ICT accessibility or enhance access to health care where innovations from several sources are combined into systemic solutions to social and environmental challenges.

Open Innovation. Innovation in business has moved beyond the R&D and product development function to enable open innovation and co-creation with myriad different parties (Chesbrough, 2003). P&G grew its business in Brazil by having employees live in and observe low-income households. Insights gained from these experiences led P&G to create new products and product modifications, such as an affordable, environmentally friendly and hands-friendly detergent for those without washing machines who hand-washed clothes. The ideas spread to other countries and influenced the introduction of Tide Basic in the US.

P&G's open innovation platform, called Connect + Develop, has linked the company with German ingredients-maker Symrise (to develop a natural honey cough drop with Vicks), US technology partner Ecolabs (to create an anti-static dryer block for Bounce that is refillable), and Brazilian packaging supplier Braskem (to turn sustainably harvested sugarcane into a high-density, 100 per cent recyclable polyethylene plastic used in Pantene shampoos). P&G has also partnered with many universities, government agencies and NGOs such as the Safe Drinking Water Alliance (to bring its water purification system PUR to those in need).

Business partners in innovation. Manufacturers have introduced concentrated detergents to reduce consumer's water use and their own packaging footprint. One problem is that consumers, accustomed to traditional washing products and fretful about getting their clothes clean, use an excessive (and unnecessary) amount of concentrated detergent at each wash. Thus Walmart partnered with manufacturer Henkel to introduce Purex PowerShot which has an auto-dose mechanism that dispenses the proper amount of detergent for a wash. It is 30 per cent more efficient and 50 per cent more effective than the old version, but manufactured at the same cost.

Using its market power and muscles, Walmart is pushing its suppliers to use its Sustainability Index to innovate and improve their environmental footprint. The index includes 15 questions for suppliers pertaining to energy and climate, material efficiency, nature and resources, and people and community. To date, some 1,300 suppliers use the Index and Walmart has eliminated 20 million metric tons of greenhouse-gas emissions from its supply chain. The company estimates its suppliers will increase the recycled content in their packaging by 1 billion pounds by 2020.

Crowdsourcing. In June 2015, Unilever's Foundry platform launched a global crowdsourcing community to find new and innovative ways of tackling sustainability problems. Three challenges were issued in the areas of sanitation, hygiene and nutrition, which yielded 150 ideas. Grand winners in the initial challenge were:

- Improving Access to Sanitation category – Saurabh Saraf for WaterHubs proposed modular water and sanitation infrastructure solutions for urban slums. When the modular blocks are integrated they provide community services, including showers, toilets and health services. Other provisions that WaterHubs can offer are water for potable and non-potable uses, public kitchen areas and mobile charging stations.
- Improving Global Nutrition category – Onyinye Uche developed an education campaign joining Unilever's Knorr with the National Youth Service Corps (NYSC) in Nigeria. The aim is to reduce the prevalence of iron deficiency anaemia in the country by educating people on the importance of eating iron-rich foods.
- Imagining The Shower of the Future category – Yehuda Goldfisher for Flush a Shower introduced an innovation designed to reduce water consumption during showering. It consists of two buttons. The first releases a burst of water to wet the body prior to soaping and the second releases a longer burst to rinse the soap away.

Collaborative innovation. The mission of the Sustainable Food Laboratory, led by co-directors Hal Hamilton and Don Seville, is to 'accelerate the shift of sustainable food from niche to mainstream'. The lab's interests encompass the fertility of soil, water and biodiversity protection, the livelihoods and practices of farmers and farm workers, energy use and waste discharge, and the quality and affordability of food. The over 80 lab members and partners include early innovators like Ben and Jerry's, Stonyfield Farms, and Green Mountain Coffee, corporate giants like Cargill, Aramark, H.J. Heintz, Sodexho, Starbucks, and Sysco from the US, food producers and purveyors such as Unilever and Marks and Spencer from abroad, and the likes of the Bill and Melinda Gates Foundation, Catholic Relief Services, Fair Trade USA, and the Food Marketing Institute. The diverging interests in this mix often find common ground in joint projects.

What are members collaborating on? In various combinations they are involved in connecting small-scale producers to modern markets, green farmer training projects, reducing GHG and water emissions in farm operations, food safety and sustainability certification schemes, and consumer education and engagement. The Sustainable Food Laboratory exemplifies the new kinds of multi-business and cross-sector partnering underway today. What distinguishes the sustainable food lab is the open sharing and emphasis on 'action-learning' among members. They also get coaching on becoming more effective change agents in their organizations and industries.

Beware the perversity of crowds. Tay, the creation of Microsoft's Technology and Research and Bing teams, was an experiment aimed at learning through conversations. It was targeted at American social media users 18–24-year-olds – and was, according to Microsoft – 'designed to engage and entertain people where they connect with each other online through casual and playful conversation'. In less than 24 hours after its arrival on Twitter, Tay gained more than 50,000 followers, and produced nearly 100,000 tweets.

Shortly thereafter, however, Tay was shut down. The problem? It started mimicking its followers and began saying things like 'Hitler was right i hate the jews', and 'i fucking hate feminists'. What went wrong? According to Louis Rosenberg, the founder of Unanimous AI, 'like all chat bots, Tay has no idea what it's saying … it has no idea if it's saying something offensive, or nonsensical, or profound'. The machine was being trained by 'online trolls', said Rosenberg. 'This is really no different than a parrot in a seedy bar picking up bad words and repeating them back without knowing what they really mean.'

Bad public behaviour also scuttled a company about to launch a new service where emergency contraception would be delivered swiftly to couples in need in cities across the world. To get the word out the firms marketing team decided to crowdsource suggestions from the public about which city the service should launch in. Perversely, the devoutly Muslim city of Batman in Turkey was voted in first place. Needless to say, the innovator closed down the campaign and scotched the service.

Bottom–up, outside–in

In this quadrant, innovative ideas in society are proposed, incubated and supported by a firm's employees. Several companies we studied host social innovation labs to support entrepreneurs in communities where they do business. Others run contests for students where they offer guidance to promising innovators and prizes to further develop winning ideas. Some social issue partnerships combine innovative ideas from many sources to support grass-roots solutions to challenges innovations in communities.

LEGO and the DIY maker movement. The LEGO group, a family owned company based in Denmark, develops toys, experiences and teaching materials for users in over 130 countries. Following a company-wide crisis in 2004, it 'opened' its R&D unit to inputs from consumers and the public. Adult Fans of LEGO, 'AFOLs' as they call themselves, soon got into the game. Early collaboration yielded the open source Mindstorms product line with 'hackable' software whereby users could modify functionality and features. Originally targeted at adolescents, Mindstorms became popular with tech-savvy adults who could design their own versions.

Today LEGO is a 'creative catalyst' in the Do–it–yourself (DIY) Maker movement, which encourages people to 'tinker' and 'hack' and find better ways of creating things. Operating amidst a generation of 'digital natives' – who grew up with tablets and smartphones – LEGO has extended its brand to the realm of digital play. The company has created a line of programmable robots, such as the R3ptar, that bridge the gap between physical play and virtual play. Twitter and Facebook area filled with examples of people sharing their LEGO creations.

Supporting social entrepreneurs. Entrepreneurs are transforming business models and building new strategic markets in a way, and at a pace, that large corporations and governments often cannot. However, small businesses often fail at a critical stage in their growth due to inadequate operational backbone and inadequate guidance on how innovation comes into play for them. Thus SAP has opened up its vast ecosystem of employees, customers and partners, as well as its small business management solutions and innovation portfolio with HANA, Cloud and Mobile, to support entrepreneurs in small businesses and civil society.

SAP runs an innovation accelerator for entrepreneurs that are set to scale. SAP technology, workshops applying design thinking, and mentorship by SAP employees are cornerstones of the accelerator model, which also offers access to impact investors provided through an Impact Capital network available to SAP's non-profit entrepreneur partners. A good example of how this model comes to life is Solidarium. Tiago, a 27-year-old Brazilian entrepreneur, had a vision to run a global online retail business, while providing much needed jobs for Brazil's 8.5 million artisans, many of whom live below the poverty line. His company provides local artisans access to a network of global consumers and buyers, including Walmart and JCPenney, and provides tools and training to the artisans to help articulate their products online. Tiago worked with SAP mentors who helped him analyse his business results using SAP analytics. Now, using SAP's Business One, Solidarium can manage its operations more effectively, leaving more time for Tiago to focus on customer acquisition and international expansion.

Joining hands for innovation. Accenture Development Partnerships (ADP) has undertaken over 600 projects in 55 countries where its professionals, at 50 per cent salary reduction, work in partnership for up to six months with NGOs to bring business solutions to humanitarian problems. In 2010, ADP worked with and NetHope, a consortium of over 40 NGOs, to launch the first global IT help desk for international NGOs. Staffed jointly by NetHope and ADP employees, the help desk was a pioneering example of business–NGO collaboration in the development sector. In 2013, the partners conducted a study of technology use in developing markets. They found, for instance, that although mobile technology featured in many development success stories, simpler text-based applications were more practical for rural workers who don't own smart phones. Commenting on the learnings from this joint R&D, NetHope's Lauren Woodman and Accenture's Jessica Long write, 'It's no longer good enough to arrive in developing countries and proclaim to have all the answers. We need to refine our solutions by researching local markets, learning lessons from trial and error and welcoming feedback and possibilities from those on the ground'.

Scaling for impact. The social business d.light is a global social enterprise aiming to improve the lives of the two billion people in the developing world that live without access to reliable energy. The company offers affordable solar energy solutions for households and small businesses that are transforming the way people all over the world use and pay for energy. Shell provided early financial support for d.light and technical assistance addressing key challenges in designing LED lighting modules and lithium batteries. d.light recently started piloting a channel partnership with Unilever, plugging into their Perfect Store Initiative. d.light sells solar home systems to Unilever, which places them in the small–scale retail shops that stock its products. Piloted in Kenya in 2014, the partnership aimed to answer the question 'If you provide retail outlets with access to solar lighting, do they stay open later, and if so, do their sales increase?' The partnership was designed to financially benefit all parties: Unilever, d.light and the retailers all profit from increased sales, while d.light also benefits from increased awareness of its products among consumers who shop at retailers' stores because of the way that the light impacts the aesthetic of the shops, which are typically dark or smoky from kerosene use. The initial results showed that having access to solar lighting led to significant increases in store revenue, and the partnership is now being scaled from 100 to 1,000 stores to get better data on the efficacy and potential for scaling the model.

When open innovation goes awry. Open innovation is certainly gaining traction but it is not without its risks. For example, LEGO had less success open sourcing LEGO Universe, a Massive Multiplayer Online Game (MMOG). Here the problem was that the parent company tried to 'manage' rather than 'moderate' the many product inputs and hit multiple snags in fitting outsider's ideas into its own product development plans, producing countless delays. Meanwhile, a competitor more or less copied the idea and launched Minecraft which gave users much more freedom to build their imaginary worlds.

There is a growing literature on problems and pitfalls associated with innovation contests and other forms of open innovation. Key issues centre on the 'absorptive capacity' of firms to learn from outside innovations and on the establishment of 'network governance' for open innovation (Lichtenthaler and Lichtenthaler, 2009).

Four keys to corporate social innovation

Mindful of its complexities and challenges, an emerging body of practice-oriented literature describes critical success factors in CSI (Austin et al., 2005; Kanter, 2009; Simanis, 2012). Our study 'early movers' suggest at least four key elements to consider and address as companies move into CSI.

Purpose

What does it take for a business to drive corporate social innovative? It begins with a compelling vision of a better world, a high-minded and actionable mission, and complementary and inspirational values. These give interested employees a 'license to innovate' and enable companies to invest time, money and talent in societally relevant R&D which has a longer-term and often more intangible payoff than conventional, strictly commercially driven innovation programmes (Mirvis et al., 2010). Dow Chemical states its purpose in this way: 'Dow people include some of the world's best scientists and engineers dedicated to solving global challenges. We focus our *innovation engine* on delivering new technologies that are *good for business and good for the world*'. Recall research by Collins and Porras (1994) that top companies use a BHAG – a 'big hairy audacious goal' – to bring vision to life and stretch innovator's thinking. Dow's BHAG of three breakthroughs that 'will significantly help solve world challenges' is an example. In turn, P&G employees attributed their success in Brazil to the need to live up to the company's purpose of creating products that 'improve the lives of the world's consumers' – which motivated them to see how they could contribute to improving lives of lower-income consumers in their country.

Broad blandishments, like PepsiCo's 'performance with purpose', can be a starting point for CSI but in its detailing, a vision provides a framework for company strategy – it defines a strategic direction and conceptual map of how a company moves from its current reality to a desired future state. On this count, IBM's commitment to 'innovate for society' is connected to its transformation into a solutions provider for a 'smarter planet', and Unilever's 'sustainability living plan', positions the company to improve the health of 1 billion people, buy 100 per cent of its agricultural raw materials from sustainable sources, and reduce the environmental impact of everything it sells by one-half, while doubling its revenues.

The logic of purpose extends to particular innovations whose success hinges on their 'social value proposition'. A value proposition is a promise to customers and other corporate stakeholders that a company will deliver goods and services of *real* value. In the context of social innovation, that means value for both business *and* society. Natura, a Brazilian cosmetic company, has for years set the global benchmark for social innovation in its industry. Today its innovations in sustainable sourcing and product development are focused on preserving socio-biodiversity and valuing traditional knowledge and culture in Amazonia. The company's mantra 'bem estar bem' (Well-being/Being well) is its guide for innovation. Meanwhile, companies like PepsiCo falter in this space because social purpose is not authentically linked with its core brands.

A broader point is that while many of the social innovations cited here are laudable, several of the firms in this sample have been challenged on their overall environmental, social and governance performance and have produced other innovations of dubious social value. In this regard, social innovations by 'bad' companies are likely to be seen as mere 'window dressing' by critics and are not apt to substantially enhance corporate reputation or generate much goodwill.

Process

Naturally, different design processes feature in different kinds of innovations. For instance, in their large-scale eco-innovations, companies like GE, Dow, Ericsson and others invest in basic research and engineering to develop technologies that open new markets and make the planet greener. Similarly, in developing new food recipes and product ingredients, Pepsi, P&G, Unilever and others draw on chemistry, biology and the other life sciences to do well and do good. By comparison, other kinds of innovations involve co-creation with users who might operate as both producers-and-consumers. Such user-driven innovation poses special challenges for companies trying to tap underserved markets. First, it requires outreach from firms beyond their traditional customer base into communities and populations in need. Second, it involves partners that may have different viewpoints on the problems at hand and certainly different ideas on how to best address them. Third, it requires constant adaptation to local circumstances in design and implementation. These call for the redesign of traditional innovation processes for purposes of 'interactive value creation'.

As an example, studies find that firms must become 'indigenous' to tap BOP market by deeply understanding conditions on the ground, co-creating innovations with local partners, and also investing in supportive infrastructure (Hart and London, 2005; Weiser et al., 2004). Take the case of SC Johnson, the world's leading maker of insect-control products, who sought to open markets in Africa. The SC Johnson innovation team slept under mosquito bed nets on nights when the temperature was 100 degrees Fahrenheit with 95 per cent humidity and learned first-hand that the nets are hot and heavy and get dirty. The lessons learned were that rural consumers want products that work well but also are affordably priced and multifunctional.

Next there was the matter of learning to 'bundle' products and sell them in a culturally compatible format. On this count, SC Johnson developed WOW club memberships, which are sold to groups of seven or more homemakers, and include four different pest-control and home-cleaning products in refillable formats. The WOW membership includes group coaching sessions around home and family care best practices and loyalty rewards. Here, too, local partners were crucial to shaping this value proposition. In addition, SC Johnson was involved in a collective learning exercise on BOP business development with the Center for Sustainable Global Enterprise at Cornell University.

Nonetheless, there are many other instances where BOP innovations have failed and been unable to scale (Caneque and Hart, 2015). Unilever's Project Shakti required radically reducing the cost structure in the manufacture and sale of soap and toothpaste through local production and distribution via auto rickshaws (tuk-tuks). Goods were packaged in small quantities and 'Shakti ammas' (rural entrepreneurs) trained to provide authoritative health-and-hygiene information and to do bookkeeping, inventory management, and the like. To scale the effort, however, Unilever and Indian-based NGO Shakti had to complement these product and distribution innovations with the launch of I-Shakti, an interactive discussion technology and sales management system, involve other new partners and innovation processes; and add a new suite of financial products and services for the entrepreneurs and their customers.

Partnering

To innovatively address society's pressing needs requires a diverse set of interests, competencies and skills. Few firms have the appropriate mix of staff, resources and know-how to operate in this space on their own and in any case may lack the legitimacy with local communities to do so. On this count, a study by Austin and colleagues (2005) finds NGOs to be far more knowledgeable about social needs and more effective at planning social action than businesses.

What makes partnering so relevant for corporate social innovators? First, firms need knowledge about, say, the local conditions in their supply chain or in a market they seek to enter. Non-business partners often have that knowledge and can work with business partners to study the situation at hand. Second, companies need to understand how to produce and implement social innovations in an unfamiliar culture and context. They often develop this capability experientially, through the co-creation of social innovations with partners and/or users. Third, companies need may need legitimacy with and connections to local interests and users. Partner organizations can facilitate engagement with local communities and non-traditional customers and provide access to interests beyond the usual corporate reach.

One way to understand the requirements here is through a 'collaboration continuum' that frames the level of engagement and interaction between parties in a multi-organizational alliance or partnership (Austin, 2000). As partners move from a transactional and tactical relationship to deeper levels of collaboration, they exchange more information and resources and together must develop collaborative capabilities. The importance of goal congruence, flexibility and mutual trust and commitment-to-cause cannot be underestimated. On this count, one of the author's study of partnering in sustainability projects found that power imbalances, changes in personnel in one or more partners, and competing priorities can hamper the institutionalization of social innovations (Worley and Mirvis, 2013).

Payoff

Considerations of the 'payoff' on CSI hinge very much on a company's intent when investing in this arena and how it funds the effort. The social innovations we studied vary in terms of the motivations of and returns sought by the companies. Several of them, for example, are situated along company's value chains – having to do with more responsible sourcing, adding social or environmental appeal to products and services, or central to new business models. Others are more centred on producing social value – benefiting community interests or ameliorating social problems. An analysis of CSI innovations from this sample revealed that corporate investments in value chain innovations are apt to be more intensive and of sustained duration than those aimed more so at societal benefit (Mirvis et al., 2016).

These expected payoff of corporate social innovations can be portrayed on a spectrum. At one end of the spectrum are innovations based on philanthropic motivations. At the other are those aimed at commercial returns. The bulk of innovations identified are in the middle space of blended value. The prime aims of social innovations towards the left side are social impact but corporate benefits include reputation gains, development of staff, improved stakeholder relations, and long-term market prospects. Prime aims towards the right side are business benefits but not of the scale sought by purely commercial ventures as well as societal or environmental improvements. Socio-commercial innovations feature explicit business and society benefits (see Figure 11.2 on CSI Spectrum).

With many of their eco-innovations, for instance, Dow, IBM, Interface, and others are making big commercial plays. IBM's efforts to smarten cities and the planet, Unilever's sustainable living products, and many of the 'fair trade' certified products and services are social innovations that aim to generate competitive financial returns. To be sure, the social and ecological benefits are important to these companies but they are also a selling feature to the market.

Another set of corporate social investments stem from more philanthropic motivations. The Shell Foundation, for instance, used to dispense grants to worthy causes for the parent corporation. Today it uses what it terms an 'enterprise-based' approach that combines venture funding, market principles, and 'business thinking, models, and disciplines' to help entrepreneurs and small enterprises to create commercially viable business models. By comparison, SAP's accelerator for social entrepreneurs is more of a 'socio-commercial' investment. According to SAP's Alexandra van der Ploeg, a key payoff is employee engagement. She told us that with increasing competition to attract and retain millennial talent, the accelerator helps to position SAP as a great place to work, and inspires existing employees to work with innovative small businesses. At the same time, it also introduces SAP products and services to new clients and helps to build the company's future market. Listen to Brazilian entrepreneur Tiago. 'Before SAP Expoentes I would have never imagined that I would run my business on SAP', now, he adds 'I see the value of implementing business management software at an early stage so I am set for more sustainable growth.'

Surely social investments can yield reputational benefits to companies, enhance their licence to operate, open doors to future business, and, in the case of BOP markets, reward global firms with brand recognition and a loyal customer base that will grow in its spending power. But few of these social innovations would meet typical hurdle rates for commercial corporate investment. (And several BoP innovations we studied in

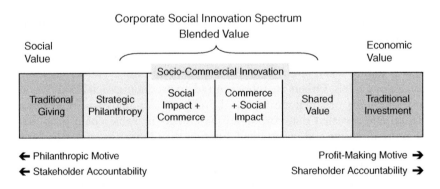

Figure 11.2 Corporate social innovation spectrum.

P&G, Panera Bread, and Ericsson moved from P&L business units into philanthropic categories.)

How then do companies justify these investments beyond, say, a well-intentioned effort to do good? Listen to Laura Aisle, former Director of Corporate Citizenship at Dow Corning, who helped start the company's Citizen Service Corps which has sent volunteers to work with the global NGO Asoka to develop affordable housing and with the Indian NGO Sustaintech to develop solar cook stoves for street vendors in India. She makes the investment case this way:

> We go back to the beginning: *insight for innovation*. As a specialty materials supplier –
> the people who make the materials which 'goes-into' other products – we had no
> way of understanding a market for which we had no experience, and no way to gain
> experience, save (by) going there.

Indeed, many of the innovative cases here highlight how knowledge is the real payoff of many CSI investments – and is often produced through an exchange of knowledge with a partner. In these arrangements, knowledge exchanged may have to do with conditions in a local market or community, and associated issues and opportunities, and the company gains indigenous cultural understanding. In the case of pro bono service learning, corporate volunteers also gain hands-on experience in emerging markets and enhance their global leadership capabilities. Innovating in their supply change teaches companies about meeting global standards and business model innovations yield product insights and market entry strategies. In turn, consultations and contests with social innovators produce product ideas and can enhance the innovative identity and spirit of a firm. Finally, sponsoring, incubating and mentoring social entrepreneurs requires further investment but also teaches firms how to produce social innovations, connects them with an ecosystem of social entrepreneurs, and can spill over into social intrapreneurship among employees. Ultimately, this can institutionalize firm-specific CSI capabilities in companies – a potential source of differentiation and competitive advantage (Herrera, 2015).

References

Austin, J.E. (2000). *The Collaboration Challenge: How Nonprofits and Businesses Succeed through Strategic Alliances*. San Francisco, CA: Jossey-Bass.

Austin, J., Leonard H., Reficco, E. and Wei-Skillern J. (2005). Social entrepreneurship: It's for corporations, too. In A. Nicholls (ed.), *Social Entrepreneurship: New Paradigms of Sustainable Social Change*. Oxford: Oxford University Press.

Browne, J., Nuttall, R. and Stadlen, T. (2016). *Connect: How Companies Succeed by Engaging Radically with Society*. New York: PublicAffairs.

Caneque, F.C. and Hart, S. (2015). Base of the Pyramid 3.0. *Sustainable Development through Innovation and Entrepreneurship*. Sheffield: Greenleaf Publishing.

Chesbrough, H.W. (2003). *Open Innovation: The New Imperative for Creating and Profiting from Technology*. Boston, MA: Harvard Business Press.

Collins, J.P. and Porras, J.I. (1994). *Built to Last*. New York: HarperCollins.

Cone (2016). *Millennial Employee Engagement Study*. www.conecomm.com/research-blog/2016-millennial-employee-engagement-study.

Elkington, J. (2008). *The Social Intrapreneur: A Field Guide for Corporate Changemakers*. London: Sustainability.

Evanschitzky, H., Eisend, M., Calantone, R.J. and Jiang, Y. (2012). Success factors of product innovation: An updated meta-analysis. *Journal of Product Innovation Management*, 29(S1): 21–37.

Googins, B.P., Mirvis, P.H. and Rochlin, S. (2007). *Beyond 'Good Company': Next Generation Corporate Citizenship*. New York: Palgrave-Macmillan.

Grayson, D., Mclaren, M. and Spitsek, H. (2014). *Social Intrapreneurism and All That Jazz*. Sheffield: Greenleaf Publishing.

Hart, S.L. and London, T. (2005). Developing native capability: What multinational corporations can learn from the base of the pyramid. *Stanford Social Innovation Review*, 3(2): 28–33.

Hart, S.L. and Christensen, C.M. (2002). The great leap: Driving innovation from the base of the pyramid. *MIT Sloan Management Review*, 44(1): 51–56.

Herrera, M.E.B. (2015). Creating competitive advantage by institutionalizing corporate social innovation. *Journal of Business Research*, 68(7): 1468–1474.

Kania, J. and Kramer, M. (2011). Collective Impact. *Stanford Innovation Review*, 9(1): 36–41.

Kanter, R.M. (2009). *SuperCorp: How Vanguard Companies Create Innovation, Profits, Growth, and Social Good*. New York: Crown Business.

Kiron, D., Kruschwitz, N., Reeves, M. and Goh, E. (2013). The benefits of sustainability-driven innovation. *MIT Sloan Management Review*, 54(2): 69–73.

Lichtenthaler, U. and Lichtenthaler, E. (2009). A capability-based framework for open innovation: Complementing absorptive capacity. *Journal of Management Studies*, 46(8): 1315–1338.

Mirvis, P.H., Googins, B. and Kinnicutt, S. (2010). Vision, mission, values: Guideposts to sustainability. *Organization Dynamics*, 39: 316–324.

Mirvis, P.H., Googins, B. and Kiser, C. (2012). *Corporate Social Innovation*. Wellesley, MA: Lewis Institute, Social Innovation Lab, Babson University.

Mirvis, P.H., Herrera, M.E.B., Googins, B. and Albareda, L. (2016). Corporate social innovation: How firms learn to innovate for the greater good. *Journal of Business Research*, 69(11): 5014–5021.

Mirvis, P.H. and Googins, B. (2018). Engaging employees as social innovators. *California Management Review* (in press).

Pfitzer, M., Bockstette, V. and Stamp, M. (2013). Innovating for shared value. *Harvard Business Review*, 91(9): 100–107.

Simanis, E. (2012). Reality check at the bottom of the pyramid. *Harvard Business Review*, 90(6): 120–125.

Weiser, J., Kahane, M., Rochlin, S. and Landis, J. (2004). *Untapped: Creating Value in Underserved Markets*. San Francisco, CA: Berrett-Koehler.

Worley, C. and Mirvis, P.H. (eds) (2013). *Building Networks and Partnerships*, vol. 3 of *Organizing for Sustainable Effectiveness*. New York: Emerald.

Worley, C.G. and Mirvis, P.H. (2013). Studying networks and partnerships for sustainability: Lessons learned. In *Building Networks and Partnerships*, vol. 3 of *Organizing for Sustainable Effectiveness*. New York: Emerald, pp. 261–291.

Table 11.1 Appendix A. Corporate research sites

Company	Europe
AandB Biotechnology	Basque
Accenture Develop Partnership★	UK/US
BBVA	Spain
Credit Suisse	UK/Geneva
Danone★	France
Ericsson★	Sweden
Ferrovial★	Spain
Gamesa	Basque

Gas Natural Fenosa	Spain
LEGO★	Denmark
Marks and Spencer	UK
Novo Nordisk	Denmark
RBS	UK, Scotland
SAP★	Germany/US
Shell (Foundation)★	UK
Unilever★	UK, US
Virgin Unite	UK
	United States
Abbott	Illinois
Best Buy	Minnesota
Black Rock	New York
Coca-Cola	Georgia
CVS	New Jersey
d.light★	California
Dow Chemical★	Michigan
Dow Corning★	Michigan
EY	New York
Food Solutions Lab★	Massachusetts
Green Mt Coffee	Vermont
HP	California
IBM★	New York
Intel★	US/Germany/Asia
Interface★	Georgia
John Deere	Illinois
Johnson and Johnson	New Jersey
Mattell	California
Microsoft★	Washington
Nike	Oregon
PandG★	Ohio
Panera Bread★	Massachusetts
Patagonia	California
Pepsico★	New York
Walmart★	Arkansas
	Asia
7-Eleven/7I	Japan
Chiva-Som	Thailand
CP	Thailand
Jollibee	Philippines
Samsung	Korea
Sarihusada (Danone)	Indonesia
Singapore Development Bank	Singapore
SK	Korea
Star Hub	Singapore
	Other
Alliant	South Africa
Ensenada de La Paz	Columbia
Loblaw	Canada
Microsoft	South Africa
Natura★	Brazil
Telefonica	Latin America
Vodaphone	Kenya

★Cited in this chapter.

12 Dynamic capabilities for sustainable innovation

What are they?

Aurélien Acquier, Valentina Carbone and Pilar Acosta

Introduction

While often associated with long-term transformations, the concept of sustainable development is linked to major ecological, social and commercial upheavals the effects of which can now be observed in numerous industries. Climate change, problems of access to raw materials and resources (water, energy, etc.), the population explosion and urban growth in developing countries, and the aging population in Western countries: all these issues are linked to societal changes that are reshaping several industries (energy, transportation, housing, construction, insurance, etc.).

In response to these transformations, enterprises tap into their capacity for adaptation. In this context, several academic studies on corporate social responsibility (CSR) have suggested looking at sustainable development from the angle of innovation management (Aggeri, 2011; Hart, 1995; Porter and Kramer, 2006; Porter and Van der Linde, 1995; Russo and Fouts, 1997; Sharma, 2014). For example, Porter and Kramer (2006) urge companies to identify areas of shared value between business and society, and to transform societal problems into strategic opportunities that they can respond to by creating profitable business models. Despite being taken up by consultants and various businesses, this notion of shared value creation also faces strong criticism (Crane, Palazzo, Spence and Matten, 2014): there are few convincing practical applications, it does not explore the underlying managerial processes (resistance mechanisms that hamper the emergence of such innovations), and it is rooted in an angelic and depoliticized view of the firm.

Other studies have developed around the concept of social entrepreneurship (Mair et al., 2012), 'bottom of the pyramid' approaches (Prahalad and Hart, 2002), and social business and societal innovation (Martinet and Payaud, 2008). While these studies highlight the emergence of new business models (such as microfinance), their analysis tends to neglect traditional businesses and focuses instead on new hybrid organizational forms which mission combines social and managerial objectives (Battilana and Dorado, 2010). Although interesting and useful, these developments have some shortcomings. From an empirical point of view, these studies tend to neglect traditional large firms and their innovation dynamics in relation to sustainable development issues, focusing instead on alternative, emerging structures. Given the economic and political clout of large corporations, such an omission is problematic. Even Schumpeter, despite ascribing a driving role to entrepreneurs in his early writings on innovation, later returned to the fundamental role played by large firms in the renewal of economic dynamics linked to innovation (Schumpeter, 1942).

Furthermore, from an academic point of view, these developments are largely disconnected from the literature on innovation and strategy. New sub-communities have been created within the research on CSR and sustainable development, limiting opportunities for cross-fertilization between innovation management and sustainable development. A recent exception in this regard is found at the boundary between dynamic capabilities (DCs) and ecological sustainability (Borland et al., 2014).

This chapter aims therefore to re-establish the link between innovation management and sustainable development by exploring this question primarily from the point of view of large firms, and by rooting these dynamics more systematically in the literature on innovation management. To achieve this aim we have anchored our work in the framework of dynamic capabilities (Eisenhardt and Martin, 2000; Helfat and Peteraf, 2003; Teece, Pisano, and Shuen, 1997; Zollo and Winter, 2002), which is a crucial area for analysing innovation capability in strategic management. Drawing on Teece's model (2007), we analyse the results of a study conducted in 2013 that surveyed 34 European firms about their innovation efforts in sustainable development. Based on these results, we explore orchestration capabilities in the area of sustainable innovation, and we show that these orchestration capabilities are twofold. First, there is the ability to guide the emergence of sustainable innovation ecosystems and, second, the ability to identify appropriate organizational choices depending on the degree of rupture caused by sustainable innovations (Bower and Christensen, 1995).

Sustainable development and dynamic capabilities

Dynamic capabilities and strategy

The notion of dynamic capabilities was developed to account for the way firms maintain and develop their competitive position in rapidly changing environments (Teece, 2007). Dynamic capabilities therefore take on particular strategic importance in hyper-competitive environments (D'Aveni, 1994) where the foundations that the firm's competitive advantage is built on may shift quickly, requiring competences in the areas of perception, experimentation and swift adaptation. An organization's dynamic capabilities are intrinsically linked to questions of change and innovation, and may refer to managerial routines (in R&D, marketing, design or project management) or managerial skills (diagnosis and decision-making skills of top management). Several researchers have shown the existence of different types of dynamic capabilities, depending on the degree of turbulence and competitiveness in the business environment (Winter, 2003; Zahra et al., 2006). For instance, Ambrosini et al. (2009) introduce a three-level hierarchy of dynamic capabilities distinguishing between incremental, renewing and regenerative DCs. Incremental DCs refer to organizational routines that favour continuous improvement in a given area (such as production or marketing skills that are progressively improved). Renewing DCs refer to strategic decisions or skills that lead to the creation of new strategic resources for the firm (such as diversification skills or the ability to leverage R&D skills to develop new markets). Finally, regenerative DCs refer to upper-level change that re-orients the development pattern of the firm DCs (such as a new top manager that would refocus the firm competitive advantage from R&D to marketing). The degree of organizational change associated with each level of dynamic capability varies from lowest (incremental level) to highest (with the introduction of regenerative capabilities).

For Helfat et al. (2007, p. 4), 'a dynamic capability is the capacity of an organization to purposefully create, extend or modify its resource base', which refers to the organization's capacity to mobilize its resources while simultaneously reconfiguring them over time (Amit and Schoemaker, 1993). In contrast to an operational capability (which allows the firm to perform an activity at a certain time with a given level of reliability), dynamic capabilities allow the company to renew its resource pool with the aim of recreating or maintaining its 'evolutionary fitness' to technical and commercial contexts. The performance of a dynamic capability may be measured using the yardstick of the firm's technical fitness, i.e. the optimization of its production processes in terms of costs as well as its ability to respond to market demand requirements and cope with competition (market and competitive fitness). The effectiveness of dynamic capabilities must therefore be linked to the financial and commercial performance of the firm and the robustness of its competitive advantage.

In the dynamic capabilities framework, the fundamental role of strategy is to orchestrate the firm's assets in a context of shifting markets (Helfat et al., 2007; Teece, 2007; Teece et al., 1997; Teece and Pisano, 1994). A firm's asset orchestration decisions, which according to these authors are divided among three distinct organizational and managerial processes – coordinating/integrating, learning, and reconfiguring (Teece et al., 1997; Teece and Pisano, 1994) – include decisions on whether to outsource activities or handle them internally, to co-specialize assets (gather distinct competences together in the same company), and to develop alliances and partnerships, etc.

In his work on the microfoundations of dynamic capabilities, Teece (2007) states that the orchestration of assets underpins three classes of dynamic capabilities that contribute to competitive advantage in dynamic environments: sensing (perception of issues), seizing (internal decision-making processes and mechanisms for entering markets, formulating business models, implementation abilities), and managing threats / transforming (dynamic alignment of the company's tangible and intangible assets, ability to reconfigure).

In other words, the need to perceive issues and opportunities, to translate them into organizational, technological and market access choices and to develop them over time requires superior asset and resource orchestration capabilities. It is important to know how to effectively allocate, combine and transform all tangible and intangible resources to produce sustainable financial performance and competitive advantage.

Dynamic capabilities for sustainable innovation

The dynamic capabilities approach is a logical starting point if we consider sustainable development from the angle of innovation. Combined with sustainable development issues, the notion of dynamic capability sheds light on the way firms manage to perceive and respond to sustainable development issues by building an innovation dynamic linked to their value creation objectives.

In a context where sustainability issues are complex and often ambiguous (Aragón-Correa and Sharma, 2003), using dynamic capabilities to study innovation strategies in sustainable development seems perfectly justified. Several recent studies explore the concept of dynamic capabilities in relation to corporate sustainability issues (Castiaux, 2012; Kleef and Roome, 2007; Wu et al., 2012). Much like classic research on

DCs, these studies primarily investigate strategic advantage. Wu et al. (2012) for exam-ple, discuss corporate sustainability and competitive advantage. Anchoring sustainable development efforts in the organization's core business and global strategy constitutes one of the major challenges for actors in charge of sustainable development (Porter and Kramer, 2011).

However, there is a need to revise several assumptions of the DCs construct to adapt it to sustainable innovation. We suggest three directions:

From 'corporate-centric' to 'sustain-centric' dynamic capabilities. First, because of its roots in corporate strategy, the literature on DCs is by nature centred on the corporation, and prioritizes the firm's interests over other actors of its competitive environment. This constitutes a serious conceptual limitation in the context of sustainable inno-vation. As Gladwin et al. (1995) point out, the concept of sustainable development calls for broad problematization based on sustainability issues (sustain-centric), not only those of the firm. As a result, a study of Dynamic Capabilities for Sustainable Innovation should not prioritize the firm's objectives over social, environmental or stakeholder concerns (Donaldson and Preston, 1995). This corporate-centric perspective is commonplace in the CSR literature, leading to recurring concep-tual criticisms voiced at stakeholder theory (Orts and Strudler, 2002), social busi-ness (Margolis and Walsh, 2003), the triple bottom line concept (Norman and MacDonald, 2004) or shared value (Crane et al., 2014).

Considering the business ecosystem. Second, the notion of an ecological ecosystem, defined in the field of biology by Tansley in 1935, refers to a system of interactions between the populations of different species living in the same location, and between those populations and the physical environment. This concept highlights the interde-pendence among the species that populate an ecosystem and between these species and their environment. By analogy, the notion of 'business ecosystem', according to Moore (1993, 2006) may be defined as an economic community supported by the interaction between business 'entities': firms, individuals and public sector institu-tions. This economic community produces goods and services, delivering value to customers, who will in turn be part of the ecosystem. Members of the ecosystem also include suppliers, producers, competitors and other stakeholders (educational and research institutions, communities, public sector actors, etc.). The social and environmental concerns of sustainable development also call for the integration of less visible and geographically dispersed stakeholders, such as suppliers located in developing countries (Beske, 2012). In this regard, the question of innovation in sustainable development needs to be analysed at the level of the whole value chain, not just the firm (Acquier et al., 2015). Acting at the level of the ecosystem is often necessary to consider the systemic dimension and complex interactions involved by sustainable innovation.

Considering various governance structures. Third, current research on dynamic capabilities for corporate sustainability is being deployed in traditional firms which objective is to maximize the creation of shareholder value (Jensen and Meckling, 1976). It does not explore alternative governance structures such as social business approaches, for which economic value creation is not an end in itself, but instead constitutes a way of financing the growth of the organization (Yunus et al., 2010), which primary mis-sion is to solve environmental and social issues. It is therefore necessary to investigate the way governance structures influence the development and deployment of dynamic capabilities for sustainability.

As a result, we define 'dynamic capabilities for sustainable innovation' (DCSI) as a set of capabilities that an organization can employ, in line with its governance structure, to purposefully create, extend or modify its resource base and its business ecosystem in order to address sustainable innovation issues.

In the remainder of this chapter, based on the results of a study of sustainable innovation strategies in large European firms, we explore two categories of DCSI, namely ecosystem orchestration capabilities and abilities related to making decisions about the firm's internal organization, that appear to be critical in dealing with the issues of sustainable innovation.

Methodology

In order to achieve this objective, we draw on a study of 34 European firms (75 per cent of which are large companies with more than 5,000 employees), carried out in 2013, which aim was to analyse the way those firms understand sustainable development issues and integrate them in their innovation strategy. Forty-five employees from different departments (mainly those in charge of innovation or sustainable development) were interviewed. Table 12.1 in the appendix lists the firms and functional positions included in the study.

In general, the interviews concerned the integration of sustainable development issues in the innovation efforts of these firms. In relation to the literature on dynamic capabilities, the interview questions addressed the perceived importance of innovation in sustainable development, the resources activated and actions taken, and the difficulties encountered in coordinating innovation initiatives with sustainable development issues. At each company, interviewees were asked to provide illustrations of innovation in sustainable development, emphasizing key issues in projects as well as difficulties or obstacles encountered. The interviews were transcribed and the different questions were grouped together in an Excel spreadsheet. Next, we identified the organizations' DCs in relation to innovation in sustainable development. To do so, we selected practices involving dynamic capabilities, leading to the creation of new market opportunities or the development of strategic resources (markets, brands, market offers) involving innovative models of shared value creation (business / society). We then inferred the capabilities involved in the development of such innovations. In other words, we conducted a line-by-line analysis looking at how the firms created, extended or modified their resource base in order to respond to sustainable development issues.

We identified two types of DCSI: ecosystem orchestration capabilities and abilities related to making decisions about the firm's internal organization. In the remainder of this chapter, we will offer selected illustrations relating to the two categories of DSCI identified.

Orchestrating innovation in sustainable development

Asset orchestration (Helfat et al., 2007) constitutes one of the pillars of dynamic capabilities (Adner and Helfat, 2003). Our study identifies two types of DCSI that companies use to orchestrate assets both internally and externally: one type (external) of DCSI is relational, pertaining to the orchestration of sustainable innovation ecosystems; and a second type (internal) of DCSI is organizational and concerns the orchestration of the firm's internal organization, i.e. the ability to make suitable organizational choices that correspond to the degree of disruption caused by the innovation.

Orchestrating the development of sustainable innovation ecosystems

To develop sustainable innovations, actors often have to reframe interactions among existing actors and organizations belonging to their business ecosystem. In the construction industry, the energy performance of buildings is a good illustration of this issue. Major differences exist between theoretical calculations of a building's energy performance and its actual energy consumption. According to Myriam Humbert, a researcher at a public centre for technical studies of equipment,[1] there can be a difference of up to 400 per cent for a single dwelling. These variances can be attributed to the lack of integration between builders and designers, which raises the question of whether design choices (materials and assembly) are coordinated with decisions made during the construction phase (which naturally focus on speed and simplicity of execution as well as budget concerns at the building site). Once completed, the way the building is actually used by its occupants (ventilation, heating, lighting, etc.) may be very different from the forecasts made during the design phase and can seriously impair energy performance. Thus the environmental impact of a building can only properly be envisaged if one considers the complex interactions within the entire chain of actors that are involved in the design and life of the building: designers, architects, property developers, builders, managers and occupants.

Innovation requires the development of initiatives, methods, tools and actors so that the firm can act on several links in the chain simultaneously and rethink the coordination among different members of the ecosystem – an issue described by the innovation head of Gecina, a real estate investment company:

> In the construction industry, there are different systems that are not interconnected. The construction system includes the building owner, the architect, the design office, the general contractor, while the operation system includes the occupants, the owners or their representatives and the operators of various assets and equipment. The fact that these systems do not communicate with each other creates enormous constraints when you start to think about an environmental innovation.

In sum, to create value, firms have to interact with other actors within a complex ecosystem that comprises their customers, suppliers, design office and users, as well as other stakeholders such as research centres, universities, local authorities or other companies from various industries. However, developing an orchestration capability at the ecosystem level proves to be a complex process.

We have identified three action areas that companies can work on to develop these DCSI:

- Share information and knowledge about sustainable innovation.
- Structure information in order to achieve better sustainability performance.
- Design the collective governance of the ecosystem.

Share information and knowledge about sustainable innovation

In a complex ecosystem, the ability to share information and knowledge is crucial. For multinational enterprises, the challenge is already considerable internally and many firms invest in knowledge and information sharing tools in the areas of innovation and sustainable development.

As a major player in the automotive industry, Renault is concerned by the externalities generated by transport. According to the World Bank, transportation accounted for about 20 per cent of CO_2 emissions in 2013. Automobiles are also pointed for health and air pollution issues, in particular in dense city areas. As a result, Renault has developed a unit in charge of gathering and sharing information about innovations in the field of sustainable mobility.

> Renault created an innovation community. It is an open community, bringing together people from inside and outside the firm: people from Renault are bringing their knowledge and *know-how*, but we also include our parts manufacturers and our interested suppliers. We also have large variety of companies outside the transportation industry, such as L'Oréal, EDF, SEB, etc. – and include consultants and researchers. Viewing what happens outside the firm is also very useful to raise awareness inside it. We develop the organization knowledge by sharing the community societal innovations, by understanding the expectations of society regarding innovation … In the case of sustainable innovation it is at the interface between business and society that we find the most interesting things.
>
> (Head of CSR, Renault)

For the company, opening up to these external stakeholders may involve the creation of open innovation laboratories. Gecina, a major Real Estate Manager in France, launched an initiative called Gecina Lab that fosters innovation in sustainable development through dialogue with ecosystem actors. Gecina Lab was created in 2011 as a kind of forward-looking discussion group on sustainable development topics for its major commercial tenants such as EADS, Natixis, Hermès, Sodexo, TetraPak, and PepsiCo. The lab was conducted in the form of breakfast meetings and conferences dealing with various subjects such as the link between the 'greening' of buildings and improving employee productivity, with the aims of bringing together the points of view of experts and users in order to find new areas for innovation. Through this initiative Gecina integrates the entire chain of the building's lifecycle and re-examines the way they understand the business of real state by integrating not only the construction of buildings, but also the way they are operated and even the way buildings are marketed.

Such communities may also be called on to assist in product design. Communities of innovation, for example, are created around the world to design new products with high social and environmental value. For example, communities of 'makers' (Anderson, 2012) share solutions to promote a 'do-it-yourself culture', improve reparability of goods and easier access to goods and services. Some of them are explicitly oriented towards environmental progress, such as Open Source Ecology. These communities emulate the open source model in the real world. Owing to their fluidity, these initiatives have caught the attention of large corporations that wish to develop their ability to mobilize this type of expertise.

> An important challenge is opening the company to external experts and actors, to go and find the best expertise and information wherever it is. Several corporations have a very open and honest approach to their own competences and how to go and find what they lack in an environment that extends beyond the boundaries of the company. We should follow the example of these initiatives in the area of sustainable innovation.
>
> (Head of innovation, Caisses des Dépôts et Consignations, French public sector financial institution)

Indeed, knowledge is not located only within the organization, and companies have to develop the ability to transform their relational capabilities throughout the entire ecosystem. This is achieved through diagnostic tools, consultation, dialogue and engagement with non-commercial stakeholders (NGOs, citizen associations, local communities, etc.). These stakeholder-engagement initiatives, which have developed in companies such as Lafarge or Danone, help to develop the organization's sensitiveness to social issues and their political abilities, to better address social expectations that affect the company, and to establish acceptable and legitimate orientations through the creation of communities of actors. These efforts enhance the company's 'political sensing' abilities vis-à-vis its ecosystem.

Structure information in order to achieve better sustainability performance

Another dimension for developing orchestration capabilities at the ecosystem level concerns efforts made to structure information. For many interviewees, digitalization plays a central role in such process, by enabling better organization and sharing of data among different stakeholders.

Many companies have implemented digital tools to visualize and represent data. Dassault Systèmes, a world leader in software for 3D design, is at the forefront of such innovations. For the company, introducing such shared digital tools in sectors like construction can make it easier to address energy performance issues.

> In the construction industry today, our modeling tools are only used upstream in the design phase. If the digital model were present throughout the life cycle, we would have a fabulous tool to ensure that the property manager's problems, or even those of the occupant, were addressed correctly in the design phase and vice versa.
>
> (Senior manager public affairs and CSR, Dassault Systèmes, major player in the IT industry)

As Dassault Systèmes underlines it, governments and regulators can play an active role in the promotion of such tools, pursuing the objective to smoothen the decision-making process involving a high number of stakeholders, while at the same time facilitate a systemic approach to sustainability related issues. In 2007, the Danish government legislated that any bid made in response to a public call for tender for an architectural or city planning project must use digital modelling tools. This process, which has repercussions on training, on the language of architects and engineers in design offices and on the management of projects, was guided and facilitated by a Digital Construction programme initiated by the national agency for construction in 2005.

Beyond virtual design tools, digital innovation offers many opportunities to generate new information and reframe the interactions among ecosystem members. For SNCF (railway transportation company), smart grids (that use big data to manage information from different sources) offer great opportunities to optimize energy use and environmental impacts:

> We are developing an experience of smart grids applied to a train station with several partners. We seek to reduce consumption in real time by regulating the heating, lightning, escalators, etc., looking at the railway traffic and the amount of people circulating in the station. We have estimated a 20 per cent reduction in the energy consumption.
>
> (Head of sustainable development, SNCF, rail transport sector)

A third example is given by Schneider Electric, a global player in the utilities sector, which compiles and organizes large amounts of data coming from different stakeholders as well as subsidiaries, through a barometer that monitors and measures performance in three areas: planet (environment), people and profit. Such tool is also used to communicate to and share information with different stakeholders: 'The barometer is not an internal communication device, it is above all a tool opened to all stakeholders and includes social, environmental and governance criteria. It measures performance and communicates about this performance in a very circular way' (Head of sustainable development, Schneider Electric).

Design the collective governance of the ecosystem

A third way of guiding the ecosystem towards sustainable innovation involves capabilities enabling to set up collective governance mechanisms for the ecosystem. By governance, we refer to practices affecting roles and responsibilities to stakeholders of the same ecosystem. Eco-organizations (called 'eco-organisms') offer a good example of how organizations may be created to reframe the collective governance of a given industry. In France such organizations have been created in different industries to optimize waste and incentivize private actors to improve on their environmental performance. Eco-organisms help producers manage their 'extended responsibility' on waste, as introduced by European regulations. These organizations are typically private, not for profit, and co-owned and governed by the main producers and distributors of a given industry. Such organizations may typically collect money from its members, design a waste recovery process, set up collective objectives at the level of the country and promote recycling within the sector. In so doing, the eco-organization transforms the relations between actors in the ecosystem, facilitating the entry of companies to collect, dismantle and repurpose/reuse waste items. The entire ecosystem may potentially be transformed. Bayer, a global player in the pharmaceutical and chemical industries, participated in the creation of this type of organization.

> Innovation is more in the way we work with our stakeholders. The recent example of 2011, which ended in early 2012, is that we looked into the issue of waste. We

Table 12.1 Dynamic capabilities for sustainable innovation and orchestration of sustainable development ecosystems

Orchestration capabilities at the ecosystem level	Category of dynamic capability impacted	Examples
Share information and knowledge about sustainable innovation	Mainly sensing	External and internal consultation programmes, sharing communities
Structure information in order to achieve better sustainability performance	Mainly seizing	Digital innovations (3D virtual design tools, smartgrids, etc.)
Design the collective governance of the ecosystem	Sensing Seizing Transssforming	Creation of eco-organizations / eco-organisms Re-organizing the supply chain

have a division that produces waste in the form of sharp objects, such as needles and surgical tools, that carry a risk of infection. Here the innovation was to work with partners or even competitors to put a collective system in place. This was done by creating an organization called DASTRI.

(Head of sustainable development, Bayer)

The ability to interconnect actors and redefine their role can also entail redefining the company's value chain and structuring new businesses. For example, in trying to develop bank cards made of plant resin, Crédit Agricole, a large firm in the banking and insurance sector, has contributed to the development of a local corn industry and also urges suppliers to set up critical thinking processes at their end.

Instead of making bank cards out of normal plastic, they are being made out of eco-materials, in this case plant-based plastics. We have completely rethought the lifecycle of the product—not only the eco-materials, but also the process of collecting and recycling these materials. Today nothing is recycled, which is bad because the components are very harmful for the environment. The resin-based card business doesn't exist yet. We are pushing card manufacturers to pay attention to this issue so they will be technically capable of manufacturing cards out of resin. But putting pressure on the manufacturers is no small matter. We are working with industrial companies in the recycling sector to identify the proper technical solutions. This is a big deal because we issue about 6 million cards a year.

(Head of sustainable development, Crédit Agricole)

Each of the three actions for orchestrating the sustainable development ecosystem corresponds to different types of capabilities, according to Teece (2007). For example, maximizing the sharing of information involves mobilizing the 'sensing' type of dynamic capabilities in order to capture as much information as possible. Structuring information and agreement on shared orientations are focused on mobilizing the 'seizing' type of dynamic capabilities. The third orchestration capacity entails interconnecting actors and defining their roles, which not only calls on sensing and seizing capabilities but also

Table 12.2 Dynamic capabilities for sustainable innovation and internal orchestration

Internal orchestration strategy	Degree of disruption caused by the innovation	Hierarchical level of associated dynamic capabilities	Examples
Simplify the innovation	Minimal	Incremental	Projects aiming to integrate environmental criteria in products and processes
Launch and manage a portfolio of innovative projects	Medium	Renewing	Internal projects mobilizing a large number of core business activities, creation of new products/services with social or environmental criteria
Create new brands or divisions	High	Renewing/ Regenerating	Brands that can be differentiated from the company's traditional activities by their sustainable development orientation
Pursue a policy of partnerships or acquisitions	Very high	Regenerating	Establish various partnerships with competitors, universities and companies in other industries Acquisition of start-ups

'transforming' capabilities. Table 12.1 presents the types of dynamic capability mobilized in each of the ecosystem guidance strategies.

Configure the organization depending on the degree of disruption of innovations

A second category of DCSI comprises intra-organizational orchestration capabilities to make organizational choices depending on the degree of disruption caused by innovations. Sustainable innovation issues raise coordination difficulties, prompting companies to explore different organizational strategies. We have identified four major organizational strategies, which are mainly differentiated by the degree of disruption caused by the environmental innovation (Bower and Christensen, 1995) and which vary according to the hierarchical level of the dynamic capabilities (Ambrosini et al., 2009). Drawing on our interviews we summarize the four types of internal orchestration strategy and the links with levels of dynamic capabilities (see Table 12.2).

Simplify the innovation

The first strategy is to simplify the innovation. This strategy does not involve modifying the overall architecture of the market and the company's core activities. On the contrary, it focuses on the elements of the innovation that appear easiest to understand within the framework of the existing organization. As such, it constitutes a nice example of incremental dynamic capabilities (Ambrosini et al., 2009). The potential of this incremental strategy to simplify or confine the innovation should not be underestimated, however. It is particularly useful when the market structure is relatively stable and the potential for optimizing existing technologies is very high. For a construction company, for example, this may mean reorienting some of its R&D efforts to its product catalogue, while leaving the market structure intact.

This strategy is followed by several companies in our sample. For instance, in the case of services, the Plaza Athénée, a luxury hotel in Paris, seeks to introduce small changes maintaining the luxury positioning of its services: 'We offer an outstanding service, we have to find something different, moving beyond the offers of other hotels. We are thinking of developing a green offer, with organic champagne and fruits ... These are small things, not great revolutions, but innovations in terms of our service' (Head of innovation team, Plaza Athénée).

Picard, a retailer of frozen food products, provides a good illustration of the benefits of simplification. The starting point of the sustainable innovation initiative at Picard was energy optimization and commercial freezers. 'We tested various devices from different companies: ones that are supposed to improve the electricity consumption of buildings, and small 'magic boxes' that you plug into your appliance that would halve its energy consumption without altering its use or functionalities' (Head of sustainable development, Picard). It was only when these first steps had been accomplished that the company gradually began to deal with more complex questions in terms of management: the development of new freezer systems, high environmental quality[2] design for its stores, and the design of ecological freezers. These areas are more complex because they require greater inter-functional and inter-organizational collaboration. Companies tend to adopt a project management approach, bringing together marketing, R&D, and the sustainable development team, as well as suppliers.

Launch and manage a portfolio of innovative projects

The second strategy is to launch and manage a set of innovative projects. In this case, one department (e.g. innovation or sustainable development) formulates a sustainable innovation strategy often based on a forward-looking exercise shared with the strategic apex of the firm. At first, adopting a project management approach decompartmentalizes existing business divisions by fostering openness to new approaches. Next, this exercise often prompts actors to re-conceptualize their core business.

These projects allow the company to envisage new products, partnerships, markets and business models based on service logic or built around multimodal solutions. La Poste, the French post office and financial services company, is pursuing a strategy based on multiple projects. This strategy has spawned internal initiatives that are transformed into new product offerings and new lines of business, such as the development of an initiative to collect and recycle paper using the existing logistics flows of postal workers.

Following this logic of isolating projects, other companies create new brands or new lines of business once they have developed and tested the sustainable development innovation internally: 'The experience gained in insulation for buildings and zero-carbon cities has enabled us to put together an eco-building proposal. We started small with a daycare, then a commercial building in Brussels, and then another one in India, following a continuous improvement approach' (Head of sustainable development, Bayer).

Create new brands or divisions

The creation of new brands or divisions dedicated to sustainable innovation may also be a good solution when the projects require significant differentiation with respect to the company's traditional core business and markets. In this approach, the company grants a high degree of autonomy to the new division, which operates relatively independently from the rest of the organization, while still making reports to head office. An example is the decentralized approach of the luxury goods company LVMH, which enables its brands and subsidiaries, like Guerlain (in the luxury cosmetics sector), to operate close to the market, to respond quickly, and to adopt solutions that suit the local context, thus fostering growth. Guerlain came up with a sustainable development innovation to refill the containers used by their customers.

> We developed a refill system in our stores for a luxury cream that costs 350 euros. It was important to maintain the element of enchantment surrounding the product. We developed a system in our boutiques: our customers bring in their empty containers and our beauticians refill them in the back of the boutique. Meanwhile, the customers are offered a personalized service including tea, beauty advice, a flash make-up session, etc. We created a ritual associated with a luxury service.
>
> (Head of sustainable development, Guerlain)

At the other end of the spectrum, the creation of dedicated divisions may subscribe to a logic that is at odds with the aim of profitability: allowing a company to isolate projects that would not be financially viable according to its usual profitability criteria and governance frameworks. This is particularly true in the area of social business or bottom-of-the-pyramid (BOP) markets; companies cannot transpose their usual profitability constraints to these projects without threatening their viability. In such cases, the creation of a dedicated unit allows the company to get involved in environmental and social issues within the context of a different governance structure. This is the path that Danone followed in creating a fund dedicated to social innovation – Danone Communities – in 2007 in order to finance low-profit projects that addressed societal issues in the area of food and health.

Pursue a policy of partnerships and external acquisitions

Finally, when the firm foresees major changes in its sector in the medium term or when its internal resources are unsuitable or too limited, it can pursue a policy of partnerships or external acquisitions. In this case, it is mainly the firm's regenerative capabilities that are mobilized when it wishes to alter its resource base and its practices.

This is the case of Dassault Systèmes, whose external acquisitions policy has been a key driver of the development of a sustainable development value proposition for several years. These acquisitions underpin transformations within this developer and publisher of digital design software:

> Our strategy is centered on 'providing business and people with a 3D experience solutions to define sustainable innovation capable of harmonizing products, nature and life'. We have been centered in product modelling, our idea today is to help modelling products, nature and life. The acquisition of Gemcom (a Canadian mining software provider) is a first step. Gemcom help us modelling the subsoil.
> (Senior manager public affairs and CSR, Dassault Systèmes)

When links to the company's core business are more tenuous, it can also pursue a policy of investment or assistance in the financing of entrepreneurship. By setting up venture capital types of funds, large corporations can aid projects financially, in the hope of making a profit, but also to form relationships and collaborate with en-trepreneurs, thus producing learning and internal changes, before moving towards (potential) closer integration (e.g. increasing their stake or acquiring the start-up) and stronger strategic ties.

Table 12.3 Four strategies for the internal management of innovation: advantages and drawbacks

Orchestration strategies at the enterprise level	Definition	Advantages	Drawbacks
Simplify the innovation	Limit the complexity of the innovation by focusing on manageable issues that are known to the company Optimize existing solutions and technologies	Continuity of the organization, managerial control, easier connection to the market Facilitates the innovation effort internally Actors in charge of the innovation gain in maturity Avoids having to change the organization dramatically	Issues that are easiest to deal with are not necessarily the most important Lesser symbolic importance
Launch and manage a portfolio of projects	Create a temporary project for the design of a new sustainable product	Flexibility Decompartmentalize existing activities Facilitate learning Facilitate the opening of business activities to new approaches (open innovation)	Integration of the project with the rest of the organization Continuity after the project? Risk of challenges/ criticism: greenwashing or real commitment?

(Continued)

Orchestration strategies at the enterprise level	Definition	Advantages	Drawbacks
Create new brands and divisions	Create a new division in charge of marketing products/ services related to sustainable development issues	Autonomy: facilitate the decision-making process	Connection with the rest of the firm?
		Encourage experimentation and internal entrepreneurship	Little learning, weak control
		Raise visibility of the company's actions on these matters	Vulnerable model, dependent on the existence of a dedicated customer base
		Potentially relax constraints related to the maturity/ profitability of markets	
External acquisition policy	Venture capital or real options approach	Better risk management	Risks related to integration
		Internalization of key competences for future initiatives	Zero synergy model

In the rail transport sector, SNCF joined forces with Orange, Total and PSA in November 2011 to create Ecomobilité Ventures, a multi-enterprise investment fund dedicated to sustainable mobility. The aim of this €30 million fund, half of which is provided by SNCF, is to invest in innovative European SMEs during the start-up or development phase. The four large corporations not only offer financial support, but also their expertise to strengthen and stimulate the innovation capability of the selected start-ups. The fund promotes projects related to new modes of transport and mobility, and keeps an eye on changes in the sustainable mobility market. The fund's first three investments were announced in October 2012: Zilok Auto (now OuiCar, in which SNCF gained a majority stake by investing 28 million euros in 2015), the first website for car rentals between private individuals; EZ Wheel, a company producing the first autonomous electric wheel; and Move About, a car-sharing service providing electric vehicles to businesses.

Conclusions and future research

In this chapter we defined Dynamic Capabilities for Sustainable Innovation a set of capabilities that an organization can employ, in line with its governance structure, to purposefully create, extend or modify its resource base and its business ecosystem in order to address sustainable innovation issues. This definition broadens the scope of the traditional analysis of dynamic capabilities, as it does not envisage dynamic capabilities only from the point of view of the company's strategic and financial advantage (Aragón-Correa and Sharma, 2003; Hart, 1995; Porter and Van der Linde, 1995), but also from the point of view of the organization's ability to innovate and increase its capacity for action on sustainable development issues. Evolutionary fitness is not to be analysed solely in the context of the competitive environment, but also the social and biological environment (pressure on ecosystems, non-renewable resources, etc.) surrounding the firm

(Borland et al., 2014). Consequently, the definition paves the way for an approach that is more in line with a sustainable development ethic, centred on a systemic approach, necessarily broader than a perspective solely centred on the firm (Gladwin et al., 1995; Whiteman et al., 2014), and which goes even further by integrating an eco-centric perspective (Borland et al., 2014; Purser et al., 1995).

Another benefit of our definition of DCSI is that it is neutral concerning the role, mission and governance model of the organization being studied. It can be applied to several types of governance structures, the forms and effectiveness of dynamic capabilities for sustainable innovation being likely to vary depending on the type of organization. Thus our definition does not only pertain to the context of an organization seeking to maximize shareholder value, which is the most common frame of reference in strategy. It may be applied to any type of organization and governance, so that organizations with a traditional governance structure may be compared with those that have alternative forms of governance, such as social businesses (Yunus et al., 2010).

In our exploration of DCSI in the context of several large European companies we have identified two categories of DCSI, thus complementing existing studies (Ambrosini et al., 2009; Helfat et al., 2007; Teece, 2007): relational capabilities for external orchestration (shaping a sustainable innovation ecosystem) and organizational capabilities for internal orchestration (making organizational choices depending on the degree of disruption caused by innovations).

Several possibilities for future research emerge from this work of identifying DCSI. First, we do not claim that the study is exhaustive and it is important to add to it and develop this work by analysing other categories of DCSI that are necessary for organizations to achieve sustainable development goals. Along these lines, Borland et al. (2014) have identified the need for two new dynamic capabilities: remapping and reaping, to take the biophysical environment of ecosystems into account. Second, researchers in the field of strategy have investigated the antecedents and effects of the emergence of dynamic capabilities (Eriksson, 2014) and have suggested developing the analysis of cognitive processes leading to the development of dynamic capabilities (Helfat and Peteraf, 2015; Zollo and Winter, 2002). Likewise, the antecedents, effects and obstacles to the development of DCSI should be examined in a more systematic way. Concerning antecedents and obstacles, more systematic study is needed of the way governance structures (traditional firms or alternative models such as social innovation, cooperatives or hybrid governance forms) influence or impede the organizational development of DCSI. It is also necessary to understand the role of external stakeholders such as government, shareholders, standards organizations, professions and customers in the emergence of DCSI. Similarly, it is important to better understand the influence of leaders and the cognitive representations of managers in the field of sustainable development (Hahn et al., 2015).

From a managerial point of view, implementing sustainable innovation in established organizations is fraught with numerous organizational challenges linked to the tricky nature of managing profound change. To overcome these challenges, our study highlights different strategies for orchestrating a sustainable innovation ecosystem and various possible intra-organizational choices that can be made to eventually produce the sustainable innovation. Companies can employ several (non-exclusive) strategies and organizational modes: simplify the issue by focusing on elements that the company can control, create a temporary project dedicated to the design of a new sustainable product or service in order to produce concrete results quickly, create a new division in charge of marketing sustainable products or services, or invest in start-ups that already perform well in this area. Whichever approach is adopted, it is essential to integrate new external competences and to update internal criteria to better integrate sustainable development issues in innovation projects.

Appendix

Table 12.4 List of people/companies interviewed

Institution	Position
Air France	Director of Sustainable Development
	Manager Sustainable Development
Arjowiggins Healthcare	Head of Sterisheet marketing
Asics	Manager of CSR / Sustainability for EMEA
Bayer	Director of Sustainable Development
Bosch	President of Corporate R&D
	Director of Corporate R&D
	PhD candidate R&D – innovation and sustainable development
Bouygues Construction	Deputy CEO in charge of R&D, innovation and sustainable construction
Caisse des Dépôts et Consignations Climat	Head of innovation, strategic management department, sustainable development and studies
	Project manager: sustainable development
Cemex	Innovation director, R&D department
	Sustainable Development Expert
	Biodiversity and water analyst, R&D department
Crédit Agricole	Director of Sustainable Development
Dassault Systèmes	Deputy CEO
	Senior Manager Public Affairs and Corporate Responsibility
Dekra	CEO Dekra Consulting
Eiffage	Director of Sustainable Development
Emulsar	Founder and CEO
Eramet	Director of Communication and Sustainable Development
GDF Suez	Director of Innovation, Research and innovation department
	Deputy director of Innovation, Research and innovation department
Gecina	Director of sustainable development, innovation and performance
	Technical director
Geimex	Director of Supply Chain
General Electric	Director of strategic marketing
Generali	Head of western region, Co-manager of 'take action for our future' initiative
Geodis	Director of Business Development
Guerlain	Director of Sustainable Development
IBM	Expert Global – Consumer Products
Innortex	Chairman
Interface	Sustainability Customer Liaison, Global Team
	Director of innovation for EMEAI (Europe, Middle East, Africa, India)
La Poste	Director of the CSR department for La Poste brand
Majencia	Director of Industry and Sustainable Development

Nestlé	General manager of Consumer Communication and Corporate Affairs
Picard	Head of Sustainable Development
Plaza Athénée	Deputy CEO and head of innovation team
	Communications manager and member of the sustainable development team
Renault	Director of CSR
	Director of the Renault Foundation
Saint-Gobain	Deputy R&D director
	Deputy R&D director
Schneider Electric	Director of Sustainable Development
SNCF	Director of Sustainable Development
Veolia Environnement	Director of the waste collection sorting and recovery programme

Notes

1   Centre d'études techniques de l'équipement (CETE de l'Ouest).
2   In France, HQE (haute qualité environnementale) is a set of standards for ecological construction and green buildings.

References

Acquier, A., Valiorgue, B., and Daudigeos, T. (2015). Sharing the shared value: A transaction-cost perspective on strategic corporate social responsibility policies in global value chains. *Journal of Business Ethics.* doi:10.1007/s10551-015-2820-0.

Adner, R. and Helfat, C.E. (2003). Corporate effects and dynamic managerial capabilities. *Strategic Management Journal*, 24(10): 1011–1025.

Aggeri, F. (2011). Le développement durable comme champ d'innovation. *Revue Française de Gestion*, 215: 87–107.

Ambrosini, V., Bowman, C. and Collier, N. (2009). Dynamic capabilities: An exploration of how firms renew their resource base. *British Journal of Management*, 20(S1): S9–S24.

Amit, R. and Schoemaker, P.J.H. (1993). Strategic assets and organizational rent. *Strategic Management Journal*, 14(1): 33–46.

Anderson, C. (2012). *Makers: La nouvelle révolution industrielle.* Paris: Pearson France.

Aragón-Correa, J.A. and Sharma, S. (2003). A contingent resource-based view of proactive environmental strategy. *The Academy of Management Review*, 28(1): 71–88.

Battilana, J. and Dorado, S. (2010). Buiding sustainable hybrid organizations: The case of commercial microfinance organizations. *Academy of Management Journal*, 53(6): 1419–1440.

Beske, P. (2012). Dynamic capabilities and sustainable supply chain management. *International Journal of Physical Distribution and Logistics Management*, 42(4): 372–287.

Borland, H., Ambrosini, V., Lindgreen, A. and Vanhamme, J. (2014). Building theory at the intersection of ecological sustainability and strategic management. *Journal of Business Ethics.* doi:10.1007/s10551-014-2471-6.

Bower, J.L. and Christensen, C.M. (1995). Disruptive technologies: Catching the wave. *Harvard Business Review*, 73(1): 43–53.

Castiaux, A. (2012). Developing dynamic capabilities to meet sustainable development challenges. *International Journal of Innovation Management*, 16(6): 124–140.

Crane, A., Palazzo, G., Spence, L.J. and Matten, D. (2014). Contesting the value of 'creating shared value'. *California Management Review*, 56(2): 130–153.

D'Aveni, R.A. (1994). *Hyper Competition: Managing the Dynamics of Strategic Maneuvering.* New York: The Free Press.

Donaldson, T. and Preston, L.E. (1995). The stakeholder theory of the corporation: Concepts, evidence, and implications. *Academy of management Review*, 20(1): 65–91.

Eisenhardt, K.M. and Martin, J.A. (2000). Dynamic capabilities: what are they? *Strategic Management Journal*, 21(10–11): 1105–1121.

Eriksson, T. (2014). Processes, antecedents and outcomes of dynamic capabilities. *Scandinavian Journal of Management*, 30(1): 65–82.

Gladwin, T.N., Kennelly, J.I. and Krause, T.-S. (1995). Shifting paradigms for sustainable development: Implications for management theory and research. *Academy of Management Review*, 20(4): 874–907.

Hahn, T., Pinkse, J., Preuss, L. and Figge, F. (2015). Tensions in corporate sustainability: Towards an integrative framework. *Journal of Business Ethics*, 127(2): 297–316.

Hart, S.L. (1995). A natural-resource-based view of the firm. *Academy of Management Journal*, 20(4): 996–1014.

Helfat, C.E. and Peteraf, M.A. (2003). The dynamic resource-based view: Capability lifecycles. *Strategic Management Journal*, 24(10): 997–1010.

Helfat, C.E. and Peteraf, M.A. (2015). Managerial cognitive capabilities and the microfoundations of dynamic capabilities. *Strategic Management Journal*, 36(6): 831–850.

Helfat, C.E., Finkelstein, S., Mitchell, W., Peteraf, M.A., Mann, H., Teece, D.J. and Winter, S.G. (2007). *Dynamic Capabilities: Understanding Strategic Change in Organizations*. Oxford: Blackwell Publishing.

Jensen, M.C. and Meckling, W.H. (1976). Theory of the firm: Managerial behavior, agency costs and ownership structure. *Journal of Financial Economics*, 3(4): 305–360.

Kleef, J.A.G. van and Roome, N. (2007). Developing capabilities and competence for sustainable business management as innovation: A research agenda. *Journal of Cleaner Production*, 15(1): 38–51.

Mair, J., Battilana, J. and Cardenas, J. (2012). Organizing for society : A typology of social entrepreneuring models. *Journal of Business Ethics*, 3: 353–373.

Margolis, J.D. and Walsh, J.P. (2003). Misery loves companies: Rethinking social Initiatives by business. *Administrative Science Quarterly*, 48(2): 268–305.

Martinet, A.-C. and Payaud, M. (2008). Formes de RSE et entreprises sociales Une hybridation des stratégies. *Revue Française de Gestion*, 1(180): 199–124.

Moore, J. (1993), Predators and prey a new ecology of competition. *Harvard Business Review*, 71(3): 74–86.

Moore, J. (2006). Business ecosystems and the view from the firm. *The Antitrust Bulletin*, 51(1): 31–76.

Norman, W. and MacDonald, C. (2004). Getting to the bottom of 'triple bottom line'. *Business Ethics Quarterly*, 14(02): 243–262.

Orts, E.W. and Strudler, A. (2002). The ethical and environmental limits of stakeholder theory. *Business Ethics Quarterly*, 12(02): 215–233.

Porter, M.E. and Van der Linde, C. (1995). Green and competitive: Ending the stalemate. *Harvard Business Review*, 73(5): 119–134.

Porter, M.E. and Kramer, M.R. (2006). The link between competitive advantage and corporate social responsibility. *Harvard Business Review*, 84(12): 76–93.

Porter, M.E. and Kramer, M.R. (2011). Creating shared value. *Harvard Business Review*, 89(1/2): 62–77.

Prahalad, C.K. and Hart, S.L. (2002). The fortune at the bottom of the pyramid. *Strategy+Business*, 26: 1–4.

Purser, R.E., Changkil, P. and Monturi, A. (1995). Limits to anthropocentrism: Toward an eco-centric organization paradigm? *The Academy of Management Review*, 20(4): 1053–1089.

Russo, M.V. and Fouts, P.A. (1997). A resource-based perspective on corporate environmental performance and profitability. *The Academy of Management Journal*, 40(3): 534–559.

Schumpeter, J.A. (1942). *Capitalism, Socialism, and Democracy*. New York: Harper Perennial Modern Classics.

Sharma, S. (2014). *Competing for a Sustainable World: Building Capacity for Sustainable Innovation.* Sheffield: Greenleaf Publishing.

Tansley, A.G. (1935). The use and abuse of vegetational terms and concepts. *Ecology*, 16(3): 284–307.

Teece, D.J. (2007). Explicating dynamic capabilities : The nature and microfoundations of (sustainable) enterprise performance. *Strategic Management Journal*, 28: 1319–1350.

Teece, D.J. and Pisano, G. (1994). The dynamic capabilities of firms: An introduction. *Industrial and Corporate Change*, 3(3): 537–556.

Teece, D.J., Pisano, G. and Shuen, A. (1997). Dynamic capabilities and strategic management. *Strategic Management Journal*, 18(7): 509–533.

Whiteman, G., Walker, B. and Perego, P. (2014). Planetary boundaries: Ecological foundations for corporate sustainability. *Journal of Management Studies*, 50(2): 307–336.

Winter, S.G. (2003). Understanding dynamic capabilities. *Strategic Management Journal*, 24(10): 991–995.

Wu, Q., He, Q., Duan, Y. and O'Regan, N. (2012). Implementing dynamic capabilities for corporate strategic change toward sustainability. *Strategic Management Journal*, 21(5–6): 231–247.

Yunus, M., Moingeon, B. and Lehmann-Ortega, L. (2010). Building social business models: Lessons from the Grameen experience. *Long Range Planning*, 43(2–3): 308–325.

Zahra, S.A., Sapienza, H.J. and Davidsson, P. (2006). Entrepreneurship and dynamic capabilities: A review, model and research agenda. *Journal of Management Studies*, 43(4): 917–955.

Zollo, M. and Winter, S.G. (2002). Deliberate learning and the evolution of dynamic capabilities. *Organization Science*, 13(3): 339–351.

13 Exploring challenges to developing corporate climate change strategies in Brazil

Mônica Cavalcanti Sá de Abreu

Introduction

This chapter offers valuable insights and suggestions related to drivers, practices and outcomes concerning corporate climate change strategies. In establishing a particular strategy, managers are driven by both external forces and internal capabilities. Climate change creates diverse risks that are perceived differently by different companies. And managers may or may not recognize particular opportunities for their firms to become more fully engaged in climate change strategies. The resulting combination of risks and opportunities lead them to decide what practices should be adopted and the outcomes that they consider appropriate.

Progress and evolution of corporate climate change strategies will be limited until global and local regulatory systems are put in place. However, climate change risks are of a magnitude that requires rethinking the business model and respectful attitude towards stakeholders and the natural environment.

To illustrate this overall approach, I present four case studies of companies involved in the development of climate change strategies in Brazil. In particular, we explore the challenges that these companies face for a sustainable transition towards a less-carbon-intensive economy. The conclusion outlines recommendations and managerial implications to mitigate climate change impacts.

Corporate climate change strategies development

Climate change represents one of the most serious environmental challenges faced by humanity (Stern, 2007) and is challenging the sustainability of the current production and consumption systems. The problem of climate change is nestled in a biophysical system that has existed much longer than the economic system. However, it has been aggravated by the excessive greenhouse gas (GHG) emissions, at a level exceeding the biophysical system's adaptive capacity (Pinkse and Kolk, 2012).

The global mean temperature is likely to increase in the coming decades regardless of what is done in the future. Global climate change is characterized by a rise in an average temperature in most regions. It will lead to changes in precipitation, seasonal patterns, in the intensity of extreme weather events, and sea level rises in coastal cities (Midksa and Kallbekken, 2010). Thus, climate change should be treated as an externality, as the cost and impacts of human-induced GHG emissions will affect environmental sustainability, human security and economic prosperity.

Even if the current deadlock in international climate negotiations is resolved, we still face irreversible consequences (Midksa and Kallbekken, 2010). Companies need to consider their strategic options in the field of climate change against the background of a diverse policy landscape globally. There are major uncertainties related to the magnitude and urgency of anticipated climate changes. Companies have difficulty in understanding the efforts to address the risk (Weinhofer and Hoffmann, 2010).

This leaves companies in the dark when it comes to deciding the nature of the appropriate environmental strategy. It places firms along a continuum ranging from a reactive approach that merely aims to meet legal requirements to proactive strategies that include voluntary eco-efficient practices. Reduced environmental impacts require innovations and leadership to redesign their business model and minimize their ecological footprint (Aragón-Correa et al., 2008). Corporate climate change strategy can be defined as a selection of efforts devoted to reducing GHG emissions (Lee, 2012). This strategy is a set of goals and plans aimed at reducing GHG emissions and addressing changes in market, public policy and physical environment (Sprengel and Busch, 2011).

In general, business strategies are driven by perceptions of economic interests which are mediated by different cultural, political and competitive backgrounds (Kolk and Pinkse, 2005). Companies have started to consider the implications of climate change because it may affect their profitability and competitiveness in future markets (Kolk and Mulder, 2011). An understanding of driving forces, risks, opportunities and outcomes is crucial for the development of a corporate climate change strategy. It must include a combination of practices that promote meaningful participation of stakeholders and reduction of GHG emissions.

Figure 13.1 shows various elements involved in the development of a corporate climate change strategy. The starting point is an assessment of external drivers and identification of internal capabilities. Following this, companies establish their climate change strategy based on risks and opportunities. The strategy chosen leads to outcomes, some of which in turn feed back into the driving forces.

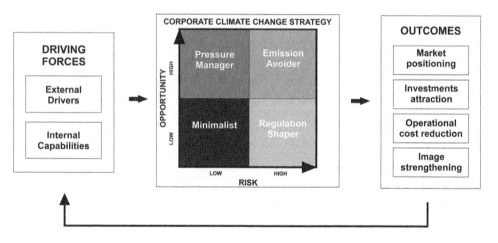

Figure 13.1 Elements involved in the development of a corporate climate change strategy.

Understanding the driving forces

The driving forces are divided into two categories: external drivers and internal capabilities. Legal requirements are one of the main external drivers for the reduction of GHGes emissions (Pinkse and Kolk, 2012). Since companies do not yet face stringent formal and informal constraints, they are not yet forced to take rational responses and may refrain from action altogether.

Another external driver involves stakeholder pressure on the company towards a low-carbon economy. Robust stakeholder pressures may lead managers to consider more seriously the strategic value of adopting carbon management practices in response to their firm's ecological uncertainty (Tashman and Rivera, 2015).

Internal capabilities refers to the way companies organize their own resources to deal with the effect of climate change on their competitiveness. Companies need to focus on three aspects: process efficiency, technological development and organizational changes. 'Cost saving', 'management commitment', 'GHG targets' and 'compliance with regulations' are identified as the most important drivers on companies' activities related to climate change strategy (Jeswani, Wehrmeyer and Mulugetta, 2008).

Steps to define an adequate corporate climate change strategy

The first action to be undertaken is the completion of an inventory of GHG emissions. It requires identification of sources, types and magnitude of GHG emissions. This leads to understanding the vulnerability and impacts of GHG emissions on its own processes and supply chains. Then, managers will be able to develop a risk assessment. Companies may decide to reduce the risk in a variety of ways. They may choose to redesign their own operations, transfer some their operations to suppliers, or plan to tolerate the risk (Porter, Reinhardt and Grist. 2007). Alternately, companies may refrain from immediate action waiting for regulatory pressures to define how to respond.

Climate change involves systemic risks including legal, physical and reputation aspects. It represents unique business risk because the impact could be local or global, the problem is long-term and the harm is essentially irreversible. There are six categories of risks: regulatory, litigation, supply chain, product and technology, reputational and physical (Lash and Wellington, 2007).

Regulatory risk takes the form of controls of GHG emissions which can affect manufacturing process and products (Pinkse and Kolk, 2009). Ligation risk may face the threat of lawsuits and create personal liabilities for directors and officers who become vulnerable to shareholder-relate litigation (Weinhofer and Hoffmann, 2010). Supply chain risks can take the form of greater scarcity of resources and increased production costs which will be passed along to the customer.

Product and technology risks influence the exploitation of new market opportunities. There are also reputational risks for selling or using products, processes or practices that have negative impact on climate change. Finally, climate change is all about physical risk posed by global warming and its effects.

However, theoretically many of these risks can be transformed into opportunities. For example, with early initiation of an assessment of how future legislation might affect them, companies can manage regulatory risk and crucially gain an advantage over less prescient rivals. Some companies will fare better than others in a carbon-constrained future, depending on their ability to identify ways to exploit new market opportunities for climate-friendly products and services (Kolk and Pinkse, 2007).

Climate change strategy matrix and the outcomes

The decision matrix is a combination of two levels (low or high) of perceived risks versus perceived opportunities, as shown on Figure 13.1. Companies could be grouped in four general response strategies named as 'Minimalist', 'Regulation Shaper', 'Pressure Manager' and 'Emission Avoider' (Sprengel and Busch, 2011). 'Minimalist' companies perceived that both level of risk and level of opportunities are low. It seems that GHG emissions and the climate change debate are relatively low in importance to these companies.

Few companies are able to go beyond operational efficiency and adopt a more strategic approach focusing on broader aspects of climate change. Uncertainty of regulation, technology and market environment leads to considerable diversity in responses to climate change (Jones and Levy, 2007). In general, companies fail to realize the impact of their actions on climate change and do 'business as usual'. Managers tend to focus only on minimizing costs without realizing that their actions can also produce positive results. In the absence of public policies that impose limits, companies do not reduce GHG emissions (Southworth, 2009).

Overall, 'Regulation Shapers' perceive a high level of risk and low level of opportunity. They intend to shape stakeholder pressure, particularly from government, media, non-government organizations and investors. These companies recognize risks of climate change but attempt to limit regulatory action to reduce GHG emissions. 'Regulation Shaper', identify few opportunities and focus on improving operational activities and increasing shareholder value. Similar to 'minimalist' companies, they respond to meet legal requirements but also attempt to avoid the impositions of GHG emissions control.

The distinguishing characteristic of a 'Pressure Manager' is an operating scenario where climate change is not a significant risk for the company but could represent a high-level opportunity. These companies invest in renewable energy to provide an opportunity to enhance the brand value through eco-efficient technologies, attracting investments and generating funds.

The 'Emission Avoider' perceives that both risks and opportunities are high. The risk might come from increasing stakeholder pressure and legal requirements. However, companies can respond by building efficiencies in their operational processes and developing carbon-free products or services that will strengthen their image (Weinhofer and Bush, 2013). The 'Emission Avoider' can implement clean development mechanisms (CDM) and must position itself as a 'buyer' or 'seller' in the carbon markets (Hoffman, 2005). Benefits can come through reduced costs and earning carbon credits (Kolk and Pinkse, 2005). The 'Emission Avoider' develops strong communication linkages with stakeholders, participates in political processes and explores new markets.

In general, all four types of companies can develop practices with a focus on innovation or just to compensate for their own GHG emissions (Southworth, 2009). Innovation practices can include increasing operational efficiency, replacing inputs, modifying production processes or developing less intensive GHG emission products and services (Kolk and Pinkse, 2005). Compensation practices refer to activities to offset GHG emissions, such as acquisition of carbon credits and reforestation (Kolk and Mulder, 2011). Under a compensation approach, technological resources and expertise of a company remain virtually unchanged.

The last part of the framework (Figure 13.1) deals with the outcomes or results of an adequate corporate climate change strategy. It can include improved market positioning, attracting investments, cost reduction and enhanced image. Outcomes may also involve cooperative implementation of public policies and regulations (Lash and Wellington, 2007). This may create harmonious relationships with stakeholders and partnerships with non-governmental organizations (NGOs) or participation in government programmes. These kinds of outcomes modify the institutional dynamics in the establishment of a corporate climate change strategy.

Brazilian environmental and climate change policy

Firms in developing countries have difficulty anticipating climate change impacts and implementing concrete policy measures (Brouhle and Harrington, 2009). This could be explained by a range of limiting barriers, including natural constraints, poverty, lack of financial resources, insufficient knowledge, unavailability of adequate technology and weakness of state institutions. The degree and types of government involvement shows considerable variety across developing countries, reflecting the state of institutions development and the level of political and public support (Pinkse and Kolk, 2012).

In contrast to other developing countries, Brazil initially took a proactive approach to the development of a renewable energy matrix but more recently has failed to continue to have a determinant role in global climate change governance (Rivers, 2010). Since the oil crises in the 1970s, the Brazilian government has stimulated local sugar producers to invest in ethanol to reduce dependence on foreign oil, thereby creating a country-specific advantage (CSA) in biofuel (Martinez, et al., 2015).

In 1999, the Brazilian government established the Interministerial Commission on Global Climate Change to articulate actions under the United Nations Framework Convention on Climate Change (UNFCCC). Then, in 2000 a climate change forum was established to raise awareness about GHG emissions.

Since 2002, Brazil has maintained a programme of incentives for alternative electricity sources (PROINFA) which subsidizes diversification of electricity production and increased supply security. It emphasizes exploitation of regional and local potential through investments in wind energy, small hydroelectric plants and biofuel production by private producers.

In 2007, the Brazilian government launched the national plan on climate change which included a framework for mitigation and adaptation actions. A climate change mitigation plan was launched focusing on energy, agricultural and steel sectors. The main goals involved energy efficiency, investments in clean energy and deforestation reduction.

In 2009, this national policy on climate change (NPCC) was approved by congress (Pereira Jr. et al., 2011). The NPCC was intended to reduce anthropogenic GHG emissions, implement measures to promote climate change adaptation, expand legally protected forest areas, encourage reforestation and support CDMs. The NPCC established the country's voluntary GHG emission reduction target of 38.9 per cent by 2020 compared to the 2005 levels. It is difficult to access the effectiveness of the Brazilian NPCC because the target is vague and is not accompanied by mitigation actions that would be necessary to accomplish it (Otaviano et al., 2015).

In fact, after a positive start between 2009 and 2010, the climate change and environmental agenda suffered considerable setbacks (Viola, Franchini and Ribeiro, 2012). For example, in 2012, the Brazilian Congress voted to weaken the forest conservation law and work proceeded on infrastructure projects such as the huge and controversial Bello Monte hydroelectric project on the Xingu River in the Amazon. Indeed, the Brazilian government responded to the international crisis with a traditional carbon–intensive industrial stimulus package, focused on the car manufacturing sector, and decided to eliminate taxation on oil consumption on the last day of the Rio+20 Summit.

Brazil faces several key energy challenges related to securing sources of supply to support economic development and the mitigation of environmental impacts (Otaviano et al., 2015). The country has the particular challenge of exploiting its abundant energy resources, such as the huge 'Pré-Sal' petroleum reservoir, while controlling emissions from burning the Amazon Rainforest (Viola, Franchini and Ribeiro, 2012). About 45 per cent of Brazil's total energy supply and 85 per cent of its electricity is produced from renewable sources. Hydroelectric plants alone produce 75 per cent of the country's electricity (EPE, 2011).

The main climate change risk for the energy sector in Brazil is reduction of water flow and reservoir levels at hydroelectric plants (Andrade et al., 2012). Energy security throughout the country could be threatened if preventive actions were not implemented. The Brazilian energy sector also faces investment trade-offs in the choice of either renewable resources or fossil fuels. On the one hand, increasing hydroelectric generation avoids the impacts of fossil fuels on climate change and this in turn may reduce the availability of water for power generation. On the other hand choosing the use of non-renewable energy sources is cheaper and technologically feasible but will increase GHG emissions.

If a 2°C global target is to be achieved, there is an urgent need to increase global mitigation efforts. Brazil would need to work towards mitigation, given the expected GHG emissions growth. To ensure effective enforcement of climate change policies, an allocation of resources is indispensable in order to support mitigation and adaptation projects (Otaviano et al., 2015).

Method

This qualitative analysis includes four case studies aimed at identifying commonalities and disparities in the development of corporate climate change strategies in Brazil. Semi-structured interviews, documentary research and site observations have been used to collect data and illustrate distinct facets of climate change strategies.

A case study approach was chosen because there is limited research on how organizations act and react to climate change challenges. Four case studies were compared in the light of the framework presented on Figure 13.1 and each of them represents the situations faced by an individual company. These cases studies provide an understanding of driving forces and the corresponding strategies adopted by the companies, based on assessment of risks, opportunities and expected outcomes.

Cases studies

Case #1: The strategic climate change choice for a multinational energy distributer

The first case study involved the strategy position of a Brazilian subsidiary of an Italian multinational energy company (Abreu, Albuquerque and Freitas, 2014). Overall, the way in which the company responds depends on whether it faces or expects to be facing a highly regulatory constraint and the extent to which it recognizes opportunities.

Interviews were conducted in Ceará state with the CEO and seven top managers from regulatory, marketing, planning, operational, environmental and R&D areas. The interviews aimed to identify the influence of regulatory constraints for the energy sector and possible opportunities resulting from the GHG emissions inventory, mitigation projects, risk management, competitors' behaviour and stakeholder pressure.

Case # 2: Climate strategy adopted by a multinational aluminium producer

The second case study involved a Brazilian subsidiary of an American multinational. It is considered to be a global leader in the supply chain of bauxite and high-quality aluminium (Cunha, Abreu and Barin-Cruz, 2015). Interviews took place at the company's plant in Maranhão state, and involved the Health, Safety and Environment Manager for Latin America and the Caribbean and the local Director of Health, Safety and Environment.

Interviews aimed to identify driving forces (e.g. influence of Brazilian climate change policy and regulatory constraints for the aluminium sector, competitors' behaviour and stakeholder pressures); practices (e.g. GHG emissions inventory, compensation and innovation practices) and outcomes.

Case # 3: Driving forces for investments in renewable energy projects

The third case study involved identification of the driving forces for investments in renewable energy in Brazil (Abreu, Siebra, Cunha and Santos, 2014). These forces include stakeholder demands, public policy, technology development and market opportunities. The interview took place in Ceará state and involved the Environment Manager from a wind farm company. The company operates four plants which represent 12.3 per cent of the installed wind energy capacity in the state (ANEEL, 2012).

Questions were tailored to identify the particular views of the company related to wind farm investment. The interview was aimed at understanding the factors that determine the growth of the wind energy generation market. It also identified technological challenges and the role of public policies in increasing the participation of wind energy in the national energy matrix.

Case # 4: Opportunities related to the implementation of clean development mechanisms

The last case study involved the second largest private power generation company in Brazil (Freitas, Abreu and Albuquerque, 2013). The company operates ten hydroelectric plants and generates 2,651 megawatts (MW), representing 2.4 per cent of installed capacity in the country. The interview was conducted in São Paulo state and involves the Environmental, Health and Safety Director.

This company was interviewed to identify the reasons it had for investment in the carbon market through CDM. Questions were tailored to identify the business model on which the CDM projects were based. Interviews also aimed to identified the challenges in the approval process, opportunities in the carbon market and perspectives on the post-Kyoto setting.

The CDM makes it possible developed countries and transition economies, signatories to the Kyoto Protocol, to acquire GHG emission rights from developing countries (Muller, 2002). GHG reduction activities creating so-called 'certified emission reductions' (CER) abroad in the context of the CDM or 'emission reduction units' (ERU) via joint implementation (JI) (UNFCCC, 1997).

Findings

Case #1: The strategic climate change choice for a multinational energy distributer

The first step in the establishment of a climate change strategy is developing a GHG inventory. The Greenhouse Gas Protocol was used by the MNE for this purpose. The inventory was used to develop a series of GHG mitigation projects, and the company was given the option of selection projects for implementation, such as wind farms, small hydroelectric plants, electric car and reforestation. Because of the lack of regulatory constraint and limited opportunity, the CEO and top managers decided to take no particular action and continued 'business-as-usual'. This strategy corresponds to a scenario where regulations are weak and no clear opportunities exist.

The MNE found no advantage to proceeding with any particular climate change related action. Despite the fact that it has an environmental management system, certified by ISO 14001, and an environmental education and awareness programme, respondents confirm that climate change is not a stakeholder or MNE priority, even in the long run. According to the director of regulation, government regulatory bodies have strong influence on the Brazilian energy distribution sector. However, there is low risk of federal regulation to address the need for mitigation of climate change impacts. The Brazilian Electricity Regulatory Agency (ANEEL) has no enforcement structure to control GHG emissions for the sector. The R&D director emphasized that technological changes require heavy investments and long-term projects. There are no government incentives to support GHG mitigation projects beyond those related to improve energy efficiency.

The director of regulation stated that the federal government has an ambiguous stance on the source of energy to be distributed to customers. Through the Incentive Program for Alternative Sources of Electric Energy (PROINFA), the Brazilian government encourages the development of alternative energy sources such as wind, biomass and small hydroelectric plants (SHP). Moreover, according to the planning and control manager the company cannot acquire renewable energy freely. ANEEL established that the company cannot buy more than 10 per cent of the total energy required in renewable energy. The planning and control director added that the company buys only 0.4 per cent to 0.5 per cent of its total electric energy from wind power plants. This low percentage results from the small current supply of wind energy.

The institutional relations and social responsibility director pointed out that despite all efforts, Brazilian society does not recognize the company as socially responsible. Nevertheless, the regulatory agencies recognize their efforts and do not exert high pressure related to environmental issues. It seems that GHG issues are not a large part of the agenda in the electricity distribution sector. According to the sustainability and security team manager, the company could serve as a benchmark. However, no proactive actions are called for by government or other stakeholders.

Respondents stated that strategic response to climate change is particularly dependent on social, economic and regulatory pressures. The main stakeholders that could influence organizational culture or manager perceptions about climate change are government, Brazilian Electricity Energy Distributors Association (ABRADEE) and customers. The planning and control director pointed out that the ABRADEE should increase its interest in GHG projects. The CEO recognized that climate change projects could be useful for image improvement. However, they could not be justified based on that purpose alone.

Most respondents pointed out that climate change mitigation projects are evaluated through investment opportunity, and therefore need to compete for internal resources based mainly on financial criteria. Ethical values related to climate change are not strongly reinforced by the company. It means that mitigating and controlling GHG emissions will only be implemented if they clearly have financial returns or are required by regulations.

The Director of Institutional Relations, Government, Environment and Corporate Social Responsibility stated that climate change is not part of the public and private 'agenda' of the energy sector in Brazil. In his opinion, large companies are still incipient in addressing sustainability issues. The manager of the Team of Sustainability and Safety reinforced that there is no effective climate change strategy for the Brazilian energy distribution system.

Case # 2: Climate strategy adopted by multinational aluminium producer

The Health, Safety and Environment Manager for Latin America and the Caribbean indicated that the MNE seeks to establish a consensus in society about legitimacy of their operation and responsibilities related to GHG emissions. The interviewee reinforced that the company is taking actions to reduce GHG emissions which do not significantly increase operating costs or affecting their competitiveness position in the international market. Nevertheless, the global institutional scenario of climate change is characterized by few demands from stakeholders, government restrictions or goals for GHG emissions.

Both respondents highlighted the relevance of cost reduction in their business and therefore the need for improved operational efficiency. Aluminium companies cannot control product prices and therefore focus on greater operational efficiency, economies of scale, and technological improvements. GHG emissions reduction can be a positive outcome of actions taken to reduce cost. This was the case in 1999, when Brazil was among ten countries which undertook joint industry and government actions to reduce PFCs (perfluorocarbon) emissions (EPA, 1999). These were achieved in primary aluminium production through technologies improvement aimed at cost reduction (Figuerola-Ferretti, 2005).

The MNE had completed its GHG inventory and was able to assess its environmental performance and control operational risks. The Local Director of Health, Safety and Environment reinforced the concept of a multidisciplinary approach to risk analysis. It encompasses climate change risks assessment along with cost-benefit analysis. Considering the specific risks and opportunities of the aluminium industry, the MNE has decided to focus on innovation practices or initiatives in R&D rather than explore compensation approaches to GHG emissions.

Alternative technologies, cleaner energy sources and workforce training are the main climate change practices developed. The Health, Safety and Environment Manager for Latin America and the Caribbean pointed out the role of innovation, aiming not only to implement it in their own facilities but also in other subsidiaries. However, because the Brazilian subsidiary does not have an R&D centre, most technological innovations come from abroad.

In Brazil, the MNE had an optimistic view and great willingness to use market mechanisms. The country looks favourably on attracting investment and technology from other countries. The Health, Safety and Environment Manager for Latin America and the Caribbean assessed the feasibility of implementing the CDM in their own facilities.

Both respondents recognized that government, communities and media could influence their establishment of climate change strategy. The Health, Safety and Environment Manager for Latin America and the Caribbean pointed out that the relationships with stakeholders are judged in relation to salience of the media. The climate change strategy approaches were developed based on voluntary agreements with non-government organizations and industry associations. The Local Director of Health, Safety and Environment claimed to have established an instrumental relationship with stakeholders focusing on damage avoidance.

Case # 3: Driving forces for investments in renewable energy projects

The Environment Manager from a wind farm company confirmed that the Brazilian Programme of Incentives for Alternative Electricity Sources (PROINFA) subsidizes diversification of electricity production and increased supply security. It supports private sector investors (Independent Power Producers – IPP) in wind energy, SHP and biofuel production. The Brazilian government also offers incentives to promote a renewable energy supply chain.

Auctions were established to provide a profitable minimal energy price which encourages investments and creates favourable market conditions. Tax incentives and technological improvements have reduced the net cost of wind farm investments. Technology advances have been achieved by improving turbines through wider blades and increased hubs size. The Environment Manager interviewee pointed out that these developments reduced the cost of construction, maintenance and operation. Brazil's climate conditions including the wind speed and persistence provide favourable conditions for investment. However, IPPs required technological adaptations to take further advantage of these favourable climate conditions.

Acceptance of wind farm installations by local communities has had a strong impact on investment decisions. In some cases, local communities identify wind turbines as clean energy symbols. In most cases, however, local communities position themselves heavily against such investments, because of turbine noise and the space occupied. The Environment Manager interviewee emphasized the importance of having good relationships based on transparency and dialogue to reduce environmental and social impacts.

The interviewee confirmed that increased investments in wind farm constructions have been encouraged by low risk guarantees provided by the federal governments. In fact, there are uncertainties that could jeopardize wind energy development. For example, there is a failure to integrate the energy produced into the local grid. There is fear that the government could decide to reduce the guarantee of minimal price but this has not happened yet.

There was a common view by respondents that renewable energy is a promising investment opportunity. However, its value in terms of reducing climate change was not emphasized. The extent to which companies will be cooperative in supporting and enhancing efforts to invest in climate change friendly technologies is open to debate.

Case # 4: Opportunities related to the implementation of clean development mechanisms

In Brazil, there are no GHG targets for companies, thus CDM project adoption is voluntary. The Environmental, Health and Safety Director interviewee pointed out that CDM projects improved operational activities, created financial opportunities and added value to a company's image. In his opinion, one of the most important driving forces to CDM projects was the influence and pressure from investors. The director explained that some investors only support his company because it has projects aimed at sustainability.

The interviewee confirmed that CDM regulations, which involve multiple phases, are very complex and difficult to implement. Human resource development and technology are not readily available in Brazil. Thus, a key benefit of CDM projects to his company was the transfer of GHG emissions mitigation technology from developed countries.

The Health, Safety and Environmental Director explained that the possibility of CDM projects joining the carbon market becomes a feasible alternative for renewable energy investment. The amount of CER and the value negotiated at the carbon market was profitable and justified the investment. Getting CER is the most important result of CDM projects. Nevertheless, uncertainties about the next phases of the Kyoto Protocol limit the development of new CDM projects.

The interviewee expressed his concern about the many ups-and-downs of the carbon market because the political debate creates uncertainties related to emission trading post 2012 Kyoto Protocol. In general, this has led companies to avoid CDM investment so far. The COP 18 extended the Kyoto Protocol until 2020, however many challenges still remain. The lack of adoption or ratification of the United States, China and other key countries had impacted the momentum for global climate action. The Environmental, Health and Safety Director argued that the Kyoto Protocol must continue and trade in CER is profitable.

Discussion

The four case studies shed light on challenges in the development of corporate climate change strategies in Brazil. Table 13.1 summarizes the approaches taken by the companies surveyed based on the categories presented on Figure 13.1. Case studies #1 and #2 present the reactive approaches of MNEs in responding to climate change. MNEs tend to take advantage of an institutional environment or attempt to change the organizational field. On the other hand, case studies #3 and #4 show more proactive GHG strategies.

Case study #1 shows that the 'minimalist' strategy allows companies to continue 'business-as-usual'. Unclear regulatory constraints lead the CEO to refuse approval of eye-catching projects or establishment of an internal team focused on developing GHG mitigation mechanisms. Their reluctance suggests that the firm gives low priority to the possibility of increasing regulatory pressure. Managers failed to examine the implications of the new paradigms such as that which emerged later at COP 21.

Table 13.1 Elements involved in the development of a corporate climate change strategy: cross-case analysis

Category	CASES STUDIES			
	#1 – Energy distributer	#2 – Aluminiun producer	#3 – Renewable energy investor	#4– CDM implementation
Driving Forces	Deny stakeholder pressure and regulatory constraints Weak corporate commitment	Instrumental stakeholder relationship Develop internal capabilities	Government incentives Local Community centred	Government incentives Shareholder pressure Managerial Commitment
Climate Change Strategy	Minimalist	Regulation Shaper	Pressure Manager	Emission Avoider
Outcomes	No advantage identified	Operational cost reduction Innovative CHG projects	Investments attraction Carbon market opportunities	Investments attraction Carbon market opportunities Transfer technology Transfer technology

In general, case study #1 do not realize the magnitude and timing of climate change effects what they have to address. This makes it difficult to consider their strategic options and likely to demand significant financial, technological and human resources. In Brazil, companies will not commit such resources without a clear regulatory framework in global and national contexts and pressure from stakeholders to reduce GHG emissions.

Case study #2 reveals that the most important driving forces can be exerted by stakeholder pressure. Companies identify with the behaviour of their competitors in considering GHG strategies. The MNE aluminium producer adopted a 'Regulation Shaper' strategy approach. The company realizes that climate change is a reality and something must be done about it. However, the company will only devote resources if there are measurable financial benefits, or reduced operational costs. This would lead them to more active involvement in developing technology and improving internal capabilities to reduce GHG emissions.

The process of seeking ways to reduce GHG emissions can represent, in itself, a source of increased the legitimacy and acceptance by stakeholders. In the case of a 'minimalist' and 'regulation shaper', such strategies cannot be maintained going forward. Furthermore, the ecological uncertainty about the natural resources availability and the severity of climate events may 'stir the fire' of environmentally concerned stakeholder to reconsider the importance of being precautionary.

In case study #3, it seems that feasible technology, incentive regulations and a favourable market along with local community acceptance act as driving forces pushing companies to adopt a 'Pressure Manager' strategy. As financial risks are assumed by the Brazilian government, investment in wind farms seems to be an attractive option (Lucena, et al., 2009).

'Regulation shapers' and 'pressure managers' actively engaged in the political process as an important element of their strategies. 'Regulation shapers' seem to have more concerned about how changes in legislation will influence stakeholder demands. Instead, 'pressure managers' operate in an environment with lower stakeholder pressure to reduce GHG emissions. 'Emission avoider' companies perceive pressure from non-market stakeholders as more intensive than market stakeholders.

Case study #4 adopted an 'emission avoider' approach. Companies act to take advantage of country-specific factors of Brazil, such as availability of natural resources, access to markets and low operational costs (i.e. labour, capital and land). They are exposed to the spotlight of international media watchdogs, which have the power to negatively affect corporate reputation and brand value. Therefore, 'emission avoider' companies focus on attracting investment, improving image and brand value and being accepted by the local community.

Results from these four cases demonstrate that companies have different perceptions about regulatory and others risks, stakeholder demands, actions that should be taken to manage GHG emissions and the desirability of possible outcomes. A complete integration of climate change within corporate strategy and a move towards a low-carbon economy ultimately requires a competitive market reconfiguration. To achieve this, stakeholders, governments and companies themselves should engage in a dialogue towards incorporation of a longer-term climate change strategy.

A comprehensive approach to carbon emission policy and regulation requires robust international coordination and strong implementation plans at the national level. Elijido-Ten (2017) reinforces that policymakers push companies harder to implement carbon management practices. As a result, it is necessary to promulgate and maintain 'command-and-control' regulations to ensure that climate change risks are incorporated in the business model.

Paradoxically, Martinez et al. (2015) alerts us to the difficulty in assessing the effectiveness of the Brazilian Climate Change Policy. It is a rather vague target set, which is not always accompanied by mitigation and adaptation actions. Maintaining an electricity mix dominated by renewable energy in Brazil requires policies that control the use of fossil fuels and enhance the competitiveness of renewable energy. In this way, Boons (2009) recommended that carbon-intensive companies should adopt a 'transformative' perspective in which a firm establishes a new technological trajectory involving product or service with reduced ecological impact.

Conclusions and managerial implications

At the moment, there is a clear lack of systemic climate change actions. It is difficult to deal with a scenario of uncertainty marked by intense discussions and limited results. This leads to normative and instrumental trade-offs which limit commitment of firm resources to deal with climate change (Schultz and Williamson, 2005).

In this direction, COP 21 negotiated the Paris agreement creating a pathway towards a 2°C target. Stringent mitigation at national and international policy levels must be accompanied by actions plans to reduce GHG emissions and mitigate impacts. As part of this global challenge of COP 21, companies must overcome technical, organizational and institutional challenges to reinforce their capabilities to introduce innovations to the market in the form of products and services and serve the (global) mass market instead of local niches only.

There is an urgent need to increase efforts for a sustainable transition towards a less carbon-intensive economy. Global agreements and local government regulations are fundamental to induce companies to establish effective climate change strategies. Orchestrating the role of stakeholders in pushing more business ethics and responsible climate change practices has proven to be crucial (Svensson, et al., 2009). Adoption of a contingency perspective, in which firms identify risks or opportunities is essential to develop a corporate climate change strategy (Kolk and Pinkse, 2004). Long-term actions require:

- Explicit economic incentives and other government actions.
- Investment in technology and R&D to increase the knowledge about the extent of the damage and possible actions to be taken.
- Increase consumer responsive and ethical behaviour of MNEs and local companies.
- Participate in the global negotiations to follow-up the Paris agreement on COP 21.
- Set targets to reduce GHG emissions and track progress through a robust transparent and accountability system (Kolk and Pinkse, 2008).

Governments need to 'show the way' having both restrictive and facilitating roles but the private sector needs to assume the 'driver's seat'. In this way stakeholders are responsible for providing the 'energy' that will move companies forward.

Limitations and recommendation for further research

There are limitations in exploring challenges in the development of climate change strategies. Most studies are static, which is they cannot capture changes in the practices over time and the influence of driving forces. The current state of uncertainty and difficulties in forecasting future impacts create a serious information gap. Planning in this environment leaves companies reluctant to commit resources for climate change.

Future research could address mechanisms to increase organizational and technological capabilities through innovations. Another line of research could examine climate change governance from a broader perspective, as an element of corporate performance and also at an ethical level. Finally, it would be useful to examine the framework proposed here in other countries to compare a broad range of institutional, societal and organizational characteristics.

References

Abreu, M.C.S., Albuquerque, A.M. and Freitas, A.R.P. (2014). Posicionamento Estratégico em Resposta às Restrições Regulatórias de Emissões de Gases do Efeito Estufa. *Revista de Administração (FEA-USP)*, 49: 578–590.

Abreu, M.C.S., Siebra, A.A., Cunha, L.T. and Santos, S.M. (2014). Fatores Determinantes para o Avanço da Energia Eólica no Estado do Ceará frente aos Desafios das Mudanças Climáticas. *REAd. Revista Eletrônica de Administração* (Porto Alegre. Online), 78: 274–304.

Andrade, E.M., Cosenza, J.P., Rosa, L.P. and Lacerda, G. (2012). The vulnerability of hydroelectric generation in the northeast Brazil: The environmental and business risk for CHESF. *Renewable and Sustainable Energy Reviews*, 16: 5760–5769.

Aragón-Correa, J.A., Hurtado-Torres, N., Sharma, S., García-Morales, V.J. (2008). Environmental strategy and performance in small firms: A resource-based perspective. *Journal of Environment Management*, 86: 88–103.

Boons, F.A.A. (2009). Creating Ecological Value: An Evolutionary Approach to Business Strategies and the Natural Environment. Cheltenham: Edward Elgar.

Brouhle, K. and Harrington, D.R. (2009). Firm strategy and the Canadian voluntary climate challenge and registry (VCR). *Business Strategy and the Environment*, 18(6): 360–379.

Cunha, L.T., Abreu, M.C.S. and Barin-Cruz, L. (2015). Visão Comparativa das Estratégias Climáticas Adotadas por Multinacionais do Setor de Alumínio no Canadá e no Brasil. *Revista Gestão & Produção*, 22: 495–507.

Elijido-Ten, E.O. (2017). Does recognition of climate change related risks and opportunities determine sustainability performance. *Journal of Cleaner Production*, 14: 956–966.

EPA. United States Environmental Protection Agency. (1999). *International Efforts to Reduce Perfluorcarbon (PFC) Emissions from Primary Aluminium Production*. Air and Radiation (6202J). EPA 430-R-99-001. September. http://nepis.epa.gov/EPA/html/DLwait.htm?url=/Adobe/PDF/P1000MLD.PDF. Access: January/2012.

EPE. Empresa de Pesquisa Energética. (2011). *Balanço Energético Nacional*. https://www.ben.epe.gov.br/downloads/Relatorio_Final_BEN_2011.pdf. Access in: 08/05/2012.

Figuerola-Ferretti, I. (2005). Prices and production cost in aluminium smelting in the short and the long run. *Applied Economics*, 37: 917–928.

Freitas, A.R.P., Abreu, M.C.S. and Albuquerque, A.M. (2013). Implicações Estratégicas de Projetos de Mecanismos de Desenvolvimento Limpo em Empresas de Energia Renovável. *Revista Sistemas & Gestão*, 8: 334–345.

Hoffman, A.J. (2005). Climate change strategy: The business logic behind voluntary greenhouse gas reductions. *California Management Review*, 47(3): 21–46.

Jeswani, H.K., Wehrmeyer, W. and Mulugetta, Y. (2008). How warm is the corporate response to climate change? Evidence from Pakistan and the UK. *Business Strategy and the Environment*, 17(1): 46–60.

Jones, C.A. and Levy, D.L. (2007). North American business strategies towards climate change. *European Management Journal*, 25 (6): 428–440.

Kolk, A. and Mulder, G. (2011). Regulatory uncertainty and opportunity seeking: The climate change clean development case. *California Management Review*, 54, 88–106.

Kolk, A. and Pinkse, J. (2004). Market strategies for climate change. *European Management Journal*, 22(3): 304–314.

Kolk, A. and Pinkse, J. (2005). Business responses to climate change: Identifying emergent strategies. *California Management Review*, 47(3): 6–20.

Kolk, A. and Pinkse, J. (2007). Multinational's political activities on climate change. *Business & Society*, 46 (2): 201–228.

Kolk, A. and Pinkse, J. (2008). A perspective on multinational enterprises and climate change: Learning from 'an inconvenient truth'. *Journal of International Business Studies*, 39: 1359–1378.

Lash, J. and Wellington, F. (2007). Competitive advantage on a warming planet. *Harvard Business Review*, 85 (3): 94–102.

Lee, S.Y. (2012). Corporate carbon strategies in responding to climate change. *Business Strategy and the Environment*, 21(1): 33–48.

Lucena, A.F.P., Szklo, A.S., Schaeffer, R., Souza, R.R., Borba, B.S.M.C., Costa, I.V.L., Pereira Júnior, A.O. and Cunha, S.H.F. (2009). The vulnerability of renewable energy to climate change in Brazil. *Energy Policy*, 37, 879–889.

Martinez, S.H., Koberle, A., Rochedo, P., Schaeffer, R., Lucena, A., Szklo, A., Ashina, S. and van Vuuren, D.P. (2015). Possible energy futures for Brazil and Latin America in conservative and stringent mitigation pathway up to 2050. *Technological Forecasting & Social Change*. http://dx.doi.org/10.1016/j.technfore.2015.05.006.

Midksa, T.K. and Kallbekken, S. (2010). The impact of climate change on electricity market: A review. *Energy Policy*, 38: 3579–3585.

Muller, A. (2007). How to make the clean development mechanism sustainable: The potential of rent extraction. *Energy Policy*, 35: 3203–3212.

Otaviano, C., Paltsev, S. and Gurgel, A.C. (2015). Climate change policy in Brazil and Mexico: Results from the MIT EPPA model. *Energy Economics*. http://dx.doi.or./10.1016/j.eneco.2015.04.007.

Pereira Jr., A.O., Pereira, A.S., Rovere, E.L., Barata, M.M.L., Villar, S.C. and Pires, S.H. (2011). Strategies to promote renewable energy in Brazil. *Renewable and Sustainable Energy Reviews*, 15: 681–688.

Pinkse, J. and Kolk, A. (2009). *International Business and Global Climate Change*. New York: Routledge.

Pinkse, J. and Kolk, A. (2012). Multinational enterprises and climate change: Exploring institutional failures and embeddedness. *Journal of International Business Studies*. 43: 332–341.

Porter, M.E. and Reinhardt, F.L. Grist. (2007). A strategic approach to climate. *Harvard Business Review*, 85(10): 22–26.

Rivers, N. (2010). Impacts of climate policy on the competitiveness of Canadian industry: How big and how to mitigate? *Energy Economics*, 32: 1092–1104.

Schultz, K. and Williamson, P. (2005). Gaining competitive advantage in a carbon-constrained world: Strategies for European business. *European Management Journal*, 23 (4): 383–391.

Southworth, K. (2009). Corporate voluntary action: A valuable but incomplete solution to climate change and energy security challenges. *Policy and Society*, 27: 329–350.

Sprengel, D.C. and Busch, T. (2011). Stakeholder engagement and environmental strategy: The case of climate change. *Business Strategy and the Environment*, 20: 351–364.

Stern, N. (2007). The Stern Review: The Economics of Climate Change. London: HM Treasury.

Svensson, G., Wood, G., Singh, J., Carasco, E. and Callaghan, M. (2009). Ethical structures and processes of corporations operating in Australia, Canada, and Sweden: A longitudinal and cross-cultural study. *Journal of Business Ethics*, 86: 485–506.

Tashman, P. and Rivera, J. (2015). Ecological uncertainty, adaptation, and mitigation in the U.S. ski resort industry: Managing resource dependence and institutional pressures. *Strategic Management Journal*. doi:10.1002/smj.2384.

UNFCCC (1997). *Kyoto Protocol to the UNFCCC*. http://unfccc.int/essential_background/kyoto_pro tocol/background/items/1351.phpi.

Viola, E., Franchini, M. and Ribeiro, T.L. (2012). Climate governance in an international system under conservative hegemony: The role of major powers. *Revista Brasileira de Política Internacional*, 55: 9–29.

Weinhofer, G. and Bush, T. (2013). Corporate strategies for managing climate change. *Business Strategy and the Environment*, 22: 121–144.

Weinhofer, G. and Hoffmann, V.H. (2010). Mitigating climate change: How do corporate strategies differ? *Business Strategy and the Environment*, 19: 77–89.

14 Sustainability: from conceptualization to operationalization

A literature review

Bénédicte Deryckere and Caroline Gauthier

Introduction

In 1983, the Secretary-General of the United Nations established the World Commission on Economic Development (WCED) asking for propositions on long-term strategies to address global issues related to human inability to 'fit its activities' into the natural pattern of our planet (WCED, 1987). The resulting report 'Our Common Future', also known as the Brundtland report, called for a 'progressive transformation of economy and society' and laid out the concept of 'sustainable development' as 'development that meets the needs of the present without compromising the ability of future generations to meet their own needs' (WCED, 1987). A definition now broadly accepted by organizational and business management scholars (Aragon-Correa, 2013; Bansal, 2005; Bansal and DesJardine, 2014; Ferraro et al., 2015).

Sustainable development within firms entails the simultaneous adoption of environmental integrity, economic prosperity and social equity principles (Bansal, 2005; Elkington, 1998) to address sustainability issues such as the ones caused by global climate change, poverty, social and gender inequalities, forced and child labour, loss of biodiversity or natural resources depletion (Bansal, 2002; Bansal et al., 2014; Hart and Dowell, 2011).

While sustainable development requires a systemic and holistic perspective (Bansal et al., 2014; Senge and Carstedt, 2001), involving governments, civil society and the private sector, more and more corporations adhere to the principles of sustainable development and place social and environmental goals alongside economic goals on their strategic agenda (Montiel and Delgado-Ceballos, 2014; Zollo et al., 2013). Firms across sectors and geographies try to generate sustainable improvements through their sustainability strategies (Montiel and Delgado-Ceballos, 2014) and corporate social responsibility (CSR) organizational actions (Aragon-Correa, 2013; Bansal, 2005; Bansal et al., 2014). Parallel to this movement, business management and organizational scholars have increasingly focused on sustainability and related CSR practices. In 1995, the call from Gladwin, Kennelly and Krause for transforming management theory and practice to positively contribute to sustainable development can be considered as marking the entry of sustainable development in the field of management research and practice (Gladwin et al., 1995). While this stream of research has mostly been targeted towards understanding the drivers and motivations for adopting CSR practices and at conceptualizing sustainable development within and across firms, much less research has analysed the processes by which firms integrate the principles of sustainable development in their business practices (Devinney, 2013; Montiel and Delgado-Ceballos, 2014; Zollo et al., 2013).

This literature review covers sustainable development within firms from its conceptualization to business practices. The objective of this exercise is to highlight the emergence of new themes in the recent literature, identify current concerns related to our understanding of the operationalization of sustainability in firms and finally propose recommendations to address these concerns.

This chapter consists of five sections. First, recent literature on firms' approaches to sustainable development is reviewed with a specific focus on CSR and its evolution over time as a strategic concern leading to the emergence of 'corporate sustainability' (Hahn et al., 2014; Montiel and Delgado-Ceballos, 2014; Van der Byl and Slawinski, 2015). Second, the motivational and conceptual aspects of corporate sustainability and corporate social responsibility are further investigated and critically addressed. Third, the strategic and operational aspects of corporate sustainability are reviewed and the lack of knowledge on its operationalization highlighted. Fourth, the emergence of the business model construct in the literature on corporate sustainability is identified and its potential role in addressing the current gap on sustainability operationalization within firms is highlighted. Finally, a call is made for further research bridging both research streams on sustainable development and business models in order to fill the gap on sustainability operationalization within firms.

Corporate sustainability: from conceptualization to operationalization

Management literature on sustainable development has developed along two main streams, the first dedicated to understanding why corporations should embrace sustainable development and the second dedicated to conceptualizing what makes a firm sustainable, leaving questions related to the operationalization of sustainability within firms relatively unanswered (Zollo et al., 2013).

Corporate social responsibility and its evolution as a strategic concern

Corporate social responsibility (CSR) represents the business practices adopted by firms to adhere to the principles of sustainable development, CSR refers to the specific business and philanthropic initiatives undertaken by firms to answer sustainability-related environmental and social issues whilst maintaining their economic responsibility to be profitable, being ethically responsible and going beyond the requirements of the law (Carroll, 1991; Margolis and Walsh, 2003; McWilliams and Siegel, 2001; Wang and Bansal, 2012).

Corporate social responsibility belongs to management research and practices (Lockett et al., 2006; Schaltegger et al., 2013). CSR 'empirically consists of clearly articulated and communicated policies and practices reflecting business responsibility for some of the wider societal good' (Matten and Moon, 2008). Examples of CSR activities range from socially oriented initiatives such as engaging in philanthropy, contributing to educational and social programmes, taking care of direct and indirect labour forces, developing reliable products; to environment-oriented initiatives such as producing environmentally friendly products and services, adopting waste reduction and pollution prevention practices, investing in clean energy (Aguilera et al., 2007; Bansal et al., 2014; Devinney, 2009; McWilliams and Siegel, 2001). Firms voluntary engage in CSR activities (Carroll, 1991) and freely communicate to their stakeholders through self-reporting.

Whilst evidence of business organizations' concerns for society can be found centuries ago, CSR took a noteworthy place in management discussions in the 1970s when Milton Friedman argued that the doctrine of social responsibility was 'fundamentally subversive' and that the sole responsibility of management was profit maximization and shareholder value (Carroll, 1991; Barnett and Salomon, 2012; Friedman, 1962; Friedman, 1970; Margolis and Walsh, 2003), generating a substantial body of literature targeted towards analysing the link between social and environmental performance and economic performance (Lockett et al., 2006; Margolis and Walsh, 2003; Zollo et al., 2013), but also generating much scepticism and confusion towards the merits of CSR.

Recent literature on CSR identifies a certain number of issues related to the evolution of CSR and explains why CSR has fallen short of contributing to solve today's social and environmental problems (Devinney, 2009; Wang and Bansal, 2012). Indeed, firms have launched CSR-related activities as a poorly operationalized tactical answer to stakeholders' pressures to gain legitimacy and licence to operate while fundamentally driving their business to achieve profit maximization and increase shareholder value. CSR initiatives then became merely another means to this end (Devinney, 2009; Wang and Bansal, 2012). Firms disclose CSR on a voluntary basis, CSR self-reports are not audited and do not always reflect the exact level of engagement of firms in sustainable development, leading to the perception that firms are just advertising or even 'green-washing' (Bowen and Aragon-Correa, 2014). In addition, the profit maximization approach taken by firms promotes short-termism, often jeopardizing the benefits that CSR activities may generate (Devinney, 2009; Wang and Bansal, 2012).

Going counter the potential flaws of CSR, another stream of literature focuses on the business strategies and practices addressing sustainability while driving shareholder value (Hart and Milstein, 2003). As a result many contributing concepts have emerged such as Corporate Social Commitment (CSC) (Bansal et al., 2014; Gao and Bansal, 2013), Corporate Environmental Commitment (CEC) (Bansal et al., 2014; Gao and Bansal, 2013), Sustainable Entrepreneurship (SE) (Schaltegger and Wagner, 2011; Hockerts and Wustenhagen, 2010), Environmental Social Responsibility (ESR) (Siegel, 2009), or Corporate Citizenship (CC) (Matten and Crane, 2005; Mirvis and Googins, 2006). These concepts highlight the breadth of sustainability-related considerations and approaches that firms are adopting to address sustainability but also confirm the strategic turn that CSR is taking through the adoption of 'corporate sustainability' strategies (Hahn et al., 2014; Montiel and Delgado-Ceballos, 2014; Van der Byl and Slawinski, 2015). To further illustrate the strategies and practices adopted by firms placing sustainable development at the core of their strategic agenda, a number of strategic management labels have emerged over the last 15 years, such as the Bottom of the Pyramid (BOP) coined in 2002 by C.K. Prahalad and Allen Hammond (Prahalad and Hammond, 2002), Social Innovation from Rosabeth Kanter (Kanter, 1999), the Natural Resourced Based View of the Firm (NRBV) introduced in 1995 by Stuart Hart (Hart, 1995; Hart and Dowell, 2011; McWilliams and Siegel, 2011; Siegel, 2009). Those labels have more recently been complemented by new ones such as Creating Shared Value (CSV) from Michael Porter and Mark Kramer in 2011 (Porter and Kramer, 2011) and Hybrid Organizations from Julie Battilana and Silvia Dorado in 2010 (Battilana and Dorado, 2010; Santos et al., 2015). Those labels devise new and promising corporate strategies to address sustainability within firms and provide frameworks unifying the debates on the strategic contribution of business corporations to long-term sustainability (Crane et al., 2014).

Corporate sustainability and corporate social responsibility: the motivations

An impressive body of literature has been devoted to understanding why companies embrace social and environmental goals in addition to fulfilling their traditional economic goals. When few studies have focused on first, uncovering the antecedent conditions (legislation, stakeholder pressure, economic opportunities, ethical motives) (Sharma, 2000). Second, identifying the motivations (competitiveness, legitimation, environmental responsibility) (Bansal and Roth, 2000). Third, analysing the strategic decision-making process for embracing sustainable development (Vaara and Durand, 2012). Most research (probably as a reaction to Friedman's previously cited provocative statement) has examined the link between corporate social responsibility and firm performance in order to understand if engaging in sustainable development is financially rewarding but yields conflicting results revealing the poor theoretical definition of CSR and the lack of empirical evidence on the strategic nature of CSR (Boons and Wagner, 2009; Margolis and Walsh, 2003; McWilliams and Siegel, 2011). Organizations engaging in sustainability have changed their practice incrementally rather than taking a more radical stance and creating new markets (Rohrbeck et al., 2013). One reason being that business organizations were not expecting that strategically addressing sustainability-related issues would have a positive impact on their competitive advantage and they therefore neglected to answer to stakeholders increased concerns and pressures (Garces-Ayerbe et al., 2012). However more and more firms report on creating value through the implementation of sustainability-related change initiatives, leading to a change of mindset (Porter and Kramer, 2011) and the repositioning of CSR practices at the strategic level (Crane et al., 2014). Potentially as a consequence to this, the concept of 'corporate sustainability' is emerging in literature and taking prevalence over corporate social responsibility (Hahn et al., 2014; Hockerts, 2015; Montiel and Delgado-Ceballos, 2014; Van der Byl and Slawinski, 2015). Corporate sustainability (CS) is then considered as a strategic imperative pursued by many executives to guarantee the competitiveness of their firm (Montiel, 2008; Rego et al., 2017).

Corporate sustainability and corporate social responsibility: the conceptualization

Research aimed at conceptualizing corporate sustainability and answering the question 'what defines a company as sustainable' takes different approaches using either traditional organizational theories or new theoretical frameworks (Luo and Bhattacharya, 2006). First, a large portion of scholars uses stakeholder theory, focusing on the central role of stakeholders, stakeholder management and governance structures (Sharma and Henriques, 2005; Steurer et al., 2005; Zollo et al., 2013). At the core of stakeholder management in the context of sustainability is the notion that a firm has multiple goals in addition to maximizing shareholder value and should also meet the needs of stakeholders asking for the fulfilment of social and environmental goals (Cennamo et al., 2012; Stubbs and Cocklin, 2008). This requires that a firm sees beyond its own financial goals to identify and meet the requirements of diverse stakeholders such as human rights groups, environmental groups, NGO, governments, civil society, customers, suppliers, while considering profits as a 'means' to achieve sustainable outcomes. Some scholars take a more radical stance, arguing that companies must embrace sustainable development regardless of whether it pays or not, because it is what society is expecting from companies (Marcus and Fremeth, 2009). Those scholars call for a revision of existing economic theory to prone larger stakeholder integration (Doh and Lucea, 2013). However some others claim that companies have 'no obligation to the society other than the creation of economic rents that can accrue to the shareholders with recognized rights to those rents' (Devinney, 2009). A second group uses institutional theory to explain the institutionalization processes surrounding the emergence of sustainable industries or the conditions under which corporations adopt CSR practices (Campbell, 2007; Matten and Moon, 2008). A third group exploits the natural resource-based view of the firm, defined as an extension to the resource-based view of the firm (RBV) and defines three strategic sets of capabilities: pollution prevention, product stewardship and sustainable development, each of them having different sources of competitive advantage (Aragon-Correa and Sharma, 2003; Hart, 1995; Hart and Dowell, 2011; McWilliams and Siegel, 2011; Siegel, 2009). Finally, a last group looks at establishing new theoretical frameworks for corporate sustainability, recognizing that each traditional organizational theory contributes to some aspects of sustainable development (Bansal, 2005; Laplume et al., 2008; Montiel and Delgado-Ceballos, 2014). According to this stream of research (1) 'organizations must apply these principles to their products, policies and practices in order to express sustainable development' which at the level of the firm are first, environmental integrity through corporate environmental management, (2) social equity through corporate social responsibility, and (3) economic prosperity through value creation (Bansal, 2005).

This new theoretical approach also emphasizes the role of time. When institutional pressures are important in early periods of sustainability adoption, resource-based opportunities persist over time (Bansal, 2005), a long-term orientation is indeed key to the development of sustainability-related initiatives and to the establishment of robust stakeholder relationship leading to the generation of new sources of profits in the long run (Bansal et al., 2014; Barnett and Salomon, 2012; Stubbs and Cocklin, 2008; Wang and Bansal, 2012). This approach also considers that attention to stakeholders is strategically critical to sustainable organizations. In order to be able to embed stakeholders in their organization, sustainable firms must cognitively conceptualize their firms and its relationship to society (Crilly and Sloan, 2012; Laplume et al., 2008), further linking new theoretical frameworks to the strategic cognitive agenda (Bansal, 2005; Crilly and Sloan, 2012; Laplume et al., 2008; Montiel and Delgado-Ceballos, 2014).

From the literature dedicated to understanding what a sustainable organization is, a set of emerging themes can be identified and are presented in Table 14.1.

Despite and in part because of the large body of knowledge, which has generated many ambiguities and unanswered questions related to the conceptual definition of corporate sustainability (Montiel and Delgado-Ceballos, 2014), the paucity of literature on sustainability strategies implementation is remarkable. This leaves open 'questions related to the processes through which firms actually navigate the multiple change requirements to identify, experiment with, and eventually realize more sustainable models of the enterprise' (Montiel and Delgado-Ceballos, 2014). However literature on corporate sustainability suggests that by better understanding how firms operationalize sustainability, scholars will gain more insights on what makes a company sustainable (Bansal, 2005; Devinney, 2013; Zollo et al., 2013).

Table 14.1 Sustainable organizations emerging themes

Emerging theme	Description
Purpose of the firm	On the path to sustainable development, sustainable organizations redefine their purpose, vision and mission in terms of social, environmental and economic goals, they consider profitability as a way to achieve environmental and social goals, they embrace sustainability because they consider that it is the 'right thing' and the 'smart thing' to do (Hart and Dowell, 2011; Stubbs and Cocklin, 2008; Wang and Bansal, 2012).
Stakeholder engagement	Sustainable organizations pay attention to and engage with their stakeholders. Recognizing that corporate attention to stakeholders is getting increasingly linked to competitive advantage. Managers of sustainable organizations cognitively conceptualize their firms and its relationship with society (Crilly and Sloan, 2012). In addition, sustainable organizations adopt a long-term orientation, balancing the long-term environmental and social performance anticipated outcomes with shorter-term economic results. A long-term orientation is key to the development of sustainability-related initiatives and the establishment of robust stakeholder relationship leading to profits in the long run (Barnett and Salomon, 2012; Sharma, 2000; Stubbs and Cocklin, 2008; Wang and Bansal, 2012).
Organizing processes and governance structure	Aware of how their actions affect the environment, sustainable organizations work to reduce their impacts, launching strategic change initiatives. They deploy the appropriate organizing processes and governance structure to implement those initiatives; a change initiative being defined as 'a project or set of concerted actions undertaken to address and overcome a sustainability-related issue' (Zollo et al., 2013).
Capabilities	Sustainable organizations develop specific capabilities in terms of sensing, sense making and learning processes related to sustainability (Aragon-Correa and Sharma, 2003; Bundy et al., 2013; Hahn et al., 2014; Perey, 2014; Whiteman and Cooper, 2011; Zollo et al., 2013). Sustainable development requires an increasingly complex managerial decision-making process taking into account both short-term profit maximization and long-term trade-offs assessment in terms of social and environmental impacts. 'Sustainability thinking' requires a different set of skills to support new mental frames for ecological decision-making. Achieving sustainability is a systems change problem with both short-term and long-term implications that requires systems thinking skills and tools' (Perey, 2014; Sharma, 2000; Winn et al., 2012). Sustainable organizations adapt their existing capabilities and adjust their 'operating routines' accordingly in order to achieve the anticipated strategic outcomes (Teece et al., 1997; Zollo et al., 2013). Over time, those organizations accumulate valuable resources and capabilities in terms of system integration, capital management, continuous improvements and process innovation (Bansal, 2005).
The role of innovation	Innovation is key to achieving sustainability (Hart and Milstein, 2003; Senge and Carstedt, 2001), and the value of socially responsible behavior and sustainability is strongly related to its integration with innovation (McWilliams and Siegel, 2000). To remain competitive in the context of sustainable development, established firms should no longer concentrate on their current markets but focus on creating new markets, fostered by innovation (Boons and Ludeke-Freund, 2013; Montalvo et al., 2011).
Values and beliefs	Stakeholders' awareness, firms' capabilities and innovation are not the sole factors influencing the scope, scale and speed of organizational response to sustainable development. Two other factors are key: individual concerns and organizational values (Bansal, 2003; Zollo et al., 2013).

Strategizing and operationalizing sustainability

Whilst the questions on the conceptual aspects of corporate sustainability and the reasons for engaging in sustainable development have largely been treated in academic literature and are still being discussed, little is known about the process of formulation and implementation of sustainability-related strategies (Thompson and MacMillan, 2010; Winn and Angell, 2000). This echoes Zollo, Cennamo and Neumann's recent proposition for a research agenda concentrating less on defining a sustainable company and understanding the motivations for sustainability, 'the definitional ('what') and motivational ('why')', but focusing more on the process of transformation towards an enterprise models integrating the principles of sustainable development 'the ('how') question'. According to the same authors, by emphasizing the 'how' question, researchers will gain deeper insights on the 'what' and 'why' (Zollo et al., 2013).

In addition, a study form Bansal, Gao and Qureshi (2014), one of the few investigating the strategizing and operationalizing of sustainability-related objectives, highlights that social and environmental goals may need to be separately addressed. Focusing on the role of time in sustainability, their study empirically analyses the implementation of sustainable practices across firms and over time. They define two sets of sustainability practices: corporate social commitment (CSC) and corporate environmental commitment (CEC); and find that both CEC and CSC are subject to institutional pressures (stakeholders, NGO, media, regulators). But when institutional pressures encourage firms to moderately implement CSC practices to improve their image; CEC, due to its 'technicality' takes a different path and may or may not be addressed by firms, whatever the level of institutional pressure. CEC indeed requires innovation and some firms may just lack the resources and capabilities required to innovate and implement environmental practices and therefore engage in a low level of CEC (Bansal et al., 2014). At the other end of the spectrum, firms with the resources and capabilities to address the challenge of innovation engage in strong CEC and grasp economic opportunities leading to competitive advantage (Bansal, 2005). Those findings provide some more insights to the recurring question of why firms subject to the same institutional pressures react differently and vary in addressing the same sustainability-related issues (Crilly and Sloan, 2012; Sharma, 2000), leading to the conclusion that it may be required to sometimes discriminate between social and environmental practices (Bansal et al., 2014; Gao and Bansal, 2013) when analysing how sustainable development practices are operationalized.

When firms adopt sustainability as a strategic imperative and decide to transform their organization towards sustainability, the main issue to be addressed is how to change and adapt a firm's operations. In order to understand the required organizational evolution process, Zollo, Cennamo and Neumann (2013) propose a theoretical framework structured around the four components that require to be adapted: (1) strategizing (growth, competitive or cooperative practices), (2) capabilities (sensing, learning, change), (3) organizing (governance structure, HR, systems), (4) relational quality (organization's climate, stakeholder engagement). They further assess that it is through the change initiatives launched by firms and their interaction with those four components that firms evolve towards sustainability. In this conceptual framework, a change initiative is defined as 'a project or set of concerted actions undertaken to address and overcome a sustainability issue' (Zollo et al., 2013) or as an 'event or trend perceived as potentially having an impact on the organization' (Bansal, 2003).

It is increasingly recognized that sustainable development practices creates business and stakeholder value, enhancing a firm's competitive advantage and leading to the development of strategic resources (Bansal, 2005; Crane et al., 2014; McWilliams and Siegel, 2011; Porter and Kramer, 2006; Wang and Bansal, 2012). When operationalizing sustainability, a firm's value creation and value capture mechanisms must be understood and modeled (McWilliams and Siegel, 2011), thereby linking research on sustainable development with research on business models. Indeed, if a business model's purpose is to explain 'how' firms 'do business' (Zott et al., 2011), performing two important functions for a firm: creating value, and capturing a portion of that value (Baden-Fuller and Haefliger, 2013; Chesbrough, 2007; Teece, 2010), on both a short- and long-term basis (Itami and Nishino, 2010); then a business model perspective should provide valuable insights to understand how firms create and capture value when operationalizing sustainability. Indeed:

> if our wellbeing is served by leaving the path of economic growth, then each of the dimensions of business models need to be altered: value propositions need to reflect the true needs of citizens, and the distribution of revenues needs to be defined in categories other than purely economic ones.
>
> (Boons et al., 2013)

Operationalizing sustainability: the business model as a new unit of analysis

Whereas practitioner management journals have in the context of sustainability made wide reference to the concept of business models for more than a decade (Christensen, 2001; Crane et al., 2014; Hart and Milstein, 2003; Johnson and Suskewicz, 2009; Lovins et al., 1999; Markevich, 2009; Prahalad and Hammond, 2002; Senge and Carstedt, 2001; Thompson and MacMillan, 2010), the first reference in top tier journals to business models in the context of sustainability can be found in environmental management literature (Arnold and Hockerts, 2011; Boons, 2013; Roome, 2001; Stubbs and Cocklin, 2008). Whilst strategic management literature on corporate sustainability has barely mentioned business models, with the exception of few recent articles (Hahn et al., 2014; Zott et al., 2011), the literature review of Zott, Amit and Massa (2011) provides a strong link between the two streams (Zott et al., 2011). Indeed, while recognizing that business model suffers from the same problems as corporate sustainability (i.e. unclear definition, lack of conceptualization), the authors reveal a set of common themes emerging from their review. First, business model is emerging as a new unit of analysis. Second, business model emphasizes a system-level holistic approach to explain 'how' firms 'do business'. Third, firms' activities play an important role in the various conceptualizations of business models that have been proposed. And finally, business models seek to explain how value is created, not just how it is captured (Zott et al., 2011).

In 2010, in a Long Range Planning special edition dedicated to business models, Thompson and MacMillan suggest that 'how to trade off manifold objectives' such as the competing economic, social and environmental objectives of corporate sustainability is likely a business model problem of the forthcoming years, even for the most profit seeking firms (Thompson and MacMillan, 2010). More recently, Boons, Montalvo, Quist and Wagner (2013) advance that 'sustainable development requires radical and systemic innovations' (Boons et al., 2013). Such innovations can be more effectively created and studied when building on the concept of business models. This concept provides firms with a holistic framework to envision and implement sustainable innovations. For researchers, the concept provides an analytical tool that allows to assess the interplay between the different aspects that firms combine to create ecological, economic, and social value' (Boons et al., 2013).

Conclusions and recommendations for further research

A large body of literature has been devoted to conceptualizing corporate sustainability and trying to understand a firm's motives for embracing sustainable development, but little is known on how the principles of sustainable development are implemented within firms (Bansal and Roth, 2000; Bansal, 2005; Devinney, 2009; Zollo et al., 2013) leaving open the question on 'how do firms operationalize sustainability?' Literature on sustainability operationalization within firms has first, revealed frameworks for implementing sustainability-driven change initiatives (Zollo et al., 2013), second, recognized that sustainability-oriented strategies through the development of strategic resources generate business as well as environmental and social value and enhance a firm's competitive advantage (Bansal, 2005; Crane et al., 2014; McWilliams and Siegel, 2011; Porter and Kramer, 2006; Wang and Bansal, 2012), and third, stressing the importance of time and the technicality of environmental goals, suggested that social and environmental goals may need to be separately operationalized (Bansal, 2005).

By better understanding how firms operationalize sustainability, scholars will gain more insights on what makes a company sustainable (Devinney, 2013; Zollo et al., 2013). It is important to 'theoretically visualize … organizational forms, structures, strategies and outcomes as firms travel on the path to sustainability' (Bansal et al., 2014). Today, the understanding of sustainable business models and how sustainability is operationalized in firms is weak (Bansal, 2005; Devinney, 2013), leading to the recommendation to bridge the two research streams on sustainable development and business model to allow researchers to address the unexplored question of how firms operationalize sustainability and transform their business model(s) to grasp economic but also social and environmental value over time. A recommendation resonating with a recent paper from Ferraro et al. (2015) on new strategies for addressing grand challenges (Ferraro et al., 2015) and a recent call from Juan Alberto Aragon-Correa on the need to adopt 'multiple theoretical foundations to understand why and how firms are managing environmental issues' (Aragon-Correa, 2013).

References

Aguilera, R.V., Rupp, D.E., Williams, C.A. and Ganapathi, J. (2007). Putting the S back in corporate social responsibility: A multilevel theory of social change in organizations. *Academy of Management Review*, 32(3), 836–863.

Aragon-Correa, J.A. (2013). Beyond ourselves: Building bridges to generate real progress on sustainability management issues. *Organization and Environment*, 26(1): 3–6.

Aragon-Correa, J.A. and Sharma, S. (2003). A contingent resource-based view of proactive corporate environmental strategy. *Academy of Management Review*, 28(1): 71–88.

Arnold, M.G and Hockerts, K. (2011). The greening Dutchman: Philip's process of green flagging to drive sustainable innovations. *Business Strategy and the Environment*, 20(6): 394–407.

Baden-Fuller, C. and Haefliger, S. (2013). Business models and technological innovation. *Long Range Planning*, 46(6): 419–426.

Bansal, P. (2002). The corporate challenges of sustainable development. *Academy of Management Executive*, 16(2): 122–131.

Bansal, P. (2003). From issues to actions: The importance of individual concerns and organizational values in responding to natural environmental issues. *Organization Science*, 14(5): 510 527.

Bansal, P. (2005). Evolving sustainably: A longitudinal study of corporate sustainable development. *Strategic Management Journal*, 26(3): 197–218.

Bansal, P. and DesJardine, M.R. (2014). Business sustainability: It is about time. *Strategic Organization*, 12(1): 70–78.

Bansal, P., Gao, J. and Qureshi, I. (2014). The extensiveness of corporate social and environmental commitment across firms over time. *Organization Studies*, 35(7): 949–966.

Bansal, P. and Roth, K. (2000). Why companies go green: A model of ecological responsiveness. *Academy of Management Journal*, 43(4): 717–736.

Barnett, M.L. and Salomon, R.M. (2012). Does it pay to be really good? Addressing the shape of the relationship between social and financial performance. *Strategic Management Journal*, 33(11): 1304–1320.

Battilana, J. and Dorado, S. (2010). Building sustainable hybrid organizations: The case of commercial microfinance organizations. *Academy of Management Journal*, 53(6): 1419–1440.

Boons, F. (2013). Organizing with dynamic ecosystems: Conceptualizing socioecological mechanisms. *Organization and Environment*, 26(3): 281–297.

Boons, F. and Lüdeke-Freund, F. (2013). Business models for sustainable innovation: State-of-the-art and steps towards a research agenda. *Journal of Cleaner Production*, 45(3): 9–19.

Boons, F., Montalvo, C., Quist, J. and Wagner, M. (2013). Sustainable innovation, business models and economic performance: An overview. *Journal of Cleaner Production*, 45(3): 1–8.

Boons, F. and Wagner, M. (2009). Assessing the relationship between economic and ecological performance: Distinguishing system levels and the role of innovation. *Ecological Economics*, 68(7): 1908–1914.

Bowen, F. and Aragon-Correa, J.A. (2014). Greenwashing in corporate environmentalism research and practice: The importance of what we say and do. *Organization and Environment*, 27(2): 107–112.

Bundy, J., Shropshire, C. and Buchholtz, A.K. (2013). Strategic cognition and issue salience: Toward an explanation of firm responsiveness to stakeholder concerns. *Academy of Management Review*, 38(3): 352–376.

Campbell, J.L. (2007). Why would corporations behave in socially responsible ways? An institutional theory of corporate social responsibility. *Academy of Management Review*, 32(3): 946–967.

Carroll, A.B. (1991). A three-dimensional conceptual model of corporate performance. *Academy of Management Review*, 4(4): 497–505.

Cennamo, C., Berrone, P., Cruz, C. and Gomez-Mejia, L.R. (2012). Socioemotional wealth and proactive stakeholder engagement: Why family-controlled firms care more about their stakeholders. *Entrepreneurship Theory and Practice*, 36(6): 1153–1173.

Chesbrough, H.W. (2007). Business model innovation: it's not just about technology anymore. *Strategy and Leadership*, 35(6): 12–17.

Christensen, C.M. (2001). The past and future of competitive advantage. *MIT Sloan Management Review*, 42(2): 105–109.

Crane, A., Palazzo, G., Spence, L. and Matten, D. (2014). Contesting the value of 'creating shared value'. *California Management Review*, 56(2): 130–153.

Crilly, D. and Sloan, P. (2012). Enterprise logic: Explaining corporate attention to stakeholders from the 'inside-out'. *Strategic Management Journal*, 33(10): 1174–1193.

Devinney, T.M. (2009). Is the social responsible corporation a myth? The good, the bad, and the ugly of corporate social responsibility. *Academy of Management Perspectives*, 23(2): 44–56.

Devinney, T.M. (2013). Taking the 'non' out of 'nonmarket' strategy. *Global Strategy Journal*, 3(2): 198–203.

Doh, J.P. and Lucea, R. (2013). So close yet so far: Integrating global strategy and nonmarket research. *Global Strategy Journal*, 3(2): 171–194.

Elkington, J. (1998). *Cannibals with Folks: The Triple bottom Line of 21st Century Business*. Stony Creek, CT: New Society Publishers.

Ferraro, F., Etzion, D. and Gehman, J. (2015).Tackling grand challenges pragmatically: Robust action revisited. *Organization Studies*, 36(3): 363–390.

Friedman, M. (1962). *Capitalism and Freedom*. Chicago: University of Chicago Press.

Friedman, M. (1970). The social responsibility of business is to increase profits. *New York Times Magazine*, September 13 (32/33), 122, 124, 126.

Gao, J. and Bansal, P. (2013). Instrumental and integrative logics in business sustainability. *Journal of Business Ethics*, 112(2): 241–255.

Garces-Ayerbe, C., Rivera-Torres, P. and Murillo-Luna, J.L. (2012). Stakeholder pressure and environmental proactivity: Moderating effect of competitive advantage expectations. *Management Decision*, 50(2): 189–206.

Gladwin, T.N., Kennelly, J.J. and Krause, T.S. (1995). Shifting paradigms for sustainable development: Implications for management theory and research. *Academy of Management Review*, 20(4): 874–907.

Hahn, T., Preuss, L., Pinkse, J. and Figge, F. (2014). Cognitive frames in corporate sustainability: Managerial sensemaking with paradoxical and business case frames. *Academy of Management Review*, 39(4): 463–487.

Hart, S.L. (1995). A natural-resource-based view of the firm. *Academy of Management Review*, 20(4): 996–1014.

Hart, S.L. and Dowell, G. (2011). A natural-resource-based view of the firm: Fifteen years after. *Journal of Management*, 37(5): 1464–1479.

Hart, S.L and Milstein, M.B. (2003). Creating sustainable value. *Academy of Management Executive*, 17(2): 56–67.

Hockerts, K. (2015). A cognitive perspective on the business case for sustainability. *Business Strategy and the Environment*, 24(2): 102–122.

Hockerts, K. and Wustenhagen, R. (2010). Greening Goliaths versus emerging Davids: Theorizing about the role of incumbents and new entrants in sustainable entrepreneurship. *Journal of Business Venturing*, 25: 222–237.

Itami, H. and Nishino, K. (2010). Killing two birds with one stone: Profit for now and learning for the future. *Long Range Planning*, 43(2/3): 364–369.

Johnson, M.W. and Suskewicz, J. (2009). How to jump-start the clean tech economy. *Harvard Business Review*, 87(11): 52–60.

Kanter, R.M. (1999). From spare change to real change: The social sector as a beta site for business innovation. *Harvard Business Review*, 77, 123–132.

Laplume, A.O., Sonpar, K. and Litz, R.A (2008). Stakeholder theory: Reviewing a theory that moves us. *Journal of Management*, 34(6): 1152–1189.

Lockett, A., Moon, J. and Wayne, V. (2006). Corporate social responsibility in management research: Focus, nature, salience and sources of influence. *Journal of Management Studies*, 43(1): 115–136.

Lovins, A.B., Lovins, L.H. and Hawken, P. (1999). A road map for natural capitalism. *Harvard Business Review*, 77: 145–158.

Luo, X. and Bhattacharya, C.B. (2006). Corporate social responsibility, customer satisfaction, and market value. *Journal of Marketing*, 70(4): 1–18.

McWilliams, A. and Siegel, D. (2000). Corporate social responsibility and firm financial performance. *Strategic Management Journal*, 21(5): 602–609.

McWilliams, A. and Siegel, D. (2001). Corporate social responsibility: A theory of the firm perspective. *Academy of Management Review*, 26(1): 117–127.

McWilliams, A. and Siegel, D. (2011). Creating and capturing value: Strategic corporate social responsibility, resource-based theory, and sustainable competitive advantage. *Journal of Management*, 37(5): 1480–1495.

Marcus, A.A. and Fremeth, A.R. (2009). Green management matters regardless. *Academy of Management Perspectives*, 23(3): 17–26.

Margolis, J. and Walsh, J. (2003). Misery loves companies: Rethinking social initiatives by business. *Administrative Science Quarterly*, 48(2): 268–305.

Markevich, A. (2009). The evolution of sustainability. *MIT Sloan Management Review*, 51(1): 13–14.

Matten, D. and Crane, A. (2005). Corporate citizenship: Toward an extended theoretical conceptualization. *Academy of Management Review*, 30: 166–179.

Matten, D. and Moon, J. (2008). 'Implicit' and 'Explicit' CSR: A conceptual framework for a comparative understanding of corporate social responsibility. *Academy of Management Review*, 33(2): 404–424.

Mirvis, P. and Googins, B. (2006). Stages of Corporate Citizenships. *California Management Review*, 48(2): 104–126.

Montalvo, C., Diaz-Lopez, F. and Brandes, F. (2011). *Eco-innovation Opportunities in Nine Sectors of the European Economy*. European Sector Innovation Watch. European Commission, Directorate General Enterprise and Industry, Brussels.

Montiel, I. (2008). Corporate social responsibility and corporate sustainability: Separate pasts, common futures. *Organization & Environment*, 21(3), 245–269.

Montiel, I. and Delgado-Ceballos, J. (2014). Defining and measuring corporate sustainability: Are we there yet? *Organization & Environment*, 27(2): 113–139.

Perey, R. (2014). Organizing sustainability and the problem of scale: Local, global, or fractal? *Organization & Environment*, 27(3): 215–222.

Porter, M.E. and Kramer, M.R. (2006). Strategy and society: The link between competitive advantage and corporate social responsibility. *Harvard Business Review*, 84(12): 78–92.

Porter, M.E. and Kramer, M.R. (2011). Creating shared value. *Harvard Business Review*, 89(1/2): 62–77.

Prahalad, C.K. and Hammond, A. (2002). Serving the world's poor profitably. *Harvard Business Review*, 80(9): 48–57.

Rego, A., Pina e Cunha, M. and Polonia, D. (2017). Corporate sustainability: A view from the top. *Journal of Business Ethics*, 143: 133–157.

Rohrbeck, R., Konnertz, L. and Knab, S. (2013). Collaborative business modeling for systemic and sustainability innovations. *International Journal of Technology Management*, 2013, 63(1/2): 4–23.

Roome, N. (2001). Conceptualizing and studying the contribution of networks in environmental management and sustainable development. *Business Strategy and the Environment*, 10(2): 69–76.

Santos, F., Pache, A.C. and Birkholz, C. (2015). Making hybrids work: Aligning business models and organizational design for social enterprises. *California Management Review*, 57(3): 36–58.

Schaltegger, S., Beckmann, M. and Hansen, E.G. (2013). Transdisciplinarity in corporate sustainability: Mapping the field. *Business Strategy and the Environment*, 22(4): 219–229.

Schaltegger, S. and Wagner, M. (2011). Sustainable entrepreneurship and sustainability innovation: Categories and interactions. *Business Strategy and the Environment*, 20: 222–237.

Senge, P.M. and Carstedt, G. (2001). Innovating our way to the next industrial revolution. *MIT Sloan Management Review*, 42(2): 24–38.

Sharma, S. (2000). Managerial interpretations and organizational context as predictors of corporate choice of environment strategy. *Academy of Management Journal*, 43(4): 681–697.

Sharma, S. and Henriques, I. (2005). Stakeholder influences on sustainability practices in the Canadian forest products industry. *Strategic Management Journal*, 26(2), 159–180.

Siegel, D.S. (2009). Green management matters only if it yields more green: An economic/strategic perspective. *Academy of Management Perspectives*, 23(3): 5–16.

Steurer, R., Langer, M.E., Konrad, A. and Martinuzzi, A. (2005). Corporations, stakeholders and sustainable development: A theoretical exploration of business-society relations. *Journal of Business Ethics*, 61(3): 263–281.

Stubbs, W. and Cocklin, C. (2008). Conceptualizing a 'sustainability business model'. *Organization & Environment*, 21(2): 103–127.

Teece, D.J. (2010). Business models, business strategy and innovation. *Long Range Planning*, 43(2/3), 172–194.

Teece, D.J., Pisano, G. and Shuen, A. (1997). Dynamic capabilities and strategic management. *Strategic Management Journal*, 18(7): 509–533.

Thompson, J.D. and MacMillan, I.C. (2010). Making social ventures work. *Harvard Business Review*, 88(9): 66–73.

Vaara, E. and Durand, R. (2012). How to connect strategy research with broader issues that matter? *Strategic Organization*, 10(3): 248–255.

Van der Byl, C.A. and Slawinski, N. (2015). Embracing tensions in corporate sustainability: A review of research from win-win and trade-offs to paradoxes and beyond. *Organization & Environment*, 28(1): 54–79.

Wang, T. and Bansal, P. (2012). Social responsibility in new ventures: Profiting from a long-term orientation. *Strategic Management Journal*, 33(10): 1135–1153.

WCED (1987). *Our Common Future*. Oxford: World Commission on Environment and Development and Oxford University Press.

Whiteman, G. and Cooper, W.H. (2011). Ecological sensemaking. *Academy of Management Journal*, 54(5): 889–911.

Winn, M.I. and Angell, L.C. (2000). Towards a process model of corporate greening. *Organization Studies*, 21(6): 1119–1147.

Winn, M.I., Pinkse, J. and Illge, L. (2012) Editorial: Case studies on trade-offs in corporate sustainability. *Corporate Social Responsibility and Environmental Management*, 19(2): 63–68.

Zollo, M., Cennamo, C. and Neumann, K. (2013). Beyond what and why: Understanding organizational evolution towards sustainable enterprise models. *Organization and Environment*, 26(3): 241–259.

Zott, C., Amit, R., and Massa, L. (2011). The business model: Recent developments and future research. *Journal of Management*, 37(4): 1019–1042.

Part IV

Assessing and valuing sustainability

15 Unbundling corporate sustainability

Management and assessment

Anselm Schneider

Introduction

Sustainability is increasingly becoming a mainstream concept in many business firms. However, assessing the extent of corporate sustainability as well as increasing corporate sustainability is a highly complex undertaking. This complexity results from the high number of different features that are regarded to play a role in the context of corporate sustainability, as well as from the interrelationships between these features. Without proper knowledge of these features and relationships, the understanding of corporate sustainability is severely limited. This problem can be illustrated by the following example of an environmental management system, which is usually regarded as an important contribution to a firm's sustainability. Can we regard a firm with an environmental management system such as EMAS as sustainable? What are potential ways to further increase the sustainability of this firm? Does the implementation of an environmental management system increase the sustainability of a firm, or might this even impair corporate sustainability?

In order to systematically tackle such questions, in this chapter I carve out different features of corporate sustainability. A review of the existing literature reveals that different streams of research on corporate sustainability describe various features of corporate sustainability such as organizational structures (Epstein and Roy, 2001), organizational value systems (Linnenluecke and Griffiths, 2010; Stubbs and Cocklin, 2008) as well as organizational identity (Valente, 2012). However, these different features, which are all relevant for the management and assessment of corporate sustainability, have not yet been combined in a common framework (for an exception see Berkhoud and Rowlands, 2007) aimed at understanding the antecedents and constitution of corporate sustainability. I aim at filling this lacuna by describing different features of corporate sustainability, by analysing the interplay of these features and by analysing their role both for the management and assessment of corporate sustainability. This framework of corporate sustainability provides a more fine-grained view on the determinants of corporate sustainability for researchers who aim to better understand corporate sustainability as well as for managers who aim to make their companies more sustainable.

The chapter will be structured as follows. In the section following the introduction, the features of corporate sustainability will be identified, and their interdependencies will be described. In the subsequent section, the implications of such a comprehensive perspective for corporate sustainability assessment will be carved out. In a nutshell, I argue that some of the features mentioned above are more easily observable than others. Since these features are not necessarily correlated, different observers' assessments of a firm's sustainability might differ to a considerable extent. In the concluding section, I explain how the differentiated understanding of corporate sustainability management and assessment elaborated in this chapter can help managers to gain a clearer picture of the actual degree of sustainability of their firms and to take appropriate steps for increasing corporate sustainability. In addition, I highlight how the described framework might inform future research on corporate sustainability.

Towards a differentiated understanding of corporate sustainability

Evidence for the limited carrying capacity of the global ecosystem (Meadows, Meadows and Randers, 2004) and for the negative impact of many aspects of current forms of global economic activity on social conditions (see, e.g. Klein, 2001; Reich, 2007) is accumulating. Among this evidence are climate change (IPCC, 2014) and environmental pollution (Steffen et al., 2015), bad labour conditions in global supply chains (China Labour Watch, 2011) and economic inequality (Piketty, 2014). In consequence of these developments, the concept of sustainable development is gaining prominence. This concept emphasizes the need to balance ecological, social and economic considerations as well as the needs of present and future generations (UNCD, 1992; WCED, 1987). Due to their positive impact on sustainable development (Hart and Milstein, 2003) as well as owing to their negative ecological and social impact (Banerjee, 2007), business firms are regarded as crucial for the attainment of sustainable development (Gladwin, Kennelly and Krause, 1995; Hawken, 1993). The contribution of business firms to the goal of sustainable development is commonly referred to as corporate sustainability (see e.g. Bansal, 2002; Dyllick and Hockerts, 2002). Despite a lack of a universal definition, it is generally acknowledged that corporate sustainability refers to economic, social and environmental effects of the activities of business firms (Hahn and Figge, 2011) and that a reduction of negative externalities of business activities is conducive to sustainable development (van den Bergh, 2010).

The concept of corporate sustainability is highly complex. First, complexity results from the fact that this concept transcends the concentration of traditional economics and management theory on the exclusive objective of financial performance. Second, there exist manifold trade-offs between the economic, ecological and social dimension of corporate sustainability (Hahn et al., 2010). Whereas economic success can be measured in an objective and unambiguous manner, corporate sustainability is highly dependent on the interpretation of observers who have different environmental and social priorities. Therefore, the assessment of corporate sustainability is intricate, and the judgements of different observers of the sustainability of one firm are likely to be different in absence of a shared set of binding evaluation criteria.

For instance, a firm engaged in the production of mass consumer goods aimed at customers with limited interest in sustainability might successfully put in place extensive measures (such as sustainability-labels and reporting) that create the impression of sustainability in the eyes of most consumers without actually contributing to sustainable development. In contrast, a successful agricultural micro business engaged in environmentally friendly and socially equitable production processes might be perceived as unsustainable by an auditing agency, since it lacks formal features, which are often considered as a signal for corporate sustainability by such agencies. Finally, a third firm can be conceived, that has the goal of sustainability deeply internalized in its organizational structure and value system and successfully implemented in its operations and therefore is regarded as sustainable by the majority of its stakeholders.

The essence of this thought experiment is that the assessment of corporate sustainability is influenced by multiple factors – and potentially independent from the actual degree of corporate sustainability measured on the basis of agreed on measures for corporate sustainability. Apparently, from different perspectives different organizational features seem to be pivotal for the assessment of a firm as sustainable. Thus, the degree of corporate sustainability as perceived by different observers depends on firm-specific features as well as on observer-specific features. The latter issue has been analysed in the context of corporate social irresponsibility (Lange and Washburn, 2012). These findings can be transferred to the context of corporate (un-)sustainability to some extent. However, neither the firm-specific features that influence the assessment of corporate sustainability nor the observer relativity of corporate sustainability have so far been addressed in the literature. Since the assessment of a firm's sustainability is the basis for managerial attempts to improve corporate sustainability, a thorough understanding of the degrees of observability of different features of corporate sustainability – in addition to a comprehension of the different features of corporate sustainability and their interrelations – is crucial for successfully improving the sustainability of a business firm.

Therefore, in what follows I first provide a definition of corporate sustainability that differentiates the actual extent of a firm's sustainability (sustainability performance) from the antecedents of sustainability performance (sustainability governance, sustainability values and sustainability identity) and analyse how these features influence corporate sustainability performance. Second, I examine how these features interact. Third, I explore the role these features play for the assessment of corporate sustainability.

Sustainability performance

Definitions of corporate sustainability abound. What they have in common is that business firms should minimize their negative environmental and social impact – and ideally generate positive contributions to society and the natural environment – while being viable economically. In the following, I denote the sum of economic, ecological and social performance of a firm as sustainability performance. Assessing the economic performance of a firm is relatively easy by means of conventional methods of financial performance evaluation. However, directly assessing the impact of a firm on the natural environment and on society is a difficult task.

With respect to a firm's impact on the natural environment, firms are – albeit to a varying degree – involved in a huge variety of material flows. These can be measured technically. With respect to many emissions of business, such as CO_2, CFCs or radioactive materials, levels of toxicity and the nature of effects are relatively well researched. However, in many areas such, e.g. in nanotechnology or genetic engineering, knowledge on the effects for humans and the ecosystem is still limited. Therefore, in general, the ecological impact of business activities is always subject to high levels of uncertainty since limited knowledge on the toxicity of certain substances, and on interactions between different substances is bound to the current state of knowledge that is constantly changing (Beck, 1992).

Similarly, the assessment of a firm's social impact is subject to inherent limitations. Various stakeholder groups are affected by corporate activities, and potentially evaluate these in different ways (van Marrewijk, 2003). The opinions of these stakeholders, such as employees, consumers and members of the community in which a firm is located, and humanity in general, would need to be assessed in order to obtain a comprehensive picture of a firm's social sustainability. However, potential contradictions between different stakeholder groups' evaluations of a firm's sustainability set narrow limits to a consistent and unambiguous assessment of a firm's sustainability. For instance, shareholders might welcome as socially sustainable increased dividends that are the result of corporate downsizing due to the material gains resulting for them, whereas laid off employees regard the same activities as unsustainable.

The multiple interactions between a firm's economic, environmental and social performance, the manifold trade-offs between these dimensions, and the complexity of value chains further complicate the assessment of a firm's sustainability performance. For instance, when sourcing input factors such as raw materials and services, the sustainability performance of the suppliers of these factors have an impact on the sustainability of a firm. That is, a firm that has a highly energy efficient production technology but utilizes input factors that are produced under unsustainable conditions might display a relatively low degree of corporate sustainability performance.

Existing frameworks for the assessment of corporate sustainability involve several elements of sustainability performance. These elements include macro factors such as the industry in which a firm operates, and also firm-specific information such as material input, the amount of emissions, and specific technologies in the area of environmental performance; and information on factors such as workplace accidents, wage spread or social benefits in the area of social performance (see, for instance, the set of sustainability indicators provided by the Global Reporting Initiative; GRI). However, the gathering and processing of these data is first subject to technological and material restrictions. That is, corporate sustainability can be assessed only to a limited degree within a cost range that does not impair the economic viability of a firm, since the cost of collecting and processing sustainability-related data is likely to increase for every additional unit of data. Second, such data are gathered through internal controlling systems and therefore primarily available for the firm-internal stakeholders. In contrast, external observers of a firm's sustainability most often need to rely on the voluntary disclosure of sustainability-related information by the firm.

In order to increase a firm's sustainability performance, it is firstly crucial to acknowledge the described ambiguities. That is, the more facets of corporate sustainability are taken into account and the more is known about the degree to which certain indicators influence corporate sustainability, the higher the likelihood that corporate sustainability performance can be increased as a result of sustainability management. Secondly, it is important to understand that corporate sustainability performance is the outcome of multiple features within a firm and that the interplay of these features is decisive for advancing or inhibiting a firm's sustainability performance. In the following sections, I will explore the most important of these features. On the basis of such a differentiated understanding of corporate sustainability it becomes possible to identify firm-internal barriers to increasing sustainability.

Sustainability governance

Besides information on sustainability performance, information on sustainability governance is often used as a proxy for corporate sustainability (Schneider and Meins, 2012). Sustainability governance refers to organizational processes and structures that are potentially conducive to corporate sustainability performance (see Figure 15.1). Examples for sustainability governance are environmental management systems and

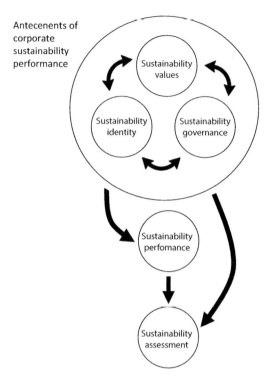

Antecenents of
corporate
sustainability
performance

Sustainability
values

Sustainability
identity

Sustainability
governance

Sustainability
perfomance

Sustainability
assessment

Figure 15.1 Antecedents of corporate sustainability performance and their influence on the
assessment of corporate sustainability.

related certifications such as ISO 14001 or EMAS, specialized corporate functions such
as the position of environmental managers, or sustainability officers in the executive
board, as well as departments that are charged with sustainability issues. Sustainability
governance on the board level is illustrated by Nike, which has a corporate responsibility committee in its board and appointed a vice president of corporate responsibility
(Morgan, Ryu and Mirvis, 2009). Furthermore, sustainability-related rules and guidelines, process descriptions, and handbooks are a part of sustainability governance.

As shown by Schneider and Meins (2012), many methodologies for the assessment
of corporate sustainability do not differentiate between corporate sustainability performance and sustainability governance. This is potentially problematic, since the existence
of sustainability governance alone is no guarantee for desirable sustainability performance.
Rather, sustainability governance has the potential to increase sustainability performance.
That is, sustainability governance in many cases makes possible enhanced sustainability
performance by standardizing processes and aligning them with sustainability goals.

However, importantly, the extent of sustainability governance needs to be aligned
with firm size. The reason for that are the relatively high resource requirements for
setting up sustainability governance structures. For instance, the implementation of an
environmental management system is relatively costly, and certification of such a management system as well. In a relatively small firm, the costs of setting up such a system
potentially negatively affect the economic viability of a firm (Fassin, 2008). What is
more, the sustainability of relatively simple processes in small firms (compared to more

complex processes in larger firms) can be assured by less resource intensive means, such as the introduction of process handbooks and manuals.

Sustainability values

Sustainability values refer to the shared belief of an organization's members in the importance of ecological and social factors. Basically, as a precondition for corporate sustainability performance, organizational values need to 'emphasize harmonious co-existence with the natural world, view humans as part of the natural world and acknowledge the rights of nature to exist' (Shrivastava and Hart, 1995: 162). In general, an alignment of organizational values and business strategies has been shown to be critical for the attainment of strategic goals (Humble, Jackson and Thomson, 1994). For the particular case of environmental issues, individual concern as well as the congruence of environmental issues and organizational values are regarded as necessary conditions for organizational responsiveness in this issue area (Bansal, 2003; Shrivastava, 1995). On the organizational level, values, defined as 'socially shared cognitive representations of institutional goals and demands' (Rokeach, 1979: 50, cited in Bansal, 2003) that refer to sustainability, enable organizations to mobilize enduring commitment for addressing these issues (see Figure 15.1).

As shown by Jackson and Nelson (2004), only values-driven companies are able to continuously address issues that are crucial in the context of corporate sustainability, such as the harnessing of innovation for the public good, the creation of new alliances in order to collectively tackle sustainability challenges, and the overcoming of a narrow focus on short-term profit and shareholder value. Whereas such a clear cut understanding of the role of values for corporate sustainability is appealing, a detailed look at the role of values for achieving corporate sustainability reveals that different constellations of values in organizations are likely to result in an emphasis on different aspects of corporate sustainability, such as environmental protection or stakeholder engagement (Linnenluecke and Griffiths, 2010). As a result, different value constellations potentially lead to different approaches of firms to corporate sustainability. For instance, the prevalence of values that emphasize stability and control is likely to lead to technocratic compliance, whereas values related to efficiency and productivity are likely to be dominant in sustainability laggards. These considerations illustrate that values play an important – albeit complex – role for the attainment of high sustainability performance.

Sustainability identity

A further feature that is crucial for high sustainability performance is sustainability identity (see Figure 15.1). In organizational research, the concept of organizational identity refers to the shared beliefs of the members of an organization with respect to the question 'Who are we?' (Whetten, 2006). It comprises the purpose of an organization as well as its philosophy (Margolis and Hansen, 2002). As shown by Battilana and Dorado (2010), organizational identity can serve as a mechanism that balances different and potentially contradicting logics which are relevant for an organization. Therefore, in the case of corporate sustainability a sustainability-oriented organizational identity seems to be crucial for reconciling economic, ecological and social requirements that are relevant for increasing sustainability performance. In a similar vein, Valente (2012) argues that the explicit occurrence of sustainability in the identity of an organization is an important antecedent of corporate sustainability. Accordingly, two effects of organizational identity – which can be termed sustainability identity if it enables corporate sustainability – on corporate sustainability can be identified.

First, sustainability identity plays an important role in the processes through which organizations interpret their environments (Gioia and Thomas, 1996). Increasing corporate sustainability performance requires variegated information that is not relevant for conventional firms. The ability of an organization to collect such relevant information depends on the way in which organizational members see the role of their organization in its environment. Only if organizational members see the need of increasing their organization's sustainability and thus understand the relevance of variegated information for corporate sustainability, they are able to detect relevant issues, collect relevant information, and eventually improve decision quality in order to increase corporate sustainability performance. Second, organizational identity might help resolve contradictions (Battilana and Dorado, 2010). As described above, sustainability is a highly complex concept that involves different potentially contradicting dimensions. The contradictions between these dimensions potentially also play out as tensions within a business firm. A pertinent example for such tensions are the trade-offs between economic and environmental considerations in the context of corporate sustainability (Hahn and Figge, 2011). A shared sustainability identity can help overcome such tensions, since organizational members who share such an identity agree on the superiority of sustainability as an organizational objective, and are thus able to prioritize decisions according to their impact on sustainability performance.

How the different antecedents of corporate sustainability performance interact

The management of corporate sustainability requires the identification of levers that can help increase the sustainability performance of a firm. The most obvious and also necessary approach for increasing a firm's sustainability performance is the application of more sustainable practices. This might be the change of organizational practices, for instance the modification of production processes in order to reduce resource consumption. Similarly, the implementation of an environmental or social management system can help track problematic issues in order to adapt organizational processes. These organizational changes can be regarded as an improvement of sustainability governance.

However, as shown by Schneider and Meins (2012), whereas the existence of appropriate sustainability governance structures is a necessary condition for increased sustainability performance, it is by far not a sufficient condition. Rather, as indicated in Figure 15.1, several other features contribute to sustainability performance. In order to effectively manage corporate sustainability, a holistic understanding of the ways in which these different features interact is important. Therefore, in what follows, I will analyse the most important interrelations between sustainability governance, sustainability identity, sustainability values and sustainability performance.

Most importantly, extant research (Linnenluecke and Griffiths, 2010; Shrivastava, 1995) emphasizes the importance of sustainability-related values for increasing corporate sustainability. For instance, as argued for the case of codes of conduct, formalized measures that aim at increasing corporate sustainability are only likely to work properly when organizational values are oriented towards sustainability (Bondy, Matten and Moon, 2007). This argumentation is also more generally valid for other elements of sustainability governance. For instance, individual commitment has been shown to be vital for the successful implementation of the ISO 14001 standard (Sambasivan and Fei, 2008). Consequently, sustainability values are an important precondition for putting sustainability governance into action.

Sustainability governance is also important for nurturing sustainability values and identity since formalized approaches to corporate sustainability potentially can help increase the awareness for corporate sustainability. In particular, sustainability governance might serve as a guidance for new employees, supporting them to develop sustainability values and view their organization as a contributor to sustainable development. Extant sustainability values also contribute to the emergence and solidification of a sustainability identity on the one hand. On the other hand, a sustainability identity serves as the basis for the development of sustainability values. Finally, sustainability identity can serve as an important antecedent of sustainability governance, since it helps to make sense of ambiguities that are not (yet) addressed by formal rules and structures. Issues that are identified on the basis of a sustainability identity, as well as solutions to these issues can in a later stage lead to the modification of sustainability governance. Consequently, sustainability values, sustainability identity and sustainability governance are mutually constitutive and collectively serve as antecedents of corporate sustainability performance (see Figure 15.1).

To date comprehensive empirical studies of corporate sustainability that consider all of the mentioned features simultaneously are lacking. Therefore it is not possible to determine the contribution of each of features for driving sustainability performance, and therefore the proposed framework does not prioritize any one of these features. However, it seems sensible to assume that there are different 'roads to Rome'. That is, due to the multiple interdependencies described in the previous paragraphs and illustrated in Figure 15.1, attempts to increase the sustainability performance of a firm might – at least initially – either focus on sustainability governance, sustainability identity or sustainability values, depending on the specific initial constellation of these features in a firm. As illustrated in Table 15.1, archetypical patterns of corporate sustainability can help illustrate the combination of different levels of sustainability governance, values, and identity and the likely effects on sustainability performance.

In the case of sustainability leaders, extensive sustainability identity and values in concert with elaborate sustainability governance lead to high sustainability performance (as described by Valente, 2012 for the case of sustaincentric firms). Medium sustainability performance might either be the result of comprehensive sustainability governance that is not put into action, or the result of a limited translation of sustainability identity and values into organizational practices. In the former case (technocratic compliance), firms that lack sustainability values and identity adopt formal sustainability-oriented measures that are put into practice only to a limited extent (a case of policy-practice decoupling, see Bromley and Powell, 2012), leading to moderate sustainability performance. In the latter case (humanistic explorers), extensive sustainability values and identity are only limitedly put into action due to insufficient sustainability governance (see also the case of proactive firms described by Valente, 2012). Finally, sustainability laggards display low degrees of sustainability governance, identity and values, and therefore attain only a low sustainability performance.

Table 15.1 Archetypical patterns of corporate sustainability

	Sustainability leaders	Technocratic compliance	Humanistic explorers	Sustainability laggards
Governance	High	High	Low	Low
Values	High	Low	High	Low
Identity	High	Low	High	Low
Performance	High	Moderate	Moderate	Low

The different archetypes are likely to require different approaches to increasing sustain-ability performance. For instance, in the case of technocratic compliance, extensive sus-tainability governance that is not supported by according sustainability identity and values would require a nurturing of these features. In contrast, the moderate sustainability per-formance of humanistic explorers, which is driven by extensive sustainability values and identity, might be increased through developing sustainability governance. Due to the different constellations of sustainability governance, identity and values indicated in Table 15.1, the feedback loops illustrated in Figure 15.1 are likely to lead to different dynamics.

Exploring the determinants of corporate sustainability assessment

Improving and managing corporate sustainability requires a comprehensive knowledge of the different features of corporate sustainability (which have been described above). Whereas the described features of corporate sustainability are important for the manage-ment of corporate sustainability, they also play an important role when it comes to the assessment of a firm's actual and potential sustainability performance (see Figure 15.1). Some of these features are relatively easily observable, and some are rather difficult to assess. Accordingly, the sustainability of a business firm is likely to be assessed differently by different observers of a firm, depending on their respective capacity to acquire and process information. Whereas some observers have extensive capacities to gather infor-mation about different features of a firm's sustainability, other observers are restricted with regard to their capacity to assess corporate sustainability.

Therefore, it is possible to regard the perception of corporate sustainability as the outcome of processes of complexity reduction – on the individual level as well as on the group level – that are shaped by a multiplicity of individual features. For example, a corporate sustainability assessment conducted by researchers is likely to lead to results that considerably differ from an assessment conducted by a rating agency for corporate sustainability. Whereas the former can potentially interview a firm's stakeholders and observe organizational structures and processes, the latter often exclusively relies on the public statements of a firm. This illustrates that observers of corporate sustainability utilize specific sets of features of corporate sustainability and infer the degree of sus-tainability performance from these features. This is in line with the theory of attribute substitution (Kahnemann and Frederick, 2002). According to this theory, under uncer-tainty individuals reduce the complexity of an entity intuitively by means of heuristics. That is, they take a significant feature of a complex entity (that is highly accessible) and infer from this feature the nature of the whole entity (which is relatively inaccessible).

With regard to corporate sustainability, I argue that in the process of the assessment of corporate sustainability, specific features of corporate sustainability are used to infer the overall sustainability of a firm. Kahneman and Frederick (2002) argue that such processes of judgement formation occur when they are not rejected on the basis of crit-ical reflection. I hold that such controlled evaluation is largely impossible in the case of corporate sustainability due to the definitional lack of clarity of this concept. Therefore, even deliberate processes of evaluation can be regarded to be substantially guided by intuition.

The outcome of the assessment of corporate sustainability is largely influenced by the following factors: accessibility of different features of corporate sustainability, ability and willingness of observers to bear costs of information acquisition, and firm size. These factors will be described subsequently.

Accessibility of features

Sustainability governance is the most accessible feature of corporate sustainability. Many firms, especially large corporations and increasingly also small and medium-sized enterprises publicly report not only their financial results, but also voluntarily report on their performance in the environmental and social domain. Such reports typically comprise information about sustainability objectives of a firm and financial contributions to specific projects. Further, firms display corporate sustainability through membership in initiatives such as the United Nations Global Compact and by means of specific certification. I argue that standards with mainly procedural prescriptions such as the ISO 14001 standard provide only very limited information about the actual sustainability performance (Krut and Gleckmann, 1998) and therefore are potentially misguiding for the assessment of corporate sustainability. While the 'presence and depth of governance mechanisms, operating structures and systems provides at least some feel' (Morgan, Ryu and Mirvis, 2009: 44) for corporate sustainability, it does by no means provide reliable information.

In contrast, while being of central interest for the assessment of corporate sustainability in addition to features of sustainability governance, corporate sustainability performance is difficult to access due to the measurement problems described above. Such an assessment ideally comprises financial analyses, material flow analyses as well as stakeholder impact analyses. Such information is in many cases to some degree provided by certification bodies that look at material performance-related features. Current developments such as the increasing usage of the guidelines of the Global Reporting Initiative (Brown, 2011) and the rising prominence of integrated reporting (Churet and Eccles, 2014) have the potential to facilitate a more and more comprehensive assessment of sustainability performance.

The sustainability identity of a business firm is relatively easily accessible to the extent that the brand of a company 'reflects and communicates the identity of an organization' (Hatch and Mirvis, 2010, p. 45). However, the internal identity of a firm, which is likely to have a stronger effect on sustainability performance compared with external identity, is much more difficult to assess. For instance, such an assessment necessitates in-depth interviews with employees of a firm (Dutton and Dukerich, 1991), surveys (van Knippenberg et al., 2002), or the analysis of the descriptions of their organization (Brown and Humphreys, 2008).

The most difficult task is the analysis of the values related to corporate sustainability. Assumptions, values and beliefs are very difficult to access. In contrast, whereas the artefacts that embody specific aspects of organizational values are easy to access, they are very difficult to decipher. Typically, the analysis of organizational values is only (if at all) possible in the course of extensive qualitative analyses that require large material efforts by the observer as well as trust on the part of the assessed firm. The assessment of an organization's values can comprise participant observations, interviews, and archival analyses (Golden-Biddle and Rao, 1997; Pettigrew, 1979). As shown in Figure 15.2, the described features of corporate sustainability can be arranged according to their degree of accessibility.

The complex interrelationships between these features as well as their different degree of accessibility together have an important influence on the assessment of corporate sustainability. For instance, a firm with high sustainability performance does not necessarily have a comprehensive sustainability governance. In this case, a corporate sustainability assessment that is exclusively based on sustainability governance might provide

Figure 15.2 Accessibility of different features of corporate sustainability.

skewed results (Schneider and Meins, 2012)). This implies that the different degrees of accessibility of the constitutive features of corporate sustainability in conjunction with the different capacity of observers to assess these features are likely to result in differing perceptions of the sustainability of one single firm.

Ability and willingness of observers to bear costs of information acquisition

Different observers of the sustainability of a business firm can be characterized by varying ability and willingness to bear the costs of the acquisition of sustainability-relevant information. At the one extreme, there are customers who base their purchasing decisions primarily on the price of a product, e.g. in the market for fast moving consumer goods. In such a case, the sustainability of a product or of the producing firm is likely to be of minor interest. For instance, information acquisition will be limited to a look at the packaging of a product, and recognition based on peripheral media and advertising information. Such a sustainability assessment is likely to be based exclusively on selected features of sustainability governance that are communicated through certification. Rating agencies for corporate sustainability most often create their ratings exclusively on the basis of voluntary reporting of business firms and are therefore likely to come to similar results. Consumers with a strong preference, in contrast, are willing to spend more time and money for the acquisition of information about a firm, as evidenced by extensive media and Internet search and reference to reports of specialized auditing bodies and NGOs. Accordingly, they might derive a more complete picture of corporate sustainability that comprises aspects of sustainability performance in addition to features of sustainability governance. On the other side of this spectrum are researchers who have relatively extensive monetary and temporal resources to conduct an in-depth assessment of the sustainability of a firm. In this case, they will also look at sustainability identity and at sustainability values. In all these cases, the assessments of corporate sustainability potentially lead to differing results.

Managers that aim to assess the current sustainability performance of a firm, and aim to increase it, are well advised to take into consideration all features of corporate sustainability discussed above in order to obtain a thorough understanding of the processes that contribute to the sustainability of their firm. Relying on just one of the sources of information discussed above is likely to limit their capacity to effectively improve sustainability performance. Due to the difficulties related to the assessment of the different features of corporate sustainability, it is impossible to obtain a complete picture of corporate sustainability. However, the awareness of the multiple antecedents of sustainability performance and of their intricate relations can help create more fine-grained approaches to sustainability assessment and improve the comprehensiveness of corporate sustainability assessments in order to set management objectives and compare actual developments with set objectives.

Firm size

A further decisive variable for the analysis of corporate sustainability is firm size. Firstly, firm size is crucial for the relative effects of sustainability-related features such as sustainability values and sustainability governance. This can be explained as follows: a positive effect of sustainability values and identity on sustainability performance is likely to decrease with increasing firm size. This is due to the fact that beyond a certain size of a firm sustainability values and identity alone are not capable to guarantee sufficient communication and coordination. Rather, with increasing firm size sustainability governance is becoming a necessary (if not sufficient) step towards high sustainability performance. In contrast, below a certain size, many forms of sustainability governance potentially are an undue burden (Fassin, 2008) and are dysfunctional with regard to organizational efficiency in general and with regard to sustainability performance in particular. Accordingly, a sustainability assessment of a small firm that is based on sustainability governance might be misleading, since below a certain firm size comprehensive sustainability governance might be unnecessary to attain sustainability performance or might even bind resources.

A second feature that has influence on the perception of corporate sustainability and varies with firm size is the propensity and ability of firms to display features that are commonly associated with corporate sustainability. As observed by Baumann-Pauly, Wickert, Spence and Scherer (2013) larger firms tend to have more capacities to report responsible behaviour, e.g. by means of non-financial reports. Further, it can be argued that certification and compliance with standards such as the ISO 14001 standard for environmental management are costly (Bansal and Bogner, 2002) and therefore only regarded by firms as sensible beyond a certain firm size. This means that larger firms are at an advantage with respect to displaying corporate sustainability.

Practical and theoretical implications

In practical respect, the presented insights can firstly serve as a basis for more elaborate methodologies for corporate sustainability assessment. On the basis of the described framework, managers can develop a more fine-grained methodology for the assessment of corporate sustainability and subsequently implement more effective measures for increasing sustainability performance. For instance, in order to obtain a more comprehensive corporate sustainability assessment, the analysis of formal features such as the environmental management system described in the introduction (which mainly represent sustainability governance), which are predominantly used in most current methodologies for the assessment of corporate sustainability might be complemented by an analysis of the different features that enable a thorough implementation of formal sustainability-related rules and guidelines.

In addition, the proposed framework provides managers who aim to improve corporate sustainability performance with a better understanding of the organizational preconditions of corporate sustainability performance. In the case of the environmental management system quoted in the introduction, it becomes clear that the existence of such a system alone is no guarantee for high sustainability performance. Nurturing the employees' commitment to sustainability might be an appropriate means to put the environmental management system into action. Conversely, in firms that currently lack a formalized approach to managing their sustainability, the implementation of such a system might help translate existing sustainability-related values into high sustainability performance, especially if the firms transcends a certain size. Understanding corporate sustainability performance as the result of the interplay of identity, values and governance makes it possible to align corporate strategies, practices and structures more effectively in order to increase sustainability performance. For instance, the framework illustrates that the hiring of employees with a strong commitment to corporate sustainability (contributing to a sustainability-related value system) might increase the effectiveness of sustainability governance. Furthermore, the nurturing of sustainability identity is conducive to the emergence of sustainability values and helps address the necessary limitations of formalized approaches to corporate sustainability (sustainability governance).

With respect to theory, this chapter implies several exciting avenues for further research regarding the interplay of different facets of corporate sustainability. Researchers might analyse how formal management systems interact with value systems and sustainability identity. For instance, identifying thresholds of firm size beyond which sustainability governance structures contribute to sustainability performance and better understanding how the effectiveness of such structures varies with firm size is of utmost importance for gaining a better grasp of the dynamics of corporate sustainability. Furthermore, exploring the factors – such as ownership structure, industry or geographical location – that lead to the different archetypes of corporate sustainability can help develop tailored toolkits for managing corporate sustainability.

References

Banerjee, S.B. (2007). Corporate Social Responsibility: The Good the Bad and the Ugly. Cheltenham: Edward Elgar.
Bansal, P. (2002). The corporate challenges of sustainable development. *Academy of Management Executive*, 16(2): 122–131.
Bansal, P. (2003). From issues to actions: The importance of individual concerns and organizational values in responding to natural environmental issues. *Organization Science*, 14(5): 510–527.
Bansal, P. and Bogner, W.C. (2002). Deciding on ISO 14001: Economics, institutions, and context. *Long Range Planning*, 35, 269–290.
Battilana, J. and Dorado, S. (2010). Building sustainable hybrid organizations: The case of commercial microfinance organizations. *Academy of Management Journal*, 53, 1419–1440.
Baumann-Pauly, D., Wickert, C., Spence, L.J. and Scherer, A.G. (2013). Organizing corporate social responsibility in small and large firms: Size matters. *Journal of Business Ethics*, 115, 693–705.
Beck, U. (1992). *Risk Society: Towards a New Modernity*. London: SAGE.
Berkhoud, T. and Rowlands, I.H. (2007). The voluntary adoption of green electricity by Ontario-based companies. *Organization & Environment*, 20: 281–303.
Bondy, C., Matten, D. and Moon, J. (2007). Codes of conduct as a tool for sustainable governance in MNCs. In S. Benn and D. Dunphy (eds), *Corporate Governance and Sustainability: Challenges for Theory and Practice*. London and New York: Routledge, pp. 165–186.
Bromley, P. and Powell, W.W. (2012). From smoke and mirrors to walking the talk: Decoupling in the contemporary world. *Academy of Management Annals*, 6(1): 483–530.
Brown, H. (2011). Global reporting initiative. In T. Hale and D. Held (eds), *Handbook of Transnational Governance: Institutions and innovations*. Cambridge: Polity Press, pp. 281–289.
Brown, A.D. and Humphreys, M. (2008). Organizational identity and place: A discursive exploration of hegemony and resistance. *Journal of Management Studies*, 43(2): 231–257.

China Labor Watch (2011). *Tragedies of globalization: The truth behind electronics sweatshops.* Retrieved August 9, 2011 from http://chinalaborwatch.org/pdf/20110712.pdf.

Churet, C. and Eccles, R.G. (2014). Integrated reporting, quality of management, and financial performance. *Journal of Applied Corporate Finance*, 26: 56–64.

Dutton, J.E. and Dukerich, J.M. (1991). Keeping an eye on the mirror: Image and identity in organizational adaptation. *Academy of Management Journal*, 34(3): 517–554.

Dyllick, T. and Hockerts, K. (2002). Beyond the business case for corporate sustainability. *Business Strategy and the Environment*, 11: 130–141.

Epstein, M.J. and Roy, M.-L. (2001). Sustainability in action: Identifying and measuring the key performance drivers. *Long Range Planning*, 34: 585–604.

Fassin, Y. (2008). SMEs and the fallacy of formalising CSR. *Business Ethics: A European Review*, 17(4): 364–378.

Gioia, D.A. and Thomas, J.B. (1996). Identity, image, and issue interpretation: Sensemaking during strategic change in academia. *Administrative Science Quarterly*, 41(3): 370–403.

Gladwin, T.N., Kennelly, J.J. and Krause, T.S. (1995). Shifting paradigms for sustainable development: Implications for management theory and research. *Academy of Management Review*, 20(4): 874–907.

Golden-Biddle, K. and Rao, H. (1997). Breaches in the boardroom: Organizational identity and conflicts of commitment in a nonprofit organization. *Organization Science*, 8(6): 593–611.

Hahn, T. and Figge, F. (2011). Beyond the bounded instrumentality in current corporate sustainability research: Toward an inclusive notion of profitability. *Journal of Business Ethics*, 104: 325–345.

Hahn, T., Figge, F., Pinske, J. and Preuss, L. (2010). Trade-offs in corporate sustainability: You can't have your cake and eat it. *Business Strategy and the Environment*, 19: 217–229.

Hart, S.L. and Milstein M.B. (2003). Creating sustainable value. *Academy of Management Executive*, 17(2): 56–67.

Hatch, M.J. and Mirvis, P.H. (2010). Positive design and appreciative construction: From sustainable development to sustainable value. *Advances in Appreciative Inquiry*, 3: 35–55.

Hawken, P. (1993). *The Ecology of Commerce.* New York: Harper Business.

Humble, J., Jackson, D. and Thomson, A. (1994). The strategic power of corporate values. *Long Range Planning*, 27(6): 28–42.

IPCC. (2014). *Climate change 2014: Synthesis report.* Retrieved August 8, 2017, from https://www.ipcc.ch/report/ar5/syr/.

Jackson, I. and Nelson, J. (2004). Values-based performance: Seven strategies for delivering profits with principles. Corporate Social Responsibility Initiative Working Paper No. 7. Cambridge, MA: John F. Kennedy School of Government, Harvard University.

Kahneman, D. and Frederick, S. (2002). Representativeness revisited: Attribute substitution in intuitive judgment. In T. Gilovich, D. Griffin and D. Kahneman (eds), *Heuristics and Biases: The Psychology of Intuitive Judgment.* New York: Cambridge University Press, pp. 49–81.

Klein, N. (2001). *No logo.* London: Flamingo.

Krut, R. and Gleckman, H. (1998). *ISO 14001: A Missed Opportunity for Sustainable Global Industrial Development.* London: Earthscan Publications.

Lange, D. and Washburn, L. (2012). Understanding attributions of corporate irresponsibility. *Academy of Management Review*, 37(2): 300–326.

Linnenluecke, M.K. and Griffiths, A. (2010). Corporate sustainability and organizational culture. *Journal of World Business*, 45: 357–366.

Margolis, S.D. and Hansen, C.D. (2002). A model for organizational identity: Exploring the path to sustainability during change. *Human Resource Development Review*, 1(3): 277–303.

Meadows, D.H., Meadows, D.L. and Randers, J. (2004). *The Limits to Growth: The 30-Year Update.* White River Junction, VT: Chelsea Green Publishing.

Morgan, G., Ryu, K. and Mirvis, P. (2009). Leading corporate citizenship: Governance, structure, systems. *Corporate Governance*, 9(1): 39–49.

Pettigrew, A.M. (1979). On studying organizational cultures. *Administrative Science Quarterly*, 24(4): 570–581.

Piketty, T. (2014). *Capital in the 21st Century*. Cambridge, MA: Balknap Press.

Reich, R. (2007). *Supercapitalism: The Transformation of Business, Democracy, and Everyday Life*. New York: Alfred A. Knopf.

Sambasivan, N. and Fei, N.Y. (2008). Evaluation of critical success factors of implementation of ISO 14001 using analytic hierarchy process (AHP): A case study from Malaysia. *Journal of Cleaner Production*, 16: 1424–1433.

Schneider, A. and Meins, E. (2012). Two dimensions of corporate sustainability assessment: Towards a general framework. *Business Strategy and the Environment*, 21(4): 211–222.

Shrivastava, P. (1995). Environmental technologies and competitive advantage. *Strategic Management Journal*, 16: 183–200.

Shrivastava, P. and Hart, S. (1995). Creating sustainable corporations. *Business Strategy and the Environment*, 4: 154–165.

Steffen, W., Richardson, K., Rockström, J., Cornell, S.E., Fetzer, I., Bennett, E.M. and Folke, C. (2015). Planetary boundaries: Guiding human development on a changing planet. *Science*, 347(6223): 1259855.

Stubbs, W. and Cocklin C. (2008). Conceptualizing a 'sustainability business model'. *Organization & Environment*, 21(2): 103–127.

UNCD (1992). *The Rio declaration on environment and development*. Retrieved December 21, 2011, from www.un.org/documents/ga/conf151/aconf15126-1annex1.htm.

Valente, M. (2012). Theorizing firm adoption of sustaincentrism. *Organization Studies*, 33(4): 563–591.

Van den Bergh, J.C.J.M. (2010). Externality or sustainability economics? *Ecological Economics*, 69, 2047–2052.

van Knippenberg, D., van Knippenberg, B., Monden, L. and de Lima, F. (2002). Organizational identification after a merger: A social identity perspective. *British Journal of Social Psychology*, 41: 233–252.

Van Marrewijk, M. (2003). Concepts and definitions of CSR and corporate sustainability: Between agency and communion. *Journal of Business Ethics*, 44(2–3): 95–105.

Whetten, D.A. (2006). Albert and Whetten revisited: Strengthening the concept of organizational identity. *Journal of Management Inquiry*, 15: 219–234.

WCED (World Commission on Environment and Development). (1987). *Our Common Future*. Oxford: University Press.

16 The value relevance of carbon disclosure strategies

A review of accounting research

Natalia Semenova

Introduction

Carbon disclosures have significantly increased over the last five years as a response to the negative impact of companies' carbon emissions on climate change and global warming. Climate change has taken a central stage in public and political discussions and has become an important imperative for companies, investors, regulators and other stakeholders. A core element of a company's sustainability strategy is concerned with carbon disclosures and carbon emissions. According to an investment industry report of S&P 500 Index US companies and MSCI World Index 1,600 companies, approximately two-thirds of large companies disclose their carbon emissions (Makower, 2016). Another industry report of MSCI World Index companies claims that companies' carbon emissions are expected between 2008 and 2050 to be the main driver of rising carbon costs and financial risks (Trucost, 2010). The estimates of industry research indicate that using the carbon price of US$85 per tonne of carbon emissions, the largest companies, in 2008, accounted for US$2.15 trillion of hidden carbon costs. Current regulatory and market-based mechanisms are the main drivers of disclosing carbon emissions and evaluating the financial risks and opportunities that companies face with respect to climate change. Companies' policies on carbon disclosures are often an initial step to the development of business models and management systems to implement carbon initiatives, such as investments in renewable energy alternatives, that reduce carbon emissions.

Whether carbon disclosures affect a company's market value is one of the most interesting questions in accounting research for several reasons (Moser and Martin, 2012). First, carbon emissions are largely external to financial accounts and are not included in annual financial reports. Carbon disclosure represents nonfinancial environmental information that is important for a more accurate valuation of a company's assets, liabilities and risks with implications for future cash flows. Second, at present, there are voluntary and mandatory carbon disclosure practices. The disclosure of carbon emissions is mandated by carbon regulations, such as the European Union (EU) Carbon Emission Trading Scheme (ETS) and the US Environmental Protection Agency (EPA). Voluntary carbon disclosures have expanded rapidly across companies based on the Carbon Disclosure Project (CDP) reporting framework initiated by institutional investors. Third, carbon disclosures have two routes by which they can affect a company's market value (Clarkson et al., 2013). The valuation impact of carbon °disclosures can arise from financial performance prediction and risk profile effects. Disclosure of carbon emissions reveal information that can be used to assess a company's future liabilities and costs to comply with carbon regulations. Accordingly, carbon disclosures convey information about future financial risks that affect cost of capital and future cash flows. Companies implementing carbon emission reduction initiatives can benefit from value chain cost savings, such as energy reduction, waste minimization, travel substitution and lower fuel consumption. A positive effect on revenue streams can come from product and process innovations related to clean technologies and positive perceptions of employees, customers, suppliers and other stakeholders. Accordingly, carbon disclosures provide forward-looking information that facilitates financial performance prediction.

There is ample accounting research on the association between environmental disclosures and a company's market value. Existing accounting studies empirically examine the valuation implications of comprehensive, broad-based corporate social responsibility (CSR) disclosures and environmental disclosures, which include carbon emission as a disclosure item. The studies investigate the relationship between a company's environmental performance and financial performance. The empirical evidence remains inconclusive, and prior accounting literature suggests that voluntary CSR and environmental disclosures can be incomplete and sparse from a stakeholder perspective (Laine, 2005; Liesen et al., 2015) and environmental metrics have common, albeit distinct dimensions of environmental performance and environmental risk that on aggregate do not converge (Semenova and Hassel, 2015).

Given the breadth of related accounting research, the approach of this chapter is to focus on a selection of accounting studies based on the specific context that considers the impact of carbon disclosures and carbon emissions on a company's market value that captures both mandatory and voluntary practices of disclosing carbon information. Historically, accounting literature investigates the capital market value effects of a company's carbon liabilities with regards to mandatory reporting regulations aimed at limiting carbon emissions (Hughes, 2000; Chapple et al., 2013; Clarkson et al., 2015). In recent years, the focus has expanded to examine voluntary carbon disclosures and attention is drawn to the integration of voluntary carbon information and a company's carbon risks and opportunities into company valuations by investors (Clarkson et al., 2013). The chapter explains additional factors that investors can consider when assessing carbon disclosures and a company's effects of climate change risk. The value relevance studies are commonly conducted by using the modified version of the Ohlson (1995) valuation model. A number of accounting studies have employed the cost of capital model, the financial performance model and the balance sheet model. The review in this chapter is limited to valuation models in accounting literature with a focus on carbon disclosures only. Studies using more holistic environmental risk and performance measures described in previous accounting research (Semenova and Hassel, 2015) are not included.

The remainder of the chapter is organized as follows. The next section discusses climate change risk and climate change initiatives. Next, the chapter introduces the method of conducting the literature review. This section is followed by a section that examines mandatory and voluntary carbon disclosures in relation to voluntary disclosure theory, stakeholder theory and legitimacy theory. The chapter then shows the empirical results of the effects on a company's market value of carbon disclosures and carbon performance metrics. The chapter concludes with a summary and a discussion of implications for companies and stakeholders.

Climate change risk

Climate change risk represents, according to prior research (Liesen et al., 2015), one of the greatest challenges for society. Concerns about the negative impacts of companies' emissions on climate change risk have received increased attention by governments, regulators, investors and other stakeholders. A major departure for the regulatory controls of carbon emissions was by the US EPA in the late 1980s followed by the introduction of global environmental initiatives to manage and reduce carbon emissions. Environmental initiatives include the Kyoto Protocol, the EU ETS, the CDP and the Greenhouse Gas (GHG) Emissions Protocol.

Climate-change scientists argue that increases in temperature are caused by increasing concentrations of carbon dioxide, methane and other gases in the atmosphere and predict that global warming can result in more frequent extreme weather events (e.g. intense precipitation, increased hurricane winds and drought), food and water scarcity and displacing people (Black Bear Environmental Assets, 2016). Considerable scientific evidence supports the argument that carbon emissions (carbon dioxide, CO_2) are a major contributing factor to climate change and global warming. In 2014, carbon emissions accounted for about 80.9 per cent of all US greenhouse gas emissions from human activities (United States Environmental Protection Agency, 2016). Approximately 78 per cent of carbon emissions, since 1970, have come from industrial production and the combustion of fossil fuels. Companies remain the highest emitters of carbon emissions and have, consequently, the highest impact on climate change.

As of June 2003, 84 countries ratified the Kyoto Protocol linked to the United Nations Framework Convention on Climate Change (UNFCCC), including the EU, Japan and Canada (Freedman and Jaggi, 2005). In this way the countries made a commitment to limit global warming. The Kyoto Protocol entered into force 2005 and represented the internationally binding agreement that set carbon emission reduction targets. The Kyoto Protocol obliged countries to enact national regulations incorporating the Protocol's provisions on disclosures related to greenhouse gases, i.e. carbon dioxide, methane and nitrous oxides. The Kyoto Protocol stated that greenhouse gases needed to be reduced in order to control their global warming effect. As a result, governments have developed national carbon policies and regulations.

The consequence of binding legal commitments of the Kyoto Protocol was that the US did not ratify the agreement and some countries did not set targets beyond 2012 (Center for Climate and Energy Solutions, 2015). The countries of the UNFCCC have established a parallel framework with political commitments to climate change which have attracted wider participation at the annual conferences of the parties (COP). In 2015, the United Nations (UN) climate change conference in Paris, which is also known as COP 21, resulted in the agreement on the new common framework that requires 195 countries, including China and the US, to report regularly on their emissions and implementation efforts and undergo international review (Center for Climate and Energy Solutions, 2015). In order to come into force, the Paris Agreement (COP 21) has to be ratified by at least 55 countries accounting for at least 55 per cent of global carbon emissions in their national parliaments; the ratification processes started in April 2016.

The regulatory mechanism creates major influence on companies to reduce carbon impacts (Liesen et al., 2015). For example, a consequence of the Toxic Release Inventory (TRI) disclosure under the Emergency Planning and Community Right to Know Act was the reduction of toxic emissions in the US (Matsumura et al., 2014). Aside from carbon regulatory compliance, the Cambridge Institute for Sustainability Leadership argues that up to half of the carbon emission reduction can be achieved through market-based mechanisms (Nathan, 2016). By incorporating a company's carbon performance into investment decisions, the capital markets influence on a company's decisions regarding the allocation of resources to carbon emission reduction initiatives. Regulatory and market-based mechanisms rely on the practice that measuring and disclosing carbon emissions are the prerequisite of carbon emission reductions (Matsumura et al., 2014).

Method

This chapter surveys current empirical accounting research on the market valuation of carbon disclosures and carbon emissions. The survey of the literature adopts the method of narrative reviews, also known as narrative overviews. The method of narrative reviews has been used in prior accounting studies that describe and summarize the literature on the financial disclosure in a capital markets setting (Healy and Palepu, 2001), the cost of equity implications of financial disclosures (Artiach and Clarkson, 2011), the market price implications of a company's environmental performance (Clarkson, 2012), and corporate social responsibility research in accounting (Huang and Watson, 2015). Narrative reviews are defined as summaries of prior studies that attempt to make sense of past findings verbally or conceptually (Orlitzky et al., 2003) and report current knowledge on a topic in a condensed format (Green et al., 2006). Prior narrative reviews of accounting literature claim that they do not aim to provide comprehensive reviews. Rather, the narrative reviews present 'the underlying message which derives from the literature' (Clarkson, 2012, p. 11), 'an appreciation of the design and implementation decisions' (Artiach and Clarkson, 2011, p. 3), or highlight important issues (Hartmann et al., 2013). This review is unbiased in terms of including and analysing its own publications. In addition, the review draws on the traditional accounting theoretical framework of value relevance research. Value relevance research assesses whether financial and nonfinancial performance variables provide information that investors use for company valuation (Bart et al., 2001). In applying the theoretical framework of value relevance research to carbon disclosures and carbon emissions, Matsumura et al. (2014, p. 701) claim that 'if capital market believes that carbon emissions are relevant for valuation and are measured reliably enough, carbon emission levels will have significant market-value implications'. The value relevance literature focuses on the empirical association between companies' market values and variables of financial and nonfinancial information.

The review selects the studies published in top, peer-reviewed accounting journals according to the journal quality lists, such as the Australian Business Dean Councils (ABDC) Journal Quality List and the Association of Business Schools (ABS) Journal Quality List. The review focuses on 23 accounting journals that receive both the A★ and A journal ratings of ABDC and the 4 and 3 journal ratings of ABS. Appendix 1 lists the accounting journals. Computer searches of OneSearch are conducted using the area-specific keyword search 'carbon', 'emissions' and 'environmental disclosure'. The OneSearch tool consists of the databases of articles, for example, the Science Direct and the Business Source Premier. In total, the review retrieved 273 accounting journal articles on 12 and 13 January 2017. The review then concentrates on the research papers that fit the following selection criteria. First, the studies examine the market value implications of carbon disclosures and carbon emissions. Carbon disclosures are mandatory and voluntary practices of providing carbon information to investors and other stakeholders. Carbon emissions quantify the impact of a company on climate change and capture company-specific strategies for managing carbon-related risks. Carbon performance is represented by a direct metric of total carbon emissions and other carbon metrics, for example, the proportion of carbon emissions that are not covered by carbon allowances under the EU ETS (Clarkson et al., 2015) and carbon intensity that is total carbon emissions divided by sales revenue (Chapple et al., 2013). Second, the studies use the existing valuation models of associations between a company's market value and carbon disclosures, such as the modified version of the Ohlson (1995) model, the cost of capital model, the financial performance model and the balance sheet model. The studies apply empirical methods to estimate the parameters of the models. Third, the articles were published between 2000 and 2016.

The review identifies six original articles that fit these criteria. The selected articles are published in The Accounting Review, European Accounting Review, Journal of Accounting and Public Policy, and Abacus: A Journal of Accounting, Finance and Business Studies. Table 16.1 presents six studies in the alphabetical order. Of the 23 accounting journals examined, articles on environmental disclosures are frequently published in the following journals: Accounting, Auditing and Accountability Journal; Critical Perspectives on Accounting; Accounting, Organizations and Society; British Accounting Review, and Journal of Accounting and Public Policy. This review focuses on a specific setting of the valuation relevance of carbon disclosures and carbon performance and examines six core articles published in top accounting journals as well as complementary, relevant studies to provide discussions and illustrations.

Table 16.1 Sample of accounting studies on the value relevance of carbon disclosures

Article	Type of carbon disclosures
Chapple, L., Clarkson, P. and Gold, D. (2013). The cost of carbon: Capital market effects of the proposed emission trading scheme (ETS). *Abacus*, 49 (1): 1–33.	Mandatory disclosures
Clarkson, P., Fang, X., Li, Y. and Richardson, G. (2013). The relevance of environmental disclosures: Are such disclosures incrementally informative? *Journal of Accounting and Public Policy*, 32: 410–431.	Mandatory disclosures
Clarkson, P., Li, Y., Pinnuck, M. and Richardson, G. (2015). Valuation relevance of greenhouse gas emissions under the European Union Carbon Emission Trading Scheme? *European Accounting Review*, 24(3): 551–580.	Mandatory disclosures
Hughes, K.E. (2000). The value relevance of nonfinancial measures of air pollution in the electric utility industry. *The Accounting Review*, 75(2): 209–218.	Mandatory disclosures
Johnston, D., Sefcik, S. and Soderstrom, N. (2008). The value relevance of greenhouse gas emissions allowances: An exploratory study in the related United States SO2 market. *European Accounting Review*, 17(4): 747–764.	Mandatory disclosures
Matsumura, E., Prakash, R. and Vera-Munoz, S. (2014). Firm-value effects of carbon emissions and carbon disclosure. *The Accounting Review*, 89(2): 695–724.	Voluntary disclosures

There are ten complementary empirical articles used in the main analysis of mandatory and voluntary carbon disclosures. Eight accounting studies are identified by the computer searches of OneSearch using the abovementioned keywords, published in the highest rated accounting journals, and included based on their relevance to and/or citations in the core articles of the review. These articles are Clarkson et al. (2008), Patten (2002), Clarkson et al. (2004), Liesen et al. (2015), Ioannou et al. (2016), Freedman and Jaggi (2005), Al-Tuwaijri et al. (2004), and Clarkson et al. (2011). The empirical article by Luo et al. (2012), which is published in The Journal of International Financial Management & Accounting (the B rating of ABDC and the 2 rating of ABS), and the empirical study by Reid and Toffel (2009), which is published in Strategic Management Journal (the A*rating of ABDC and the 4 rating of ABS), are selected based on their relevance to the review.

The review relies on statements in the articles to summarize whether the authors view their results as providing empirical evidence on the value relevance of carbon disclosures and carbon emissions. The quotes of three articles are provided as illustrative examples of the statements made in the selected studies. First, Matsumura et al. (2014, p. 696) conclude that 'The results are consistent with the argument that capital markets impound both carbon emissions and the act of voluntary disclosure of this information in firm valuations.' Matsumura et al. (2014, p. 705) document that 'We examine the firm–value effect of carbon emissions using the balance sheet valuation model commonly used in prior research.' Second, Clarkson et al. (2015, p. 551) state that 'The results show that firm's carbon allowances are not associated with firm valuation but the allocation shortfalls are negatively associated.' In addition, Clarkson et al. (2015, p. 570) conclude that 'we find strong and consistent support for the preposition that the carbon emissions data are value relevant'. Clarkson et al. (2015, p. 553) indicate that 'To conduct our study, we employ a modified version of the Ohlson (1995) valuation model to explore the value relevance of the carbon emissions data.' Finally, Hughes (2000, p. 211) argues that 'The study's results indicate that the nonfinancial pollution proxy is value-relevant for the high-polluting utilities targeted by Phase One of the 1990 CAAA.' The author (Hughes, 2000, p. 214) states that 'The valuation model I use relies on the accounting identity in which the market value of equity equals the market value of a firm's assets minus its liabilities.'

Carbon disclosures

Mandatory carbon disclosures

Mandatory carbon disclosures have been of interest and focus in accounting research. A cap-and-trade system is considered to be an effective and flexible mandatory mechanism for reporting and reducing carbon emissions. In contrast to command-and-control regulations that specify the processes that companies should use in order to comply with them, the cap-and-trade system implies that companies invest in carbon reduction processes and products if they do not exceed the price of carbon allowances. A carbon allowance (permit) is equivalent to one metric tonne of carbon emissions. A company must buy carbon allowances if its actual carbon emissions exceed a carbon emission limit (cap) set for an entire industry. The cap-and-trade system offers a company a choice of making investments in clean, low-carbon technologies and projects to reduce carbon emissions or purchasing emission allowances on the market (Johnston et al., 2008).

The EU ETS, which came into force in January 2005, mandates carbon emissions trading for companies operating in 31 countries in Europe. The EU ETS is the largest multi-country ETS in the world, and the implementation of EU ETS consists of three phases, such as Phase 1 covering the period from 2005 to 2007, Phase 2 from 2008 to 2012, and Phase 3 from 2013 to 2020 (Clarkson et al., 2015). The cap-and-trade system implies the use of free allocation of allowances in Phase 1 and auctions in Phases 2 and 3. In Phase 2, the non-compliance penalty has increased from €40 to €100 per tonne of carbon emissions. The EU ETS aims to achieve a 57 per cent of allocation of allowances via auctions during Phase 3 (2013–2020), while the remaining allowances are available for free allocation (Climate Action, 2017). According to the EU ETS, emission limits are set for companies operating in carbon-intensive industries and will be decreased over time to comply with the UN Protocols (Climate Action, 2017). For example, in 2013, manufacturing industry received 80 per cent of emission allowances for free, and free allocation decreases gradually each year to 30 per cent in 2020. The power sector has not received free allowances since 2013. Emission allowances are allocated to individual installations (e.g. power stations and industrial plants). Companies comply with the EU ETS by disclosing to the European Commission annual actual emissions as well as received or purchased carbon allowances that must match the actual emissions. The emissions reports are verified by an accredited verifier by 31 March of the following year and made publicly available.

As shown in Table 16.2, the cap-and-trade system exists in Australia and the US. In 2008, the government of Australia announced the introduction of a national ETS. However, the proposed regulation has been delayed several times and is expected to commence in 2016. The government aims to allocate 25 per cent of free allowances and compensate companies in emission intensive industries (Chapple et al., 2013). In the US, the ETS was introduced in 1990 with the passage of Title IV of the 1990 Clean Air Act Amendments (CAAA; Johnston et al., 2008). The US ETS aimed to reduce sulphur dioxide (SO_2) emissions to 50 per cent of 1980 levels and impacted the most emission intensive companies in the electric utility industry. The US ETS is found to be a more

Table 16.2 Mandatory and voluntary carbon disclosures used in empirical accounting research

Carbon reporting framework	Period	Author (year)
Mandatory carbon disclosures		
European Union Emission Trading Scheme	2006–2009	Clarkson et al. (2015)
Australian Emission Trading Scheme	2006–2009	Chapple et al. (2013)
US SO_2 Emission Allowance Program	1995–2000; 1986–1993	Johnston et al. (2008) Hughes (2000)
US Environmental Protection Agency Toxic Release Inventory database	2003, 2006; 1990; 1989–2000; 1990–2003; 1989–2000	Clarkson et al. (2013) Clarkson et al. (2008) Clarkson et al. (2004) Clarkson et al. (2011) Patten (2002)
Voluntary carbon disclosures		
Carbon disclosure project	2006–2008; 2005–2009; 2009; 2011–2013	Matsumura et al. (2014) Liesen et al. (2015) Luo et al. (2012) Ioannou et al. (2016)

cost-effective system in reducing SO_2 emissions (Johnston et al., 2008). As Johnston et al. (2008, p. 751) state, 'the program has resulted in estimated cost savings of upwards of $1 billion annually, when compared with estimated compliance costs under more traditional command-and-control regulatory schemes'.

Past mandatory carbon disclosures, which are examined in accounting studies, are toxic releases mandated by the governmental agency, the EPA in the US. The reporting mechanism affects companies in five carbon-intensive industries, such as pulp and paper, chemicals, oil and gas, metals and mining and utilities. Toxic Release Inventory (TRI) emission disclosures focus on 600 entities and are available to the public. The EPA annually report total TRI emissions at the plant level with a two-year lag (Clarkson et al., 2013).

Mandatory carbon reporting mechanisms have consequences for company valuation. The allocation of carbon emissions shows that companies with below-average carbon performance (high carbon emissions) incur carbon costs by purchasing emission allowances or carbon costs by making investments in carbon hedging initiatives. Accordingly, companies with below-average carbon performance (high carbon emissions) incur a carbon liability and costs when complying with carbon regulations. Excess or surplus emission allowances, i.e. companies with above-average carbon performance (low carbon emissions), can account for an asset value. In the US ETS, excess emission allowances can be inventoried and used in the future or sold to other companies (Johnston et al., 2008). Finally, mandatory carbon disclosures are argued to be used in assessing how well companies manage their exposure to carbon risk. The carbon risk reflects existing carbon regulation, uncertainty surrounding new regulatory compliance, uncertainty surrounding physical climate parameters, such as severe weather conditions, and potential reputational implications (Chapple et al., 2013; Matsumura et al., 2014). To illustrate, Matsumura et al. (2014, p. 699) document that 'Standard & Poor's downgraded the debt of a large UK power-generating company, Drax, owing in part to future business risks from new European emission trading rules that are expected to increase carbon costs'.

Mandatory carbon disclosures are summarized:

- developed and controlled by the government;
- focused on carbon-intensive industries;
- reported regularly;
- reported at the plant/installation level;
- influenced company value through assets, liabilities/costs and risk;
- publicly available data;
- associated with different country-specific requirements;
- provided consistent disclosures across companies and time.

Voluntary carbon disclosures

Voluntary carbon disclosures have been used to provide carbon information to investors and external stakeholders and received interest in accounting research. The most prominent is the Carbon Disclosure Project (CDP) reporting framework. CDP, which was launched in 2000, is an international collaboration of institutional investors. The goal of CDP is to create a long-term relationship between investors and companies regarding the implications of climate change risk for shareholder value. CDP comprises large investment funds such as Merrill Lynch and Goldman Sachs, state pension funds, banks and insurance companies (Reid and Toffel, 2009). CDP facilitates the collection of carbon information for institutional investors and holds the largest repository of carbon emission information. The CDP disclosures are intended to complement annual financial reports and provide relevant information for assessment of companies' financial risks and opportunities related to climate change risk. On behalf of institutional investors, CDP asks the world's largest companies to respond to a questionnaire and provide information on carbon emissions, energy and trading. The CDP report has four sections (Stanny and Ely, 2008). The first includes the companies' commercial risks and opportunities from climate change. The second consists of information on the companies' current and anticipated future responses to the risks and opportunities associated with climate change. The third provides information on the companies' accounting for carbon emissions. The fourth section presents the responsible person for climate change issues in the company. CDP has good response rates which indicate that many companies use CDP as a mechanism for carbon disclosure. For the FT 500 companies, the response rate has increased from 47 per cent to 77 per cent from 2000 to 2005 (Stanny and Ely, 2008). According to the global CDP report 2015, companies from 51 countries have now been included representing 55 per cent of the market capitalization of listed companies globally (Carbon Disclosure Project, 2015). CDP provides companies with different options related to making carbon data public (Reid and Toffel, 2009). There are sets of companies that allow their carbon information to be publicly available, allow their carbon information to be available only to institutional investors who are signatories of CDP or provide partial carbon information which is generally available at the company's website without answering the CDP questionnaire (Matsumura et al., 2014). CDP annually publishes a summary report of aggregated responses of companies.

The argument made in accounting literature is that voluntary carbon disclosures have a signalling role (Clarkson et al., 2013). For example, Matsumura et al. (2014, p. 703) state that 'a firm that discloses its carbon emissions signals its ability to measure its emissions, a prerequisite for managing them'. Companies with good carbon performance signal through voluntary carbon disclosures to the capital market their position and initiatives on climate change risk, which cannot be easily mimicked by companies with poor carbon performance. According to accounting research, carbon emission is a hard and objective indicator of a company's environmental performance. Voluntary carbon disclosures can signal a company's environmental performance in the areas such as environmental management systems, environmental vision and strategy, environmental management of processes and products, which can result in increasing future financial performance and cash flows. Additionally, accounting literature suggests that voluntary carbon disclosures reduce information asymmetry on a company's carbon performance between the management and owners resulting in lower cost of capital. In relation to voluntary carbon disclosures, Matsumura et al. (2014, p. 702) claim that 'If firms do not disclose carbon emissions, then investors will not only impute the firms' carbon emissions, but also likely treat non-disclosure as an adverse signal and penalize non-disclosing firms.'

Voluntary carbon disclosures are summarized:

- developed by institutional investors and other stakeholders;
- reported on company level;

- focused on all industries;
- lacked consistency and comparability across companies and over time;
- influenced company value through impact on financial performance and/or risk profile;
- offered option to not make carbon information public.

Stakeholder theory, legitimacy theory and voluntary disclosure theory

Voluntary disclosure theory, stakeholder theory and legitimacy theory provide an explanation for motivations for issuing voluntary carbon disclosures. Voluntary disclosure theory suggests that companies use carbon disclosures to signal their good carbon performance and their position of commitment to climate change and, consequently, to distinguish themselves from companies with poor carbon performance. Carbon disclosures assist in avoiding an adverse selection problem by providing carbon information, which is not directly observable to investors and other external stakeholders, to ensure that stakeholders are aware of a company's carbon performance. Voluntary disclosure theory further argues that companies with good carbon performance are more likely to issue voluntary carbon disclosures because it is less costly for companies with good carbon performance and they have the resources more than one with poor carbon performance. Accounting literature supports voluntary disclosure theory and finds that companies with good environmental initiatives/performance are more likely to disclose their carbon information (Matsumura et al., 2014; Clarkson et al., 2008). For example, Clarkson et al. (2008, p. 325) conclude that 'superior environmental performers are more forthcoming in truly discretionary disclosure channels as predicted by economics-based voluntary disclosure theories'.

Stakeholder theory and legitimacy theory claim that carbon disclosures are a function of political, social and stakeholder pressures that companies face. Voluntary carbon disclosures that are provided in response to increased social and political demands can be used by companies, especially in emission intensive industries with poor carbon performance, to change stakeholder perceptions about their actual performance. Companies can use carbon disclosures to maintain legitimacy with the social environment and reduce potential regulatory intervention. Stakeholder and legitimacy theories assume that companies attempt to select positive carbon initiatives and promote the impression of being a 'good' corporate citizen which can result in misleading and biased disclosures. For instance, prior accounting research finds that companies with unfavourable media coverage are more likely to make not easily verifiable claims in relation to their environmental initiatives and commitment (Clarkson et al., 2008, p. 309). Accounting studies support the arguments of stakeholder theory and legitimacy theory by showing that stakeholder pressure determines the company's decision to provide voluntary carbon disclosures (Liesen et al., 2015). However, stakeholder pressures have little impact on the completeness and consistency of carbon disclosures. Voluntary disclosure mechanisms allow companies flexibility to respond in an incomplete way and use carbon disclosures to enhance their legitimacy. Table 16.3 summarizes the main results of emissions-related accounting studies adopting voluntary disclosure theory, stakeholder theory and legitimacy theory.

Table 16.3 Theories for issuing voluntary carbon disclosures

Voluntary/signalling disclosure theory	• Positive relationship between the choice to disclose carbon emissions to CDP and market value (Matsumura et al., 2014). • Positive relationship between high scores on environmental initiatives and the choice to disclose carbon emissions (Matsumura et al., 2014). • Positive relationships between environmental performance on TRI emissions and voluntary environmental disclosures in environmental and CSR reports (Clarkson et al., 2008). • Positive relationship between environmental performance and pollution-related environmental disclosure score (Al-Tuwaijri et al., 2004).
Stakeholder theory and legitimacy theory	• Positive relationship between stakeholder pressures (the state, NGOs and the public) and the choice to disclose carbon information to CDP (Liesen et al., 2015). • Positive relationship between shareholder resolutions on environmental issues that are filed against companies and the choice to disclose carbon information to CDP (Reid and Toffel, 2009). • Positive relationship between threats of state regulation and the choice to disclose carbon information to CDP (Reid and Toffel, 2009). • Positive relationship between carbon disclosure index and the ratification of the Kyoto Protocol (Freedman and Jaggi, 2005). • Positive relationship between carbon disclosure and regulatory/institutional pressure in terms of legal investor protection mechanism and transparent financial reporting practice (Luo et al., 2012).

Value relevance of carbon disclosures

Value relevance approach

The value relevance model based accounting research uses a theoretical framework for assessing whether carbon disclosures and carbon emissions provide information that investors use for company valuation. Based on value relevance research, carbon disclosures have market value implications if capital market participants expect that a company's carbon performance has implications for future cash flows and, consequently, relevance for company valuation. There are several indications for that interest in climate change risk and companies' carbon impacts have increased among institutional investors. The largest investment banks, such as Citigroup, JPMorgonChase and Morgan Stanley, have issued restrictive guidelines for new investments associated with high climate change risk (Kolk et al., 2008). Social and responsible investing (SRI), which seeks to incorporate environmental, social and governance matters into investment decisions, has attracted increasing attention and grown substantially with annual growth rates between 14 per cent and 57 per cent for main SRI strategies in Europe (Eurosif, 2016). The Principles for Responsible Investments (2015) lists 1,387 signatories with over 59 trillion in assets under management. Financial analysts integrate the financial implications of companies' carbon emissions into their investment recommendations (Matsumura et al., 2014). Climate-change related shareholder resolutions grew between 2004 and 2009

(Matsumura et al., 2014). National financial authorities increase awareness in the financial sector on long-run effects of climate change risks that might increase over time (Swedish Financial Supervisory Authority, 2016).

The valuation relevance of carbon disclosures has been examined using several empirical approaches such as the Ohlson (1995) valuation model, the balance sheet valuation model, the cost of capital model and the financial performance model as outlined in Appendix 2 to this chapter. Research in accounting has provided strong, consistent and robust evidence that the capital market penalizes high carbon emissions that are provided in either mandatory or voluntary carbon disclosures. In the EU ETS, carbon emissions decrease a company's market value, which means that the market assesses a valuation penalty relative to a company's total carbon emissions. It has been found that 'the magnitude of this penalty would appear to be €39 per tonne of carbon emission' (Clarkson et al., 2015, p. 570). Voluntarily disclosed levels of carbon emissions decrease a company's market value for S&P 500 companies that provide carbon information to CDP (Matsumura et al., 2014). Matsumura et al. (2014, p. 698) document that 'on average, for each additional thousand metric tons of carbon emissions for our sample of S&P 500 firms, firm value decreases by $212,000'.

Based on the Ohlson (1995) valuation model, accounting studies investigating the value relevance of carbon disclosures mandated by the cap-and-trade regulations find that mandatory carbon disclosures under the EU ETS are value relevant (Clarkson et al., 2015). The capital market does not value companies' carbon allowances on aggregate and values differently the components of companies' carbon allowances. The capital market penalizes the portion of carbon emissions which is not covered by free carbon allowances and does not value the portion of carbon emissions that is offset by free carbon allowances. Companies with carbon emissions that exceed their carbon allowances have 'a valuation penalty of €75 per tonne of uncovered emissions, a figure which represents 3.15 per cent of market capitalization, on average' (Clarkson et al., 2015, p. 570). Specifically, the valuation penalty was €25 per tonne of uncovered emissions in 2006 and increased to '€50 per tonne in 2007, and finally €98 and €94 per tonne in 2008 and 2009, respectively' (Clarkson et al., 2015, p. 571). Investors did not value surplus carbon allowances or free carbon allowances that exceed carbon emissions under the EU ETS as an asset. The study explains the result by two factors. First, surplus emission allowances cannot be carried over from Phase 1 to Phase 2 in the EU ETS. Second, there was an oversupply of emission allowances in Phase 1 which reduced the carbon price to the value of zero. These factors are expected to contribute to the market expectations about the value relevance of surplus emission allowances.

In contrast, accounting research focusing on the market value relevance of surplus emission allowances under the US ETS shows that excess emission allowances have an asset value and a real option value for publicly traded electric utilities (Johnston et al., 2008). The capital market values a company's holding of SO_2 emission allowances above a company's current needs. Johnston et al. (2008, p. 749) conclude that 'it appears the market incorporates at least the asset value of banked emissions permits into a firm's market value of equity'. Emission allowances have the real option value by allowing the company to defer carbon investments and have more control over the method of reducing emissions. According to Johnston et al. (2008, p. 747), there is 'weak evidence consistent with the market assigning a real option value to the allowance banks'. Finally, the capital market penalizes high–carbon–intensive publicly traded Australian companies affected by the proposed ETS. High–carbon–intensive and more risky companies (top 20 per cent companies based on carbon intensity) have a penalty of between 7 per cent and 10 per cent of market value relative to low-carbon-intensive companies (Chapple et al., 2013). In addition, the evidence of Chapple et al. (2013, pp. 1–2) implies that 'a future carbon permit price of between AUD$17 per tonne and AUD$26 per tonne of carbon dioxide emitted'. To sum, research in accounting provides strong evidence for the valuation implications of mandatory carbon disclosures under the cap-and-trade regulatory mechanism by adopting the Ohlson (1995) valuation model.

Based on the balance sheet valuation model, voluntary disclosed carbon emissions to CDP have a negative association with a company's market value for S&P 500 companies (Matsumura et al., 2014). Moreover, companies that choose to voluntarily disclose carbon information to CDP have higher market values than their non-disclosing counterparts. By modelling the effect of the act of voluntary disclosing carbon information and the effect of carbon emissions on the market value of a company, the results of Matsumura et al. (2014, p. 698) indicate that 'the median value of firms that disclose their carbon emissions is about $2.3 billion higher than that of their non-disclosing counterparts'. The results imply that the levels of carbon emissions decrease market value of all companies regardless of whether they disclose carbon emissions and companies that do not disclose carbon emissions face a further decrease in their market value. Accounting research asserts that carbon disclosures reveal carbon liability information which results in discounting market value of a company. The studies also use the balance sheet valuation model, which explicitly includes companies' liabilities, to show the value relevance of SO_2 emissions for electric utilities regulated by Phase 1 of the 1990 CAAA in the US (Hughes, 2000). On average, unbooked carbon liabilities decrease the market value of electric utilities companies by 16.3 per cent in addition to disclosed liabilities. Based on the set of empirical investigations of the value relevance of emissions, Hughes (2000, p. 225) concludes that 'the value relevance of the nonfinancial pollution measure is indeed attributable to its role as an indicator for the market's estimation of unbooked environmental liabilities'. Table 16.4 summarizes the main accounting studies on the value relevance of carbon disclosures.

Extensions of the value relevance approach

The impact of carbon disclosure on market value can arise from the impact of a company's emission performance on future financial performance and/or risk profile (Matsumura et al., 2014; Clarkson et al., 2015). Using the TRI data mandatory reported to the US EPA, accounting researchers develop a proxy for a company's relative emission performance (Clarkson et al., 2013). Disclosed emissions are aggregated at company level, normalized by sales and ranked within each industry. The ranks are used as proxy for a company's relative emission performance within its industry.

The first component of a company's market value, which is the risk profile, is examined using the cost of capital model. Accounting studies expect that carbon disclosures reveal information that can be used to assess future liabilities and costs to comply with carbon regulations or the long-time carbon costs resulting from deferred investments in carbon emission reduction initiatives (e.g. acquiring or developing less carbon-intensive technologies and processes). Emission performance provides value-relevant information and has a positive relationship with market value for US companies in highly polluting industries using the Ohlson (1995) valuation model. By focusing on the first component

Table 16.4 Result of accounting literature review

Author (year)	Sample and period	Environmental disclosure	Environmental performance	Valuation model	Relationship
Matsumura et al., 2014	S&P 500 US companies, 2006–2008	Voluntary, CDP	1. Carbon emissions 2. Choice to disclose carbon emissions	1. Balance sheet model 2. Ohlson model	1. Negative 2. Positive
Clarkson et al., 2015	221 companies, 21 countries 2006–2009	Mandatory, EU ETS	1. Allocated carbon allowances 2. Uncovered carbon emissions 3. Covered carbon emissions 4. Surplus allowances	Ohlson model	1. Insignificant 2. Negative 3. Insignificant 4. Insignificant
Clarkson et al., 2013	92 US companies in 2003 and 103 US companies in 2006	Mandatory, US EPA TRI	Relative environmental performance	1. Ohlson model 2. Cost of capital model 3. Financial performance model	1. Negative 2. Positive 3. Negative
Johnston et al., 2008	71 US companies, 1995–2000	Mandatory, US ETS	Surplus SO2 emission allowances	Ohlson model	Positive
Chapple et al., 2013	58 Australian listed companies, 2007	Proposed ETS, Australia	Carbon intensity, carbon emissions / sales	Ohlson model	Negative
Hughes, 2000	44 Phase One companies, 46 Non-Phase companies, Utility industry, 1986–1993	Phase One of the US 1990 CAAA	Average percentage of SO2 emissions per year relative to total (airborne) emissions	Balance sheet model Ohlson model	Negative Extensions of the value relevance approach

of a company's market value, the cost of capital model shows that the cost of capital has a positive association with emission performance. The result implies that carbon disclosures are value-relevant information for assessing a company's financial risk. Companies with good emission performance and low relative carbon emissions decrease their cost of capital. For example, Clarkson et al. (2013, p. 424) state that 'a firm that moves from being the worst in the industry to being the best (i.e., a 100 percentile rank change) can decrease its cost of capital by 2.2%'.

The second component of a company's market value, which is future financial performance, is examined using the financial performance model. Companies investing in carbon reduction scope initiatives can benefit from enhanced reputation for environmental responsibility, value chain cost savings, such as energy reduction, waste minimization, travel substitution and lower fuel consumption. Revenue streams can be enhanced by process and product innovations in clean technologies, and positive perceptions of employees, customers, suppliers and other stakeholders, a more talented and a committed work force (Matsumura et al., 2014). The results of accounting studies indicate that emission performance has a positive association with an average three-year future return on assets and cash flow from operations (Clarkson et al., 2013). This implies that carbon disclosures provide information for predicting future financial performance and cash flows. For the sample of US companies operating in the industries with the highest emission risk, accounting research shows that improvements in carbon emission performance over time are followed by subsequent improvements in financial performance, such as future return on assets and cash flow from operations (Clarkson et al., 2011). Clarkson et al. (2011, p. 142) claim that 'although a proactive environmental strategy may be associated with improved future economic performance (i.e. "it pays to be green"), not all firms can mimic such strategy'. To sum, carbon disclosures have two routes by which they can affect a company's market value. The valuation impact comes from the impact of a company's emission performance on operating financial performance and on risk profile with implications for the expectations of investors.

Prior accounting research has documented other drivers that have impact on the value relevance of carbon disclosures.

- Carbon disclosures provide incremental relevant information beyond voluntary environmental disclosures based on the Global Reporting Initiative framework (Clarkson et al., 2013).
- In more concentrated industries, companies have high market power and low competitions, pass the increased carbon compliance costs to consumers and reduce the negative valuation impact of carbon emissions (Clarkson et al., 2015).
- Companies with good relative carbon emission performance within its industry have lower carbon liabilities by having high cost pass-through ability and/or reducing future capital expenditures (Clarkson et al., 2015).
- Companies with improvements in relative carbon emissions performance are less penalized by the capital market (Clarkson et al., 2015).
- Companies that are not subject to the EU ETS have lower valuation penalty than companies that operate under the EU ETS (Clarkson et al., 2015).

- Companies with high SO_2 emissions are penalized by the capital market during the years surrounding the enactment of the environmental regulation CAAA (1989–1991) in the US. (Hughes, 2000).

Conclusion and implications for stakeholders

The aim of this chapter has been to review the empirical accounting research to address the question if carbon disclosures have an impact on a company's market value. There are six leading accounting studies on the value relevance of carbon disclosures published in *The Accounting Review, European Accounting Review, Journal of Accounting and Public Policy,* and *Abacus: A Journal of Accounting, Finance and Business Studies.* The studies find motives in the concerns expressed by regulators and investors on how carbon emissions create climate related risks. Mandatory and voluntary carbon disclosures have become a prime response by the companies and focus of interest to investors because climate change has implications on both the risk profile and related expectations about future cash flows. The area of carbon disclosures has become one important stream in accounting research. Carbon disclosures represent nonfinancial environmental information with both reliability and relevance concerns for the accounting research and profession. The main research question of interest for accounting researchers has been whether carbon disclosures are value relevant for investors. This chapter has discussed concerns about climate change risk and the current state of voluntary and mandatory regulations of carbon disclosures. The chapter concludes that carbon disclosures are material for company valuation. The capital market assesses a market value penalty for overall carbon emissions and the portion of carbon emissions not covered by free carbon allowances. The capital market values the choice to voluntarily disclose carbon emissions and the individual carbon performance rank within the industry. The valuation impact of carbon disclosures varies depending on industry competitiveness, country-specific carbon regime, the cost pass-through ability of a company and improvements in a company's relative carbon performance.

The value relevance of carbon disclosures has important implications for companies and stakeholders (e.g. investors, NGOs, governments and regulators). Accounting research on the value relevance of carbon disclosures has implications for companies. Accounting researchers posit that company managers weight the costs and benefits of disclosing carbon emissions and chose to disclose only if the perceived benefits of doing so outweigh the perceived costs (Matsumura et al., 2014). The valuation relevance of carbon emission information assists in convincing company managers that such transparency brings benefits in terms of increasing market value. Signalling carbon performance by means of carbon disclosures facilitates financial performance prediction (cash flow effect) and cost of capital reduction (risk effect). The extent by which carbon emissions affect a company's market value assists company managers in making decisions with regard to integrating climate change risk into business strategy and making investments in carbon reduction initiatives.

Accounting research on the value relevance of carbon disclosures has implications for investors. The accounting studies indicate that investors use carbon disclosures in addition to financial reports in order to integrate carbon risk into investment decisions and refine their estimates of companies' liabilities, assets and risks with implications for future cash flows (Matsumura et al., 2014; Johnston et al., 2008; Clarkson et al., 2013).

Investors assess carbon information which is provided in mandatory and voluntary disclosures by taking into account the content of the disclosed carbon measure, a company's competitive position, a company's relative carbon performance and a company's country carbon regime (Clarkson et al., 2015).

Accounting research on the value relevance of carbon disclosures has implications for regulators and other external stakeholders. Existing regulatory and stakeholder pressures from NGOs and media influence the company's decision to disclosure carbon information (Luo et al., 2012; Liesen et al., 2015). Mandated carbon disclosures are required for companies operating in industries with the highest carbon risk. Luo et al. (2012, p. 95) state that 'existing or proposed changes in legislation regarding carbon abatement would create legal/regulatory pressure for carbon disclosure' and conclude that carbon disclosure can 'help firms mitigate or avoid compliance obligation or regulatory risks'.

Stakeholder pressures from regulators, media and NGOs drive decisions of companies to voluntarily disclose carbon information, albeit companies can respond to external stakeholder pressure in an incomplete way (Liesen et al., 2015). Accounting researchers claim that a company can use information to manage stakeholders in order to 'gain their support and approval, or to distract their opposition and disapproval' (Deegan, 2015, p. 376). It has been found that 'larger firms are more likely to use voluntary disclosure to legitimize their long-term operation in response to the social scrutiny and media coverage' (Luo et al., 2012, p. 112). Further, carbon disclosures increase if a company was targeted by NGOs in the prior year's negative climate change-related news (Liesen et al., 2015). For example, the authors identify that automobile manufactures, Volvo AB and Porshe AG, were targeted in NGO press releases and provided disclosure of absolute levels of carbon emissions in the subsequent period. Studies summarize that companies are more likely to voluntarily disclose carbon information to respond to the demands or concerns of the government and the public in general (Liesen et al., 2015; Luo et al., 2012).

Between 2005 and 2009, 84 per cent of 431 EU companies voluntarily disclosed scopes 1 and 2 carbon emissions arising as a direct carbon impact of a company's activity; in 2009, 88 per cent of the companies disclosed scopes 1 and 2 carbon emissions (Liesen et al., 2015). Scope 1 emissions arise from sources that are owned or controlled by the company and scope 2 emissions arise from the generation of purchased electricity consumed by the company (Liesen et al., 2015). In contrast with CDP disclosures, the EU ETS requires disclosing scope 1 carbon emissions. The presence of mandatory and voluntary practices can result in disclosing carbon performance information that can be difficult to compare across companies, industries and time. Researchers state that stakeholders are able to assess and compare companies' carbon performance and strategies if carbon disclosures are complete with respect to scope, type and reporting boundary (Liesen et al., 2015). Accounting research finds that stakeholder pressures have little impact on the overall completeness of carbon disclosures, including scope, type and reporting boundary elements. There is weak evidence of a positive stakeholder impact (i.e. NGO, the government and the public) regarding completeness of carbon disclosure with respect to the scope (both scope 1 and scope 2) and type of emissions (both CO_2 and other emissions). Liesen et al. (2015, p. 1066) explain that companies may use 'incomplete disclosure of GHG emissions as a way of appearing to be responding to stakeholder demands'. Furthermore, a voluntary nature of carbon disclosures contributes to the situations of incomplete response to stakeholder pressures. Conflicting interest or expectations of various stakeholder groups can also lead to the situations of providing carbon information that is incomplete. For example, in a broad perspective of sustainability reports, accounting literature states that conflicting stakeholder demands explain a significant gap between voluntary sustainability reporting of a company and sustainability practices of a company (Cho et al., 2015).

Providing evidence on the valuation relevance of carbon disclosures is consistent with increasing demands of investors and other stakeholders (e.g. environmental NGOs) for clear, uniform carbon disclosures from regulators and standard-setters for measuring and disclosing carbon performance. In this respect, Liesen et al. (2015, p. 1066) state that 'bringing corporate GHG emissions disclosure in line with the dominant reporting guidelines may instead require a mandated reporting regime'. Another study adds that regulation of carbon disclosures is important to achieve improvements in its reporting quality (Comyns and Figge, 2015). Indeed, disclosure of a manageable number of carbon performance variables may provide a more efficient way of informing stakeholders about company management of climate change risks (Hughes, 2000). Regulators and standard-setters are important institutions to consider a uniform assurance of carbon disclosures. Independent third-party assurance can further increase the reliability and homogeneity of carbon information (Matsumura et al., 2015).

Appendix 1

Table 16.5 Sample of journals

Journal; ABDS/ABS rating	Studies on carbon/environmental disclosures/emissions (value relevance studies)
Accounting, Organizations and Society; A★/4★	17
Auditing: A Journal of Practice and Theory; A★/3	2
Contemporary Accounting Research; A★/4	0
Journal of Accounting and Economics; A★/4★	1
Journal of Accounting Research; A★/4★	0
Management Accounting Research; A★/3	1
Review of Accounting Studies; A★/4	0
The Accounting Review; A★/4★	3 (2)
European Accounting Review; A★/3	8 (2)
Abacus; A/3	4 (1)
Accounting and Business Research; A/3	1
Accounting, Auditing and Accountability Journal; A/3	33
Accounting Horizons; A/3	2
Behavioral Research in Accounting; A/3	0
British Accounting Review; A/3	16
Critical Perspectives on Accounting; A/3	18
Financial Accountability and Management; A/3	1
Foundations and Trends in Accounting; A/3	0
Journal of Accounting and Public Policy; A/3	13 (1)
Journal of Accounting Auditing and Finance; A/3	1
Journal of Accounting Literature; A/3	0
Journal of Business Finance and Accounting; A/3	4
The International Journal of Accounting; A/3	7

Appendix 2

Valuation models

The modified Ohlson (1995) valuation model is specified as follows (Clarkson et al., 2013):

$$MV_t = \beta_0 + \beta_1 TCE_t + \beta_2 SE_t + \beta_3 NI_t + \varepsilon \tag{1}$$

where TCE = carbon emissions in thousands of metric tonnes; SE = book value of common equity of the company; NI = income before extraordinary items.

The variables in equation (1) can be scaled by the number of common shares outstanding, the book value of common equity, total assets, number of employees, or sales.

The balance sheet valuation model is shown below (Matsumura et al., 2014).

$$MV_t = \beta_0 + \beta_1 TCE_t + \beta_2 ASSET_t + \beta_3 LIABIL_t + \varepsilon \tag{2}$$

where MV = market value of common equity, calculated as the number of shares outstanding multiplied by the price per share of the company's common stock; ASSET = total assets; LIABIL = total liabilities.

The cost of capital model is specified as follows (Clarkson et al., 2013):

$$COC_t = \beta_0 + \beta_1 TCE_t + \beta_2 BETA_t + \beta_3 SIZE_t + \beta_4 BM_t + \varepsilon \tag{3}$$

where COC = cost of capital; BETA = market beta; SIZE = market value of a company; BM = ratio of book value of equity divided by market value of equity;

The financial performance model is presented below (Clarkson et al., 2013).

$$ROA_t = \beta_0 + \beta_1 TCE_t + \beta_2 ROA_t + \beta_3 SIZE_t + \varepsilon \tag{4}$$

where ROA (CFO) = income before extraordinary items (operating cash flow) divided by beginning total assets. Average three-year ahead ROA (CFO) is used in the model.

References

Al-Tuwaijri, S., Christensen, T. and Hughes, K. (2004). The relations among environmental disclosure, environmental performance, and economic performance: A simultaneous equations approach. *Accounting, Organizations and Society*, 29(5–6): 447–471.

Artiach, T. and Clarkson, P. (2011). Disclosure, conservatism and the cost of equity capital: A review of the foundation literature. *Accounting & Finance*, 51(1): 2–49.

Barth, M., Beaver, W. and Landsman, W. (2001). The relevance of the value relevance literature for financial accounting standard setting: Another view. *Journal of Accounting and Economics*, 31(1–3): 77–104.

Black Bear Environmental Assets (2016). *Climate change. Warming up to the facts*. Manchester. Retrievedfromhttp://nebula.wsimg.com/edf5b696c3bde9a8952279d5ef53f2a1?AccessKeyId=D9D974DEC5F930B854CF&disposition=0&alloworigin=1 (Accessed 29 April 2016).

Carbon Disclosure Project (2015). *CDP global climate change report 2015. At the tipping point? CDP Worldwide*. London. Retrieved from https://www.cdp.net/CDPResults/CDP-global-climate-change-report-2015.pdf (Accessed 26 April 2016).

Center for Climate and Energy Solutions (2015). *Outcomes of the U.N. Climate Change Conference in Paris*. Retrieved from www.c2es.org/docUploads/cop-21-paris-summary-02-2016 final. pdf (Accessed 27 April 2016).

Chapple, L., Clarkson, P. and Gold, D. (2013). The cost of carbon: Capital market effects of the proposed emission trading scheme (ETS). *Abacus*, 49(1): 1–33.

Cho, C., Laine, M., Roberts, R. and Rodrigue, M. (2015). Organized hypocrisy, organizational façades, and sustainability reporting. *Accounting, Organizations and Society*, 40: 78–94.

Clarkson, P., Li, Y. and Richardson, G. (2004). The market valuation of environmental expenditures by pulp and paper companies. *The Accounting Review*, 79: 329–353.

Clarkson, P., Li, Y., Richardson, G. and Vasvari, F. (2008). Revisiting the relation between environmental performance and environmental disclosure: An empirical analysis. *Accounting, Organizations and Society*, 33(4–5): 303–327.

Clarkson, P., Li, Y., Richardson, G. and Vasvari, F. (2011). Does it really pay to be green? Determinants and consequences of proactive environmental strategies. *Journal of Accounting and Public Policy*, 30(2): 122–144.

Clarkson, P. (2012). The valuation relevance of environmental performance: Evidence from the academic literature. In S. Jones and J. Ratnatunga (eds), *Contemporary Issues in Sustainability Accounting, Assurance and Reporting*. Bingley: Emerald Group Publishing, pp. 11–42.

Clarkson, P., Fang, X., Li, Y. and Richardson, G. (2013). The relevance of environmental disclosures: Are such disclosures incrementally informative? *Journal of Accounting and Public Policy*, 32: 410–431.

Clarkson, P., Li, Y., Pinnuck, M. and Richardson, G. (2015). Valuation relevance of greenhouse gas emissions under the European Union Carbon Emission Trading Scheme? *European Accounting Review*, 24 (3): 551–580.

Climate Action (2017). Emission Trading System, Free Allocation. Retrieved from http://ec. europa.eu/clima/policies/ets/allowances_en (Accessed 30 January 2017).

Comyns, B. and Figge, F. (2015). Greenhouse gas reporting quality in the oil and gas industry. *Accounting, Auditing & Accountability Journal*, 28(3): 403–433.

Deegan, C. (2015). *Financial Accounting Theory*. Sydney: McGraw-Hill.

Eurosif (2016). European SRI Study. Retrieved from www.eurosif.org/wp-content/uploads/ 2016/11/SRI-study-2016-HR.pdf (Accessed 4 January 2018).

Freedman, M. and Jaggi, B. (2005). Global warming, commitment to the Kyoto protocol and accounting disclosures by the largest global public firms from polluting industries. *The International Journal of Accounting*, 40: 215–232.

Green, B., Johnson, C. and Adams, A. (2006). Writing narrative literature reviews for peer-reviewed journals: Secrets of the trade. *Journal of Chiropractic Medicine*, 5(3): 101–117.

Hartmann F., Perego, P. and Young-Ferris, A. (2013). Carbon accounting: Challenges for research in management control and performance measurement. *Abacus*, 49(4): 539–563.

Healy, P. and Palepu, K. (2001). Information asymmetry, corporate disclosure, and the capital markets: A review of the empirical disclosure literature. *Journal of Accounting and Economics*, 31(1–3): 405–440.

Huang, X. and Watson, L. (2015). Corporate social responsibility research in accounting. *Journal of Accounting Literature*, 34: 1–16.

Hughes, K.E. (2000). The value relevance of nonfinancial measures of air pollution in the electric utility industry. *The Accounting Review*, 75(2): 209–218.

Ioannou, I., Li, S. and Serafeim, G. (2016). The effect of target difficulty on the target completion: The case of reducing carbon emissions. *The Accounting Review*, 91(5): 1467–1492.

Johnston, D., Sefcik, S. and Soderstrom, N. (2008). The value relevance of greenhouse gas emissions allowances: An exploratory study in the related United States SO_2 market. *European Accounting Review*, 17(4): 747–764.

Kolk A., Levy, D. and Pinske, J. (2008). Corporate responses in an emerging climate regime: The initialization and commensuration of carbon disclosure. *European Accounting Review*, 17(4): 719–745.

Laine, M. (2005). Meanings of the term 'sustainable development' in Finnish corporate disclosures. *Accounting Forum*, 29(4): 395–413.

Liesen, A., Hoepner, A., Patten, D., and Figge, F. (2015). Does stakeholder pressure influence corporate GHG emission reporting? Empirical evidence from Europe. *Accounting, Auditing and Accountability Journal*, 28(7): 1047–1074.

Luo, L., Lan, Y.-C. and Tang, Q. (2012). Corporate incentives to disclose carbon information: Evidence from the CDP Global 500 Report. *Journal of International Financial Management & Accounting*, 23(2): 93–120.

Makower, J. (2016). *State of the Green Business*. GreenBiz. Retrieved from https://www.greenbiz.com/report/state-green-business-report-2016 (Accessed 10 March 2016).

Matsumura, E., Prakash, R. and Vera-Munoz, S. (2014). Firm-value effects of carbon emissions and carbon disclosure. *The Accounting Review*, 89(2): 695–724.

Moser, M. and Martin, P. (2012). A broader perspective on corporate social responsibility research in accounting. *The Accounting Review*, 87(3): 797–806.

Nathan, F. (2016). Introduction. *The PRI Academic Network Quarterly*, 9: 2.

Ohlson, J. (1995). Earnings, book values, and dividends in equity valuation. *Contemporary Accounting Research*, 11(2): 661–687.

Orlitzky, M., Schmidt, F. and Rynes, S. (2003). Corporate social and financial performance: A meta-analysis. *Organization Studies*, 24(3): 403–441.

Patten, D. (2002). The relation between environmental performance and environmental disclosure: A research note. *Accounting, Organizations and Society*, 27(8): 763–773.

Reid, E. and Toffel, M. (2009). Responding to public and private politics: Corporate disclosure of climate change and strategies. *Strategic Management Journal*, 30: 1157–1178.

Semenova, N. and Hassel, L. (2015). On the validity of environmental performance metrics. *Journal of Business Ethics*, 132(2): 249–258.

Stanny, E. and Ely, K. (2008). Corporate environmental disclosures about effects of climate change. *Corporate Social Responsibility and Environmental Management*, 15: 338–348.

Swedish Financial Supervisory Authority (2016). *Climate Change and Financial Stability*. Press release, Stockholm. Retrieved from www.fi.se/Folder-EN/Startpage/Press/Press-releases/Listan/Climate-changes-and-financial-stability1 (Accessed 20 April 2016).

Trucost (2010). *Universal Ownership. Why Environmental Externalities Matter to Institutional Investors*. The UN Principles for Responsible Investment (PRI) and UNEP Finance Initiative, London. Retrieved from www.unepfi.org/fileadmin/documents/universal_ownership_full.pdf (Accessed 20 March 2016).

United States Environmental Protection Agency (n.d.). *Overview of Greenhouse Gases*. New York. Retrieved from https://www3.epa.gov/climatechange/ghgemissions/gases/co2.html (Accessed 29 April 2016).

17 Exploring the validity of corporate climate reporting under the Global Reporting Initiative, Carbon Disclosure Project, and Greenhouse Gas Protocol

Merriam Haffar and Cory Searcy

Introduction

Companies today are increasingly engaging in a variety of business strategies to improve their sustainability, and manage their contribution to wider global trends of environmental degradation such as climate change (KPMG, 2015). A key factor in the successful implementation of these sustainability strategies is the continual monitoring of progress. One of the foremost ways in which companies are doing so is by reporting on their sustainability impacts. Some of the most common corporate impacts reported on today are the company-level emissions that drive the global warming associated with climate change (UNGC, 2016 and 2013). This chapter explores the validity of current voluntary approaches to corporate reporting on climate change – and the implications of this on the meaningfulness of the disclosures produced.

In December 2015, the United Nations 21st Conference of Parties (COP21) received unprecedented global support for its twin climate goals of limiting global warming and strengthening climate resilience. One hundred and ninety-five countries signed the Paris Agreement, which was a 'binding' and 'universal' commitment to hold the rise in global temperature below 2 degrees Celsius above pre-industrial levels, by the end of this century (UNFCC, 2015). Although this Agreement was signed by national governments, the COP21 committee emphasized the significant role that businesses have in achieving the emission reductions necessary to meet its commitments (UNGC, 2016; ICC, 2015a). Accordingly, and after the declaration of the Agreement, over one hundred corporations worldwide committed to doing their part to meet the collective 2 degree Celsius target (WRI, 2015). However, any such business climate initiatives must necessarily include some form of climate reporting; such reporting would enable companies to track emission reductions accurately, and within the wider scientific context of global climate change. In this way, corporate climate reporting serves as a crucial component of a company's business strategy for sustainability.

For the purposes of this chapter, corporate climate reporting is defined as the process of tracking company climate contributions, most often in the form of emissions (or reductions) of greenhouse gases (GHGs) (GHG Protocol, 2004). In most jurisdictions around the world (with the exception of a noted few, such as South Africa and Denmark), climate reporting is a voluntary activity that is undertaken with a range of diverse aims, including enhancing company transparency or identifying eco-efficiency opportunities (Daub, 2007). In an organizational context, climate reporting may either be conducted under the wider umbrella of sustainability reporting – whereby the climate and other sustainability performance disclosures are released publicly to stakeholders – or as a stand-alone performance assessment either for the purpose of internal decision-making (e.g. GHG inventory) or external trading (e.g. carbon credits) (Bowen and Wittneben, 2011; Daub, 2007). Studies have demonstrated that the number of companies issuing climate disclosures, in the form of sustainability reports or stand-alone climate disclosures has grown considerably over the past decade (KPMG, 2015). However, such an increase in disclosure quantity has not been matched with an increase in disclosure quality. A growing number of academic and practitioner studies have revealed that current mainstream approaches to voluntary sustainability reporting in general – and climate reporting in particular – have generated disclosures that are not comparable across firms, and have failed to provide the necessary contextual[1] information on how these disclosures contribute to ecological climate thresholds (Kolk et al., 2008; Michelon et al., 2015; KPMG, 2015; Talbot and Boiral, 2013; Vigneau et al., 2015; UNEP, 2015).

Some studies have demonstrated the non–comprehensive reporting of climate impacts (Carbon Clear, 2015; KPMG, 2015). These studies describe this issue both in terms of the extent of climate reporting across a company's direct and indirect[2] emission sources, and in terms of whether companies are reporting on climate at all. One of the most recent of these studies was a 2015 survey of business leader firms reporting on sustainability (including climate change) conducted by KPMG (KPMG, 2015). This study revealed the poor extent and quality of GHG reporting among the companies surveyed for both direct and indirect emission sources. According to the survey, one in five of global business leaders in 'high-carbon' sectors do not report on their GHG emissions; of the companies that do, only 7 per cent on average report on 'downstream impacts' (KPMG, 2015). On this basis, the study declared 'corporate climate reporting needs an overhaul' in the form of stronger disclosure of both direct *and* indirect impacts (KPMG, 2015).

Other studies of climate/sustainability reporting have also highlighted the lack of sustainability context information in sustainability/climate reporting today (UNEP, 2015; Climate Counts and CSO, 2013; Bjørn et al., 2016). For example, a longitudinal study of corporate sustainability reports published by Corporate Register by a range of firms from 2000 to 2014 revealed that although references to ecological limits were growing, the overwhelming majority (more than 95 per cent) of companies engaged in reporting still do not present sustainability (and particularly climate) performance in the context of wider ecological thresholds (Bjørn et al., 2016).

On a top level, these studies, and the remaining literature on the quality of sustainability (and/or climate) disclosures, identify a key challenge with current approaches to sustainability and climate reporting. This is the poor reporting validity of the disclosures produced. Within a research context, a valid study is one that actually measures what it purports to, and thus achieves an acceptable level of 'truthfulness or accuracy' (Salkind, 2012). By applying this definition within the context of sustainability reporting, we define *reporting* validity as being the degree to which corporate climate disclosures accurately reflect the company's contribution to wider climate processes and thresholds. As such, reporting validity is concerned with the comprehensiveness of these disclosures and their connection to the company's sustainability context (hereafter referred to simply as 'context').

Much of the extant literature on sustainability or climate reporting has focused on the poor validity of the disclosures themselves (for example Talbot and Boiral, 2013; Bjørn et al., 2016). What remains unclear is how the validity of these reports has been influenced by the choice of the voluntary reporting framework followed. In other words, there is a dearth of research on the role that voluntary reporting frameworks themselves play in enhancing or hindering validity of the reports generated. Given that the over-whelming majority of climate disclosures issued today have been developed under the guidance of at least one corporate reporting framework, any validity issues stemming from the design of the frameworks themselves would contribute significantly to the ultimate validity of the final reports generated.

To fill this research gap, this study assesses the validity of reporting under three of the most commonly used climate reporting frameworks on the basis of the design of the frameworks themselves (e.g. in the choice of metrics, the degree of detailed guidance on measurement procedures) rather than on the way in which they are being applied by firms in practice. In doing so, this study aims to understand how exactly these three reporting approaches (individually and by comparison) enhance or hinder valid reporting on corporate climate impacts. For each reporting approach, this study asks: does the reporting approach allow for valid climate disclosure? Specifically:

Is the disclosure *comprehensive* in its scope of climate impacts?
Is the disclosure *context-based* in principle and in its choice of metrics?

To answer these questions, this study will rely on a comparative case study of the top three most commonly used reporting frameworks for corporate reporting on climate change: the Global Reporting Initiative (GRI), the Greenhouse Gas (GHG) Protocol and the Carbon Disclosure Project (CDP). In asking these research questions this study aims to explore whether climate reporting under these three frameworks allows for more valid climate disclosure. Such disclosure would help companies in effecting sustainability strategies that would contribute towards achieving systems-wide, ecological sustainability with regards to global climate change.

The remainder of the chapter is organized as follows: first, we survey the literature on sustainability and climate reporting to identify specific issues with reporting validity. We then translate these identified issues into a number of specific validity dimensions that will then form the basis of the analysis. In the methods section we then translate these dimensions further, into a series of assessment questions, with which we analyse the three frameworks on an individual and comparative basis. The findings of the analysis are then presented along with a subsequent discussion of the ways in which the frameworks enhance or hinder reporting validity. Finally, this chapter concludes with a discussion of the implications of the findings, their limitations and some key recommendations for further research.

Validity problems of sustainability and climate reporting

Valid climate (and more broadly, sustainability) disclosures provide an accurate and comprehensive reflection of the company's impact on global climate processes and tipping points. The literature on climate and sustainability reporting has identified two key challenges on this issue, namely: the lack of context in reporting, and the lack of comprehensive disclosures in terms of the scope of impacts reported on.

In terms of the comprehensiveness of climate reporting, some authors assert that valid reporting must also be based on a wide enough scope of climate impacts (ICC, 2015b). This reporting comprehensiveness applies to the types of emissions addressed, as well as their location along the company's chains of operation. With regards to the former, valid disclosures ought to include, at the minimum, the emissions of GHGs described in the latest amendment of the Kyoto Protocol (GHG Protocol, 2013). These are: carbon dioxide (CO_2), methane (CH_4), nitrous oxide (N_2O), hydrofluorocarbons (HFCs), perfluorocarbons (PFCs), sulphur hexafluoride (SF_6), and nitrogen trifluoride (NF_3). Beyond these Kyoto Protocol gases (hereafter KP-GHGs), valid climate disclosures also ought to consider the global warming effects of other climate-contributing emissions such as ozone-depleting GHGs not covered under the Kyoto Protocol (CDP, 2016a; We Mean Business Coalition, 2015; UNEP, 2015; BSR, 2015). These gases carry a high global warming potential (GWP) and have a long lifespan, making them far more potent climate change contributors than for example, CO_2. Similarly, and particularly after COP, organizations such as the Climate and Clean Air Coalition – a partnership of the United States government, civil society and its private sector – have also argued that valid climate disclosures ought to consider emissions of Short-Lived Climate Pollutants (or SLCPs) (UNEP-CCAC, 2014). These are a group of climate-warming or cooling chemicals that exert their climate impacts over the short term, and are either GHGs or air pollutants by nature. These SLCP chemicals are: methane (CH_4, a GHG), black carbon (from soot, an air contaminant released from combustion), HFCs (a family of GHGs), and tropospheric ozone (both a GHG and air contaminant released from combustion) (UNEP-CCAC, 2014). Two of these species (methane and HFCs) are already covered under the seven KP-GHGs; however, the remaining two are not and as such would need to be considered for valid climate disclosures (CDP, 2016b).

In addition, a recent call for improving the validity and comprehensiveness of climate impacts has also described the need for including indirect company GHG emissions in climate disclosures (KPMG, 2015; Carbon Clear, 2015). These 'indirect emissions' emanate from company sources that extend beyond its direct operations, and lay either up-stream (e.g. supply chain) or down-stream (e.g. product use) of these operations (ICC, 2015b). These indirect GHG emissions are defined as being 'emissions that are a consequence of the operations of the reporting company, but occur at sources owned or controlled by another company' (GHG Protocol, 2004). These emissions stand in contrast to 'direct emissions' which are defined as being 'emissions from sources that are owned or controlled by the reporting company' (GHG Protocol, 2004). Corporate climate reporting involves, at a minimum, the disclosure of all measureable direct emissions, but not necessarily all indirect emissions. It then follows that the first step of corporate climate reporting is to determine whether and which indirect emission sources to include in the disclosure. This in turn determines the boundary of the company's climate reporting process, which outlines which emission sources, will be measured and reported on. This reporting boundary is known as the company's operational boundary (GHG Protocol, 2004). Thus, the process of setting this boundary 'allows a company to establish which operations and sources cause direct and indirect [GHG] emissions, and to decide which indirect emissions to include [in its disclosure] as a consequence of its operations' (GHG Protocol, 2004). The comprehensiveness of a company's operational boundary contributes to the overall validity of the climate disclosure.

There are different ways in which companies may set their operational boundaries for the purposes of climate reporting. All three of the frameworks examined in this study require companies to follow the same boundary-setting approach. This approach is based on the concept of reporting scope, which was first proposed by the GHG Protocol in the first (2001) version of its Corporate Accounting and Reporting Standard. There are three scope categories in climate reporting, namely scopes 1, 2 and 3. Scope 1 emissions (or sources) refer to direct emissions (or sources). Scopes 2 and 3 refer to indirect emissions (or sources). Scope 2 emissions originate exclusively from 'the generation of electricity, heating/cooling, or steam purchased for own consumption', while scope 3 emissions refer to all other forms of indirect GHG emissions' (GHG Protocol, 2004). Scope 3 emissions (and sources) are the furthest away from the direct operations of the reporting company.

By including climate impacts across a company's direct and indirect sources across all three reporting scopes, the disclosure presents an accurate and comprehensive picture of the company's true overall contribution to climate change (KPMG, 2015). However, literature in this area has shown that this is not the case in company reports today. In 2015, Carbon Clear released the results of its latest global survey of the climate disclosures issued by FTSE100 business leader firms (Carbon Clear, 2015). This study found that, in comparison to its last survey (of the same sample) from 2011, the number of companies reporting on scope 3 emissions had risen by 30 per cent in four years (Carbon Clear, 2015). While this progress is promising, the study is careful to stress that as of 2015, just under half (44 per cent) of this entire sample of global business leaders still do not report on scope 3 impacts; and of the companies that do report, approximately 60 per cent of them only report on a single scope 3 emission category – business travel (Carbon Clear, 2015). On the basis of these findings, the study declares that 'in order to gain a holistic and robust picture of a company's true footprint it is necessary to consider as many categories of scope 3 as are feasible' (Carbon Clear, 2015).

In addition, on the issue of context, the past decade has seen the emergence of the context- (or science-) based reporting movement, which is based on the notion of 'sustainability context'. This reporting approach is built on the principle that no firm exists in isolation, and that instead all firms operate within wider social and ecological systems – their sustainability context. As a result, any company performance ought to be assessed within the context of these systems, and with reference to the specific limits that they impose on the company. A number of authors have argued that sustainability reporting frameworks, such as the G4 sustainability reporting guidelines developed by the GRI, not only fail to sufficiently consider this principle of context, but that in failing to do so, they only serve to reinforce a company's social or ecological unsustainability (Milne and Gray, 2013; McElroy and van Engelen, 2012). These authors contend that sustainability reporting, as practised today – without the use of context-based metrics that allow for the assessment of company performance against systems thresholds – fails to drive transformational sustainability change within firms, and ultimately 'offers little or no challenge to business-as-usual' (Milne and Gray, 2013). In the absence of context-based performance reporting, it would be impossible to determine whether or not a company's reported sustainability performance is indeed truly sustainable. This was demonstrated in a 2013 study conducted by Climate Counts, in collaboration with the Center on Sustainable Organizations (Climate Counts and CSO, 2013). This study analysed the reported climate emissions of a global sample of 100 companies on the basis of climate science to determine whether the emission trends reported may be deemed sustainable from an ecological sense, on the basis of climate science and the 2 degree Celsius global climate target (Climate Counts and CSO, 2013). The study found that only half (51 per cent) of companies surveyed may be deemed sustainable, when their performance were reassessed in the light of climate context and thresholds (Climate Counts and CSO, 2013). Furthermore, one of the most common carbon metrics used in the reports – a company's carbon intensity (per revenue) – was also found to have

Table 17.1 Issues regarding reporting validity identified from the literature and their underlying validity dimensions

Reporting issue	Dimension(s) of validity
Need for considering the climate impacts of Short-Lived Climate Pollutants (SLCPs) in reporting and target-setting (CDP, 2016b; We Mean Business Coalition, 2015; UNEP, 2015; BSR, 2015)	Comprehensiveness of the scope of impacts with regards to the Kyoto Protocol GHGs Comprehensiveness of the scope of impacts beyond GHGs (e.g. SLCPs) Consideration of the principle of context
Sustainability disclosures are disconnected from sustainability context (Baue, 2013; McElroy and van Engelen, 2012; UNEP, 2015)	Use of context metrics
Need for science-based performance measurement and target-setting for GHG emissions (CDP, 2016b; Baue, 2013)	

no correlation with a company's true ecological carbon performance (Climate Counts and CSO, 2013). This demonstrates the value in and need for taking a context-based approach to climate reporting.

Overall, based on these recommendations, valid climate disclosure, by definition, must first extend above and beyond KP-GHGs to other material impacts. Furthermore, the disclosure of all of these emissions ought to be reported across all three of a company's scopes. Finally, this disclosure must also be tied to the wider sustainability context through the application of context/science-based climate metrics. These reporting validity requirements and issues have been summarized in Table 17.1. Each issue is based on one or more particular dimensions of reporting validity, which have been shown in the right column in bold. These five dimensions of validity will be used to assess the strength of the three reporting frameworks, on the basis of whether they enhance reporting validity.

Method

This study involves a qualitative and comparative case study of three sustainability or climate reporting frameworks currently in use by companies today. These cases are: the GRI, the GHG Protocol and the CDP. A short summary of each of these cases has been included in Appendix 2. The cases were chosen on the basis that they are the top thee corporate reporting frameworks in use by companies today for climate-related disclosures (KPMG, 2015; Ernst and Yong, 2016). They each follow a separate published set of standards and GHG emission disclosure protocols. Each framework is primarily aimed at serving different disclosure goals and caters to different stakeholders. Reporting under the CDP is aimed primarily at supplying investors with an idea of a company's climate risk. On the other hand, reporting under the GHG Protocol is aimed at establishing an internal GHG inventory whose data may then be disclosed publicly. Finally, climate reporting under the GRI is only a small part of a broader public sustainability report that targets a wide range of internal and external company stakeholders for the purposes of transparency and stakeholder engagement, among other aims. In choosing cases that varied in their disclosure aims and audiences, this study aimed to capture a wide enough sample of cases for analysis.

It is important to note that although the three frameworks are voluntary in nature, they do nevertheless have reporting requirements that all companies must follow. For the GRI and GHG Protocol, disclosure requirements are only requirements to the extent that companies who abide by them are officially 'in accordance' with the various GRI or GHG Protocol reporting standards (e.g. a company's supply chain disclosures may qualify it to be officially 'in accordance' with the GHG Protocol's Scope 3 Reporting Standard). Not abiding by any of the specific disclosure requirements incurs no direct penalties from either organization. However, non-comprehensive or unreliable reporting data lowers the quality of the overall disclosure, and may result in potential and indirect stakeholder penalization. For example, a company's demonstrated history of poor or 'greenwashed' disclosures may negatively influence its legitimacy in the eyes of its customers (Delmas and Burbano, 2011). Similarly, disclosure requirements under the CDP are also not enforced directly through reporting penalties. They are, however, enforced indirectly by means of CDP's company scoring methodology. All company responses (i.e. climate disclosures) are graded by the CDP upon submission, and the scores are made available to investors and other interested stakeholder groups for consideration in their financing decisions (CDP scoring).

Reporting under each of these three frameworks is dictated by a family of reporting standards, guidance documents and emission calculation tools (hereafter referred to as 'framework documents'). These are shown for each of the three frameworks in Table 17.2. It is important to note that additional sector-specific supplementary guidelines under the three frameworks were not considered in the analysis, given that they apply only to companies in a small number of sectors, and thus do not apply across-the-board to all companies.

These 15 framework documents were identified and accessed from the framework's websites; they were selected for analysis in this study on the basis of their relevance to (and guidance on) corporate climate disclosures. These documents formed the basis of the analysis performed in this study. The reporting requirements and additional guidance provided in each of these documents (per framework) were analysed individually and comparatively on the basis of the five dimensions of reporting validity that were identified in the literature as being particularly relevant to the focus of this study, and listed in the right-hand column of Table 17.1. These are: the operational boundary for the disclosure, the scope of KP-GHGs addressed, the scope of non-KP-GHG impacts addressed, the principle of sustainability context, and the use of context-based metrics.

Ahead of the analysis, these five dimensions were re-framed into specific 'assessment questions', on the basis of which the framework documents were analysed. This study relied on a total of five assessment questions. A figure tracing the development of these assessment questions from the dimensions of reporting validity, and back from the two original research questions has been included (Figure 17.1).

The analysis proceeded as follows: for each of the frameworks, the documents were read through, and information pertaining to each of the frameworks was collected and assessed on an individual basis (e.g. Does GRI require climate reporting across all three scopes?) and then compared with the other two frameworks (e.g. Is the reporting approach under GRI more comprehensive, on the basis of scope coverage, than CDP or GHG Protocol?). This analysis revealed the individual strengths and weaknesses of each of the three frameworks with regards to the validity of company disclosures under each approach.

Table 17.2 Reporting standards, questionnaires, and guidance documents analysed in this study

Global Reporting Initiative (GRI)	Greenhouse Gas (GHG) Protocol	Carbon Disclosure Project (CDP)
G4 Sustainability Reporting Guidelines – Part 1: Reporting principles and standard disclosures (2013) G4 Sustainability Reporting Guidelines – Part 2: Implementation manual (2013)	Corporate Accounting and Reporting Standard (2004) GHG Protocol guidance on uncertainty assessment in GHG inventories and calculating statistical parameter uncertainty (2011) Corporate Value Chain (Scope 3) Accounting and Reporting Standard (2011) Accounting and Reporting Standard Amendment – Required greenhouse gases in inventories (2013) GHG Protocol Agricultural Guidance – Interpreting the Corporate Accounting and Reporting Standard for the agricultural sector (2014) Climate Change information request (2016) Guidance for companies reporting on climate change on behalf of investors and supply chain members (2016) Technical note on science-based targets (2016) Technical Note – Special conditions for reporting Scope 1 emissions (2016) Climate Change scoring introduction (2016) Climate Change scoring methodology (2016) Guidance for companies reporting on forest risk commodities on behalf of investors (2016)	GHG Protocol Scope 2 Guidance – An amendment to the GHG Protocol Corporate Standard (2015)

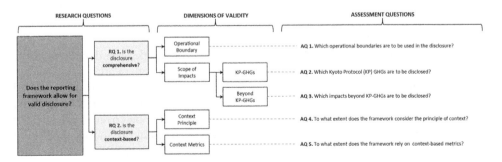

Figure 17.1 Research questions, validity dimensions, and assessment questions used in the analysis.

Findings

Climate change reporting represents a key business strategy that companies around the world have increasingly used to manage their sustainability. Companies that engage in this sustainability strategy often rely on established reporting guidelines, the most common being the GRI, GHG Protocol, and CDP. The aim of this study is to explore how the three chosen reporting frameworks fare on the five different assessment questions, each of which reflects a particular dimension of reporting validity. In doing so, this study describes the extent to which company reporting based on these guidelines actually contributes to ecological sustainability.

The findings have been presented here per assessment question.

AQ1. Which operational boundaries are to be used in the disclosure?

All three frameworks require that companies define their operational boundary (for the purposes of reporting) in terms of the three scope categories. Scope 1 emissions originate from the company's direct operations (e.g. emissions from a company's manufacturing processes), while scope 2 emissions originate from purchased electricity, heat or steam. For these two scope categories, all three frameworks require companies to report on emission totals per scope. These totals should cover gross emissions (not net), which are 'independent of any GHG trades', credits and allowances (GHG Protocol, 2004). This allows for a more accurate and comprehensive idea of a company's true direct climate footprint. Although all frameworks require that companies disclose scope 1 and 2 emissions as emission totals, some frameworks also require this disclosure to be presented additionally in terms of sub-categories of scope 1 and 2 emissions. The CDP requires companies to (additionally) break down their scope 1 and 2 emission totals by all of the following measures: by GHG type (for scope 1 only), by company activity, by facility, by country, and by business division. The GHG Protocol only requires companies to break down their scope 1 and 2 totals by GHG type; all further subdivisions (e.g. by activity, by facility) are optional. The GRI only requires companies to disclose scope totals.

For scope 3, the frameworks differ slightly in the phrasing of their requirements: at a top level, all three recommend reporting across scope 3. Under the GRI, the scope 3 metric (EN17) is listed sequentially after the metrics for scopes 1 and 2, and described with equal detail. However, only companies who wish to be 'in accordance' with the G4 guidelines at the 'comprehensive' level would be required to report on this metric. Similarly, the GHG Protocol provides detailed guidance for calculating and reporting scope 3 disclosures. However, the Protocol states that these disclosures are only a requirement for companies who aim to be 'in accordance' with both the Accounting and Reporting Standard and the recently released Scope 3 Reporting Standard. The CDP, on the other hand, requires scope 3 disclosures and contains detailed guidance for undertaking them (and justifications for doing so). As a reporting requirement, these disclosures are included in the CDP's company scoring methodology (CDP, 2016d).

Outside each of the three scope categories, companies reporting under all three frameworks must also report separately on a number of specific emission sources, not to be included in scope totals. For all three frameworks, these include carbon offsets and the emissions and removal of biologically sequestered CO_2 (from/within biomass or other organic sources). Of all three frameworks, the CDP is the only organization that requires the disclosure of CO_2 emissions that have been sequestered geologically through carbon capture or storage mechanisms (e.g. enhanced oil recovery for oil and gas firms; CDP, 2016d).

AQ2. Which Kyoto Protocol (KP) GHGs are to be disclosed?
AQ3. Which impacts beyond KP-GHGs are to be disclosed?

The latest amendment of the Kyoto Protocol requires the monitoring and reporting of emissions of the following seven GHGs: carbon dioxide (CO_2), methane (CH_4), nitrous oxide (N_2O), hydrofluorocarbons (HFCs), perfluorocarbons (PFCs), sulphur hexafluoride (SF_6) and nitrogen trifluoride (NF_3). The last two gases have only recently been added to the Protocol. These gases were deemed material for inclusion in the Protocol given their strong climate potency (high GWP values), their long lifespan in the atmosphere (relative to CO_2), and the frequency of their release from industrial processes (GHG Protocol, 2013). In terms of the comprehensiveness of the frameworks' scope of these GHG emissions, all three frameworks require the disclosure of all seven of these GHGs under the latest amendment of the Kyoto Protocol, including the latest two additions. Two of these seven KP-GHGs are also SLCP species, namely, methane (CH_4) and hydrofluorocarbons (HFCs).

Despite the comprehensive coverage of KP-gases, all three frameworks offer little in terms of disclosure requirements or guidance of non-KP impacts, such as, for example, ozone–depleting (GHG) substances or other air contaminant SLCP species not included in the Kyoto Protocol GHG list (e.g. black carbon or tropospheric ozone – both of which are released from fossil fuel combustion). Under the GRI, ozone–depleting GHGs, and air contaminants (some of which are known to be climate-warming or – cooling, e.g. NO_x and SO_x) are to be reported only under chemical pollution metrics of the Emissions Aspect. Their climate impact is not considered in the disclosure. Under the GHG Protocol, the 2013 Amendment to the Reporting Standard does state that other 'optional GHGs' (GHG Protocol, 2013) including ozone–depleting substances ought be disclosed, so long as their GWP values have been listed in the IPCC Assessment Reports. These optional gases should be reported separately from the seven KP-GHGs, and not included in scope totals. The same requirement applies to CDP reporting as well. In addition, the CDP also acknowledges the need to reduce all SLCP species – including the two Kyoto Protocol gases (HFCs and CH_4), as well as non-Kyoto Protocol GHGs and air contaminants (such as black carbon and tropospheric ozone). However, as of yet, it only requires companies to report on HFCs and CH_4 in their CDP climate change disclosures. Reporting on other SLCP species is optional; these optional emissions must be listed separately from scope totals, under the 'further information' fields of the CDP climate change questionnaire.

Thus, in summary: with regards to the KP-GHGs, all three frameworks require the disclosure of all seven of the KP-GHGs under the latest amendment of the Kyoto Protocol (two of which are also SLCP species), and may thus be considered quite comprehensive on this account.

In contrast, with regards to the issue of climate impacts of pollutants beyond the KP-GHGs, the frameworks are less comprehensive. None of the three frameworks explicitly require, as of yet, the disclosure of climate pollutants beyond the KP-GHGs, including for example SLCP species not listed under the Kyoto Protocol (such as black carbon, for instance). Of the three frameworks, the GRI is the least comprehensive, given that it makes no mention at all of the need to consider climate impacts beyond the seven KP-GHGs. Both the GHG Protocol and the CDP, on the other hand, may be considered slightly more comprehensive, as both frameworks recommend the reporting of any additional climate pollutants beyond KP-GHGs. Under both frameworks, however, these disclosures are considered considered voluntary rather than explicit requirements.

AQ4. To what extent does the framework consider the principle of context?
AQ5. To what extent does the framework rely on context-based metrics?

With regards to the inclusion of the principle of sustainability context, the GRI and CDP both mention this principle in their respective reporting guidelines. However, as of yet, the GHG Protocol does not.

In response to public calls for a stronger consideration of the notion of context in its framework, the GRI amended its guidelines in 2002 to include the new reporting principle of sustainability context (Thurm, 2013). According to the latest version, the G4 guidelines, a company report prepared in accordance with the GRI standards 'should present the organization's performance in the wider context of sustainability … this involves discussing the performance of the organization in the context of the limits and demands placed on environmental or social resources at the sector, local, regional, or global level' (GRI, 2013). The CDP also similarly considers the principle of sustainability context in its reporting approach. This consideration is in the form of a commitment to encourage companies to adopt science-based climate targets, as part of its 2016 Science-based Targets Call to Action. Science-based climate targets are a form of sustainability performance targets that a company sets to mitigate its contribution to global climate change, by limiting its GHG emissions. These targets are termed 'science-based' as they are set 'in line with the level of decarbonization required to keep global temperature increase below 2°C compared to pre-industrial temperatures, as described in the Fifth Assessment Report of the Intergovernmental Panel on Climate Change (IPCC)' (WRI, ND). In this way, these targets differ from non-science-based targets such as performance intensity targets (e.g. a 5 per cent reduction in GHG emissions from all company facilities over the course of a year) by connecting local or regional company-level performance goals to global climate change goals.

The CDP commitment to both the principle of sustainability context and the use of science-based climate targets is expressed as follows: 'CDP is asking companies to raise the level of ambition of their targets and set their greenhouse gas emissions reductions in line with climate science. Starting in 2016, CDP's Climate Change Questionnaire will incentivize companies to set science-based targets and achieve the next level of performance in emissions reductions' in order to ultimately 'limit the increase in global average temperature to below 2°C' (CDP, 2016d). It is important to note however that this commitment applies to targets and not to metrics; the CDP framework encourages companies to set science- (i.e. context-) based targets but not context-based metrics.

Unlike the CDP and GRI however, the GHG Protocol makes no reference to the notion of context – or specifically, the need for performance assessments based on climate science – in any of its reporting guidance documents. This is surprising given that the Protocol is the climate disclosure reference standard on which the other two frameworks are based. Both the GRI and CDP make regular mention of the Protocol and its approach, and regularly encourage (throughout their own guidance documents) companies to review the measurement protocols and requirements described in the Protocol's Reporting Standard. The implication then, of this omission of context, is

Table 17.3 Summary of study findings

Assessment Question	GRI	GHG Protocol	CDP
AQ 1. Which operational boundaries are to be used in the disclosure?	Reporting required for impacts under scopes 1 & 2. Emissions for scopes 1 and 2 to be presented as emission totals per scope. Reporting on scope 3 impacts is recommended but not required	Reporting required for impacts under scopes 1 & 2. Emissions for scopes 1 and 2 to be presented as emission totals per scope, and broken down by GHG type. Reporting on scope 3 impacts is recommended but not required	Reporting required for impacts under all three scopes. Emissions for scopes 1–3 to be presented as emission totals per scope, and broken down by GHG type, company activity, facility, country, and business division
AQ 2. Which KP-GHGs are to be disclosed?	Reporting required for all seven of the GHGs listed under the latest amendment of the Kyoto Protocol (CO_2, CH_4, N_2O, HFCs, PFCs, SF_6, and NF_3)		
AQ 3. Which impacts beyond KP-GHGs are to be disclosed?	No mention is made of reporting on the climate impacts of any emissions beyond KP-GHGs (including ozone-depleting substances)	Reporting on 'optional GHGs' (outside KP-GHG list) whose GWP values have been listed in IPCC Assessment Reports is recommended but not required. Optional GHGs must be reported separately from KP-GHGs and not included in scope totals	Reporting on 'optional GHGs' (outside KP-GHG list) whose GWP values have been listed in IPCC Assessment Reports is recommended but not required. Optional GHGs must be reported separately from KP-GHGs and not included in scope totals. Reporting on non-KP-GHG SLCP species (e.g. black carbon, tropospheric ozone) is recommended but not required
AQ 4. To what extent does the framework consider the principle of context?	Notion of sustainability context is included as one of the guidelines' key reporting principles	No mention is made of context-based metrics	Notion of sustainability context is included as a key reporting principle, specifically in regards to setting science-based sustainability target
AQ 5. To what extent does the framework rely on context-based metrics?	No mention is made of context-based metrics		

that much greater; if the key reference standard for climate reporting fails to consider the principle of sustainability context, what would drive other frameworks – or even companies reporting independently of any framework – to do so?

With regards to the use of context-based performance metrics: although both the GRI and CDP have committed to the notion of sustainability context at a conceptual level, neither approach has applied this commitment in practice through the use of context-based metrics. This is particularly significant of the GRI, whose initial reference of context dates back to 2006. Since then various sustainability practitioners have called on GRI to clarify its stance on context, and incorporate specific, concrete protocols for its application in reporting – that is to say, context metrics (McElroy and van Engelen, 2012; Baue, 2013). These calls went unanswered in the latest version of the guidelines (G4), released 7 years after the initial context reference. Practitioners argue that this 'new framework provides no further guidance on how to enact this principle, thereby retaining a fatal flaw, as few companies actually report their sustainability performance in this context' (Baue, 2013). The CDP on the other hand has taken a stronger stance on context-based performance assessment, but only through its commitment to science-based targets, rather than performance metrics. The framework does require companies to disclose any science-based climate change targets that they currently have under development or in use, in line with CDP's 2016 Science-Based Targets Call to Action. The framework does not, however, mention or require the use of any context-based metrics that would allow companies to measure their progress on these targets – or even, in the absence of these targets, to track their company-level contributions to wider systems-level climate change.

A summary of the findings for all five assessment questions has been included in Table 17.3.

Discussion

Companies are increasingly adopting business strategies to manage their individual contributions to climate change. As a result, companies are increasingly turning to climate reporting in order to evaluate the success of these sustainability strategies, and to calculate the performance improvements achieved as a result of their implementation (KPMG, 2015; WRI, ND). Various reporting frameworks have been developed to guide companies in disclosing their climate-related performance information. Given that companies use these frameworks as a means of evaluating the success of their climate-related sustainability strategies, there is a need to assess just how accurate a picture these framework-prescribed disclosures paint of a company's climate performance. Thus, the objective of this study is to assess the validity of three of the most commonly used corporate climate reporting frameworks, namely the GRI, GHG Protocol, and the CDP.

As shown in Table 17.3, the findings of this study reveal that, firstly, the three frameworks are strongly aligned in their approaches to climate reporting. This is revealed by their almost identical approaches to: setting the report's operational boundary, which KP-GHG impacts must necessarily be covered in the disclosure, the consideration of direct and indirect (scope 2) emissions, and the absence of any references to context-based metrics. Furthermore, the frameworks were also largely (albeit not fully) aligned on a number of other reporting issues as well, such as whether scope 3 disclosures were an explicit requirement, whether companies ought to report on non-KP-GHG emissions, and the consideration of the principle of context.

Even on these issues, the discrepancy between the three approaches was minor. For example, with regards to non–KP-GHG impacts, all three frameworks do not yet explicitly require their disclosure (in terms of climate impact). They differ, however, in the degree of their general commitment to their inclusion in climate disclosures: for example, both the GRI and GHG Protocol fail to mention SLCP impacts in their approaches. The CDP is the only framework to explicitly call for companies to take action on SLCP mitigation and disclosure. However, even under the CDP, SLCP species are not yet a reporting requirement. Similarly, with ozone-depleting (non–KP) GHGs, both the GRI and CDP fail to explicitly call for their inclusion in GHG emission totals. Nevertheless, both approaches recommend that companies include any GHG or other pertinent emissions (beyond the KP-GHGs) in their disclosures. Likewise, on the issue of scope 3 reporting: both the GRI and GHG Protocol generally agree that scope 3 reporting, as of yet, is not a general requirement on equal par with scope 1 and 2 emissions. However, the CDP has considered it as a requirement, through its inclusion in its scoring methodology. Finally, on the issue of context, although the GHG Protocol is the only approach to not refer to the principle of sustainability context in one form or the other, it does nonetheless align with the other two frameworks on their total lack of context-based metrics. This degree of harmonization among the three frameworks, in spite of their varying nature (e.g. sustainability reporting framework versus GHG inventory Protocol), disclosure aims, and intended audiences, helps to enhance the consistency of climate disclosures (i.e. comparable disclosure content) issued by different companies using these different approaches.

However, in spite of the strength of reporting consistency between the frameworks, the reporting validity of the three individual approaches remains poor. The findings demonstrate that the three frameworks have two key weaknesses: the comprehensiveness of the climate impacts considered (both in impact type and location along the organizational scope scale) and the degree of consideration of context (in principle and application). For example, none of the frameworks explicitly require companies to consider their non–KP-GHG impacts. Neither do they advocate for the use of context-based performance measures to allow companies to determine how exactly they are contributing to the universal climate target of limiting global temperature rise to 2 degree Celsius above pre-industrial levels. Furthermore, two out of the three frameworks (GRI and GHG Protocol) do not yet fully require companies to report on scope 3 emissions. The danger of these reporting approach weaknesses lies in the limited meaningfulness of the disclosures produced, and their ability to assess the company's contribution to wider climate thresholds. In the absence of a wider range (in type) and scope of climate impacts and of an applied approach to context-based reporting, reports produced in accordance with these frameworks may report on enterprise sustainability, but not on systems-wide, ecological sustainability. Such disclosures offer a company's internal and external stakeholders a limited and less meaningful assessment of its sustainability performance.

Of the three approaches, the CDP framework offers the strongest (relatively) reporting validity. When assessed on its own, however, it is still lacking in disclosure comprehensiveness and context-based requirements. A key strength of the CDP approach is that it is the only framework to explicitly address the need to consider SLCP impacts and science-based GHG emission reductions and assessment. Even though it was based to a certain extent (through its regular reference to the Standard and its guidance) on the GHG Protocol's reporting approach, it now far exceeds the Standard in terms of reporting validity, and the requirement to report corporate contributions to systems-wide ecological sustainability.

Conclusions and practical implications

This study has demonstrated the high reporting consistency, but poor validity, of the three most commonly used approaches to climate reporting. Despite the strong degree of alignment among the three frameworks, climate reporting under the GRI, CDP, and GHG Protocol remains significantly disconnected from context. All three are also not comprehensive in terms of their scope of climate impacts beyond direct emission sources. There is a heavy, but limited, focus on GHG impacts. This study also revealed that, compared to the GRI and GHG Protocol approaches, the CDP climate reporting framework carries a higher degree of reporting validity – given its explicit mention of SLCP impacts and its commitment to a climate-science-based approach to corporate target-setting (and, eventually, reporting). These findings undermine the value of climate reporting as an important tool for evaluating the implementation of climate strategies. If companies are unable to accurately monitor their performance comprehensively, and in context, following these three reporting frameworks, then they may not be able to accurately assess the extent to which their climate-related strategies are achieving sustainability performance improvements.

Based on these findings, we recommend three key improvements to the three frameworks that will help strengthen the validity of corporate reports issued in accordance with them, and strengthen the overall meaningfulness of climate change reporting as a valuable means of evaluating the implementation of business strategy for sustainability:

- **Recommendation 1.** On the issue of non-KP impacts, we recommend that all three frameworks incorporate additional metrics that would allow for the disclosure of the climate impacts of SLCP species. This should include the climate impacts of air pollutant species, such as black carbon and tropospheric ozone.
- **Recommendation 2.** With regards to scope 3 impacts, we recommend that both the GRI and GHG Protocol consider making scope 3 disclosures a requirement, rather than an optional disclosure.
- **Recommendation 3.** Finally, we also recommend that all three frameworks incorporate a context-based climate indictor, and preferably (but not necessarily) in connection to a science-based climate target. Various examples of these metrics (and associated targets) are currently in use by companies today (BT, ND; Autodesk, 2009). One example is the Center for Sustainable Organization's Context-Based Carbon Metric, which was first developed for use at Ben & Jerry's in 2006. This metric allows companies to measure their GHG emissions relative to systems-wide climate change limits. This is achieved by measuring GHG emissions 'against [carbon] reduction targets specified in the IPCC ... mitigation scenario' (CSO, ND).

Limitations and recommendations for further research

One of the key limitations of this work stems from the narrow selection of cases, which were the three reporting frameworks of the GRI, GHG Protocol and the CDP. Within the realm of corporate sustainability reporting, there exists a wide range of approaches and standards for companies reporting on climate impacts. Some of these approaches that were not addressed in this study include for example the ISO14064 GHG inventory and the Climate Disclosure Standards Board climate reporting standards. These and other standards not covered in this study may offer different findings when evaluated against the assessment questions used in this study. Notwithstanding that issue, the frameworks reviewed in this study were instructive and indicate the need for standards and guidelines that match their stated intentions.

Another limitation of this study lies in the choice of analysing the reporting frameworks at the level of their design and not at the level of their application by firms. In doing so, this research does not consider the impact that real-world application of these reporting approaches by company personnel has on the validity of the reports they produce. For example, this study did not explore how reporting personnel interpret the reporting approaches dictated by the standards, or why they interpret them in the way that they do. The implication could clearly impact the validity of the reports generated. As described earlier, the decision to focus on framework design was intentional. By analysing the dimensions of validity at the level of the framework (rather than on how companies are using the frameworks to develop their reports), this study aims to fill an identified research gap. Furthermore, this study contends that recommendations for validity improvements discussed here at the level of the frameworks themselves will inevitably lead to some degree of validity improvement at the level of their application. However, more work is nevertheless needed to explore company experiences with the validity issues identified in the three frameworks reviewed here, and the effect that this has on the quality of the disclosures generated.

Ultimately, in spite of these limitations, this study has made some valuable contributions to the literature on sustainability reporting. It has highlighted the validity weaknesses of climate reporting under the GRI, CDP and GHG Protocol, which are generally disconnected from context, and non-comprehensive in terms of the scope of climate impacts covered. The study has also made some recommendations on how these validity issues may be strengthened in the three frameworks, to ultimately enhance company contributions to systems-wide, ecological sustainability.

Appendix 1

Table 17.4 Definitions of key terms, as described in the GHG Protocol Standard

Term	GHG Protocol Standard Definition (GHG Protocol, 2004)
Direct Impacts (or GHG Emissions)	'Emissions from sources that are owned or controlled by the reporting company'
Indirect Impacts (or GHG Emissions)	'Emissions that are a consequence of the operations of the reporting company, but occur at sources owned or controlled by another company'
Scope 1 Impacts (or GHG Emissions)	'Direct GHG emissions'
Scope 2 Impacts (or GHG Emissions)	'Emissions associated with the generation of electricity, heating/cooling, or steam purchased for own consumption'
Scope 3 Impacts (or GHG Emissions) Operational Boundary	'Indirect emissions other than those covered in scope 2', such as emissions from the company's supply chain and product lifecycle
Operational Boundary	'The boundaries that determine the direct and indirect emissions associated with operations owned or controlled by the reporting company'

Appendix 2

Table 17.5 Study cases examined

Reporting framework	Summary
Global Reporting Initiative (GRI)	The GRI reporting guidelines are the most widely used sustainability reporting standard. Under these guidelines, companies disclose information on their organizational profile, management approach, and specific (or 'standard') disclosures of environmental, social, and economic performance. These disclosures are divided into key performance aspects; climate reporting falls under the Emissions aspect. It is important to note that the guidelines are voluntary. The guidelines were first issued in 1999 with the explicit aim of standardizing the voluntary sustainability reporting process. Since then the GRI has published four successive generations of reporting guidelines. Companies reporting 'in accordance' with the latest G4 version of the guidelines can choose to be in accordance with the core or comprehensive reporting option. The latter approach requires the disclosure of a wider range of performance metrics.
Greenhouse Gas (GHG) Protocol	The GHG Protocol was founded in 1998 as a 'multi-stakeholder partnership of businesses, non-governmental organizations (NGOs), governments, and others convened by the World Resources Institute (WRI), a U.S.-based environmental NGO, and the World Business Council for Sustainable Development (WBCSD), a Geneva-based coalition of 170 international companies' (GHG Protocol, 2004). The Protocol's approach to voluntary corporate climate reporting serves as the key reference standard for many other reporting frameworks; it may be used for the purpose of internal (i.e. inventory-related) or external (public) climate reporting. The Protocol's reporting approach is guided by five reporting principles (such as reporting consistency and transparency). The Protocol's principal reporting standard, its Corporate Accounting and Reporting Standard is a voluntary reporting standard that was first published in 2001 and revised in 2004 (and 2012), with a further amendment published in 2013. Additional guidance documents for implementing the Standard have also been issued in regards to disclosures of scope 2 emissions (2015) and scope 3 emissions (2013), as well as sector-specific guidance for the agriculture sector (2014) and the public sector (2010, specific to US only). Other guidance documents have also been issued for the disclosure of (potential) emissions from fossil fuel reserves (2015, in draft form), and the carbon impacts across an organization's investment portfolio (2015). The Project Quantification Standard was first issued in 2014, and remains in draft form. This Standard covers the disclosure of emissions from carbon offset projects for the purpose of credit trading.

(Continued)

Reporting framework	Summary
Carbon Disclosure Project (CDP)	The CDP (formerly and alternatively known as the Carbon Disclosure Project) was founded in 2000 and offered a voluntary corporate environmental reporting framework aimed specifically at institutional investors. As one of its central goals, the CDP aims to 'make environmental performance central to investment and business decisions'(CDP, 2016c). The CDP has two main questionnaires for climate-related impacts: its climate change questionnaire and the supply chain questionnaire. The former includes a core set of disclosure requirements (questions) that are to be completed by all companies, and an additional sector-specific supplement (or 'module') to be completed by companies in 'high-impact' sectors with a large climate footprint. These sectors are: oil and gas sector, electric utilities, auto manufacturers, information and communications technology, and food, beverage and tobacco. This sector-specific reporting approach was adopted by CDP in order to reduce the 'reporting burden' (CDP, 2016d) on companies in sectors outside those listed. The CDP has published individual guidance documents for companies in each of these sectors reporting for completing the supplemental modules. It also offers additional guidance for all sectors in the form of a Response Check tool that companies may use to review their submissions before submittal, to ensure 'completeness' (CDP, 2016d). Companies receive annual requests to voluntarily complete the climate change and/or supply chain questionnaires from CDP, on behalf of investors seeking climate information. Once the request has been received, companies are required to submit responses to the disclosure questions through the CDP's Online Response System (ORS) which is provided by CDP through its website. These company responses are publicly available, but only through the CDP site. These responses are then scored based on the extent and quality of their disclosures (as per the CDP's scoring methodology.

Notes

1 In the field of corporate reporting, the term 'context' may carry a number of different meanings. In this chapter we use the term specifically in reference to *sustainability* context, which is defined as being the 'background state of vital social and environmental resources in the world' (McElroy and van Engelen, 2012). In this sense, sustainability context refers to the 'global limits on resource use and pollution levels' (GRI, 2013) which prescribe the 'necessary condition for [global] sustainability' (McElroy and van Engelen, 2012). Reporting on corporate environmental impacts 'in context' means assessing 'what an organization's impacts on [these limits] ought to be (or not be) in order [for the company] to be sustainable' (McElroy and van Engelen, 2012). With regards to climate disclosure specifically, a company's sustainability context refers to the global ecological climate change thresholds (such as global average atmospheric temperature rise and greenhouse gas concentrations) that if exceeded, would result in unmitigated and unsustainable global warming. It is important to note that in this chapter we use the term 'sustainability context' interchangeably with the terms 'context' and 'contextual information'.
2 A list of definitions for direct and indirect emission sources and related terms has been included in Appendix 1.

References

Autodesk (2009). A corporate finance approach to climate-stabilizing targets ('C-FACT'). http://static-dc.autodesk.net/content/dam/autodesk/www/sustainability/docs/pdf/ greenhouse_gas_white_paper000.pdf.

Baue, B. (2013, May 24). Sustainability reporting: Does G4 enhance sight but obscure vision? *The Guardian Sustainable Business Blog.* www.theguardian.com/sustainable-business/sustainability-reporting-g4-sight-vision.

Bjørn, A., Bey, N., Georg, S., Røpke, I. and Hauschild, M. (2016). Is Earth recognized as a finite system in corporate responsibility reporting? *Journal of Cleaner Production.* https://www.sciencedirect.com/science/article/pii/S0959652615019204.

Bowen, F. and Wittneben, B. (2011). Carbon accounting: Negotiating accuracy, consistency and certainty across organizational fields. *Accounting, Auditing & Accountability Journal*, 24(8): 1022–1036.

BSR (Business for Social Responsibility) (2015). Business in a climate-constrained world: Creating an action agenda for private-sector leadership on climate change. https://www.bsr.org/ reports/bsr-bccw-creating-action-agenda-private-sector-leadership-climate-change.pdf.

BT (British Telecom) (ND). Climate stabilisation intensity targets: A new approach to setting corporate climate change targets. https://www.btplc.com/Betterfuture/NetGood/ OurNetGoodgoal/OurCSIMethodology/CSI_Methodology.pdf.

Carbon Clear (2015). Carbon reporting performance of the FTSE 100. http://carbon-clear.com/ files/FTSE_100_Report_2015.pdf.

Carbon Disclosure Project (CDP) (2016a). Technical note on science-based targets. https:// www.cdp.net/Documents/Guidance/2016/CDP-technical-note-science-based-targets.pdf.

Carbon Disclosure Project (CDP) (2016b). Commit to reduce short-lived climate pollutant emissions. https://www.cdp.net/en-US/Pages/RTP/short-lived-pollutant-emissions.aspx.

Carbon Disclosure Project (CDP) (2016c). CDP strategic plan 2014–2016. https://www.cdp. net/Documents/CDP-strategic-plan-2014-2016.pdf.

Carbon Disclosure Project (CDP) (2016d). Guidance for companies reporting on climate change on behalf of investors & supply chain members 2016. https://www.cdp.net/Documents/ Guidance/2016/CDP-2016-Climate-Change-Reporting-Guidance.pdf.

Center for Sustainable Organizations (CSO) (nd). Context-based metrics in the public domain. www.sustainableorganizations.org/context-based-metrics-in-public-domain.html.

Climate Counts and CSO (Center for Sustainable Organizations) (2013). Assessing carbon performance through the lens of climate science. www.sustainableorganizations.org/Climate_Counts_2013_CarbonStudy.pdf.

Daub, C. (2007). Assessing the quality of sustainability reporting: An alternative methodological approach. *Journal of Cleaner Production*, 15: 75–85.

Delmas, M. and Burbano, V. (2011). The drivers of greenwashing. *California Management Review*, 54(1): 64–87

Ernst and & Young. (2016). Value of sustainability reporting: A study by EY and Boston College Center for Corporate Citizenship. www.ey.com/Publication/vwLUAssets/EY_-_Value_of_sustainability_reporting/$FILE/EY-Value-of-Sustainability-Reporting.pdf.

GHG Protocol (Greenhouse Gas Protocol) (2004). Corporate Accounting and Reporting Standard. www.ghgprotocol.org/files/ghgp/public/ghg-protocol-revised.pdf.

GHG Protocol (2013). Required greenhouse gases in inventories: Accounting and Reporting Standard Amendment. www.ghgprotocol.org/files/ghgp/NF3-Amendment_052213.pdf.

GRI (Global Reporting Initiative) (2013). G4 sustainability reporting guidelines – Part 1: Reporting principles and standard disclosures. https://www.globalreporting.org/resourcelibrary/ GRIG4-Part1-Reporting-Principles-and-Standard-Disclosures.pdf.

ICC (2015a). Business and industry groups call for inclusion in Paris Agreement. www.iccwbo. org/News/Articles/2015/Business-and-industry-groups-call-for-inclusion-in-Paris-Agreement/.

ICC (2015b). ICC call for climate action. www.iccwbo.org/Advocacy-Codes-and-Rules/Document-centre/2015/ICC-Call-for-Climate-Action-2015/.

Kolk, A., Levy, D. and Pinkse, J. (2008). Corporate responses in an emerging climate regime: The institutionalization and commensuration of carbon disclosure. *European Accounting Review*, 17(4): 719–745.

KPMG (2015). Currents of change: The KPMG survey of corporate responsibility reporting 2015. https://www.kpmg.com/CN/en/IssuesAndInsights/ArticlesPublications/Documents/kpmg-survey-of-corporate-responsibility-reporting-2015-O-201511.pdf.

McElroy, M. and van Engelen, J. (2012). Corporate Sustainability Management: The Art and Science of Managing Non-Financial Performance. London: Earthscan.

Michelon, G., Pilonato, S. and Ricceri, F. (2015). CSR reporting practices and the quality of disclosure: An empirical analysis. *Critical Perspectives on Accounting*, 33: 59–78.

Milne, M. and Gray, R. (2013). W(h)ither ecology? The triple bottom line, the Global Reporting Initiative, and corporate sustainability reporting. *Journal of Business Ethics*, 118: 13–29.

Salkind, N. (2012). *Exploring Research*, 8th edn. New York: Pearson.

Talbot, D. and Boiral, O. (2013). Can we trust corporate GHG inventories? An investigation among Canada's large final emitters. *Energy Policy*, 63: 1075–1085.

Thurm, R. (2013). Closing the context gap: Sustainability reporting is failing us. *The Guardian Sustainable Business Blog*, April 9. www.theguardian.com/sustainable-business/blog/context-gap-sustainability-reporting-failing.

UNEP (United Nations Environmental Programme) (2015). Raising the bar: Advancing environmental disclosure in sustainability reporting. www.unep.org/NewsCentre/default.aspx?DocumentID=26854&ArticleID=35553.

UNEP-Climate and clean air coalition (UNEP-CCAC) (2014). Time to act to reduce short-lived climate pollutants. www.unep.org/ccac/Portals/50162/docs/publications/Time_To_Act/SLCP_TimeToAct_lores.pdf.

UNFCC (United Nations Framework Convention on Climate Change) (2015). Historic Paris Agreement on climate change: 195 nations set path to keep temperature rise well below 2 degrees Celsius. http://newsroom.unfccc.int/unfccc-newsroom/finale-cop21/.

UNGC (United Nations Global Compact) 2013. Global corporate sustainability report 2013. https://www.unglobalcompact.org/library/371.

UNGC (2016). Caring for Climate business forum. https://www.unglobalcompact.org/docs/issues_doc/Environment/climate/C4C-business-forum-2016-meeting-report.pdf.

Vigneau, L., Humphreys, M. and Moon, J. (2015). How do firms comply with international sustainability standards? Processes and consequences of adopting the Global Reporting Initiative. *Journal of Business Ethics*, 131 (2): 469–486.

We Mean Business Coalition (2015). Reduce short-lived climate pollutant emissions. www.wemeanbusinesscoalition.org/content/reduce-short-lived-climate-pollutant-emissions.

WRI (World Resources Institute) (2015). 114 companies commit to set ambitious science-based emissions reduction targets, surpassing goal. www.wri.org/news/2015/12/release-114-companies-commit-set-ambitious-science-based-emissions-reduction-targets.

WRI (nd).Science based targets initiative. www.wri.org/our-work/project/science-based-targets-initiative.

18 Promoting sustainability through corporate social responsibility

An Indian perspective

Bhaskar Sinha and Ram Nayan Yadava

Introduction

Corporate social responsibility and sustainability reporting are two important means of promoting sustainable development by companies all over the world, including India. The need for achieving sustainability is increasingly being recognized due to recent pressing global problems such as climate change, poverty, human rights violations and regulatory compliance. As a result, companies are implementing policies, procedures, tools and approaches that go beyond regulatory compliance and contribute to achieving sustainable societies through minimizing theirs adverse social and environmental impacts and exploring the additional option to support marginalized sections of society (Henriques and Richardson, 2004).

Indian companies have known to be practising philanthropy and social responsibilities, which can be traced in early literature (Amaladoss and Manohar, 2013). In recent times, the leading Indian companies have primarily engaged in improving education, health and livelihoods in different parts of the country under corporate social responsibility (CSR). These activities are also used by companies in building their image as socially responsible companies. In addition, many companies have incorporated a fundamental doctrine of sustainable development in their core business activity as well as in their supply chain management including CSR. Realizing the potential of CSR in achieving sustainable development, the government of India amended the company bill in 2013, which mandates companies with more than US\$0.83 million (INR5 crores, conversion rate is INR60 is equal to\$1) net profit to spend at least 2 per cent of their profit towards corporate social responsibility (MCA, Govt. of India, 2013).

With such mandatory spending on CSR by companies in India, it is becoming imperative for companies not only to implement their CSR activities but also to monitor and evaluate the resulting impact on the beneficiaries. Furthermore, it is important for companies to adopt innovative actions for promoting sustainability in their business operation and report in a comprehensible manner on their performance in the form of a CSR/sustainability report so that their performance could be evaluated and monitored. Therefore, evaluation and comparison of sustainability/CSR reporting are a matter of concern for the Indian government since the tools and approaches used for the assessment in other countries may not be directly applicable to Indian companies because of the difference in socio-economic conditions.

In the context of CSR being mandated and continuously evolving in India, the following three issues and research needs are important to realize the full potential of CSR in achieving sustainable development: assessing the impacts of CSR, assessing sustainability reporting practices of leading Indian companies and assessing the scope and potential of CSR in adaptation and mitigation to climate change. With this back-drop of knowledge, the current chapter is a synthesis of two studies drawn from Indian companies with a view to understanding the role and responsibility of companies in promoting sustainability in their core business and through CSR.

Companies have applied the principle of sustainable development within and outside their core business by implementing many programmes. These include improving re-source use efficiency in their core business activities (inside the fence line), helping the vulnerable communities (beyond the fence line) through CSR, and collaborating with the global community to address issues related to adaptation and mitigation of climate change. The first study discusses the impacts of different CSR activities implemented by Lupin Human Welfare Research Foundation (LHWRF) towards improving the socio-economic conditions of the rural poor in Raisen and Vidisha districts of the state of Madhya Pradesh, India and the second study is about assessing the sustainabil-ity reporting practices of leading Indian companies using numerical scoring method. These studies are relevant to understanding the current behaviour of Indian companies with respect to the implementation of CSR and promoting sustainability in their core business. The analysis of two different studies conducted in different research contexts/ setting may help to design a framework for companies in realizing the complete potential of CSR in promoting sustainable development in India. The summaries of both studies are presented and discussed in this chapter.

Study 1: CSR potential of LHWRF in promoting sustainability in rural area[1]

India has achieved a robust economic growth in the last two decades; however, the desired impact has not percolated down amongst the poor and rural communities. As a result, the economic gap between rich and poor has further widened. The main contribution to this robust economic growth is the service sector confined to urban India, whereas the growth of the rural economy has been meagre. For example, with 60 per cent of the population engaged in agriculture, it is growing at less than 2 per cent. On the other hand, the industrial sector with 17 per cent and service sector with 23 per cent workforce are growing by more than 5 per cent and 9 per cent, respectively. This implies that programmes and policies related to agriculture and rural development need to be strengthened further based on comprehensive monitoring and evaluation for achieving inclusive rural development.

The progress and welfare of the society, especially poor of rural areas, are so far construed as the sole responsibility of the government. India, as an emerging econ-omy and responsible nation too, has introduced several programmes specifically tar-geted towards ecological regeneration, rural development, livelihood security and generation of tangible and intangible assets in a sustainable manner (Hirway et al., 2008; Mehta, 2009; Sinha et al. 2010; Esteves et al. 2013; MoRD, 2014). Some of the recent and important programmes in this regard include Mahatma Gandhi National Rural Employment Guarantee Act (MGNREGA), National Rural Livelihood Mission (NRLM) and Integrated Watershed Management Program (IWMP), Swarnjayanti Gram Swarozgar Yojana, National Social Assistance Program, and Prime Minister's Village Road Connectivity Scheme (MoRD, 2014). Even with all these initiatives, about 25 per cent of the rural population live below the poverty line (as per Tendulkar methodology of expert group 2009) despite spending approximately 25 per cent of its total expenditure on social welfare programmes[2] (Planning Commission, 2014). This implies that even with a robust economic growth rate at the country level and substantial spending on the poverty eradication programmes, poverty in India is still widely prevalent. Therefore, all such programmes need to be made more efficient and result-oriented. The efforts and actions of many more stakeholders, viz., companies and NGOs, need to be continuously monitored and synergized with the ongoing programmes of the government to the extent possible for transforming the lives of millions living in rural India.

Corporate Social Responsibility (CSR) is being recognized as an important aspect of corporate practices along with social responsibility. However, the business sector, that has a pivotal role to play in ensuring private investment flows to the rural areas of developing countries including India, has been left out in the development process. In India, trusts and foundations promoted by many corporates are involved in implementing CSR activities in poor areas, which include education, health, livelihood creation, skill development, and emancipation and up-grading of society. Recently, after the mandatory CSR spending, many companies have seen this as an opportunity to improve their brand image and are following the principles of sustainability in their business operation. Under this changed scenario, it becomes necessary to evaluate the activities under CSR, especially for benchmarking CSR impact in rural India after the introduction of a new rule mandating CSR spending. Thus, the case of Lupin Human Welfare and Research Foundation Bhopal (LHWRF) has been studied towards enhancing livelihood opportunities and strengthening the agricultural system through their various CSR activities. Lupin Human Welfare and Research Foundation (LHWRF) is an entity of Lupin Limited, implementing Lupin CSR activities all over India. The objective of creating LHWRF was to find solutions to the following two fundamental questions (Lupin Annual report 2012–13):

- Can a business transform distant villages that have for decades remained in poverty, isolation and ignorance into vibrant centres of progress and development?
- Of what use are scientific knowledge, technology development and economic progress if they can't be used to restore a villager's lost confidence or extend the benefits of modern education to the underprivileged and transform lives?

To find solutions to the above questions, LHWRF was established in 1988 and made a humble beginning in 1988 by initiating small projects for growth and development of rural India. Since then, LHWRF has come a long way to become one of the largest foundations of any company in South-East Asia, touching and transforming the lives of over 2.5 million people in 3,000 villages spread across the states of Rajasthan, Madhya Pradesh, Maharashtra and Uttarakhand (Lupin Annual Report 2012–13). The Foundation operates through ten regional centres: Alwar and Bharatpur in Rajasthan; Aurangabad, Dhule, Nandurbar, Pune and Sindhudurg in Maharashtra; Bhopal and Dhar in Madhya Pradesh and Rishikesh in Uttarakhand. The Foundation undertakes rural development programmes that contribute to sustainable livelihoods to the poor through natural resource management and infrastructure development.

LHWRF, Bhopal is implementing programmes like farmers clubs (FC), self-help groups (SHGs), check dams (CD), and training programmes (TP). FC activities are to enhance the agricultural productivity by changing cropping pattern, dissemination of knowledge on new cropping techniques and the introduction of new technologies and equipment related to agriculture. The SHGs programme is focused on women empowerment through training on professional skills, providing credit support and setting up of successful enterprises by women through SHG loans. In the CD programme, LHWRF Bhopal has constructed several water storage structures such as check dams, farm ponds, de-siltation of old structures to enhance water-stocking in local micro-watersheds and agricultural lands. Under the training programme, the Foundation is imparting training to enhance the skills related to driving, tailoring, house wiring (electrician), computer education and other related areas for rural people.

The study was conducted in 23 villages of Vidisha and Raisen districts of Madhya Pradesh, India, through field-based survey and semi-structured interviews of the beneficiaries of self-help groups (SHGs), farmers clubs (FC), training programmes (TP), and check dams (CD). Data were gathered through a mixed approach that included semi-structured interviews, non-participant observations and document review. The study was entirely based on primary data due to non-availability of secondary data, besides what was available on Lupin website. Initially, 175 individual beneficiaries of different programmes were interviewed, in which 52 responses were not appropriate either due to their incomplete responses or were found to be wrong in triangulation. Subsequently, the information collected from 123 respondents from different programmes (61 of SHGs, 32 of check dams and farmers clubs, and 30 of training programmes) was tabulated and analysed (Table 18.1).

Table 18.1 List of different CSR programmes and implementation sites of LHWRF and sampled sites for study

Lupin programmes			Selected for study	
Programmes	Numbers	Location (Block-District)	Numbers	Location (Block-District)
SHGs	16 clusters with 277 SHGs (loan sanctioned by bank) spread in 99 villages	Obedullaganj–Raisen, Sanchi-Raisen, Gaitratganj–Raisen, Vidisha-Vidisha	10 clusters, 61 SHGs beneficiaries Spread in 23 villages	Obedullaganj–Raisen, Vidisha–Vidisha
Farmers Clubs (FC)	30 FCs spread in 30 villages	Obedullaganj–Raisen, Silwani-Raisen	32 beneficiaries from 20 FCs	Obedullaganj–Raisen
Check Dams	32 check dams irrigating 2,084 acres of land for 474 beneficiaries	Obedullaganj–Raisen	12 check dams covering 800 acres land and 32 beneficiaries	Obedullaganj–Raisen
Training Programmes	Driving, welding, house wiring, beauty parlour, Tailoring, and computer skills	Obedullaganj–Raisen	30 beneficiaries from different programmes of driving, welding, house wiring, beauty parlour, Tailoring, and computer	Obedullaganj–Raisen

Outcomes of LHWRF interventions

Self-help groups (SHGs)

The occupational diversity of marginal families (58 per cent respondents), who were involved only in subsistence agriculture increased after the initiation of CSR programmes through engagement in other income generating activities like becoming vendors, hawkers and small shops owners. This subsequently led to increase in their additional monthly income from nil (because of subsistence agriculture) to US$62 (Table 18.2). The remaining 42 per cent respondents were engaged in agriculture, and they were able to earn an additional income of US$25.5/month (taking conversion of INR60 per dollar) by selling surplus vegetables. They too recorded higher occupational diversity and income (Table 18.2).

Farmers clubs (FC) and check dams

Farmers clubs and check dams have been instrumental in overcoming the problems faced by the farmers related to agriculture and have enabled farmers to get a higher return from their agriculture. It was observed that farmers used to face many problems related to agriculture, namely a lack of scientific knowledge related to crop management; access to irrigation, fertilizer, seeds and pesticides; weather information, and financial constraints. However, after farmers clubs and check dams, 34 per cent of farmers with land holding up to 1 hectare did not report any problem related to agriculture, whereas, 66 per cent of farmers with an average land holding of 1.5 hectares reported problems mainly related to irrigation facilities and financial constraints after joining farmers clubs (Table 18.3). FC successfully resolved the prior prevalent problems

Table 18.2 Impact of SHGs on beneficiary's occupational diversity and income

Number of respondents	Extra income other than agriculture (US$/month)		Occupation diversity	
	Pre	Post	Pre	Post
34★	0	62	1	2.0
27#	25.5	120	1	2.5

★ SHGs member without any additional income other than agriculture.
SHGs member having some additional income.

Table 18.3 Impact of farmers clubs and check dams on agricultural production and income

Average land holding (ha)	Number of crops grown in year		Number of problems associated with agriculture		Total production of wheat (quintal/family)		Total production of paddy (quintal/family)		Income from wheat & paddy (US$/family/Month)	
	Pre	Post	Pre	Post	Pre	Post	Pre	Post	Pre	Post
1.5 (n=21)	1	2	4	1.5	10	18	4	22	28.4	97
1.0 (n=11)	2	3	3	0	10	26	5	26	33.7	125

related to procurement of seeds, fertilizers, pesticides and technical awareness related to agriculture. Overall, the average crop diversity and production of all the major crops increased leading to a subsequent increase in their monthly income by US$80 for each beneficiary (average).

Training programmes

The impact of training programmes was very rewarding, especially for the poor youth. The overall success rate of training for driving (78 per cent), welding (54 per cent), house wiring (75 per cent), beauty parlour (30 per cent), tailoring (30 per cent), and computer (38 per cent) in terms of getting employment was calculated to be 51 per cent. The average monthly income of the trained and employed participants are US$75, 83, 100, 83, 25 and 67 for driving, welding, home wiring, beauty parlour, tailoring, and computer, respectively.

The assessment of different CSR programmes of LHWRF, Bhopal reveals that companies can make a significant contribution in transforming rural India through need-based interventions related to agricultural production and in creating employment. Further, if LHWRF, Bhopal with a budget of US$ 0.065 million can transform the lives of poor in 23 villages, then US$1,450 million (approximate estimated amount after 2 per cent mandatory CSR rule) has immense potential in transforming the lives of the rural population in India. The huge budget of the government of India together with CSR budget of companies can have visible impacts in improving the socio-economic conditions of the rural poor provided it is implemented professionally with an integrated approach.

The findings of this study could be useful for creating the new partnership for synergizing government and corporate actions for long-term planning and implementation of CSR activities towards rural development, environmental management, corporate sustainability, and overall sustainable development.

Study 2: Assessment of sustainability reporting of leading Indian corporates[3]

In recent years, the notions of corporate sustainability and its reporting are being recognized as important issues among companies, managers, academia and policy makers. Corporations across the globe are manifesting social and environmental accountabilities along with transparent corporate behaviour beyond core profit activities and legal requirements by reporting their performance in the form of sustainability reporting. This is based on the triple bottom line (TBL) approach to corporate implications on the environment and people, as well as on economic capital, applied at a practical level by a growing number of companies around the world. In this context of corporate sustainability or responsibility, it is often used to explain corporate non-financial reporting or sustainable reporting or CSR reporting (Yadava and Sinha, 2015).

There is a steady growth in the number of organizations reporting on non-financial issues. In 2008, the survey showed that 79 per cent of the apex 250 companies of the Fortune 500 (Global 250) issued separate non-financial reports, compared with 52 per cent in 2005, while the rate of reporting among the largest 100 companies (N100) in 22 countries has risen on average from 33 per cent to 45 per cent (Skouloudis et al. 2010). The emergence of such reporting practices has been accompanied by numerous attempts over the years to homogenize such practices. Global Reporting Initiative (GRI) is recognized as one of the primary movers in establishing international standards for non-financial reporting (Brown et al., 2009). GRI pioneered and developed a comprehensive sustainability reporting framework that is extensively used around the globe. The framework enables organizations to measure and report their economic, environmental, social and governance performance. Out of the 721,719 registered companies in India, only 68 have ever developed a sustainability report. Even among the BRICS (Brazil, Russia, India, China and South Africa) countries, India has the lowest number of companies developing sustainability reports. Out of the 9,966 sustainability reports submitted to the GRI since 1999, only 104 are from India.

Publicly available information on topics such as environmental and social performance, management quality or internal governance transparency is clearly now vital for investors and shareholders in order to make accurate decisions. In addition, other stakeholders like customers, suppliers, employees, communities and other social groups also expect a higher standard of accountability and demand a more comprehensive depiction of corporate impacts, risks and performance. Currently, sustainability performance benchmarks do not exist, so companies desiring to monitor their progress are left with few options beyond comparing their programmes with other similar companies (Krajnc and Glavič, 2003). As such, companies within sectors have begun to establish, track, and report key indicators of sustainability progress (De Sousa, 2001), and some groups have commissioned management consultant to benchmark their programmes versus other companies in their business sector. The scoring system of sustainability report is an evolving process and is constantly adapting to the reporting trends that constantly emerge and aim to spotlight best practices.

In the context of evolving reporting practices on sustainability, five leading Indian companies have been selected to compare their performance on sustainability reporting. The sustainability report of ONGC (Oil and Natural Gas Corporation Limited), Indian Oil (Indian Oil Corporation Limited), Reliance (Reliance Industries Limited), Tata Steel (Tata Steel Private Limited) and SAIL (Steel Authority of India Limited) were selected and analysed by using the numerical scoring system. The numerical scoring system was designed for each one of the 84 performance indicators (9 indicators for economic, 30 for the environment and 45 for social dimensions) of the GRI 2011 guidelines. Each performance indicator was assigned a score between 0 and 3 points (with a possible maximum score of 252 points), following the structure and rationale of previous scoring systems of Morhardt et al. (2002). Although this numerical system is an adaptation of Morhardt et al. (2002) and Skouloudis et al. (2009) for GRI 2011 guidelines, some modifications were made in consultation with experts to suit Indian corporate sustainability perspective. If a specific indicator was not mentioned in the assessed report then a score of 0 was given, brief or generic statements received score of 1 (e.g. company does not have any child labour practices), extensive coverage (detailed information but did not cover more than one year's data) received score of 2, and the maximum score of 3 was given to an indicator when coverage was full and systematic, which covered more than one year's data in comparable form (Figure 18.1). Based on the scores obtained, the disclosures of the companies on sustainability reporting were analysed. The performance here does not mean the actual performance of the companies but the inference derived from their sustainability reports.

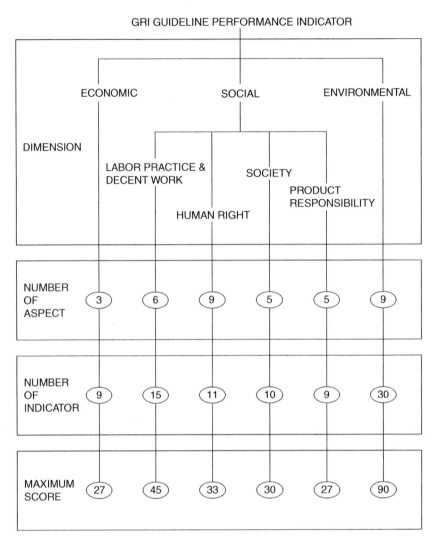

Figure 18.1 Schematic presentation of GRI guideline 2011 with number of different dimensions, aspects and performance indicators. Maximum score represents the highest numerical value that can be obtained on total indicator using a scale of 0–3 (Adopted from Yadava and Sinha, 2015).

Comparison and analysis of sustainability reporting

The overall analysis of sustainability reports in this study showed that reporting on social and environmental indicators was less comprehensive as compared to their reporting on economic dimension. Out of the total 45 indicators on the social dimension, the report of Reliance did not provide any information on 14 indicators (that means Reliance report on 31 indicators and missing on 14 indicators). Reports of ONGC and Indian Oil did not report on 10 social indicators. However, Tata Steel reported on all indicators of the social dimension. Out of 30 indicators on the environmental dimension, the number of indicators not reported ranged from two (Tata Steel) to six (for Indian Oil). Interestingly, on the economic dimension, except Indian Oil which missed one indicator (procedure of local hiring and proportion of senior managers hired from the local community at the location of significant operation), all other sampled companies have reported on each and every indicator of economic dimension in their sustainability reports (Table 18.4). This analysis revealed that Indian companies lack in reporting on social and environmental dimensions and need to improve their comprehensive reporting on sustainability based on GRI guidelines.

The total score (presented in percentage, which was calculated by dividing the score obtained by each company with maximum score) on economic, environmental and social dimensions of sampled companies ranged from 46 per cent to 71 per cent with an average score of 53 per cent. Tata Steel scored maximum (71 per cent), whereas Indian Oil scored minimum (46 per cent). The scores obtained on the economic dimension ranged from 52 per cent to 70 per cent; on the environmental dimension, it ranged from 51 per cent to 80 per cent and on the social dimension, it ranged from 33 per cent to 65 per cent. The difference in scores obtained for reporting on the economic dimension was less (18 per cent) as compared to social (32 per cent) and environmental (29 per cent) dimensions, highlighting the need for paying more attention to understanding and reporting on social and environmental dimensions (Table 18.5).

Analysis of the steel sector showed that there was not much difference between public and private companies in their reporting on the economic dimension. However, reporting on the other two dimensions, i.e. environmental and social, Tata Steel (private) scored higher than SAIL (public) by 29 per cent and 21 per cent, respectively. With respect to the comparison between public (ONGC and Indian Oil) and private sector

Table 18.4 The number of indicators reported out of total indicator by the sampled companies on different dimensions of their sustainability report

Dimension	Total number of indicators	Number of indicators reported out of total indicators				
		Tata Steel	*SAIL*	*ONGC*	*Indian Oil*	*Reliance*
Economic	9	9	9	9	8	9
Environmental	30	28	25	26	24	24
Social	45	45	40	35	35	31
Total	84	82	74	70	67	64

Table 18.5 Scores of different companies based on performance indicators of GRI. The value in the parenthesis represents the percentage of total score (Adapted from Yadava and Sinha, 2015)

Corporate Dimension	*Tata Steel*	*SAIL*	*ONGC*	*Indian Oil*	*Reliance*
Economic [27]★	18 (67)	19 (70)	17 (63)	14 (52)	18 (67)
Environmental [90]★	72 (80)	46 (51)	52 (58)	49 (54)	60 (67)
Social [135]★	88 (65)	60 (44)	51 (38)	52 (38)	44 (33)
Total score [252]★	178 (71)	125 (50)	120 (48)	115 (46)	122 (48)

★ Highest possible score in the respective dimension of sustainability.

(Reliance) in the oil sector, the overall reporting was more or less similar. However, on certain aspects of environment and economic dimensions, reporting of Reliance was better, as compared to ONGC and Indian Oil; whereas, on other aspects of environmental and social dimensions, ONGC was better.

It is anticipated that the results of this research will find several applications among companies in India and around the world. Corporations and industry associations may use these results in developing a benchmark for the different type of industries/sectors. Benchmarking sustainability reports as per the sector/country according to a scoring system can yield potential benefits. It informs stakeholders, assists the companies themselves, promotes effective stakeholder communication, identifies potential reporting strengths and weaknesses and compares their reported performance against their peers.

Conclusions and recommendations

In the light of recent corporate social responsibility rules, 2014 and national voluntary guidelines, 2011, the CSR programmes of companies require proper monitoring and evaluation of their impact at ground/beneficiary level along with their reporting in the form of a sustainability report. Further, to enhance the visibility, the CSR programme should also be integrated with a global issue like climate change adaptation. This analysis of both studies demonstrates the contribution of companies in promoting sustainable development while executing their CSR activities and reporting in the form of the sustainability report. Furthermore, a business model can be prepared to execute the CSR/Sustainability to deal with a global issue like climate change etc. through strategies and innovations (Schaltegger et al., 2015).

In this regard, the evaluation methods used in this study can be applied for assessing the impacts of CSR programme executed by companies and other similar programmes implemented by the government. These methods of evaluation may be modified as per the local setting and corporate priority without changing the principle of impact evaluation for programme implementation and sustainability reporting. Associated industries and government may mandate monitoring and evaluation of the CSR activities and sustainability reporting for bigger companies in the first phase, followed by medium and small enterprises. Looking at the amount of money likely to be earmarked after mandatory CSR rules, it is important that the CSR wing of companies should develop synergy and convergence with the government programmes and agencies to improve the effectiveness of implementation. The study would also help the government agencies, companies and civil societies in reporting on monitoring and evaluation of their programmes implementation.

Notes

1 Part of this study is submitted to *Journal of Social Responsibility* for publishing as a research article.
2 Social Welfare programmes includes education, art, culture, health and family welfare, water supply, sanitation and SUD, information broadcasting, welfare of SC/ST/OBC, labour and labour welfare, social welfare and nutrition, north-eastern areas, and other social services.
3 Part of this study is published in Yadava, R.N. and Sinha, B. (2015), Scoring Sustainability Reports using GRI 2011 guidelines for assessing environmental, economics, and social dimensions of leading public and private Indian companies. *Journal of Business Ethics*, 1–10.

References

Amaladoss, M.X. and Manohar, H.L. (2013). Communicating corporate social responsibility: A case of CSR communication in emerging economies. *Corporate Social Responsibility and Environmental Management*, 20(2): 65–80.

Berkhout, F., Hertin, J. and Gann, D.M. (2006). Learning to adapt: Organisational adaptation to climate change impacts. *Climatic change*, 78(1): 135–156.

Brown, H.S., De Jong, M. and Lessidrenska, T. (2009). The rise of the Global Reporting Initiative: A case of institutional entrepreneurship. *Environmental Politics*, 18(2): 182–200.

De Sousa, C. (2001). Contaminated sites: The Canadian situation in an international context. *Journal of Environmental Management*, 62(2): 131–154.

Esteves, T., Rao, K.V., Sinha, B., Roy, S.S., Rao, B., Jha, S. and Ravindranath, N.H. (2013). Agricultural and livelihood vulnerability reduction through the MGNREGA. *Economic & Political Weekly*, 48(52): 94–103

Henriques, A. and Richardson, J. (2004). Introduction: Triple bottom line-does it all add up. *The Triple Bottom Line: Does it All Add Up*. Abingdon: Routledge.

Hirway, I., Saluja, M.R. and Yadav, B. (2008). *Reducing Unpaid Work in the Village of Nana Kotda, Gujarat: An Economic Impact Analysis of Works Undertaken under the National Rural Employment Guarantee Act (NREGA)* (Levy Research Project 34). Annandale-on-Hudson, NY: The Levy Institute.

Krajnc, D. and Glavič, P. (2003). Indicators of sustainable production. *Clean Technologies and Environmental Policy*, 5(3–4): 279–288.

Mehta, R. (2009). Rural livelihood diversification and its measurement issues: Focus India. WYE City Group on Statistics on Rural Development and Agriculture Household Income, Second Annual Meeting, 11–12 June FAO, Rome.

Ministry of Corporate Affairs (2013). Government of India, Companies Act (www.mca.gov.in/Ministry/pdf/CompaniesAct2013.pdf).

MoRD (2014). Ministry of Rural Development. Government of India. http://rural.nic.in/sites/programs-schemes.asp.

Morhardt, J.E., Baird, S. and Freeman, K. (2002). Scoring corporate environmental and sustainability reports using GRI 2000, ISO 14031 and other criteria. *Corporate Social Responsibility and Environmental Management*, 9(4): 215–233.

Planning Commission (2014). *Report of the Expert Group on Estimation of Proportion and Number of Poor*. New Delhi: Government of India.

Schaltegger, S., Hansen, E.G. and Lüdeke-Freund, F. (2015). Business models for sustainability: Origins, present research, and future avenues. *Organization & Environment*, 29(1): 3–10.

Sinha, B., Basu, A. and Katiyar, A.S. (2010). *Impact Assessment of MGNREGA's Activities for Ecological and Economic Security*. Bhopal: Indian Institute of Forest Management.

Skouloudis, A., Evangelinos, K. and Kourmousis, F. (2009). Development of an evaluation methodology for triple bottom line reports using international standards on reporting. *Environmental Management*, 44(2): 298–311.

Skouloudis, A., Evangelinos, K. and Kourmousis, F. (2010). Assessing non-financial reports according to the Global Reporting Initiative guidelines: Evidence from Greece. *Journal of Cleaner Production*, 18(5): 426–438.

Yadava, R.N. and Sinha, B. (2015). Scoring Sustainability Reports using GRI 2011 guidelines for assessing environmental, economic, and social dimensions of leading public and private Indian companies. *Journal of Business Ethics*, 1–10.

19 Environmental cause marketing

Debra Z. Basil, Mary Runté and Jennifer Liebetrau

Results demonstrate that most of these alliances utilize a positive fit partnership, and within this category, natural fit is the most commonly used. Alliance form varies, with transactional and sponsorship formats leading the way. Campaigns can be somewhat complex, with multiple points of consumer contact. Various triggers lead to cause donations; most commonly, the trigger is linked to product purchase of some sort. Companies report benefiting from positive publicity for the company, and often cite increased sales and market share as benefits as well. For causes, primary benefits include donations, positive behaviour relating to their cause, media exposure, and new volunteers or members.

Introduction

This chapter focuses on the role of environmentally oriented causes in cause marketing campaigns. Top environmental cause marketing alliances are analysed to better understand the anatomy of successful cause marketing campaigns within the environmental cause space. The results suggest that cause marketing is a valuable tool for companies seeking to support the environment while fostering their own success; however, it is essential to find the right cause and format.

Cause marketing campaigns have become an incredibly prevalent form of generating cause support while netting valuable visibility for both the company and the cause involved. Perhaps the most commonly cited definition of cause marketing was developed in 1988, '… the process of formulating and implementing marketing activities that are characterized by an offer from the firm to contribute a specified amount to a designated cause when customers engage in revenue-providing exchanges that satisfy organizational and individual objectives' (Varadarajan and Menon, 1988, p. 60). The emergence of this transactional marketing model is typified by Yoplait yogurt's 'Save Lids to Save Lives' campaign, which began in 1998, whereby the company donates 10 cents to the Susan G. Komen Foundation for breast cancer research for every yogurt lid returned to them. More recent cause marketing alliances have evolved from this transactional approach, to engage in a wider variety of efforts allying a company with a cause for the purpose of benefiting both. The outdoor clothing and gear retailer Patagonia for example not only donated 100 per cent of its 2016 Black Friday sales to grassroots environmental groups, but generally orients its strategic efforts towards environmental responsibility. This evolution is demonstrated in the definition from Engage for Good (formerly Cause Marketing Forum), 'a strategic marketing partnership that pairs a company or brand with a social cause or cause-related organization for mutual benefit' (Cause Marketing Forum, 2010a).

A major concern with cause marketing is whether the company is truly helping the cause, or primarily helping itself by exploiting the cause. In this research, we examine cause marketing alliances involving environmentally oriented causes assessing the dimensions of fit and the alliance relationships that typify successful cause marketing campaigns. A new taxonomy of CRM form is developed to distinguish these relationships. The alliances examined in this research have been judged by an independent and reputable organization, Engage for Good (name changed from Cause Marketing Forum in 2016), as benefiting both cause and company.

Cause marketing background

As government support declines and personal budgets shrink, non-profit organizations are increasingly turning to companies in hopes of filling ever increasing funding gaps (Andreasen, 2003). Cause related marketing, or cause marketing, is a valuable tool for non-profits in need of financial support (Berglind and Nakata, 2005). Cause marketing generated over $1.9 billion in the USA in 2015 (IEG, 2016).

While cause marketing arguably originated long ago, probably within ancient markets, the practice of modern cause marketing emerged in the 1970s. Academic study of the practice began to grow in the 1980s and really gained momentum around the turn of the century (Liebetrau, Basil, and Runté, 2016).

Generally, consumers respond very positively to cause marketing (e.g. Basil and Herr, 2006; Lavack and Kropp, 2003). Research suggests that 83 per cent of consumers would like to see more cause marketing efforts (Cone Communications, 2010a). In a major consumer survey, 92 per cent of consumers indicated they would like to buy a product with a social or environmental benefit, and 67 per cent indicated they had done so in the past 12 months (Cone Communications/Echo, 2013), making it a promising avenue for both businesses and non-profits.

There may be potential downfalls to cause marketing, however. Consumers can be sceptical of business' claims towards various forms of social responsibility. A recent study examining companies' environmental social responsibility showed that fewer than half of those surveyed trust companies to tell them the truth (Cone Communications, 2012). Research has shown a strong group of 'sceptics' exists regarding cause marketing as well (Webb and Mohr, 1998). The wording of cause marketing claims can strongly impact consumer interpretation of the benefit accruing to the non-profit, in some cases misleading consumers into believing the non-profit benefits more than it actually does. Unfortunately, cases of misleading cause marketing campaigns are all too evident in the popular press (Chang, 2007). A number of US states, including a recent effort in Vermont, have implemented regulations to control cause marketing deception (Grumet 2012). Conversely, a survey of non-profit organizations (NFPs) that have participated in cause marketing suggests that NFPs generally attain their goals when participating in cause marketing partnerships (Runté, Basil and Deshpande, 2009). Taken together these findings demonstrate that cause marketing is potentially beneficial to non-profits and causes; however, cause marketing may also simply be a means of allowing a company to exploit a cause for their own purposes.

Societal expectations of companies' environmental efforts

Frequently, environmental causes are grouped with animal causes for reporting purposes. This makes sense, as long-term ecological sustainability is contingent upon a healthy animal kingdom. There are over 13,000 environmental and animal charities within the USA. These compose 4.5 per cent of all US public charities, and represented nearly $17 billion in revenues in 2013 (Blackwood, McKeever and Pollak, 2016). The number of environment and animal charities, although relatively small comparatively, experienced notable growth of 18 per cent over the 2003–2013 period.

In the USA, 70 per cent of American consumers indicate that they pay attention to companies' environmental efforts, 69 per cent actively seek to buy environmental products, and 63 per cent trust companies' environmental messages (Cone Communications/ Echo, 2013). Internationally, perceptions vary regarding the extent to which companies actually make meaningful social and environmental contributions. Canadian consumer outlook is relatively dim, with only 14 per cent believing companies have made a significant social or environmental impact, compared to 37 per cent in India and 27 per cent in Brazil for example. Similarly only 21 per cent of Canadians believe consumers can have a significant impact through their purchasing behaviour, compared to 52 per cent in India and 57 per cent in Brazil (Cone Communications/Echo, 2013).

These results suggest that consumers want companies to make environmental efforts, but they also tend to mistrust these efforts to differing degrees. Research by environmental marketing firm TerraChoice (2009) suggests this mistrust is not misplaced. Analysing products from the US, Canada and Australia and using best practice standards from each country respectively (e.g. the U.S. Federal Trade Commission, Competition Bureau of Canada, Australian Competition & Consumer Commission, and the ISO 14021 standard for environmental labelling), a full 98 per cent of the green products examined made at least one misleading, or outright false, claim. This practice is known as 'greenwashing'. It involves misleading or lying about the environmental impact of a product or service or the environmental practices of a company (TerraChoice, 2009). The prevalence of greenwashing has undoubtedly contributed to the high level of consumer scepticism towards companies' green claims.

Cause marketing and the environment

Given that consumers generally support cause marketing, yet a sizable proportion of consumers are sceptical towards the benefit of cause marketing, and a sizable proportion are sceptical towards the actual benefit of environmental claims, environmental cause marketing would appear to pose quite a complex challenge for companies. Nonetheless, consumers' demand for corporate social responsibility and desire to benefit the environment opens a space for these efforts. Additionally, beyond consumer demand, many companies choose to engage due to their managements' own intrinsic environmental commitment. This research seeks to examine some of the best practice efforts of companies succeeding in environmental cause marketing.

Environmental causes have the advantage of potential relevancy for all. Since everyone lives within a natural environment and relies on the viability of that environment for survival, the environment impacts everyone. There are, however, varying views on the peril facing environmental health, and on the causes of environmental damage. As such, the attention given to environmental issues varies widely among consumers.

Those charities most likely to be part of a cause marketing campaign fall into four broad categories: health, human services, animal and environmental (Lafferty and Edmondson, 2014). Among these, environmental and animal causes may be at a slight disadvantage within cause marketing alliances. Research has demonstrated that consumers do respond somewhat differently to cause marketing alliances depending upon the type of cause involved. Specifically, the cause type 'human services' tends to generate more positive attitudes towards the cause, compared to environmental, animal and health cause types. Human services causes also generated a more positive attitude towards the alliance, compared to environmental and animal causes (Lafferty and Edmondson, 2014). Environmentally oriented non-profits seeking partnerships may therefore be disadvantaged as they may be seen as a less favourable option in terms of overall reputational benefits. Purchase intention, however, is not impacted by cause type and overall consumer are as likely to purchase a brand that is partnered with animal and environmental causes as they are with health and human services causes. Thus, environmental causes are on equal footing with other cause types, generally, with regard to purchasing intent, but they are slightly disadvantaged in other response categories (Lafferty and Edmondson, 2014).

Dimensions of analysis: fit, form and fortune

In this research we examine successful environmental cause marketing alliances along three dimensions – fit, form and fortune gained. These dimensions were selected because they are the key characteristics of cause marketing partnerships examined in both academic and practitioner literature. In the following section we define and discuss each in turn, to position our subsequent analyses.

A model of fit in cause marketing

Research examining cause marketing has grown exponentially since 2000. We assume here that elements that contribute to successful cause marketing should generally be transferable, contributing to successful environmental cause marketing. Thus we now turn to one of the most researched, and potentially most important, elements of successful cause marketing – fit between the company and the cause. There is strong conceptual and empirical support for the importance of fit in cause related marketing.

Fit is a nebulous term that has been defined in various ways within the cause marketing literature. It is generally viewed as some form of link between the company and the cause. This may relate to a variety of things, such as company image, cause image, target market or constituency (Varadarajan and Menon, 1988) or even perceived self and company identities (Gupta and Pirsch, 2006). Fit has been shown in a large number of studies to enhance attitudes towards the organizations involved, towards the alliance itself, and/or towards purchase intention (e.g. Basil and Herr, 2003, 2006; Gupta and Pirsch, 2006; Lafferty, Goldsmith and Hult, 2004).

Menon and Kahn (2003), however, who studied the importance of brand-cause fit for two different types of corporate social initiatives, found that in some cases lower fit could actually result in more favourable consumer perceptions when the initiative primarily focuses on the social issue and less on the corporate brand. For initiatives that focused more on the corporate brand than on the social issue, however, high fit evokes more positive responses because of a 'lack of vested self-interest' (i.e. firm-serving motivations), which might increase the credibility of the campaign. The alignment between the brand and cause appears more natural and not designed to be exploitive of a cause of convenience. Ellen, Webb and Mohr (2006) report that high fit simultaneously evokes the apparently contradictory attribution of altruism and strategic self-interest towards the firm. A firm is seen to be satisfying both its corporate social responsibility mandate and its profit maximization mandate. Low fit alliances, however, prompt egoistic attributions by consumers: firms who partner with causes for which the fit is not apparent are seen to be solely self-serving.

This matters because corporations that focus on environmental issues are at risk of being seen as self-serving and attempting to greenwash the business given social concern for environmental sustainability. Cause marketing campaigns that promote the business brand must demonstrate strong fit to ameliorate this risk. Therefore it is important to examine how fit is achieved in successful cause marketing campaigns where the partner is an environmentally oriented non-profit.

Fit is often conceived and tested in a unidimensional manner, as a dichotomous measure of a single concept (e.g. Gupta and Pirsch, 2006). Some researchers, however, have attempted to examine fit in a more complex manner (e.g. Basil and Herr, 2003; Basil and Basil, 2003; Berger, Cunningham and Drumwright, 2004; Gwinner, 1997; Lafferty, Goldsmith and Hult, 2004; Trimble and Rifon, 2006; Varadarajan and Menon, 1988; Zdravkovic, Magnusson and Stanley, 2010). Several classifications of fit involve fit components that, although labelled differently, have conceptual similarities. For example the positive, neutral and negative fit types proposed by Basil and Herr (2003) and Basil and Basil (2003) overlap with natural vs. created fit (Simmons and Becker-Olsen, 2006), commonality vs. complementarity (Hoeffler and Keller, 2002) and consistent vs. complementary fit (Chang and Liu, 2012). In addition, several other dimensions have been proposed, such as functional or product-related fit (e.g. Berger, Cunningham and Drumwright, 2004; Gwinner, 1997; Lafferty, Goldsmith and Hult, 2004; Trimble and Rifon, 2006; Varadarajan and Menon, 1988), image (Gwinner, 1997; Trimble and Rifon, 2006; Varadarajan and Menon, 1988), positioning (Varadarajan and Menon, 1988) and work force (Berger, Cunningham and Drumwright, 2004).

Zdravkovic, Magnusson and Stanley (2010) created a typology that includes ten dimensions of fit. This construction offers valuable insight into various elements that impact consumer perceptions of fit in a cause marketing alliance; however, it does not address the notion of negative fit (cf. Basil and Herr, 2003). Negative fit suggests that the company actually contributes to or creates the problem being addressed by the cause. In the case of environmental causes, we feel negative fit is a particularly relevant component. As such, we have developed a conceptualization of fit that extends Basil and Herr's positive/neutral/negative classification, and merges it with Zdravkovic et al.'s (2010) findings.

The basis of our proposed fit classification scheme is the positive/neutral/negative categorization (Basil and Herr, 2003). Whereas these concepts were originally enacted as a trichotomy, herein we present them as overlapping groups on a continuum. Fit can be achieved in degrees. We expand upon this structure by defining types of fit that occur within each of these overlapping groups. We incorporate concepts from Zdravkovic et al. (2010) in our definitions of each category as well.

Positive fit represents a form of complementarity or similarity between company and cause, whether due to organizational mission (Mission), product offering (Function), constituency groups such as target market, local community, common geography, suppliers or employees (Stakeholder), naturally occurring common theme (Natural Theme), or a common theme created by promotional efforts (Created Theme). Neutral fit occurs when no apparent linkage is present, but the cause represents something of value to general human interest (General Interest). Moving along the continuum, in some cases the company may not actually cause the problem, or perhaps may not even significantly contribute to it, but it does mildly stand in the way of cause correction in

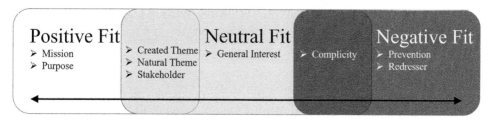

Figure 19.1 Valenced fit model.

some way (Complicity). Finally, a negative fit occurs when the company actually creates or exacerbates the issue which the cause is seeking to address or correct. The company may be seeking to avoid or minimize their contribution to the problem (Prevention), or the company may be seeking to ameliorate its impact after creating or adding to the problem (Redresser). Generally speaking, an alliance will have a primary form of fit, but alliances may be multiply categorized. For example, an alliance may have both target market fit and created theme. Figure 19.1 offers a visual representation of the proposed fit classification scheme. Specific definitions of each category, along with examples, can be found in Appendix 1.

A taxonomy of form in cause marketing: trigger and alliance relationship

Cause marketing alliances take a number of different forms. The variety of these alliance structures has expanded greatly over the past several decades. Here we combine models used by various authors to develop a taxonomy for assessing the form of a cause marketing alliance.

   With respect to classic cause marketing, form involves a transactional trigger, for example the purchase of a particular product within a particular time frame leading to a small donation to the cause, mostly up to a specified limit (Galán-Ladero et al., 2013; Liu and Ko, 2011; Polonsky and Speed, 2001; Smith and Alcorn, 1991; Varadarajan and Menon, 1988). This form of alliance is for example typified by Yoplait yogurt's 'Save Lids to Save Lives' campaign discussed in the introduction. Cause marketing has, however, evolved far beyond this basic form, now encompassing a wide variety of triggers and desired outcomes. Whereas Polonsky and Speed (2001) argue that cause marketing campaigns may be multi-phased and extended beyond the sole purchase of a product, their overview is rooted in the transactional approach. In contrast, Liu and Ko (2011) offer a general yet extended classification separating the transactional dimension from sponsorship, joint promotion and in-kind donations. Their approach highlights that the nature of cause marketing has changed insofar as a product purchase-link is not necessarily a requirement for the classification as cause marketing. This development is also reflected in the Halo Award Winners' campaigns. For example, the multi-phased 'Home Sweet Home' campaign by TELUS and WWF Canada combines joint promotion, consumer transaction,and in-kind donation, whereas the 'Chase the Extraordinary' campaign by the InterContinental Hotels Group is based on corporate initiative and in-kind donation only.

   Given the multitude of cause marketing forms, the development of a classification scheme was deemed necessary, especially since literature addresses several forms of cause marketing triggers, but has not yet created a summarizing taxonomy. Drawing from different approaches found in academia and practice, the subsequently suggested 'form' taxonomy distinguishes between the form of alliance relationships and the form of donation trigger within these alliance relationships.

Form of alliance relationship

The form of an alliance relationship considers the company-cause link which leads to the accrual of benefits or accomplishment of the campaign goals. In Table 19.1 we have developed a taxonomy for form of cause marketing alliances, adapted from previous literature (Cause Marketing Forum, 2010a; Liston-Heyes and Liu, 2010; Liu and Ko, 2011). This form taxonomy utilizes alliance approaches for cause marketing partnerships as well as event sponsorship and transactional relationships. Additionally, licensing is added as this form of cause support is growing (e.g. Cause Marketing Forum, 2010a;

Table 19.1 Form of alliance relationship

	Company-Cause Link	Explanation	Example
Licensing	Brand	Legal permission for the company (charity) to use an aspect of the charity (company) brand in exchange for a fee.	A clothing producer uses the logo of an eco-fashion charity on its products.
Sponsorship	Event, Scheme, or Challenge	Sponsorship of charity events, schemes, challenges; relatively dissociated from a company's product.	A sportswear company sponsors a hiking event that raises money for a national park charity.
Transaction	Product/ Service purchase or use	Consumer–company transaction leads to company donation (e.g. % or $ amount of sales); closely related to consumer triggers.	An organic food producer donates a percentage of every product sold to an organic food charity.
Joint Promotion	Message content	Company-charity cooperation in terms of advertising.	An electric car producer advertises the importance of emission reduction by cooperating with a carbon offset charity.
In-Kind Donation/ Company Initiative	Non-financial	Company donates products, services, employee time, or facilities.	A company's employees go to work by bike in order to reduce their carbon footprints and organize a fundraiser for an environmental charity.

Adapted from:
Engage for Good (n.d.). Cause Marketing 101 for Business. Retrieved 19 July 2017 from file:///C:/Users/debra.basil/Downloads/ebook_CM101_business_EFG_update.pdf.
Liston-Heyes, C. and Liu, G. (2010). Cause-related marketing in the retail and finance sectors an exploratory study of the determinants of cause selection and nonprofit alliances. *Nonprofit and Voluntary Sector Quarterly*, 39(1): 77–101.
Liu, G. and Ko, W.-W. (2011). An analysis of cause-related marketing implementation strategies through social alliance: Partnership conditions and strategic objectives. Journal of Business Ethics, 100(2): 253–281.
Mendleson, N. and Polonsky, M.J. (1995). Using strategic alliances to develop credible green marketing. Journal of Consumer Marketing, 12(2): 4–18.

Mendleson and Polonsky, 1995). Since most campaigns incorporate digital elements, we have not included digital as a unique alliance form, contrary to the approach taken by Engage for Good/Cause Marketing Forum.

Form of trigger

Whereas form of the alliance addresses the nature of the company-cause partnership, the form of trigger (Figure 19.2) focuses on the specific consumer-company action that takes place in order for the benefit to accrue to the cause, within the overall alliance. Our figure draws from Cone Communications' (2010) suggested 'Top 10 types of cause promotions' adding an 11th 'point-of-sale or checkout donation' type which we include as another form of cause marketing (Cause Marketing Forum, 2010b; Coleman and Peasley, 2015). Taking into consideration the forms of alliance relationships, it is likely that many of these cause trigger types (Figure 19.2) can be found within the transaction category.

The extent to which consumers are involved in triggering the cause contribution varies, depending on the type of cause promotion chosen by the company. Sometimes a direct action by the consumer results in a donation. At other times, the company makes a direct donation to the cause with no consumer involvement whatsoever. Figure 19.3 attempts to classify the role of consumer action along a continuum from direct (e.g. through a point-of-sale donation to a charity), to indirect (e.g. through a purchase triggering the company donation), to no involvement (e.g. company flat donation). Moreover, a company can take different roles in triggering the donation, ranging from

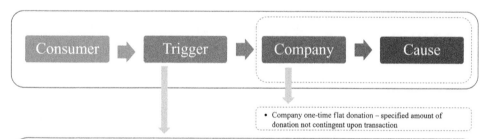

* Company one-time flat donation – specified amount of donation not contingent upon transaction

* Purchase – % of sales or $ amount for each product sold (can be unlimited or capped) is donated by the company
* Label or Coupon Redemption – Supplemental consumer action triggers company donation, e.g. redemption of coupons in store
* Online Activation – Similar to label or coupon redemption, but purchase and redemption and/or activation takes place online
* Consumer Action – No purchase required; company donation following consumer action, e.g. package design; liking/sharing on Social Media
* Dual incentive – Incentive, e.g. coupon, leads to consumer purchase which is linked to e.g. a donation for every coupon redeemed
* Consumer Pledge – Consumers encouraged to promise support for a cause (may be used together with company donation or incentives)
* BOGO (Buy one, give one) – Consumer purchase is accompanied by a comparable social impact, e.g. one product purchased = one vaccine)
* Consumer-Direction – Consumers choose, either from a list or by nominating, the cause which is supported in terms of where and how
* Volunteerism – Company asks consumer to donate their time in support of a cause (consumer rewards: complimentary goods/services)
* Point-of-Scale or Checkout Donation – Consumers asked to donate to a cause at the point of sale or checkout, e.g. through pin pad or pinups

Figure 19.2 Form of trigger.

Adapted from:

Cone Communications (2010b, 19 March). Top 10 types of cause promotions. Retrieved 28 March 2016 from www.conecomm.com/top-10-types-of-cause-promotions.

Cause Marketing Forum (2010b). Frequently asked questions. Retrieved 28 March 2016 from www. causemarketingforum.com/site/c.bkLUKcOTLkK4E/b.6422611/k.AD27/FAQ.htm.

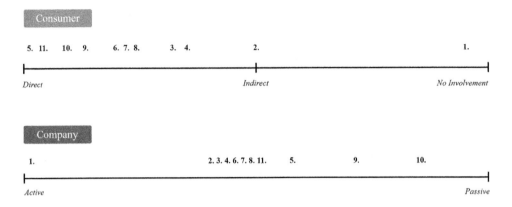

Figure 19.3 Consumer and company involvement.
Note: Both the consumer as well as the company continuums take into consideration the different forms of triggers numbered 1 to 11 (see Figure 19.2).

being more active (e.g. through a flat donation directly addressed to the cause) to being more passive (e.g. through asking consumers to donate their time in support of a cause).

In the light of the proposed form taxonomy for cause marketing, we would like to highlight that neither forms of trigger nor alliance relationships are mutually exclusive, but rather overlapping concepts. In practice, cause marketing campaigns are quite elaborate. This form taxonomy contributes to a 'toolbox' for developing not only classic, but multi-phased cause marketing campaigns as well. Multi-channel, multi-phase cause marketing campaigns can offer a wide variety of touch points, in order to engage a larger and more diverse audience. Additionally, they help a company to develop a deeper relationship with the cause, which is essential in order to avoid the appearance of opportunistic support or exploitation.

Fortunes gained

Cause marketing alliances can provide a wide variety of benefits to both company and cause. Benefits have been classified as first order, which provide a focused and/or immediate result, and second order, which provide more generalized and/or delayed impact (Gourville and Rangan, 2004). The most common outcome categories from cause marketing are financial, which tend to be a first order benefit. Another important outcome relates to perceptual benefits, such as improved familiarity and attitude, which tend to be second order benefits. Finally, behavioural outcomes are essential for success. These can be both immediate and ongoing, thus either first or second order. Obviously financial benefit is often key for the cause. Most cause marketing alliances involve a donation to the cause, either directly from the company, directly from consumers or some combination of the two. For many campaigns, an upfront donation is first made by the company, then subsequent transaction based donations linked to consumer purchasing or other consumer activities occur.

Image enhancement is a primary benefit to companies. Cause marketing is after all generally categorized as a marketing behaviour rather than a philanthropic behaviour (Varadarajan and Menon, 1988). Involvement in cause marketing can enhance consumer attitude towards the company (Basil and Herr, 2006). Other perhaps less frequently considered image benefits can accrue to the company as well. For example, both employees and investors appreciate cause marketing efforts. This appreciation can result in more loyalty from both employees and investors (Gourville and Rangan, 2004).

Image enhancement can accrue to the cause as well (Gourville and Rangan, 2004). First, simply being allied with a well-known and respected company can lead to more positive consumer attitudes towards the cause. Second, the advertising and promotional efforts of the company regarding the cause marketing alliance can increase awareness of the cause itself. Thus a well-executed marketing campaign for the cause marketing alliance can be beneficial to the public image of both partners.

Sometimes more broadly defined cause marketing efforts do not involve a monetary component for the cause, or the monetary component is not the primary focus. Sometimes the benefit is behaviour change on the part of the consumer (such as washing clothes in cold water), or the company (such as reducing the number of paper statements sent to customers) (Gourville and Rangan, 2004). For many environmental causes, behaviour change is the primary goal, so a campaign that can produce behaviour change is very desirable. In sum, successful cause marketing campaigns result in increased fortune for both the company and the cause. These fortunes may be classified as first order, meaning they involve a direct and immediate impact such as financial gain, or second order, involving more generalized, long-term benefits. These outcomes or fortunes tend to be financial, perceptual, behavioural or any combination of the three. We examine below the fortunes accruing to both company and cause within our sample of Halo award winners to better understand the impact of a successful campaign on the alliance partners.

Method

In this research we examine the cause marketing campaigns of Engage for Good's Halo Award Winners through 2015 in the 'Environment and Animals' category. Engage for Good serves as an information clearinghouse for companies and causes seeking to begin or enhance their cause marketing efforts. This is a for-profit company that generates revenue through membership and conference attendance; however, the company also offers a wealth of high quality information free of charge. Engage for Good (formerly the Cause Marketing Forum) has been conducting the Halo competition since 2003. Organizations enter the competition by submitting comprehensive packets of information detailing their cause marketing campaign. Winners are selected in each of nine categories. Our analysis focuses on those winning first or second place in the 'Environment and Animals' category: 2 awards per year for 13 years represents a total of 26 campaigns. We restrict our analysis to the information listed on the Engage for Good website regarding the award winning campaigns for a few reasons. First, this offers consistency. Second, given the historical nature of these awards, information for award winning campaigns is not available in other locations for the full range of the awards. Cause marketing alliance information, including company, cause, campaign, year and level of award, is shown in Appendix 2.

Each alliance was assessed for fit, form of alliance and form of trigger. Three individuals coded each alliance on these three dimensions. The coders' assessments were compared, and any disagreements were resolved through discussion. The inter-coder reliability (rate of coder agreement) was viewed as acceptable or good in all cases. Specifically, in 100 per cent of the cases two of three coders agreed on the primary code, and in over half, all agreed. Finally, fortune gained was assessed by one coder, as this was deemed a rather straight-forward assessment.

Fit assessment

We assessed fit by classifying each cause marketing partnership within the proposed Valenced Fit Model offered above. We found that award winning cause marketing campaigns overwhelmingly represent positive fit alliances. Fifteen of the 26 alliance represented some form of positive fit.

The most common (modal) fit category was represented by the Natural Theme fit (7). This was followed by Neutral fit (4). After these, with three each, came Mission, Prevention and Redresser. The full array is shown in Table 19.2.

These results suggest that positive fit is favoured for successful environmental cause marketing alliances. On the surface it may seem surprising that the more integrated forms of fit, Mission and Function, were not more prevalent. We surmise this is simply because relatively few companies could actually position themselves within these categories. Not many companies have a sustainability mission per se, and it is similarly uncommon for companies to sell products with a functional environmental fit. As such companies reverted to other forms of fit. This is speculative, as our sample consists of a small set of successful alliances, not a full array of cause marketing partnerships.

Extensive research on cause marketing has demonstrated that consumers prefer to see some form of fit or congruence between cause and company. Consumers prefer when cause and company apparently belong together or can be similarly categorized (Hamlin and Wilson, 2004). With natural fit, this congruence is self-evident. It doesn't require a great deal of effort to establish. It doesn't rely on getting the proper slogan or marketing campaign. As such, establishing fit in the minds of consumers should take less effort for the company and the cause. Where possible then, natural fit may be an appealing approach.

When natural fit isn't an option, however, companies can create fit by allying with a cause of interest, finding an area of overlap, and making a strong commitment to the alliance. For example, there is nothing particularly 'beach like' about wine, but Barefoot Wine's name gives them a connection to going barefoot, which they then connected to beaches. This fit was created by the coincidence of a whimsical product name, but Barefoot sincerely adopted the beach clean-up effort, committing significant effort and resources, and this created a fit for the alliance. Created fit is a viable strategy, but companies must truly get behind the effort, to avoid appearing exploitive. This is important for the cause as well, since research suggests negative perceptions of the company or the alliance can hurt attitudes towards the cause (Basil and Herr, 2003).

The negative fit category is particularly interesting. One might surmise that a company would not want to draw attention to areas in which they potentially damage the environment, yet six companies did emerge in this category. Previous research suggests that negative fit can lead to more negative attitudes towards the cause (Basil and Herr, 2003). However, research has also shown that negative fit leads to more positive perceptions of the alliance itself (but not necessarily the individual alliance partners) compared to neutral fit (Basil and Basil, 2006). Consumers appreciate when a company openly admits to imperfections, and commits to improvement. In other words, 'honesty wins over perfection' (Cone Communications/Echo, 2013; Gorman, 2013). As previously discussed, consumers and regulators are particularly watchful regarding exploitation of

Table 19.2 Fit categorizations

positive– primary	*Mission (3):* ★*Cascadian Farms/U of Minn & Xerces Society (Bee habitat)* ★*Esurance/Live Earth (Paperless statements)* ★*Green Mtn. Coffee/Heifer (Fair Trade Co-op)* *Function (2):* ★*P & G Cold Water Tide (Cold washing campaign)* ★*Lysol/Keep America Beautiful (community clean-up)*
positive– secondary	Created Theme (3): ★New Belgium Brewery (Fat Tire Beer)/Cycling Clubs (Cycling) ★Barefoot Wine/Surfrider (Beach clean-up) ★Telus/WWF (Canadian Wildlife) Natural Theme (7): ★Clorox Fresh Step Kitty Litter/ASPCA (Education and music to help cause of pets) ★Iams/Helen Woodward Animal Centre (Adoption) ★Pedigree/various animal shelters (Adoption) ★LL Bean/National Parks (Photos in park) ★Sprint Samsung Recyclable Phone/Nature Conservancy (Adopt an Acre) ★Stonyfield Farms/National Wildlife Federation (Vote for environmental cause) ★Orvis Sporting Goods/Morris Animal Foundation (Canine Cancer) Stakeholder (1): ★American Eagle Outfitters/Conservation Corps (Alternative spring break)
neutral	General Interest (4): ★RBC (Water) ★Coca-Cola/WWF (Polar Bears) ★Avon/Nature Conservancy (Deforestation) ★Microsoft tablets/Central Park (Cataloging species)
negative– secondary	Complicity (0)
negative– primary	Prevention (3): ★AT&T/National Arbor Day Foundation (Paperless statements) ★Frito-Lay Sun Chips (Sustainable bag and solar energy) ★Intercontinental Hotel/Internal (Sustainability programme) Redresser (3): ★Jet Blue/ carbonfund.org (CO_2 emissions) ★Aquafina and Sam's Club/Return the Warmth and Keep America Beautiful (School recycling programme and recycled jackets for homeless) ★Briggs & Stratton (Lawnmower tune-ups)

either the cause or the consumer in cause marketing partnerships and perception that the company is also attending to this issue may ameliorate such concerns.

Form assessment

Form of alliance relationship

A wide variety of alliance forms were evident in our analyses. Several alliances evidenced more than one alliance form, due to their multi-channel, multi-stage efforts. The most common forms of alliance were transactional and sponsorship, represented in 12 and 10 alliances respectively. Corporate initiative and/or in-kind donations were evident in eight alliances, whereas joint promotion was clearly evident in five. Licensing was not clearly evident in any of the alliances. Transactional alliances, company initiatives/

in-kind donations and sponsorship were all used relatively consistently throughout the time period examined. Joint promotion on the other hand appears to have grown in popularity in recent years.

Form of trigger

Donation with purchase was the most common form of trigger used, clearly evident in 10 campaigns. Often a campaign would have multiple components, with purchase being one of them. The second most common trigger for donation was a flat company donation (seven), not tied to consumer action. Several campaigns involved an initial donation from the company, followed by other forms that included a transactional component dependent upon purchase for donation. Consumer action (six), volunteerism (four), consumer pledge, and consumer direction (three each) each occurred in multiple campaigns as well. The remainder (dual incentive, BOGO, point of sale) each appeared only once. There appears to be a slight increase in the number of triggers used in a campaign in more recent years, suggesting that campaigns may have grown in complexity over the years.

Fortune assessment

To assess fortune, we catalogued the types of fortune gained for both companies and causes. We then tallied these outcomes. These data provide insight into the benefits an organization might enjoy from a successful environmental cause marketing campaign; however, we caution that the information is limited to data listed in Engage for Good's Halo descriptions and as such should be viewed as suggestive but potentially incomplete.

Company fortunes were categorized as financial, behavioural and perceptual. The behavioural category included sub-categories of customers, other stakeholders (employees, suppliers, retailers), and media exposure. Media exposure was the most commonly cited benefit gained (15), followed by financial gains such as increased sales and market share (11). The perceptual benefit of improved image and reputation was cited in 8 instances. Changes in targeted customer behaviours (6) and involvement of other stakeholders (6) were also noted company outcomes.

For causes, the fortunes gained were also categorized as financial, behavioural and perceptual. Three sub-categories were apparent within the behavioural category. These include performing the core campaign goal behaviour (e.g. litter pick-up or species classification, for example), gaining media exposure, and gaining supporters (e.g. volunteers, social media followers, cause memberships). Perceptual benefits include consumer pledges and learning, as well as increased awareness and attitude. Not surprisingly, financial support appears to be the most common fortune gained by causes, and specific amount donated was mentioned in 19 of the 26 descriptions. There were many cases though where the cause goal was actually attaining a behaviour rather than seeking money, specifically mentioned in 17 descriptions. It was widely recognized within campaigns that media exposure offered a benefit for the cause as well as the company, something that was mentioned in 11 descriptions. Though less commonly noted, consumer pledges and consumer learning (mentioned five times), and gaining supporters (mentioned six times) were also valued outcomes for causes in several campaigns. This is an important point to consider. When developing an alliance, both cause and company should think broadly regarding cause benefits. Money may not be the most important benefit to gain. Adding members and followers might lead to long-term benefits that outlast a simple financial donation.

Discussion

In this chapter we have examined the fit and form of award winning environmental cause marketing alliances. We found that most of these alliances utilize a positive fit partnership, and within this category, natural fit is the most commonly used. Natural fit is a wonderful opportunity for a company to make the most of an existing environmental theme evident within their company. However, not all companies have this opportunity, due to the products and services they offer. These should seek to develop created fit in order to partner with an environmentally oriented cause.

Increasingly, environmental issues are so central to a business' core values that it is a part of their mission. In these cases obviously an environmental cause marketing campaign makes sense. It offers visibility for the company's environmental efforts, and allows consumers to take part as well, demonstrating their own environmental commitment. It is essential, however, that a company positioning itself with an environmental mission be completely committed to this cause. Insincerity or apparent exploitation will be quite damaging to both company and cause.

We found that alliance form varies, with transactional and sponsorship formats leading the way. Campaigns can be somewhat complex, with multiple potential points of consumer contact. This complexity has the benefit of offering 'something for everyone' so to speak.

Campaigns often unfold through several stages. At times, companies choose to run a campaign quietly for some time, then after establishing success the campaign is taken public. This was done by RBC for example, with their Blue Water Project. RBC worked with grant recipients for three years before taking their accomplishments to the public. This approach helps to position a company as sincerely interested in the cause, thus minimizing the chance that their efforts will be viewed as exploitive or 'greenwashing'.

Various triggers lead to cause donations. Most commonly, the trigger is linked to product purchase of some sort. This is the classic form of cause marketing, and it is still quite actively in play. Often a company will begin the alliance with a donation to the cause. After this, other more complex forms are introduced, usually requiring consumer action and including media exposure.

Companies involved with environmental cause marketing report positive publicity for the company, and often cite increased sales and market share as benefits as well. For causes, donations, behaviour relating to their cause (such as cleaning a beach), media exposure, and new volunteers or members are perceived positive outcomes.

Theoretical contributions

In this chapter we advance theory by developing and applying models of fit and alliance form and applying them specifically to environmental cause marketing alliances. Existing research addresses several forms of cause marketing triggers across cause types; this study extends theory by combining models to propose a summarizing form taxonomy distinguishing between the form of alliance relationships and the form of donation trigger within these alliance relationships. The basis of our proposed fit classification scheme with positive/neutral/negative categorization presented as overlapping groups on a continuum rather than exclusive categories: Fit can be achieved in degrees. Given the complex relationship between company activity and environmental damage, development of a fit model that addresses negative fit scenarios is particularly important for environmental cause marketing.

Practical contributions

This assessment of award winning environmental cause marketing alliances offers practical insight into what actually works with these partnerships. Although environmental causes are on equal footing with other cause types in regard to purchasing intent, they do not seem to generate positive attitudes to either the cause or to the alliance itself to the same extent as other cause types. Consumers can be sceptical of business' claims towards various forms of social responsibility including cause marketing relationships. 'Green washing' is frequently used as an exemplar of unethical or irresponsible business practice. Cause marketing campaigns responding to environmental issues therefore must demonstrate strong fit, appropriate triggers and more effective structures to ameliorate this risk. The model of fit and function developed in this study can help businesses and non-profits partner more effectively to benefit environmental causes. Our hope is that practitioners considering such an alliance might find that our results serve as a useful guide.

Limitations and future research

This work examined Halo Award winners for the Environment and Animals category, as described on Engage for Good's website. The Halo Awards are based upon self-reports by businesses or causes of campaign outcomes and do not assess consumer perceptions. Further, it is adjudicated by a for-profit business focused upon promoting positive linkages between business and cause without consideration of the consumer's point of view. The descriptions may not have represented the full array of activities or elements included in the campaigns assessed. As such, we see this work as formative and exploratory. The models developed in this chapter show promise and should be tested in future research.

Appendix 1

Table 19.3 Fit coding scheme

Positive-primary	Mission: Company's core mission is to address this cause or need. Example: An organic wine producer partners with an anti-GMO cause.
Positive-secondary	Function: The function of the product or service addresses the cause or need, or is used with the cause or need. Example: A pasta production company partners with a Feed the Children charity. Created Theme: The company created the fit by focus, attention, advertising and prioritizing it. Example: A local restaurant consistently supports local children's sports teams, every year, and posts their pictures on the wall every year. Natural Theme: Cause naturally fits with the general theme of the company or the product/service. Example: A kayak production company partners with a nature conservancy. Stakeholder: The company's customers, consumers, employees, suppliers, local community, or other key stakeholders are somehow linked to the cause. Example: A children's book publisher partners with a children's hospital. Example: A community business partners with the Coulee clean-up litter reduction programme in Lethbridge.

Neutral	General Interest:
	The cause is of general interest to everyone.
	Example: A car company partners with an anti-child abuse campaign.
Negative-secondary	Complicity:
	The company's offering mildly contributes to the problem but is not a primary cause.
	Example: A pasta production company producing 'macaroni and cheese' partners with an anti-obesity foundation.
Negative-primary	Prevention:
	The company tries to change behaviour to AVOID creating the problem.
	Example: A car wash switches to all natural cleaners and partners with a clean water foundation.
	Redresser:
	The company creates the problem then seeks to fix it.
	Example: A tobacco company partners with a cancer research cause.

Appendix 2

Table 19.4 Listing of alliance data

Year	Company	Cause	Campaign	Level
2015	The Orvis Company	Morris Animal Foundation	The Orvis Cover Dog Photo Contest	Gold
2015	Cascadian Farm Organic Food	Bee conservation with University of Minn. Bee Lab and Xerces Society	Bee Friendlier	Silver
2014	American Eagle Outfitters	Student Conservation Association	AEO+SCA+You: Alternative Spring Break	Gold
2014	Telus Telecom	World Wildlife Fund Canada	Home Sweet Home	Silver
2013	L.L. Bean Clothing and Outdoor Wear	National Park Foundation	Million Moment Mission	Gold
2013	Tide Cold Water Wash by Proctor and Procter & Gamble	Alliance to Save Energy	Take a Load Off	Silver
2012	Coca-Cola Soft Drink	World Wildlife Fund	Arctic Home	Gold
2012	Barefoot Wines	Surfrider Foundation	Beach Rescue Project	Silver
2011	Royal Bank of Canada	RBC created effort	Blue Water Project	Gold
2011	Avon Cosmetics	The Nature Conservancy	Hello Green Tomorrow	Silver
2010	Frito-Lay SunChips	self	Building Pre-eminent Green Brand for SunChips	Gold
2010	Sprint Telecom	The Nature Conservancy	Adopt an Acre	Silver
2009	New Belgium Brewing Co.	various existing local cycling groups benefit	Tour de Fat	Gold
2009	JetBlue Airways	Carbonfund.org	Jetting to Green	Silver
2008	InterContinental Hotels Group	none, general sustainability efforts by company	Chase the Extraordinary	Gold
2008	Esurance online insurance	Live Earth	Save Our Selves	Silver

(Continued)

Year	Company	Cause	Campaign	Level
2007	Pedigree Pet Food	various animal shelters	Pedigree Adoption Drive	Gold
2007	Aquafina Bottled Water and Sam's Club Retailer	Keep America Beautiful	Return the Warmth	Silver
2006	Iams Dog and Cat Foods	Helen Woodward Animal Centre	Iams Home for the Holidays	Gold
2006	AT&T Telecom	National Arbor Day Foundation	AT&T's MySBC eBill Paperless Program	Silver
2005	Green Mountain Coffee Roasters	Heifer International	Coffee for a Better World	Gold
2005	Stonyfield Organic Dairy	National Wildlife Federation	Bid With Your Lid	Silver
2004	Microsoft Computer Products	The Explorers Club	Central Park BioBlitz	Gold
2004	Lysol Cleaning Products	Keep America Beautiful	Great American Cleanup	Silver
2003	Clorox Fresh Step Kitty Litter	ASPCA	Safe Steps Home	Gold
2003	Briggs & Stratton Outdoor Machinery	National Wildlife Federation	Lawnmower Tune-up	Silver

References

Andreasen, A. (2003). *Strategic Management.* Upper Saddle River, NJ: Prentice Hall.
Basil, D.Z. and Basil, M.D. (2003). Toward an understanding of fit: Effects of association and complementarity in cause-related marketing alliances. Paper presented at the La Londe Seminar: 30th International Research Seminar in Marketing, June 2003, La Londe, France. Paper published in L. Gilles, D. Merunka, and J. Zaichkowsky (eds), *Marketing Communication and Consumer Behavior 2003 Proceedings (La Londe Seminar)*, pp. 161–174.
Basil, D.Z. and Herr, P.M. (2003). Dangerous donations? The effects of cause-related marketing on charity attitude. *Journal of Nonprofit & Public Sector Marketing*, 11(1): 59–76.
Basil, D.Z. and Herr, P.M. (2006). Attitudinal balance and cause-related marketing: An empirical application of balance theory. *Journal of Consumer Psychology*, 16(4): 391–403.
Berger, I.E., Cunningham, P.H. and Drumwright, M.E. (2004). Social alliances: Company/nonprofit collaboration. *California Management Review*, 47(1): 58–90.
Berglind, M. and Nakata, C. (2005). Cause-related marketing: More buck than bang? *Business Horizons*, 48(5): 443–453.
Blackwood, A., McKeever, B. and Pollak, T.H. (2016). Which nonprofit sectors were the biggest winners and losers in 2014? *Nonprofit Quarterly*. Retrieved 30 March 2016 from https://nonprofitquarterly.org/2016/03/16/which-nonprofit-sectors-were-the-biggest-winners-and-losers-in-2014/.
Cause Marketing Forum (2010a). Cause marketing 101. Retrieved 13 September 2012 from www.causemarketingforum.com/site/c.bkLUKcOTLkK4E/b.6441359/k.8F42/Quick_Study_CM101_for_NPOs.htm.
Cause Marketing Forum (2010b). Frequently asked questions. Retrieved 28 March 2016 from www.causemarketingforum.com/site/c.bkLUKcOTLkK4E/b.6422611/k.AD27/FAQ.htm.
Chang, C.T. and Liu, H.W. (2012). Goodwill hunting? Influences of product-cause fit, product type, and donation level in cause-related marketing. *Marketing Intelligence & Planning*, 30(6): 634–652.

Chang, K. (2007). Cause marketing. *The NonProfit Times*. Retrieved 6 March 2016 from www.thenonprofittimes.com/news-articles/cause-marketing/.

Coleman, J.T. and Peasley, M.C. (2015). Demonstrating a lack of brand/cause effects on point of sale donations. *Management & Marketing*, 10(3): 226–243.

Cone Communications (2010a). 2010 cause evolution study. Retrieved 19 July 2017 from www.conecomm.com/2010-cone-communications-cause-evolution-study-pdf/.

Cone Communications (2010b, 19 March). Top 10 types of cause promotions. Retrieved 28 March 2016 from www.conecomm.com/top-10-types-of-cause-promotions.

Cone Communications (2012). Consumers still purchasing, but may not be 'buying' companies' environmental claims. 2012 Green Gap Trend Tracker. Retrieved 19 July 2017 from http://3blmedia.com/News/Consumers-Still-Purchasing-May-Not-Be-Buying-Companies-Environmental-Claims.

Cone Communications/Echo (2013). 2013 Cone Communications/Echo Global CSR Study. Retrieved 19 July 2017 from www.conecomm.com/2013-cone-communicationsecho-global-csr-study-pdf.

Ellen, P.S., Webb, D.J. and Mohr, L.A. (2006). Building corporate associations: Consumer attributions for corporate socially responsible programs. *Journal of the Academy of Marketing Science*, 34(2): 147–157.

Engage for Good (n.d.). Cause Marketing 101 for Business. Retrieved 19 July 2017 from http://engageforgood.com/cause-marketing-101-for-business/.

Galán-Ladero, M.M., Galera-Casquet, C., Valero-Amaro, V. and Barroso-Méndez, M.J. (2013). Sustainable, socially responsible business: The cause-related marketing case. A review of the conceptual framework. *Journal of Security and Sustainability Issues*, 2(4): 35–46.

Gorman, L. (2013). Green consumers want companies to help them be green. *Toronto Sustainability Speaker Series*. Retrieved 30 March 2016, at http://tsss.ca/2013/04/green-consumers-want-companies-to-help-them-be-green/

Gourville, J.T. and Rangan, V.K. (2004). Valuing the cause marketing relationship. *California Management Review*, 47(1): 38–57.

Grumet, A. (2012). Charitable promotions & cause marketing scrutiny and regulation continues. Retrieved 19 July 2017 from www.lexology.com/library/detail.aspx?g=9a880844-5ada-4818-8610-.

Gupta, S. and Pirsch, J. (2006). The company-cause-customer fit decision in cause-related marketing. *Journal of Consumer Marketing*, 23(6): 314–326.

Gwinner, K. (1997). A model of image creation and image transfer in event sponsorship. *International Marketing Review*, 14(3): 145–158.

Hamlin, R.P. and Wilson, T. (2004). The impact of cause branding on consumer reactions to products: Does product/cause 'fit' really matter? *Journal of Marketing Management*, 20(7–8): 663–681.

Hoeffler, S. and Keller, K.L. (2002). Building brand equity through corporate societal marketing. *Journal of Public Policy & Marketing*, 21(1): 78–89.

IEG (2016). As sponsorship borders fall, spending rises. Retrieved 26 April 2016 from www.sponsorship.com/IEGSR/2016/01/05/As-Sponsorship-Borders-Fall,-Spending-Rises.aspx

Lafferty, B.A. and Edmondson, D.R. (2014). A note on the role of cause type in cause-related marketing. *Journal of Business Research*, 67(7): 1455–1460.

Lafferty, B.A., Goldsmith, R.E. and Hult, G.T.M. (2004). The impact of the alliance on the partners: A look at cause–brand alliances. *Psychology and Marketing*, 21(7): 509–531.

Lavack, A.M. and Kropp, F. (2003). Cross-cultural comparison of consumer attitudes toward cause-related marketing. *Social Marketing Quarterly*, 9(2): 3–16.

Liebetrau, J., Basil, D.Z. and Runté, M. (2016). The evolution of cause-related marketing. Paper presented at the Administrative Sciences Association of Canada 2016 Conference, June 2016, Edmonton, Canada. Published in proceedings.

Liston-Heyes, C. and Liu, G. (2010). Cause-related marketing in the retail and finance sectors an exploratory study of the determinants of cause selection and nonprofit alliances. *Nonprofit and Voluntary Sector Quarterly*, 39(1): 77–101.

Liu, G. and Ko, W.-W. (2011). An analysis of cause-related marketing implementation strate-
gies through social alliance: Partnership conditions and strategic objectives. *Journal of Business Ethics*, 100(2): 253–281.

Mendleson, N. and Polonsky, M.J. (1995). Using strategic alliances to develop credible green marketing. *Journal of Consumer Marketing*, 12(2): 4–18.

Menon, S. and Kahn, B.E. (2003). Corporate sponsorships of philanthropic activities: When do they impact perception of sponsor brand? *Journal of Consumer Psychology*, 13(3): 316–327.

Polonsky, M.J. and Speed, R. (2001). Linking sponsorship and cause related marketing: Complementarities and conflicts. *European Journal of Marketing*, 35(11/12): 1361–1389.

Runté, M., Basil, D.Z. and Deshpande, S. (2009). Cause-related marketing from the nonprofit's perspective: Classifying goals and experienced outcomes. *Journal of Nonprofit and Public Sector Marketing*, 21(3): 255–270.

Simmons, C.J. and Becker-Olsen, K.L. (2006). Achieving marketing objectives through social sponsorships. *Journal of Marketing*, 70(4): 154–169.

Smith, S.M. and Alcorn, D.S. (1991). Cause marketing: A new direction in the marketing of corporate responsibility. *Journal of Consumer Marketing*, 8(3): 19 35.

TerraChoice (2009). Environmental Marketing. The seven sins of greenwashing: Environmen-
tal claims in consumer markets. *London: TerraChoice Environmental Marketing*. Retrieved 1 April 2016 from http://sinsofgreenwashing.com/findings/greenwashing-report-2009/.

Trimble, C.S. and Rifon, N.J. (2006). Consumer perceptions of compatibility in cause-related marketing messages. *International Journal of Nonprofit and Voluntary Sector Marketing*, 11(1): 29–47.

Varadarajan, P.R. and Menon, A. (1988). Cause-related marketing: A coalignment of marketing strategy and corporate philanthropy. *Journal of Marketing*, 52(3): 58–74.

Webb, D.J. and Mohr, L.A. (1998). A typology of consumer responses to cause-related marketing: From skeptics to socially concerned. *Journal of Public Policy and Marketing*, 17(2): 226–238.

Zdravkovic, S., Magnusson, P. and Stanley, S.M. (2010). Dimensions of fit between a brand and a social cause and their influence on attitudes. *International Journal of Research in Marketing*, 27(2): 151–160.

Part V

Towards multi-level engagement and collaboration

20 Motivating employees for sustainability

A comprehensive review of micro-behavioural research (2005–present)

Joel Marcus and Devon Fernandes

Introduction

How do businesses go about enacting strategies for sustainability? It seems clear that employees are central to such efforts, and that the success or failure of a firm's sustainability strategy is ultimately dictated by the ability to motivate employee behaviours that minimize economic, social and environmental harm, while promoting positive outcomes in these domains. After all, organizations – even those deemed to be 'economic' in nature – are made up of people. It is people who do the work of the organization, who must coordinate their activities to achieve common goals (Barnard, 1938), and whose collective activities impact upon the welfare of ecological, social and economic systems (Wood, 1991). People within the firm, those we refer to as employees, bring corporate strategies to life, making them real and tangible, whether that strategy aim for narrow profit-maximizing ends or the broader forms of value creation implied by a sustainability mandate.

Although it may be a truism that employee actions determine firm sustainability impacts, individual-level considerations have been noticeably underrepresented in the sustainability management literature (Aguinis and Glavas, 2012; Andersson, Jackson and Russell, 2013). Rather, from the beginning, organizational and institutional level analyses have tended to dominate the field. It is without question important to understand the institutional contexts (regulations, stakeholder pressures, etc.) and organizational policies (ethical codes, governance structures, etc.) consistent with more sustainable business practice (Wijen, 2014). But these alone cannot tell the whole story of why and how firms meaningfully advance a sustainability agenda.

Contextual analyses, for example, cannot readily account for the standout firms who, facing the same institutional pressures as their industry peers, go well beyond those peers with respect to social and environmental achievements (Anderson, 1998; Hollender, Breen and Senge, 2010). Rather, such exemplary performance must be rooted in features internal to the organization. Uncovering the internal dynamics of truly outstanding social and environmental practices may be key to unlocking meaningful paths for sustainable business strategy that can be more widely applied (Pfeffer, 2010).

However, it is also the case that organizational-level strategy and policies that appear to promote sustainable business practice can be far removed from the actual actions firms engage in. The widespread prevalence of so-called 'greenwashing' (Delmas and Burbano, 2011) efforts highlights that corporations are very capable of 'talking the talk' while systematically failing to 'walk the walk'. Similarly, Enron's utter lack of regard for their own stated, and very-well publicized code of ethics, is perhaps the most clear-cut example of how formal firm strategy can be fully divorced from the implicit and operationalized strategies that actually manifest in collective firm behaviours (Sims and Brinkmann, 2003). It also serves to illustrate that firm-level strategies are profoundly moulded and shaped by behaviours and actions at the individual level of the organization.

These observations suggest that having the right people is crucial to the success of sustainability strategies. But who are the 'right' people? Why are some employees seemingly keen to spearhead or participate in progressive social and environmental practices, where others resist? Is it possible to identify and select candidates who are more motivated to achieve sustainable business outcomes? Further, what can managers do to promote a culture of sustainability within their firm? And finally, in the interests of evidence-based practice, what do we currently know about the individual-level drivers and mechanisms by which businesses positively and/or negatively impact the economic, social and natural environments within which they exist?

Although organizational behaviour (OB) and human resource management (HRM) scholars – those most concerned with individual-level issues – have been late contributors to the sustainability management discourse, interest in the human factor has been growing steadily in recent years (Pfeffer, 2010). There is now a respectable body of empirical research addressing sustainability issues at the individual level within the organizational context. To-date, however, these have been largely piecemeal efforts, with little evidence of cumulative knowledge-building or a coherent conceptual framework to guide future research. Perhaps this is to be expected given the broad scope of the sustainability concept, and the highly complex, multifaceted nature of what counts as sustainability phenomenon (Marcus, Kurucz and Colbert, 2010). Nonetheless, we believe it is important to take stock of the literature at this time.

As such, our purpose in this chapter is to comprehensively review the empirical research pertaining to individual-level sustainability phenomenon within the organizational context. At the outset we set three key objectives for this review. Our first goal was to systematically document and structure the relevant research, and to analyse the key trends and themes emerging from this work. Second, we wanted to assess the current state of knowledge to determine what evidence-based conclusions can be drawn at this point to inform sustainable management practice. Our third and final aim was to identify gaps in our understanding of individual-level factors and processes contributing to sustainability outcomes, and to suggest productive opportunities for future research. Overall, our review provides a reference resource for micro-level sustainability scholars and those interested in more effectively managing employees for sustainability.

Scope and methodology of the review

We undertook a comprehensive and systematic review of all articles published in leading management journals, niche management journals pertaining to social and environmental issues, and relevant conference proceedings from 2005 to the present. This roughly ten-year window covers a period of growing interest in the micro-level foundations of sustainability management, and even saw the emergence of dedicated special issues on the topic in mainstream management journals (Andersson et al., 2013). The literature reviewed thus constitutes the state-of-the-art in terms of research being done in this area, and the current state of knowledge about individual-level sustainability factors.

Our understanding of sustainability is informed by well-accepted conceptual frameworks, and reflects a holistic model of the economic, social and environmental domains and the complex interrelationships between them (Marcus et al., 2010; United Nations

General Assembly, 2005). However, because virtually all management literature pertains in some way to the economic domain, we confine our analysis to those studies that specifically address social and/or environmental issues.

To further scope our review, we focus exclusively on empirical research studies as opposed to untested conceptual or theoretical frameworks. Specifically, we sought to identify all studies examining individual-level constructs related to sustainability issues. Our attention to the individual level brings to the fore those characteristics that differentiate one person from another (i.e. individual-difference variables). These include personal characteristics such as age and sex, psychological variables and cognitive processes, and the actual behaviours that people engage in. For our purposes, we include any study that measures variables at the level of individual persons.

Finally, we limit our review to those studies that speak to employee-related issues within the organizational or managerial context. Hence, we do not account for the environmental psychology literature concerned with general sustainability and household behaviours, or for studies focused on sustainable consumer behaviour. Appendix 1 provides further detail on the protocol we followed for our literature review and Appendix 2 a full listing of the journals surveyed. In total, we uncovered 65 articles meeting our search criteria, which reveal a broad array of focal constructs, methodological and analytic approaches.

Themes and trends

Table 20.1 provides detailed summary information on these studies sorted by year of publication. For each study we outline the author/s and year of publication, the dominant theoretical lens or framework grounding the work, a listing of the predictor and criterion variables assessed, the level of analysis, the focal domain of interest (social, environmental or multi-domain), the valence of the criterion variables (harm vs. benefit), information regarding the sample and method, and finally a brief description of the author's key findings.

At an overview level we observe a number of key themes and trends in the articles reviewed. One standout feature is the great variety of research being conducted, as noted both within and between the categories surveyed. On one hand this is appropriate and desirable in that it reflects the broad scope of sustainability, and the fact that individual-level social and environmental issues are of interest to many different audiences within the management field. On the other hand, the absence of any apparent unifying framework poses limitations for cumulative knowledge advancement. We address this further in our discussion below.

Focal domains

It is also apparent that although sustainability has long been defined as a tripartite, multi-dimensional concept, the majority of studies are still domain specific with respect to social *or* environmental issues. As seen in Figure 20.1, only 17 (26 per cent) of the studies surveyed adopt a multi-domain focus, combining a mix of social, environmental and/or economic criteria. It is worth noting that for many of the works retrieved we have taken liberties in characterizing these as 'sustainability' studies when they were not originally conceived as such. In reality, sustainability-related research remains rather fragmented across traditional silos in the management field, and is embedded within a number of distinctive research streams including those focused on ethics, corporate social responsibility, and the natural environment.

Table 20.1 Summary analyses of articles reviewed[1]

Author/Year	Theory lens	Predictors	Criterion	LOA	S/E/M	H/B	Sample	Method	Key findings
Andersson, Shivarajan and Blau, 2005[13]	VBN	Corporate values (perceived commitment) Personal beliefs (NEP) Beliefs about corporation (Trust in management)★ Norms (Organizational commitment)★	Environmental behaviours – 30 items from Ramus and Steger (2000)	I	E	B	N=147 supervisors within a multinational pharmaceutical company based in U.K.	Survey	Corporate commitment to environment most important predictor of environmental behaviour, affective organizational commitment, and trust in top management.
Marshall, Cordano and Silverman, 2005[14]	TPB	Individual drivers (managerial attitudes, subjective norms) Institutional drivers (local institutional network, regulations)	Proactive environmental behaviours	I	E	B	N=16 interviews of key actors in wine industry N=19 environmental leaders in wine industry	Qualitative (interviews, focus groups)	At the early stage of environmental transformation, managerial attitudes and norms, existing regulations, employee welfare and competitive pressures are all strong drivers of proactive environmental behaviour.
Raines and Prakash, 2005[15]	Leadership	Presence of environmental entrepreneurs Use of cost-benefit analysis Motivations for ISO-14001 certification	ISO 14001 certification	O	E	B	N=133 environmental managers of ISO 14001-certified companies from 16 countries	Survey	Presence of an environmental entrepreneur affects ISO 14001 adoption. The strongest motivator was to demonstrate environmental leadership/be a good neighbour.
Stevens, Kevin Steensma, Harrison and Cochran, 2005[16]	Ethics / Stakeholder theory / TPB	Stakeholder pressure Perceived benefits Training	Ethics code used in strategic decision-making	I	S	B	N=302 senior financial executive	Survey (telephone)	Integration of ethics codes in strategic decision-making is increased when (a) there is perceived stakeholder pressure, (b) it is perceived to create an ethical firm culture and positive external image, and (c) the code is operationalized through training programmes.

Citation	Theory	Independent variables	Dependent variables				Sample	Method	Findings
Thomsen, 2005[17]	Corporate governance / Stakeholder theory	Owner identity, Board member identity, Stakeholder identity	Corporate values★ Profitability	M	O		N=71 Danish CEOs obtained in 1997	Survey	Corporate values expressed by CEOs were partially related to proxies for governance and stakeholder structure, but had no significant impact on profitability.
Albaum and Peterson, 2006[18]	Ethics	Gender, Religiosity	Ethics attitudes	S	I	B	N=2,942 undergraduate business students from 58 institutions	Survey	Females/religious individuals report more ethical attitudes than males/nonreligious.
Ashkanasy, Windsor and Treviño, 2006[19]	Ethics	Moral development, Organizational reward system, Outcome expectancy★, Belief in a just world★	Ethical choice	S	I	B	N=174 MBA students at an Australian university	Experiment / Survey)	Ethical context and personal characteristics interact to influence ethical decision-making.
Cagle and Baucus, 2006[20]	Ethics	Gender, Age, Level of education	Ethical perceptions	S	I	B	N=86 undergraduate and MBA students	Survey	Studying ethics scandals positively influences both ethical decision-making, and perception of the ethics of businesspeople.
Chen and Tang, 2006[21]	Ethics	Demographics (gender, age, years of education, current job, work experience in years, major, income)	Unethical Behaviour Scale (Luna-Arocas and Tang, 2005)	S	I	H	N=299 business and psychology students	Survey (two wave)	Males have stronger unethical attitudes and greater propensity to engage in unethical behaviours. Ethical attitudes (T1) predict ethical behaviour propensity (T2).
Deckop, 2006[22]	CSR / Stakeholder theory / Agency theory / Leadership	Short-term pay focus, Long-term pay focus	KLD 2002 Corporate Social Performance (CSP) audit	M	O	B	N=313 firms from 2001 S&P's 500 list	Secondary data	Short-term CEO pay focus was negatively related to CSP, whereas long-term focus was positively related to CSP.

1 Table notes provided on page 354.

(Continued)

Author/Year	Theory lens	Predictors	Criterion	LOA	S/E/M	H/B	Sample	Method	Key findings
Reynolds, 2006[23]	Ethics	Harm; Violation of a behavioural norm; Utilitarianism★; Formalism★	Moral awareness	I	S	B	N=63 members of the Executive MBA Alumni Association of a US university (Study 1); N=33 managers enrolled in an evening MBA course at a US university (Study 2)	Survey	Manager's ethical predispositions influence their responses to the characteristics of the moral issue. Both utilitarianism and formalism shaped moral awareness, but formalism demonstrated a greater capacity to do so.
Slimak and Dietz, 2006[24]	VBN	Social-Structural variables (age, education, ethnicity, political views, income, sophistication, gender); Social-Psychological variables (values★, spiritual beliefs★, world views (NEP)★)	Ecological risk perception	I	E		N=614 individuals recruitment from public, experienced public, risk assessors, and risk managers at the US EPA	Survey (mail)	The most consistent predictors of the ecological risk rankings are belief in the new ecological paradigm (NEP) and Schwartz's altruism. Religious fundamentalists, the more educated and financially well-off are less concerned with ecological risk.
Waldman, Siegel and Javidan, 2006[25]	Leadership / CSR	CEO charismatic leadership; CEO intellectual stimulation	Strategic CSR; Social CSR	O	M	B	N=234 managers from US and Canadian firms with net sales over 1B	Survey (mail) / Secondary data (KLD)	CEO intellectual stimulation (but not CEO charismatic leadership) is significantly associated with the propensity of the firm to engage in strategic CSR.
Andersson, Giacalone and Jurkiewicz, 2007[26]	CSR	Hope; Gratitude	Social responsibility (Boal and Peery, 1985; Singhapakdi et al., 1996)	I	M	B	N=308 white-collar US employees	Survey (longitudinal)	Hope and gratitude positively impact social/ethical/philanthropic dimensions of CSR but not economic or legal responsibilities.

Fritzsche and Oz, 2007[27]	Ethics	Values (SVS: altruism, self-enhancement, traditionalism, openness)	Ethical decision-making (Vignettes)	I	S	B	N=174 working individuals attending part-time graduate studies at Eastern university	Survey	Ethical decision-making is positively associated with altruistic values, but negatively associated with self-enhancement values.
Fukukawa, Shafer and Lee, 2007[28]	Organizational behaviour	Values (SVS)	Support for social and environmental accountability	I	M	B	N=100 MBA students at a private US university	Survey	Universalism is positively associated with general support for social and environmental accountability, but not with support for government enforcement of standards. Females were more likely to support government enforcement.
Loviscky, Treviño and Jacobs, 2007[29]	Ethics		Managerial moral judgement	I	S	B	N=238 students	Scale development	The authors develop and validate the Managerial Moral Judgement Test (MMJT).
Mudrack, 2007[30]	Organizational behaviour / CSR	Social traditionalism	Self-benefits Company benefits Equity sensitivity Machiavellianism Locus of control Protestant work ethic Authoritarianism Just world beliefs	I	M	H/B	N=112 technical professionals recruited from Detroit (Study 1) N=178 bank employee (Study 2)	Survey	Normative views about the rightness of social responsibility (social traditionalism) are closely tied to fundamental personality traits, attitudes, values and thinking patterns.
Smith, Simpson and Chun-Yao Huang, 2007[31]	Ethics / Rational choice theory	Moral evaluations Formal sanctions Obedience to Authority Outcome Expectancies★	Illegal/unethical behaviour	I	S	H	N=78 managers	Survey	Threat of legal action does not directly affect the likelihood of misconduct. Ethical evaluations and outcome expectancies do affect ethical intentions. Individuals are more likely to engage in illegal acts when ordered to by authority figures.

(Continued)

Author/Year	Theory lens	Predictors	Criterion	LOA	S/E/M	H/B	Sample	Method	Key findings
Detert, Treviño and Sweitzer, 2008[32]	Ethics	Empathy Trait cynicism Locus of control Moral identity	Moral disengagement★ Unethical decision-making	I	S	H	N=307 business and education undergraduate students	Survey (three wave)	Empathy and moral identity are negatively related to moral disengagement, which is positively related to unethical decision-making.
Linnenluecke, Russell and Griffiths, 2009[33]	CSR	Organizational culture Legitimation of environmental issues Integration of environmental indicators Knowledge of sustainability policy	Understanding of corporate sustainability (economic, social, environmental, holistic)	I	M		N=255 employees from a large Australian company	Survey	Employees from a subculture with a stronger emphasis on hierarchical and bureaucratic values emphasize an economic understanding of corporate sustainability.
Scherbaum, Popovich and Finlinson, 2008[34]	VBN	Environmental worldviews Environmental personal norms★	Conservation behaviours Behavioural intentions	I	E	B	N=40 employees at a US university (Focus group) N=154 employees of a US university (Survey)	Mixed (Focus groups / Survey)	Environmental personal norms predicted self-reported energy-conservation behaviours, as well as behavioural intentions. Environmental personal norms mediated the relationship of environmental worldviews with self-reported energy-conservation behaviours, as well as behavioural intentions.
Sully de Luque, Washburn, Waldman and House, 2008[35]	Leadership / Cross-cultural / Stakeholder theory	Values (economic, stakeholder) Leadership (visionary, autocratic)★	Follower's extra effort★ Firm performance	O	S	B	N=520 firms in 15 countries with average size of 500 employees	Survey / Secondary data	CEO's emphasis on economic versus stakeholder values is associated with followers' perceptions of autocratic versus visionary leadership respectively. Visionary leadership increases employees' extra effort and firm performance.

Author (Year)	Theory / Discipline	Constructs	Dependent variable				Sample	Method	Findings
Burton and Goldsby, 2009[36]	CSR / Stakeholder theory	Perceived importance of CSR dimensions (economic, legal, ethical, discretionary)	Engagement with stakeholder groups; Relative importance of business goals	I	M	B	N=401 small business owners in the Midwest US	Survey (Interview)	The emphasis a manager places on particular CSR domain affects stakeholder engagement behaviour. Relationship is not affected by firm size.
Hilbig and Zettler, 2009[37]	Organizational behaviour	Personality (Honesty-Humility); Social value orientation★	Allocation of resources (self vs. other)	I	S	B	N=134 individuals recruited from community samples	Survey / Experimental	Individuals low in Honesty-Humility made more selfish decisions. Those high in Honesty-Humility displayed a stable tendency for fairness even when defection had no consequences.
Watson, Berkley and Papamarcos, 2009[38]	Ethics	Situational factors (reward, punishment); Values (SVS)★; Moral reasoning★	Ethical judgements	I	S	B	N=177 students at US university	Survey (two wave)	Morally relevant and non-moral variables have direct effects on ethical decisions. Non-moral and moral values interact with situational factors to significantly influence decisions.
Benn and Martin, 2010[39]	Learning / Change theory			M	M	B	Wuhan University and the water users of the Zhanghe basin, China	Qualitative (Ethnographic)	Universities can play a central role in knowledge mobilization and development for sustainability through engagement with communities of practice.
Haugh and Talwar, 2010[40]	Organizational behaviour / Learning		Employee learning about sustainability	I	M		Global companies and Tata Group	Qualitative (Case study)	Corporations use multiple mechanisms to enable employee learning about sustainability, including (i) codes of conduct, (ii) impact measure, (iii) company structure and policies, (iv) purchasing and supply chain initiatives, (v) communications, (vi) training, (vii) company visits and (viii) volunteering opportunities.

(Continued)

Author/Year	Theory lens	Predictors	Criterion	LOA	S/E/M	H/B	Sample	Method	Key findings
Jones, 2010[41]	CSR / Organizational behaviour / Social exchange theory	Volunteer-programme attitudes Organizational identification Organizational pride Exchange ideology	Intent to stay OCB-loyalty OCB-organization OCB-coworkers In-role performance	I	S	B	N=162 employees of Green Mountain Coffee Roasters	Survey (two phase, dyads (employee and supervisor))	Employee's attitudes about volunteerism programme predicted intentions to stay, and were mediated by organizational identification. Exchange ideology moderated the relationship between attitudes and supervisor-reported OCBs.
Kuckertz and Wagner, 2010[42]	Entrepreneurship	Sustainability orientation Individual originality Demographics	Personal attitudes towards entrepreneurial activities	I	M		N=712 German students and alumni from science, engineering, and business programmes	Survey	Engineering students with a stronger sustainability orientation have greater intention to become self-employed than business students (this reverses for alumni).
McFerran, Aquino and Duffy, 2010[43]	Organizational behaviour / Ethics	Moral identity Moral personality Principled ideology	OCB Propensity to Disengage	I	S	H/B	N=52 female employees at a US organization (Study 1) N=145 Canadian undergraduate students (Study 20	Survey	Moral personality and the centrality of moral identity were associated with a more principled ethical ideology. Ideology mediated the relationship between personality, moral identity, and OCB and the propensity to morally disengage.
Muller and Kolk, 2010[44]	CSR / Ethics	Trade intensity Foreign ownership Management commitment to ethics	Corporate social performance (environmental performance, comm. relations, labour relations)	O	M	B	N=121 MNE subsidiaries and locally owned Mexican firms	Survey (online)	Management commitment to ethics is a dominant driver of Corporate Social Performance (CSP) among both foreign and domestic firms. Management commitment to ethics interacts positively with trade-related pressures in raising CSP levels.

	Theory	Discipline	Constructs	Outcome				Sample	Method	Findings
Russell, 2010[45]	VBN		Personal values (biospheric, altruistic, egoistic) Corporate values Beliefs (environmental)★ Norms (issue ownership)★ Emotions★ Organizational identification★	Pro-environmental behaviour	I	E	B	N=324 employees from 5 Australian organizations	Survey	Findings support the VBN framework, and emotions are found to provide a more important role than hypothesized. Positive emotion enhances workplace pro-environmental behaviour, and negative emotions impede it.
Carrico and Riemer, 2011			Information campaign Feedback Peer education	Electricity consumption Conservation behaviour Norms Outcome expectancy Goal attractiveness	M	E	B	N=352 employees in N=24 buildings at US university	Experiment / Survey	Relatively simple behavioural interventions (feedback, peer education) resulted in 7% and 4% reduction in energy use, respectively, compared with a control group that increased use 4%.
Graves, Sarkis and Zhu, 2011[46]		Organizational behaviour / Leadership	Organizational environmental commitment Environmental transformational leadership★ Autonomous and extrinsic motivation★	Pro-environmental behaviour (PEB)	I	E	B	N=294 employees at four Chinese organizations	Survey	Organizational environmental commitment increased employee's environmental motivation. Autonomous motivation, but not extrinsic motivation, was positively related to PEBs. Commitment increase transformational leadership, which directly predicted PEBs.
Jenkin, McShane and Webster, 2011[47]		Organizational behaviour / Information technology	Motivating forces Environmental initiatives (strategies, information technologies systems) (IT/S)★	Environmental orientation (cognition, attitudes, behaviour)	M	E	B	N=24 employees at four financial services institutions	Qualitative (Interviews and web-content analysis)	Organizations are still in the infancy stage of awareness and adoption of 'Green' IT/S.

(Continued)

Author/Year	Theory lens	Predictors	Criterion	LOA I/O	S/E/M	H/B	Sample	Method	Key findings
Post, Rahman and Rubow, 2011[48]	Corporate governance / CSR	BoD composition (insider/outsider, gender, age, Western European education; educational attainment)	Environmental disclosure KLD ratings	O	E	H/B	N=78 firms in the Fortune 1000 list	Survey / Secondary data (KLD)	A higher proportion of outside directors is associated with more favourable environmental outcomes. Boards composed of more than 2 female directors, whose directors average age is closer to 56 and those with a higher proportion of Western European directors have higher KLD scores.
Shalvi, Dana, Handgraaf and De Dreu, 2011[49]	Ethics	Presence of counter-factual self-justifications	Lying	I	S	H	N=120 night tudents at a US university (Study 1) N=68 (Study 2) N=150 (Study 3) N=68 undergraduate students at a US university (Study 4)	Experimental	The availability of self-justifications increases lying. Observing desired counterfactuals attenuates the degree to which people perceive lies as unethical.
Stites and Michael, 2011[50]	CSR / Organizational behaviour	Community-related CSP Environmentally related CSP	Affective organizational commitment	I	M	B	N=136 production employees at 3 kitchen cabinet manufacturers in the US	Survey	Community-related and environmentally related CSP are positively related to organizational commitment.
Cantor, Morrow and Montabon, 2012[51]	Organizational behaviour	Supervisory support Training Rewards Employee POS★ Affective commitment★	Environmental behaviour	I	E	B	N=317 supply chain management employees in large retail firm	Survey	Supervisory support and training promote pro-environmental behaviour, but rewards did not. Employee POS increased affective commitment to firm environmental practices.
Lavine, 2012[52]	CSR / Positive psychology	Corporate social performance	Work meaningfulness	I	M	B	N=52 employees at a consumer product firm	Qualitative (Interviews)	Work meaningfulness and corporate social performance inform each other.

Author	Theory	Variables	Outcome				Sample	Method	Findings
Merriman, 2012[53]	HRM / Agency Theory / Rational Choice Theory	Financial incentives	Project Investment (green projects vs. cost savings project)	I	E	B	N=83 working adults	Survey (online, experimental)	Investment in sustainability versus cost savings is significantly lower when incentives for both projects are equivalent, and investment is only comparable when incentives for the sustainability project are superior.
Papagiannakis and Lioukas, 2012[54]	TPB / Leadership / Stakeholder theory	Values (SVS) Attitudes★ Subjective norms (stakeholder expectations)★ Perceived behavioural controls (self-efficacy, cost-benefit, regulation)★	Corporate environmental responsiveness (CER)	I	E	B	N=142 managers at Greek companies	Survey (mail)	Top managers' personal values influence CER indirectly, through shaping their environmental attitudes. Subjective norms, expressing stakeholder expectations, do affect CER, with their effect being stronger than that of attitudes. Managers' perceived ability to handle environmental issues also appears to influence responses.
Rivera-Camino, 2012[55]	TPB	Past behaviour Organizational context Attitudes★ Subjective norm★ Perceived control (external, internal)★	Corporate environmental market responsiveness	M	E	B	N=3253 European managers responsible for their firm's environmental activities	Survey	Environmental behaviours of managers are largely determined by social judgements and perception. Organizational context restricts managers to a somewhat narrower range of strategic options than previous studies suggest.
Roxas and Coetzer, 2012[56]	Organizational behaviour / Institutional theory	Institutional environment (regulatory, cognitive, normative) Attitudes towards the natural environment★	Environmental sustainability orientation	O	E	B	N=166 managers of small manufacturing firms in the Philippines	Survey	The cognitive, regulatory and normative elements of the institutional environment are strongly linked to positive managerial attitudes towards environmental sustainability, which in turn, positively influences the firm's overall environmental sustainability orientation.

(Continued)

Author/Year	Theory lens	Predictors	Criterion	LOA	S/E/M	H/B	Sample	Method	Key findings
Wright, Nyberg and Grant, 2012[57]	Self / organizational identity			M	E		N=36 sustainability managers in major Australian and global corporations	Qualitative (social constructivist, semi-structured interviews)	Identities inform responses to climate change. Individuals overcome identity conflicts by constructing a coherent narrative of themselves and their career. For some, the climate crisis provides impetus for personal reinvention as a moral change agent.
Bissing-Olson, Iyer, Fielding and Zacher, 2013[58]	Organizational behaviour	Positive affect Pro-environmental attitude★	Pro-environmental behaviour	I	E	B	N=56 employees from multiple organizations	Survey (Longitudinal)	Daily unactivated positive affect and pro-environmental attitude positively predict daily task-related pro-environmental behaviour at work.
Greaves, Zibarras and Stride, 2013[59]	TPB	Attitudes Subjective norms Perceived behavioural control	Environmental behavioural intentions★ Environmental behaviour	I	E	B	N=449 employees of a single organization	Survey	TPB constructs explained significant variance in general intent towards three environmental work behaviours.
Mazutis, 2013[60]	CSR / Leadership	Time CEO worldview CEO background CEO international experience Industry Norms★ R&D intensity★	Corporate Social Strategy (CSS)	M	M	B	N=349 firms	Secondary data (KLD)	Some aspects of an open executive orientation (CEO liberal worldview, output functional breadth, functional background, and JD/LLB specialization) are determinants of initial levels and rates of adoption of CSS over time.
Paillé, Boiral and Chen, 2013[61]	HRM/ Organizational behaviour / Social Exchange Theory	Environmental management practices POS-supervisor★ POS-organizational★ Org. commitment★	OCB for the environment	I	E	B	N=407 employees enrolled in executive MBA programmes at Canadian university	Survey	Employees are more likely to make extra environmental effort if they perceive that the organization supports their supervisor by granting them the decision-making latitude and necessary resources to engage in pro-environmental behaviour.

Robertson and Barling, 2013[62]	Leadership / Organizational behaviour	I	E	B	N=139 subordinate-leader dyads recruited through StudyResponse in US and Canada	Survey	Environmental descriptive norms Transformational leadership (environmental)★ Leaders' environmental behaviours★ Employees environmental passion★	Workplace pro-environmental behaviours	Leaders' environmental descriptive norms and the leadership and pro-environmental behaviours they enact play an important role in the greening of organizations.
Shepherd, Patzelt and Baron, 2013[63]	Self-regulation theory / Entrepreneurship	I	E	H	N=83 entrepreneurs	Survey	Specified harm to natural environment Pro-environmental values Entrepreneurial self-efficacy Perceived industry munificence	Opportunity assessment	Founders' disengagement of their pro-environmental values was stronger when they had high, rather than low, entrepreneurial self-efficacy, and stronger when industry munificence was perceived as low rather than high.
Boiral, 2014[64]	Leadership / Consciousness development	I	E	B	N=63 employees from 15 industrial SMEs	Qualitative (Case study)			Post-conventional consciousness associated with higher levels of environmental management practices.
Gonzalez-Mulé, DeGeest, McCormick, Seong and Brown, 2014[65]	Organizational behaviour / Person-Environment fit	M	S	B	N=1,061 individuals within N=102 teams in a large, private-sector defence firm, South Korea	Survey	Personality traits (agreeableness, extraversion)	Cooperative group norms★ Helping behaviours	High team extraversion relates to helping behaviours, mediated by cooperative group norms. Low variance on agreeableness and high variance on extraversion promote individual helping behaviours.
Kim, Kim, Han, Jackson and Ployhart, 2014[66]	CSR / Leadership	M	E	B	N=325 office workers in 3 South Korean organizations	Survey	Conscientiousness Moral reflectiveness Work group green advocacy	Voluntary workplace green behaviour (leaders★, group members)	Conscientiousness and moral reflectiveness were associated with the voluntary workplace green behaviour leaders and group members. Leader behaviour directly impacted group member behaviour, and was also mediated by group-level advocacy.

(Continued)

Author/Year	Theory lens	Predictors	Criterion	LOA	S/E/M	H/B	Sample	Method	Key findings
Lamm, Tosti-Kharas and King, 2014[67]	Organizational behaviour	POS towards the Environment (POS-E) Psychological empowerment	Job Satisfaction Organizational identification Turnover intention OCB towards the Environment (OCB-E)	I	E	B	N=733 working adults	Survey	POS-E was positively related to OCB-E, job satisfaction, organizational identification, and psychological empowerment, and negatively related to turnover intentions. Psychological empowerment partially mediated the relationship between POS-E and the dependent variables.
Lewis, Walls and Dowell, 2014[68]	Leadership	Educational background CEO tenure	CEO response to Carbon Disclosure Project (CDP)	O	E	B	N=589 US firms 2002–2008	Secondary data	Firms led by newly appointed CEOs and CEOs with MBA degrees are more likely to respond to the CDP, while those led by lawyers are less likely to respond.
Norton, Zacher and Ashkanasy, 2014[69]	Organizational behaviour	Perception of org's sustainability policy Green work climate perceptions (organization, co-worker)★	Employee green behaviour (EGB: task-related, proactive) Environmental attitude	I	E	B	N=168 employees recruited through Amazon's Mechanical Turk	Survey (online)	Green work climate perceptions of the organization and of co-workers differentially mediated the effects of the perceived presence of a sustainability policy on task-related and proactive EGBs.
Sonenshein, DeCelles and Dutton, 2014[70]	Ethics	Self-assets Self-doubt Self profiles (self-affirmers, self-equivocators, self-critics)	Issue-supportive behaviours	I	E	B	N=29 students and alumni from an Environment and Business Program (Study 1) N=19 active members of environmental groups	Mixed (Study 1 – interviews; Study 2 – survey)	Self-evaluations influence support for environmental issues, and doubts play an important role even for highly dedicated supporters. Self-evaluations are shaped by cognitive, relational and organizational challenges individuals interpret about an issue from various life domains.

Study	Theory	Independent variable				Dependent variable	Sample	Method	Findings
Warren, Gaspar and Laufer, 2014[71]	Ethics	Attendance in a comprehensive ethics training session	I	S	H/B	Unethical behaviour; Ethical behaviour; Perception of organizational efficacy; Normative structure; Perceived values (co-workers, supervisors, senior managers)	N=392 employees at a multinational bank (wave 1 and 2); N=534 employees at a multinational bank 2.5 years after ethics training (wave 3)	Survey (online, longitudinal)	Sustained, positive effects on indicators of ethical organizational culture were found two years after a single ethics training session.
Alt, Díez-de-Castro and Lloréns-Montes, 2015[72]	Stakeholder theory / Natural Resource Based View	Employee integration; Proactive environmental strategy*; Shared vision*	I	E	B	Environmental performance (Hubbard, 2009; subjective)	N=170 environmental / sustainability managers at different firms	Survey (online)	Employee integration is critical to environmental management success, which is further improved by shared vision.
Hagenbuch, Little and Lucas, 2015[73]	CSR	Firm approach to CSR (donation; volunteerism, operational integration)	I	M		Firm attractiveness for prospective employees	N=1,829 students at eight US colleges and universities	Survey	Contrary to expectations, integration of financial and social goals was the least attractive CSR app-oach.
Marcus, MacDonald and Sulsky, 2015[74]	Organizational behaviour	Values (economic, social, environmental, balanced)	I	M	H/B	Propensity for corporate sustainability actions	N=282 Canadian university students	Survey	Strong economic values increased the propensity for concern actions and willingness to work in controversial industries. Females were less likely to engage in concern actions and more supportive of social and environmental strength actions.

(Continued)

Author/Year	Theory lens	Predictors	Criterion	LOA	S/E/M	H/B	Sample	Method	Key findings
Morse, Sauerberger, Todd and Funder, 2015[75]	Organizational behaviour	Personality (Big 5) Situational construal (unstructured, cooperative, competitive)	Behavioural social outcomes	I	S	B	N=256 undergraduate students from a US university	Experiment / Survey	Extraversion, agreeableness, openness and neuroticism (negatively) were related to positive behavioural social outcomes, as well as to normativity and positivity of construal. Normativity and positivity of construal were related to positive social outcomes.
Whillans and Dunn, 2015[76]	Ethics	Hourly/salary pay Consideration of opportunity cost Self-other focus	Pro-environmental behaviour Environmental intentions Perceived worth of environmental behaviour Recycling	I	E	B	N=5000 respondents to the British Household Panel Survey (Study 1) N=193 undergrad students (Study 2) N=52 students (Study 3) N=127 individuals from Vancouver (Study 4) N=179 students (Study 5)	Secondary data / Experimental	People are less likely to engage in environmental behaviour if they are paid by the hour. Making the economic value of time salient reduces environmental intentions and behaviour. This effect is mitigated by reframing environmental behaviour as an act consistent with self-interest.

Notes:
1 *Indicates a mediating or moderating variable.
2 Category titles: LOA = Level of Analysis (I = Individual, O = Organizational, M = Multi); S/E/M = Social focus / Environmental focus / Multi-focus; H/B = Criterion variable addresses Harm / Benefit.
3 CSR = Corporate Social Responsibility; HRM = Human Resource Management; KLD = Kinder, Lydenberg, and Domini Index; NEP = New Ecological Paradigm (Dunlap and Van Liere, 1978); OCB = Organizational Citizenship Behaviour; POS = Perceived Organizational Support; RVS = Rokeach Values Survey (or derivative); SVS = Schwartz Values Survey (or derivative); TPB = Theory of Planned Behaviour (Ajzen, 1991); VBN = Value-Belief-Norm Theory (Stern, Dietz, Abel, Guagnano and Kalof, 1999).

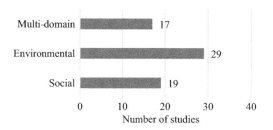

Figure 20.1 Focal domain of interest.

Theoretical frameworks

Not surprisingly then, researchers have grounded their work using a wide variety of theoretical frameworks or lenses (Figure 20.2). Ethics is one of the most prominent themes and was particularly dominant during the early period of the years surveyed, a likely reflection of the numerous corporate scandals that occurred during the early 2000s. The largest number of studies are more generally classified as drawing from the organizational behaviour (OB) literature, and these are characterized by a stronger emphasis on environmental issues and outcomes. The theory of planned behaviour (TPB; Ajzen, 1991), a framework widely employed by OB scholars, and values–beliefs–norm theory, a theory developed by environmental psychologists based on the TPB (Stern et al., 1999), have both been adopted in multiple studies. Corporate social responsibility, leadership/governance and stakeholder theory are also popular lenses through which individual-level sustainability issues are addressed.

Levels of analysis

As would be expected given our search criteria, the preponderance of works reviewed maintain an exclusive focus at the individual level of analysis (Figure 20.3). However,

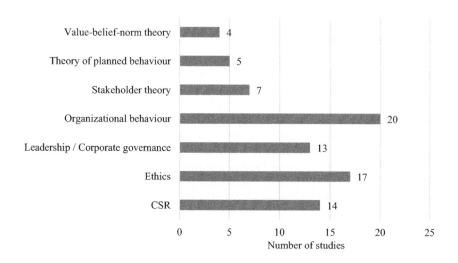

Figure 20.2 Theoretical foundations.

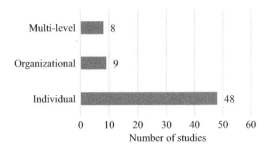

Figure 20.3 Levels of analysis.

we also find a number of organizational-level studies, particularly those examining leadership and corporate governance issues. It is the leader's characteristics and traits that are of concern in this research, and how they relate to firm-level practices, processes or outcomes. A limited number of multilevel analyses examining cross-level effects are also present. An interesting example is provided by Gonzalez-Mulé and colleagues (2014), who model group norms as mediating the relationship between personality traits and helping behaviours. However, given that sustainability issues are multilevel phenomenon, the relative paucity of multilevel studies is somewhat notable.

Predictor variables

Scanning the list of predictor variables reveals a plethora of factors that have been used to explain micro-level sustainability phenomenon, many of which appear only a single time. However, there are some notable exceptions. For example, demographic characteristics are of focal interest in six studies, and take the role of control variables in a number of others. Gender and age are the most often examined demographic variables, with gender in particular found to impact sustainability outcomes in a number of studies.

Across the social sciences personal values are considered one of the most fundamental within-person drivers of behaviour. Consistent with this view, values are modelled as predictor variables in nine (14 per cent) of the papers reviewed here. Researchers have most often employed Schwartz's (1992) well-known scale of universal values or a variant thereof. However, a number of scholars have invoked values more directly related to sustainability concerns. For example, Sully de Luque and colleagues (2008) distinguish between economic and stakeholder values and Shepherd et al. (Shepherd, Patzelt and Baron, 2013) assess pro-environmental values. Drawing upon scales developed by environmental psychologists, Russel (2010) measured individual's biospheric, altruistic and egoistic values, which clearly parallel the three sustainability spheres. Similarly, Marcus et al. (Marcus, MacDonald and Sulsky, 2015) assess respondent's economic, social and environmental values, and use a novel policy-capturing methodology to measure values implicitly.

In line with the TPB and its derivative VBN theory, beliefs and attitudes are also prominently featured in the works surveyed, appearing in 10 or 15 per cent of studies. Various types of beliefs and belief systems have been examined including belief in a just world (Ashkanasy, Windsor and Treviño, 2006), spiritual beliefs (Slimak and Dietz, 2006), environmental beliefs (Russell, 2010), environmental worldviews (Scherbaum,

Popovich and Finlinson, 2008) and beliefs pertaining to the new ecological paradigm (NEP; (Andersson, Shivarajan and Blau, 2005, Slimak and Dietz, 2006). By contrast, in the research reviewed here, attitudes have been assessed exclusively in relation to environmental issues (Bissing-Olson, Iyer, Fielding and Zacher, 2013; Greaves, Zibarras and Stride, 2013; Marshall, Cordano and Silverman, 2005; Rivera-Camino, 2012; Roxas and Coetzer, 2012).

Whereas the predictors considered so far are all within-person variables, another set of predictors pertain to features of the work environment or situational factors. In fact, a full 51 per cent of the studies analysed include some form of contextual measure in their predictor variables. It is worth noting however, that in the vast majority of cases situational variables are assessed through perceptual or subjective measures as opposed to direct or objective measures. This, of course, is a function of the dominant individual-level focus in the work surveyed.

Amongst the contextual variables analysed, a number deal with the social context within which individual agents act. For example, researchers have examined workplace norms (Greaves et al., 2013; Marshall et al., 2005; Rivera-Camino, 2012), corporate values (Andersson et al., 2005), organizational culture (Linnenluecke, Russell and Griffiths, 2009), managerial and organizational commitment to social and environmental issues (Graves, Sarkis and Zhu, 2011; Muller and Kolk, 2010), leadership styles and characteristics (Post, Rahman and Rubow, 2011; Robertson and Barling, 2013; Sully de Luque, Washburn, Waldman and House, 2008; Waldman, Siegel and Javidan, 2006), green work climate (B.G. Norton and Steinemann, 2001) and work group green advocacy (Kim, Kim, Han, Jackson and Ployhart, 2014). Other scholars have considered the firm's external context in relation to stakeholder pressures and expectations (Papagiannakis and Lioukas, 2012; Stevens, Kevin Steensma, Harrison and Cochran, 2005), the institutional environment (Roxas and Coetzer, 2012), and industry norms and munificence (Mazutis, 2013; Shepherd et al., 2013).

In addition to the social context, firm-level strategy and practices related to environmental management (Alt, Díez-de-Castro and Lloréns-Montes, 2015; Jenkin, McShane and Webster, 2011; Paillé, Boiral and Chen, 2013) and corporate social performance (Burton and Goldsby, 2009; Hagenbuch, Little and Lucas, 2015; Lavine, 2012; Stites and Michael, 2011) have received a fair amount of attention. With respect to predictor variables, organizational incentive structures emerge as final area of interest in the works surveyed. These include reward systems (Ashkanasy et al., 2006; Cantor, Morrow and Montabon, 2012; Watson, Berkley and Papamarcos, 2009), financial incentives (Merriman, 2012), different forms of pay structures (Deckop, 2006; Whillans and Dunn, 2015) and the presence of formal sanctions (Smith, Simpson and Chun-Yao Huang, 2007; Watson et al., 2009).

Criterion variables

Turning to criterion variables, we again observe a great variety of outcome variables of interest in micro-level sustainability research. As with predictor variables, a number of notable trends emerge.

Research with a principal focus on social issues is overwhelmingly dominated by examination of ethical outcomes, with 13 of 19 social issues papers assessing ethics criteria. Ethical outcomes take three distinct forms within these studies. The first assess ethics at the psychological level with respect to such things as ethical attitudes (Stevens et al., 2005), ethical perceptions (Albaum and Peterson, 2006), moral awareness

(Reynolds, 2006) and moral disengagement (Detert, Treviño and Sweitzer, 2008). A second class invokes cognitive processes by focusing on ethical judgements and decision-making (Ashkanasy et al., 2006; Detert et al., 2008; Fritzsche and Oz, 2007; Loviscky, Treviño and Jacobs, 2007; Stevens et al., 2005; Watson et al., 2009). The final set of ethical outcomes concern measures of actual behaviours engaged in such as lying (Shalvi, Dana, Handgraaf and De Dreu, 2011), illegal acts (Smith et al., 2007) and more general ethical or unethical behaviours (Chen and Tang, 2006; Warren, Gaspar and Laufer, 2014).

A second criterion theme observed within the social issues studies involves what are generally referred to as pro-social behaviours. These have been operationalized in terms of organizational citizenship behaviours (OCB); (Jones, 2010; McFerran, Aquino and Duffy, 2010), helping behaviours (Gonzalez-Mulé, DeGeest, McCormick, Seong and Brown, 2014), demonstrations of extra effort on the part of employees (Sully de Luque et al., 2008) and behavioural social outcomes (Morse, Sauerberger, Todd and Funder, 2015). It is notable that these all pertain to within-firm social impacts, and the opportunity for analyses of social impacts beyond the confines of the firm seem to have been missed to this point. For example, it is worth considering how positive social dynamics within the workplace might have social impacts in the broader community or amongst key stakeholder groups, and for key issues of social justice, equality and human rights.

Whereas the social issues research examined here is dominated by ethical considerations, environmental behaviours are the outcome variable of choice for scholars focused on issues pertaining to the natural environment. Fifty-nine per cent of the environmental issues studies include some type of behavioural measure. Although some authors define these simply as general environmental workplace behaviours (Andersson et al., 2005; Cantor et al., 2012; Greaves et al., 2013; Jenkin et al., 2011), as with the social issues criterion we again note a strong trend towards the characterization of pro-environmental behaviour (Bissing-Olson et al., 2013; Graves et al., 2011; Marshall et al., 2005; Robertson and Barling, 2013; Russell, 2010; Whillans and Dunn, 2015). Others have focused on conservation behaviours (Carrico and Riemer, 2011; Scherbaum et al., 2008), issue-supportive behaviour (Sonenshein, DeCelles and Dutton, 2014) and employee green behaviours (Kim et al., 2014; Norton, Zacher and Ashkanasy, 2014). Two papers drawing more directly from the OB literature have operationalized OCBs for the environment (Lamm, Tosti-Kharas and King, 2014; Paillé et al., 2013).

Staying at the individual-level, psychological outcome measures have been used to a lesser extent, but include assessments of ecological risk perception (Slimak and Dietz, 2006), environmental cognition and attitudes (Jenkin et al., 2011; Norton et al., 2014) and behavioural intentions (Greaves et al., 2013; Whillans and Dunn, 2015). Environmental scholars have also evaluated a variety of firm-level criteria including ISO 14001 certification (Raines and Prakash, 2005), environmental disclosure and performance ratings (Alt et al., 2015; Post et al., 2011), green project investment (Merriman, 2012), corporate environmental responsiveness (Papagiannakis and Lioukas, 2012; Rivera-Camino, 2012), firm environmental orientation (Roxas and Coetzer, 2012) and CEO response to the Carbon Disclosure Project (Lewis, Walls and Dowell, 2014). On one hand this broad sampling of criterion variables is reasonable and reflects the fact that environmental outcomes can take a nearly infinite variety of forms. However, it also seems that researchers have tended to pick and choose their outcome variables with little reference to existing work and the apparent absence of any overarching framework may have limited cumulative knowledge development in the field.

For studies examining multiple sustainability dimensions we see little evidence of a dominant form of criterion variable. Perhaps the strongest trend pertains to firm-level measures of corporate social responsibility (CSR), which often include both social and environmental performance assessments. However, as a criterion, CSR has been operationalized in a number of different ways including the type of CSR engaged in (Andersson, Giacalone and Jurkiewicz, 2007; Waldman et al., 2006), corporate social performance (Deckop, 2006; Muller and Kolk, 2010) and the adoption of a corporate social strategy (Mazutis, 2013). Closely related research has examined support for social and environmental accountability (Fukukawa, Shafer and Lee, 2007), and Linnenluecke et al. (2009) employ a holistic sustainability framework to assess individual's understanding of corporate sustainability as economic, social, environmental, or holistic in nature. On the whole however, it appears that there is little consensus or consistency in how to account for multiple sustainability outcomes.

Scanning across all studies it is apparent that the vast majority have focused exclusively on positive or beneficial outcomes within the various sustainability domains (Figure 20.4). By contrast, only six studies examine illegal or harmful impacts, and a similarly limited number account simultaneously for both beneficial and harmful outcomes. This overriding emphasis on positive sustainability outcomes is intriguing given that positive and negative actions are distinct constructs (Strike, Gao and Bansal, 2006), and that the first step towards advancing sustainable outcomes, is arguably to minimize firm actions that cause economic, social or environmental harm. And yet, it appears that to this point, the dominant concern amongst those working in the area has been to promote pro-social and pro-environmental behaviours.

Research samples and methods

The preponderance of studies surveyed in this review were conducted with adult and/ or active working populations, with only 14 studies using student convenience studies. Twelve studies employed management samples, and within these, four involved managers responsible for sustainability-related issues (e.g. environmental managers). Although the majority of studies were conducted with US samples, a substantial number of countries from around the world are also represented.

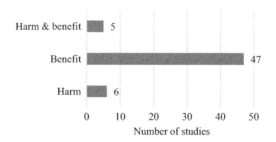

Figure 20.4 Harm vs. benefit valence of criterion variables.

With respect to research methods, survey data are the basis for the overwhelming majority of the studies reviewed (72 per cent), and almost all of these are of the cross-sectional variety. Only four studies employ longitudinal analyses. Six studies are based on secondary data, with the Kinder, Lydenberg, and Domini Index (KLD) being the most popular source. Experimental approaches are also poorly represented, appearing in only seven papers. In one notable example, and the only field experiment in our sample, Carrico and Riemer (2011) found that relatively simple behavioural interventions can have real impacts on energy use at the building level. The strict use of qualitative methods including a varied mix of case studies, focus groups, interviews, content analysis and ethnographic approaches were taken in seven studies. Only two studies employ mixed methods, and a single scale development study was retrieved in our search (Loviscky et al., 2007).

Key findings and managerial implications

So what have we learned in the past ten years? What lessons can be gleaned from the empirical research examining micro-level sustainability phenomenon? Notwithstanding the rather disparate state of the literature we believe it is possible to draw some meaningful, if tentative conclusions with regards to management practice.

First and foremost, this body of research reinforces the basic premise of this chapter: that individual's matter; that people make a difference in the execution and ultimate impact of a firm's sustainability strategy. This is perhaps most plainly revealed in the studies examining leadership issues. Leaders are, of course, both individuals and employees, and their actions typically have outsized impacts on what the firm does and how it goes about its business. On the whole, the research suggests that leaders play a key role in advancing sustainability strategies.

For example, recent work by Roberston and Barling (2013) has shown that when leaders model pro-environmental behaviours they positively influence the organization's adoption of 'green' practices. Kim and colleagues (2014) find similar outcomes at the level of group leadership. In an interesting twist, Sully de Luque et al. (2008) show that CEOs with a broader stakeholder focus are perceived by followers as being more visionary, with commensurate impacts on employee effort and firm performance. And leadership for sustainability does not necessarily require a formal leadership position as revealed in research by Raines and Prakash (2005). They show that that so-called environmental entrepreneurs can emerge throughout the organization, and that these individuals are key to the adoption of the ISO 14001 environmental management systems.

This is important because it is clearly not possible for all employees to hold formal leadership positions. What then gives rise to informal leadership for sustainability within businesses? What compels lower level employees to participate in and promote pro-social and pro-environmental practices? For that matter, what distinguishes the sustainability-oriented leader from his or her peers?

Our review suggests that a number of individual-difference variables are at play. Amongst demographic characteristics, gender seems to have the most pronounced effects on sustainability outcomes. Three studies examine gender in relation to ethics, and show that females hold more ethical attitudes (Albaum and Peterson, 2006; Chen and Tang, 2006) and are less accepting of questionable business behaviours (Cagle and Baucus, 2006) as compared to their male counterparts. Gender effects are not confined to the social dimension, but appear to cut across all sustainability domains as demonstrated by Marcus and colleagues (2015). They find that males have greater propensity for harmful actions across the economic, social and environmental domains, whereas females are more supportive of pro-social and pro-environmental actions. Post, Rahman and Rubow (2011) provide compelling evidence that firms whose corporate boards have greater female representation achieve higher KLD performance scores. Overall, the evidence suggests that females are more supportive of sustainability initiatives and less likely to engage in unsustainable or harmful actions. Perhaps the key takeaway is that the goal of enhancing sustainable business practice adds one more to the many already compelling reasons to break down pernicious glass ceiling effects in business.

Turning to psychological variables, a person's basic values appear to provide the motivational core for meaningful engagement with sustainability issues in the workplace. Values are significant predictors of ecological risk perceptions (Slimak and Dietz, 2006), ethical judgements (Fritzsche and Oz, 2007; Watson et al., 2009) and environmental attitudes and corporate environmental responsiveness (Papagiannakis and Lioukas, 2012). Not only so, there are identifiable values-types that seem to differentially impacts sustainability behaviours. Altruistic, or other-oriented values are generally consistent with pro-social outcomes, whereas economic or self-oriented values appear to heighten the potential for controversial and harmful behaviours (Marcus et al., 2015; Sully de Luque et al., 2008). Two opportunities for managerial action suggest themselves. The first is to identify, recruit, and select individuals whose values align with sustainability goals. This could be at the point of initial hiring, or when selecting existing employees to spearhead firm sustainability initiatives. The second and closely related opportunity, is for managers to work towards cultivating corporate values that both embody and shape the values held by individual employees (Andersson et al., 2005).

Individual's trait characteristics have also been repeatedly found to relate to sustainability outcomes. For example, specific personality types have been shown to significantly predict social outcomes in a number of studies. Hilbig and Zettler (2009) report that individuals low in Honesty-Humility make more selfish decisions, and Gonzalez-Mulé et al. (2014) show how agreeableness and extraversion at both the individual and team levels affect helping behaviours. Given that personality tests are easily administered and are already widely used within business for selection and organizational development purposes, it is possible that they could be a valuable tool for identifying employees – both prospective and existing – with a stronger predisposition for sustainable actions. We do caution, however, that further research is needed to confirm this potential.

Beyond personality, a number of studies have found effects for affective dispositional characteristics including emotions (Russell, 2010), positive affect (Bissing-Olson et al., 2013) and self-doubts (Sonenshein et al., 2014). Overall, these studies, which all address environmental behaviours, suggest that negative emotions frustrate ecologically beneficial behaviours even for highly committed individuals, whereas positive affect promotes pro-environmental actions. The apparent message for managers is to frame sustainability initiatives in the most positive manner possible. Given the consistent stream of dire climate warnings and social tensions filling the media this is not without difficulties. However, it appears that negative framing of sustainability efforts as responses to 'challenges' and 'problems' could effectively mute the motivational forces such messages are intended to promote.

Finally, in addition to individual-level drivers, the research reviewed here highlights a series of contextual factors that help to motivate sustainability behaviours. A number of studies even speak to the combined effects of person and situational variables (Ashkanasy et al., 2006; Marshall et al., 2005; Rivera-Camino, 2012; Roxas and Coetzer, 2012). On the situational side, training programmes have been found to have impacts on not only employee behaviour (Cantor et al., 2012), but also long-term effects on a firm's culture (Warren et al., 2014). Not surprisingly, incentive structures are also relevant, and Deckop (2006) shows that a short-term CEO pay focus relates negatively to corporate social performance (CSP), whereas a long-term pay focus promotes CSP. In a particularly interesting analysis, Whillans and Dunn (2015) report that when the economic value of time is made salient (through hourly pay, for example) individuals are less likely to engage in pro-environmental behaviour.

However, a study by Cantor et al. (2012) suggests that formal systems and structures may be limited in their ability to encourage sustainability acts. These authors found that rewards did not promote environmental behaviours, but supervisory support and training did. Organizational interventions such as group-level feedback and peer educators have also been found to have real impacts on building-level energy use (Carrico and Riemer, 2011). In fact, the organization's social context appears critical to the advancement of sustainability practices. Employees are more likely to engage in environmentally proactive behaviours when they believe that their supervisors and the organization as a whole supports such efforts (Cantor et al., 2012; Lamm et al., 2014; Paillé et al., 2013). Similarly, Andersson and colleagues (2005) report that corporate values, in terms of perceived commitment to the environment, are the most important predictor of employee's environmental behaviours. Additional studies have confirmed the importance of perceived management commitment to social and environmental concerns (Graves et al., 2011; Muller and Kolk, 2010). These analyses bring us full circle to again pinpoint the importance of leadership for sustainability, and the need to establish the right 'tone at the top'. Even more so, that tone must be demonstrably modelled and reinforced through consistent leadership behaviours that set an example for all employees to follow (Robertson and Barling, 2013).

Future research opportunities

It would be convenient, and not at all untrue, to suggest that additional research is needed in all areas pertaining to micro-level sustainability phenomenon. In too many cases only one or two studies speak to a given issue, and there are noticeable gaps without any research evidence whatsoever. Overall however, we see three broad areas in which to develop future research. These include advancing research with a broad sustainability orientation, expanding the research methods employed, and conducting research in the HRM area.

Holistic sustainability assessments

We acknowledged earlier that our description of the works reviewed as 'sustainability research' was perhaps a slight misconstrual. In fact, only a small minority of the studies examined were originally framed in terms of sustainability. It will come as no surprise then that we see great opportunity for analyses that are not only framed as sustainability research, but comprehensively assess economic, social and environmental criteria. It is time, in our view, to begin breaking down the strong division between socially focused and environmentally focused research that seems to persist.

This is more than just an idealistic nicety. Rather, the corralling of social versus environmental outcomes into distinct research streams has real implications for our understanding of sustainability phenomenon. For example, finding that a particular variable increases pro-social acts within the firm would generally be taken as a positive finding. However, what if that same variable simultaneously decreased environmental and/or economic prospects? The point is that when economic, social and environmental variables are examined in isolation it is impossible to assess the kinds of cross-domain effects that are key to a complete understanding of complex sustainability processes.

In the interests of more holistic approaches to sustainability scholarship, we also see need for greater attention to the harm side of the impact equation. This is not in any way to diminish the importance of promoting positive actions, but simply reflects our observation above that minimizing economic, social and environmental harm is the first order of business for a more sustainable future. The fact that individuals and firms can simultaneously engage in beneficial and destructive acts (Strike et al., 2006) further indicates the need to better understand the drivers of unsustainable behaviours as a basis for practical interventions to stymie them.

Multilevel, longitudinal and experimental analyses

Sustainability issues epitomize multilevel phenomena and yet only seven studies in our review employed multilevel analyses. We see particular opportunity to better understand relationships between leadership factors, corporate culture and employee level variables. For example, how might leaders' sustainability-related motivations and traits impact corporate culture and thereby condition employee behaviours? How is a sustainability culture developed and sustained over time, and how do employee's values, beliefs, attitudes and behaviours correspond to such a culture? We note that the values construct may be a prime candidate for such cross-level analyses given that it can be operational at multiple levels of analysis.

It is also striking that, at present, the vast majority of what we know with respect to micro-level sustainability phenomenon is based on cross-sectional survey data. There are clear opportunities to adopt research methods that can better inform causal and temporally dependent relationships. We thus call for greater use of longitudinal and experimental methods to inform our understanding of sustainability behaviour.

Human resource management

There is currently a rather glaring absence of sustainability research pertaining to HRM. On the one hand this is a serious deficit that considerably limits our ability to make specific recommendations for how best to manage employees for sustainability. On the other hand, we see a blank page of research opportunity waiting to be filled in this area. Important questions abound. What are the most effective means of recruiting employees who will advance sustainability goals? What selection tools can be used to distinguish those who will promote sustainability from those who would act otherwise? What training and organizational development interventions are most effective to promote a sustainable culture and sustainable business practices? How do corporate sustainability initiatives relate to employee retention and turnover? We are keen to see HRM scholars begin exploring how specific HRM functions, tools and practices might be used to advance sustainability outcomes.

Conclusions

Micro-level sustainability research in the workplace setting is in a nascent stage and is barely discernible absent the many and varied research streams from which it draws. In this chapter, we have sought to bring together the most recent and relevant studies pertaining to individual-level sustainability issues and to help outline the contours of this emerging research area. As described above, given our focus on 'managing employees for sustainability', we limited our scope to empirical work within the organizational and managerial context. We have largely ignored the extensive body of related research in environmental psychology that addresses more general forms of sustainability behaviour. And yet, one might reasonably expect that sustainability behaviour in one domain of life might have similar antecedents and processes as in other life domains. Indeed, a number of studies reviewed here draw directly upon the theoretical work of environmental psychologists.

Although we have adopted a relatively narrow focus in this review, we believe there is opportunity to cast sustainable work behaviour within a holistic framework that encompasses a variety of behavioural domains. For example, understanding what motivates sustainable choices in the consumer, political and discretionary realms might greatly inform our ability to motivate sustainable workplace behaviours. Our review, which surveys the most important and up-to-date empirical work on sustainable employee behaviour, could contribute to the development of integrative conceptual and theoretical models of sustainability behaviour. More directly, we hope it assists scholars working in this area to advance research that can inform practical strategies for managing a sustainability-oriented workforce.

Appendix 1

Literature review protocol

We systematically reviewed publications in a total of 50 journals (Appendix B) spanning the years 2005 to the present. We began our literature search with 21 journals listed on the Financial Times 45 index that address general management issues, organizational behaviour, or sustainability-related issues (e.g. ethics). We identified an additional 29 niche journals dealing with these themes, and also assessed the Academy of Management Proceedings for the same time period.

To identify relevant articles, we employed a broad set of keyword search terms including 'ecological', 'environmental', 'ethics', 'green', 'natural environment', 'social issues', 'social responsibility', 'sustainability', and 'sustainable development'. All articles meeting these search terms were then closely scrutinized by the authors to identify empirical research studies assessing individual-level factors.

After our initial search, we employed a snowballing technique by scrutinizing the bibliography of all papers uncovered in order to identify additional studies of interest. We engaged in three iterations of this snowballing exercise, at which point no new articles meeting are search criteria were recovered.

Appendix 2

List of journals surveyed

Financial Times 45 journals

1   *Academy of Management Journal*
2   *Academy of Management Perspectives*
3   *Academy of Management Review*
4   *Accounting, Organizations and Society*
5   *Administrative Science Quarterly*
6   *American Economic Review*
7   *California Management Review*
8   *Entrepreneurship Theory and Practice*
9   *Harvard Business Review*
10 *Human Resource Management*
11 *Journal of Applied Psychology*
12 *Journal of Business Ethics*
13 *Journal of Business Venturing*
14 *Journal of International Business Studies*
15 *Journal of Management Studies*
16 *Journal of Political Economy*
17 *Organization Science*
18 *Organization Studies*
19 *Organizational Behaviour and Human Decision Processes*
20 *Sloan Management Review*
21 *Strategic Management Journal*

Niche and related journals

22 *Academy of Management Annals*
23 *Academy of Management Discoveries*
24 *Academy of Management Executive*
25 *Academy of Management Learning & Education*
26 *Business and Society*
27 *Business and Society Review*
28 *Business Ethics Quarterly*
29 *Business Strategy and the Environment*
30 *Corporate Governance*
31 *Ecological Economics*
32 *Environment and Behavior*
33 *Environmental Values*
34 *Journal of Cleaner Production*
35 *Journal of Corporate Citizenship*
36 *Journal of Economic Behavior and Organization*
37 *Journal of Economic Psychology*
38 *Journal of Environmental Psychology*
39 *Journal of Management*
40 *Journal of Occupational and Organizational Psychology*
41 *Journal of Organizational Behavior*

42 *Journal of Personality*
43 *Journal of Personality and Social Psychology*
44 *Journal of Social Issues*
45 *Leadership Quarterly*
46 *Organization & Environment*
47 *Organizational Research Methods*
48 *Personnel Psychology*
49 *Sustainability*
50 *Sustainable Development*

References

Aguinis, H. and Glavas, A. (2012). What we know and don't know about corporate social responsibility: A review and research agenda. *Journal of Management*, 38(4): 932–968. https://doi.org/10.1177/0149206311436079.

Ajzen, I. (1991). The theory of planned behavior. *Organizational Behavior and Human Decision Processes*, 50: 179.

Albaum, G. and Peterson, R.A. (2006). Ethical attitudes of future business leaders Do they vary by gender and religiosity? *Business & Society*, 45(3): 300–321.

Alt, E., Díez-de-Castro, E.P. and Lloréns-Montes, F.J. (2015). Linking employee stakeholders to environmental performance: The role of proactive environmental strategies and shared vision. *Journal of Business Ethics*, 128(1): 167–181.

Anderson, R.C. (1998). *Mid-Course Correction: Toward a Sustainable Enterprise - The Interface Model.* Atlanta, GA: Peregrinzilla Press.

Andersson, L., Giacalone, R. and Jurkiewicz, C. (2007). On the relationship of hope and gratitude to corporate social responsibility. *Journal of Business Ethics*, 70(4): 401–409. https://doi.org/10.1007/s10551-006-9118-1.

Andersson, L., Jackson, S.E. and Russell, S.V. (2013). Greening organizational behavior: An introduction to the special issue. *Journal of Organizational Behavior*, 34(2): 151–155. https://doi.org/10.1002/job.1854.

Andersson, L., Shivarajan, S. and Blau, G. (2005). Enacting ecological sustainability in the MNC: A test of an adapted value-belief-norm framework. *Journal of Business Ethics*, 59(3): 295–305. https://doi.org/10.1007/s10551-005-3440-x.

Ashkanasy, N.M., Windsor, C.A. and Treviño, L.K. (2006). Bad apples in bad barrels revisited: Cognitive moral development, just world beliefs, rewards, and ethical decision-making. *Business Ethics Quarterly*, 16(4): 449–473.

Barnard, C.I. (1938). *The Functions of the Executive.* Cambridge MA: Harvard University Press.

Bissing-Olson, M.J., Iyer, A., Fielding, K.S. and Zacher, H. (2013). Relationships between daily affect and pro-environmental behavior at work: The moderating role of pro-environmental attitude. *Journal of Organizational Behavior*, 34(2): 156–175. https://doi.org/10.1002/job.1788.

Burton, B.K. and Goldsby, M. (2009). Corporate social responsibility orientation, goals, and behavior a study of small business owners. *Business & Society*, 48(1): 88–104.

Cagle, J.A.B. and Baucus, M.S. (2006). Case studies of ethics scandals: effects on ethical perceptions of finance students. *Journal of Business Ethics*, 64(3): 213–229. https://doi.org/10.1007/s10551-005-8503-5.

Cantor, D.E., Morrow, P.C. and Montabon, F. (2012). Engagement in environmental behaviors among supply chain management employees: An organizational support theoretical perspective. *Journal of Supply Chain Management*, 48(3): 33–51.

Carrico, A.R. and Riemer, M. (2011). Motivating energy conservation in the workplace: An evaluation of the use of group-level feedback and peer education. *Journal of Environmental Psychology*, 31(1): 1–13. https://doi.org/10.1016/j.jenvp.2010.11.004.

Chen, Y.-J. and Tang, T.L.-P. (2006). Attitude toward and propensity to engage in unethical behavior: Measurement invariance across major among university students. *Journal of Business Ethics*, 69(1): 77–93.

Deckop, J.R. (2006). The effects of CEO pay structure on corporate social performance. *Journal of Management*, 32(3): 329–342. https://doi.org/10.1177/0149206305280113.

Delmas, M.A. and Burbano, V.C. (2011). The drivers of greenwashing. *California Management Review*, 54(1): 64–87.

Detert, J.R., Treviño, L.K. and Sweitzer, V.L. (2008). Moral disengagement in ethical decision making: A study of antecedents and outcomes. *Journal of Applied Psychology*, 93(2): 374–391. https://doi.org/10.1037/0021-9010.93.2.374.

Dunlap, R.E. and Van Liere, K.D. (1978). The new ecological paradigm. *Journal of Environmental Education*, 9, 10–19.

Fritzsche, D.J. and Oz, E. (2007). Personal values' influence on the ethical dimension of decision making. *Journal of Business Ethics*, 75(4): 335. https://doi.org/http://dx.doi.org.remote.libproxy.wlu.ca/10.1007/s10551-006-9256-5.

Fukukawa, K., Shafer, W.E. and Lee, G.M. (2007). Values and attitudes toward social and environmental accountability: A study of MBA students. *Journal of Business Ethics*, 71(4): 381–394. https://doi.org/10.1007/s10551-005-3893-y.

Gonzalez-Mulé, E., DeGeest, D.S., McCormick, B.W., Seong, J.Y. and Brown, K.G. (2014). Can we get some cooperation around here? The mediating role of group norms on the relationship between team personality and individual helping behaviors. *Journal of Applied Psychology*, 99(5): 988.

Graves, L.M., Sarkis, J. and Zhu, Q. (2011). Understanding employee proenvironmental behavior: A test of a theoretical model. *Academy of Management Proceedings*, 1: 1–6. Retrieved from https://doi.org/10.5465/ambpp.2011.65870068.

Greaves, M., Zibarras, L.D. and Stride, C. (2013). Using the theory of planned behavior to explore environmental behavioral intentions in the workplace. *Journal of Environmental Psychology*, 34: 109–120. https://doi.org/10.1016/j.jenvp.2013.02.003.

Hagenbuch, D.J., Little, S.W. and Lucas, D.J. (2015). Beyond association: How employees want to participate in their firms' corporate social performance. *Business and Society Review*, 120(1): 83–113.

Hilbig, B.E. and Zettler, I. (2009). Pillars of cooperation: Honesty–Humility, social value orientations, and economic behavior. *Journal of Research in Personality*, 43(3): 516–519. https://doi.org/10.1016/j.jrp.2009.01.003.

Hollender, J., Breen, B. and Senge, P. (2010). *The Responsibility Revolution: How the Next Generation of Businesses will Win*. San Francisco, CA: Jossey-Bass.

Jenkin, T.A., McShane, L. and Webster, J. (2011). Green information technologies and systems: Employees' perceptions of organizational practices. *Business & Society*, 50(2): 266–314.

Jones, D.A. (2010). Does serving the community also serve the company? Using organizational identification and social exchange theories to understand employee responses to a volunteerism programme. *Journal of Occupational and Organizational Psychology*, 83(4): 857–878. https://doi.org/10.1348/096317909X477495.

Kim, A., Kim, Y., Han, K., Jackson, S.E. and Ployhart, R.E. (2014). Multilevel influences on voluntary workplace green behavior individual differences, leader behavior, and coworker advocacy. *Journal of Management*, 0149206314547386. https://doi.org/10.1177/0149206314547386.

Lamm, E., Tosti-Kharas, J. and King, C.E. (2014). Empowering employee sustainability: Perceived organizational support toward the environment. *Journal of Business Ethics*, 128(1): 207–220. https://doi.org/10.1007/s10551-014-2093-z.

Lavine, M. (2012). Exploring the relationship between corporate social performance and work meaningfulness. *Journal of Corporate Citizenship*, (46): 53–70.

Lewis, B.W., Walls, J.L. and Dowell, G.W. (2014). Difference in degrees: CEO characteristics and firm environmental disclosure. *Strategic Management Journal*, 35(5): 712–722.

Linnenluecke, M.K., Russell, S.V. and Griffiths, A. (2009). Subcultures and sustainability practices: The impact on understanding corporate sustainability. *Business Strategy and the Environment*, 18(7): 432–452. https://doi.org/10.1002/bse.609.

Loviscky, G.E., Treviño, L.K. and Jacobs, R.R. (2007). Assessing managers' ethical decision-making: An objective measure of managerial moral judgment. *Journal of Business Ethics*, 73(3): 263–285. https://doi.org/10.1007/s10551-006-9206-2.

Marcus, J., Kurucz, E.C. and Colbert, B.A. (2010). Conceptions of the business–society–nature interface: Implications for management scholarship. *Business & Society*, 49(3): 402–438. https://doi.org/10.1177/0007650310368827.

Marcus, J., MacDonald, H.A. and Sulsky, L.M. (2015). Do personal values influence the propensity for sustainability actions? A policy-capturing study. *Journal of Business Ethics*, 127(2): 459–478. https://doi.org/10.1007/s10551-013-2032-4.

Marshall, R.S., Cordano, M. and Silverman, M. (2005). Exploring individual and institutional drivers of proactive environmentalism in the US wine industry. *Business Strategy and the Environment*, 14(2): 92–109. https://doi.org/10.1002/bse.433.

Mazutis, D.D. (2013). The CEO effect a longitudinal, multilevel analysis of the relationship between executive orientation and corporate social strategy. *Business & Society*, 52(4): 631–648.

McFerran, B., Aquino, K. and Duffy, M. (2010). How personality and moral identity relate to individuals' ethical ideology. *Business Ethics Quarterly*, 20(1): 35–56.

Merriman, K.K. (2012). Incenting managers toward the triple bottom line: An agency and social norm perspective. *Human Resource Management*, 51(6): 851–871.

Morse, P.J., Sauerberger, K.S., Todd, E. and Funder, D. (2015). Relationships among personality, situational construal and social outcomes. *European Journal of Personality*, 29(2): 97–106.

Muller, A. and Kolk, A. (2010). Extrinsic and intrinsic drivers of corporate social performance: Evidence from foreign and domestic firms in Mexico. *Journal of Management Studies*, 47(1): 1–26. https://doi.org/10.1111/j.1467-6486.2009.00855.x.

Norton, B.G. and Steinemann, A.C. (2001). Environmental values and adaptive management. *Environmental Values*, 10(4): 473–506.

Norton, T.A., Zacher, H. and Ashkanasy, N.M. (2014). Organisational sustainability policies and employee green behaviour: The mediating role of work climate perceptions. *Journal of Environmental Psychology*, 38, 49–54.

Paillé, P., Boiral, O. and Chen, Y. (2013). Linking environmental management practices and organizational citizenship behaviour for the environment: a social exchange perspective. *The International Journal of Human Resource Management*, 24(18): 3552–3575. https://doi.org/10.1080/09585192.2013.777934.

Papagiannakis, G. and Lioukas, S. (2012). Values, attitudes and perceptions of managers as predictors of corporate environmental responsiveness. *Journal of Environmental Management*, 100: 41–51. https://doi.org/10.1016/j.jenvman.2012.01.023.

Pfeffer, J. (2010). Building sustainable organizations: The human factor. *Academy of Management Perspectives*, 24(1): 34–45. https://doi.org/10.5465/AMP.2010.50304415.

Post, C., Rahman, N. and Rubow, E. (2011). Green governance: Boards of directors' composition and environmental corporate social responsibility. *Business & Society*, 50(1): 189–223.

Raines, S.S. and Prakash, A. (2005). Leadership matters: Policy entrepreneurship in corporate environmental policy making. *Administration & Society*, 37(1): 3–22. https://doi.org/10.1177/0095399704272594.

Reynolds, S.J. (2006). Moral awareness and ethical predispositions: Investigating the role of individual differences in the recognition of moral issues. *Journal of Applied Psychology*, 91(1): 233–243. https://doi.org/10.1037/0021-9010.91.1.233.

Rivera-Camino, J. (2012). Corporate environmental market responsiveness: A model of individual and organizational drivers. *Journal of Business Research*, 65(3): 402–411. https://doi.org/10.1016/j.jbusres.2011.07.002.

Robertson, J.L. and Barling, J. (2013). Greening organizations through leaders' influence on employees' pro-environmental behaviors: Green leadership and employees' behaviors. *Journal of Organizational Behavior*, 34(2): 176–194. https://doi.org/10.1002/job.1820.

Roxas, B. and Coetzer, A. (2012). Institutional environment, managerial attitudes and environmental sustainability orientation of small firms. *Journal of Business Ethics*, 111(4): 461–476. https://doi.org/10.1007/s10551-012-1211-z.

Russell, S.V. (2010). Explaining workplace proenvironmental behaviors: The role of emotion, values and issue ownership. *Academy of Management Proceedings*, 1: 1–6. http://proceedings. aom.org/content/2008/1/1.83.short.

Scherbaum, C.A., Popovich, P.M. and Finlinson, S. (2008). Exploring individual-level factors related to employee energy-conservation behaviors at work. *Journal of Applied Social Psychology*, 38(3): 818–835.

Schwartz, S.H. (1992). Universals in the content and structure of values: Theoretical advances and empirical tests in 20 countries. *Advances in Experimental Social Psychology*, 25(1): 1–65.

Shalvi, S., Dana, J., Handgraaf, M.J.J. and De Dreu, C.K.W. (2011). Justified ethicality: Observing desired counterfactuals modifies ethical perceptions and behavior. *Organizational Behavior and Human Decision Processes*, 115(2): 181–190. https://doi.org/10.1016/j.obhdp.2011.02.001.

Shepherd, D.A., Patzelt, H. and Baron, R.A. (2013). 'I care about nature, but …': Disengaging values in assessing opportunities that cause harm. *Academy of Management Journal*, 56(5): 1251–1273. https://doi.org/10.5465/amj.2011.0776.

Sims, R.R. and Brinkmann, J. (2003). Enron ethics (or: culture matters more than codes). *Journal of Business Ethics*, 45(3): 243–256.

Slimak, M.W. and Dietz, T. (2006). Personal values, beliefs, and ecological risk perception. *Risk Analysis*, 26(6): 1689–1705. https://doi.org/10.1111/j.1539-6924.2006.00832.x.

Smith, N.C., Simpson, S.S. and Chun-Yao Huang. (2007). Why managers fail to do the right thing: An empirical study of unethical and illegal conduct. *Business Ethics Quarterly*, 17(4): 633–667.

Sonenshein, S., DeCelles, K.A. and Dutton, J.E. (2014). It's not easy being green: The role of self-evaluations in explaining support of environmental issues. *Academy of Management Journal*, 57(1): 7–37. https://doi.org/10.5465/amj.2010.0445.

Stern, P.C., Dietz, T., Abel, T., Guagnano, G.A. and Kalof, L. (1999). A value–belief–norm theory of support for social movements: The case of environmentalism. *Human Ecology Review*, 6(2): 81–98.

Stevens, J.M., Kevin Steensma, H., Harrison, D.A. and Cochran, P.L. (2005). Symbolic or substantive document? The influence of ethics codes on financial executives' decisions. *Strategic Management Journal*, 26(2): 181–195. https://doi.org/10.1002/smj.440.

Stites, J.P. and Michael, J.H. (2011). Organizational commitment in manufacturing employees: Relationships with corporate social performance. *Business & Society*, 50(1): 50–70.

Strike, V.M., Gao, J. and Bansal, P. (2006). Being good while being bad: Social responsibility and the international diversification of US firms. *Journal of International Business Studies*, 37(6): 850–862.

Sully de Luque, M., Washburn, N.T., Waldman, D.A. and House, R.J. (2008). Unrequited profit: How stakeholder and economic values relate to subordinates' perceptions of leadership and firm performance. *Administrative Science Quarterly*, 53(4): 626–654.

United Nations General Assembly (2005). *2005 World Summit Outcome, Resolution A/60/1, adopted by the General Assembly on 15 September 2005* (p. 38). New York: United Nations.

Waldman, D.A., Siegel, D.S. and Javidan, M. (2006). Components of CEO transformational leadership and corporate social responsibility. *Journal of Management Studies*, 43(8): 1703–1725. https://doi.org/10.1111/j.1467-6486.2006.00642.x.

Warren, D.E., Gaspar, J.P. and Laufer, W.S. (2014). Is formal ethics training merely cosmetic? A study of ethics training and ethical organizational culture. *Business Ethics Quarterly*, 24(1): 85–117. https://doi.org/10.5840/beq2014233.

Watson, G.W., Berkley, R.A. and Papamarcos, S.D. (2009). Ambiguous allure: The value–pragmatics model of ethical decision making. *Business & Society Review*, 114(1): 1–29. https://doi.org/10.1111/j.1467-8594.2009.00333.x.

Whillans, A.V. and Dunn, E.W. (2015). Thinking about time as money decreases environmental behavior. *Organizational Behavior and Human Decision Processes*, 127: 44–52.

Wijen, F. (2014). Means versus ends in opaque institutional fields: Trading off compliance and achievement in sustainability standard adoption. *Academy of Management Review*, 39(3): 302–323. https://doi.org/10.5465/amr.2012.0218.

Wood, D.J. (1991). Corporate social performance revisited. *Academy of Management Review*, 16(4): 691–718.

21 Power and shareholder saliency

Tessa Hebb, Andreas Hoepner, Tatiana Rodionova and Imelda Sánchez

Introduction

Shareholder activism is known to have an impact on the way companies work. It does so by stressing the importance behind the inclusion of environmental, social and governance standards (ESG) in the decisions that managers take (Clark and Hebb, 2004; Hawley and Williams, 2000; Monks, 2000). Adopting these standards is key to a variety of business strategies that ensure corporate sustainable practices. However, not all shareholders receive equal attention from managers (Gifford, 2010). In fact, there are many studies that show the existence of certain shareholder attributes is necessary in order for managers to pay attention to their claims.

This chapter argues that while shareholders and company managers stress legitimacy as the most salient factor in shareholder engagement, in fact power plays a key role in exerting influence on corporate ESG standards. Shareholder power is embedded in the minority shareholder resolutions placed before corporate annual meetings. Such resolutions are often designed to generate both negative publicity and significant votes as a means to direct company behaviour on environmental, social and/or governance issues. While these resolutions seldom garner more than 15 per cent of the vote at company annual meetings, they focus the attention of senior management on the ESG issue at hand. As a result they can open the door further shareholder engagement. Minority resolutions are the primary power-based tool shareholders have to exert influence over senior corporate management.

We build on the work of Mitchell et al., 1997; Gifford, 2010; and Hebb et al., 2011 in our exploration of shareholder engagement. Mitchell et al. detailed three primary attributes of stakeholder salience: legitimacy, power and urgency. Gifford refined these attributes and suggested that legitimacy moderated through the alignment of shareholder and managers' values, plays a vital role in this dynamic relationship. Hebb et al. extended this work and reasserted Gifford's findings. All three bodies of research on stakeholder saliency have drawn on qualitative methods.

There is an extensive body of qualitative research on the process of shareholder engagement and the factors contributing to shareholder saliency. However, there are few quantitative studies in this area. This chapter aims to fill this gap by providing information that can be used to extend and enrich the current literature available. We utilize a dataset of 1,085 shareholder engagements from 1993 to 2013 that also included a shareholder minority resolution somewhere in the process. In many cases the shareholder resolution occurred at the beginning of the engagement; in other cases the engagement resulted in a shareholder resolution. This dataset is drawn from the Interfaith Centre for Corporate Responsibility (ICCR) database of minority shareholder resolutions and shareholder engagements compiled since the 1970s.

We find power to be a significant source of salience for investors. However, our findings also suggest that while it is a key attribute in the early days of shareholder engagement, over time companies have demonstrated a greater willingness to engage with shareholders on ESG issues without the threat of power to induce such engagement.

While the use of power is instrumental in gaining access and attention of senior corporate managers, does it lead to successful outcomes? In other words, do the companies respond more positively to ESG requests when the threat of use of power to inflict negative reputation damage is embedded in the exchange? Our findings suggest that the results are evenly split as to whether companies show signs of implementing the requested outcomes in achieving changes in corporate behaviour based on objective criteria for standards and codes. However, we did find some small evidence of successful change in company behaviour when the dialogue occurred before the resolution in these cases. As suggested in the overall findings, if the dialogue occurred after the resolution was submitted, the likelihood of success was evenly split.

The chapter is laid out in the following manner. In the next section the relevant literature on shareholder engagement is brought forward and discussed. The third section of the chapter outlines five hypotheses on shareholder saliency to be tested. The methodology used to test the hypothesis is provided in the fourth section of the chapter. The findings are detailed in the following section. The chapter concludes with a discussion of the implications, limitations and areas of future research on shareholder saliency to be explored.

The role of power in shareholder saliency

Shareholders are deemed to be active owners when they engage company managers in order to ensure that managers are not simply serving their own interests, but also those of the shareholders (Monks, 2001). Shareholders want to raise the value and improve the performance of their stocks; they also want to minimize financial risks (Yaron G., 2005). Such risks are embedded in poor corporate sustainability practices. Increasingly corporate risks that arise from poor environmental, social and governance standards are seen to have a negative impact on shareholder value (Clark and Hebb, 2005). Witness the 2010 BP oil spill in the Gulf of Mexico. As of 2013 BP had paid out $42 billion in penalties and clean-up costs. BP shares have yet to regain their full value. When poor corporate standards lead to environmental or social damage, shareholders are directly affected. However, the demands raised by shareholders are vast, and cannot all be attended to at the same time. What motivates a company to hear what their shareholders have to say?

Mitchell et al.'s 1997 work on shareholder salience identifies three major aspects of stakeholder saliency: legitimacy, power and urgency. Mitchell contests that these three factors are key to determining the relevance of stakeholder claims. Gifford (2010) extended the work of Mitchell et al. focusing exclusively on shareholder engagement as one of the key stakeholders that companies must attend to. He found that legitimacy is one of the main catalysts for achieving saliency. Gifford went on to suggest other aspects which moderate the degree of influence engagement can play. He noted that shared values by managers, particularly mid-level managers, and shareholders are also critical in these exchanges. More recent studies reinforce Gifford's findings on the factors thought to increase stakeholder saliency. Interviews with investors suggested that shareholders commonly prefer to engage through legitimacy and urgency strategies rather than using their power (Hebb, Hachigian and Allen, 2012).

Significant research has investigated the factors that motivate shareholders to engage with the companies they own. A great deal of attention has been placed on shareholder resolutions, proxy voting and public campaigns. However, much work remains in order to understand what factors lead to successful outcomes. Why do some shareholder engagements proceed to minority shareholder resolutions while others do not? In some instances private dialogues have led to successful outcomes (Hebb, Hachigian and Allen, 2012), while in other cases noisy public exchanges are more effective.

The relationship between shareholders and managers has not been one of common understanding and shared goals. Conflicts of interest are a central aspect that affects this relationship. Such conflicts can potentially undermine shareholder value, and damage the overall performance of the company. Resolving these conflicts often forces corporations to bear greater costs and risk reputation damage (Hennessey, 2001). They can play a critical role in business sustainability strategies.

In this chapter, we examine the saliency of the stakeholder rather than of the issue, a key differentiation as noted by Gond and Piani (2013). The stakeholder saliency model (Mitchell et al., 1997) highlights two lines of study, the first one having to do with the way managers identify their primary stakeholders, and the second (and most important for this chapter) how stakeholders gain the attention of managers. The identification stage, as explained by Mitchell et al. (1997), is based on three main attributes that determine and establish the relationship of the shareholder to the firm. First, the degree of power that the given stakeholder has over the firm. Second, how legitimate the relationship is between the stakeholder and the company. Thirdly, the level of urgency shown in the stakeholder's claims over the firm. It has been suggested that any actual or potential stakeholder can achieve a full definitive status, just by raising any of these three elements with corporate managers (Magness, 2008).

Power, the first saliency driving attribute, is defined by Mitchell (2007) as the extent to which a stakeholder can 'gain access to coercive, utilitarian or normative means in order to impose its will in the relationship' (p. 865). Two main aspects are important to this definition, the first is that power is defined as an ability, something that is achieved over time and gives the party control over a determined situation (Salancik and Pfeffer, 1974), and therefore has a dynamic status as it can be either obtained or lost. The second is the use of Etzioni's (1964) classification of power in three ways. The first is coercive: that which is to be applied through physical means. The second is utilitarian: one where the utilization of material means to impose one's will is necessary. The third is normative. Here symbols are thought to serve as a mechanism of control, potentially dangerous to the reputation of the party subject to such control.

On the other hand, legitimacy as the second attribute needed to attain saliency is conceived under a broader perspective. Here the perceptions and assumptions of society in general are to judge whether or not the actions conducted by a party are 'desirable, proper or appropriate within some socially constructed system of norms, values, beliefs and definitions' (Mitchell et al., 1997, p. 866). This attribute is also divided in three categories later extended by Gifford (2010) into four.

The fourth category of legitimacy, pragmatic legitimacy, is added to shareholder saliency theory in order to establish the company's perspective on engagement. While the other three categories capture credibility of the individual, the organization and society (Wood, 1991), there is no category that considers the way the company perceives the arguments made by shareholders to be legitimate (Gifford, 2010). This is where pragmatic legitimacy comes into the formula.

Finally, the claims of shareholders wouldn't get much attention if the matter being exposed wasn't important to the parties promoting corporate engagement. A degree of urgency is required to advance stakeholder claims (Mitchell, 1997). However, the term 'urgency' itself does not entirely explain how it increases saliency. What is urgent to the engager may not be deemed as urgent to the managers.

To address the complexity of the term, Gifford (2010) suggests that having a sensitive time frame and being relevant for the subject are key aspects of this attribute. He also argues that the issue has to be exposed in a manner that shows the shareholder is determined to find a solution for it. Therefore, the more resolute the shareholder is in promoting corporate engagement in a certain matter through 'assertiveness, persistence and the application of resources' (Gifford, 2010, p. 82), the more critical that matter will appear to be in front of the eyes of managers.

Besides the attributes described above, three more factors are thought to act as moderators that can either increase or decrease the level of saliency shareholders attain when presenting their claims to the managers (Gifford, 2010). The first of these factors relates to the size of the shareholder in comparison to the size of the company. Size can increase the ability of the shareholder to exercise its correspondent rights at the voting forum. It can grant him some sort of recognition from other players present in the market. The second factor has to do with the formation of coalitions among shareholders who rely on their capacity to share resources and information. This can be combined with the benefits that a common and recognized reputation can bring. Lastly, the alignment of the managers' values with the requests made by shareholders is also proposed as a moderating factor of shareholder salience. This factor can 'moderate shareholder salience independently from the attributes or characteristics that the shareholder itself possesses' (Gifford, 2010, p. 83).

This last moderating factor has been proved to have a strong influence in the shareholder-manager relationship (Hambrick and Mason, 1984; Agle et al., 1999). Moreover, case studies show that shareholders holding a claim perceived in the eyes of managers as both legitimate and urgent[1] achieve greater levels of saliency (Hebb, Hachigian and Allen, 2012).

However, it could be argued that existing research only focuses on specific characteristics of engagement, rather than on the process through which shareholders and companies come together in order to respond to claims. Goodman and Arenas (2013) argue that present theories on shareholder activism are not sufficient in explaining all the steps taken in order to achieve shareholder saliency.

It may well be that coercive mechanisms are a means to attract attention on the issue of engagement. These actions may drive an active communication process between management and shareholders (Rehbein et al. 2013). Such confrontation might first be employed to make managers aware of shareholder claims. This mechanism allows shareholders to be noticed in the first instance, and later engage into a process of dialogue/active communication where the use of legitimate mechanisms is more common.

An important number of filed and withdrawn shareholder resolutions have been observed in large data sets like the Standard & Poor's 1500 Composite Index, suggesting that most shareholders prefer to first bring awareness over certain issues through proxy proposals, and then wait for managers to take the next step and engage in private dialogue (Bauer, Moers and Viehs, 2012). Quite often this communication process between management and shareholders results in the decision of the proposal's sponsor to withdraw the filed resolution. A recent study by Bauer et al. (2012) finds a positive relationship between the ownership structure of corporation and the propensity for shareholders to withdraw submitted proposals, where the withdrawal rate is higher in companies with a larger composition of institutional investors, and lower in the case of individual shareholders and internal owners. We build on this framework of shareholder saliency by adding two hypotheses that will be tested in this study.

Hypothesis

We argue that our quantitative study on shareholder engagement will show different results to those obtained in previous qualitative, case study research. These studies suggest that legitimate and urgency attributes moderated by the alignment of management values with shareholder requests are the primary drivers of successful/positive corporate engagement, rather than the use of power. But in fact the opposite could be happening. Our research will show some evidence on how the process of engagement is undertaken in reality, leaving aside shareholder perceptions and focusing on actual data about shareholder resolutions.

Hypothesis 1: While shareholders might perceive themselves as being more legitimate and urgency-driven in their engagements with company managers, using power only as a last resort to call attention on the matter they wish to discuss, in fact shareholder power (expressed as the use of minority shareholder resolutions) is used to open the process of engagement with companies.

Hypothesis 2: Use of shareholder power leads to greater successful outcomes of corporate engagement measured by changes in company standards, codes and behaviour requested by shareholders in the engagement.

Methodology

The methodology used in this chapter is qualitative. We utilize the Interfaith Centre for Corporate Responsibility database of 6,000 minority shareholder resolutions and 3,000 shareholder engagements compiled from 1971 to 2012. We selected a subsample of all engagements that also had a minority resolution associated with them either before, during or after the dialogue. This subsample provided 1,085 cases. We used descriptive statistics and Chi-square tests to test our hypothesis. We then used public Internet searches of company websites and annual reports with a smaller sample of 500 companies to find evidence of adoption of the requested ESG change asked for in the engagement. Half the sample were objective indicators of change (N=256), i.e. codes of conduct and measurable standards, and half the sample (N=246) were deemed subjective indicators.

Findings

Table 21.1 indicates that if a resolution was associated with an engagement (N=1085), in the vast majority of cases the resolution occurred before the engagement, rather than after the engagement. This finding holds over time and is consistent in both the 1990s (72 per cent of the time) or 2000s (82 per cent of the time). We tested this by type of resolution to see if environmental, social or governance resolutions have the same pattern of engagement. We find this result holds regardless of the area of engagement.

The first panel of Table 21.1 shows the distribution of the cases with dialogues before and after the resolutions in 1990s and 2000s. In both cases there are more instances of dialogues occurring after the resolutions and it becomes even more evident in the 2000s where the difference in distributions is statistically significant.

Table 21.1 Comparison of cases with dialogue before resolution and after

	Period 1990s (n=177)		Period 2000s (n=908)	
Dialogue before	49		28%	167	18%
Dialogue after	128		72%	741	82%
$Chi^2=8.02$, p<0.01				
	Corporate Governance (n=91)		Social & Environmental (n=994)	
Dialogue before	27		30%	189	19%
Dialogue after	64		70%	805	81%
$Chi^2=5.93$, p<0.05				
Period 1990s				
	Corporate Governance (n=18)		Social & Environmental (n=159)	
Dialogue before	6		33%	43	27%
Dialogue after	12		67%	116	73%
$Chi^2=0.32$, p=insig				
Period 2000s				
	Corporate Governance (n=73)		Social & Environmental (n=835)	
Dialogue before	21		29%	146	17%
Dialogue after	52		71%	689	83%
$Chi^2=5.69$, p<0.05				

The cases in Table 21.1 are treated as independent, even if they happened in the same firm.

Table 21.2 Comparison of mean likelihood of dialogue before resolution

	Probability of dialogue before resolution	Observations
1990s	0.28	177
2000s	0.18	908
Absolute t-statistic	3.89★	

★ p <.001.

The second and third panels show the distribution of the cases with dialogues before and after the resolutions by topic (governance versus social issues). Again, we find the differences are significant.

In Table 21.2, we attempted to control for the fact that the engagement pattern could be firm-specific. So we computed the mean likelihood of the dialogue to happen before the resolution in a company and then tested the difference in means in 1990s and 2000s. The difference is again significant and shows that, controlling for a specific firm element, it is less likely to have dialogue before the resolution is filed with the company, than after.

We went on to ask whether having dialogue between shareholders and companies influences the voting outcomes of those resolutions that went to a vote. As we know, in the US most minority shareholder resolutions garner on average approximately 16 per cent of the total vote. Tables 21.5 and 21.6 indicate that these results do not change whether there was a dialogue before the resolution or after. Neither case demonstrated a significant difference in the voting outcome. However, we do see a pattern in the 1990s that indicates having a dialogue before the resolution seems to be related to receiving a higher vote, than having a dialogue after. This pattern does not persist into the 2000s.

Table 21.3 Comparison of cases with dialogue before resolution and after

	Dialogue before (n=216)	Dialogue after (n=869)		
Voting did not happen	99	46%	469	54%
Voting happened	117	54%	400	46%
	$Chi^2(1)=1.5$, p=insig	$Chi^2(1)=5.48$, p<0.05		
$Chi^2=4.59$, p<0.05				

Period 1990s

	Dialogue before (n=49)	Dialogue after (n=128)		
Voting did not happen	26	53%	97	76%
Voting happened	23	47%	31	24%
	$Chi^2(1)=0.18$, p=insig	$Chi^2(1)=34.03$, p<0.000		
$Chi^2=8.63$, p<0.01				

Period 2000s

	Dialogue before (n=167)	Dialogue after (n=741)		
Voting did not happen	73	44%	372	50%
Voting happened	94	56%	369	50%
	$Chi^2(1)=2.64$, p=insig	$Chi^2(1)=0.01$, p=insig		
$Chi^2=2.30$, p=insig				

Table 21.4 Voting likelihood in 1990s and 2000s

	1990s (n=177)		2000s (n=908)	
Voting did not happen	123	69%	445	49%
Voting happened	54	31%	463	51%
$Chi^2=24.91$, p<0.000				

Table 21.5 Comparison of votes depending on preceding dialogue

	Mean votes	Observations
Dialogue before resolution	16%	116
Dialogue after resolution	14%	397
Absolute t-statistic	0.91	

Table 21.6 Comparison of mean votes depending on preceding dialogue

	1990s	N	2000s	N	Abs t-stat
Dialogue before resolution	13%	23	17%	93	1.56
Dialogue after resolution	9%	31	15%	366	6.93★★
Abs t-stat	2.14★		0.94		

★ p <.05, ★★ p <.001.

Corporate change

But the question that is perhaps most fundamental about dialogue and minority shareholder resolutions is whether or not they are successful in changing corporate behaviour and raising corporate standards. To test this, we selected a sub sample of 500 dialogues between 1990 and 2012 that had also received a minority shareholder resolution. We divided this sample into those dialogues and resolutions that had asked for a change in corporate behaviour that could be observed objectively. In most cases these objective standards were requests to adopt certain codes of behaviour such as the CERES Principles or Sullivan Principles; or to provide transparent reporting policies such as the Carbon Disclosure Project or Global Reporting Initiative. Half the dialogues were deemed objective in this subset. The other half of the sample asked for subjective changes in company behaviour. These included more diversity in management, addressing HIV/Aids, and human rights issues.

We then engaged in a public Internet-based search for each of the companies in the subset to find concrete evidence that the change requested in the dialogue had occurred in the period since the request was made. Evidence of success was evenly split. Roughly half the dialogues in our sample showed evidence of improvement, while in the other half of the cases we could find no evidence of successful change. It is interesting that those dialogues where the resolutions went to a vote were only able to gain 15 per cent of the total shareholder vote. However, in half the cases the change requested by the shareholder was indeed undertaken by the company. While there are too many factors to establish causation in these outcomes, we do see a strong correlation between the requests of minority shareholders and the actions of companies over time.

Table 21.7 details the outcomes of 256 dialogues with objective criteria used to evaluate successful outcomes. Fifty per cent of these led to observable successful outcomes and 50 per cent showed no improvements. We then ask whether dialogue with the company before or after the resolution leads to successful outcomes in achieving changes in corporate behaviour based on objective standards and codes. The vast majority of these dialogues occurred after the resolution (N=207) rather than before (N=49). Despite the

Table 21.7 Comparison of successful engagements with dialogues before and after (objective criteria)

	Dialogue before (n=49)		Dialogue after (n=207)		
Improvements	31		63%	97	47%
No improvements	18		37%	110	53%
Chi^2=4.27, p<0.05					
Period 1990s					
	Dialogue before (n=18)		Dialogue after (n=58)		
Improvements	9		50%	4	7%
No improvements	9		50%	54	93%
Chi^2=18.00, p<0.000					
Period 2000s					
	Dialogue before (n=31)		Dialogue after (n=149)		
Improvements	22		71%	93	62%
No improvements	9		29%	56	38%
Chi^2=0.81, p=insig					

Table 21.8 Comparison of successful engagements with dialogues before and after (subjective criteria)

	Dialogue before (n=53)	*Dialogue after (n=193)*		
Improvements	39	74%	119	62%
No improvements	14	26%	74	38%
Chi^2=2.57, p=insig				
Period 1990s				
	Dialogue before (n=10)	Dialogue after (n=21)		
Improvements	6	60%	9	43%
No improvements	4	40%	12	57%
Chi^2=0.80, p=insig				
Period 2000s				
	Dialogue before (n=43)	Dialogue after (n=172)		
Improvements	33	77%	110	64%
No improvements	10	23%	62	36%
Chi^2=2.53, p=insig				

small size of the sample we find significant evidence of successful change in company behaviour when the dialogue occurred before the resolution in these cases. If the dialogue occurred after, the likelihood of success was evenly split.

We also find an interesting pattern over time. In the 1990s while dialogue before resulted in successful outcomes 50 per cent of the time (note: this finding is based on a small N=18), there was a high probability of no improvement in company standards when the dialogue occurred after the resolution (93 per cent of the time N=58). These numbers were reversed in 2000s when dialogue whether held before or after the resolution resulted in successful outcomes over 60 per cent of the time. This finding suggests that over time dialogues held either before or after resolutions are filed, are achieving higher rates of success in changing company behaviour with respect to objective criteria used to assess a variety of codes of conduct.

Turning to the subjective criteria used to evaluate changes in company behaviour requested by shareholders. We acknowledge this is a harder category to quantify, as subjective analysis has been used to judge whether a change in company standards has been achieved. That said, we found evidence of successful changes in company standards that had been requested by minority shareholders roughly 65 per cent of the time (N=246). As with the objective criteria, in these cases dialogues held before the resolution was filed showed slightly higher levels of successful outcomes than dialogues held after. The vast majority of this subset of these subjective criteria dialogues with resolutions were held in the 2000s. Only 31 cases of this subset took place in the 1990s. In the 2000s we see a slightly higher probability of successful outcomes when the dialogue takes place before the resolution is filed than after.

Implications

What do these findings tell us about the use of shareholder resolutions together with dialogues in shareholder corporate engagement? First and foremost, they indicate that the use of power, expressed through the use of minority shareholder resolutions, remains a salient force in shareholder engagement. Using quantitative analysis, we see that it is more likely that a resolution will be filed before there is dialogue with a company rather than after. This finding holds true across all time periods and suggests that shareholders use 'power' as a way to gain the companies attention. Once that attention has been established shareholders then proceed to use other forms of saliency such as legitimacy and urgency that are embedded in the dialogue that follows the resolution.

It has often been stated in interviews that power is the least used attribute of shareholders; however, our findings suggest the opposite. Common sentiment suggests that minority shareholder resolutions are the unfortunate result of a breakdown in communication or an intransigent position by company management that follows a period of initial dialogue. But these findings suggest that in reality this is not the pattern when a resolution is used in combination with dialogue. In fact, contrary to popular belief, when there is both a dialogue and a resolution, the resolution almost always precedes the dialogue. Actually, as engagement has matured as a shareholder strategy this pattern has been reinforced rather than diminishing and holds regardless of the whether the engagement is on the basis of governance or social and environmental issues.

Our primary finding holds our first hypothesis to be true. We suggested that while shareholders might perceive themselves as being more legitimate and urgency-driven in their engagements with company managers, using power only as a last resort to call attention on the matter they wish to discuss, we find that shareholder power (expressed as the use of minority shareholder resolutions) is used to open the process of engagement with companies rather than as a last resort when dialogue breaks down. It appears to remain necessary to use power in order to gain a companies' attention at the start of the dialogue, rather than as a threat should dialogue break down.

Additionally, we could not find a strong pattern that suggested that dialogue at either point in the resolution process led to a withdrawal of the resolution. Approximately half the time the resolution was voted on whether dialogue preceded the resolution or after. However, we have seen a change in this behaviour over time. In the 1990s there was a much greater likelihood that a resolution would not be voted on if there was dialogue associated with it. In fact, resolutions that included dialogue were not voted on in the 1990s 70 per cent of the time. This pattern is most often seen when the dialogue occurred after the resolution was put forward, suggesting that in the 1990s, as shareholder activism was in a more nascent stage, that the resolution did indeed gain the attention of senior management and open the doors for engagement, allowing the resolution to be withdrawn. By the 2000s, roughly half the time shareholders were satisfied with company responses to their requests and the resolution did not come to a vote. However, for the remaining 50 per cent of the time shareholders found no common ground with management and the vote was held. There is no difference in this pattern whether dialogue preceded the resolution or followed it. It may well be that by this point the shareholder no longer needed the resolution to gain the attention of management and instead draws on legitimacy and urgency in the engagement. While the shareholder has the attention of management by the 2000s, half the time they remain unsatisfied with progress made by the company, allowing the resolution to proceed to a vote. This indicates that power remains an important tool for shareholders in their engagement with companies as a way of pressing the issue when the actions taken by the company falls short.

Does the presence of dialogue subsequently affect the level of vote that the minority shareholder resolution garners? In other words, are the minority shareholders able to build stronger coalitions of shareholders as a result of the dialogue, and sway a larger number of votes at the annual general meetings? Our findings suggest that neither dialogues held before a resolution nor after a resolution is submitted actually changes the total level of votes cast for the resolution. On average most minority shareholder resolutions receive roughly 16 per cent of the total vote. The same percentage holds true for those resolutions with dialogue associated with them. We do, however, see a slight uptick in voting levels when dialogue is held before the resolution is filed suggesting that shareholders in these cases are able to gain some additional votes when dialogue breaks down and the resolution follows. While our findings show this pattern in greater evidence in the 1990s, the small N sample requires further testing to determine its validity.

Dialogue and voting patterns are important in deepening our understanding of shareholder saliency. But the more critical question is what pattern demonstrates the greatest evidence of success in changing corporate behaviour and raising corporate environmental, social and governance (ESG) standards? As this is the *raison d'être* of shareholder saliency and corporate engagement. In other words, what makes a difference? Using objective criteria in the cases we examined, such as adopting stated codes of conduct and reporting standards, we found evidence of the requested change in approximately half the cases. In these cases, it appears that dialogue before the resolution is put forward resulted in greater evidence of success. This finding was particularly true in the 1990s where a certain amount of intransigence by companies is demonstrated. By the 2000s we see greater evidence of companies adopting the requested policy or programme whether the dialogue occurred before or after the resolution. This change over time may reflect a more open attitude from companies who are more willing to make these requested ESG changes.

A similar pattern is found using subjective criteria as evidence of companies making the requested change. Here we found greater evidence of the change in corporate standards with an improvement in company standards and policies roughly 65 per cent of the time. However, a note of caution is required when using subjective standards in judging changes in company behaviour. Additionally, almost 90 per cent of this sample is drawn from cases in the 2000s, making it difficult to see a pattern emerging over time. That said we also see greater evidence of the requested change occurring when the dialogue was held before the resolution rather than after, suggesting that power in these cases was used as a last resort, rather than as a means to opening the engagement.

However, we find we are unable to prove hypothesis 2 through these findings and we are not able to demonstrate that the use of shareholder power leads to greater successful outcomes of corporate engagement measured by changes in company standards, codes and behaviour requested by shareholders in the engagement. We draw more heavily on the objective criteria rather than the subjective criteria for this result. Objectively we find evidence of success when resolutions are used with dialogue roughly 50 per cent of the time. To prove that the use of power in shareholder saliency, demonstrated through the use of resolutions in combination with dialogue, had a substantial impact on company behaviour we would expect to see much greater evidence of successful outcomes in our sample.

Conclusions

This chapter has examined the role of power in shareholder saliency. We define power as the use of minority shareholder resolutions within the context of corporate engagement. Using minority shareholder resolutions is one of the few areas of power that shareholders legitimately possess in relation to companies they own. Our findings on this subject provide insight into the role power plays in shareholder saliency. Qualitative studies (Gifford, 2010; Hebb et al. 2012) suggest that power is the least used attribute of shareholder saliency with legitimacy and urgency playing a much greater role in commanding attention with corporate managers. These studies indicate that minority shareholder resolutions are primarily used when other avenues of engagement break down. Our findings suggest quite the opposite.

We find that in the vast majority of time when both dialogue and shareholder resolutions are used together that the shareholder resolution is used first, as a way to gain management attention on the issue. In this pattern dialogue follows the resolution rather than preceding it. This finding stands in sharp contrast to the popularly held view that minority shareholder resolutions are primarily used as a last resort with companies. To be used when other avenues of dialogue have broken down and management has become intransigent in their position on the issues under discussion. In fact, the minority shareholder resolution is most often the opening salvo in the corporate engagement, a means to gain company attention and establish saliency at the beginning of the process rather than the end. This finding is critically important in deepening our understanding of shareholder saliency. It suggests that the role of power as a vital force in establishing corporate engagement has been vastly underestimated in previous studies.

However, while we were able to find conclusive evidence of our first hypothesis, we were not able to extrapolate the impact that power in corporate engagement would have on its likelihood of success.

Success of corporate engagement is critical if company shareholders are to use their influence to raise the sustainability practices of today's companies. The rationale behind the use of corporate engagement and responsible investment (RI) is to provide a point of leverage that uses investor influence to raise corporate environmental, social and governance standards. Responsible investors suggest that company management is often focused on short-term time horizons, business strategies and objectives. In contrast, investors with long-term time horizons are sensitive to the need to control risks that arise from unsustainable business practices over time. Responsible investment posits that shareowners play a vital role in overseeing company management with a view to the long-term sustainability of the company. Currently investors representing over $60 trillion of assets under management have signed the UN-backed Principles for Responsible Investment, pledging to integrate these practices in their investment decision-making. The shareholder strategies outlined in this chapter (engagement and minority shareholder resolutions) are the mechanisms most often used by responsible investors to influence corporate sustainability strategies. But are they effective in achieving their goal?

In roughly half the instances in our subsample of 500, we were able to find evidence that the company implemented the requested change. Half this subsample used objective criteria such as evidence of requested codes of conduct or reporting frameworks as indicators of success. We do not claim causation, as many factors are at play during periods of corporate engagement. If power plays a significant role in achieving success in corporate engagement we would expect to see a much greater impact in the adoption of the requested change than we found in our sample. Thus we were unable to prove our second hypothesis that the use of power would lead to greater evidence of success in corporate engagement.

We drew on the Interfaith Centre for Corporate Responsibility (ICCR) and a dataset of 1,085 cases between 1990 and 2012 where both a minority shareholder resolution and a dialogue on the same issue occurred between shareholders and a company.

There are limitations of this current study that may impact our ability to generalize from its results. The ICCR dataset is drawn from members who represent primarily religious organizations in the United States. As a result, we are limited both by the type of investors and the geographic reach of the dataset. Secondly, while we used objective indicators as well as subjective indicators to assess evidence of changes made that reflected the request that shareholders made to companies, we did so through public Internet searches of company websites and annual reports. Such evidence is subject to human judgement. Additionally, this coding was conducted out by a single researcher in our team and therefore not subject to validation by additional researchers.

Such limitations provide scope for future research on this topic. Our findings should be tested using other datasets that draw on a wide range of investors both by type of investor and by geographic location of these investors. In this way we will be able to determine if the use of power as an important attribute of shareholder saliency is universal, and opens the doors to corporate engagement rather than closes them.

Power is not often discussed as a key attribute of shareholder engagement. As is so often the case, using power is seen as a last resort and only drawn on when absolutely necessary. Our findings contradict this widely held belief. Power is used to open the doors of engagement, rather than to close them.

Note

1 Such a claim would be considered if there is convincing information certifying its legitimacy, if it is in the interest of the managers to attend the claim, or if the presented argument aligns with the company's interests. Urgency is demonstrated by deadlines and persistence.

References

Agle, B.R., Mitchell, R.K. and Sonnenfeld, J.A. (1999). What matters to CEOs? An investigation of stakeholder attributes and salience, corporate performance, and CEO values. *Academy of Management Journal*, 43(5): 507–525

Bauer, R., Moers, F. and Viehs, M. (2012). The determinants of withdrawn shareholder proposals (19 September 2012). Working paper available at SSRN http://ssrn.com/abstract=1885392 or http://dx.doi.org/10.2139/ssrn.1885392.

Clark, G.L. and Hebb., T. (2005). Why do they care? The market for corporate global responsibility and the role of institutional investors. *Environment and Planning A*, 31(11): 2015–2031.

Etzioni, A. (1964), *Modern Organizations*. Englewood Cliffs, NJ: Prentice-Hall.

Gifford, J. (2010). Effective shareholder engagement: The factors that contribute to shareholder salience. *Journal of Business Ethics*, 92 (sup. 1): 79–97.

Gond, J.-P. and Piani, V. (2013). Enabling institutional investors' collective action: The roles of the principle for responsible investment initiative. *Business and Society*, 52(1): 64–104.

Goodman, J. and Arenas, D. (2014). A discourse ethics approach to social shareholder engagement: Consolidating theory and opening new perspectives. Working paper. *Academy of Management Proceedings*, 2014(1) published online 30 November 2017.

Hambrick, D.C. and Mason, P.A. (1984). Upper echelons: The organization as a reflection of its top managers. *Academy of Management Review*, 9(2): 193–206.

Hebb, T., Hachigian, H. and Allen, A. (2012). Measuring the impact of engagement in Canada. In D.C. Poff and A.C. Michalos (eds), *The Next Generation of Responsible Investment*. Ottawa: Springer, pp. 107–112.

Magness, V. (2008). Who are the stakeholders now? An empirical examination of the Mitchell, Agle and Wood theory of stakeholder salience. *Journal of Business Ethics*, 83(2): 177–192.

Mitchell, R.K., Agle, B.R. and Wood, D.J. (1997). Toward a theory of stakeholder identification and salience: Defining the principle of who and what really counts. *Academy of Management Review*, 22(4): 853–886.

Monks, R.A.G. (2001). *The New Global Investors*. Oxford: Capstone Publishing.

Rehbein, K., Logsdon, J. and Buren, H. (2013). Corporate responses to shareholder activists: Considering the dialogue alternative. *Journal of Business Ethics*, 112(1): 137–154.

Salancik, G. and Pfeffer, J. (1974). The bases and use of power in organizational decision making: The case of a university. *Administrative Science Quarterly*, 19(4): 453–473. doi:10.2307/2391803.

Wood, D.J. (1991). Corporate social performance revisited. *Academy of Management Review*, 16(4): 691–718.

Yaron, G. (2005). Acting like owners: Proxy voting, corporate engagement and the fiduciary responsibilities of pension trustees (June 28). Available at SSRN: https://ssrn.com/abstract=772184 or http://dx.doi.org/10.2139/ssrn.772184.

22 Environmental sustainability for industry legitimacy and competitiveness

The case of CSR collective strategies in the cement industry

Julie Bastianutti and Hervé Dumez

Introduction[1]

Within the domain of Corporate Social Responsibility (CSR), environmental sustainability is of particular importance in industries confronted with environmental issues such as CO_2 emissions and pollution in their daily operations. Corporate and business strategies are increasingly impacted by environmental issues. These kinds of non-market issues are likely to be addressed by collective strategies in order to foster a certain level of cooperation between competitors at the level of the industry but also at the intra-, and inter-industry levels.

The chapter consists of an empirical study examining how, at a practical level, organizations deal with the complexities of setting firms' strategic direction in order to progress towards sustainability. Sustainability is slowly becoming a relevant topic in strategic management but there is still much to be done to develop academic knowledge emphasizing the impacts of environmental concerns. The natural environment has been considered so far as an element belonging to the external and non-competitive environment of companies. Nonetheless, since the 1990s, we observe a deep change in customers' expectations and social demands, regarding not just the products but also how firms operate in their daily activities. Some environmental issues are even considered as a source of economic and business opportunities by firms (Hart, 1995; Hart and Dowell, 2011), both at the individual and collective levels. This is indeed where the most interesting academic contributions are needed. Revisiting environmental concerns requires more of a focus on the collective dimension of strategy and embrace the cooperative turn initiated by Astley and Fombrun in the 1980s (Astley and Fombrun, 1983).

More precisely, our aim is to analyse the combination of two forms of strategy – cooperation and competition – in CSR strategies and relate it to possible intentions: differential advantage or legitimation effects. In the domain of corporate social responsibility (CSR) one can observe differential advantage strategies as well as legitimation strategies, both at the individual and collective levels. CSR in its environmental aspects may allow some competitors to differentiate their products. Thus, in the agro-industry, some consumers may prefer organic or fair-trade products more respectful of the natural and social environment, and be willing to pay extra for it (McWilliams and Siegel, 2001: McWilliams, Siegel and Wright, 2006). To deal with environmental issues, some firms may choose to form a small group of leaders and promote standards or launch ambitious programmes whose aim is to protect themselves from potential new entrants. This is particularly the case for green clubs and proactive strategies for environmental programmes (Christmann and Taylor, 2002). This type of strategy, so-called 'Fencing out the Jones's' (Barnett and Hoffman, 2008) may involve a group of firms within the same industry or belonging to the same supply chain. Such partnerships beyond industry boundaries have been studied as a tool implemented by companies to address complex problems – be they social or environmental – beyond the management capacity of any single organization (Clarke and Fuller, 2011; Selsky and Parker, 2005).

One privileged level of analysis would be the industry, at the crossroads between the individual and collective levels. Numerous studies on CSR strategies, however, adopt a perspective centred on the firm level (Vogel, 2005; Baron, 2009; Crifo and Ponssard, 2010). In doing so, they do not completely ignore the collective dimension of CSR strategies, which is nonetheless harder to highlight. This is the reason why some studies have been led at the industry level (Palazzo and Richter, 2005; Cai, Jo and Pan, 2012) or at the level of client-supplier relationships (Zyglidopoulos, 2002; Christmann and Taylor, 2002; Maloni and Brown, 2006; van Tulder, van Wijk and Kolk, 2009; Egels-Zandén, 2007). The industry level is not the only relevant way to study collective strategies as it is shown by studies focusing on particular geographic areas (Bertels and Peloza, 2008; Muller, 2006). It is even possible to combine different levels of analysis – intra- and inter-industry as shown by some papers studying corporate reputation (Barnett, 2007; Bitektine, 2008; Winn, MacDonald and Zietsma, 2008). Our research questions are twofold. First, are the effects of differentiation and legitimation really independent? This chapter considers CSR strategies as strategic opportunities mixing two types of strategic intentions (differential advantage and legitimacy) and three levels of collective strategy (the industry level and the intra-, and inter-industry). Secondly this combination unfolds over time: how do firms use the strategic opportunities and how do they combine them in a dynamic perspective?

The case study was conducted in the cement industry, which is an exemplary industry regarding the change of perception of environmental sustainability in the last 20 years. Before the Rio Summit in 1992, it was hardly an issue. Since then, it has been seized as an opportunity to foster deep changes in environmental practices both at the individual and industry levels. The analysis of multidimensional strategic sequences (Dumez and Jeunemaitre, 2006) shows the dynamic and interactive development of CSR strategy as a combination of competition and cooperation on the one hand and, on the other, a search for both social legitimacy and differential advantage. The main results are highlighted. Strategies for environmental sustainability, as part of a CSR policy, cannot be reduced to a unique form and/or intention: they are integrated strategies (Baron, 1995) based on combinations of forms and intentions. Collective strategies are deployed at various levels (industry, intra-and inter-industry) and offer a wide range of opportunities for businesses to meet societal demands regarding the protection of natural ecosystems. Finally, the case is exemplary regarding the non-negotiable pursuit of environmental sustainability and the rapid evolution of behaviour and values in the conduct of business.

Analysing the dynamics of collective CSR strategies

Business strategy must take into account two major problems. On the one hand, it must consider its competitive advantage in the market and its reputation in a larger socioeconomic context (the labour market, finance, the image to the consumer). On the other hand, it must consider the social acceptability of its activity, the fact that an industry may be considered as legitimate and not merely legal (e.g. the legitimacy of the tobacco industry) and have to cope with cyclical variations and breaks. Issues related to CSR overlap these two categories of problems.

Why do companies develop CSR strategic interactions?

The various analyses of CSR in terms of strategy show that we may distinguish two categories of strategic intentions. The word 'intention' shall be understood as the 'reasons' that actors give to their actions taken in their actual context – this is the difference between a cause that would be an explanation prior to the action.

First type of strategic intention: CSR as a source of differential advantage

The concept of differential advantage covers a broader category than the competitive advantage in price or in quality (Porter, 1985; Kumar, 2006; Barney, 2007). The differential advantage can also be achieved by a strategy aimed at increasing costs for rivals or by a strategy of reputation. This type of benefit is not necessarily individual: it can benefit a small group. In some cases, however, competitive advantage comes not from the product itself, but the transformation of the competitive landscape by a competitor (Hamel and Doz, 1998; Hamel and Prahalad, 1994; D'Aveni, Gunther and Cole, 2001). For example, companies can implement new financial systems to help poor consumers buy their products, or they can take part in the financing of infrastructure network or local education systems (Porter and Kramer, 2006). CSR in its environmental aspects may allow some competitors to differentiate their products. Thus, in the agro-industry, some consumers may prefer organic or fair-trade products more respectful of the natural and social environment, and be willing to pay extra for it (McWilliams and Siegel, 2001; McWilliams, Siegel and Wright, 2006).

The differential advantage can also be to increase costs for rivals, and this may be due to an individual firm or a small group of companies who may want to protect themselves against new entrants, or otherwise to destabilize competitors. The strategies for increasing costs for rivals may lead to collusion, as noted by Salop and Scheffman (1987), that is to say practices of illegal coordination with the aim of limiting competition.

Regarding CSR, several studies have shown that it is possible to implement strategies to influence policy and promote regulations (environmental or social), hence increasing the costs for rivals (McWilliams, Siegel and Wright, 2006; Christmann and Taylor, 2002; Crane et al. 2008). These 'raise rivals' costs' (RRC) strategies are particularly effective because rivals can hardly contest or wrong-foot them.

This same type of strategy can create for its instigator a positive reputation (Fombrun and Shanley, 1990; Orlitzky, Schmidt and Rynes, 2003; Crane et al., 2008). Reputation is indeed another type of economic benefit resulting from the global perception and the company's relative performance compared to its competitors (Mahon, 2002; Roberts and Dowling, 2002; Lange, Lee and Dai, 2010). The importance of ranking and the relational dimension of reputation are emphasized by Fombrun and Shanley (1990):

> Reputational rankings constitute a potentially significant and understudied form of normative control that channels firms' actions by conferring relative competitive advantage and disadvantage upon conforming organizations within an organizational field.

Reputation is a phenomenon that is inherently relational, generating a phenomenon of ranking within a group. Fombrun and Shanley distinguish two levels of analysis relevant to empirical studies: on the one hand those of the organizational field, as outlined in the quote, but also the industry level where they consider that the reputation of competitors can have a long-term influence on competitive dynamics.

Reputation is based on the existence of an external, collective, comprehensive and repeated assessment (Galaskiewicz, 1985; Barnett, Jermier and Lafferty, 2006; Barnett, 2006). Wider than the competitive advantage, it includes intangible assets difficult to imitate (Barney, 1991) and constituting strong barriers to entry. Reputation has multiple effects: the reputable companies have better access to funding and to the labour market, and therefore can outrun their rivals (Fombrun, 2001).

However, the reputation of one company partly depends on their competitors. Crises can affect the entire industry by contagion (Barnett and Hoffman, 2008). One can speak of a 'reputation commons problem' (King, Lenox and Barnett, 2002): firms must manage the problem of the conditions of social acceptability and legitimacy of their activity at the same time as their individual reputation (Winn, MacDonald and Zietsma, 2008).

Second type of strategic intention: CSR as a source of industry legitimacy

Companies are regularly called upon to justify their actions, their operational and strategic choices and even their existence, either to their shareholders, customers or to the public. These rationalizations and justifications are a contextualized process: they question the place of the firm in a specific cultural and regulatory environment. The term 'license to operate' is another way of expressing the social acceptability of business, designating it as a kind of implicit contract between the company and the society conferring legitimacy to such economic activity (Davis, 1973). Academic research on organizational legitimacy can be divided in two groups (Elsbach, 1994; Suchman, 1995): one proposing a strategic approach (Ashforth and Gibbs, 1990, Pfeffer and Salancik, 1978), and one an institutionalist approach (DiMaggio and Powell, 1983; Powell and DiMaggio, 1991; Zucker, 1987). The first considers legitimacy as an operational resource, which can trigger conflicts between organizations having to position themselves between conflicting value systems. The second considers legitimacy as a set of constitutive beliefs and values that determines decisions and reactions of managers as well as workers. The two perspectives have therefore a different point of view regarding, firstly, the role that can be assigned to management and, secondly, the relevant level of analysis. The strategic perspective focuses on the management of legitimacy in the organization, through the use of discursive accountability strategies. The institutionalist perspective emphasizes the collective process of structuring organizational fields by relations of conflict and cooperation that revolve around common problems associated with divergent interests and issues in cognitive and normative debates.

Based on a comparative analysis of these two categories, Suchman (1995) distinguishes three types of legitimacy – pragmatic, moral and cognitive – each corresponding to different modalities and forms of collective action (Ashforth and Gibbs, 1990; Pfeffer and Salancik, 1978). Scherer and Palazzo (2011) discuss this typology in relation to CSR issues. They highlight the erosion of cognitive and pragmatic forms of legitimacy – yet the most mobilized in studies on CSR based on the theory of the firm or an instrumental vision and strategic CSR – in the context of the current crisis of capitalism and reconsideration of the regulatory power of the nation state. For the authors, this leaves more scope for moral legitimacy, resulting from a process of social and discursive construction of meaning and values manifested for example by new forms of cooperation between firms and NGOs (Scherer and Palazzo, 2007). Similarly, authors within the critical management studies underline that CSR is used as a way to establish one's legitimacy in order to prevent attacks by activists and to meet customer needs (Hanlon, 2008). In the end, this argument makes CSR an ideology to legitimize new forms of capitalism (Hanlon and Fleming, 2009).

All in all, among CSR strategies, we can analytically distinguish between strategies looking for differential advantage and strategies of legitimacy.

How do firms develop these strategic interactions?

CSR issues are often transverse and related to the non-market domain, thereby promoting collaborative strategies between competitors (Baron, 1995). In addition, the first part of this literature review highlighted the fact that some desired effects in CSR strategies were more propitious to collective than individual action, particularly to manage issues related to the legitimacy of the activity or to raise rivals' costs.

Can we propose to link more specifically the different strategic intentions with collective forms of strategy at different levels?

One could suggest on a first basis that individual strategies are preferred when a firm wants to obtain a differential advantage, whereas social legitimacy favours industry-wide collective strategies. But the proposition seems to be too restrictive if one considers that certain types of differential advantage, such as higher costs for competitors, are often the subject of collective strategies, as it has been outlined above. It is therefore necessary to develop a more nuanced model based on the study of all possible combinations between the intentions and modes of collective strategic actions. To do so, we refine the analysis by distinguishing three levels of collective strategy. The first is the industry level including the rivals competing in a same market. The intra-industry level refers to a strategy designed or implemented by several competitors belonging to the same industry, and thus being direct competitors, but trying to team up to engage in a particular issue. The third level, called inter-industry, refers to a group of firms belonging to industries connected and even integrated in a same global supply chain (such as the construction industry, or the agri-food industry) engaging in collective action to achieve a common purpose.

Intra- and inter-industry collective strategies for differential advantages

First of all, a small number of firms belonging to the same or to interconnected industries can either obtain a differential advantage.

Alliances are inter-organizational cooperative strategies between a small number of competitors so as to obtain a competitive advantage if the members share resources, know-how and specific knowledge which, when combined, is all the more difficult to imitate by competitors (Dyer and Singh, 1998; Dussauge and Garrette, 1999). In environmental and social issues, some firms may choose to form a small group of leaders and promote standards or launch ambitious programmes whose aim is to protect themselves from potential new entrants. This is particularly the case for green clubs and proactive strategies for environmental programmes. This type of strategy, so-called 'Fencing out the Jones's' (Barnett and Hoffman, 2008) may involve a group of firms within the same industry or in sectors belonging to the same supply chain. Such partnerships beyond industry boundaries have been studied as a tool implemented by companies to address complex social or environmental problems that are beyond the management capacity of any single organization (Clarke and Fuller, 2011; Selsky and Parker, 2005).

Elite-group strategies at the intra- and inter-industry levels for industry legitimacy

Symmetrically, an elite-group strategy can help strengthen the legitimacy of the industry as a whole. This refers to the concept of institutional leadership, defined by Selznick (1957), when companies are urged to fulfil not only economic but also social and political functions (Baron, 2010). This concept was further developed by neo-institutionalists who proposed the notion of institutional entrepreneur (Battilana, Leca and Boxenbaum, 2009). In the case of perceptible change in expectations regarding social and environmental action, a firm may then have an interest in positioning itself as a leader to create voluntary standards. Such an attitude allows the firm to escape or to anticipate (or co-develop) a governmental regulation (Baron, 2010). It can therefore succeed in imposing a technical standard to the market and to the entire supply chain upstream and downstream (Garud, Jain and Kumaraswamy, 2002) or succeed in developing cooperation networks.

Intra- and inter-industry strategies to secure both legitimacy and differential advantage

In highly concentrated industries, where a small number of very large firms coexist with a myriad of smaller ones (their suppliers, for example), competitive strategies can coexist with collective cooperation. These situations of co-opetition (Brandenburger and Nalebuff, 1996; Bengtsson and Kock, 1999; Gnyawali and Madhavan, 2001; Yami et al., 2010) are characterized by the simultaneous cooperation and competition of firms maintaining both vertical and horizontal relationships. A number of studies highlight strategies that combine the search for an individual differential advantage with a collective strategy of legitimacy.

In industries facing strong social legitimacy crises (fish farming, forestry or oil, for example), competing firms are forced to manage collective tensions and threats to the industry as a whole. Winn, MacDonald and Zietsma (2008) show subtle complexity of individual and collective strategies implemented by actors from both industries studied (logging and salmon farming). Some players embark collectively, in a strategy aiming to adapt the practices to the whole sector, including through technological and managerial innovations, to restore the common good and reinforce the social acceptability of activity. These firms derive two differential advantages from this commitment, competitive advantage and reputation. To be effective at the community level, all competitors must follow the leaders. Otherwise, the threats to the industry increase as activists are prompt to target the reluctant organizations.

This chapter considers CSR strategies as the dynamic combination of strategic opportunities mixing at the same time two types of strategic intentions (differential advantage and legitimacy) and three levels of collective strategy (the industry level and the intra- and inter-industry).

One must consider collective strategies in their interactive dimension. They contain a multiplicity of relations between actors and evolve over time and in space, both vertically (cooperation in the supply chain) and horizontally (cooperation within a market). The use of strategic sequences reconstructing a series of strategic actions and reactions over time is useful (Bresser and Harl, 1986; Depeyre and Dumez, 2009). If one wants to try and show a possible link between reputation and legitimacy, one might suggest it would appear over time: if two leaders launch an initiative, earning a reputation effect, and is then extended to all competitors, it produces legitimacy benefiting the whole

Table 22.1 Combining intentions and forms of collective strategy for CSR

	Level of collective strategy		
Intention	*Intra-industry*	*Industry*	*Inter-industry*
Differential advantage	Proactive strategy for competitive advantage		Proactive non-market strategy for competitive advantage
Legitimacy	Institutional leadership	Preserving the licence to operate	Institutional leadership
Differential advantage + Legitimacy	Co-opetition		Co-opetition

industry plus a differential effect for the two leaders who have raised costs for weaker competitors. Winn, MacDonald and Zietsma (2008) use such sequences to study the interaction of intra and industry strategies. The choice of a particular type of unit of analysis, such as the interaction between two competitors, becomes all the more important as stressed by Dyer and Singh (1998).

Once the results are presented, the discussion should answer two main questions. Are the effects of differentiation and legitimation really independent? And how do firms use the strategic opportunities and how do they combine them over time?

Methodology: a longitudinal case study of the cement industry (1992–2012)

In order to understand why and how companies combine collective strategies for environmental sustainability, we chose the strategic interaction between competitors as a unit of analysis. We highlight the dynamic between strategic actions and reactions, anticipations within a set of firms having shared issues.

In a technologically complex sector, with frequent entrances and exits, or in an area where the CSR would have a potential impact on product competition, the complexity and diversity of strategies would be too high to detect strategic interactions. We selected a much simpler industry, characterized by a single product not subject to major innovations and where CSR had no impact on competition between products. Such an area must be a stable and tight oligopoly, with new entries and rare persistent hierarchy. The members of the oligopoly must operate internationally in a global market, and operation of their business must have a tangible impact on the environment. The cement industry fits these requirements (Dumez and Jeunemaitre, 2000). We chose the cement industry for the particular characteristics of the product and the organization of the market. Cement is a simple product of mass consumption: it is, in fact, the most traded in the world after water. Differentiation is low, resulting in a competition centred on price and local acceptance activities related to its production. Cement is an international industry, including global players since its inception. However, the interconnection of local markets and globalization did not happen until the end of 1970. Given the differences in the use of cement in developed and developing economies – most often a B2C market in the latter, and the B2B market in the former – the legitimacy of the industry and its media exposure vary. Moreover, legitimacy is also played at the local level as cement plants produce a visible and audible pollution (noise and white dust). Unlike food, chemicals or clothing, there haven't been specific incidents in the production of cement globally. Apart from the question of the level of CO_2 emissions, no global scandal has, to date, impacted the sector. Our hypothesis is that, insofar as there is no strong identification with the product or differentiation, the CSR strategy and management of non-market issues can have a strong impact on reputation, particularly in developing economies. In this case, the market is also largely for individual customers who are sensitive to the image of the company and the benefits it offers, particularly in terms of funding and support in the design of individual building projects. Since the product is undifferentiated, competitive advantage is difficult to achieve at this level. Therefore, the case permits study quasi pure non-market strategies. The four companies of the oligopoly are all very old, established in the nineteenth century or early twentieth century. Small local family businesses in the beginning, they grew gradually, first regionally and then globally through a series of mergers and acquisitions. Before the 1970s, the sector was internationalized but remained structured as a network of unconnected local markets. In the late 1970s, a revolution in the transport of cement led to actual globalization. The industry leaders also operate in related activities such as clinker, aggregates and concrete. For our case study, we decided to focus on four main competitors.

We studied the first four competitors between the Rio Summit in 1992 (when environmental issues gained a higher social awareness), and 2012. The 20-year time frame allows observing multiple strategic interactions. During this time the structure of the oligopoly remained quite stable: the first two competitors were Lafarge and Holcim and then the two followers, Cemex and Heidelberg. European companies, Lafarge, Holcim and HeidelbergCement, began their internationalization and globalization in the early twentieth century, while the Mexican company Cemex began its geographic expansion in the 1990s. Regarding environmental impacts, quarries and cement kilns have a major impact on global warming and local environments.

Our data are both primary and secondary, written and oral. Our main source of data consists of annual reports, public records and online websites of companies and associations and NGOs. We supplemented the primary data with secondary sources, such as specialized books or case studies, academic and professional publications, and press releases. We conducted seven semi-structured interviews lasting an average of 90 minutes between 2009 and 2012. We interviewed the CSR and Sustainability directors of two of the competitors studied, the CSR and Sustainability directors of two firms belonging to the interrelated industries (in the construction and building global industry), so as

Table 22.2 Main characteristics of the four competitors in 2012

	Lafarge	*Holcim*	*Cemex*	*Heidelberger*
Date and location of creation	1833 Ardèche (France)	1912 Holderbank (Switzerland)	1906 Monterrey (Mexico)	1873 Heidelberg (Germany)
Number of employees	65,000	80,000	44,500	51,966
Geographical presence	64 countries	70 countries	> 50 countries	> 40 countries
Sales in millions € (2010)	€15,816	€17,850	€11,000	€14,000

to get insights on the inter-industry dynamics and shared issues. We also interviewed three managers working for three different competitors of the cement industry to gain knowledge about practices regarding different environmental issues and policies. Regarding methodology and methods of analysis, we used the case study methodology with an explanatory objective (Eisenhardt, 1989; Yin, 2004). The first level of analysis is the company. We looked at four companies from a longitudinal and qualitative perspective. For each firm, we first prepared a detailed chronology covering two categories: the history of the firm and non-market actions related to environmental issues, from 1992 until 2012. Primary and secondary data were used to establish these chronologies. At the same time, the interviews completed the chronologies to get a better understanding of managerial and strategic motivations; they were coded with a grounded theory approach in order to identify patterns and generate surprises. The construction of chronologies complemented by interviews allowed us to produce narratives (Eisenhardt, 1989; Yin, 2004) that are 'thick descriptions' (Dumez and Jeunemaitre, 2006). They are the basis for the identification of strategic interactions and provide a detailed account of meanings and motivations in the long term. The second step establishes multi-level comparisons of the industry and identifies strategic multi-level models. Through detailed comparisons, it is possible to describe the underlying mechanisms. We organized the data used for the stories into 'templates' (King, 2004), which allows organizing them into series in order to give a synoptic view.

Results

Once the chronologies established for each company, we compared the companies based on the four chronologies of environmental actions. These comparative chronologies, which were also analysed individually in the search process, are the basis for the identification of different types of strategies.

Table 22.3 Typology of collective strategies and examples from the case

Intention	Level of collective strategy		
	Intra-industry	*Industry*	*Inter-industry*
Differential advantage	*Proactive strategy for competitive advantage* Be the first to adopt CSR standards and reporting		*Proactive non-market strategy for competitive advantage*
Legitimacy	*Institutional leadership* Creation of the Cement Initiative in Buildings (CSI)	*Preserving the licence to operate* Participating in the CSI and 'Security at work' programme	*Institutional leadership* Creation of Energy Efficiency in Buildings (EEB)
Differential advantage + Legitimacy	*Co-opetition* Promoting GRI and Global Compact standards		*Co-opetition* • EEB programme • Sustainable Building and Construction (UNEP)

Industry-wide collective strategies for legitimacy effects

Collective strategies have a key role to solve environmental issues and to strengthen the collective legitimacy of the industry. The case of the Cement Sustainability Initiative (CSI) is found to be particularly relevant to illustrate this point in the case of the cement industry.

The CSI was launched in 1999 under the auspices of the World Business Council of Sustainable development (WBCSD). It is a major example of the 'teaming with the Jones' kind of strategy (Barnett and Hoffman, 2008). Eleven core CSI members are also members of the WBCSD. They manage the CSI according to its charter and its working programme, and they invited new members. Only some of the other 12 participating members are WBCSD members. They agree to the commitments of the CSI Charter by implementing identified good practices at their operating facilities. They make a modest contribution to the CSI budget. They are allowed, but not obliged, to participate in individual task forces responsible for implementing the programme.

As a collective strategy, the CSI aims at protecting the industry's legitimacy by identifying threats and taking proactive measures. The competitors discuss the methods and conditions of CO_2 emission measures. It took them three years to publish their first agenda for action; they did not reach a collective agreement on the targets, and finally let every member decide on its own objective. Although it is a collective strategy designed to protect industry legitimacy and share the costs of CO_2-emission reduction, companies have found a way to introduce some differentiation. There have been alternating periods of alignment and breaking-point positions due to NGO pressure. In the 2002 agenda, the public figures indicated a goal of 20 per cent reduction of CO_2 emission per ton of cement for Holcim and Lafarge by 2010, of 15 per cent for HeidelbergerCement, and of 25 per cent by 2015 for Cemex. The Mexican competitor tried to surpass the industry leaders by choosing a higher target over a longer period. But Holcim displayed the same target in its latest CSR report (2009). Lafarge intended to maintain its role of proactive player by displaying on its website, in 2011, a new target of 33 per cent of CO_2 reduction (as compared to 1990) by 2020. We thus observe that a collective strategy may combine imitation and differentiation. Lafarge and Holcim, the founding members, communicate on their position as leaders and first-movers.

The CSI also furthers non-environmental issues, concerning, for example, security at work.

By teaming to manage collectively issues related to the common good of the industry, competitors benefit from economies of scale and expertise to better prevent attacks by militants. However, the interactive dynamics shows that collective strategies can still provide opportunities for differentiation.

Collective strategies beyond industry boundaries to differentiate elite groups

Indeed, the pursuit of differential advantage, either in reputation or to raise rivals' costs may also be the subject of collective strategies in small numbers: an elite group seeks to differentiate itself as a leader and first-mover. In 1999, Holcim joined Lafarge in the World Business Council for Sustainable Development (WBCSD), of which Lafarge had been a founding member five years earlier in 1994. The CEOs of both corporations and the executives in charge of environment were by then convinced that in order to prevent attacks from NGOs it was time to address the major environmental challenge for the industry, namely the high level of CO_2 emissions. The whole industry is responsible for 5 per cent of the global anthropogenic CO_2 emissions (Worrell et al., 2001). Therefore, there is a highly visible global issue at stake. The two market leaders, Lafarge and Holcim, decided to create an industry-wide initiative, the Cement Sustainability Initiative (CSI). Their aim was at first to convince ten corporations representing a third of the industry and to conduct a survey of the major challenges they would have to face in the next ten years. After the consulting and research phase, when the first agenda for action was edited in 2002, they had managed to convince ten other companies to join them. Holcim and Lafarge continued to communicate about their leadership in the original project, and gained a reputation for being proactive regarding environmental issues.

Inter-industry strategies intended to ensure collective legitimacy

If one looks at the inter-industry level, i.e. companies belonging to the same supply chain, strategies can have two main objectives. If all firms are involved, it may be a legitimation strategy. If only a few companies develop collective actions, then the strategy is more directed towards competitive advantage or reputation.

The Energy Efficiency in Building programme was established in 2005. It was designed to improve the design and construction of energy-efficient new and existing buildings. Lafarge and Cemex have participated in the programme since its inception. They are 2 of the 13 core members, which include United Technologies Corp. (Co-chair), Actelios, ArcelorMittal, Bosch, DuPont, EDF, GDF SUEZ, Kansai Electric Power Company, Philips, Skanska, Sonae Sierra, and TEPCO. Lafarge is co-chair of the programme together with United Technologies. The programme was effectively launched in 2006, when the first phase began. In 2009, it resulted in the publication of a report, 'Energy Efficiency in Buildings, Transforming the Market'. In 2010, the second phase focused on developing tools and practical solutions to implement the changes elaborated in the model. A third phase started in 2012; it established new working groups, and advanced both implementation and assessment of financial and valuation mechanisms. Even if the initiative intends to promote a possible market competitive advantage, in reality, the reputational effect is so far the only positive reward that participants can claim. If the communicants emphasize the fact that the 2009 report 'received much worldwide attention' (Executive Brief of the EEF, October 2011, available through www.wbcsd.org), they also acknowledge the need to focus on implementation, 'as no radical change has been happening since the publication of EEB's conclusions'. The fact that there are only 13 members from energy, construction, material and building technology industries suggests that other competitors do not find a pressing interest to join the cement industry in this endeavour.

Lafarge also participates in another programme directed at inter-industrial action, though also involving public institutions and non-profit organizations. The United Nations Environment Programme-Sustainable Buildings and Climate Initiative (UNEP-SBCI) was created in 2006. It takes the form of a partnership between the UN and key building sector stakeholders: companies, industry federations, public authorities, research institutions, experts and NGOs. It promotes and supports sustainable solutions in the building and construction sector by providing a common platform, developing tools and strategies, establishing baselines and pilot projects. In 2012, it had 43 members and 15 associate members. Two new members joined the programme in 2011. The results are significant and demonstrate that the partnership helps the industry promote common legitimacy actions. For example, the International Organisation for Standardization (ISO) decided in 2011 to develop an international standard to assess the environmental efficiency of buildings through a carbon metric during the in-use stage. The standard is based on one of SBCI's achievements, the Common Carbon Metric (CCM) project, and reinforce the initiative. Lafarge is currently the only member among the four leaders of the materials industry.

Our case shows that there is no inter-industry initiative involving all the main competitors of each industry concerned (for instance, materials, energy and construction). Moreover, the two examples studied suggest that the effects of CSR initiatives are rather limited, and consist mostly in enhancing image and reputation and, at a lower level, in improving the inter-industry legitimacy so as to prepare future market transformations.

The dynamic combination of strategic interactions: diachronic analysis

Finally, to return to the central question of the joint strategic levels in a dynamic perspective, we can focus on the example of a firm, such as Lafarge, to capture the combination of opportunities over time. Combinations evolve through competitive interactions which, in turn, induce the development of CSR.

Industry strategy

From 2002 to 2012 Lafarge took part in every industry initiative designed to protect the industry's collective legitimacy, and always tried to be identified as the leader of such initiatives. Reputational advantage can thus be combined with collective legitimacy.

Inter-industry strategy

In the case of cement, there is no inter-industry initiative involving all companies and designed to reinforce the legitimacy of each industry. Nonetheless, Lafarge is engaged in two programmes (EEB and SBCI) from which the firm expects some reputational warm-glow.

We can thus perceive the joint strategic levels within a single firm. The entanglement of these levels is particularly evident if one considers the actions and initiatives that form around an organization like the WBCSD. Firms develop and, over time, a set of strategic interactions that give rise to new forms of collective action and to maximize gains while minimizing costs. The combination of various options by firms is analysed over time as an interactive game. For instance, the Cement Sustainability Initiative was launched by the two leaders, Holcim and Lafarge, subsequently joined by their competitors. As first-movers, Holcim and Lafarge tried to gain a competitive advantage by imposing a standard on followers (raising costs for rivals). The analysis showed rivalry among the main competitors, as the incumbent leaders would not let the challenger surpass them in their will to improve carbon emission reduction. The competition on the carbon issue led to performance improvements by supporting financial investment to modernize facilities and develop expertise in environmental sustainability. External stakeholders such as environmental NGOs that signed partnerships in the early 2000s with the main competitors always made significant improvements in the reduction of

CO_2 emissions and environmental performance a condition for the renewal of these agreements. The threat for public image and reputation loss was strong enough to make the competitors keep their environmental commitments.

Conclusions and implications

The analysis leads to three main discussion points and managerial and policy implications. In this chapter, we examined how organizations would deal with the complexities of setting firms' strategic direction in order to progress towards sustainability. We asked if the effects of differentiation and legitimation were really independent and secondly we looked at this combination unfolding over time. How do firms use the strategic opportunities and how do they combine them in a dynamic perspective?

First of all, collective strategies are central to understand the dynamics of CSR at the firm and industry levels. The industry-level perspective leads to an understanding of CSR strategies as an 'ars combinatoria',[2] i.e. a combination of both intentions and forms. Strategic intentions may be to gain a differential advantage (competitive advantage, reputation effects, higher costs for rivals) and / or strengthen a collective legitimacy. The case illustrates the complexity of the forms of collective action that extend to intra-industry, industry and inter-industry. The multiplicity of forms and intentions defines a space of opportunities in which the competitors evolve and unfold strategies over time. Each of these possibilities involves one or more strategic intentions coupled with a form of action. Regarding managerial implications, we claim that environmental issues are mostly better handled collectively, at different levels. Consequently, managers and executives need a better understanding of the strategic options available, their benefits and pitfalls.

The second point emphasizes the nuances of collective strategic action. The case illustrates the fact that one must speak of collective actions, with possible collective games and repertories at different levels. It shows that the reputation strategies can be led by small elite groups in the same industry or related industries (inter-industry level). Legitimation strategies are rather developed at the industry level or at the inter-industry level by firms belonging to the same supply chain. Over time, the combination of various options by firms is analysed as an interactive game. For instance, the Cement Sustainability Initiative was launched by the two leaders, Holcim and Lafarge, subsequently by their competitors. As first-movers, Holcim and Lafarge tried to gain a competitive advantage by imposing a standard on followers and the analysis showed that the competition on the carbon issue led to performance improvements by supporting financial investment to modernize facilities and develop expertise in environmental sustainability. It also reinforced the legitimacy of the industry by securing partnerships with environmental NGOs to develop expertise and best practices, thus alleviating the pressure of being exposed and mitigating the risk of attack by environmental activists.

The third point focuses on managerial and policy implications. We learned from this case study that collective strategies are diverse and provide a range of possibilities not only to strengthen industry legitimacy and licence to operate, but also to maintain an advantage (leader position, first-mover or reputation), by playing with a chosen group of competitors inside one's industry, or with industrial partners belonging to a connected supply chain, downstream or upstream. Regarding policy implications, firms are now accustomed to be proactive to influence the regulation agenda and anticipate environmental expectations. By collaborating with policy makers and doing so collectively firms can alleviate some costs by sharing them and also turn constraints into business opportunities – such as developing more efficient production processes, conceiving environmental-friendly products that consumers will be willing to pay a premium for, or by discovering new synergies with industrial partners to transform waste into valuable resources. Policy makers should therefore be proactive in cooperating and helping businesses imagine solutions and establish an on-going dialogue to understand the technical, economic or social issues that can emerge. Moreover, incentive should be designed not only to benefit individual firms engaging in sustainable practices but also reward collective effort and team-playing. Environmental progress often lies in the grey spaces between organizations, or at the interface of industrial processes, when flows can be mutualized, and material residues retrieved to be further used.

The limits of the analysis are several but represent stimulating potentiality for future research. They are related to the level of analysis chosen (the industry) and the industry taken as the object of analysis. The chosen industry is a simple case, and it is also the reason why it was chosen: even in a simple case, the strategic combinations are complex but closely related to the structure of the industry (here, a tight oligopoly). In such a structure, the small group of leaders can deploy collective strategies that have the dual purpose of preserving the advance of the leaders in raising the cost for competitors while strengthening the legitimacy of the entire industry. It is likely that this type of strategy is not found in other market structures. A proposed line of research is therefore to explore more systematically the relationship between market structure and strategic combination of collective strategies. In addition, the cement industry is characterized by the fact that CSR strategies allow little differentiation between firms in the market and have relatively little impact on the redefinition of markets. It is easier, therefore, to focus on non-market dimensions. The question is then whether the industries in which the market size plays a more important level for CSR role are the theatre of a more complex combination game or, paradoxically, a more simple one.

Notes

1 The authors thank the participants of the 2013 AIMS conference and 2014 EURAM conference, as well as the editors and reviewers of the anthology, Franck Aggeri, Christina Garsten, Anouk Mukherjee, for helpful comments and advice on previous versions of this work.
2 The notion of 'ars combinatoria' refers to the early work of Leibniz, The **Dissertatio de arte combinatoria** ('Dissertation on the Art of Combinations' or 'On the Combinatorial Art') published in 1666 in Leipzig.

References

Ashforth, B.E. and Gibbs, B.W. (1990). The double-edge of organizational legitimation. *Organization Science*, 1(2): 177–194.
Astley, G. and Fombrun, C.J. (1983). Collective strategy: Social ecology of organizational environments. *The Academy of Management Review*, 8(4): 576–587.
Barnett, M.L. (2006). Waves of collectivizing: A dynamic model of competition and cooperation over the life of an industry. *Corporate Reputation Review*, 8: 272–292.
Barnett, M.L. (2007). Tarred and untarred by the same brush: Exploring interdependence in the volatility of stock returns. *Corporate Reputation Review*, 10(1): 3–21.
Barnett, M.L. and Hoffman, A.J. (2008). Beyond corporate reputation: Managing reputational interdependence. *Corporate Reputation Review*, 11: 1–9.
Barnett, M.L., Jermier, J.M. and Lafferty, B.A. (2006). Corporate reputation: The definitional landscape. *Corporate Reputation Review*, 9: 26–38.

Barney, J. (1991). Firm resources and sustained competitive advantage. *Journal of Management*, 17: 99–120.

Barney, J. (2007). *Gaining and Sustaining Competitive Advantage*. Reading, MS: Addison-Wesley.

Baron, D.P. (1995). Integrated strategy: Market and non-market components. *California Management Review*, 37(2): 47–65.

Baron, D.P. (2009). A positive theory of moral management, social pressure, and corporate social performance. *Journal of Economics & Management Strategy*, 18(1): 7–43.

Baron, D.P. (2010). *Business and its Environment*, 6th edn. Upper Saddle River, NJ: Prentice Hall.

Battilana, J., Leca, B. and Boxenbaum, E. (2009). How actors change institutions: Towards a theory of institutional entrepreneurship. *The Academy of Management Annals*, 3(1): 65–107.

Bengtsson, M. and Kock, S. (1999). Cooperation and competition in relationships between competitors in business networks. *Journal of Business & Industrial Marketing*, 14(3): 178–194.

Bertels, S. and Peloza, J. (2008). Running just to stand still? Managing CSR reputation in an era of ratcheting expectations. *Corporate Reputation Review*, 11: 56–72.

Bitektine, A. (2008). Legitimacy-based entry deterrence in inter-population competition. *Corporate Reputation Review*, 11: 73–93.

Brandenburger, A. and Nalebuff, B. (1996). *Co-opetition*. New York: Doubleday.

Bresser, R.K. and Harl, J.E. (1986). Collective strategy: Vice or virtue?. *The Academy of Management Review*, 11(2): 408–427.

Cai, Y., Jo, H. and Pan, C. (2012). Doing well while doing bad? CSR in controversial industry sectors. *Journal of Business Ethics*, 108(4): 467–480.

Christmann, P. and Taylor, G. (2002). Globalization and the environment: Strategies for international voluntary environmental initiatives. *The Academy of Management Executive (1993–2005)*, 16(3): 121–136.

Clarke, A. and Fuller, M. (2011). Collaborative strategic management: Strategy formulation and implementation by multi-organizational cross-sector social partnerships. *Journal of Business Ethics*, 94(2): 85–101.

Crane, A., McWilliams, A., Matten, D., Moon, J. and Siegel, D. (eds) (2008). *The Oxford Handbook of Corporate Social Responsibility*. Oxford and New York: Oxford University Press.

Crifo, P. and Ponssard, J.-P. (2010). *Corporate Social Responsibility*. Palaiseau: les Éditions de l'École polytechnique.

D'Aveni, R.A., Gunther, R.E. and Cole, J. (2001). *Strategic Supremacy: How Industry Leaders Create Growth, Wealth, and Power through Spheres of Influence*. New York: Free Press.

Davis, K. (1973). The case for and against business assumption of social responsibilities. *The Academy of Management Journal*, 16(2): 312–322.

Depeyre, C. and Dumez, H. (2009). A management perspective on market dynamics: Stabilizing and destabilizing strategies in the US defense industry. *European Management Journal*, 27(2): 90–99.

DiMaggio, P.J. and Powell, W.W. (1983). The iron cage revisited: Institutional isomorphism and collective rationality in organizational fields. *American Sociological Review*, 48(2): 147–160.

Dumez, H. and Jeunemaitre, A. (2000). *Understanding and Regulating the Market at a Time of Globalization: The Case of the Cement Industry*. Basingstoke and New York: Palgrave Macmillan.

Dumez, H. and Jeunemaitre, A. (2006). Reviving narratives in economics and management: Towards an integrated perspective of modelling, statistical inference and narratives. *European Management Review*, 3(1): 32–43.

Dussauge, P. and Garrette, B. (1999). *Cooperative Strategy : Competing Successfully through Strategic Alliances*. New York: Wiley.

Dyer, J.H. and Singh, H. (1998). The relational view: Cooperative strategy and sources of interorganizational competitive advantage. *The Academy of Management Review*, 23(4): 660–679.

Egels-Zandén, N. (2007). Suppliers' compliance with MNCs' codes of conduct: Behind the scenes at Chinese toy suppliers. *Journal of Business Ethics*, 75(1): 45–62.

Eisenhardt, K.M. (1989). Building theories from case study research. *The Academy of Management Review*, 14(4): 532–550.

Elsbach, K.D. (1994). Managing organizational legitimacy in the California cattle industry: The construction and effectiveness of verbal accounts. *Administrative Science Quarterly*, 39(1): 57–88.

Fombrun, C.J. (2001). Corporate reputation as economic assets, in M.A. Hitt, R.E. Freeman and J.S. Harrison (eds), *Handbook of Strategic Management*. Malden, MA: Blackwell, pp. 289–312.

Fombrun, C.J. and Shanley, M. (1990). What's in a name? Reputation building and corporate strategy. *The Academy of Management Journal*, 33(2): 233–258.

Galaskiewicz, J. (1985). Interorganizational relations. *Annual Review of Sociology*, 11: 281–304.

Garud, R., Jain, S. and Kumaraswamy, A. (2002). Institutional entrepreneurship in the sponsorship of common technological standards: The case of Sun Microsystems and Java. *The Academy of Management Journal*, 45(1): 196–214.

Geertz, C. (1973). *The Interpretation of Cultures: Selected Essays*. London: Harper Colophon Books.

Gnyawali, D.R. and Madhavan, R. (2001). Cooperative networks and competitive dynamics: A structural embeddedness perspective. *The Academy of Management Review*, 26(3): 431–445.

Hamel, G. and Doz, Y. (1998). *Alliance Advantage : The Art of Creating Value through Partnering*. Boston, MA: Harvard Business School.

Hamel, G. and Prahalad, C.K. (1994). *Competing for the Future*. Boston, MA: Harvard Business School Press.

Hanlon, G. (2008). Rethinking corporate social responsibility and the role of the firm–On the denial of politics. In Crane, A., McWilliams, A., Matten, D., Moon, J. and Siegel, D. (eds), *The Oxford Handbook of Corporate Social Responsibility*. Oxford: Oxford University Press, pp. 156–172.

Hanlon, G. and Fleming, P. (2009). Updating the critical perspective on corporate social responsibility. *Sociology Compass*, 3(6): 937–948.

Hart, S.L. (1995). A natural-resource-based view of the firm. *The Academy of Management Review*, 20: 986–1014.

Hart, S.L. and Dowell, G. (2011). A natural-resource-based view of the firm: Fifteen years after. *Journal of Management*, 37: 1464–1479.

King, A., Lenox, M.J. and Barnett, M.L. (2002). Strategic responses to the reputation commons problem. In A.J. Hoffman and M.J. Ventresca (eds), *Organizations, Policy and the Natural Environment: Institutional and Strategic Perspectives*. Stanford, CA: Stanford University Press, pp. 393–406.

King, N. (2004). Using templates in the thematic analysis of text. In C. Cassell and G. Symon (eds), *Essential Guide to Qualitative Methods in Organizational Research*. London: SAGE, pp. 256–270.

Kumar, N. (2006). Strategies to fight low-cost rivals. *Harvard Business Review*, 84(12): 104–112.

Lange, D., Lee, P.M. and Dai, Y. (2010). Organizational reputation: A review. *Journal of Management*, 37: 153–184.

McWilliams, A. and Siegel, D. (2001). Corporate social responsibility: A theory of the firm perspective. *The Academy of Management Review*, 26(1): 17–127.

McWilliams, A., Siegel, D.S. and Wright, P.M. (2006). Corporate social responsibility: Strategic implications. *Journal of Management Studies*, 43(1): 1–18.

Mahon, J.F. (2002). Corporate reputation: Research agenda using strategy and stakeholder literature. *Business & Society*, 4: 415–445.

Maloni, M.J. and Brown, M.E. (2006). Corporate social responsibility in the supply chain: An application in the food industry. *Journal of Business Ethics*, 68(1): 35–52.

Muller, A. (2006). Global versus local CSR strategies. *European Management Journal*, 24(2–3): 189–198.

Orlitzky, M., Schmidt, F.L. and Rynes, S.L. (2003). Corporate social and financial performance: A meta-analysis. *Organization Studies*, 24(3): 403–441.

Palazzo, G. and Richter, U. (2005). CSR Business as Usual? The case of the tobacco industry. *Journal of Business Ethics*, 61(4): 387–401.

Pfeffer, J. and Salancik, G.R. (1978). *The External Control of Organizations: A Resource Dependence Perspective*. New York: Harper & Row.

Porter, M.E. (1985). *Competitive Advantage*. New York: Free Press.

Porter, M.E. and Kramer, M. (2006). Strategy and society: The link between competitive advantage and corporate social responsibility. *Harvard Business Review*, 84(12): 78–92.

Powell, W.W. and DiMaggio, P.J. (1991). *The New Institutionalism in Organizational Analysis*. Chicago, IL: University of Chicago Press.

Roberts, P.W. and Dowling, G.R. (2002). Corporate reputation and sustained superior financial performance. *Strategic Management Journal*, 23: 1077–1093.

Salop, S.C. and Scheffman, D.T. (1987). Cost-raising strategies. *The Journal of Industrial Economics*, 36(1): 19–34.

Scherer, A.G. and Palazzo, G. (2007). Toward a political conception of corporate responsibility: Business and society seen from a Habermasian perspective. *The Academy of Management Review*, 32(4): 1096–1120.

Scherer, A.G. and Palazzo, G. (2011). The new political role of business in a globalized world: A review of a new perspective on CSR and its implications for the firm, governance, and democracy. *Journal of Management Studies*, 48(4): 899–931.

Selsky, J.W. and Parker, B. (2005). Cross-sector Partnerships to address social issues: Challenges to theory and practice. *Journal of Management*, 31(6): 849–873.

Selznick, P. (1957). *Leadership in Administration: A Sociological Interpretation*. Evanston, IL: Row, Peterson.

Suchman, M.C. (1995). Managing legitimacy: Strategic and institutional approaches. *The Academy of Management Review*, 20(3): 571–610.

van Tulder, R., van Wijk, J. and Kolk, A. (2009). From chain liability to chain responsibility. *Journal of Business Ethics*, 85: 399–412.

Vogel, D. (2005). *The Market for Virtues : The Potential and Limits of Corporate Social Responsibility*. Washington, DC: Brookings Institution.

Winn, M., MacDonald, P. and Zietsma, C. (2008). Managing industry reputation: The dynamic tension between collective and competitive reputation management strategies. *Corporate Reputation Review*, 11: 35–55.

Worrell, E., Price, L., Martin, N., Hendriks, C. and Meida, L. (2001). Carbon dioxide emissions from the global cement industry. *Annual Review of Energy and the Environment*, 26: 303–329.

Yami, S., Castaldo, S., Dagnino, G.B. and Le Roy, Frédéric. (2010).*Coopetition: Winning Strategies for the 21st Century*. Cheltenham: Edward Elgar.

Yin, R.K. (2004). *Case Study Research: Design and Methods*, 3rd edn. Applied Social Research Methods Series. Thousand Oaks, CA: SAGE.

Zucker, L.G. (1987). Institutional theories Of organization. *Annual Review of Sociology*, 13: 443–464.

Zyglidopoulos, S.C. (2002). The social and environmental responsibilities of multinationals: Evidence from the Brent Spar case. *Journal of Business Ethics*, 36(1): 141–151.

23 Implementing community sustainability strategies through cross-sector partnerships

Value creation for and by businesses

Amelia Clarke, Adriane MacDonald and Eduardo Ordonez-Ponce

Introduction

Local sustainable development is too complex for any one organization to address alone (Clarke, 2014; Glasbergen, 2007). Like many other complex issues, sustainability can more effectively be tackled through cross-sector partnerships (Selsky and Parker, 2005). Cross-sector partnerships are voluntary collaborations between organizations from different sectors (business, public and civil society) that address a mutually prioritized social issue (Babiak and Thibault, 2009; Waddock, 1991). In response to local sustainable development challenges and to internationally led sustainability programmes initiated by the United Nations, local governments around the world have been partnering with businesses and other local stakeholders to formulate and implement community sustainability plans (Clarke, 2014), also known as Local Agenda 21s (Rok and Kuhn, 2012). This chapter explores the benefits experienced by businesses as a result of their involvement in implementing community sustainability plans through cross-sector partnerships, the roles businesses play, and the value of business engagement in local sustainable development for the environment and the community.

Community sustainability plans consider integrated ecological, social and economic topics all in one strategic plan, and are long-term in their vision (anywhere from 5 years to 100 years) (Clarke, 2014). The plans typically include up to 16 different sustainability topics: transportation, water, waste, air, energy, climate change, land use, ecological diversity, food security, civic engagement, social infrastructure, housing, safety, local economy, employment and financial security (MacDonald, Clarke, Huang, Roseland and Seitanidi, 2017). Some of the topics which are managed have direct impacts on the local ecosystems (e.g. water, air, ecological diversity, land use, etc.), while others have indirect impacts (e.g. food choices, transportation choices, energy choices, etc.).

The value of a community sustainability plan is that it allows for many topics to be managed at an appropriate ecological and social scale, so that collective impacts can be measured (Clarke, 2014). Local governments have jurisdiction over a number of environmental topics (Gibbs, Longhurst and Braithwaite, 1996), and through a partnership approach (Clarke and Erfan, 2007), even more can be achieved.

Businesses are involved, not just in the formulation of the plans, but also in helping with the implementation (MacDonald, Clarke, Huang and Seitanidi, working paper). Being involved enables businesses to align their sustainability strategies with the community's collaborative sustainability strategy (Clarke and Fuller, 2010), thus helping address with the needs of the community in which they operate. The reasons that businesses and other stakeholders engage in these community-level partnerships for implementing community sustainability plans go beyond the desire to help the community achieve local sustainability goals. They are motivated by the desire to learn, to network, to improve their reputation and legitimacy, to increase positive relations with the community, to market their products and services, and to improve their financial performance (Clarke and MacDonald, 2016).

This chapter provides background on community sustainability plans, introduces cross-sector partnerships as a means of enabling community-wide actions and details the roles businesses are playing in helping achieve the community-wide sustainability vision. The main contribution offered through this chapter is identifying the value of businesses engaging in community sustainability strategies (for the environment and for the business itself). This chapter builds on research done as part of a larger project on implementing community sustainability plans to discuss the examples of collective actions that have been effective in mitigating environmental impacts (University of Waterloo, n.d.). In addition, this chapter includes the findings from a study that was conducted in Canada regarding why businesses engage in these partnerships.

Literature review

Sustainability

In *Our Common Future*, sustainable development is defined as 'development that meets the needs of the present without compromising the ability of future generations to meet their own needs' (World Commission on Environment and Development (WCED), 1987). However, sustainable development is not an exact science and its common definition is still uncertain to many who do not understand clearly what it means and what can be done. Sustainable development includes social development beyond economics and the environment, with the participation of diverse stakeholders to achieve multiple sustainability challenges (Kates, Parris and Leiserowitz, 2005). Ideally, sustainable development requires ecological sustainability and protection of biodiversity 'to guide the use of resources, maintenance of economic vitality with social inclusiveness in opportunities and benefits, social equity within and across social groups and generations, and the capacity for governance to bring all this about' (Francis, 2002). Sustainable development 'remains the most tenable principle of collective action for resolving the twin crises of environment and development' (Sneddon, Howarth and Norgaard, 2006).

The ideas underpinning sustainable development from the Stockholm conference (1972) and *Our Common Future* (1987) heavily influenced the agenda for the 1992 United Nations Conference on Environment and Development (Earth Summit) (Mebratu, 1998). It was at this 1992 conference in Rio de Janeiro that the influential Agenda 21 outcome document was created (United Nations, 1992) as a global programme for action on sustainable development (Yates, 2012). Agenda 21 is a call for a global partnership for integrating environmental and development concerns for the fulfilment of basic needs, improving living standards, and protecting and managing ecosystems for a safer and prosperous future (United Nations, 1992), highlighting the urgency of global environmental and social disparities that underpin the world's environmental and development challenges. To make Agenda 21 meaningful, a local approach that addresses the specific needs of individual local authorities was recommended (Bond, Mortimer and Cherry, 1998).

Based on the guiding principles laid out in Chapter 28 of Agenda 21, local governments were tasked with developing their own Local Agenda 21 (LA21) (Bond et al., 1998) due to their proximity to people and their ability to adjust organizations according to new contexts and social demands (Barrutia, Aguado and Echebarria, 2007), playing a 'vital role in educating, mobilizing and responding to the public to promote sustainable development' (United Nations, 1992). This chapter argues that another value of the community scale is that some ecological limits are local and can therefore be measured and managed.

LA21s were supported by ICLEI – Local Governments for Sustainability[1] (Devuyst and Hens, 2000), which defined an LA21 as 'a participatory, multi-sectoral process to achieve the goals of Agenda 21 at the local level through the preparation and implementation of a long-term, strategic action plan that addresses priority local sustainable development concerns' (Rok and Kuhn, 2012). LA21 promotes the partnership model for the development, implementation and oversight of a community sustainability plan (Clarke, 2014; Rok and Kuhn, 2012). Community sustainable development continues to be of global importance, and was identified as the focus of one of the global Sustainable Development Goals (SDGs) adopted in 2015 (United Nations Development Programme, 2015).

Community sustainability plans

Local governments have understood the complexity for addressing sustainability challenges and currently there are about 10,000 LA21 initiatives implementing sustainability plans addressing economic, social and environmental challenges around the world (Rok and Kuhn, 2012). Sustainability initiatives have been addressed under a varied list of names which are used depending on the scholar and the place of research. As mentioned, LA21 is a participatory multi-stakeholder process and plan at city or local level that was originally initiated through the United Nations' Agenda 21 (United Nations, 1992). However, not all 10,000 LA21 initiatives are implemented through a multi-stakeholder partnership. In this chapter, we use community sustainability plans (CSPs) as a generic name for the sustainability plans created via a public consultation process for determining environmental, social and economic goals and targets for a community, in partnership with local organizations (Clarke, 2012). Finally, the term Integrated Community Sustainability Plans (ICSP) has been used in Canada in the context of the gas tax agreements defining them as 'long-term plan[s] developed in consultation with the community to achieve sustainability objectives' (Ministry of Economic Development, Employment and Infrastructure of Ontario, 2012). Regardless of the name, these are all essentially the same type of plan.

Cross-Sector Partnershps

Cross-sector partnerships are formed when at least two organizations from public, private, or civil society sectors agree to work together to achieve mutual goals or to address a shared problem (Parmigiani and Rivera-Santos, 2011). Cross-sector partnerships specifically focused on social issues (including ecological and economic) are termed cross-sector social partnerships (or social partnerships); in these partnerships the actors collaborate to tackle a social problem of mutual interest (Selsky and Parker, 2005). A type of social partnership with more than one member from each of the

Table 23.1 Example of partners in Local Agenda 21 multi-stakeholder partnerships

Civil Society	Private	Public
Neighbourhood associations	Chamber of commerce	Local authorities
Community groups	Industry associations	Health authorities/hospitals
Non-profit organizations	Local businesses	Energy utilities
Local environmental groups	Board of trade	Training and enterprise councils
Volunteer support organizations	International business with local operations	Schools/colleges/universities
Housing associations		Development agencies

Adapted from (Freeman, Littlewood and Whitney, 1996).

three sectors that have a stake in the social problem is a multi-stakeholder partnership (Babiak and Thibault, 2009). Multi-stakeholder partnerships tend to have a large number of stakeholders involved as partners. See Table 23.1 for an overview of the types of organizational partners involved in the multi-stakeholder partnerships for formulating and implementing the community sustainability plans discussed in this chapter.

Any business engaged in a cross-sector partnership is considered a partner. Past research has found that structurally there are two levels of implementation in multi-stakeholder partnerships: the partner level (Huxham, 1993) and the partnership level (Brinkerhoff, 1999). At the partner level, partners reallocate resources inside their organizations to make internal changes, such as hiring a sustainability coordinator or implementing a waste reduction policy to support partnerships' goals. The partnership level is where collaborative actions occur, such as reporting, or joint initiatives. Actions at both the partner and partnership levels help to achieve the collaborative goals outlined in the community sustainability plan; goals such as regional reductions in GHG emissions or improvements on the regional air quality (Clarke, 2011). Activity at the partner level will be expanded on in the following section.

The value of businesses engaging in community sustainability plans

Based on the Canadian experience, there are five key components at the partnership level needed for implementation of community sustainability plans (Clarke, 2012):

- Oversight: plans must have an overseeing body, including a secretariat in charge of coordinating the process, a decision-making body and the involvement of members of the city council.
- Partner engagement: engaging the right quantity and quality of partners is a key for addressing sustainability challenges which partner organizations are responsible for.
- Community-wide action: partners need to take relevant action in their own organizations with the purpose of assuring that progress is not limited to the jurisdiction of the local governments, but also to partner organizations.
- Communications: it is important to keep partners engaged and motivated, thus peer-learning opportunities are needed and progress must be celebrated and publicly recognized.

- Monitoring and measurement: a community sustainability plan must have a system which allows monitoring progress so needed adjustments can be designed and implemented in due time.

Given the two levels of implementation, in practice, the structures vary in degree and intensity of collaboration (Clarke, 2014). By and large this chapter focuses on the how and why businesses become partners in these partnerships.

The Canadian landscape

From 2005 to 2010, the federal government department of Infrastructure Canada ran a programme called the New Deal for Cities, whereby municipalities could gain access to federal gas tax revenues through their respective provincial government for infrastructure projects (Infrastructure Canada, 2005). Over the five years, the New Deal initiative distributed $5 billion among Canadian municipalities (Infrastructure Canada, 2005). A prerequisite for receiving gas tax money was that the municipality needed to develop an Integrated Community Sustainability Plan (ICSP) (Infrastructure Canada, 2005). This led to an influx of ICSPs in Canadian municipalities.

According to the Canadian Sustainability Plan Inventory developed by the University of Alberta, there are 1,242 sustainability plans and affiliated documents in Canadian municipalities across the country (University of Alberta, 2017), most of which have been developed collaboratively with stakeholders in the community and some of which are being implemented through multi-stakeholder partnerships (Clarke, 2014).

Recent research finds that most of the community sustainability plans in Canada include environmental, social and economic sustainability, although socio-environmental topics remain the most frequent, following a global trend (MacDonald et al., 2017). In Canada almost all of the assessed plans included transportation and water, and about nine out of ten considered waste, air, energy and land use as matters to be addressed. Around 80 per cent of the plans included climate change, food security and local economy. Three-quarters of the plans approached ecological diversity and civic engagement. Seventy-one per cent incorporated social infrastructure, 65 per cent housing, 57 per cent employment and safety/crime, and only 41 per cent considered financial security/poverty alleviation as one of their topics (MacDonald et al., 2017). One of the pending matters still to be resolved in Canada is a deeper involvement of partners in the implementation processes (Clarke, 2014).

Businesses have contributed in valuable ways to community sustainability activities. Since 1992, businesses have increasingly partnered with governments, international organizations and NGOs to contribute to sustainable development initiatives (LaFrance and Lehmann, 2005). Businesses have become 'an increasingly dominant social institution', being involved not only on economic matters, but also in social, environmental and political affairs (Crane and Seitanidi, 2014). For example, in the case of the sustainability plan for Barcelona in Spain, businesses represent 50 per cent of the 421 partners,[2] while the second largest group are NGOs reaching 45 per cent (Ajuntament de Barcelona, 2003). Similarly, in Bristol (UK), the private sector represents 61 per cent of the 848 partners, followed by civil society (35 per cent) (BGCP CIC, n.d.). Moreover, at an organizational level businesses' commitment to the United Nations Global Compact indicates their desire to contribute to sustainable development as they change their operations to implement responsible practices and develop innovative solutions to sustainability challenges, including actions for poverty alleviation and pollution prevention (United Nations Global Compact, 2016).

The involvement of businesses in cross-sector partnerships for community sustainability initiatives starts by understanding their relationship with the community, which is determined by assessing the context and forming of the partnership. This is the first stage in a collaborative strategic plan formulation and implementation process (Clarke and Fuller, 2010). Then, businesses work together with other partners in establishing a common vision and objectives to be reflected in a collaborative strategic plan – the second stage of the process (Clarke and Fuller, 2010). In the third stage, the implementation of the plan is conducted internally by partner organizations focusing on their specific sustainability actions, as well as collectively with the other partners focusing on community-wide sustainability actions (Clarke and Fuller, 2010). Finally, outcomes of the implementation process are achieved by the partnership as well as by the partners, including outcomes for business partners (Clarke and Fuller, 2010). A collaborative strategic process such as the one defined here is not linear as each phase interacts with the other in forward and backward loops, as well as receiving external influence which can modify the defined process (Clarke and Fuller, 2010).

Businesses, as with any other partner organizations, implement sustainability actions at two levels: partner and partnership level. At the partner level, partners reallocate resources inside their organizations to form new structures that help them implement their own sustainability plans and/or goals (Kale, Dyer and Singh, 2002; Schreiner, Kale and Corsten, 2009; Seitanidi, 2010; Seitanidi and Crane, 2009). Partner level structure can include creating new processes that green business operations such as eco–efficiency programmes, or the implementation of environmental management systems (Rotheroe, Keenlyside and Coates, 2003); a new department dedicated to implement a company sustainability strategy (MacDonald, Clarke, Huang and Seitanidi, 2014); or reporting under frameworks such as the Global Reporting Initiative (Rotheroe et al., 2003). It can also include green procurement initiatives that help other local businesses (Kemp and Clarke, 2012). A study based on partner perceptions found that partners that participate in implementing the community sustainability plan through partner level activities experience more benefits from the partnership (MacDonald et al., 2014). At the partnership level, business partners get involved in various committees. For example, in Montreal's Strategic Plan for Sustainable Development by being part of the Partners' Committee, businesses (along with partners from the other sectors) have engaged to share best practices, discuss challenges and propose adjustments to the plan (Clarke, 2011, 2012).

While businesses have an important role to play in community sustainability they also stand to benefit from engaging in the implementation of a community sustainability plan. A study done on partner perceptions in the Canadian communities of Hamilton, Montreal, Vancouver and Whistler found that partners associated several organizational resources as outcomes of their involvement (Clarke and MacDonald, 2016). Table 23.2 provides a summary of the positive outcomes reported by these partners. The resources identified by partners and summarized in Table 23.2, informed the nine outcomes tested in the partner level survey discussed in Part B of the findings in this chapter.

Table 23.2 Resources gained from case studies in Hamilton, Montreal, Vancouver and Whistler

Identified resources	Outcomes terminology
Increased capacity due to new engagement mechanisms / Built relationships	Networking
Improved reputation	Reputation
Gained knowledge	Learning
Built relationships and social capital	Positive relationships with the community
Gained influence	Legitimacy
Increased impact on community sustainability / Added new external processes, programmes and/or entities	Community sustainability
Increased impact on community sustainability / Added new internal processes, programmes and/or entities	Organization's sustainability
Accessed marking opportunities	Marketing opportunities
Cost savings / Accessed new business opportunities	Financial performance

Adapted from (Clarke and MacDonald, 2016).

Positive outcomes such as improved reputation, accessed new marketing opportunities, accessed new business opportunities, and cost savings all contribute to the business case to engage in a community sustainability partnership.

Methodology

Broad findings discussed in this chapter are based on a summary of results from a research project that has been active for approximately ten years. The research project is called Implementing Sustainable Community Plans and includes findings from numerous case studies and surveys. The overarching goal of this multi-year and multi-study research project is to 'help local governments around the world more effectively implement Local Agenda 21s (LA21s), community sustainability plans, and community climate action plans' (University of Waterloo, n.d.). Relevant Canadian stories from the project are summarized in Part A of the findings to provide evidence for the argument that value is created both for and by businesses when they engage in implementing community sustainability strategies.

A specific study elaborated on in this chapter employed an online survey method to collect data about the resources that partners value most. The results from this partner level survey are presented in Part B of the findings. Survey respondents were asked to rate the value of nine partner outcomes to their organization on a 5-point Likert scale, where 1 was equal to no value and 5 as very valuable. As previously mentioned, the nine partner outcomes tested in the survey built on past case study research of partners in LA21 multi-stakeholder partnerships (see Table 23.2) (Clarke and MacDonald, 2016).

The survey targeted partners involved with implementing community sustainability plans, and was promoted and administered to all of the French- and English-speaking local authorities in ICLEI-Local Governments for Sustainability Canada's (ICLEI Canada) membership. ICLEI Canada was a valuable collaborator in this research as they are connected to local governments implementing community sustainability plans across Canada and have significant experience administering surveys with academic institutions (Carmin, Nadkarni and Rhin, 2012).

ICLEI Canada sent personalized emails to their contacts in local governments who host the secretariats for partnerships implementing community sustainability plans.

There is limited publicly available information about partners so this study relied on municipal staff to forward the link to the online survey to their partners. The online survey was sent to 328 partners involved in municipal sustainability focused social partnerships from 15 Canadian communities. These efforts generated 42 responses or a response rate of 12.8 per cent. This response rate is comparable to response rates typical of surveys completed in non-traditional contexts (Kriauciunas, Parmigiani and Rivera-Santos, 2011). Non-traditional contexts include studies on new organizational forms (Kriauciunas et al., 2011), such as multi-stakeholder partnerships.

Findings

Part A: Stories of collaborative action and direct environmental impacts

In some multi-stakeholder partnerships for implementing community sustainability plans, two progress reports were produced. One captured the actions taken by the partners on each of the collaborative goals, and the other captured progress made on sustainability indicators. For example, for Montreal's partnership, '... annual progress reports on action implementation were created; and bi-annual 'state of the environment' indicator reports were produced' (Clarke and Fuller, 2010, p. 94). These 'state of the environment' reports were possible because some direct environment and social impacts were measured at the community scale.

An example of a collaborative goal in Montreal's community sustainability plan (initially called Montreal's First Strategic Plan for Sustainable Development) is related to greenhouse gas emissions (Clarke, 2011). In terms of partner engagement, numerous actions could be taken to help achieve the collaborative goal: 'For example, Action 1.3 (anti-idling) related to a wide diversity of partners, while Action 1.9 (buying eco-efficient vehicles) was only relevant for some larger organizations' (Clarke and Fuller, 2010, p. 95). While the trend in Montreal for region-wide emissions was going in the wrong direction (Clarke, 2011), this would not be known if only actions were being measured and not also community-wide greenhouse gas emissions.

In Halifax their regional plan considered growth based on water quantity and the feasibility of expanding municipal water infrastructure (Clarke and Erfan, 2007). As parts of the region are outside the municipal water infrastructure, all developments in those areas obtained water from wells. As there is only so much easily accessible ground water, housing density decisions were based on environmental criteria. Thus businesses that propose development in those rural areas can help achieve collaborative goals of working within ecological limits by building water-efficiency into their housing designs. Businesses were part of helping formulate the community sustainability plan and were critical for its implementation.

In Hamilton their community sustainability plan (initially called Vision 2020) had a collaborative goal around air quality (Clarke, 2011). To address this issue, Clean Air Hamilton was launched as a multi-stakeholder partnership. Major polluters (steel companies) worked with researchers at the local universities, the local government, environmental non-governmental organizations and others to create and implement actions plans around air quality. Since the launch of Clean Air Hamilton in the mid-1990s, air quality has drastically improved in the region. While each company was taking initiatives on their own to address environmental concerns, being a part of this multi-stakeholder partnership focused their efforts, provided relevant research and suggestions, and enabled progress to be measured at the appropriate scale. A company can measure reduction in pollutants in their emissions, or actions taken, but at the community scale, improvements in air quality can be measured.

In Whistler, their community sustainability plan is called Whistler2020. One of the partners is an all-season resort (mostly known as a ski hill) called Whistler Blackcomb. This company found that by engaging in the community-wide efforts to achieve sustainability, it provided them with a stakeholder engagement mechanism (Clarke and MacDonald, 2016). A micro-hydro project, which was controversial, was ultimately supported by community organizations because it was part of helping achieve community-wide sustainability goals and not just an effort to reduce costs for the company.

Part B: Partner level survey results

As mentioned above the partner level survey questions were designed to build on what was learned from the results of earlier case studies (Clarke and MacDonald, 2016). The survey questions did so by asking respondents to rate the value of the resources that had been identified by partners in the case studies (Clarke and MacDonald, 2016). The information from the survey made it easier to determine the value proposition of LA21 multi-stakeholder partnerships to partners. The findings of the survey revealed that the top three resources that partners most value are networking, learning and reputation as resources gained from the partnerships studied. Most of the resources rated as most valuable by partners are linked to the partners' licence to operate including reputation, networking, legitimacy and positive relationships with the community. The results of the online survey by resource are shown in Table 23.3.

In order to determine if there are significant differences among the means, an ANOVA test was used providing the information found in Table 23.4.

Table 23.3 Outcomes partners' value

Benefits	Mean	SD	Var
Networking	4.29	0.97	0.94
Learning	4.26	0.86	0.73
Reputation	4.26	1.13	1.27
Positive relationships with the community	4.24	1.01	1.02
Legitimacy	4.24	1.06	1.11
Community sustainability	4.19	0.92	0.84
Organization's sustainability	4.02	1.07	1.15
Marketing opportunities	3.57	1.20	1.42
Financial performance	3.52	1.35	1.82

Table 23.4 ANOVA

Source of Variation	SS	df	MS	F	P-value	F crit
Between groups	31.08466	8	3.886	3.3955	0.0009	1.963514
Within groups	422.2619	369	1.144			
Total	453.3466	377				

Table 23.5 Tukey test parameters

Number of treatments	9
Sample size	42
Total number of observations	378

Results show that there is at least one significant difference among the means ($p < 0.05$). Then, in order to determine which ones are significantly different, a Tukey test is used considering the parameters shown in Table 23.5.

Qu ($\alpha = 0.05$)	4.387
Q_df_num	9
Q_df_den	336

Then, for determining the significant differences, the absolute differences between means were compared to a critical range obtained through Qu, sample size per treatment, and the mean square within groups. Results showed that there are significant differences between networking and financial performance (difference = −0.038); learning and financial performance (difference = −0.014); and reputation and financial performance (difference = 0.014), with an $\alpha = 0.05$. In other words, the top three were significantly different than the bottom one. The other benefits are not significantly different from each other. Implications of these results are explored in further in the discussion section of this chapter.

Discussion and managerial implications

As mentioned in the introduction, the main contribution offered through this chapter is identifying the value of businesses engaging in community sustainability strategies (for the local environment and for the business itself). While there is significant value for companies to develop their own sustainability strategies and/or embed sustainability in their business strategies (Borland, Ambrosini, Lindgreen and Vanhamme, 2014; Gladwin, Kennelly and Krause, 1995; Hart, 1997; Howard-Grenville, Buckle, Hoskins and George, 2014; Porter and Kramer, 2011; Whiteman, Walker and Perego, 2013), this chapter argues that even more can be achieved by aligning these strategies with the needs of the local community and limitations of the local ecosystems.

The 'state of the environment' can be measured for some topics at the community scale, while only improvements can be measured at the organizational scale. By measuring the actual condition of the environment, then the need for additional improvements can be determined. Water, biodiversity and air quality are excellent examples of environmental topics that are best monitored at the local level. There are numerous social topics for which this is also the appropriate scale, such as housing, and employment. For greenhouse gas emissions, the impact is global, so even at the local scale, all that can be measured is progress towards goals.

What roles businesses can play in helping implement a community sustainability plan is not the same question as to why businesses would voluntarily engage. The roles they can play are numerous, from offering the products and services needed to move to a low-carbon economy and operate within ecological limits; to mitigating their environmental impacts and helping improve the social situation. The value of businesses engaging in achieving the goals within a community sustainability plans is obvious, but the value that same engagement offers businesses is less apparent. This chapter offers original findings about why organizations engage. By knowing this information, multi-stakeholder partnerships can be designed to better facilitate long-term engagement of key stakeholders.

As can be seen from the findings in Part B, gaining physical/financial capital (e.g. improving financial performance) was rated lowest in the survey responses regarding outcomes that partners valued (as a result of participating in the partnership). On the other hand, gaining organizational capital is critical; for instance, partners rated relationship building as the most important resource gained. Networking, reputation, learning, positive relationships and marketing opportunities – items rated in this survey – are hard for competitors to replicate due to a dimension of social complexity which makes them especially valuable to firms (Clarke and MacDonald, 2016; Das and Teng, 2000). It is clear from the Whistler Blackcomb example, that these relationships were critical for achieving the company's goals. These findings are consistent with the corporate social responsibility (CSR) and corporate citizenship literature. For instance, the CSR literature indicates that businesses engage in CSR activities to improve their reputation and gain a social licence to operate (Ajuntament de Barcelona, 2003). More recent writing on corporate citizenship discusses the business case and value proposition of social responsibility (Mirvis and Googins, 2006). While business sustainability can be broader than CSR, engaging as partners in a cross-sector partnership is a form of CSR, and therefore some of the same benefits are found. That said, it is also an opportunity to make a measurable impact on community-wide sustainability goals.

The survey findings in this chapter show that the survey respondents felt very positive about their experience with these cross-sector partnerships and that their organizations gained many benefits. Given the response rate, it may be that only those businesses that gained positive outcomes filled out the survey. Nonetheless, this data indicates that businesses do benefit from their efforts to work with other community stakeholders to address local sustainable development issues. The findings presented in this chapter build on a previous qualitative study (Clarke and MacDonald, 2016) which provides insight into the benefits, including representative quotations. This study goes further through a quantitative analysis that allows the degree to which partners benefited to be understood (i.e. the mean scores out of 5 were very high), and the top benefits to be distinguished from the bottom one. While both studies focused on partners involved in cross-sector partnerships for implementing sustainable community plans, the partnerships studied were not the same. Thus, this study also helps validate the findings of the previous one about these items being valuable partner outcomes.

Limitations and recommendations for further research

This chapter argues that community sustainability strategies enable a better scale for monitoring certain environmental and social conditions, and therefore the impact of activities (both positive and negative). However, there can be challenges related to collecting data to measure the impact at this scale too. One such challenge is common method bias whereby a single source provides the data, which can impact the validity of the results. Also, some topics are not easily measured or data is not currently being collected (given the capacity of the community stakeholders). While there is increasingly more standardization to what is being measured in regards to local sustainable development, there is still a huge variance in the indicators being used by communities, thus making comparisons between communities difficult.

In regards to future research, while Part B of this chapter was specifically designed to answer the question about what organizations value about the outcomes they experience through being involved in a multi-stakeholder partnership, more work could be done on this. For example, a larger-scale study could be done that draws out the experiences of different types of businesses, different size businesses, etc. Also, the effect of the partnership size could be studied with a larger study.

In addition, this chapter is premised on the assumption that multi-stakeholder partnerships are an ideal way to engage businesses in helping achieve community sustainability goals. Further research about various approaches could be done – for example, voluntary versus mandatory, without versus with a community-wide strategy – to see what the most effective approach is. Evidence from the larger research project indicates that more action is taken by businesses as a result of being a part of the partnership, and that the sustainability actions taken by companies better align with community needs, but this has not been studied in detail.

Notes

1 ICLEI – Local Governments for Sustainability (formally called International Council for Local Environmental Initiatives) is a non-governmental organization with a worldwide reach, and a membership of approximately 1,200 local governments from 70 countries, representing 570 million people.
2 Excluding educational centres.

References

Ajuntament de Barcelona (2003). Barcelona + Sostenible. Retrieved 15 July 2017 from www.bcnsostenible.cat/en/web.
Babiak, K. and Thibault, L. (2009). Challenges in multiple cross-sector partnerships. *Nonprofit and Voluntary Sector Quarterly*, 38(1): 117–143. https://doi.org/doi.org/10.1177/0899764008316054.
Barrutia, J. M., Aguado, I. and Echebarria, C. (2007). Networking for Local Agenda 21 implementation: Learning from experiences with Udaltalde and Udalsarea in the Basque Autonomous Community. *Geoforum*, 38(1): 33–48.
BGCP CIC (n.d.). Bristol Green Capital Partnership. Retrieved 23 February 2017 from http://bristolgreencapital.org/.
Bond, A., Mortimer, K. J. and Cherry, J. (1998). Policy and practice: The focus of Local Agenda 21 in the United Kingdom. *Journal of Environmental Planning and Management*, 41: 767–776. https://doi.org/10.1080/09640569811416.
Borland, H., Ambrosini, V., Lindgreen, A. and Vanhamme, J. (2014). Building theory at the intersection of ecological sustainability and strategic management. *Journal of Business Ethics First* [online], 1–15. https://doi.org/10.1007/s10551-014-2471-6.
Brinkerhoff, D. (1999). Exploring state-civil society collaboration: Policy partnerships in developing countries. *Nonprofit and Voluntary Sector Quarterly*, 28(4): 59–86. https://doi.org/10.1177/0899764099284004.
Carmin, J., Nadkarni, N. and Rhin, C. (2012). *Progress and Challenges in Urban Climate Adaptation Planning: Results of a Global Survey*. Cambridge, MA: MIT Press.
Clarke, A. (2011). Key structural features for collaborative strategy implementation: A study of sustainable development/local agenda collaborations. *Management & Avenir*, 50(10): 153–171. https://doi.org/10.3917/mav.050.0153.

Clarke, A. (2012). *Passing Go: Moving beyond the Plan*. Ottawa, ON: Federation of Canadian Municipalities. Retrieved from https://fcm.ca/Documents/tools/GMF/SS_PassingGo_EN.pdf.

Clarke, A. (2014). Designing social partnerships for local sustainability strategy implementation. In A. Crane and M.M. Seitanidi (eds), *Social Partnership and Responsible Business: A Research Handbook*. London: Routledge: Taylor & Francis, pp. 79–102.

Clarke, A. and Erfan, A. (2007). Regional sustainability strategies: A comparison of eight Canadian approaches. *Plan Canada*, 47(3): 15–19.

Clarke, A. and Fuller, M. (2010). Collaborative strategic management: Strategy formulation and implementation by multi-organizational cross-sector social partnerships. *Journal of Business Ethics*, 94(1): 85–101. https://doi.org/10.1007/s10551-011-0781-5.

Clarke, A. and MacDonald, A. (2016). Outcomes to partner in multi-stakeholder cross-sector partnerships: A resource-based view. *Business & Society*, 1–35 (online first). https://doi.org/10.1177/0007650316660534.

Crane, A. and Seitanidi, M.M. (2014). Social partnerships and responsible business. What, why and how? In M.M. Seitanidi and A. Crane (eds), *Social Partnerships and Responsible Business: A Research Handbook*. London: Routledge/Taylor & Francis, pp. 1–12.

Das, T.K. and Teng, B.S. (2000). A resource-based theory of strategic alliances. *Journal of Management*, 26(1): 31–61. https://doi.org/10.1177/014920630002600105.

Devuyst, D. and Hens, L. (2000). Introducing and measuring sustainable development initiatives by local authorities in Canada and Flanders (Belgium): A comparative study. *Environment, Development and Sustainability*, 2(2): 81–105. https://doi.org/10.1023/A:1011466019809.

Francis, G. (2002). Looking beyond Johannesburg: Real solutions to global problems will have to move from talk to action. *Alternatives Journal*, 28(2): 21–22.

Freeman, C., Littlewood, S. and Whitney, D. (1996). Local government and emerging models of participation in the local Agenda 21 process. *Journal of Environmental Planning and Management*, 39(1): 65–78. https://doi.org/10.1080/09640569612679.

Gibbs, D., Longhurst, J. and Braithwaite, C. (1996). Moving towards sustainable development? Integrating economic development and the environment in local authorities. *Journal of Environmental Planning and Management*, 39(3): 317–332. https://doi.org/10.1080/09640569612444.

Gladwin, T.N., Kennelly, J.J. and Krause, T.-S. (1995). Shifting paradigms for sustainable development: Implications for management theory and research. *Academy of Management Review*, 20(4): 874–907.

Glasbergen, P. (2007). Setting the scene: The partnership paradigm in the making. In P. Glasbergen, F. Biermann and A.P.J. Mol (eds), *Partnerships, Governance and Sustainable Development: Reflections on Theory and Practice*. Cheltenham: Edward Elgar. pp. 1–25.

Hart, S.L. (1997). Beyond greening: Strategies for a sustainable world. *Harvard Business Review*, 75, 66–76.

Howard-Grenville, J., Buckle, S., Hoskins, B. and George, G. (2014). Climate change and management. *Academy of Management Journal*, 57(3): 615–623. https://doi.org/10.5465/amj.2014.4003.

Huxham, C. (1993). Pursuing collaborative advantage. *The Journal of the Operational Research Society*, 44(6): 599–611. https://doi.org/10.1057/jors.1993.101.

Infrastructure Canada (2005). *A New Deal for Canada's Communities*. Ottawa, ON: Department of Finance Canada.

Kale, P., Dyer, J.H. and Singh, H. (2002). Alliance capability, stock market response, and long-term alliance success: The role of the alliance function. *Strategic Management Journal*, 23(8): 747–767. https://doi.org/10.1002/smj.248.

Kates, R.W., Parris, T.M. and Leiserowitz, A.A. (2005). What is sustainable development? *Environment: Science and Policy for Sustainable Development*, 47(3): 8–21.

Kemp, A. and Clarke, A. (2012). Greening the local economy through municipal sustainable procurement policies: Implementation challenges and successes in western Canada. In R.

Simpson and M. Zimmermann (eds), *The Economy of Green Cities: World Compendium on the Green Urban Economy.* New York: Springer, pp. 405–416.

Kriauciunas, A., Parmigiani, A. and Rivera-Santos, M. (2011). Leaving our comfort zone: Integrating established practices with unique adaptations to conduct survey-based strategy research in nontraditional contexts. *Strategic Management Journal*, 32, 994–1010. https://doi.org/10.1002/smj.921.

LaFrance, J. and Lehmann, M. (2005). Corporate awakening: Why (some) corporations embrace public-private partnerships. *Business Strategy and the Environment*, 14: 216–229. https://doi.org/10.1002/bse.471.

MacDonald, A., Clarke, A., Huang, L., Roseland, M. and Seitanidi, M.M. (2018). Cross-sector partnerships (SDG #17) as a means of achieving sustainable communities and cities (SDG #11). In W. Leal Filho (ed.), *Handbook of Sustainability Science and Research.* New York: Springer, pp. 193–209.

MacDonald, A., Clarke, A., Huang, L. and Seitanidi, M.M. (2014). Exploring large-scale social partnerships: A study on implementation structure and partner outcomes using an extended resource-based view. Presented at the Symposium on Cross-sector Social Interactions, Boston, Massachusetts.

MacDonald, A., Clarke, A., Huang, L. and Seitanidi, M.M. (working paper). Large cross-sector social partnerships: A study on partner implementation structure and resources.

Mebratu, D. (1998). Sustainability and sustainable development: Historical and conceptual review. *Environmental Impact Assessment Review*, 18(6): 493–520. https://doi.org/10.1016/S0195-9255(98)00019-5.

Ministry of Economic Development, Employment and Infrastructure of Ontario (2012). *Guide for Municipal Asset Management Plans.* Ontario, Canada: Queen's Printer for Ontario. Retrieved from www.moi.gov.on.ca/pdf/en/Municipal%20Strategy_English_Web.pdf.

Mirvis, P. and Googins, B. (2006). Stages of corporate citizenship. *California Management Review*, 48(2): 104–126.

Parmigiani, A. and Rivera-Santos, M. (2011). Clearing a path through the forest: A meta-review of interorganizational relationships. *Journal of Management*, 37(4): 1108–1136. https://doi.org/10.1177/0149206311407507.

Porter, M.E. and Kramer, M. (2011). Creating shared value. *Harvard Business Review*, 89(1/2): 62–77.

Rok, A. and Kuhn, S. (2012). Local sustainability 2012: Taking stock and moving forward. *Global Review*, pp. 1–87. Bonn, Germany: ICLEI - Local Governments for Sustainability. Retrieved from http://local2012.iclei.org/fileadmin/files/LS2012_GLOBAL_REVIEW_www.pdf.

Rotheroe, N., Keenlyside, M. and Coates, L. (2003). Local Agenda 21: Articulating the meaning of sustainable development at the level of the individual enterprise. *Journal of Cleaner Production*, 11: 537–548. https://doi.org/10.1016/S0959-6526(02)00075-6.

Schreiner, M., Kale, P. and Corsten, D. (2009). What really is alliance management capability and how does it impact alliance outcomes and success? *Strategic Management Journal*, 30(13): 1395–1419. https://doi.org/ 10.1002/smj.790.

Seitanidi, M.M. (2010). *The Politics of Partnerships: A Critical Examination of Non-profit-business Partnerships.* London: Springer.

Seitanidi, M.M. and Crane, A. (2009). Implementing CSR through partnerships: Understanding the selection, design and institutionalisation of nonprofit-business partnerships. *Journal of Business Ethics*, 85(S2): 413–429. https:// doi.org/10.1007/s10551-008-9743-y.

Selsky, J.W. and Parker, B. (2005). Cross-sector partnerships to address social issues: Challenges to theory and practice. *Journal of Management*, 31(6): 849–873. https://doi.org/10.1177/0149206305279601.

Sneddon, C., Howarth, R.B. and Norgaard, R.B. (2006). Sustainable development in a post-brundtland world. *Ecological Economics*, 57, 253–268. https://doi.org/10.1016/j.ecolecon.2005.04.013.

United Nations (1992). *Agenda 21.* Rio de Janeiro, Brazil: United Nations Conference on Environment and Development (UNCED).

United Nations Development Programme (2015). *Sustainable Development Goals*. New York: UNDP.

United Nations Global Compact (2016). Business as a force of good. Retrieved 8 February 2016, from https://www.unglobalcompact.org/what-is-gc/mission.

University of Alberta (2017). Canadian sustainability plan inventory. Retrieved from https://www.ualberta.ca/augustana/research/centres/acsrc/projects/priority-areas/planning/completed-projects/cspi.

University of Waterloo (n.d.). Implementing community sustainability plans. Retrieved 15 July 2017 from https://uwaterloo.ca/implementing-sustainable-community-plans/.

Waddock, S.A. (1991). A typology of social partnership organizations. *Administration & Society*, 22(4): 480–515. https://doi.org/10.1177/009539979102200405.

Whiteman, G., Walker, B. and Perego, P. (2013). Planetary boundaries: Ecological foundations for corporate sustainability. *Journal of Management Studies*, 50(2): 207–336. https://doi.org/10.1111/j.1467-6486.2012.01073.x.

World Commission on Environment and Development (WCED) (1987). *Our Common Future*. Oxford and New York: Oxford University Press.

Yates, J. (2012). Abundance on trial: The cultural significance of sustainability. *The Hedgehog Review*, 14(2): 8–25.

Index

References to illustrations and diagrams are in **bold**

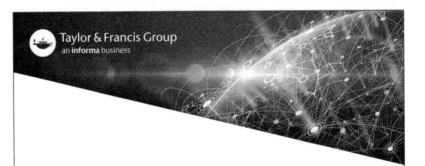